The Generalist Model of Human Services Practice

Grafton H. Hull, Jr.

University of Utah

Karen K. Kirst-Ashman

University of Wisconsin–Whitewater

THOMSON

⸻ ✦ ⸻ ™

BROOKS/COLE

Australia • Canada • Mexico • Singapore • Spain
United Kingdom • United States

Handwritten annotations:

Joy Graham
Jan 2015
$ 560

Dr. Richard Bumpers
ph4-330-1820
Richard.Bumpers@point.edu

"this is the House that Prayer Builts"

MW01235012

THOMSON
BROOKS/COLE
™

Editor: *Lisa Gebo*
Assistant Editor: *Alma Dea Michelena*
Editorial Assistant: *Sheila Walsh*
Marketing Manager: *Caroline Concilla*
Project Manager, Editorial Production: *Tom Novack*
Print/Media Buyer: *Kristine Waller*
Permissions Editor: *Sue Ewing*
Production Service: *Heckman & Pinette*
Text Designer: *John Edeen*

Photo Researcher: *Pat Quest*
Copy Editor: *Margaret Pinette*
Illustrator: *Jennifer Mackres*
Cover Designer: *Lisa Berman*
Cover Image: *Stephen Daigle*
Cover Printer: *Phoenix Color Corporation*
Compositor: *New England Typographic Service*
Printer: *Phoenix Color Corporation*

Printed in the United States of America
2 3 4 5 6 7 06 05 04

For more information about our products, contact us at:
Thomson Learning Academic Resource Center
1-800-423-0563
For permission to use material from this text, contact us by:
Phone: 1-800-730-2214   **Fax:** 1-800-730-2215
Web: http://www.thomsonrights.com

Library of Congress Cataloging-in-Publication Data

Hull, Grafton H.
  The generalist model of human services practice / Grafton Hull, Jr.,
    Karen Kirst-Ashman.
        p. cm.
  Includes bibliographical references and index.
  Casebound ISBN 0-534-51273-9
  Advantage ISBN 0-534-59207-4
  1. Social service. 2. Human services. I. Kirst-Ashman, Karen Kay.
    II. Title.

HV40 .H7812 2003
3610—dc21   2002038579

Brooks/Cole–Thomson Learning
511 Forest Lodge Road
Pacific Grove, CA 93950
USA

Asia
Thomson Learning
5 Shenton Way #01-01
UIC Building
Singapore 068808

Australia/New Zealand
Thomson Learning
102 Dodds Street
Southbank, Victoria 3006
Australia

Canada
Nelson
1120 Birchmount Road
Toronto, Ontario M1K 5G4
Canada

Europe/Middle East/Africa
Thomson Learning
High Holborn House
50/51 Bedford Row
London WC1R 4LR
United Kingdom

Latin America
Thomson Learning
Seneca, 53
Colonia Polanco
11560 Mexico D.F.
Mexico

Spain/Portugal
Paraninfo
Calle Magallanes, 25
28015 Madrid
Spain

to Susan L. Spielman,

Gary S. Kirst,

Joseph Frisbie,

and

Jannah J. Mather

Mezz systems eg. co-workers

Macro the Large company
you work for and the state

Brief Contents

Contents

CHAPTER 8
Evaluation and Termination in Generalist Practice   **230**

PART THREE:
Intervention with Multiple Systems   **265**

CHAPTER 9
Working with Individuals   **266**

x   Contents

Preface

Written as a guide to generalist human services practice, this book is specifically oriented toward students. It provides them with a generalist perspective from which to view the world and their own work in human services. The text pursues two primary goals. First, it aims to teach students the relationship-building, interviewing, and problem-solving skills necessary for them to work with individual clients. The perspective is assumed that group (i.e., mezzo) skills are built upon a firm foundation of individual (i.e., micro) skills. Likewise, skills involved in community organization and social planning (i.e., macro skills) rest upon a solid base of both micro and mezzo skills.

The text's second major goal is to introduce students to generalist practice. It orients them to think not only in terms of individual needs but also of group and community needs. The book's intent is to structure how students think about clients and their problems so that they automatically explore alternatives beyond the individual level. Links are clearly made among these three levels of practice. A systems approach aids students' understanding of how perspectives shift when changing from one practice level to another. The text provides knowledge and skills needed by the entry-level practitioner while helping students recognize that all practice is governed by ethical guidelines. As Woodside and McClam (2002) note, today's generalist possesses the ability to work in numerous positions and with clients ranging from micro systems (individuals) to macro systems (organizations and communities). The generalist professional is employed in agencies ranging from substance abuse programs to child welfare and from juvenile justice to nursing homes. They work with the elderly and children, adults and adolescents. Problems they encounter can range from domestic and child abuse to criminal behavior and disabilities. This diversity of problems, settings,

and system levels means that the generalist professional must have developed the competency to work with individuals as well as with communities. Professionals must possess knowledge and skills that cover the responsibilities of engaging clients, assessing their needs, planning, implementing the plan, evaluating the outcomes, and terminating with them. This text seeks to provide a comprehensive approach to generalist human services practice accompanied by numerous case examples that capture the dynamic nature of work in this field. To this end, each chapter provides specific content to ensure that the student will be able to function effectively in the human services arena. In the paragraphs below, we will identify the salient concepts and issues that form the basis of each section and chapter in the book.

The first section of the book is devoted to addressing the model of practice that will be followed throughout the book while recognizing two factors that will always have an impact on the practice. The factors are professional ethics and human diversity.

Chapter 1 introduces the Generalist Intervention Model that is used throughout the text. It highlights the wide array of skills and knowledge needed for human services practice and discusses the many roles played by the professional. It also reviews the importance of thinking critically about what human services professionals do.

The second chapter provides a solid introduction to the importance of values and ethical behavior of the professional. All human services practitioners operate within a framework of guidelines or principles that govern what is, and what is not, ethically appropriate. Chapter 2 emphasizes that the human services professional has obligations to many individuals and groups. These include *clients, community and society, one's own colleagues, the profession, employers, one's self.* In addition, it discusses what happens when two or more of these obligations collide, presenting the practitioner with an ethical dilemma. Students are provided with models for resolving such situations. Specific examples of ethical challenges are given to help students anticipate situations they may encounter in practice.

Chapter 3 addresses culturally competent human services practice and recognizes the enormous diversity that professionals will encounter. It provides information on the context of practice, describes how cultural competence is integrated into the Generalist Intervention Model, and identifies specific practice knowledge and skills applicable to people of color and those with disabilities.

Chapter 4 completes this section by echoing the importance of diversity with a focus on gender-sensitive practice. The chapter looks at the unique challenges facing women from stressful life events to domestic violence, rape, and poverty. The emphasis, however, is on strengths and the importance of macro-level prevention.

The second section of the book, which includes Chapters 5 through 8, addresses the steps in the planned change approach used in the Generalist Intervention Model. Chapter 5 looks in detail at the tasks and activities required to engage the client system and to perform a competent assessment that takes into account micro through macro dimensions.

Chapter 6 discusses the planning process in detail by helping students develop skills in prioritizing problems, evaluating levels of intervention, establishing goals and objectives, specifying action steps, and contracting. Again, micro, mezzo, and macro aspects of planning are addressed.

Chapter 7 reviews the implementation phase of planned change with examples drawn from child abuse, crisis intervention, and alcohol and substance abuse. Implementation at all levels of practice, micro through macro, is considered.

Chapter 8 concludes this section by preparing students to evaluate their own practice and to terminate the professional–client relationship. Specific evaluation approaches are identified for both direct practice and entire programs. Major issues and problems in evaluation are reviewed to help students plan for and effectively examine their interventions. Termination is discussed with a focus on ethical considerations, tasks of termination, and managing reactions to endings.

The third section of the book is devoted to providing knowledge and skills for specific areas of practice. This includes work with individuals, families, groups, organizations, and communities, as well as the roles of advocacy, brokering, and case management.

Chapter 9 focuses on the skills needed to work with individuals. This includes interviewing, building relationships, verbal and nonverbal behavior, warmth, empathy, and genuineness. It also covers client self-determination and empowerment while addressing steps and challenges in the interview process.

Chapters 10 and 11 address understanding and working with families. The goal is to provide the students with knowledge needed for accurate family assessment as well as the skills required to intervene effectively.

Chapter 12 looks at human services practice with various groups. This includes both treatment and task groups. Topics covered include understanding the development process in groups, assessing groups, and leadership skills needed by the human services professional.

Chapter 13 is concerned about preparing students to function effectively in organizations while acquiring skills needed to bring about change in larger systems. The chapter looks at a variety of macro skills that the professional might employ as well as micro and mezzo skills that are applicable to working with large systems. Topics covered including fund-raising, budgeting, negotiating, mediating, needs assessments, and working with coalitions. Professional roles in the organizational and community venues are also discussed.

Chapter 14 provides an in-depth look at the human services professional as advocate. It looks at different types of advocacy and its goals and targets. It also identifies knowledge required to be an effective advocate and some of the practice skills helpful when engaging in the advocate role.

The last chapter in the book covers both brokering and case management. Because these are both major roles for the human services practitioner, it is essential that students be prepared to carry out the responsibilities of each effectively. Attention is given to the knowledge required of a broker as well as application of the planned change process to brokering.

Case management is reviewed with a goal of helping students become adept at this important role. Definitions of case management and the application of the planned change process to this role are addressed.

Each chapter in this book concludes with a section on the Brooks/Cole InfoTrac system. This resource allows students to acquire additional knowledge about topics covered in chapters as well as the opportunity to explore related issues.

There is also a list of Internet sites that can be helpful to the student.

Finally, an added feature of this book is its accompanying Web site, which provides students with a thorough discussion of professional writing and record keeping in human services. This add-on can be accessed by interested students or be made a part of the course at the discretion of the instructor. In addition, an *Instructor's Manual* includes multiple test questions for each chapter.

In summary, we hope that *The Generalist Model of Human Services Practice* will be a practical and flexible tool for students. Finally, we hope students will find its content interesting and even enjoy it.

Acknowledgments

No book is produced without the help, support, and cooperation of many people. We would like to express our sincere appreciation to those who have assisted with the continued success of this book. They include Lisa Gebo of the Wadsworth Group, who initially supported and encouraged us to pursue the book and whose enthusiasm and energy keeps us improving our efforts. Several people played key roles in the preparation of the manuscript, and we thank each of them. They include Sheila Walsh of the Wadsworth Group, whose conscientious work and assistance greatly facilitated the writing process; Becky Lubbers (University of Utah), who helped with the individual chapters and the reference list; and our great friend and colleague, Vicki Vogel (University of Wisconsin–Whitewater), who continually exceeds our expectations in her support and talents. We would also like to acknowledge those colleagues who took the time to review drafts of this manuscript and provide suggestions and recommendations for improvement. They include Mary Davidson, Columbia-Greene Community College; Kathleen Dotter, Springfield College; Chris Faiver, John Carroll University; Sharon Hall, University of Houston–Clear Lake; Mary Kay Kreider, St. Louis Community College–Meramec; Wm. Lynn McKinney, University of Rhode Island; and Joyce Shepherd, Henderson State University.

Finally, we wish to acknowledge our spouses, Nick Ashman and Jannah Mather, whose incredible support, encouragement, and patience continue to sustain us.

Grafton H. Hull, Jr.
Karen K. Kirst-Ashman

Photo Credits

PART ONE

An Introduction to the Generalist Intervention Model

CHAPTER 1
Introducing the Generalist Model of Human Services Practice

CHAPTER 2
Values and Ethics in Human Services Practice

CHAPTER 3
Culturally Competent Human Services Practice

CHAPTER 4
Gender-Sensitive Human Services Practice

CHAPTER 1

Introducing the Generalist Model of Human Services Practice

A 15-year-old can hardly make it through the morning until he can meet with his dealer and get some crack. He thinks briefly that it didn't used to be this bad, that he didn't used to "need" it this much. But he doesn't want to think about that for very long. It's too uncomfortable. He rationalizes that life is short, and he wants to make the most of it. Besides, all of his friends use drugs, too. He's no different.

Forlorn homeless people are starving in the streets. Public funding for a community mental health program has been drastically cut back. That program had provided a halfway house where people could stay, receive counseling, and have their medication monitored. Years ago the long-term, inpatient mental institution had been shut down. It was much too expensive. Now with the cutbacks, the community program can barely survive. People with serious mental and emotional problems have been turned away and are roaming the streets with nowhere to go.

A family of four—the fifth generation to live on their family farm—is dispossessed. They had several years of crop failures and were unable to pay back the loans they so desperately needed to survive at the time. They're living in their '94 Chevy van now. They can't find any housing they can possibly afford even though both parents work full-time, minimum-wage jobs.

Introducing Generalist Practice

The previous situations confront generalist human services practitioners daily. Human services workers do not pick and choose which problems and issues they would like to address. They see a problem, even a difficult problem, and try to help people solve it.

This book is about generalist practice and what human services professionals do to help people with problems in virtually any setting. There are many ways to describe what practitioners do. They work with individuals, families, groups, organizations, and communities. Their work is based on a body of knowledge, practice skills, and professional values. They work in settings that focus on children and families, health, justice, education, and economic status. As a consequence of this breadth of responsibilities, human services workers must have infinite flexibility, a solid knowledge base about the human condition, and a wide range of skills at their disposal.

Proposed here is a model of planned change based on a specific definition of generalist practice. It views practice from a systems perspective. The intent is to clarify in a practical manner what occurs in generalist human services practice. This chapter emphasizes that the human services planned change approach can be applied virtually to any situation, no matter how difficult or complex. Finally, the model integrates an orientation to advocacy and a focus on more than just an individual as the target of change. Mezzo systems such as small groups and families (the latter of which we consider to lie somewhere between the micro and mezzo levels of generalist practice), in addition to macro systems such as communities and large organizations, are also potential targets of intervention.

Integral links exist among micro, mezzo, and macro practice. Generalist practice skills are built upon each other in a progression from micro to mezzo to macro levels. Relating to individuals in groups (mezzo practice) requires basic micro skills. Likewise, macro practice requires mastery of both micro and mezzo skills for relating to and working with individuals and groups of individuals in organizational and community (macro) settings. As an introduction to generalist practice, this book establishes a framework for analyzing issues and problems from a generalist perspective. It then describes and discusses the micro skills necessary to formulate the foundation for the ongoing development of mezzo and macro skills. Linkages with mezzo and macro practice are emphasized throughout.

This chapter will:

- define and explain generalist practice, thoroughly discussing each concept involved;
- propose a Generalist Intervention Model that employs a seven-step planned change focus;
- briefly introduce content for the remainder of the text.

Defining Generalist Practice

Generalist practice may involve almost any helping situation. A generalist practitioner may be called upon to help a homeless family, a physically abused child, a pregnant teenager, a sick elderly person unable to care for him- or herself any longer, an alcoholic parent, a community that is trying to address its drug abuse problem, or a public assistance agency struggling to amend its policies to conform to new federal regulations. Therefore, generalist practitioners must be well prepared to address many kinds of difficult situations.

For our purposes, we will define generalist practice as: the application of an *eclectic knowledge base,*[1] *professional values,* and a *wide range of skills to target systems of any size,* for change within the context of four primary processes. First, generalist practice involves working effectively within an *organizational structure* and doing so *under supervision.* Second, it requires the assumption of a *wide range of professional roles.* Third, generalist practice involves the application of *critical thinking skills to the planned change process.* Fourth, it emphasizes *client empowerment.*

This chapter will address ten key concepts inherent in this definition. The order in which the concepts are presented does not imply their relative importance—each is significant. They are outlined in Highlight 1.1. A later portion of the chapter will describe details outlined under some of the ten major concepts, such as "fields of practice" and "systems theory" under the first concept, "acquisition of an eclectic knowledge base."

Figure 1.1 illustrates how these various concepts involved in the definition of generalist practice fit together. The large square in the top half of the figure portrays the *organizational structure.* An organization (or agency) will employ you to do a human

---

1. The term *eclectic* refers to selecting concepts, theories, and ideas from a wide range of perspectives and practice approaches.

HIGHLIGHT 1.1

An Outline of Concepts Involved in the Definition of Generalist Practice

1. **Acquisition of an eclectic knowledge base**
   A. Fields of practice
   B. Systems theory
   C. Ecological perspective
   D. Curriculum content areas
      i. human growth and development
      ii. helping relationships
      iii. research and program evaluation
      iv. social and cultural diversity
      v. professional identity, ethics, and ethical dilemmas
      vi. field practicum/internship
2. **Application of a wide range of skills**
   A. Micro
   B. Mezzo
   C. Macro
3. **Targeting any size system**
   A. Micro
   B. Mezzo
   C. Macro
4. **Working in an organizational structure**
5. **Appropriate use of supervision**
6. **Assumption of a wide range of professional roles**
7. **Employment of critical thinking skills**
8. **Use of a planned change process**
   A. Engagement
   B. Assessment
   C. Planning
   D. Implementation
   E. Evaluation
   F. Termination
9. **Emphasis on client empowerment**

services job. Organizational structure involves how lines of authority and communication operate within an agency. It also entails how the administration runs the organization and what the agency environment is like. As a generalist practitioner, you will work within this environment with all its constraints, requirements, and rules. Thus, Figure 1.1 pictures you as a generalist practitioner represented as a smaller rectangle within this large square.

In that same square you see the terms *knowledge, values,* and *skills.* These terms illustrate how you bring to your job position a broad knowledge base, professional values, and a wide range of skills so that you can do your work effectively. Also, in the large square at the top of the figure is another rectangle labeled *supervision.* An arrow runs from the supervision rectangle to the rectangle representing you. Part of working as a generalist practitioner involves receiving and using supervisory input appropriately.

The large square at the bottom of Figure 1.1 illustrates your potential *target system.* We have established that generalist practitioners may choose to work with a micro, mezzo, or macro system as the target of their change efforts. These three systems are arbitrarily portrayed in concentric squares to reflect their respective sizes.

An arrow flows from the organizational structure square down to the target system square. This arrow refers to how, as a generalist practitioner, you will apply your knowledge, skills, and values to help change a micro, mezzo, or macro system. Likewise, there are four smaller, curved arrows leading from concepts listed to the right of the application arrow into the application process. These arrows depict how you as a generalist practitioner will use a *wide range of professional roles, critical thinking skills, the planned change process,* and *client empowerment* as you work to solve a problem or help a system improve its functioning. The following sections will define and explain more thoroughly each concept portrayed in Figure 1.1.

Defining Generalist Practice: An Eclectic Knowledge Base

Acquisition of an eclectic knowledge base is the first dimension involved in the definition of generalist practice. Human services has a growing and progressive knowledge base. More and more is being researched and written about how practitioners can become increasingly effective in helping people solve problems. Additionally, the field has borrowed

Figure 1.1   *The Definition of Generalist Practice: A Pictorial View*

most significant and useful theories, information, and methods for generalist practice.

An Eclectic Knowledge Base: Fields of Practice

There are a number of ways to classify the kinds of knowledge generalist practitioners need. One is by fields of practice, which are broad areas in human services that address certain types of populations and needs. Each field of practice is a labyrinth of typical human problems and the services attempting to address them. Some fields of practice currently characterizing the profession include families and children, mental health, schools, aging, and substance abuse (Gibelman, 1995). Other fields of practice are occupational human services (focusing on work in employee assistance programs or directed toward organizational change), rural human services (addressing the unique problems of people living in rural areas), police human services (emphasizing work within police, courthouse, and jail settings to provide services to crime victims), and forensic human services (dealing with the law, educating lawyers, and serving as expert witnesses).

Generalist practitioners require information about people who need help in each of these areas. Workers also must be knowledgeable about the services available to meet needs and the major issues related to each area. On one hand, a practitioner may be called upon to work with a problem that clearly falls within one field of practice. On the other hand, a problem may involve several of these fields.

For example, the Stubs family comes to a practitioner's attention when a neighbor reports that Curran, a 5-year-old child, is frequently seen with odd-looking bruises on his arms and legs. The neighbor suspects child abuse. Upon investigation, the practitioner finds that the parents are indeed abusive. They often grab the child violently by a limb and throw him against the wall. This problem initially falls under the umbrella of family and children's services.

However, the practitioner also finds a number of other problems operating within the family. The mother, Grenda Stubs, is seriously depressed and frequently suicidal. She needs mental health services. Additionally, the father, Johann Stubs, is struggling with a drinking problem that is beginning to affect his performance at work. A program is available at his place of employment where an employee assistance practitioner helps employees deal with such problems.

There is a maternal grandmother, Lottie, living in the home with the Stubs family, whose physical health is failing. She is also overweight and finds

much knowledge from other fields like psychology and sociology. Human services workers then apply this knowledge to practice situations.

Knowledge involves understanding the dynamics of people's situations and recognizing the skills that work best in specific situations. We have emphasized that generalist practitioners need a broad knowledge base because they are called upon to help people solve such a wide variety of problems. Some important content areas discussed here include fields of practice, theoretical foundations (such as systems theory and the ecological perspective), and curriculum content. These are areas selected as some of the moving around by herself increasingly difficult. As a result, she is demanding more and more physical help and support from Grenda, who has back problems herself and finds helping her mother increasingly burdensome. Although she dreads the idea of nursing home placement, Grenda knows the issue must be addressed. Finally, Videla, the 12-year-old daughter in the family, is falling behind in school. Truancy is becoming a major problem. This last issue falls under the school's umbrella.

Most of the problems that practitioners face are complex. They may involve a variety of practice fields all at one time. In order to understand clients' needs, practitioners must know something about a wide range of problems and services.

An Eclectic Knowledge Base: Systems Theory

Systems theory provides practitioners with a conceptual perspective that can guide how they view the world. A *system* is a set of elements that are orderly and interrelated to make a functional whole. A person, your class, your family, and your college or university are all systems. Each involves many components that work together in order to function.

Understanding systems theory is especially important because generalist practice targets systems of virtually any size for change. Regardless of your field of practice, having a sound knowledge base in systems theory is helpful. As a generalist, you will evaluate any confronting problem from multiple perspectives. You will determine whether change is best pursued by individual, family, group, organizational, or community avenues. You might decide that any of these systems should be the target of your planned change efforts.

In order to understand how a systems model can provide the framework for intervention, one must understand some of the major concepts involved. These concepts include the terms *system, dynamic, interaction, boundary, subsystem, interface, input, output, homeostasis,* and *equifinality* (Zastrow & Kirst-Ashman, 2001).

We defined a *system* as a set of elements that forms an orderly, interrelated, and functional whole. Several aspects of this definition are important. The idea that a system is a "set of elements" means that a system can be composed of any type of things as long as these things have some relationship to each other. Things may be people, or they may be mathematical symbols. Regardless, the set of elements must be orderly and arranged in some pattern that is not simply random.

The set of elements must also be interrelated. They must have some kind of mutual relationship or connection with each other. Additionally, the set of elements must be functional. Together, they must be able to perform some regular task, activity, or function and fulfill some purpose. Finally, the set of elements must form a whole, a single entity. Examples of systems include a large nation, a public social services department, a Girl Scout troop, and a newly married couple.

Other concepts important in understanding systems are boundaries, subsystems, and interfaces. *Boundaries* are the repeatedly occurring patterns of behavior that characterize the relationships within a system and give that system a particular identity. You might think of boundaries as resembling your skin, which maintains you as a separate entity apart from the rest of your environment.

A boundary may exist between parents and their children. Parents maintain family leadership and provide support and nurturance to their children. A boundary may also exist between the protective service workers in a large county human services department and those who work in financial assistance. These orderly and interrelated groups set apart by specified boundaries in terms of their designated job responsibilities and the clients they serve. Yet, each group is part of the larger human services agency system.

A *subsystem* is a secondary or subordinate system. It may be thought of as a smaller system within a large system. Obvious examples of subsystems are the parental and sibling subsystems within a family. The group of protective services workers in a large human services agency forms one subsystem and the financial assistance workers another. These subsystems are set apart by designated boundaries, yet still are part of the larger, total system.

An *interface* is the point at which two systems or subsystems come together to communicate or interact. For example, one interface is the written contract established between a field instructor in an adoption agency and a student intern placed under his or her supervision. At the beginning of the semester, they discuss plans and goals for the semester. What tasks will the student be given, and what levels of performance are expected? With the help of the student's field liaison (that is, the student's college instructor), a written contract is established that clarifies these expectations. Contracts generally involve written, oral, or implied agreements between persons regarding expectations for the behaviors, actions, commitments, and responsibilities of each.

Systems concepts help practitioners focus on a target for intervention. The system may be an individual or a state government. The fact that the target is conceptualized as a system means that an understanding of the whole system and how its many elements work together is necessary. View, for example, an individual named Keung as a functioning system. Keung says he is depressed. The psychological aspects are only one facet of the entire functioning system; physical and social aspects are among numerous other system characteristics. A worker who looks at the person as a total system would inquire further about the individual's health and social circumstances. The worker finds that Keung is suffering both from a viral flu infection that has been "hanging on" for the past three weeks and from a chronic blood disease. Both of these elements affect his psychological state. Additionally, the worker discovers that Keung has recently been divorced and, since he has only partial custody, misses his three children desperately. (These three children might be thought of as a subsystem of Keung's family system.) These aspects, too, relate directly to Keung's depression.

Thus, a systems approach guides practitioners to look beyond a seemingly simplistic presenting problem. Workers view problems as being interrelated with all other aspects of the system. Many aspects work together to affect the functioning of the whole person.

A systems perspective also guides workers to view systems as *dynamic*—that is, having constant dynamic movement because problems and issues are forever changing. This perspective provides workers with an outlook that must be flexible. They must be ready to address new problems and apply new intervention strategies. For instance, a worker's assessment of the situation and intervention strategies would probably change if the man were fired from his current job or was reunited with his ex-wife.

Systems are constantly involved in *interaction* with each other. A system can be an individual, a group, or a large organization. A systems focus provides the worker with a framework that extends far beyond that of the individual as the sole target of intervention. A systems perspective diverts the attention from the individual to the interaction between that individual and the environment (Hartman, 1970). There is a constant flow of input and output among systems. *Input* is the energy, information, or communication flow received from other systems; *output* is the same flow emitted from a system to the environment or to other systems.

Reconsider Keung, the depressed man. His relationship with his ex-wife and children is seriously affecting not only him but also his interactions at work. Coworkers who were once his friends are tired of hearing him complain about how hard life is. They no longer like to associate with him.

Keung feels that he is in a dead-end, low-level, white-collar job that requires a minimal level of skill. Even worse, his boss has cut back his hours so he no longer can work any overtime. Now he can barely scrape by financially. The courts have mandated support payments for his children, which he has not been able to make for three months. His ex-wife is threatening not to let him see his kids if he does not get some money to her soon. This important focus of interaction serves as the interface between Keung and his ex-wife, Susana.

Of course, one should note that Susana views the situation from a totally different perspective. She attributes the divorce to the fact that Keung had a long series of affairs throughout their marriage. She had sacrificed her own employment and career in order to remain the primary caretaker of home and children. She just could not stand the infidelity any longer and filed for divorce. Her serious financial situation is magnified by the fact that she has neither an employment nor credit history of her own. She remains extremely angry at Keung and feels demanding support payments is her right. At this point in her life, she maintains clear-cut boundaries between herself and Keung.

Keung, on the other hand, is expending much energy to hold his life together. This situation is his output. However, he is receiving little input in return. As a result, he is unable to maintain his *homeostasis*, which refers to the tendency for a system to maintain a relatively stable, constant state of equilibrium or balance.

A systems perspective takes these many aspects of Keung's life into account. It focuses on his input, output, and homeostasis with respect to the many systems with which he is interacting. Sitting in an office with this man for 50 minutes each week and trying to get him to talk his way out of his depression will not suffice in generalist practice. His interactions with his family and impinging mezzo systems (e.g., his coworkers) and macro systems (e.g., the large company he works for and the state that mandates his support payments) provide potential targets of intervention and change. Can visits with his children and his support payment schedule be renegotiated? Can reconciliation with Susana be pursued? Are the policies mandating his support payments and controlling his visitation rights fair? Are there any support groups available that he could join whose members had similar situations to his own and from whom he could gain support? Is there any potential for job retraining or perhaps a job change?

Equifinality refers to the fact that there are many different means to the same end. In other words, there are many ways of viewing a problem and, thus, many potential means of solving it. Keung's interaction with friends, family, coworkers, governmental offices, and health care systems all affect his psychological state. Therefore, targets of intervention may involve change or interaction with any of these other systems.

Conceptualizing Workers and Clients as Systems

A helpful orientation for practice is to conceptualize yourself and your clients in terms of systems. We have already established that a target system or target of change is the system that practitioners need "to change or influence in order to accomplish (their) goals" (Pincus & Minahan, 1973, p. 58). Targets of change may be individual clients, families, formal groups, administrators, or policymakers, depending on what you need to change. At the micro level, a 5-year-old child with behavior problems might be the target of change, the goal being to improve behavior. At the mezzo level, a support group of people with eating disorders might be the target of change, aiming to control their eating behavior. Finally, at the macro level an agency director might be the target of change if your aim is to improve some agency policy and she is the primary decision maker capable of implementing that change.

Three other systems critical to the planned change process are the client, target, and action systems (Pincus & Minahan, 1973; Resnick, 1980a, 1980b). A *client system* is any individual, family, group, organization, or community that will ultimately benefit from generalist human services intervention. Your clients are client systems. The *change agent system* is the individual who initiates the planned change process. This book assumes you will function as the change agent system while helping your client systems.

You might gain support of and join in coalitions with others who also believe in the proposed change, especially when you work for changes at the macro level. Then you as a single change agent might become part of a larger system. Whether you undertake macro change by yourself or join together with others, you are or are part of an *action system.* The action system then includes those people who agree and are committed to work together in order to attain the proposed change. An action system might undertake the planned change process to change an agency policy, develop a new program, or institute some project like evaluating intervention methodology or setting up agency in-service training sessions.

An Eclectic Knowledge Base: The Ecological Perspective

The ecological perspective is another relevant part of human services' knowledge base. Like systems theory, it provides a useful framework for generalist practice. This text assumes a systems theory approach; however, it takes and utilizes selected concepts from the ecological perspective that are exceptionally useful in describing human interaction with other systems. For instance, the concept of social environment is grounded in the ecological perspective. Generalist practitioners work with clients within the context of their social environments.

The Relationship between Systems Theory and the Ecological Perspective

There exists some debate regarding the relationship between systems theory and the ecological perspective. That is, to what extent are the theoretical approaches similar and dissimilar? The ecological approach assumes a person-in-environment focus. Each perspective has, at various times, been described as being a theory, model, or a theoretical underpinning.

First, a number of major concepts involved in the ecological perspective will be explained. Subsequently, some similarities and differences will be briefly discussed. Finally, the question of which approach is best will be addressed.

Ecological Concepts

In order to understand similarities and differences between the two perspectives, you need to know the terms and principles involved in each. We have already reviewed some systems theory terminology, including system, dynamic, interaction, input, output, homeostasis, and equifinality. The following are some commonly used ecological concepts.

The *social environment* involves the conditions, circumstances, and human interactions that encompass human beings. Persons are dependent on effective interactions with this environment in order to survive and thrive. The social environment includes the types of homes people live in, the types of work they do, the amount of money available, and the laws and social rules they live by. The social environment also includes all the individuals, groups, organizations, and systems with which a person comes into contact.

A *person-in-environment* focus sees people as constantly interacting with various systems around them. These systems include the family, friends, work, social services, politics, religion, goods and services, and educational systems. The person is portrayed as being dynamically involved with each. Human services practice then is directed at improving the interactions among the person and the various systems. This focus is referred to as improving person-in-environment fit.

People communicate and interact with others in their environments. The ecological perspective refers to such dynamic interactions (stressed in systems theory) as *transactions* (i.e., something is communicated or exchanged). These interactions or transactions may be positive or negative. A positive transaction may be the revelation that the one you dearly love loves you in return. A negative transaction may involve being fired from a job you have held for 15 years.

The ecological perspective stresses the concept of *energy* as the natural power of active involvement among people and their environments. Energy can take the form of input or output (concepts also emphasized in systems theory). *Input* is a form of energy coming into a person's life and adding to that life (e.g., an elderly person in failing health may need substantial physical assistance and emotional support in order to continue performing necessary daily tasks) or output.

Output, on the other hand, is a form of energy going out of a person's life or taking something away from it. For instance, a person may volunteer time and effort to work on a political campaign.

As in systems theory, the *interface* is the exact point at which the interaction between an individual and the environment takes place. During an assessment of a person-in-environment situation, the interface must be clearly in focus in order to target the appropriate interactions for change. For example, a couple entering marriage counseling may first state that their problem concerns disagreements about how to raise the children. On further exploration, however, their inability to communicate their real feelings to each other surfaces. The actual problem—the inability to communicate—is the interface at which one individual affects the other. Each person is part of the other's social environment. If the interface is inaccurately targeted, much time and energy will be wasted before getting at the real problem.

Adaptation is the capacity to adjust to surrounding environmental conditions. It implies change. A person must change or adapt to new conditions and circumstances in order to continue functioning effectively. As people are constantly exposed to changes and stressful life events, they need to be flexible and capable of adaptation. Practitioners frequently help people in this process of adaptation. A person may have to adapt to a new significant other,

a new job, or a new neighborhood. Adaptation usually requires energy in the form of effort. Practitioners often help direct people's energies so that they are most productive.

People are affected by their environments and vice versa. People can and do change their environments in order to adapt successfully. For instance, a person would find surviving a Montana winter in the natural environment challenging without shelter. Therefore, those who live in Montana change and manipulate their environment by clearing land and constructing heated buildings. They change their environment so they are better able to adapt to it. Therefore, adaptation often implies a two-way process involving both the individual and the environment.

Coping is a form of human adaptation and implies a struggle to overcome problems. Although adaptation may involve responses to new positive or negative conditions, coping refers to the way we deal with the problems we experience. For example, a person might have to cope with the sudden death of a parent or the birth of a baby.

Interdependence is the mutual reliance of each person on each other person. Individuals are interdependent as they rely on other individuals and groups of individuals in the social environment. Likewise, these other individuals are interdependent on one another for input, energy, services, and consistency. People cannot exist without each other. The business executive needs the farmer to produce food and customers to purchase goods. Likewise, the farmer must sell food products to the executive in order to get money to buy seeds, tools, and other essentials. People—especially in a highly industrialized society—are interdependent and need each other in order to survive.

Similarities between Systems Theory and the Ecological Perspective

Some basic similarities exist between systems theory and the ecological perspective. Both emphasize systems and focus on the dynamic interaction among many levels of systems. Some of the terms and concepts (e.g., the terms *input, output,* and *interface*) are similar. Additionally, each provides practitioners a framework with which to view the world. Finally, both perspectives emphasize external interactions instead of internal functioning. In other words, from a human services point of view, both emphasize helping people improve their interactions with other systems. As a result, these two perspectives are different from a focus on fixing or curing the individual.

Differences between Systems Theory and the Ecological Perspective

In the simplest sense, there are two major differences between systems theory and the ecological perspective. First, the ecological approach refers to living, dynamic interactions. The emphasis is on active participation. People, for example, have dynamic transactions with each other and with their environments. Systems theory, on the other hand, assumes a broader perspective. It can be used to refer to inanimate, mechanical operations such as a mechanized assembly line in a pea-canning plant. It can also be used to describe the functioning of a human family.

A second difference between the ecological perspective and systems theory concerns how different terms are emphasized. Systems concepts focus on boundaries, subsystems, homeostasis, and equifinality. Ecological concepts, on the other hand, stress the social environment, adaptation, coping, and interdependence. Table 1.1 summarizes some of the differences and similarities involved in concepts characterizing each.

Which Perspective Is Best?

Both systems theory and the ecological perspective provide major tools for human services (Iatridis, 1995). The important thing is that both emphasize interactions with the environment. Depending on the circumstance, one perspective might be more helpful to employ than the other. For example, systems theory might be more helpful when addressing problems within a family. Using concepts like subsystems and boundaries helps practitioners understand the ongoing dynamics. Likewise, analysis of a particular family system using these concepts provides cues for how to proceed to improve family functioning.

On the other hand, an ecological perspective can also be useful. The concept of transactions with the social environment helps provide focus when a homeless family is not getting the resources it needs. A focus on the interface between family and environment leads a practitioner to emphasize getting the family the services and support it requires to survive.

An Eclectic Knowledge Base: Curriculum Content Areas

There is another way of classifying what bodies of knowledge practitioners need: One can look at the educational content of human services programs. Commonly required areas of content currently include human growth and development, helping relationships, practice skills, research, social and cultural diversity, values and ethics, and field practica.

Curriculum Content Area: Human Growth and Development

Knowledge about human growth and development is an essential foundation on which to build practice skills. Accurate assessment of the person, problem, and situation is a critical step in effective intervention. The environment, however, is also vitally important in the analysis and understanding of human behavior. As human services has a person-in-environment focus, the interactions between individuals, systems, and the environment are critical (Sheafor, Horejsi, & Horejsi, 2000). Such a conceptual perspective provides practitioners with a symbolic representation of how to interpret the world. It provides ideas for how to assess clients' situations and identify their alternatives.

People are constantly and dynamically involved in social transactions. There is ongoing activity, communication, and change. Human services assessment

Table 1.1   *Major Concepts in Systems Theory and the Ecological Perspective*

Systems Theory Concepts	Ecological Perspective Concepts	Similar Concepts in Both
System	Social Environment	Dynamic Interaction (Transactions)
Boundaries	Person-in-Environment	Interface
Subsystem	Energy	Input
Homeostasis	Adaptation	Output
Equifinality	Coping	
	Interdependence	

seeks to answer the question, "What is it in any particular situation that causes a problem to continue despite the client's expressed wish to change it?" A person-in-environment perspective allows practitioners to assess many aspects of a situation. Assessment may involve not only individual, personal characteristics and experiences (micro events) but also mezzo and macro events (Kirst-Ashman, 1989). These concepts are grounded in systems theory.

Mezzo events involve interactions with other people in the immediate environment. These experiences often concern relationships with peer groups and immediate work groups. Family events lie somewhere between the micro and mezzo levels of generalist practice. Because of the intimacy and intensity of family relationships and the importance of the family context to individuals, families deserve special status and attention.

Macro events involve people's transactions with large organizations and systems around the individual. An individual's place within the total scheme of things can be analyzed. Such macro events may include poverty, discrimination, social pressures, and the effects of social policies. These events mean that clients' problems are not viewed solely as each client's own fault. The forces surrounding the client frequently cause or contribute to problems. Thus, practitioners must focus their assessment on many levels. How the client and the problem fit into the larger scheme of things is critically important.

For instance, consider Keno, a 15-year-old inner-city gang member. The gang is involved in drug dealing, which, of course, is illegal. However, when assessing the situation and what might be done about it, a broader perspective is necessary. Looking at how the environment encourages and even supports the illegal activity is critical in understanding how to solve the problem. Keno's father is no longer involved with Keno's family. Now only Keno, his mother, and three younger brothers remain. Keno's mother works a six-day-per-week, nine-hour-per-day second shift job at the Road Kill Diner, a local all-night restaurant where she cooks. Although she loves her children dearly, she can barely make ends meet. She has little time for their supervision, especially Keno's, as he is the oldest.

It must be understood that adolescence is a turbulent period of growth and development. Keno is undergoing puberty, experiencing significant physical changes and maturing sexually. He is striving desperately to achieve his own sense of self and identity. Fitting in and being accepted by peers is also critically important during this period.

All of the neighborhood kids seem to belong to one gang or another, which gives them a sense of identity and importance and provides social support, where, in many instances, such support is otherwise almost completely lacking. Easy access to drugs offers a readily available chance to escape from impoverished, depressing, and apparently hopeless conditions. Finally, gang membership gives these young people a source of income. In fact, they can get relatively large amounts of money in a hurry.

The gang members' alternatives appear grim. There are few, if any, positive role models to show them other ways of existence. They do not see their peers or adults close to them becoming corporate lawyers, brain surgeons, nuclear physicists, or editors. In fact, they do not see anyone who is going or has gone to college. Finishing high school is considered quite a feat. Neighborhood unemployment runs at more than 50 percent. A few part-time, minimum-wage jobs are available—cleaning washrooms at Bug Butler's Burger Palace or hauling heavy packages off trucks at Freddie's Fabulous Food Center. These options are unappealing alternatives to the immediate sources of gratification provided by gang membership and drug dealing. Even if another minimal source of income could be found, the other rewarding aspects of gang membership would be lost. Also, there's the all-consuming problem of having no positive future to look forward to. The future looks pretty bleak, so the excitement of the present remains seductive.

This situation is not meant to imply that joining vicious gangs and participating in illegal activities is right for people like Keno. Nor does it mean that Keno's plight is hopeless. Going beyond a focus on the individual to assess the many environmental impacts and interactions gives the practitioner a better understanding of the whole situation. The answer might not be to send Keno to the state juvenile correctional facility for a year or two and then put him back in the same community with the same friends and same problems. That focuses on the individual in a limited manner.

A generalist human services practitioner views Keno as a person who's acting as part of a family and a community. Keno is affected, influenced, supported, and limited by his immediate environment. Continuing along this line of thought, other questions can be raised. For example, how might Keno's environment be changed? What other alternatives are available to him? Many potential alternatives would involve major changes in the larger systems around him. Neighborhood youth centers with staff serving as positive role models could be developed as an alternative to gang membership. Keno's school system could be evaluated. Does it have enough resources to give Keno a good education? Is there a teacher who could single Keno out and serve as his mentor and enthusiastic supporter? Can a mentor system be established within the school? Are scholarships and loans available to offer Keno a viable alternative of college or trade school? Can positive role models demonstrate to Keno and his peers that alternative ways of life may be open to them? Where might the resources for implementation of any of these ideas come from?

Concerning Keno's family environment, can additional resources be provided? These resources might include food and housing assistance, good day care for his younger brothers, and even educational opportunities for Keno's mother so that she, too, could see a brighter future. Is there a Big Brother organization to provide support for Keno and his siblings? Can the neighborhood be made a better place to live? Can crime be curbed and housing conditions improved?

There obviously are no easy answers. Scarcity of resources remains a fundamental problem. However, this illustration is intended to show how a generalist practitioner would look at a variety of options and targets of change—not just at Keno.

In summary, knowledge about human growth and development is essential in generalist practice. Only then can the total picture be better understood and a wider range of possible options identified.

Curriculum Content Area: Helping Relationships

A second typical curriculum area is helping relationships and practice skills. Courses in this area focus on a variety of professional activities that impact on our work with clients. This includes interpersonal relationship and interviewing skills, how to establish an effective professional relationship, and acquiring the knowledge needed to work effectively with individuals, families, groups, and larger systems. These courses also cover the helping process, practice techniques, and appropriate theories including systems theory. Students learn how to use various assessment tools, understand basic principles that affect assessment, and ethical implications of assessments.

Curriculum Content Area: Research and Program Evaluation

Knowledge about human services research is important for two basic reasons. First, it can help practitioners to evaluate their effectiveness. Framing human service interventions so that they can be evaluated through research provides information about which specific techniques work best with which problems. Evaluation of practice throughout the intervention process can help to determine whether or not a worker is really helping a client.

The second reason is that accumulated research helps to build a foundation for planning effective interventions. Knowledge about what has worked best in the past provides guidelines for approaches and techniques to be used in the present and in the future. Research forms the basis for the development of whole programs and policies that affect large numbers of people. Such knowledge can also be used to generate new theories and ideas to further enhance the effectiveness of human services.

The content of human services research tends to fall within four major categories (Reid, 1995). First, many studies involve the behavior of individual clients and their interactions with others close to them, including families and small groups. Second, much research focuses on how services are provided to clients, what specifically such services involve, and how successfully they accomplish their goals. Third, studies address practitioners' attitudes and educational backgrounds, in addition to major trends in the entire human service profession itself. The fourth research category involves the study of "organizations, communities, and social policy" (1995, p. 2044). This latter category emphasizes the importance of the larger social environment and its effects on clients' behavior and conditions.

Thus, research is important to human services practice. Research informs and supports intervention approaches, identifies theories and programs that are more likely to be effective, and helps workers ensure that the client is being helped, rather than hurt, by what workers do.

Each practitioner must master three dimensions of basic research skills. First, practitioners need research skills to evaluate effectively the work they do with clients on all levels. Evaluation is the fifth step of the planned change process emphasized in this book. It involves determining whether what you do as a practitioner is effective or not. On a micro level, are your clients' needs being met? Are they generally attaining their goals? On a mezzo level, is the group you are running effective? Are individual members and the entire group as a whole accomplishing their respective goals?

The second dimension of basic research skills necessary for generalist practice involves the evaluation of macro system effectiveness. On a macro level, is your agency generally effective in its provision of services? Are clients really getting what they need? Practitioners, thus, need research competence in evaluating the effectiveness of service provision at all three levels of practice.

A third dimension is the ability to understand, analyze, and critically evaluate human services literature and research. Wide varieties of competing intervention approaches and techniques are available. Practitioners require research competence to make effective choices in their own generalist practice. How much faith can you place in some specific research findings, considering the research methodology used? How useful is the research for your particular client population? How relevant are the findings for your own generalist practice?

Curriculum Content Area: Social and Cultural Diversity

Social and cultural diversity refers to the vast range of differences among people, including those related to race, ethnicity, cultural background, place of origin, age, physical and mental ability, spirituality, values, sexual orientation, and gender. Human services by nature addresses virtually any type of issue posed by any type of person from any type of background. Practitioners must be open minded, nonjudgmental, knowledgeable, and skilled in order to work with and help any client.

Membership in groups that differ from the young white male heterosexual mainstream can place people at increased risk of discrimination and oppression. *Discrimination* is "the prejudgment and negative treatment of people based on identifiable characteristics such as race, gender, religion, or ethnicity" (Barker, 1999, p. 132). *Oppression* involves putting extreme limitations and constraints on the members of some identified group. Discrimination and oppression often result from *stereotypes,* fixed mental images of members belonging to a group based on assumed attributes that portray an overly simplified opinion about that group. Stereotypes neither consider nor appreciate individual differences.

One might envision a number of scenarios concerning potential discrimination and oppression based on stereotypes. For instance, think of an African American family moving into a virtually all-white,

small midwestern town. Picture a 55-year-old woman applying for a job in a software production center where all employees are under age 30. Or consider a gay couple expressing affection in a primarily heterosexual bar.

Membership in any diverse group provides a different set of environmental circumstances. A wealthy Asian American middle-aged man who just immigrated to Los Angeles from Tokyo experiences a very different world from an elderly woman of Scandinavian heritage living in Michigan's economically depressed upper peninsula.

Promotion of Social Justice. *Social justice* involves the idea that in a perfect world, all citizens would have identical benefits, opportunities and rights. In real life, social justice is a hard goal to attain. Rarely are rights and resources fairly and equitably distributed. Even the definitions of *fair* and *equitable* are widely debated. What does *fair* mean? Does it mean that all people should receive the same income regardless of what work they do or even whether or not they have jobs at all? The point is that practitioners must be vigilantly aware of the existence of injustice. It is our ethical responsibility to combat injustice whenever it is necessary and possible to do so.

Cultural Competency. Another critical concept related to social justice and cultural diversity is *cultural competency*, or the knowledge and skills practitioners require to work effectively with diverse clients (Lum, 1999a). *Culture* is "the sum total of life patterns passed on from generation to generation within a group of people and includes institutions, language, religious ideals, habits of thinking, artistic expressions, and patterns of social and interpersonal relationships" (Hodge, Struckmann, & Trost, 1975; Lum, 1999a, p. 2). Aspects of culture are often related to people's ethnic, racial, and spiritual heritage. People from different cultural backgrounds may be populations-at-risk due to discrimination and oppression from other dominating groups. Cultural competency, strongly supported by many ethical codes, involves the following six dimensions for practitioners (Arredondo et al., 1996; Lum, 1999a; NASW, 1996, 1.05):

1. Development of an awareness of personal values, assumptions, and biases.
2. Establishment of a "positive orientation toward multiculturalism," an appreciation of other cultures, and a nurturance of attitudes that respect differences.

3. Understanding of how their own cultural heritage and belief system differs from and may influence interaction with clients who have a different cultural background.
4. Recognition of the existence of stereotypes, discrimination, and oppression on various diverse groups.
5. Commitment to learning about clients' cultures.
6. Acquisition of effective skills for working with people from other cultures.

Curriculum Content Area: Identity and Ethics

Another curriculum content area in human services' knowledge base is identity and ethics. The human service practitioner has an identity that includes membership in a professional organization and adherence to a set of ethical standards. Because of their profound significance, professional ethics also compose the second major concept in the definition of generalist practice (see Highlight 1.1).

Ethics. Ethics involve principles that specify what is good and what is bad and clarify what should and should not be done. Practitioners have a specific set of ethical standards that is based on professional values. Ethics and values are clearly related, although they are not synonymous. Loewenberg, Dolgoff, and Harrington explain that "[e]thics are deduced from values and must be in consonance with them. The difference between them is that values are concerned with what is *good* and *desirable,* while ethics deal with what is *right* and *correct*" (2000, p. 22). Values determine *what* beliefs are appropriate. Ethics address what to *do* with, or how to *apply,* those beliefs.

Human services values focus on "a commitment to human welfare, social justice, and individual dignity" (Reamer, 1987, p. 801). This focus frames the perspective with which practitioners view their work with people. In other words, the well-being of people is more important than making the largest business profit or becoming the most famous actor. Practitioners care about other people and spend their time helping people improve the conditions of their lives.

Human services values address individual needs and concerns, those of communities, and those of society in general. Professional values are interwoven throughout micro, mezzo, and macro levels of practice. The individual well-being of a person with a severe physical disability is critical, as is the way public services and laws generally treat such persons.

Ethical codes address several aspects of professional responsibility. These areas include practitioners' ethical responsibilities to clients, colleagues, the pro-

fession, society, and oneself (National Organization for Human Service Education, 2000).

Superficially, this situation appears simple. The profession provides ethical guidelines for how to help people. Theoretically, then, all you should have to do is closely adhere to those guidelines, and ethical practice should be easy. You are simply supposed to look out for the well-being of your clients, right?

To say that people are complicated, as is life in general, is a cliché. However, one can also say that the application of ethics to actual decision making is often tremendously complicated. Many times, ethical conflict will arise. In these situations, adherence to one ethical standard will effectively contradict adherence to another ethical standard.

For example, clients' privacy rights must be respected and confidentiality of all client-related information protected. However, some situations may require that confidences be shared with others and that privacy can't be maintained.

Consider the situation in which a client, Bob, reveals that he has recently been given the diagnosis that he is HIV positive. This condition is usually fatal in the long run, and the practitioner, Mia, knows that Bob has been having unprotected sexual relations with several people over the past months. During their meetings, Bob has specifically named these people. After discussing options, he refuses to tell his sexual partners about his diagnosis. Additionally, for a variety of reasons, Mia doubts that Bob will begin to use precautions against spreading the disease. Agency policy mandates that practitioners may not violate clients' confidentiality, which means that according to policy a practitioner may not tell anyone about the HIV-positive diagnosis without Bob's clearly expressed written permission. Mia worries that, among other things, prior sexual partners unaware of the HIV diagnosis and their potential exposure may continue to spread the disease.

Which ethical concepts are more important: respect for Bob's privacy, compliance with agency policy, or the general welfare of society and the well-being of other people? The worker cannot fulfill all her responsibilities. Human services workers also owe an obligation to their employers, but this can pose a problem when that obligation conflicts with the client's rights. In such cases, practitioners must exercise their own best judgment.

Ethical dilemmas are numerous, and the potential variety of ethical dilemmas is endless. Professional values and ethics do provide some basic guidelines. However, many times, a practitioner have to make choices about what is more more critical to do. Chapter 2 addresses making ethical decisions. Suggestions for evaluating problems, breaking down potential solutions, and prioritizing ethical principles will be discussed. Highlight 1.2 provides a further example of how complex ethical dilemmas can be.

Professional Identity. Professional identity is another aspect of curriculum that applies to the human services practitioner. For example, we are expected to understand the history of the profession, various roles helpers play, and the professional organizations that offer membership and provide ethical guidelines for practitioners. Licensing and other forms of professional credentialing are also covered at some point in the curriculum because they have a direct impact on our practice. Finally, the effect of public policy on the human services worker is likely to be addressed. The goal of the identity emphasis is on informing the potential human services helper of "all aspects of professional functioning" (Council for Accreditation of Counseling and Related Educational Programs, 2000, p. 7).

Curriculum Content Area: Field Practicum

Field practicum is another curriculum area in human services' knowledge base. As the culmination of their education, most students find their field practicum a valuable and challenging experience. The student engages in supervised practice and is provided opportunities to apply classroom learning in an agency setting. Goals of the field practicum include: expanding practice experiences; developing, integrating, and applying practice knowledge, skills, and values; providing opportunities for students to integrate what they've learned from other curriculum content areas; and enhancing commitment to and identification with the profession.

Defining Generalist Practice: Application of a Wide Range of Skills to Target Systems of Any Size

We have reviewed the knowledge base practitioners need as part of their foundation for generalist practice

---

HIGHLIGHT 1.2

Ethical Dilemmas

One of the ethical dilemmas commonly faced by practitioners is deciding who is to get help when there are limited resources. In many instances, there is a given amount of money, and a practitioner must choose regarding who will and will not receive help.

The following is an exercise designed to help you understand how difficult ethical dilemmas can be. (Later, Chapter 2 will help you work through some of the dilemmas practitioners commonly face. It will also provide suggested structures for making difficult decisions.)

The exercise

You have $35,000 to spend. You must choose one situation where it will be spent from ten possibilities. Each situation requires the full amount of $35,000 in order to do any good. Dividing the money up would be useless and would help no one. You must decide where to spend the money.

Which of the following persons should have the $35,000 made available to help him or her?

1. A premature infant (born three months early), who needs to be maintained in an incubator and receive medical benefits.
2. A 52-year-old man, who needs a heart transplant in order to survive.
3. Your 52-year-old father, who needs a heart transplant.
4. A 5-year-old child, who is HIV positive.
5. You, who recently graduated and have been out of work for six months.
6. A divorced single mother with three children, a tenth-grade education, and nothing but the clothes on her back.
7. A person who has a cognitive disability (formerly referred to as mental retardation), who needs the money to live in a group home with others who have similar disabilities.
8. A 14-year-old runaway, addicted to cocaine and alcohol, who has been prostituting herself to survive and needs the money to enter a drug treatment program.
9. A convicted child sexual abuser, who was himself sexually abused as a child and seeks rehabilitation.
10. A dispossessed urban family—a couple in their late 20s with three small children.

There are no easy answers.

and emphasized the significance of human services values and ethics. The third and fourth concepts in the definition of generalist practice are the *wide range of skills* needed to implement the planned change process and the use of these skills to target virtually a *system of any size*. These two dimensions are so intertwined that we will address them together.

Common Generalist Skills

Specific skills characterize different levels of practice. However, six core activities are also necessary, regardless of the type of intervention (Sheafor & Landon, 1987, p. 668). First, generalist practitioners must *prepare* for the intervention before they begin. They need to get information and make plans, not just rush in haphazardly and "do something." What they do must be based on professional knowledge, skills, and values.

Second, generalist practitioners must know how to *communicate*. Knowing how to form a relationship and talk to clients is essential, whether they are single teen mothers receiving public assistance, state senators, an agency's Board of Directors, or a crowd of 900 people marching to gain resources for persons living with AIDS. Effective communication involves understanding the issues and problems. Communication allows you to make your intent clear to others. Words must be used in such a way that others can understand. Both verbal and nonverbal communication (for example, posture, eye contact, and gestures) must coincide to help deliver the intended message.

Finally, communication involves good listening skills. Not only must you hear what others are saying to you, but you must also listen to what they mean.

Third, generalist practitioners need to *analyze* the problem situation regardless of whether individuals, groups, or communities are involved. This skill concerns "sorting and thinking through the various factors that have an impact on the client system and selecting the appropriate intervention approach" (Sheafor & Landon, 1987, p. 668).

The fourth skill common to all levels of practice is formulating a *contract* with the client system. Problems must be clearly identified and goals established with clients. Procedures to attain goals—including who is to do what and when—should be clearly specified.

Fifth, the generalist practitioner may need to assume a variety of *roles* when addressing a problem. A professional role is behavior and activity involved in performing some designated function for a specified purpose. For example, if the client desperately needs help, the worker may need to function as an advocate. Other roles might include educator, mobilizer, broker, counselor, mediator, and facilitator (these roles will be defined later in the chapter).

The sixth skill needed, regardless of level of practice, is *stabilizing*. The practitioner needs to continually guide and monitor the intervention and its progress. Goals may need modification when relevant conditions change. New roles may be assumed in order to continue progress. Additionally, workers must evaluate the effectiveness of their interventions. Evaluation is necessary whether clients are individuals, groups, or entire communities. Likewise, workers need to identify when goals are attained and termination achieved.

Micro Skills for Generalist Practice.   We mentioned earlier that generalist practice skills are to some extent built upon each other as we move from micro to mezzo to macro levels. Human services obviously involves working with people. In order to work with people, basic interpersonal skills, including good communication skills, need to be mastered. These basic skills are the same regardless of whether you are working with one individual, a group of people, or representatives of a large organization or community.

Endless scenarios come to mind that illustrate the use of micro skills. Practitioners counsel people addicted to alcohol or other drugs. They try to find places to live and other resources for homeless families. They manage service provision for elderly people who are ill or for people who have developmental disabilities and require numerous resources. They investigate potential child abuse situations. They help displaced homemakers and their families who are survivors of domestic violence.

Chapter 9 will focus on these micro-level skills. Relationship-building skills will be explained. The importance of displaying warmth, empathy, and genuineness will be discussed. Various aspects of communication will be examined, including verbal and nonverbal and the discrepancies between the two. Basic interviewing skills with a planned change orientation will be explained. A broad range of possible verbal responses to clients will be reviewed. Finally, a number of challenges in interviewing will be examined.

Mezzo Skills for Generalist Practice.   Practitioners use mezzo skills with a wide range of groups. They run support groups for people who are HIV positive and for those who are primary caregivers of elderly patients. They run staffings to evaluate progress and establish treatment recommendations for young people with serious emotional and behavioral problems living in group homes and residential treatment centers. They participate in educational groups in schools to talk about birth control. They facilitate activity groups in nursing homes for the elderly. They run agency meetings aimed at developing new treatment programs or a new policy manual.

Building upon the basic interpersonal skills established in Chapter 9, we will examine skills used in mezzo practice in Chapter 12. First, basic group dynamics (that is, what tends to go on within any actively functioning group) will be explored. Before group work skills can be applied, how groups form rules and expectations, select leaders, and distribute power must be understood.

The application of micro-level relationship building and communication skills will then be specifically applied to group settings. We will review the types of groups practitioners frequently encounter and explain common human service roles. Finally, we will discuss specific skills practitioners often need to help groups function and effectively work toward achieving their goals. For instance, how can goals be formulated to satisfy the needs of all group members? How can conflict among group members be managed?

Macro Skills for Generalist Practice. In order to solve problems involving organizations or communities, mastery of both micro- and mezzo-level skills is necessary. Working with macro-level problems requires working with other individuals and working with groups of individuals. Chapter 13 will introduce you to the types of situations practitioners frequently encounter in working with larger systems and organizations. The relationship between micro- and mezzo-level skills for those involved in macro-level interventions will be described. Finally, we will examine the specific skills useful in macro practice and the roles practitioners frequently assume.

Macro practice most frequently involves issues concerning a number of people or a specific group of people. For example, illegal drug use might be identified as a major difficulty in an urban neighborhood. Violence over drug sales is escalating. More and more people, including teens, are being shot as dealers and users squabble. The incidence of persons diagnosed as HIV positive is abruptly increasing as addicts share needles and contaminate each other. Child neglect and abuse in the community are skyrocketing. Truancy rates are soaring. Parents on a "high" fail to attend to their young children. Parents' anger at themselves, at unsatisfied needs, and at the world in general is taken out on the easiest scapegoats: their children.

Approaches to solving these problems may reach far beyond helping an individual break a drug habit. Drug rehabilitation programs may be needed. Policies regarding the treatment of dealers may need to be addressed. Alternatives to a drug-related lifestyle may need to be pursued and developed for community residents. A youth center may be needed as a place for younger people to socialize, participate in activities, and have fun. Community residents may need job training and help in finding adequate employment.

The list of needs and possibilities is endless. A practitioner involved in the community needs skills for organizing residents to come together and plan solutions. Skills in approaching community leaders and policy makers are important so that they may be persuaded to support and help finance needed services. Fund-raising skills are often necessary when other funding sources are unavailable. Skills are needed for a variety of macro practice roles, including: initiating action, negotiating solutions, advocating on the behalf of clients when they are unable to do so adequately for themselves, speaking on behalf of groups to make their issues and needs clear to those in decision-making positions, organizing people into groups that seek to have their own needs met, mediating among parties so that differences will be resolved, and, finally, providing consultation to people in need of information. Highlight 1.3 illustrates some case scenarios where macro practice skills may be useful.

Defining Generalist Practice: Working in an Organizational Structure under Supervision

As a human services practitioner, you are most likely to *work within an organizational structure* (or agency context) under *supervision*. These are the fifth and sixth concepts in the definition for generalist practice. *Organizational structure* is the formal and informal manner in which tasks and responsibilities, lines of authority, channels of communication, and dimensions of power are established and coordinated within an organization. Understanding organizational structure involves knowing how decisions are made and what chain of command is followed, what procedures regulate service provision to clients, and how your own job expectations fit into the larger scheme of things.

Supervision is the process by which a designated supervisor watches over a worker's performance, directs activities, and provides feedback. A good supervisor can be invaluable in helping you get your work done effectively within an agency setting.

HIGHLIGHT 1.3

The Macro-Level Approach

It's very easy for practitioners, especially when they are just beginning in practice, to focus on changing the individual. Using interviewing and planned change techniques with an individual in a practice situation is exciting. Figuring out how an individual client thinks and functions is fascinating. Additionally, the individual is right in front of you. The other systems with which the individual client is involved are much more abstract. Their interactions and effects may seem vague and distant. Because of the complexity of outside systems, pinpointing targets of change often seems more difficult.

However, generalist human services practitioners must also think in terms of needed changes beyond the individual client system. The individual is only one focus for potential change.

Macro system changes are seldom easy. They often involve influencing large numbers of people or key decision makers. Sometimes conflict is necessary and may open up multitudes of new planned change alternatives.

The following three scenarios put you in various situations. For each one, think in terms of how the problem might be solved through macro-level changes. For this exercise, do not change or move the individual. Think in terms of what major organizations or community groups can do to effect change. What policies might be changed? What community services might be developed? What strategies might achieve these changes? Remember, do not change the individual— focus only on macro system change.

What Might You Do When:

1. You are a public social services worker in a rural county. Your job includes doing everything from helping the elderly obtain their Social Security payments to investigating alleged child abuse. Within the past six months, six farm families in the county have filed for bankruptcy. Government farm subsidies that used to be available have been with-drawn, and the past two years have been hard on crops. Now the banks are threatening to foreclose on the farm mortgages. Thus, the six families will literally be put out in the cold with no money and no place to go. What do you do?

2. You are a practitioner for Pinocchio County Social Services. It is a rural county with a few towns and no large cities. Your job as intake worker is to do family assessments when people call up with problems (anything from domestic violence to coping with serious illnesses). Your next task is to make referrals to the appropriate services.

    You have been hearing about a number of sexual assaults in the area. Women are expressing fear for their safety. People who have been assaulted do not know where to turn. The nearest large cities are over 80 miles away. You have always been interested in women's issues and advocacy for women. Now what do you do?

3. You have a 70-year-old client named Harriett who lives in an old, near inner-city neighborhood in a large city. Since her husband died seven years ago, she has been living alone. She has no children, is still in good health, and likes to be independent.

    The problem is that her house has been condemned for new highway construction. The plans are to tear it down within six months. There is no public housing available for the elderly within five miles of where she lives. She would like to stay in the area because she has a lot of elderly friends there. Now what? (Remember, don't move Harriett.)

A Commentary

The scenarios above are difficult to solve. They are not designed to frustrate you but rather to encourage you to think about interventions beyond the micro and mezzo levels. Sometimes, macro system service provision is inadequate, ineffective, or simply wrong. The generalist practitioner's unique perspective is one of potential system change at all levels.

This text is designed to help you clarify that perspective and assimilate a wide variety of practice skills. The dimension of macro skills focuses on targeting the environment, not the person, for change.

Defining Generalist Practice: A Wide Range of Roles

Assuming a wide range of professional roles is the seventh concept in the definition of generalist practice. We have emphasized that generalist practitioners can tackle a wide range of problems by using many different methods. Another way of making this point is that you will assume many roles. We have established that a professional role is behavior and activity involved in performing some designated function. Some of the roles characterizing generalist practitioners, which include counselor, educator, broker, case manager, mobilizer, mediator, facilitator, and advocate, are briefly summarized:

- *Counselor:* one who provides guidance to clients and assists them in a planned change or problem-solving process. For example, a worker might help a teenager decide which form of contraception is best for her.
- *Educator:* one who gives information and teaches skills to other systems (Kirst-Ashman & Hull, 2001; Yessian & Broskowski, 1983). For instance, a practitioner might teach parents child management skills.
- *Broker:* one who links client systems to needed resources (Connaway & Gentry, 1988; Kirst-Ashman & Hull, 2001). For example, a worker might refer a client to a substance abuse treatment center for inpatient treatment.
- *Case manager:* a practitioner who, on the behalf of a specific client, coordinates needed services provided by any number of agencies, organizations, or facilities. For instance, a worker might coordinate the many services needed by a quadriplegic living in a group home.
- *Mobilizer:* one who identifies and convenes community people and resources to identify "unmet community needs" and "effect changes for the better in their community" (Halley, Kopp, & Austin, 1998, p. 179). For example, a practitioner might encourage community residents to band together and start a drug education program for residents' children.
- *Mediator:* one who resolves arguments or disagreements among micro, mezzo, or macro systems in conflict (Kirst-Ashman & Hull, 2001; Yessian & Broskowski, 1983). For instance, a worker might serve as a go-between to establish an agreement between an agency wanting to start a group home for people with developmental disabilities and neighborhood residents who violently oppose having the facility in their neighborhood.
- *Facilitator:* one who guides a group experience. For instance, a practitioner might run a support group for young women with eating disorders.
- *Advocate:* one who steps forward and speaks out on the behalf of clients in order to promote fair and equitable treatment or gain needed resources. For example, a worker might meet with an administrator on the behalf of a client to change an agency policy on that client's behalf.

Defining Generalist Practice: Critical Thinking Skills

Not only do generalists have an *eclectic knowledge base, professional values,* and many *different practice skills* to work with *systems of various sizes,* as well as assuming a *wide range of roles,* but they also must have the ability to *think critically* as they pursue the planned change process. The eighth component in the definition of generalist practice involves critical thinking skills.

Critical thinking is the ability to use intellectual and "affective processes which evaluate statements, arguments, and experiences by judging the validity and/or worth of those statements, arguments, and experiences" (Lindsay, 1995, p. 20). In other words, critical thinking entails the ability to carefully evaluate the validity of an assumption and even of a so-called "fact."

Gibbs and colleagues (1994) state that critical thinking usually involves four dimensions. First, practitioners should be predisposed to ask questions about how their clients are served and treated. Second, they should be inquisitive about how interventions are supposed to work and whether or not they are really effective. Third, workers should carefully examine any assertions made as facts by evaluating arguments on both sides of an issue. Fourth, practitioners should use "scientific reasoning" to analyze arguments, keeping their eyes open for inconsistencies and deviations from the truth.

In other words, do not believe everything you hear. Rather, critically evaluate for yourself whether what you hear is true or not.

For example, Carlene, a colleague, tells you that the most effective child management technique ever is to "bonk the misbehaving child on the nose with a flyswatter." She swears that it immediately and permanently curbs obnoxious behaviors such as swearing, hitting other children, or sticking fingers into various facial orifices. Critical thinking would lead you to ask some serious questions about the validity of Carlene's statements. What are the theoretical underpinnings of the flyswatter approach to behavior management? How has it been proven effective, with whom, and under what conditions? What are some potential negative consequences of this technique? Of course, we are being facetious when talking about the flyswatter approach to child management. The point is that critical thinking concerns not necessarily accepting situations or stories at face value. Rather, it entails using your own judgment to seriously consider their worth and relevance.

Defining Generalist Practice: Planned Change

The ninth concept inherent in the definition of generalist practice is planned change. *Planned change* is the development and implementation of a strategy for improving or altering "some specified condition, pattern of behavior, or set of circumstances that affects social functioning" (Sheafor et al., 2000, p. 119). Planned change is a process whereby practitioners engage a client; assess issues, strengths, and problems; and establish a plan of action, implement the plan, evaluate its effects, terminate the process, and do subsequent follow-up to monitor the client's ongoing status. The Generalist Intervention Model proposed in the next section of this chapter explores this process much more thoroughly. The model's six primary steps are engagement, assessment, planning, implementation, evaluation, and termination.

Note that another term often used to describe what generalist practitioners do is *problem solving*. Essentially, problem solving refers to the same process as planned change, although many debate the nuances of difference. Human services' more recent emphasis on client strengths may be at odds with the more negative connotations of the word *problem*. The term *change* may have more positive connotations, despite the fact that most human services intervention deals with problem situations. As there is some evidence that the term *planned change* is more frequently used in generalist practice, we will use it here (Hoffman & Sallee, 1993; Landon, 1995).

Defining Generalist Practice: Empowerment

The final concept emphasized in our definition of generalist practice is empowerment. *Empowerment* helps systems of all sizes increase their resources and strength in order to improve their lives. Empowerment means increasing, emphasizing, developing, and nurturing strengths and positive attributes. It aims at enhancing individuals', groups', families', and communities' power and control over their destinies.

Cowger maintains that human services historically has focused on dysfunction, pathology, and "individual inadequacies" (1994, p. 262). He states that "if assessment focuses on deficits, it is likely that deficits will remain the focus of both the worker and the client during remaining contacts. Concentrating on deficits or strengths can lead to self-fulfilling prophecies" (1994, p. 264). However, a strengths perspective can provide "structure and content for an examination of realizable alternatives, for the mobilization of competencies that can make things different, and for the building of self-confidence that stimulates hope" (1994, p. 265).

Saleebey articulates a strengths perspective that is essentially based on empowerment. He also cites at least five primary underlying principles:

1. "Every individual, group, family, and community has strengths."
2. "Trauma and abuse, illness, and struggle may be injurious but they may also be sources of challenge and opportunity."
3. "Assume that you do not know the upper limits of the capacity to grow and change and take individual, group, and community aspirations seriously."
4. "We best serve clients by collaborating with them."
5. "Every environment is full of resources" (2002, pp. 14–16).

 ### The Generalist Intervention Model (GIM)

Our definition of generalist practice provides the foundation for the Generalist Intervention Model (GIM). GIM is a practice model providing step-by-step direction concerning how to undertake the planned change process, which is generally directed at addressing problems.

Practitioners help people deal with problems ranging from personal relationships to lack of resources to blatant discrimination. A practitioner may need to address the problem of a battered woman who is economically and emotionally dependent on her abusive husband and who also has three children to protect. In another instance, a practitioner might have an adolescent client who has committed a number of serious crimes and is heavily involved with an urban gang. At yet another time, a practitioner may need to advocate and fight for change in a public assistance policy—one that discriminates against people who speak little to no English and are unable to follow an intricate, exasperating application process in order to receive benefits. Regardless of what problem is addressed, the planned change effort follows the same course of action.

Three major features characterize GIM. First, GIM assumes that workers acquire an eclectic knowledge base, a wide range of skills to target any size system, and a professional values base. Earlier parts of this chapter describe the major concepts involved (summarized in Highlight 1.1).

GIM's second major feature is its core six-step planned change process that emphasizes the assessment of client strengths. The steps, illustrated in Figure 1.2, are engagement, assessment, planning, implementation, evaluation, and termination. This

and later chapters will define these steps and break them down into smaller substeps or action steps to help guide you through the change process.

GIM's third major feature is its generalist approach, which means that virtually any problem may be analyzed and addressed from multiple levels of intervention. GIM is oriented toward addressing problems and issues that involve not only individuals but also groups, organizations, and even major social policies. In other words, the model involves micro, mezzo, and macro systems as targets of change. Figure 1.3 illustrates this approach.

We have established that a target of change or target system is one that practitioners need "to change or influence in order to accomplish (their) goals"

Figure 1.2   *Planned Change Steps in the Generalist Intervention Model (GIM)*

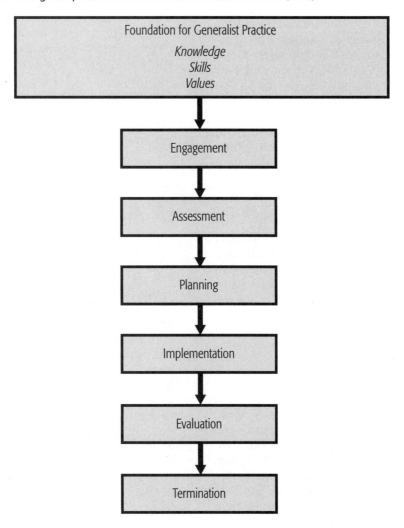

(Pincus & Minahan, 1973, p. 58). Micro systems are individuals, and mezzo systems are small groups. Families, because of their intimate nature, arbitrarily lie somewhere between micro and mezzo systems. Finally, macro systems are large systems that include organizations and communities.

For example, suppose you are a practitioner for Upbeat, a large, urban diagnostic and treatment center serving children who have various physical, speech, and psychological disabilities. Upbeat is a private agency funded primarily by private insurance payments, medical assistance reimbursement, voluntary donations, and government grants. Your job description specifies that you are responsible for providing help to families, educating parents about behavior management techniques, and brokering resources.

You receive a new case referral, Tanaka, a 5-year-old boy who has severe speech and behavioral problems. He stutters and has difficulty enunciating words and formulating sentences. He frequently refuses to obey his parents at home, often lashing out in violent temper tantrums. At school he has poor communication and relationship-building skills with his peers. He is unable to play with peers without acting out aggressively, such as hitting them in the stomach or poking them in the eye. Such behavior causes serious problems for him with his kindergarten teacher.

Unfortunately, his parents have indicated that their insurance will not pay for Tanaka's treatment. They are not receiving any public assistance and will be hard pressed to pay for services by themselves.

As a generalist practitioner you can assess and proceed with this case on several levels, considering the possibility of micro, mezzo, or macro intervention. First, on a micro level, Tanaka requires speech and behavioral assessments to determine a treatment plan. To what extent are his speech difficulties physiologically based? What speech therapy goals might be established? How do Tanaka's speech problems affect his ability to interact with others? How are his parents and other family members reacting to and handling his speech and behavior problems?

On a mezzo level, Tanaka is having difficulty interacting with family members, peers, and other adults. Remember that we arbitrarily consider the

Figure 1.3   *Initiating Micro, Mezzo, or Macro Change during Assessment*

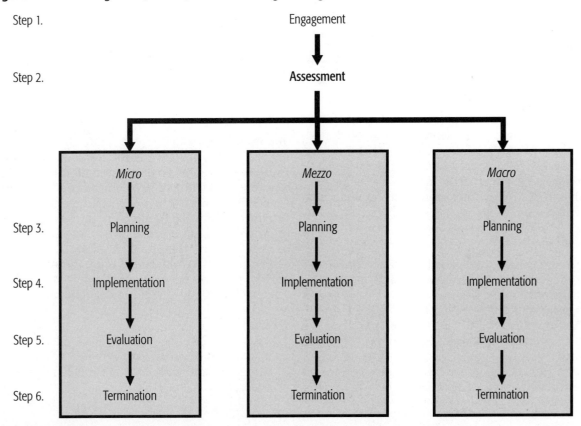

family as placed between the micro and mezzo levels of practice because of its special personal significance and the importance of group dynamics. Tanaka's parents may require family counseling and education about behavior management techniques. Mezzo-level intervention also may address Tanaka's peer relationships. His teacher may need consultation regarding behavioral control in the classroom. Tanaka might benefit from membership in a treatment group with other children experiencing similar difficulties. Group involvement might include discussing feelings and behavior, providing role models for improved behavior, and encouraging positive interaction among group members.

Macro-level intervention investigates and promotes changes in the broader macro environment. Tanaka's parents indicate that paying for his treatment by themselves will be difficult, if not impossible. Can agency policy be changed so that families in financial need like Tanaka's may receive services based on a sliding fee scale based on their ability to pay? Can a special fund based on private donations be established for families in financial need? Should a fund-raising drive for such a cause be initiated? Should the school be expected to provide speech therapy and behavioral counseling in view of Tanaka's inability to function in the academic environment? Potential macro-level interventions, then, might involve changes in community services or agency policies and practices to make needed resources more readily available.

Planned Change Steps in the GIM

Regardless of what kind of problem is addressed, the planned change process presented here involves six major steps. We will define each step briefly now; later chapters will provide more extensive elaboration. Planned change steps include engagement, assessment, planning, implementation, evaluation, and termination.

Step 1: Engagement

Engagement is the initial period where practitioners orient themselves to the problem at hand and begin to establish communication and a relationship with others also addressing the problem. Regardless of whether you pursue micro, mezzo, or macro change, you must establish rapport or a harmonious relationship with clients and target systems in order to communicate and get things done. Engagement is based on the acquisition of a range of micro skills. Both the words you speak (verbal communication) and your

coinciding actions and expressions (nonverbal communication such as tone, posture, and gestures) can act to engage others in the helping process.

Many other dimensions are involved in engagement. Your overall demeanor, including your ability to convey warmth, empathy, and genuineness, can enhance engagement. (*Conveying warmth* involves enhancing the positive feelings of one person toward another by promoting a sense of comfort and well-being in that other person. *Empathy* involves not only *being in tune* with how a client feels but also *conveying to that client* that you understand how the client feels. This process involves "sharing of self by relating in a natural, sincere, spontaneous, open and genuine manner" [Hepworth & Larsen, 1987, p. 998]. *Genuineness* simply means that you continue to be yourself, despite the fact that you are working to accomplish goals in your professional role. Chapter 9 discusses these qualities more thoroughly.) Likewise, how you introduce yourself and arrange an initial meeting's setting affects the engagement process. Other engagement skills include alleviating initial client anxiety and introducing your purpose and role. Chapter 5 will describe more thoroughly engagement and how it relates to micro practice skills.

Step 2: Assessment

According to Siporin, assessment is the "differential, individualized, and accurate identification and evaluation of problems, people, and situations and of their interrelations, to serve as a sound basis for differential helping intervention" (1975, p. 224). Meyer defines assessment simply as "knowing, understanding, evaluating, individualizing, or figuring out" (1995, p. 260). For our purposes, assessment is the investigation and determination of variables affecting an identified problem or issue as viewed from micro, mezzo, or macro perspectives. In the first place, assessment refers to gathering relevant information about a problem so that decisions can be made about what to do to solve it. Secondly, assessment can involve preparation for intervention at any level of practice. As Figure 1.4 indicates, assessment includes the following four substeps:

1. Identify your client.
2. Assess the client-in-situation from micro, mezzo, macro, and diversity perspectives.
3. Cite information about client problems and needs.
4. Identify client strengths.

Figure 1.4   *Assessment in the Generalist Intervention Model (GIM)*

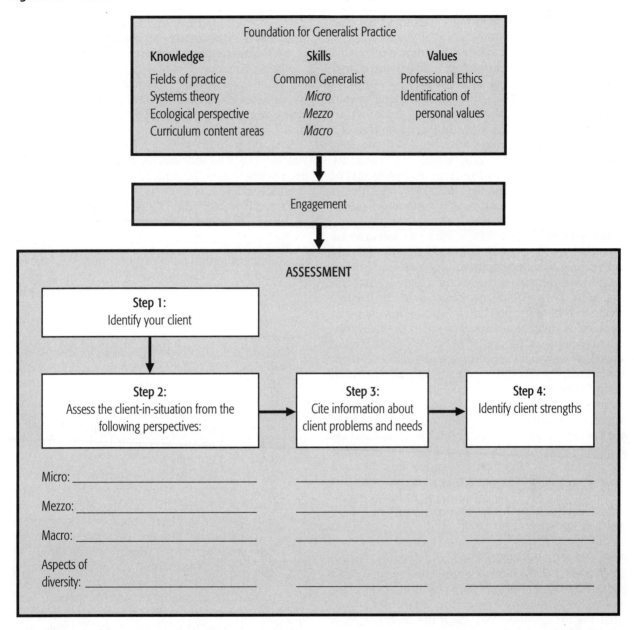

Identify Your Client.   The first step in assessment is to determine who your client is. At first glance, this method may sound overly simplistic. To say your clients are those people cited on your client list (i.e., your caseload) seems logical. However, we have already established that people, their lives, and their problems are often complicated. The designation of who is really your client and who is not may become blurred and vague.

For example, say you are a probation officer. Jerrad, age 15, is a client on your caseload. He was adjudicated delinquent because he had stolen over a dozen cars. Because Jerrad is clearly listed on your caseload, he is your client, right? However, you determine that Jerrad needs support and guidance from his parents. He currently lives at home with them, and both parents are currently using illegal drugs. Both also have conviction records for drug dealing. Additionally, Jerrad has three younger siblings also living in the home. You worry that they are likely to follow in Jerrad's footsteps and become involved in theft and other illegal activities.

Who is your client? Whom do you need to help? Is it just Jerrad? Or is his entire family your client? Is your client really the community that employs you to monitor lawbreakers and help them fit into the community more appropriately?

To answer these questions, thinking in terms of a *client system* is helpful, which we define as "the individual, family, group, organization, or community that, in addition to being the expected beneficiary of service, is a system that asks for help and engages the services of a [practitioner] as a change agent" (Pincus & Minahan, 1973, p. 56).

The probation officer may decide that Jerrad alone is the client system or that Jerrad and his entire family will become the client system. Whoever is identified as "those who have sanctioned (or asked for) his services, are expected to be beneficiaries of the change efforts, and have entered into a working agreement or contract" with the practitioner becomes the client system (Pincus & Minahan, 1973, p. 57). One should note, however, that clients may be voluntary or involuntary. Jerrad surely did not choose to have a personal probation officer. His family may not be thrilled with the idea either. Rather, society forced the probation situation upon Justin and his family in response to the boy's behavior. Nonetheless, in this case Jerrad and his family are intended to receive the benefits of the intervention effort. Additionally, the probation office will make agreements with whomever is identified as part of the client system by establishing a contract with them. This situation fits the definition of client system that was provided earlier.

Assess the Client-in-Situation and Identify Issues.

After the client system is established, a generalist practitioner will continue with the assessment. This process of gathering information is tied directly to what the practitioner does about the problem. How practitioners intervene is based on the information they have and on the judgments they have made about that information.

Assessment in generalist practice focuses on understanding the many aspects of a problem. Information is needed about the client and about those aspects of the client's environment that the worker feels are significant.

For example, a worker in a rural county receives a call about Haley from Haley's neighbor. Haley, 84, lives in an old farmhouse in the country where she has lived for most of her life. Her health is deteriorating; as a result, she is falling more frequently, and her eyesight is failing. The neighbor worries that Haley may fall, break something, and lie helpless and alone for days.

The worker visits Haley and does an assessment of her and her situation. The worker needs information to make decisions about what he and Haley can do. Haley may need some supportive services or even health care center placement.

The information needed falls into four major categories. These include micro, mezzo, and macro levels of assessment in addition to consideration of elements of human diversity. In each category, problems must be defined and strengths identified.

Micro Aspects.

First, the worker needs to explore the micro aspects of the situation. What are Haley's most critical problems? What things about Haley contribute to her problems? On the other hand, what are Haley's strengths? What does she do well? What aspects of her life does she consider important?

The worker explores both biological and psychological aspects of Haley's situation. In Haley's case, the biological aspects primarily involve her current health problems. Yes, Haley admits she falls occasionally, but she thinks that a cane might help. Her failing sight is especially difficult for her. She talks of how she is not eating very well lately because she cannot see well enough to cook.

Also, from the micro perspective the worker explores Haley's psychological situation. How does Haley feel about herself and her situation? The worker discovers that Haley, too, finds taking care of herself increasingly difficult. She loves her home and expresses the strong desire to remain in it. However, she feels she could use some help, especially with food purchase and preparation. The worker finds that Haley expresses herself well. Although Haley is somewhat discouraged about her eyesight, she appears to be emotionally stable.

Micro/Mezzo Aspects: Families.

The worker asks Haley about her family. Does she have any relatives in the immediate vicinity? Does she have children who are available to help out? What are her relationships with relatives who might be accessible?

The worker discovers that Haley has three children in the area. They call and visit frequently but haphazardly. They occasionally take her shopping or to visit their homes.

Mezzo Aspects.   The worker then pursues questions about the other mezzo aspects of Haley's situation. Does she have friends she can talk to? Do people visit her? How often? Does she have opportunities to get out of the house at all?

The worker establishes that Haley has a number of friends in the area. However, she rarely sees them because of the transportation difficulties for both her and them. She is, however, affiliated with a church and participates in church activities as frequently as she can. Spirituality can provide a beneficial means of support.

Macro Aspects.   Thirdly, the worker explores the macro aspects of the situation. What services might be available to help Haley with her identified problems? Is there a Meals-on-Wheels program available? Meals-on-Wheels provides regular delivery of hot meals to elderly people throughout a designated area. Is there a Visiting Friends program through which paraprofessionals regularly visit elderly residents in their homes and help them with shopping, paying bills, making medical appointments, and so on?

The worker determines that no such services are readily available at this time. He decides that the system is not designed to meet Haley's needs or the needs of other elderly people in similar positions.

Aspects of Diversity.   The worker needs to consider a fourth dimension while assessing Haley and her situation: Are there any significant aspects of diversity? Human diversity refers to "the range of differences between peoples in terms of race, ethnicity, age, geography, religion, values, culture, orientations, physical and mental health, and many other distinguishing characteristics" (Barker, 1999, p. 223). The worker finds that Haley is of German heritage. This aspect of ethnic and cultural diversity is relevant. She also feels strongly about her membership in a local Lutheran church that many other elderly people of similar heritage also attend. For many reasons, Haley's church involvement is important to her.

Another aspect of diversity is Haley's age. Is Haley being treated differently or in a discriminatory manner because of ageism? *Ageism* refers to discrimination based on predisposed notions about older people, regardless of their individual qualities and capabilities. The worker closely evaluates his own attitudes. For instance, is he tempted to make assumptions about Haley's mental capability because of the stereotype that older people can no longer think as clearly as they could when they were younger?

Likewise, the worker must be aware of any sexist biases he might harbor. Sexism refers to predisposed notions about a person based on that person's gender. For instance, does the worker feel that Haley is a dependent person who needs to taken care of simply because she is a woman? Such a bias fails to take into account the client as a unique individual with particular strengths and weaknesses.

Assessment and Planning.   After reassessing the client and her situation, the worker and Haley together establish the following plan. First, regarding micro intervention, Haley needs a cane. Haley also needs some supportive care related to micro/mezzo (family) and macro interventions. The worker and Haley decide to meet with Haley's children and their families to work out a schedule for visitation and assistance. In this way, her relatives can regularly check to make certain Haley is all right. Haley feels strongly about remaining in her home as long as possible. The worker, Haley, and Haley's family agree that until her health deteriorates further, they will try to maintain her in her own home.

The macro intervention in Haley's case involves the lack of supportive services available to her. The worker and his supervisor bring Haley's situation to the attention of the social services department's administration. On further investigation, a substantial number of other elderly people are found to be in positions similar to Haley's. Thus, the change process is initiated to pursue funding for new resources to help elderly people.

Haley's example provides only a brief summary of the worker's assessment. However, it does highlight the basic categories of information needed in virtually every assessment. As Figure 1.4 indicates, four general categories of information should be considered: *micro information*, which includes both biological and psychological aspects; *mezzo information*, which involves immediate groups with which clients have interaction; *macro information*, which concerns the impact of the broader social environment, organization, laws, and policies upon the client(s); and finally, *aspects of diversity*, which focus on special qualities or characteristics that may place clients in a designated group. Concerning the last category, the potential for discrimination must also be considered.

The crucial task of generalist practice is to look beyond the individual and examine other factors that impinge on the client's environment. In any individual case, the emphases upon one or the other assessment categories may vary. However, each category must still be reviewed and considered for its potential contribution to the problem.

For instance, a couple may come to a practitioner for help in their marital relationship. Thus, assessment of the mezzo aspects or relationship issues of the situation would be emphasized. However, a generalist practitioner would also consider both the micro aspects—such as the strengths, needs, and issues of each partner—and the macro aspects impinging upon their situation. Macro aspects might involve the fact that both spouses have been laid off their jobs at the local Truly Tremendous Tractor factory. They have held these jobs for over ten years, and the layoff was due to a serious depression in farm prices. In this case, the practitioner might not be able to do much about the current economy, but the economic impact on the couple is vital in an assessment of the current conflictual situation.

We have already established that the problems practitioners deal with are seldom easy to solve. We have also identified an underlying theme in generalist practice that provides a whole new array of potential alternatives: The generalist practitioner focuses on how clients are integrally involved with their social environments, on both the mezzo and macro levels.

Many specific assessment instruments and techniques are available. They vary by agency, clientele, and problem area. Within the framework of the GIM, Chapter 5 will discuss a variety of more specific assessment methods and issues commonly encountered during the assessment process. Specific case examples will illustrate the application of assessment principles.

Step 3: Planning

The third step in the GIM involves planning what to do. Planning follows assessment in the problem-solving process. Assessment sets the stage for the intervention, and planning specifies what should be done. Chapter 6 elaborates on the planning process in greater depth. As shown in Figure 1.5, planning involves the following eight substeps:

1. Work with the client.
2. Prioritize problems.
3. Translate problems into needs.
4. Evaluate levels of intervention for each need.
5. Establish goals.
6. Specify objectives.
7. Specify action steps.
8. Formalize a contract.

Work with the Client.   The generalist practitioner follows eight substeps in the planning process. Figure 1.5 illustrates these substeps. First, working *with* the client is important, not *at* the client. The client must be involved in problem definition and must agree as to which problems merit attention. Additionally, the planning process should take advantage of the client's strengths.

Prioritize Problems.   The second substep in planning is to prioritize the problems. Again, the client must be a partner in this process. Many times, what the worker feels is important differs drastically from what the client thinks is most significant. For example, a practitioner may be most concerned about Carol's potential for abusing her small children and about her alcohol consumption. Carol, on the other hand, may be most interested in solving her financial problems. Her work schedule has been cut back on the hours she works, so she now works only part-time. Meanwhile, her rent is rising astronomically, she owes growing debts on her credit cards, and she sees herself as a failure because she cannot take adequate care of her family. Part of the worker's job is to examine the various aspects of the problems at hand and to focus on problems and issues considered significant by the client and the worker.

Translate Problems into Needs.   Substep 3 in the planning process involves translating problems into needs. Clients come to you because they are suffering from problems. The way you can help them is to establish what they *need* to solve the problem. This relatively simple step in planning helps to restructure how you look at the situation so that it is easier to decide on solutions.

Evaluate Levels of Intervention (Micro, Mezzo, and Macro).   Substep 4 in the planning process involves first focusing on one client need at a time, beginning with those of highest priority. Possible alternative solutions should be discussed with the client.

Alternative solutions may focus on the micro, mezzo, or macro level of change. The proposed alternative thus may involve what the individual can do at the micro level. For instance, one alternative solution aims at having Carol change her own behavior. She might enter an alcohol and drug treatment program. Another tack might be to help her find a new, more suitable job.

Or the worker and client might address the problem at a mezzo level. Carol could join a support group for people dealing with similar issues. Still another option

Figure 1.5   *Planning in the Generalist Intervention Model (GIM)*

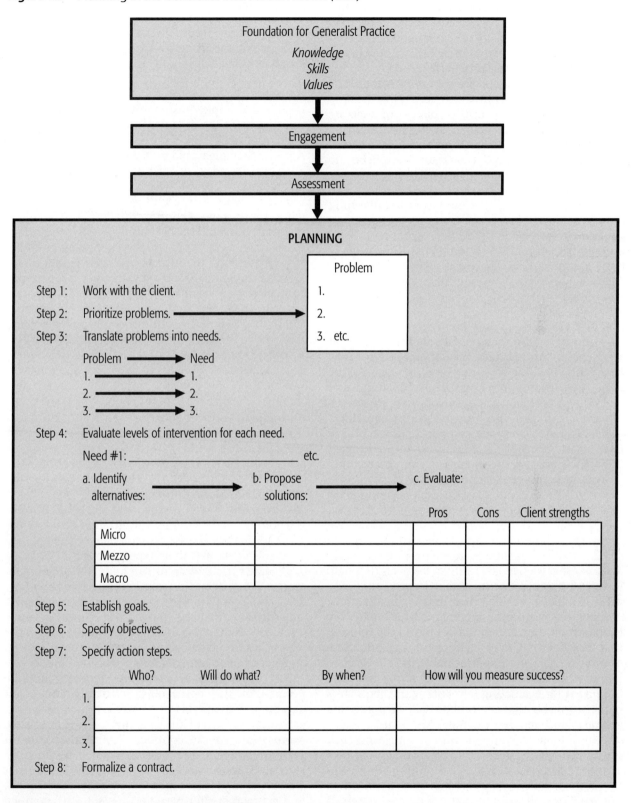

may involve proposed change at the macro level. The worker might advocate to get Carol into low-rent housing. Another strategy might be to develop a plan for instituting rent control in the community. This last idea would make life more affordable for people facing financial conditions similar to Carol's.

Each proposed alternative solution should be evaluated regarding its pros and cons. How feasible or doable is it? What are the chances of success? How long will it take? Client strengths should be constantly kept in mind and involved in the solutions whenever possible. One result should be the selection of an alternative plan of action.

Establish Goals.   The fifth substep in the planning process is to establish goals. Goals provide you and your client with general direction regarding how to proceed with the intervention. What do you really want to accomplish? How can your client's major needs be met? What are your primary and necessary end results?

Specify Objectives.   Goals are often not very specific. In fact, many times clients identify goals that are vague or unclear and that do not let us know when they have or have not been attained. At the same time, clients' initial goals give an important sense of the problems and needs they are experiencing. For example, think of the following client-stated goals: "I want to improve communication with my husband" or "I need to find housing." By themselves, these goals are not specific enough to do anything more than state a general direction for our work with the client. They do not give you a clue regarding *how* to achieve them or where you would go to meet these needs. It is the worker's task to help move vague goals statements into more explicit ends or *objectives,* the sixth substep in the planning process.

Think of objectives as clearly stated goals that help identify what steps we must take to proceed. Using the goals above, our objectives might look like this: "Reduce the number of arguments I have with my husband" or "locate affordable and clean housing that has at least three bedrooms." Each of these objectives is specific and measurable and allows us to know whether we succeeded. As such, they are important for evaluating our work with clients. It is entirely possible that one broad goal might generate several objectives. For example, Ms. Schultz might also like to spend one hour with her husband each week, talking over their week. This would then be a second objective under the goal of improving communication with her husband. However, objectives don't tell us who will do what nor do they necessarily contain a time frame in which activities should be accomplished. Further, they don't really tell us how things will get done. This is the role of *action steps.*

Specify Action Steps.   Action steps are detailed listings that specify *who* will do *what* by *when,* and *how* that individual should do it. They represent tasks that must be completed in order to move toward achieving the objective and ultimately the client's goals. For example, "Ms. Schultz will maintain a chart listing each of the arguments she had with her husband this week and bring it to our next session." Another example would be "I will contact the housing authority Monday and get a list of three-bedroom apartments or houses." Each objective might have multiple action steps, each specifying how things are going to get done. Action steps allow us to monitor our work with clients. For example, if Ms. Schultz fails to maintain a chart, quits midweek, or does not bring it to the session, we must reassess whether our action steps are appropriate. Perhaps other means are needed to help move toward her objective of reducing arguments with her husband. Similarly, if you do not get a list from the housing authority, you and the client can't move forward with locating housing. Failure to complete important action steps can lead to failure to attain objectives. Needless to say, if we don't achieve our objectives, we also won't reach the client's goals.

Formalize a Contract with the Client.   "A contract is a working agreement that usually is negotiated by the client, the worker, and other service personnel who will be involved in the service process" (Seabury, 1987, p. 343). The contract is the final substep in the planning process. It can be used to specify the many ways in which the worker and client are going to work together toward their goals. A contract formalizes the agreement between client and worker and clarifies their expectations.

A wide variety of items can be included in a contract. These items include specific aspects of the plan—such as who will do what by when, intended goals, fees or financial responsibility, meeting times, types of services provided, and virtually any other condition involved in the intervention. As in other aspects of the planned change process, having "the client to be actively involved in developing the terms" of the contract is critically important (Seabury, 1987, p. 344). The worker must make certain that the client understands all of the specific words used in the contract. Technical jargon (or "psychobabble," as a business major friend once labeled it) must be clearly explained to the client or paraphrased in words the client readily understands.

Contracts are flexible agreements. In this manner, they are strikingly different from legal contracts, which require that all parties concur with their terms. This latter type of contract cannot be easily altered. Contracts with clients must be formal enough to clarify expectations but informal enough to let the worker respond flexibly to the client's changing needs or conditions.

Step 4: Implementation

The fourth step in the GIM involves carrying out the plan. Client and worker follow their plan to achieve their goals. Progress during implementation must be constantly monitored and assessed. Sometimes, new issues, situations, and conditions require that the plan be changed (see Figure 1.6).

For example, consider a case in which the intervention plan involves the goal of determining custody and visitation rights following a divorce. The couple suddenly decides to stay together. Determining custody rights is no longer relevant. However, new goals might need to be developed concerning more effective behavioral management

of the children to prevent family feuding and future disruptions of the marital relationship.

Chapter 7 will examine the implementation of the GIM. It includes assessment of and treatment for child maltreatment, assessment and treatment of alcohol and other drug abuse, and crisis intervention. Other issues addressed are empowerment of the elderly and managed care.

Step 5: Evaluation

Evaluation of implementation, step five in the GIM, is important for accountability. Practitioners must be accountable. That is, they must prove that their interventions have been effective. Each goal is evaluated in terms of the extent to which it has been achieved. The decision then must be made about whether the case should be terminated or reassessed to establish new goals (see Figure 1.7).

Evaluation techniques are becoming increasingly more sophisticated. They involve the application of research principles to generalist practice. Chapter 8

Figure 1.6   *Implementation in the Generalist Intervention Model (GIM)*

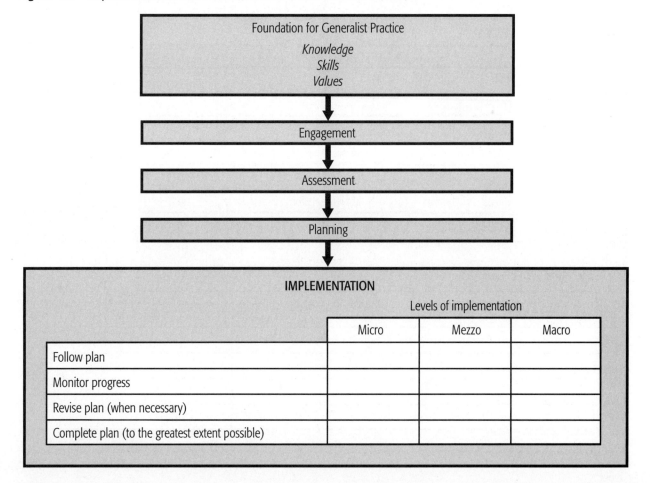

will explore a variety of evaluation designs both for direct service practitioners and for whole programs. Evaluation issues commonly faced by practitioners will also be addressed.

Step 6: Termination

Step six in GIM concerns termination. The worker/client relationship must eventually come to an end. To get up one day and, out of the clear blue sky, say "Well, good-bye" is not a good ending for a worker. Termination in generalist practice involves specific skills and techniques. This fact is true regardless of the level of intervention (see Figure 1.2).

Appropriate timing of the termination is important. Fortune cites at least five basic reasons for termination. First, termination may occur at the end of a "planned, time-limited service. . . . [p]articipants know how long their contact will last and use that sense of time to frame their work, to maintain a focus, and to increase motivation" (Fortune, 1995, pp. 2398–2399).

Second, termination may occur with ongoing "open-ended" service "by mutual agreement." Goals may have been achieved, and the clients should take what they have learned and go out on their own. Other times, participants unfortunately determine that success has not been achieved or that the necessary energy to achieve success would not be worth it.

A third reason for termination is unanticipated occurrences, which include "the practitioner

Figure 1.7   *Evaluation in the Generalist Intervention Model (GIM)*

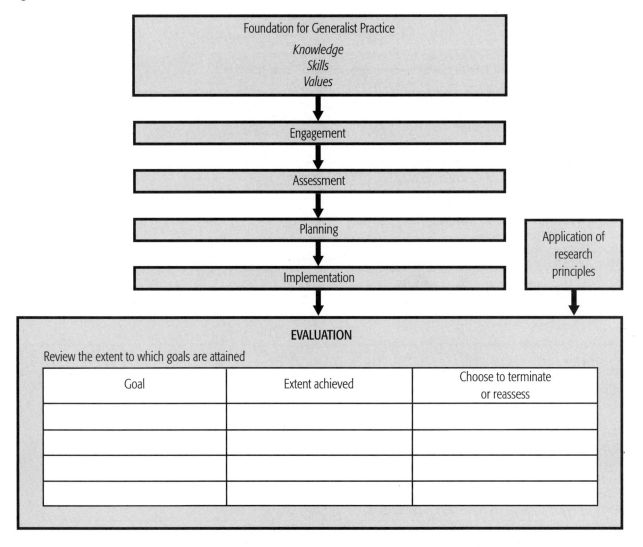

(or human service student) leaving an agency, changes in the client's schedule, the client's move to another geographic area, agency policies about the duration of service, limits imposed by insurers, and agency constraints such as excessive caseloads" (Fortune, 1995, pp. 2398–2399).

A fourth explanation for termination is transfer to another practitioner. The worker may leave for another job, or the client may qualify for other services or funding.

The fifth reason for termination is "dropping out." Without warning, clients simply do not come back. Clients may feel the intervention is not working, or they no longer feel the discomfort initially causing them to seek help. The family moves. The client is no longer motivated to return. Other aspects of a client's life take precedence over the problem he or she came to the practitioner to solve.

The most effective terminations follow a process of disengagement and stabilization. Chapter 8 discusses this process. Practitioners need to acknowledge that endings are near before they abruptly occur. They must encourage clients to share feelings about the termination and in turn share their own. Additionally, practitioners must clearly identify whatever progress has been made. This process increases the chance that the client will use what has been learned during this intervention to help solve other problems in the future.

As noted earlier, the client may be an individual, a group member, or a large agency. Regardless, each needs help in the transition from dependence on the worker for support or guidance to making decisions and functioning independently.

Other Practical Generalist Skills: A Perspective on the Rest of the Text

This text introduces a generalist perspective to human service practice, one that is directed at practitioners working primarily in micro settings. It emphasizes a wide range of micro skill acquisition and relates the use of these skills to mezzo and macro levels of practice.

The next chapter will examine the role that values and ethics play in human services work. It discusses the worker's ethical obligations, codes of ethics, and ethical dilemmas.

Chapters 3 and 4 will consider, respectively, culturally competent and gender-sensitive human services practice, aspects of diversity that affect the quality of care we provide for our clients. Chapter 3 will look at diversity in the United States, explore barriers to cultural competence, and identify ways to increase a worker's skill when working with different groups. Chapter 4 will similarly look at gender issues in the United States and discuss the relationship between feminist theory and human services practice. It will also identify common problems encountered in this arena.

Chapters 5 through 8 will describe in detail the various steps in the planned change process discussed initially in this chapter. Chapters 9 through 13 focus on acquiring the knowledge and skills needed for work with all size systems—individual through community.

Finally, Chapters 14 and 15 will look at three specific roles in depth—advocacy, brokering, case management.

 ## InfoTrac College Edition

In this chapter we discussed the importance of generalist practice. Concepts basic to generalist practice were reviewed along with the Generalist Intervention Model. For more information on these topics, please enter the following search terms:

counseling
psychology
systems theory
ecological perspective
human diversity
discrimination
oppression
social justice
economic justice

 ## On the Internet

Because of the very dynamic nature of the Web, URLs are subject to change. Therefore, be sure to check out the companion Website for this book at http://www.humanservices.wadsworth.com, where links will be updated periodically.
latino.sscnet.ucla.edu
alabanza.com
aad.english.ucsb.edu
www.progress.org
www.nmef.org
www.50years.org

CHAPTER 2
Values and Ethics in Human Services Practice

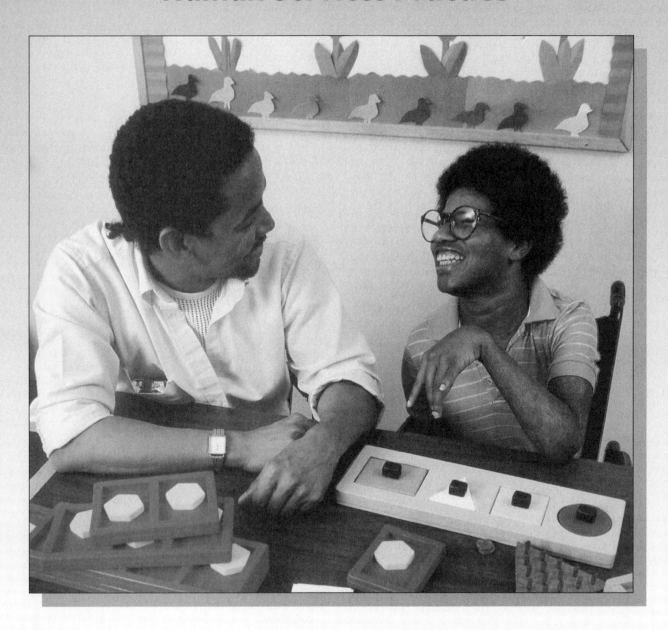

Two sisters, Keisha, 5, and Reshea, 7 months, are placed in a temporary foster home when both parents are killed in a car crash. Tona Lisa, their human service worker, must decide whether they should be placed for adoption separately or together. The problem is that placing infants is much easier than older children. Reshea's chances of adoption are excellent if placed alone. The chances of placing both girls together are much slimmer. However, Tona Lisa feels strongly that there are many positive reasons to keep the sisters together. What should she recommend (Rothman, 1998)?

David's kidneys are failing. At age 31, he is extremely sick from regular renal dialysis. His health is rapidly deteriorating, and he has become extremely depressed. Chances of receiving a kidney transplant are slim due to his rare tissue type and poor general health. David knows he cannot live like this much longer. He begs his hospital human service worker, Tomas, to help him pull the plug and discontinue his treatments. David is in such excruciating pain that he cannot stand it anymore (Rothman, 1998).

David's parents are mortified about his wish to "commit suicide," which is how they see his request. They sincerely love their son and want to hold on to him as long as possible. They desperately cling to the hope of a kidney transplant and vehemently disagree with David's request, beseeching Tomas to tell David it is ridiculous. What should Tomas do? Who is right?

Bart, 17, tells his school counselor, Cat, that he intends to steal his father's car and any money he can get hold of and take off for San Francisco. For the past several weeks, Cat has been seeing Bart, who has a case of mild depression and family problems. She knows if she reports Bart's plan, he will never talk to her again. On the other hand, if she pretends she does not know about the plan, she fears what will happen if he really does take off. What will happen to him? To his parents? To her? What should she do?

Aurelia is a human services worker providing substance abuse at a community center. The agency primarily serves low-income clients and relies heavily on grants to keep it going. Suddenly, one of its primary grant-funding agencies announces that it requires access to client records to monitor the appropriate use of funds. On her clients' behalf, Aurelia is outraged. Clients use the center and its services with the understanding that their involvement will be kept confidential. Many clients have much to lose if private information becomes public. For example, a number of clients are HIV positive. They are terrified of losing jobs and any health insurance they do have. If this funding stops, the number of clients the agency serves will be reduced by about one-third. However, if the funding agency gets access to client records, the results may be harmful to clients and a violation of their right to confidentiality. What should Aurelia do?

These examples are just a few of the many ethical dilemmas human services workers frequently encounter in practice. How can practitioners evaluate these scenarios? What guidelines can help them decide what to do? Values and ethics provide a major foundation of practice. This chapter addresses such issues.

 ## *Introduction*

Chapter 1 introduced the concepts of values and ethics. Along with knowledge and skills, professional values comprise the third basis for the foundation of generalist human services practice. Values involve what you consider important and what you do not. They concern what is considered worth having and what is not. They also involve making judgments or decisions about relative worth, that is, what is more valuable and what is less valuable. Common human services values include promotion of client well-being and individual dignity, self-determination, client empowerment, and human diversity (National Organization for Human Service Education, 2000).

Ethics involve principles that specify what is good and bad. They clarify what should and should not

be done. As you should know by now, human services workers have ethical codes based on professional values. Ethics and values are clearly related, although they are not the same thing. Loewenberg and colleagues state that "[e]thics are deduced from values and must be in consonance with them. The difference between them is that values are concerned with what is *good* and *desirable,* while ethics deal with what is *right* and *correct*" (2000, p. 22). Values then deal with what beliefs are appropriate. Ethics address what to *do* with or how to *apply* those beliefs.

Cournoyer clearly summarizes the momentous importance of professional ethics:

Every aspect of practice, every decision, every assessment, every intervention, and virtually every action you undertake . . . must be considered from the perspective of your professional ethics and obligations. This dimen-

sion supersedes all others. Ethical responsibilities take precedence over theoretical knowledge, research findings, practice wisdom, agency policies, and, of course, [our] own personal values, preferences, and beliefs. (2000, p. 67)

From a superficial perspective, professional judgments may look like a simple matter of common sense. However, in real-life decisions, values and ethical principles conflict constantly. These conflicts can result in ethical dilemmas, namely, problematic situations whose possible solutions all offer imperfect and unsatisfactory answers. For example, your client informs you of an activity such as dealing drugs that you are required to report. How can you maintain confidentiality and report at the same time? Or you find that your agency's eligibility requirements cut off services to some clients who are in dire need. You are ethically responsible for serving these clients effectively, yet you are also professionally committed to your employer as its agent.

This chapter deals with making ethical decisions within a wide range of generalist practice contexts. It focuses on those decisions you must make when there is no absolutely clear *right* thing to do.

This chapter will:

- examine the National Organization for Human Service Education Ethical Standards point by point;
- provide examples of how practitioners might conform to or violate various aspects of the standards;
- formulate an eight-step decision-making model for conceptualizing and addressing ethical dilemmas;
- discuss a model for ethical decision making;
- identify a range of ethical dilemmas commonly observed in generalist human services practice;
- analyze these dilemmas, raise questions, and propose some solutions.

Professional Ethical Standards

The National Organization for Human Service Education has established a set of ethical standards designed to guide human services professionals in their decision making. This section provides a summary of basic principles. (The standards are provided in their entirety on the Web at http://www.nohse.com/ethstand.html.) The standards recognize that human services workers play many roles and are designed to be used in a large variety of professional situations. Two audiences are targeted in the standards, the human services professional and the human services educator. This book focuses on the former. The standards stress that human services professionals have responsibility to several stakeholders (clients, community and society, colleagues, the profession, employers, and self). Each of these areas is addressed and examples of its primary dimensions provided below. Some examples of violations of and compliance with the standards are also described.

Human Services Professionals' Obligations to Clients

Practitioners' responsibility to their clients takes many forms. In the following pages, we will cite the ethical obligations required by the NOHSE standards with a particular emphasis on the six primary dimensions of the standards—respect for clients' welfare, confidentiality, dual relationships, sexual relationships with clients, clients' rights to self-determination, and building on clients' strengths.

Respect for Clients' Welfare

NOHSE Statement 1: Human service professionals negotiate with clients the purpose, goals, and nature of the helping relationship prior to its onset as well as inform clients of the limitations of the proposed relationship.

NOHSE Statement 2: Human service professionals respect the integrity and welfare of the client at all times. Each client is treated with respect, acceptance, and dignity. (NOHSE, p. 1)

Workers should hold clients in high regard and listen carefully to what they have to say. Practitioners should be dedicated to their clients' well-being and put their clients' best interests first. This means that a client's welfare is always foremost among the various obligations that professionals undertake. As major participants in the client–professional relationship, clients must be informed about the risks, obligations, and purposes of our efforts. Client participation in the relationship is the result of negotiation with the professional rather than a one-sided imposition.

Example of a Violation. Cathy is a counselor at a domestic violence shelter. She attends a case staffing where counselors discuss current residents, their plans, and their progress. Daffodil is a client with three children who has left her extremely abusive husband and fled to the shelter four different times. After each time, she returned to her abusive partner. She is wavering once again in her determination to leave her abusive home situation. She says she really loves her husband and feels her children need a father, even one who is abusive. During the staff meeting, Cathy states, "Daffodil is such a wuss. She just doesn't have the guts to leave that jerk and get on with her life! When I see her this afternoon, I'm going to lean on her a bit to try to get her to stay here."

Confidentiality

> *NOHSE Statement 3: Human service professionals protect the client's right to privacy and confidentiality except when such confidentiality would cause harm to the client or others, when agency guidelines state otherwise, or under other stated conditions (e.g., local, state, or federal laws). Professionals inform clients of the limits of confidentiality prior to the onset of the helping relationship.*
>
> *NOHSE Statement 4: If it is suspected that danger or harm may occur to the client or to others as a result of a client's behavior, the human service professional acts in an appropriate and professional manner to protect the safety of those individuals. This may involve seeking consultation, supervision, and/or breaking the confidentiality of the relationship. (NOHSE, p. 1)*

One aspect of our demonstrated respect for the client governs the right to privacy and confidentiality. Practitioners should uphold client privacy and confidentiality. *Privacy* is the condition of being free from unauthorized observation or intrusion. *Confidentiality* is the ethical principle that workers should not share information provided by a client or about a client unless the client has given explicit permission to do so. Human services professionals are obligated to guard against revealing information shared by the client unless there are compelling reasons for breaching confidentiality. Compelling reasons might occur when clients threaten harm to themselves or others, when mandated by state or federal law, or when clear agency policies limit confidentiality. Clients should be informed of such limitations and restrictions at the beginning of the professional–client relationship.

Sometimes human services professionals must breach client confidentiality when clients threaten to harm themselves or others. Such situations can pose difficult dilemmas for professionals. On the one hand, a human services worker is supposed to maintain confidentiality. On the other, someone may be at risk of great harm if the professional doesn't reveal the threat and seek outside help. Although the ethical guidelines do not specifically mention how to treat threats, it is imperative for human services professionals to warn victims or report dangerous situations to authorities. Note that when facing an ethical dilemma, it is often desirable to seek consultation from colleagues or a supervisor to help determine the best course of action.

Example of Compliance. A 21-year-old single mother, Naomi, confides in her public assistance worker, Herbert, that she is planning to shoot her boyfriend. Herbert must report Naomi's intentions to the proper authorities because the potential harm to Naomi's boyfriend supersedes Herbert's commitment to Naomi. Herbert explains his serious concerns and informs Naomi that he is required by law to inform authorities of her threats. Herbert then informs the designated authorities and warns Naomi's boyfriend.

Safeguarding Client's Records

> *NOHSE Statement 5: Human service professionals protect the integrity, safety, and security of client records. All written client information that is shared with other professionals, except in the course of professional supervision, must have the client's prior written consent. (NOHSE, p. 1-2)*

It is also the professional's responsibility to safeguard client records. This means that the client must give written consent before records may be shared with other professionals. The only exception to this guideline involves the need to share records with one's professional supervisor.

There is much more to confidentiality and safeguarding clients' records than is superficially apparent. Maintaining confidentiality requires workers not to solicit unnecessary information; to inform clients about the limitations of confidentiality with respect to agency policy, interagency work, legal requirements, and funding requirements; and to expend substantial effort safekeeping confidential information.

Example of a Violation. Huey and Dewey are counselors at a group home for adolescent boys with emotional and behavioral problems. They and their significant others occasionally have dinner with a mutual friend, Jerry, a county social services worker, along with his significant other. The three workers regularly compare "battle stories" about their most difficult cases, despite the fact that their caseloads are all different and their significant others are present. Sometimes, after a few cocktails, voices elevate, and other diners can overhear.

Dual Relationships

NOHSE Statement 6: Human service professionals are aware that in their relationships with clients power and status are unequal. Therefore they recognize that dual or multiple relationships may increase the risk of harm to, or exploitation of, clients, and may impair their professional judgment. However, in some communities and situations it may not be feasible to avoid social or other nonprofessional contact with clients. Human service professionals support the trust implicit in the helping relationship by avoiding dual relationships that may impair professional judgment, increase the risk of harm to clients or lead to exploitation.

NOHSE Statement 7: Sexual relationships with current clients are not considered to be in the best interest of the client and are prohibited. Sexual relationships with previous clients are considered dual relationships and are addressed in Statement 6 (above). (NOHSE, p. 2)

The relationships between clients and professionals are inherently unequal, a point the standards recognize. This difference in power and status has several implications. For example, professionals must not engage in dual or multiple relationships with clients because these may lead to harm or exploitation of the client. A *dual relationship* is one where a worker engages in a relationship other than that of professional with a client, supervisor, student, or other party in a work setting. The dual (or additional) role might include "friend, employer, teacher, business associate, or sex partner" (Kagle & Giebelhausen, 1994, p. 213). A related term to dual relationship is *multiple relationships,* as many types of such associations can occur including those where a worker assumes more than two roles at one time (Corey, Corey, & Callanan, 1998). For example, a client might offer to provide a service to the professional such as house cleaning or lawn mowing. The relationship of client–worker now has another intertwined role, that of employer–employee.

Another example of dual relationships occurs when clients and workers engage in personal relationships. The ethical standards for human services professionals and for many other helping professionals are clear

about this. Sexual relationships with current clients are strictly prohibited. Even relationships with previous clients are suspect because they can exploit the client. Dual and multiple relationships will be discussed later in the chapter in the context of ethical dilemmas.

Ethical practice strongly suggests that any kind of sexual contact between the professional and the client is unethical and harmful to the client because of the power differential, potential for exploitation, and confusion of roles. By its very nature, a client–counselor sexual relationship is an extreme type of dual relationship. For the same reasons, human services workers should not provide clinical services to clients with whom they were formerly sexual partners. The seriousness of these situations is illustrated by the comments from Cox, Erlich, Rothman, and Tropman:

Great damage has been done to clients who have been exploited by trusted physicians, therapists and other "helping persons," and to the professions (especially in the mental health field) which have seen public confidence in their motives, competence, and integrity steadily eroded. (1987, p. 426)

Example of a Violation.   Shelley, age 24, is a counselor at a community-based halfway house for men on parole who are also recovering substance abusers. *Parole* is the "conditional release of a prisoner serving an indeterminate or unexpired sentence," usually for good behavior or the promise of good behavior, under the supervision of a designated parole officer (*Merriam Webster's Collegiate Dictionary,* 1994). Most of the clients are in their 20s and early 30s. Sheila finds herself physically attracted to Terrell, a good-looking, charming, 26-year-old parolee who resides in the house. She fights her feelings but finally gives in. When he asks her for a date, she assents and begins an intimate relationship with Terrell "on the sly." Agency policy clearly forbids any such relationships with current clients or anyone who has been a client within the past six months.

Clients' Right to Self-Determination

NOHSE Statement 8: The client's right to self-determination is protected by human service professionals. They recognize the client's right to receive or refuse services. (NOHSE, p. 2)

As we mentioned earlier, clients also have a right to self-determination. *Self-determination* is each individual's right to make his or her own decisions. Applied to human services this means that practitioners are responsible for: (1) informing clients about available resources; (2) helping them define and articulate their alternatives; and (3) assisting them in evaluating the consequences of each option. This means that clients may choose to accept or refuse services. Practitioners should nurture and support client self-determination. The point is to assist clients in making the best, most informed choices possible.

Example of a Violation. Lulabelle is a job coach for a county social services department. Stephanie, age 19, is one of Lulabelle's clients. Stephanie emphasizes how she would like to get a clerical job such as being a secretary or administrative assistant. She says she is generally shy with people and would like a job where she could work in a more solitary manner. She also states she has always been good at typing. Lulabelle knows that Stephanie never graduated from high school and cannot believe that Stephanie's typing or writing skills are anywhere near adequate for such a position. Therefore, Lulabelle decides not to inform Stephanie about available clerical alternatives. Rather, she steers Stephanie to think about becoming a sales clerk.

Example of Compliance. DeShawn is a counselor at a group home for people with cognitive disabilities (formerly and more negatively referred to as mental retardation). One of his clients, Vincent, age 23, has a mild to moderate disability and has been a group home resident for two months. He is a pleasant individual who likes to socialize and participate in the home's activities (such as playing games, going bowling, seeing movies, or occasionally eating out). Additionally, Vincent conscientiously attends to his responsibilities. For example, he eagerly does dishes, folds clothes, or mops floors when given clear instructions. He obviously takes pride in such accomplishments as they make him feel like a "normal" person who can do useful work. Vincent can read at the third grade level. When talking, he has some difficulty putting sentences together, and his speech is difficult to understand.

DeShawn feels that Vincent has much more to offer than sitting around the group home all day long watching television. When DeShawn asks Vincent if he would like to get a job, Vincent enthusiastically agrees. DeShawn and Vincent focus on Vincent's strengths including his ambition, conscientiousness, responsiveness to supervision, and ability to get along

well with others. DeShawn successfully arranges for Vincent to get a part-time maintenance job at a local drug store. Vincent readily assumes work responsibilities and takes pride in his job. DeShawn also gets Vincent involved with the local Boys Club. As Vincent loves to play games, he now volunteers at the Club regularly, teaching children games and supervising their activities.

Building on Clients' Strengths

NOHSE Statement 9: Human service professionals recognize and build on client strengths. (NOHSE, p. 2)

Finally, human services professionals are committed to recognizing and building upon client strengths. This helps empower clients to develop and foster their capacities to problem solve and manage their own lives.

Human Services Professionals' Responsibilities to Community and Society

NOHSE Statement 10: Human service professionals are aware of local, state, and federal laws. They advocate for change in regulations and statutes when such legislation conflicts with ethical guidelines and/or client rights. Where laws are harmful to individuals, groups or communities, human service professionals consider the conflict between the values of obeying the law and the values of serving people and may decide to initiate social action.

NOHSE Statement 11: Human service professionals keep informed about current social issues as they affect the client and the community. They share information with clients, groups, and community as part of their work.

NOHSE Statement 12: Human service professionals understand the complex interaction between individuals, their families, the communities in which they live, and society.

NOHSE Statement 13: Human service professionals act as advocates in addressing unmet client and community needs. Human service professionals provide a mechanism for identifying unmet client needs, calling attention to these needs, and assisting in planning and mobilizing to advocate for those needs at the local community level. (NOHSE, p. 2)

As you can see, a human services professional's obligations to the community and society cover several areas. First is a responsibility to stay abreast of laws and regulations that have an impact on our profession and on client rights. When needed, we must engage in appropriate social action to bring about changes that are consistent with the profession's ethical obligations, address client unmet needs, and ensure the rights of all society's members. This includes forming coalitions and working with client groups to achieve desired ends. As part of their professional responsibility, workers should pursue social and political action seeking fair and equal access to resources and opportunities. They should actively support policies to improve the human condition and promote social justice for all. *Social justice* is a condition that exists when all members of society have similar rights, opportunities, and access to resources. Similarly, human services professionals should work to prevent and eliminate conditions, policies, rules, and regulations that discriminate against or exploit vulnerable populations such as people of color, those with disabilities, and others.

As professional helpers, human services workers must be constantly aware of how the larger society impacts on the individual and vice versa. All areas in which clients operate, such as families, groups, and educational and economic systems, affect individuals and, in turn, affect these same systems. For example, a client thrown out of work by a recession may be experiencing depression, financial problems, lower self-esteem, or other social/psychological difficulties. As he is affected by the economic system, he simultaneously affects his own family.

Professional Qualifications

NOHSE Statement 14: Human service professionals represent their qualifications to the public accurately.

NOHSE Statement 15: Human service professionals describe the effectiveness of programs, treatments, and/or techniques accurately. (NOHSE, p. 2)

We will always accurately represent our professional qualifications to the public as well as factually describe the effectiveness of programs, treatments, and services we provide. This also requires that we practice within our area of competence while being honest with clients about what kinds of help we may be able to offer.

Cultural Competence and Nondiscrimination

NOHSE Statement 16: Human service professionals advocate for the rights of all members of society, par-

ticularly those who are members of minorities and groups at which discriminatory practices have historically been directed.

NOHSE Statement 17: Human service professionals provide services without discrimination or preference based on age, ethnicity, culture, race, disability, gender, religion, sexual orientation or socioeconomic status.

NOHSE Statement 18: Human service professionals are knowledgeable about the cultures and communities with which they practice. They are aware of multiculturalism in society and its impact on the community as well as individuals within the community. They respect individuals and groups, their culture and beliefs.

NOHSE Statement 19: Human service professionals are aware of their own cultural backgrounds, beliefs, and values, recognizing the potential for impact on their relationships with others.

NOHSE Statement 20: Human service professionals are aware of sociopolitical issues that differentially affect clients from diverse backgrounds.

NOHSE Statement 21: Human service professionals seek the training, experience, education and supervision necessary to ensure their effectiveness in working with culturally diverse client populations. (NOHSE, pp. 2–3)

Recognizing the multicultural world in which we live, we are committed to nondiscriminatory services, culturally relevant helping relationships, and sensitivity to populations that have historically been discriminated against. We recognize how those from diverse backgrounds may be negatively affected by social, political, and economic issues in society. We also acknowledge the importance of learning about the cultures of others and understanding one's own cultural background and how it affects our relationship with others. A lack of understanding of the cultural experiences of others reduces significantly our effectiveness with multicultural clients.

Example of Compliance. Gschu, a counselor at a homeless shelter, is seeing an increasing number of Haitian immigrants enter the shelter. She determines that she must enhance her knowledge of their cultural values in order to work with them more effectively. As she develops an understanding, she begins to understand that "the plight of Haitian immigrants is noteworthy because of its complexity and because of their flight from political and economic oppression" (J. A. Allen, 1995, p. 125). Gschu discovers that a local organization exists primarily to assist immigrants of Caribbean origin socially, economically, and politically. Some of the organization's goals include "contributing to the economic welfare of the community through the stimulation of businesses, promoting the housing needs of their constituents, and assisting their members in securing employment" (1995, p 125). Seeking information about Haitian immigrants from this organization enhances both Gschu's understanding of their culture and her ability to communicate with her clients. It also makes her aware of a whole new orb of resources potentially available to clients.

Human Services Professionals' Obligations to Colleagues

NOHSE Statement 22: Human service professionals avoid duplicating another professional's helping relationship with a client. They consult with other professionals who are assisting the client in a different type of relationship when it is in the best interest of the client to do so.

NOHSE Statement 23: When a human service professional has a conflict with a colleague, he or she first seeks out the colleague in an attempt to manage the problem. If necessary, the professional then seeks the assistance of supervisors, consultants or other professionals in efforts to manage the problem.

NOHSE Statement 24: Human service professionals respond appropriately to unethical behavior of colleagues. Usually this means initially talking directly with the colleague and, if no resolution is forthcoming, reporting the colleague's behavior to supervisory or administrative staff and/or to the professional organization(s) to which the colleague belongs.

NOHSE Statement 25: All consultations between human service professionals are kept confidential unless to do so would result in harm to clients or communities. (NOHSE, p. 3)

Human services professionals have four basic responsibilities to colleagues. First, they should avoid duplicating other professionals' helping relationships with clients. Whenever possible they work in consort with other professionals to further client well-being. Second, in the event of a conflict with a colleague, professionals are obligated to address the problem directly with the individual. This includes seeking outside assistance in doing so, if needed.

Third, if we perceive a colleague's actions to be unethical we raise this concern with that person

seeking to resolve it. If this fails, we are committed to reporting the colleague's behavior to appropriate supervisory or professional authorities.

Finally, human services professionals are obligated to keep all confidences that arise in the process of seeking consultation from others. Failure to do so can harm clients and others just as much as any other breach of confidentiality.

Example of Compliance. Kloua and Marci are both workers for a rural social services agency. They also have been working together for several years. Lately, Marci has been asking Kloua to cover for her on Friday afternoon so that she can spend time with her new boyfriend. Initially, Kloua agreed to this arrangement but is beginning to resent the fact that Marci departs at noon on Friday leaving Kloua to handle both her work and Marci's. Finally, Kloua sits down with Marci to discuss the situation and assertively express her concern about what has happened.

Human Services Professionals' Obligations to the Profession

NOHSE Statement 26: Human service professionals know the limit and scope of their professional knowledge and offer services only within their knowledge and skill base.

NOHSE Statement 27: Human service professionals seek appropriate consultation and supervision to assist in decision-making when there are legal, ethical or other dilemmas.

NOHSE Statement 28: Human service professionals act with integrity, honesty, genuineness, and objectivity.

NOHSE Statement 29: Human service professionals promote cooperation among related disciplines (e.g., psychology, counseling, social work, nursing, family and consumer sciences, medicine, education) to foster professional growth and interests within the various fields.

NOHSE Statement 30: Human service professionals promote the continuing development of their profession. They encourage membership in professional associations, support research endeavors, foster educational advancement, advocate for appropriate legislative actions, and participate in other related professional activities.

NOHSE Statement 31: Human service professionals seek out new and effective approaches to enhance their professional abilities. (NOHSE, p. 3)

Human services workers are obligated to serve as competent professionals who preserve their integrity and continuously pursue their own professional development. Workers should represent the profession in a positive light by demonstrating objectivity in their decision making and honesty and genuineness in their interactions with others. They should also be committed to cooperating with other professionals, supporting the goals of the human service profession, and participating in professional activities. It is a professional obligation to continue developing and improving one's skills as a human services worker, thereby enhancing one's ability to serve clients.

Professionals must know the limits of their own knowledge and skill and practice only within the realm of their competence. Competence involves having adequate knowledge and skills to effectively complete one's work and accomplish goals. Practicing beyond your knowledge or skill level endangers clients and our own professional reputation.

Example of a Violation.   Hank is an adult protective services worker for an urban county. His clients are older adults who may be victims of physical or psychological maltreatment. Living arrangements vary from staying with relatives to being homeless. Services Hank's unit provides include "preliminary investigation of medical and psychiatric care, social casework, goods and services that allow the client to remain at home, respite care, emergency care, placement in a rest or residential home, referral to legal assistance, . . . referral for medical assessment, transportation, and other services" (Austin, 1995, p. 91).

Hank has begun working with one case that especially interests him. Lois, 82, lives with her daughter, Grizelda, 57, who appears to have a serious alcohol abuse problem. Hank feels this problem is directly related to her alleged abuse of her mother. Hank has no training in alcohol and other substance abuse. However, he thinks to himself, "How hard can it really be?" He proceeds to "counsel" Grizelda regarding her abuse.

When needed, human services professionals seek consultation or supervision to help resolve issues that pose ethical or legal dilemmas. In the human services context, *supervision* is the process of overseeing and directing the work of employees. *Good* supervision also involves being readily available to help when needed, supporting workers, evaluating their job performance, and facilitating their development of new skills. *Consultation* is provision of special help when

needed and sought from an outside expert source. For instance, workers might go to their immediate supervisor for help when that supervisor is available and knowledgeable. However, they might seek outside consultation to help solve a problem when their supervisor is unavailable or unable to provide help. They, along with their supervisor and others, might also seek consultation from an outside source for needed expertise when neither they nor their supervisor have the necessary knowledge or skills.

One example of a problem that might require help involves a worker who must deal with a client's mental condition or health issue about which the worker knows little. Another scenario where workers might need help from a supervisor or consultant concerns addressing extremely difficult situations such as those posed by multiproblem families (those facing problems in many arenas of life including poverty, housing, health, behavioral problems, disabilities, and emotional problems).

Ethical standards require that practitioners seek out help, even when they're overwhelmed. Ignoring the problem or adopting an "out of sight, out of mind" attitude is inappropriate. Rather, workers should attack problems to the best of their ability and seek out additional help when needed.

Finally, it is also important to represent the profession in a positive light by demonstrating objectivity and integrity in decision making and honesty and genuineness in interactions with others. We also are committed to cooperating with other professionals, working for development of the human services profession, and participating in professional activities. As professionals we continually seek new, more effective ways of helping clients and carrying out our duties.

Example of Compliance.   Emanuel has accepted a new position with the homeless coalition that involves advocacy and development of resources to serve the homeless. Although he is well informed about many aspects of his role as a human services professional, Emanuel does not feel very competent with respect to grant writing, one of his new responsibilities. He enrolls in a local university course on grant writing and reads several books and articles on this topic.

Human Services Professionals' Responsibility to Employers

NOHSE Statement 32: Human service professionals adhere to commitments made to their employers.

NOHSE Statement 33: Human service professionals participate in efforts to establish and maintain employment conditions which are conducive to high quality client services. They assist in evaluating the effectiveness of the agency through reliable and valid assessment measures.

NOHSE Statement 34: When a conflict arises between fulfilling the responsibility to the employer and the responsibility to the client, human service professionals advise both of the conflict and work conjointly with all involved to manage the conflict. (NOHSE, pp. 3–4)

Because most human services work occurs within organizations of various sizes, we have a responsibility to our employing agencies. First and foremost of these is to adhere to commitments that we have made to the employer. We also work to ensure employment conditions that are humane, contribute to quality client services, and engage in evaluation efforts to improve agency services. When conflicts occur between our obligation to the employer and to the client, professionals share this dilemma with both parties and work with them to manage the conflict.

Example of a Violation. Hargrove, a human services worker at a day care center, is angry with the administration. He feels the administration is unfair to the center's workers and is not treating clients the way they should be treated. He calls parents to complain to them about the agency's other workers and administrators.

Human Services Professionals' Responsibility to Self

NOHSE Statement 35: Human service professionals strive to personify those characteristics typically associated with the profession (e.g., accountability, respect for others, genuineness, empathy, pragmatism).

NOHSE Statement 36: Human service professionals foster self-awareness and personal growth in themselves. They recognize that when professionals are aware of their own values, attitudes, cultural backgrounds, and personal needs, the process of helping others is less likely to be negatively impacted by those factors.

NOHSE Statement 36: Human service professionals recognize a commitment to lifelong learning and continually upgrade knowledge and skills to serve the populations better. (NOHSE, p. 4)

You may be puzzling over this one. What kind of responsibility do we have to ourselves? Well, to start with, we must work to develop those characteristics

that are the mark of a competent professional. Empathy, respect for others, and genuineness are all crucial abilities for developing and maintaining professional relationships with others. We must also develop our ability to be accountable for what we do and say and to be practical in what we suggest or propose. For example, recommending the agency increase its staff by 50 percent when it is already facing serious financial problems is impractical, at best.

We must develop a level of self-awareness that ensures we will not be dealing with our own issues when we are trying to help clients. To do this requires an ongoing awareness of all aspects of our lives—culture, values, needs, and beliefs. It also means that we have to resolve our own life challenges to the extent that they don't interfere with our efforts to assist clients. Finally, we must recognize that our need for new knowledge expands continually and that we must be committed to seeking new learning throughout our professional life. It is this commitment that will help ensure clients receive the most effective and relevant services possible.

 ## Ethical Dilemmas

In human services practice, one encounters a wide range of ethical dilemmas. A dilemma is a situation where one must make a difficult choice between two alternatives. Ethical dilemmas usually involve problematic situations whose possible solutions all offer imperfect and unsatisfactory answers. In other words, your ethical guidelines conflict with each other. There is no one perfect answer that can conform to all the ethical principles in the professional standards. You are stuck with deciding what to do.

Thankfully, we have established professional values to help guide us through the difficult decision-making process when solving an ethical dilemma. Rarely, if ever, does an ethical dilemma involve being faced with bad alternatives that are exactly equal. Rather, we can use values to carefully examine and weigh the pros and cons of each alternative to determine the best course of action.

An ethical dilemma, then, involves being faced with a situation where a decision must be made under circumstances where ethical principles are in conflict. For example, perhaps you cannot abide by the ethic of confidentiality and save a suicidal person's life at the same time. However, because we have professional values, we can formulate some guidelines for making tough choices. We can establish a hierarchy to decide what aspect of any particular ethical dilemma is more important than another and then act on that decision. The following sections will first establish a process for conceptualizing an ethical dilemma, review a procedure for ethical decision making, and then examine a range of ethical dilemmas common in human service practice.

Conceptualizing and Addressing an Ethical Dilemma: Decision-Making Steps

The first step in determining what to do about an ethical dilemma is to establish the fact that one actually exists. There are a series of variables to consider as you first conceptualize the potential problem. Figure 2.1 illustrates eight steps in the decision-making process.

Step 1: Recognize the Problem

The first step in confronting a potential ethical dilemma is to begin recognizing the problem (Corey et al., 1998). The seed might be a gut reaction, that is, an unarticulated emotional feeling that something is not right. Something does not fit together or make any sense. You must determine that an ethical dilemma exists before going any further.

Case Scenario.   To illustrate how to proceed when you first become aware of an ethical dilemma's possibility, we will take you through an example by following the proposed step-by-step conceptualization process. The scenario's intent, however, is not to provide you with a recipe for how to approach ethical dilemmas. In reality, each dilemma is different.

Figure 2.1   *Conceptualizing an Ethical Dilemma*

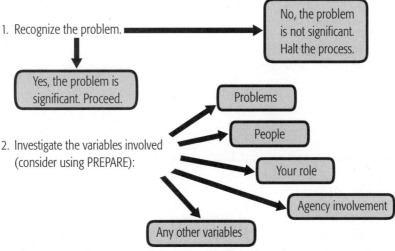

3. Get feedback from others.

4. Appraise what values and ethical standards apply to the dilemma.

5. Evaluate the dilemma on the basis of established ethical principles.

6. Identify and think about possible alternatives to pursue:

7. Weigh the pros and cons of each alternative.

8. Make your decision.

Each worker may perceive the dilemma differently, focus upon different variables, and eventually make a different choice. This scenario only depicts one worker's situation and thought process. There is not necessarily one uniquely best solution.

The dilemma involves Tombi, a worker who runs a series of secondary school support groups for troubled teens. One of her 16-year-old clients, Tolemy, faithfully attends a support group for young people suffering from depression. Through no fault of his own, Tolemy has had a turbulent history, having lived in eight different foster homes. His biological parents were tragically killed in a car accident when he was only 4. As there were no relatives available to take Tolemy and his siblings in, they were shifted from foster home to foster home. Sometimes, some of them were placed together; more often than not they were separated. Tolemy was virtually never to blame for his displacement. For instance, one foster father developed cancer and could no longer care for foster children. Another foster family moved out of state when the parents got new and better jobs. Yet another foster mother became pregnant with triplets, and the couple decided they could no longer adequately care for foster kids.

Tolemy struggles with many issues. Although a bright, good-looking young man, he thinks very little of himself. He has limited self-confidence and is shy. Without good reason, he tends to blame himself for having such a troubled history. He has had thoughts of harming himself and getting it over with many times.

Tolemy currently resides with his 21-year-old sister Bebi, her 6-month-old daughter Alicia, and her 24-year-old boyfriend Mark. Tolemy is extremely grateful for this haven, finally feels somewhat settled, and wants to remain there.

One day after group sessions, Tolemy lingers in Tombi's office pretending to look at some algebra homework. After the other group members leave, he asks Tombi if he could talk to her a minute. She replies that of course he can, and Tolemy begins his story. It turns out that his sister and her boyfriend fight a lot. Sometimes, after arguments, Mark stomps out on his own to go drinking, leaving Bebi to stew in unresolved anger. At such times, Bebi has little patience. When Alicia cries, Bebi can become infuriated. She takes out her frustration by putting Alicia's head under the faucet and dousing it with either very cold or very hot water. Tolemy is greatly worried about his niece. Thus, Tombi *recognizes that a serious problem exists.*

Step 2: Investigate the Variables Involved

The second step in the conceptualization process concerns investigating the complex matrix of variables that encompass the dilemma (Corey et al., 1998; Loewenberg et al., 2000). What problems are involved? What is your agency's involvement? Roll the dilemma around in your mind. Think deeply about what it is and why it exists. What other variables are concerned that might provide you with clues to a workable solution?

Case Scenario. Consider how you might apply this step to the case vignette concerning Tombi and Tolemy. Tombi needs more information, so she *investigates the variables involved.* She urges Tolemy to proceed with his explanation of his home environment. Tolemy emphasizes his dilemma: If he causes any trouble, Mark has warned that he will kick Tolemy out. Where would Tolemy go then? He has nowhere to go. If Bebi and Mark find out Tolemy told someone, Tolemy is certain they will get rid of him. Yet if nothing's done, he is terrified that Alicia will be seriously hurt.

Tombi knows that Tolemy has a foster care worker, Pedro, who monitors Tolemy's placement with Bebi. Tolemy feels that if he tells Pedro about the abuse, the same thing will happen—he will lose his home. Tombi also knows that reporting any suspected abuse or neglect is mandatory for human service workers in her state. Tolemy also knows this law. Tombi told Tolemy's support group members during their first group session what types of information she is required to report and, thus, be unable to keep confidential.

Step 3: Get Feedback from Others

If at all possible, talk to other people about your concerns (Corey et al., 1998; Sinclair, 1993). Bounce your ideas off of them to more firmly establish your objectivity. Brainstorm with them, looking for different ways of viewing and eventually handling the dilemma. A trusted supervisor or colleagues familiar with the dilemma's context would be helpful.

Case Scenario. Tombi *gets feedback from others.* She talks with her supervisor about Tolemy's situation. She also solicits ideas from a trusted coworker who has worked for the school system for 20 years.

Step 4: Appraise What Values and Ethical Standards Apply to the Dilemma

Assess and choose what values and ethical standards might best apply to the dilemma (Corey et al., 1998; Loewenberg et al., 2000). What specific aspects of the ethical standards do you feel are being violated? You may discover that there is really no ethical *dilemma*, only a more straightforward ethical *problem*. A problem can have some clear solution, while a dilemma, by definition, has competing, imperfect solutions. If the standards provide you with a clear answer, then use them to follow steps toward the problem's resolution.

Case Scenario. Tombi *determines that a number of professional values and ethical standards apply to the dilemma.* Values include service, dignity and worth of the person, importance of human relationships, and integrity. Tombi's responsibility is to serve both Tolemy and Alicia as people who are in great need. She must also consider the dignity of both. She respects Tolemy's right to make his own choices. She also respects the value of Alicia's health and well-being. Tombi knows her relationship with Tolemy is important. To some extent, he depends on her to help him work on his self-confidence and his ability to look more objectively at himself and his life. Tombi also realizes that Tolemy's relationship with his sister is critical. If at all possible, she would certainly choose to strengthen rather than weaken their bonds. Finally, Tombi must maintain her integrity. She must make an ethical decision to produce the least harm and enhance people's well-being to the best of her ability.

Ethical standards involved in this case include commitment to clients, self-determination, and confidentiality. Tombi must maintain her commitment to her client Tolemy and his well-being. Yet, she also must be concerned with Alicia's welfare. Child abuse is certainly at odds with society's and the individual's welfare. Tombi must respect Tolemy's privacy and confidentiality as much as possible. Likewise, to the greatest extent possible, Tolemy should be able to make his own decisions about what he will do.

Step 5: Evaluate the Dilemma on the Basis of Established Ethical Principles

Making conscious decisions about what values are more important than others is possible. One can establish a hierarchy of principles based on values that can guide you through the process of confronting an ethical dilemma. Remember that ethical dilemmas always involve situations with imperfect solutions. Each dilemma involves some conflict among ethical principles so that abiding by them all is impossible for you. For example, you might determine that staying alive is more important than telling the truth. Telling the truth is the ethical thing to do. However, what if you are in a situation where telling the truth and keeping someone (perhaps yourself) alive at the same time is impossible? Your arbitrarily best course of action might then be not to tell the truth.

Case Scenario. Tombi *evaluates the dilemma on the basis of established ethical principles.* This process is getting difficult to discuss because a suggested hierarchy of principles for ethical decision making will not be explained until the next section. Suffice it to say that the ethical principle assuming the highest priority involves the sanctity of human life. Ethical choices must be made to allow people to survive and thrive, existing with their basic needs met. Other principles in order of their priority include fair and equal treatment, free choice and freedom, least harm, good quality of life, confidentiality, and access to information. In this hierarchy, confidentiality is significantly less critical than the right to life or even the right to protection from harm.

Step 6: Identify and Think about Possible Alternatives to Pursue

What can you do in your job to solve the dilemma? What creative ideas can you come up with? What other people might help you with their consultation, support, or action to solve the problem?

Case Scenario. Tombi *identifies a number of alternative plans of action.* First, she could simply report the abuse, and repercussions would result as they may. Second, Tombi could ignore the fact that Tolemy shared the information with her and go on with her own business. Third, Tombi could work with Tolemy to determine a way to alert authorities to the problem more indirectly.

Step 7: Weigh the Pros and Cons of Each Alternative

Weighing the pros and cons of each alternative is a common perspective in various aspects of human services practice. This approach is also useful in resolving ethical dilemmas (Corey et al., 1998). What course of action is best for the client? What alternative is most likely to succeed? How might you best proceed?

Case Scenario.   Tombi *weighs the pros and cons of each alternative.* Her first option is to call the authorities and report the abuse. Tolemy would have to suffer whatever consequences transcend upon him. It is likely that Alicia would be removed from the home. Bebi and Mark might evict Tolemy from their home. Tolemy would then need someplace else to go. A major question concerns how this eviction would affect his depression, overall mental health, and his relationship with Tombi.

Tombi's second alternative is to ignore the situation entirely. This alternative is irresponsible in that she then fails to help Alicia, who is in great danger of harm. This choice is also illegal as her state requires reporting of alleged abuse.

Tombi's third option is to figure out another way of informing authorities without directly implicating Tolemy. This would both protect Tolemy and address Alicia's situation.

Step 8: Make Your Decision

Finally, make a decision regarding what is the best route for you to take. The main thing about confronting an ethical dilemma is to do some serious thinking about it.

Case Scenario.   Tombi *makes a decision.* She works on her third option, namely notifying authorities while protecting Tolemy. She talks with Tolemy about this possibility. They decide to contact Tolemy's foster care worker Pedro and discuss the problem with him. Together they determine that a viable option would be to keep Tolemy's report of the abuse anonymous. His name would not enter into the issue at all. Anonymous reports can originate from neighbors, concerned friends, or other family members. Pedro as a foster care worker is responsible for Tolemy's well-being while residing in the foster placement. Any suspected abuse might also involve Tolemy as a victim. Thus, Pedro can legitimately involve himself in the situation and work with a protective services worker. Pedro can help to protect Tolemy, yet focus on the real problem, the abuse.

Ranking Ethical Principles: Loewenberg, Dolgoff, and Harrington's "Ethical Principles Screen"

There are various ways of addressing ethical dilemmas and making decisions regarding how to proceed. The following section will focus on one prominent method, Loewenberg and colleagues' "Ethical Principles Screen" (2000, pp. 68–72). This approach proposes a hierarchy of ethical principles with which to evaluate the potential courses of action possible for any ethical dilemma. A hierarchy is a ranked order in which a principle takes precedence over the principles below it. In other words, abiding by the first principle is more important than principles two through seven, the second principle than principles three through seven, and so on.

Principle #1: People Have the Right to Have Their Basic Needs Met

This principle stresses that people have a basic right to life. Therefore, workers should abide by this principle before any other ethical principle. When an ethical dilemma involves a life-or-death variable, choose an action to save the life, even if this means breaking confidentiality with a client or suppressing the rights of others. Sustaining life takes precedence.

Principle #2: People Have the Right to Fair and Equal Treatment

The second ethical principle guarantees fair and equal treatment. Human services workers should make decisions to abide by this principle except in those cases where life or death is involved. Ethical principle #1 is the only condition that takes precedence.

Principle #3: People Have the Right to Choice and Freedom

Ethical principle #3 maintains that people's right to be free is the third priority in addressing an ethical dilemma. We all know the value that human services places on the principle of self-determination. Making their own decisions is people's basic right. The "Ethical Principles Screen" indicates that only people's right to survival or their right to equal treatment takes precedence over their freedom.

Principle #4: People Have the Right to be Protected from Harm

This principle states that people have the basic right to be protected from injury. In the event of potential harm, people have the right to experience the least initial injury possible, the least lasting harm or injury, and, finally, "the most easily reversible harm" (Loewenberg et al., 2000, p. 71).

Principle #5: People Have the Right to a Good Quality of Life

People have the right to seek and attain a "better quality of life" than they currently have (Loewenberg et al., 2000, p. 71). This principle applies to individuals, groups, neighborhoods, communities, states, and nations. Only principles #1 through #4 take precedence over this right.

Principle #6: People Have the Right to Secure Their Privacy and Confidentiality

Human services practitioners should strive to secure people's privacy and confidentiality. People have the right not to have their private information made public. We have established that confidentiality is the ethical principle that workers should not share information provided by a client or about a client unless that worker has the client's explicit permission to do so. Such information might include clients' names, what they say, professional beliefs and findings about clients, and anything written about the clients. Confidentiality is a principle strongly stressed in human services practice. Why, then, is it #6 of seven in the Ethical Principles Screen's list? Later portions of the chapter focusing on ethical dilemmas will discuss this issue more thoroughly.

Principle #7: People Have the Right to the Truth and All Available Information

Ethical Principle #7 states that people have the right to the truth. They have the right to accurate information. Having the truth and nothing but the truth unveiled to you all of the time would be nice. When possible, this axiom is important for workers to follow. However, if you are legally forbidden to disclose information to clients, what do you do? Or, should you be forced to tell them everything you think about them, even when your thoughts and ideas are negative? Must you always show people all your notes about them and the issues concerning them?

A Postscript Concerning Ethical Guidelines

You may or may not personally agree with Loewenberg and colleagues' proposed ethical guidelines. They provide one example of an ethical guide to decision making in practice. Regardless of what ethical guidelines you use in practice, you will continue to be responsible for your own behavior and decisions.

Discussion and Resolution of Ethical Dilemmas in Generalist Practice Contexts

There is an endless array of ethical dilemmas encountered in generalist human services practice. Addressing them all, however, is beyond the scope of this text. Even so, we will discuss some of the most significant ones, including: confidentiality and privileged communication; self-determination and paternalism; dual relationships; laws, policies, and regulations; whistle-blowing; and personal and professional values (Reamer, 1995a, pp. 897–989).

Confidentiality and Privileged Communication

Confidential information includes personal details about the client's identity, records of verbal statements made by the client, professional reports or professed opinions concerning the client, and content from other records (e.g., employment, health, or educational). Typically, professionals respect and protect clients' privacy and confidentiality. This principle sounds simple enough, but what if a client tells you that he is sexually abusing his 5-year-old child, that he cannot control himself, and that he does not want anyone to know about it? Or, what if a client tells you that she made $2,500 last week in her cocaine dealings? Or, what if a married client tells you he is really gay, has had numerous unprotected sexual encounters with other men over the past 15 years, worries about having contracted AIDS, but absolutely does not want to tell his wife about his fears? Highlight 2.1 addresses some of the concerns involving AIDS and confidentiality.

Confidentiality is not a simple concept. Actually, two dimensions are involved: relative confidentiality and privilege. Confidentiality, often referred to as *relative confidentiality,* is "a broader term that exists for the protection of the individual client but may allow a limited amount of disclosure, especially to those co-workers, superiors, and subordinates whose knowledge of certain communications is required to aid in the therapy [or planned change process] of the

HIGHLIGHT 2.1

Confidentiality and Persons Living with AIDS

AIDS has posed some special problems of confidentiality that differ from those of any other illness. Unlike many other diseases, people with AIDS face discrimination "in many spheres, including housing, employment, insurance, and health care" (Taylor-Brown, 1995, p. 1293).

Abramson (1990) interviewed practitioners who spent from 20 to 100 percent of their caseload time working with persons diagnosed with AIDS. She found that secrecy was by far the most dominant problematic issue addressed by these workers.

This secrecy primarily concerned three areas. First, secrets were kept from those diagnosed with AIDS. Second, there were secrets kept from people close to those with AIDS who were unknowingly at risk of contracting the disease. Third, secrets about the AIDS diagnosis were kept from society at large.

Evident were numerous dilemmas concerning confidentiality. Some involved not telling people about their own positive diagnosis because of the negative emotional ramifications. Others involved not telling people at risk of contracting AIDS from the client in order to keep the client's confidentiality. Still others concerned hiding the diagnosis from other staff, agencies, and organizations. For example, such information might be kept confidential in order to allow the client continuity of health insurance benefits.

Abramson emphasized what a horrible quandary secrecy imposed for practitioners. Although secrecy might maintain an individual's confidentiality, there are numerous negative effects. She continued that:

> . . . on a practical level, secrets can impede understanding, foster isolation, prevent access to services, increase stigma, and interfere with a sense of

community, keeping society separated into "us" and "them." More important, the energies that should be invested in finding a cure, changing behaviors, and fighting discrimination are drained by the demands of secrecy by patients, families, and health providers. (1990, p. 172)

Some states have enacted laws aimed at regulating knowledge about HIV-infected people (Gothard, 1995). For example, one law required people knowingly infected with HIV to inform sexual partners of the status. Whether such laws actually encourage telling partners for fear of lawsuits or negative legal repercussions is doubtful. Still, other states have established laws forbidding others knowing about a person's HIV-positive status from disclosing that information. A general trend appears to place responsibility on the infected person to notify partners of risks (1995). These conflicting laws do not necessarily help with the worker's dilemma concerning confidentiality when clients choose not to inform.

People are often terrified by AIDS. They want no one to know about it. They fear, often realistically so, that they will be ostracized and discriminated against (Corey et al., 1998; Lloyd, 1995; Loewenberg et al., 2000). Fear may force them to cling doggedly to confidentiality.

However, questions must be raised about the well-being not only of the client but also of those interacting with the client and of society at large. People who are positively diagnosed need to know about their condition in order to maximize the treatment and prevention aspects that maximize longevity. People who are at risk of contracting AIDS need to know in order to prevent contraction. Finally, society, with its many facets and organizations, must know in order to combat the disease and help those afflicted. Confidentiality concerning AIDS becomes a most complex and difficult issue. There are some laws that now restrict the amount of information that can be shared about a person with AIDS. These laws further restrict and affect confidentiality and the worker's freedom.

client" (Gothard, 1995, p. 1580). Relative confidentiality involves the professional's ethical responsibility to keep information as confidential as possible.

Privilege, on the other hand, refers to legal rights (Gambrill, 1997). Privilege means that what has transpired between the worker and client is protected by law and cannot be revealed without that client's expressed permission (Barker, 1999; Gothard, 1995).

However, in most, if not all, states even legal privilege is vulnerable (Gothard, 1995). Circumstances usually exist where workers must disclose privileged communication. For example, consider child or elderly maltreatment cases or situations where clients threaten to hurt themselves or others. In such instances, laws often maintain that protecting victims takes precedence over worker–client privilege

(Gothard, 1995; Hepworth, Rooney, & Larsen, 1997). Gambrill (1997) reports numerous other situations when privilege might be waived; these include when a client sues his worker, "a minor is involved in criminal activity," "a client is using certain types of drugs," "the court orders a professional examination," "a professional needs to collect fees for services rendered," or "the client dies" (1997, p. 52).

A landmark California court decision, *Tarasoff* v. *The Regents of the University of California* (1976), was the first "to recognize the duty of a psychotherapist to protect a third party from the foreseeable harm of a client" (Polowy & Gorenberg, 1997, p. 182). The case involved a student who told his therapist at a university outpatient clinic that he planned to murder his former girlfriend, who had dropped him. The therapist notified the campus police of the threat but failed to contact the young woman or her parents. As a result, the police apprehended the man but let him go shortly because he "appeared rational" and promised not to hurt her (1997, p. 182). About two months later he killed her. Subsequently, the woman's parents sued the therapist for failing to warn her of the potential danger. The California Supreme Court determined that the client–therapist relationship was "special" (1997, p. 182). Therefore, the therapist was responsible for taking "protective action by releasing confidential information about the client to those who are capable of preventing the threatened harm"; such responsibility "can include warning an outpatient's caregiver or family, involving the police, warning the potential victim, or involuntarily committing the client" (1997, p. 182). This case clearly accentuates human service workers' responsibility to notify potential victims of ensuing harm.

Compton and Galaway (1999) question the overall emphasis on confidentiality. They indicate that "[w]ith so many limitations on confidentiality, practitioners might seriously reconsider whether to offer it at all"; although they do believe that "you do have an obligation . . . to clearly discuss with the client what information you will be sharing, with whom you will be sharing it, and the reasons for such disclosures" (p. 162).

When workers are legally required to break confidentiality and are unable to gain the client's consent, it is advisable to notify the clients regarding the disclosure of confidential information and the potential consequences. This suggestion, at least, allows clients to prepare for the disclosure's potential repercussions.

When disclosure is required with or without consent, sharing the least amount of information is an appropriate means of maintaining some level of confidentiality. In other words, say no more than is absolutely necessary to fulfill the disclosure requirement.

Even before situations arise that require disclosure of confidential information, workers should inform clients about their limitations concerning confidentiality. For example, you might inform a minor as soon as possible in the intervention process that you must report any statement she makes concerning using drugs or violating other state laws. Additionally, mandatory reporting includes clients' reports of intention to harm themselves or others. Making these limitations early in the interviewing and intervention process places the responsibility on the client for maintaining confidentiality. They let clients know that they should not tell you specific types of information that they do not want reported.

Workers should also discuss with clients limitations on confidentiality within the agency setting. Clients should be aware that records may be viewed by secretaries who have access to records, supervisors for consultation, administrators for monitoring practice, other colleagues involved with the case, or students in field internships.

Workers should take great care in handling records. To the greatest extent possible, you should store records where unauthorized persons are least likely to secure access. Practitioners should take special care when using various electronic systems of storage and transmission which can be accessed by others not authorized to see a client's records. This includes fax machines, e-mail, computers, and answering machines. Workers should minimize the risk of unauthorized persons accessing confidential information.

Practitioners should also exercise extreme caution concerning talking about clients in both professional and personal settings. A worker should not talk about a case in front of colleagues unless there is some specific reasons for doing so. Likewise, workers should not informally share information about clients with friends or family or in public places where others might overhear. Consider the information serious and avoid using it as juicy tidbits in social conversation.

In summary, a generalist practitioner should make every effort to keep information about the client confidential. However, the worker should also be aware that, depending on the particular situation, there are many constraints about what really can and cannot be kept secret. Constraints include those imposed by the agency and other legal restrictions regarding what must be shared. Therefore, the worker should clarify to the client what these constraints are in order to maximize client understanding and control.

The following case provides an example of an ethical dilemma concerning confidentiality. Both the steps for conceptualizing an ethical dilemma and the Ethical Principles Screen will be applied.

Case Vignette.   Uranus, a 12-year-old, develops a life-threatening bronchial infection. As a result, she is rushed to the hospital and remains there for several days to recuperate. Uranus's condition gradually improves. On several occasions, nurses observe her curling up into a fetal position and crying softly to herself. They ask her what's wrong, but she refuses to answer. She shakes her head when asked if something physically related to her illness is bothering her. To find out what's going on, the nurses refer Uranus to Joni, the hospital human services worker who visits Uranus. At first, Uranus barely utters a word, but gradually she warms to Joni. Uranus hesitantly confesses that she is two and a half months pregnant. Hence, Joni *recognizes the problem* and *begins investigating the variables involved* (steps one and two in conceptualizing an ethical dilemma). Uranus desperately pleads with Joni not to tell her parents but to help her make plans so she can have and keep the baby.

At this point, several ethical dilemmas confront Joni (Loewenberg & Dolgoff, 1996). First, considering to keep the baby without her parents knowing is unrealistic for Uranus. Second, the potential negative social, emotional, and physical ramifications for Uranus are huge if she has and keeps the baby. Third, questions must be raised about Uranus's competence concerning making such a significant decision. To what extent is Uranus capable of understanding the consequences? Finally, Joni must question the extent to which she can influence Uranus one way or another. She surely has no right to pressure Uranus to have an abortion.

Joni *appraises values that apply to these dilemmas* (step four in conceptualizing an ethical dilemma). Joni is unable to pursue step three, *getting feedback from others,* because of her stringent time constraints. Applying the values of service, social justice, dignity and worth of the person, the importance of human relationships, integrity, and competency is difficult. Clients have the right to self-determination. However, to what extent does Uranus have adequate decision-making capacity? What are her parents' rights and responsibilities?

Joni proceeds to *evaluate the dilemma on the basis of established ethical principles* (step five in conceptualizing an ethical dilemma). Consideration of such a

situation involves several facets (Loewenberg et al., 2000). Ethical Principle #6 emphasizes the client's right to privacy and confidentiality. Ethical Principle #3 focuses on one's right to have free choice and freedom. Both principles underscore Uranus's right to make her own decisions and follow her directive of not contacting her parents. However, Principle #1 emphasizes people's right to life and having their basic needs fulfilled. Joni carefully considers Uranus's well-being, including the physical variable related to her health and the risks assumed in bearing a child at such an early age.

Joni *identifies possible alternatives* and *weighs the pros and cons of each* (steps six and seven in conceptualizing an ethical dilemma). One choice is to ignore the pregnancy revelation and pretend Uranus never informed her. Pros might include avoiding the worrisome issue. On the other hand, cons include failing to assume professional responsibility in looking after her client's welfare.

Another alternative, of course, is to inform Uranus's parents about the pregnancy. Cons include breaking Uranus's confidentiality and probably losing her trust. Pros include looking out for Uranus's well-being and involving her guardians in the decision-making process.

Joni decides that Ethical Principle #1, looking out for what Joni determines is Uranus's best interest, must take precedence. Joni *makes her decision* (step eight in conceptualizing an ethical dilemma) and, after informing Uranus of her plans, immediately calls Uranus's parents.

Self-Determination and Paternalism

The Ethical Standards requires that human services practitioners demonstrate respect for and promote the client's right to self-determination in pursuing their goals. *Self-determination* is an ethical principle that acknowledges people's right to make their own decisions and choices. Maintaining a commitment to client self-determination has been shown to enhance a positive relationship between worker and client (Kadushin, 1995).

Maximizing client self-determination to whatever extent possible is the practitioner's responsibility. For example, Abramson (1988) found that to varying degrees self-determination is possible for elderly patients in their own discharge planning from acute care hospitals. Most patients "participated actively in their own discharge planning process, and many controlled the discharge decisions" (1988, p. 446). Those with the poorest levels of mental and physical functioning participated the least. People with moderate to severe, although not mild, dementia found determining courses of action more difficult. (*Dementia* is a condition of seriously impaired mental ability, including loss of memory, diminished judgment, inability to think abstractly, alterations in personality, and, often, disturbed behavior.) Abramson concludes:

> *Workers should assess the capacity of each individual and provide choices at whatever level the patient can respond to them. For example, encouraging someone to pick the hour for discharge (a task within the capacity of many demented individuals), or the clothing or other possessions to bring to a new setting, might have significant effects on postdischarge outcome. Although such strategies do not provide true client self-determination, they do enhance individual perceived control, which in itself has been found to be beneficial. (1988, p. 446)*

Paternalism is action that interferes "with a client's wishes or freedom 'for his own good'" (Reamer, 1995a, p. 897). Examples include preventing clients from harming themselves, providing necessary services that clients do not want, failing to provide information to clients, or providing clients with censored, inaccurate, or altered information (1995a). The worker's underlying motive consistently concerns making a decision that supersedes the client's wishes on behalf of the client's well-being. Highlight 2.2 addresses ethical issues concerning self-determination and paternalism when working with people who have physical disabilities.

Ethical dilemmas involving self-determination and paternalism often focus on two other concepts, informed consent and clients' decision-making capacity (Reamer, 1995a). *Informed consent* means that workers should clearly inform clients about the purposes, risks, limitations, possible costs, alternatives, right of refusal, and time frames concerning the services provided. A potential problem is that a client may be unable to make an informed decision. For example, lacking maturity and experience, a child client may not be capable of making an informed decision (Abramson, 1982). Likewise, a client who lacks mental competence (e.g., an individual with serious cognitive impairment or mental disability) may be unable to grasp the implications of a decision (1982).

The client's decision-making capacity can also induce ethical dilemmas. Examples of such dilemmas abound. A pregnant 13-year-old living in a foster home whose parents are deceased insists that she will keep the baby and bring it up by herself. A man in his 50s with a crippling, progressive, and severely painful disease explores ways to commit suicide. An elderly woman with increasing forgetfulness and lack of mental clarity demands that she remain alone in her own home, despite the fact that she has already started two minor fires by forgetting to turn off her stove burners. A young man with AIDS boasts about having numerous sexual conquests without informing partners about their potential infection.

The variations regarding the concepts of informed consent and clients' decision-making capacity and their involvement in ethical dilemmas are endless. The following two cases provide examples. The steps conceptualizing an ethical dilemma will be applied (note that steps are printed in italics).

Case Example 1. Edna is a worker for a homeless shelter in a northern inner-city neighborhood. Her job involves counseling residents regarding future plans, job training, employment possibilities, resource acquisition, empowerment, and self-confidence issues. She also does some outreach to homeless people in the community, offering them the shelter's services.

One January day Edna is walking through the shelter's neighborhood, which has many deserted buildings often frequented by homeless people. She sees a woman dressed in rags and hauling a large green garbage bag filled with some kind of stuffing. Edna calls out to the woman, but the woman scurries away around the corner of a building. Although Edna tries to follow her, the woman abruptly disappears from view. Edna *recognizes that there is a problem:* This woman appears alone and homeless on a cold winter day. Yet, she flees from Edna's overtures. Edna decides to *investigate the variables involved* and *gets feedback from others.*

Edna talks to other neighborhood and shelter residents about the woman. She finds out that the woman is a 27-year-old named Bobbi who has a cognitive disability (mental retardation), has been diagnosed with schizophrenia, and is homeless. (*Schizophrenia* is "a disturbance that lasts for at least six months and includes at least one month of active-phase symptoms [i.e., two (or more) of the following: delusions, hallucinations, disorganized speech, grossly disorganized or catatonic behavior, and negative symptoms]" (American Psychiatric Association, 1994, p. 273). Edna discovers that Bobbi has refused help from shelter employees, police officers, and others on numerous occasions.

Edna considers the values that apply to this dilemma. Her duty is to serve people in need. Additionally, Bobbi deserves to maintain dignity and worth, which is very difficult when homeless. Bobbi deserves to receive supportive help and services.

HIGHLIGHT 2.2

Self-Determination and People with Physical Disabilities: An Empowerment Approach

The concept of self-determination has special ethical implications for adults having physical disabilities. Major (2000) indicates that "[c]lient self-determination is closely linked with the concept of autonomy," a person's ability to function independently (p. 9). Depending on the type and degree of the disabilities, people with physical disabilities often experience greater difficulties maintaining autonomy than do able-bodied people. For example, a person with a serious visual impairment may have great difficulty getting around in an unfamiliar neighborhood without assistance.

Gilson, Bricout, and Baskind (1998) interviewed six people with physical disabilities who felt that human services workers tended to focus more on their health status and limitations than on themselves as unique individuals. Ethical concerns included stereotyping people based on the disability label and clearly visible disabilities, ignoring strengths, accessing personal information without receiving client permission, and not consulting clients as expert resources for information about their disabilities and issues. Although limited in scope due to small sample size, this study and its implications of paternalism raise serious ethical questions regarding whether we are maximizing client self-determination. It apparently is easy for practitioners to make assumptions about people with disabilities that emphasize weakness instead of strength.

The following are recommendations for improving service provision to this population-at-risk.

Human Services Workers Should Adopt a Consumer-Oriented Approach (Mackelprang & Salsgiver, 1996; Major, 2000)

Treating people as consumers involves assuming that they are knowledgeable about their own needs and are capable of making intelligent decisions about services. This approach contrasts sharply with that of making decisions about what's best for clients without their input, recommendations, and consent.

Three facets are especially important. First, listen very carefully to what the client is saying instead of jumping to conclusions based on the disability label. Second, ask the client to clarify when you don't understand. Third, carefully scrutinize any possible assumptions you may be making about your client and his or her disability. Face your stereotypes and work to get rid of them.

Practitioners Should Learn about Services and Resources (Major, 2000)

People with physical disabilities have the same needs and wants as able-bodied people. They just have more obstacles in the way of getting what they need. Services include rehabilitation, employment, and health, residential, recreational, and personal care. Financial resources include various sources of public funding, such as Disability Insurance, Workers' Compensation, Supplemental Security Income (SSI), and other forms of public assistance (Asch & Mudrick, 1995).

Major (2000) urges that workers familiarize themselves with various advocacy and resource groups. For example, the Self-Determination Movement, funded by grants from the Robert Wood Johnson Foundation, "is an attempt on the part of people with disabilities to guarantee client autonomy in their quest for services" (Major, 2000, p. 11). It provides an information network, advocacy, and a range of supportive services. Additionally, supporters encourage public policy changes that incorporate self-determination initiatives.

The Self-Determination Movement is founded on four primary principles (National Program Office on Self-Determination [NPOSD], 1998). First, *freedom* concerns people with disabilities having the same rights as other citizens. They should be able to choose where they want to live and how to spend their time just like anybody else.

The second concept, *authority,* involves people with disabilities having control over their own finances, prioritizing where their money should be spent, and developing their own budgets. Major (2000) cites the following example:

> *[A] married couple who had been previously receiving supports and services from two different agencies "frequently sought psychiatric hospitalizations to be together" (NPOSD, 1998). After implementing a self-determination program, the couple now lives together and is served by one agency. Because the couple can supply each other with many of the supports they need, they are much more comfortable and content with their situation. What is equally important to note here is that the overall cost of providing their services has decreased significantly. (p. 12)*

Support, the third foundation principle for the Self-Determination Movement, involves having people with disabilities make decisions about where their support comes from. Instead of being given "supervision," people with disabilities should be able to seek out their own support systems for companionship. Similarly, they should be able to determine what specific tasks necessitate formal assistance from paid staff and others.

The final concept is *responsibility,* which involves the wise use of public funding. Resources used by people with disabilities should be considered as investments in the person's quality of life instead of a list specifying purchase of specific services. Just as all citizens should be responsible for the efficient and effective use of resources, so should they. Similarly, people with disabilities should be able to contribute to their communities' well-being in meaningful ways (e.g., volunteering, voting, or running for public office).

Workers Should Advocate for Clients with Disabilities Whenever Possible (Major, 2000)

Clients may need expanded services or additional resources. Practitioners should work with clients to determine their needs. Strive to make changes in agency policy and laws governing resources to benefit people with physical disabilities.

Sometimes, political advocacy is necessary. The Americans with Disabilities Act of 1990 (ADA) is a good example of positive legislation on the behalf of people with disabilities. The ADA intends "to provide America's 49 million . . . people [with physical or mental disabilities] with access to public areas and workplaces" and to blast away barriers keeping these people isolated from "the mainstream of public life" (Smolowe, 1995, p. 54). The ADA defines people with disabilities as those who have substantial physical or mental difficulties that significantly hinder at least one primary life activity, have an established record of such hindrances, or are regarded by other people as demonstrating such difficulties (Asch & Mudrick, 1995; Kopels, 1995). Major ADA provisions include prevention of job and employment discrimination and enhanced access to transportation and other community services.

The ADA "has legitimized the idea that the fundamental problems facing people are less medical than social and structural" (Renz-Beaulaurier, 1998, p. 81). It redefines problems as belonging to the *community,* not to people with disabilities living in the community. For example, "the problem of how to get up the steps (problem with the individual) changes to how to get a ramp installed (problem outside the individual)" (Renz-Beaulaurier, 1998, p. 80).

Bobbi also has the right to self-determination and to control her own path in life. Finally, there is the question regarding whether or not Bobbi is competent to make decisions in her best interest.

Edna proceeds to *evaluate the dilemma on the basis of established ethical principles.* Ethical Principle #3 relates to Bobbi's right to choose how she will live, which takes precedence over Ethical Principle #4, the right to experience the least harm possible. Bobbi would be safer, warmer, and better fed if she would accept services. Principle #3 also takes precedence over Ethical Principle #5, a person's right to attain a good quality of life. Bobbi has the right to choose her life path, even if it is not the one providing the best quality of life she might have possible. However, Edna decides that Ethical Principle #1 is the key. People have the right to have their basic needs met. Scurrying from one empty, dilapidated, unheated building to another between biting, snowy gales poses too great a risk to Bobbi's survival. Edna also considers Bobbi's ability to make competent decisions in view of her mental and emotional disabilities.

Edna *identifies the possible alternatives to pursue* and *weighs their respective pros and cons.* First, she can forget about Bobbi and allow her to lead whatever life she chooses. A pro of this is that Edna may then stop worrying about the dilemma and invest her energies elsewhere in other productive ways. A con of this alternative is that Bobbi may likely suffer severe consequences, including frostbite, starvation, and possible death.

Edna's second alternative is to call Adult Protective Services and inform them about Bobbi. Such social services include "social, medical, legal, residential, and custodial care" provided for adults who are unable to take adequate care of themselves and have no significant other who might provide necessary care (Barker, 1999, p. 11). In Edna's city, Adult Protective Services can pick up people like Bobbi and take them to a facility for assessment and treatment.

Edna *makes her decision.* She calls Adult Protective Services and explains to them about Bobbi.

Do you agree with Edna's decision? Why or why not? What would you have done in her place?

Case Example 2. Edward is a 42-year-old who is HIV positive. He is suffering from more frequent and more serious bouts of a variety of painful infections. Alvin, one of Edward's workers, works for an agency that provides supportive services for eligible elderly and sick people. Alvin helps clients accomplish daily activities and make decisions so that they may remain in their homes as long as possible. Alvin usually visits Edward three times a week, although more when necessary. During one visit, Edward bluntly announces to Alvin that he intends to kill himself. Alvin quickly *recognizes that a problem exists.*

Alvin further *investigates the variables involved* and explores Edward's perceptions and feelings. Edward, responding in a monotone to Alvin's probing questions, explains that because he has been too sick he has not been able to go to his accounting job for quite some time. As a result, his savings are almost depleted. Within days he will lose his condo home of 13 years. He does not want to leave his home and move into whatever public housing assistance might provide. Edward hates the hospital and only goes when absolutely necessary. He is in continuous excruciating pain and has become extremely depressed.

When Alvin leaves Edward, he *gets feedback from others.* He talks to his supervisor, who refers him to the local AIDS Support Project. A physician there informs Alvin that there is a new mixture or "cocktail" of drugs available that has helped many other HIV-positive patients. The physician urges Alvin to encourage Edward to try them.

Alvin thanks the physician and once again visits Edward with some rays of hope. Edward thanks Alvin for his efforts but declares they are of no use. He has made up his mind—to him life is not worth living.

What human services values might apply to this dilemma? How might Alvin evaluate this dilemma using ethical principles? What possible alternatives might Alvin pursue? What are the pros and cons of each? Finally, what should Alvin do?

 ## Dual Relationships

Dual relationships are those situations where a worker engages in a relationship other than that of professional with a client, supervisor, student, or other party in a work setting. The relationship may be one of ". . . worker and friend, employer, teacher, business associate, or sex partner" (Kagle & Giebelhausen, 1994, p. 213). In other words, such

relationships occur when workers assume more roles either concurrently or consecutively than that of professional practitioner in practice, work, or educational settings. Another term for dual relationships is *multiple relationships,* as many types of such associations can occur including those where a worker assumes more than two roles at one time (Corey et al., 1998; NASW, 1996).

Dual relationships involve *boundary issues.* In this context, boundaries are invisible barriers that separate various roles and limit the types of interaction expected and considered ethically appropriate for each role. For example, a practitioner and his client might attend the same church. Here the worker assumes roles of both professional practitioner and congregational member with respect to this client.

There is an almost endless configuration of dual relationships that workers might assume in practice and in life. Our discussion here focuses on some of those between workers and clients and between supervisors and supervisees.

Practitioners' Dual Relationships with Clients

We have established that practitioners should avoid dual or multiple relationships with clients or former clients that place the client at risk of harm or exploitation. Yet, boundary violations including sexual relationships are a common cause for practitioners to be cited for unethical conduct and for loss of their professional license (Strom-Gottfried, 2000). While the prohibition on sexual contact should be obvious, less clear are other types of relationships and scenarios. Congress (1999) comments that "while most . . . workers believe that sexual relationships with current clients are unethical, they are much more divided when it comes to social, occupational, or educational relationships with current clients" (p. 110). Reamer (1998) comments:

> *Dual or multiple relationships can assume many forms, not all of which are ethically problematic. At one extreme are dual and multiple relationships that are not typically problematic, for example, when a [practitioner] and client coincidentally attend the same play and have adjacent seats. The boundary issues are temporary and, most likely, manageable. There may be awkward moments, particularly when the client meets the human service worker's spouse or partner during intermission, but this kind of unanticipated boundary issue may not unleash complex issues in the therapeutic relationship. This is not to*

say that an unanticipated social contact should be ignored—it may be useful to address the client's feelings about the encounter. However, in the long run this is not the kind of dual relationship that is likely to have harmful, long-standing consequences. (pp. 50–51)

One scenario comes to mind. Kelly, a therapist at a day-treatment center for adolescents with behavioral and emotional problems, attended the Fourth of July fireworks, a colossal annual display shot off over Lake Michigan in downtown Milwaukee. She was with 23 other people including her parents, siblings and their spouses, nieces, nephew, aunt, uncle, grandmother, and neighbor's family of six. Suddenly, Bruce, 16, one of her clients, popped into view with a huge grin on his face. This setting was very different than where their typical interactions took place in her office, his classroom, or the halls of the treatment center. Kelly was happy to see him, returned a big smile, and said a welcoming hello. Three seconds of silence followed. Then Bruce said,

"Well, aren't you going to introduce me to everyone?" Kelly, taken aback, nonetheless began the complicated introductions of who each person was. It took about 15 minutes.

This is the kind of impromptu interaction that might happen to any practitioner. It was important to Bruce to be treated respectfully and warmly. There was really no harm in the simple interaction, even though it peripherally involved Kelly's roles in her personal life. Other scenarios unlikely to be problematic include living in the same neighborhood as a client, participating in the same community activities, taking continuing education classes with a client's parent, or attending the same fitness center as do clients (Reamer, 1998). Highlight 2.3 discusses scenarios where boundaries are more blurred.

At the same time, there is significant disagreement about what is ethically appropriate in social relationships with clients (Congress, 1999; Loewenberg et al., 2000). Jayaratne, Croxton, and Mattison (1997) surveyed a sample of practitioners in Michigan and found that 21 percent of respondents

---

HIGHLIGHT 2.3

Critical Thinking: What Would You Do?

Three examples illustrate gray areas where solutions involving interpersonal boundaries are a bit less clear (Reamer, 1998). What do you think is the most ethical and *right* thing for the workers to do in each of the following cases?

1. Ferdinand, a substance-abuse counselor, had been working with his client Tricia for several years. Tricia attributes much of her success in maintaining sobriety to Ferdinand's help and efforts. Ferdinand receives an invitation to Tricia's wedding with a note saying how much it would mean to her for him to attend. Should Ferdinand attend? To what extent might such an action blur boundaries and harm the therapeutic relationship?

2. Kashena is a hospice worker. (A hospice is a place of rest or a system of services proving care for people who are terminally ill. The idea is to make people as comfortable as possible in the little time they have before they die.) She visits her 72-year-old hospice client Leonard weekly to provide supportive counseling and link him with needed resources. One week Leonard invites Kashena to have lunch with him. Should Kashena politely decline in order to maintain clear professional boundaries? To what extent might such a refusal hurt Leonard's feelings? What are the pros and cons of accepting or declining the invitation?

3. Dilbert is a private practitioner in a rural area, who provides counseling on a range of issues. Gomez, his client for two years, addressed serious self-esteem issues during the course of counseling. Partially as a result of the counseling, Gomez went back to school and earned undergraduate and graduate degrees in the human services. Six years after his counseling ended, Gomez approaches Dilbert and asks him to provide clinical supervision. Gomez expresses how much he respects Dilbert and how no other licensed therapists are available in the area. To what extent would this dual relationship be appropriate? To what extent does it matter that several years have passed since Gomez was Dilbert's client? What are the implications of Dilbert knowing a lot about Gomez's personal life? What should Dilbert do?

felt that it was appropriate to "develop a friendship with a former client"; 39.3 percent to "touch a client as a regular part of the therapy process"; 30.2 percent to "participate in recreational or social activities with clients", and 57.3 percent to "provide your home telephone number to clients" (p. 192).

Kagle and Giebelhausen (1994) maintain that

> . . . dual relationships [including nonsexual] are potentially exploitive, crossing the boundaries of ethical practice, satisfying the practitioner's needs, and impairing his or her judgment. . . . They cross the line between the therapeutic relationship and a second relationship, undermining the distinctive nature of the therapeutic relationship, blurring the roles of practitioner and client, and permitting the abuse of power. (pp. 213, 217)

Robison and Reeser (2000) make an interesting analogy:

> A physician who giggled when examining you would be acting unprofessionally, no matter how funny you might look. A [practitioner] who made friends with clients would have crossed the same sort of boundary. These boundaries can be difficult to draw or maintain, but both parties to the relationship have obligations that come from being in a professional relationship. (p. 92)

Boundary issues can be complex. What is considered appropriate behavior can be confusing. Highlight 2.4 poses a number of questions for you concerning the ethical behavior of workers with clients.

Recommendations for Addressing Dual Relationships

Any type of dual relationship requires serious scrutiny and thought. The following are suggestions for reflecting on, avoiding, or handling potential dual-relationship problems with clients.

1. Think about boundary issues and establish clear professional boundaries from the beginning of involvement with a client (Corey et al., 1998).
2. Consult with supervisors and professional colleagues about how to deal with potentially problematic dual relationships (Corey et al., 1998; Kagle & Giebelhausen, 1994; Reamer, 1998). You need to carefully consider the potential consequences of your actions upon clients and your professional relationship with them.
3. Carefully scrutinize your own motivations, wants, and needs (Reamer, 1998). It's critical always to keep in mind that you are there for the client, not the other way around.
4. In the event that dual relationships occur involuntarily, discuss these issues frankly with clients, identify risks, and consider how to deal

---

 HIGHLIGHT 2.4

Critical Thinking— What Is Ethical?

Below are several questions concerning how human services practitioners should act with respect to their clients. In view of this chapter's discussion about ethical human services practice and dual relationships, answer the following questions regarding what you think is the right thing for them to do.

With current clients, to what extent is it appropriate and ethical for a professional human services worker to:

1. Become friends with a client while working with that client?
2. Accept an invitation to a special event (e.g., wedding or graduation) from a current client?

3. Accept a gift from a client (e.g., as a thank you or for Christmas or birthday)?
4. Go out to lunch or dinner with a client after a counseling session?
5. Invite a client to a personal party or social event?
6. Invite clients to an agency function such as an open house?

What are the reasons for each of your answers?

Now ask yourself the same questions while considering *former* instead of *current* clients. What do you think? Do your answers change much?

Answer one more question with respect to former clients. *To what extent do you feel it is appropriate and ethical for a worker to become involved in a sexual relationship with a former client?*

with such occurrences in the future (Corey et al., 1998; Reamer, 1998).

5. If you feel attracted to a client and tempted to get sexually involved, address your feelings as early as possible. The ethical guideline is simply to *not* do it. Talk the issue over with your supervisor or get counseling help. Face and evaluate the serious negative consequences for both you and the client. Corey et al. (1998) suggest that "when necessary, refer clients to another professional," although this is not always possible or practical (p. 230).

   A related issue concerns getting sexually involved with former clients or relatives of clients. In either case, it is the worker's responsibility to evaluate the potential effects on the client, on others involved, and on the treatment process. The worker assumes all risk and the substantial burden of any negative consequences (Reamer, 1998).

6. Distribute fliers on client rights and professional ethics to clients to educate them about these issues (Kagle & Giebelhausen, 1994).

A related issue, dual relationships between supervisors and supervisees, is discussed in Highlight 2.5.

Laws, Policies, and Regulations

Most practitioners believe they should carefully obey laws and comply with agency policies and regulations. However, such rules do not always coincide with professional values (Loewenberg et al., 2000). What does a practitioner do in such instances? The following cases are examples of potential ethical dilemmas regarding laws, policies, and regulations that may confront you in practice. Place yourself in each of the following three workers' shoes.

Case Example 1. You are a financial assistance worker. Agency policy requires you to report any extra income clients may earn. The exact amount of such income is then deducted from their financial assistance checks. An excited client with four children bursts out, "I'm so happy! My neighbor is going to pay me to take care of her two children while she works. This will do wonders for my grocery bill."

As her case worker, what should you do? Should you report the additional income and thereby decrease her financial assistance check? If so, will you tell her what you plan to do? What do you think her reaction might be? Or should you keep her statement confidential, thereby disobeying agency policy? What is the ethical thing to do?

Case Example 2. You work for a social services agency serving almost all Hispanic and African American clients. All the human service workers and administrators are white. None of the professional staff speaks Spanish (Cournoyer, 2000).

How might clients be better served? What are the agency's needs? What options might you consider pursuing? What is the ethical thing to do?

Case Example 3. You are a counselor at a shelter and treatment center for runaways. The center typically uses volunteers to serve many of its functions, including counseling youth and families. Although volunteers receive 20 hours of training, you feel this does not make them competent to counsel young people and their families.

What, if anything, is wrong with this agency's volunteer policy? What might you do to make changes? What might those changes be? What is the ethical thing to do?

Whistle-Blowing

Whistle-blowing is the act of informing on another or making public an individual's, group's or organization's corrupt, wrong, illegal, wasteful, or dangerous behavior. Within an organizational context, it can involve inefficient or unethical policies. Whistle-blowing can occur within an organization when an employee reports a problem to higher levels of administration. It can also happen when an employee informs entities outside of the organization, such as a regulatory agency or the general public, about an internal problem. Of course, someone entirely outside of an organization can also whistle-blow to internal administration, outside agencies, or the public.

Some organizations, such as the federal government, provide established means for whistle-blowing to occur, while maintaining the anonymity of the person reporting the problem. Likewise, laws do exist to protect the whistle-blower from retaliation of supervisory and administrative personnel whose positions are threatened by the whistle-blower's unappealing revelations.

HIGHLIGHT 2.5

Dual Relationships between Supervisors and Supervisees

Supervisors have substantial power over supervisees, including what discretion supervisees have in making decisions, what responsibilities they must assume, how they must accomplish their assigned tasks, what vacation times they take, and what merit they earn. Therefore, the potential for the abuse of power is significant when a supervisor assumes a dual relationship. Any kind of exploitation of a person with less power is unethical (Loewenberg et al., 2000). Of course, sexual relationships are obviously unethical, but what about other types of dual relationships?

Consider Earhardt, a county social services supervisor, who took his supervisee Cathy, a relatively new practitioner with one year's experience, under his wing. Earhardt genuinely liked Cathy, her enthusiasm, and her serious desire to do the best job possible. He took her on home visits to provide a role model for how these should be done. At her request, he helped her develop counseling techniques and write efficient, effective reports. In some ways, he assumed the role of friend with her. For example, when he held a party for all his supervisees and coworkers, he asked her to help him with the arrangements, which she gladly did. Cathy respected and admired Earhardt. At one point, she felt she was even falling in love with him, although Earhardt never felt any reciprocal romantic feelings toward her (they were both single). Eventually, Earhardt left the agency for another position. Twenty-five years later Cathy still thinks fondly of Earhardt and appreciates all he taught her. Cathy, by the way, is happily married to somebody else.

To what extent was this a dual relationship? To what extent was it ethical? Why or why not?

Critical Thinking

What do you think is the appropriate ethical behavior between a human service worker and his or her super-

visor? Answer the following questions. Is it appropriate and ethical for a worker to:

1. Become friends with a current supervisor?
2. Accept an invitation to a special event (e.g., wedding or graduation) from a current supervisor?
3. Accept a gift from or give one to a current supervisor (e.g., as a thank you or for Christmas or birthday)?
4. Go out to lunch or dinner with a current supervisor?
5. Invite a current supervisor to a personal party or social event?
6. Become involved in a sexual relationship with a current supervisor?

Now answer the same questions considering a *former* instead of a *current* supervisor. To what extent do your answers change?

Suggestions for Addressing Dual Relationships between Supervisors and Supervisees

Congress (1999) makes the following suggestions for determining whether a potential dual relationship between supervisor and supervisee is appropriate or ethical:

1. Clearly define the nature of the dual relationship involved.
2. Examine carefully the risk of exploitation and harm to the most vulnerable person.
3. Anticipate possible consequences, positive and negative, of proceeding with a dual relationship.
4. Discuss with colleagues and ... [others] the advisability of developing a dual relationship.
5. Ascertain which other part of the code, in addition to the section on dual relationships, might help determine whether a dual relationship is inappropriate.
6. Affirm the responsibility of the professional human services worker to avoid even the possibility of exploiting the most vulnerable persons involved. (p. 115)

However, despite the fact that sometimes there is some protection, whistle-blowing is usually risky. Whistle-blowing carries a degree of risk that varies in direct proportion to the seriousness of the allegations, which only makes sense. Going over the head of someone in your own agency and informing

those with greater power about bad, inappropriate, or unethical behavior can anger and intimidate the person in question. Similarly, airing "dirty laundry" outside of an agency can be threatening to people who run the agency. All agencies have problems of one sort or another, just as all individual people have problems. However, people responsible for agency activity do not like the negative aspects of this activity to be obtrusively displayed for all to see. Such exposure reflects badly on those who run the agency. The implication, perhaps rightly so, is that the administration is at fault. As a result, whistle-blowers have been fired, reassigned to insignificant responsibilities at remote locations, and harassed into quitting. In short, administrators and other people in power can make a whistle-blower's life extremely miserable.

Whistle-blowing can have many consequences that affect the whistle-blower personally. Those in the organizational administration or others who resent the allegations can attack the whistle-blower personally. Others can seek to pinpoint and emphasize the whistle-blower's faults. We know that *everyone* has faults. Colleagues may ostracize whistle-blowers, thus making them feel tremendously isolated and alone. They may receive threats to themselves or loved ones. They may even lose their jobs. Perhaps, worse yet, they may be blacklisted as troublemakers in the professional community. Thus, they may discover that finding new employment—unless they undertake a major relocation—is virtually impossible.

Yet, sometimes whistle-blowing is necessary, especially after other less extreme measures (such as working through the agency administration) have already been tried and failed. Sometimes, whistle-blowing is an ethical imperative "when the violations of policy or law seriously threaten the welfare of others" (Reamer, 1990, p. 219).

Levy addresses the choice of whether to blow the whistle or not:

> *The choice must be based upon the seriousness and the consequences of the organization's failing; the relationship of the failing to the organization's obligations to others; and the relationship and responsibility of the ... worker to both. Whistle-blowing is not always justifiable, but is often necessary in the interest of fairness and justice, and in the interest of institutional responsibility (1982, p. 57)*

Most cases involving potential whistle-blowing are ambiguous; there is frequently a fine line between breaking the rules and only bending them (Reamer, 1990). Therefore, we continue to stress that the decision to act be an extremely serious one. Before blowing the whistle on an agency or colleagues, consider four questions (1990):

1. How great is the threat to the potential victims? Is it life-or-death? Or is it only a minor infraction of the rules? Is it worth the time, energy, and risk to blow the whistle?

2. What type and quality of proof are available that the wrongdoing has occurred or is going on? How solid is the evidence? Do you have written documentation? Do you have witnesses? Or do you only have some ideas based on minor informal observations and hearsay?

3. Are there less severe alternative measures you might take to remedy the problem? Are there established agency channels through which you can work? How difficult would navigating through these channels be? How much resistance do you anticipate encountering? Can you confront the abuser personally before trying other more severe measures? Can you solicit support from colleagues? Will your supervisor help?

4. Can you assume the burden of risk? How much do you really have to lose? Is it worth the risk? Is whistle-blowing really the only way you can attack the ethical problem? Or are there other less risky alternatives you can pursue?

The decision to blow the whistle, whether it be to higher levels of administration beyond an immediate supervisor or to someone outside the agency, is a tough one. Depending of the worker's own individual situation, it requires weighing numerous pros and cons. If the ethical dilemma concerns literally life and death, attacking the problem in some way is essential. However, which of many courses of action is best? Whistle-blowing is probably only one of them.

If a worker does choose to blow the whistle because there is no other choice, there are several recommendations to follow. First, be certain that you clearly define the variables and issues involved. What, specifically, is the problem? What documentation can you employ as proof of your allegations? What ethical standards or rules are being violated? Exactly in what ways are these standards and rules being breached?

The second suggestion for blowing the whistle involves knowing what your rights are. Do you work for a public agency whose policy sanctions employees' right for free speech? On the other hand, is it part of agency policy to address procedural issues internally and internally only? Is there an available grievance or complaint procedure that you could utilize? How easy is it for your agency to fire you? Do you belong to a union on which you could depend for help? Is the union strong in actuality or is it relatively weak?

The third recommendation for whistle-blowing entails being prepared for the consequences. What is the worst thing that could happen to you? Might it be that your supervisor would put a note of reprimand in your permanent file, barring you from future promotions? Would such a note work against your potential for a positive letter of recommendation? Might you be fired as a result of your actions? Would blowing the whistle ruin your reputation in the professional community, thereby branding you as a troublemaker no other agency wants to hire? In the event that the worst would happen to you, what would you be prepared to do?

The fourth suggestion for whistle-blowing concerns following the chain of command. Going over your supervisor's head almost always puts you at risk of his or her resentment and wrath. By doing so, you appear to negate the supervisor's authority and competence, which usually threatens supervisors. It probably would be threatening to you, too, were you in their same position. At any rate, if at all possible, before pursuing the whistle-blowing option, try to follow the agency's predetermined, sanctioned chain of command. If that route does not work, then you might consider more extreme options such as whistle-blowing.

Finally, the fifth recommendation for blowing the whistle involves establishing a clearly defined plan of action. Whom do you plan to tell about the problem? In what order will you tell people? What will you do if they react positively? How will you proceed if they respond negatively? Whom can you solicit as allies? Are other workers and administrators willing to support you? Are there external organizations, such as professional associations or licensing bodies, that would aid you or even advocate on your cause's behalf? Can you beseech experts to support your case? What specific goals do you hope to attain? What is your time frame for achieving them?

In summary, considering the whistle-blowing alternative carefully is extremely important. Weigh potential gains against risks and negative consequences. There is no crystal ball. All you can do is act as your conscience dictates and do the best you can.

Personal and Professional Values

Values involve "one's belief about how things ought to be and what is right and worthwhile" (Sheafor,

Horejsi, & Horejsi, 1997, p. 41). We all have the right to our personal values. We have ideas about how we personally feel things should be. We have personal opinions about the death penalty, capital punishment, and abortion. We have personal values and beliefs concerning spirituality, state and federal tax rates, and whether a woman should change her last name to that of her spouse upon marriage.

Conflicts between personal and professional values frequently pose ethical dilemmas for workers. Put yourself in the place of a human services practitioner and consider the following scenarios:

1. Your personal value might be that abortions, although legal in your state, are morally wrong. However, you have an adult client who asks you to help her seek one.

2. You have an adult client with a life-threatening disease who desperately needs surgery to ensure survival. However, the client refuses such medical help because it conflicts with his strong religious beliefs. You personally feel this perspective is stupid.

3. You believe strongly in the equality of men and women and in their right to equal choices and chances. You work with a family who culturally maintains a patriarchal perspective where female family members are given much less respect, allowed less input, and generally have significantly less power than male members.

At this point in your education, you should be regularly addressing the concept of personal values and how they must stand apart from professional values. Each dilemma requires workers to "weigh the competing obligations of the client, the employee, the profession, and third parties against the requirements of their own conscience" (Reamer, 1995a, p. 898). For each client and each case, workers must conduct an ongoing evaluation of personal values and how these might affect their ability to intervene effectively.

InfoTrac College Edition

This chapter reviewed in depth the NOHSE Ethical Standards of Human Service Professionals and identified principles for resolving ethical dilemmas. A model of ethical decision making was provided, along with a discussion of the values that underpin ethical practice. For further information on these and related areas, enter the following search terms:

professional ethics
professional values
ethical dilemmas
ethical conflicts
confidentiality

 On the Internet

Because of the very dynamic nature of the Web, URLs are subject to change. Therefore, be sure to check out the companion Website for this book at http://www.humanservices.wadsworth.com, where links will be updated periodically.
www.nohse.com/ethstand.html
www.asbh.org
php.indiana.edu/~appe/home.html

CHAPTER 3
Culturally Competent Human Services Practice

Jane Edgewood was mystified. In talking with Lana Black Bear, mother of a family on her caseload, she learned that Mr. Black Bear's two nephews were coming to live with the family for a while. The Black Bear family already had great trouble getting by on their meager income from the sawmill. How could they afford to care for two more children? In addition, Lana Black Bear had serious medical problems stemming from a car accident two years ago. Why would she want to take on this extra burden on top of raising her own three children? "It seems crazy," Jane thought to herself. "I guess I'll have to talk to the Black Bears about this."

John Martin, counselor for the Dinh Phuc Van family, had just walked into the waiting room of the human services department. This meeting was to be his first with the family, which had been recently referred to him by the Salvation Army human services. The couple were recent Vietnamese refugees and had just arrived in the city. "Hello, Dinh, how are you today?" He smiled and shook Dinh Phuc Van's hand. He greeted the wife similarly, shaking her hand and motioning them both toward his office.

Although John expected the family to be somewhat hesitant in asking for help, he was very surprised when the couple seemed both distant and uncommunicative. During the brief interview, John learned nothing that would help him decide how to help the family. The interview concluded when the husband apologized for bothering John and said they had to leave.

Introduction

The United States is a pluralistic nation composed of, except for Native Americans, immigrants or the descendants of immigrants. With a total population of over 275 million, the United States is a diverse society. Over 35 million people are of African American heritage, 11.1 million are from Asian American or Pacific Islander backgrounds, and 32.4 million are of Hispanic or Latino extraction. An additional 2.4 million are Native Americans (U.S. Bureau of the Census, 2000a).

The white population is a similarly diverse amalgam of peoples from Western and Eastern Europe, sometimes representing cultures with long histories of enmity and conflict. The traditional American view of this amalgam was that the differences and animosities that many people from many countries felt toward each other became submerged in what we liked to call the melting pot. The melting pot idea has been used repeatedly to suggest that all peoples who come to America figuratively get stirred into a giant pot and come out looking, thinking, and acting alike. As a concept, it was an attractive way for a nation to see itself—a country where all people could go and become as one.

Yet the reality of America is vastly different from the image of the melting pot, as we will discuss in this chapter. For example, we will look at the two cases that opened this chapter, identifying problems caused by human services workers who lacked cultural competency. In addressing the reality of human services practice in a diverse society, this chapter will:

- explore the general experiences of minorities in the United States;
- examine the ways in which various forms of racism affect human services practice with people of color;
- consider how diversity issues influence each stage in the Generalist Intervention Model;
- propose culturally competent practice skills that can be effective tools for working with ethnically and racially different groups;
- formulate assessment strategies for culturally diverse groups;
- evaluate ways in which human services institutions can be more effective in delivering service to people of color.

 Diversity in the United States

Race and Ethnicity

In the introduction to this chapter, we noted that the United States is an enormously diverse society. Over 25 percent of our current population is descended from people who did not come from the European backgrounds that characterized immigrants in the eighteenth, nineteenth, and first half of the twentieth centuries. The U.S. Bureau of the Census (2000b) projects that by 2050 almost one-half the U.S. population will come from the four traditional people-of-color groups. The melting pot concept is not applicable to the experiences of these people of color. It does not adequately address the history of white immigrants to America, who often maintained their values, beliefs, traditions, and behavior through successive generations, and ignores enormous diversity within Anglo (white) culture. Worse, it completely fails to address the experiences of people of color. Unfortunately, it has been a popular notion and still has vestiges of support. This support compounds the difficulties already experienced by racial and ethnic groups in our society.

Even the terminology we use to discuss diversity is fraught with problems. For example, the term *minority* is offensive to many who believe it connotes inferiority and reflects racism. Others point out that the term is meaningless because throughout the world, those traditionally labeled minorities (e.g., people of color) compose the majority of the population. The term is sometimes used to convey subordinate social, political, or economic status, at which point it can apply to women, children, gays and lesbians, and others experiencing social and economic injustice. Using this definition, any group oppressed by another could be considered a minority even if numerically superior in numbers. This situation was the case in South Africa under apartheid where power was held by a relatively small group of whites over vast numbers of South Africans.

Similar concern is raised about the term *race*. While *race* is used routinely in our legal system, the concept is more social than biological in importance (Spickard, Fong, & Ewalt, 1995). Geneticist James King recognizes this viewpoint in his book *The Biology of Race* (1981, pp. 156–157) when he notes that cultural factors determine both race and racial differences. Issues such as "history, tradition, and personal training and experiences" are what individuals use to designate themselves as members of particular groups (1981, p. 156). He concludes that "there are no objective boundaries to set off one subspecies from another" (1981, p. 197). Similar conclusions are echoed by Marks (1995) and Fraser (1995).

The increase in populations involving mixed ancestry or race confounds attempts to categorize or pigeonhole people. The potential of this change is enormous (see Highlight 3.1). The U.S. Bureau of the Census uses the familiar categories of race but is now faced with finding ways to accommodate the millions of individuals who recognize and celebrate their mixed heritage. Laws, rules, and regulations exist prohibiting discrimination based on race and asking individuals to select a single group to which they belong. The changes these accommodations would evoke in everything from preschool applications to official government documents are fascinating to consider.

Whenever possible, this chapter will use the term *multicultural group* to replace common but sometimes objectionable terms such as minority group, diverse groups, ethnic group, and similar phrases (Takahashi, 1994). Customary

---

HIGHLIGHT 3.1

Common Terminology

Ableism

"Ableism assumes the superiority of the person who is nondisabled and views persons with disabilities who have different physical and mental characteristics as somehow inferior. Along with this assumption is a low expectation of the level of performance and responsibility of persons with disabilities." (Mackelprang & Salsgiver, 1998, p. 202)

Cultural Competence

Culture competence is the ability to apply knowledge and skills to human services practice with diverse groups. Cultural competence includes specific knowledge about individual cultures, valuing of and sensitivity to cultural differences, awareness of the patterns of oppression experienced by those cultures, and the skill to utilize culturally appropriate interventions (Lum, 1999a; NASW, 1996).

Ethnocentrism

A belief that one's own group, whether racial, ethnic, or cultural, is superior to all others is called ethnocentrism. This belief, epitomized in Hitler's belief in a "master race," led to the extermination of millions of Jews during and prior to World War II. It is also characteristic of apartheid in South Africa and of the extremist views of such groups as the Ku Klux Klan.

Individual Racism

Individual racism is characterized by "the negative attitudes one person has about all members of a racial or ethnic group, often resulting in overt acts such as name-calling, social exclusion, or violence" (Barker, 1999, p. 239). Often, racism rests on an assumption of racial superiority. It is difficult, though not impossible, for individual racism to flourish without legitimization by institutionalized racism (Osborne et al., 1983).

Institutional Racism

Barker defines institutional racism as "those policies, practices, or procedures embedded in bureaucratic structures that systematically lead to unequal outcomes for people of color" (1999, p. 244). For example, college admission standards that admit only students receiving extremely high scores on the Scholastic Aptitude Test (SAT) or other similar tests systematically exclude many minorities who, as a group, may not do as well on such tests.

Minority

The term minority is "one term for a group, or a member of a group, of people of a distinct racial, religious, ethnic, or political identity that is smaller or less powerful than the community's controlling group" (Barker, 1999, p. 304).

People of Color

People whose skin color differs from that of the community's predominant group are called people of color. Typically, this includes Native Americans, Asian Americans, African Americans, as well as some other groups.

racial groups will be discussed when needed to convey conceptual approaches to understanding individual and group differences as well as the consequences of oppression and social and economic injustice. However, we will try to emphasize that differences within individual groups often are greater than those between groups. We also caution in advance that individuals and families from mixed racial backgrounds may share all, some, or none of the characteristics, values, and beliefs commonly attributed to the groups with which they identify.

Disabilities

Between 32 and 43 million Americans suffer from disabilities (Mackelprang & Salsgiver, 1999; Stoddard et al., 1998). This includes people with motor impairments, visual or hearing deficits, psychological disorders, cognitive disabilities, and many others. The Americans with Disabilities Act (ADA) defines disability as a "physical or mental impairment that substantially limits one or more of the major life events of such an individual" (EEOC, 1991, p. I-25). It also includes individuals who have a record of impairments as well as those who are considered by others to have such an impairment. The ADA goes on to define physical or mental impairment to include

> . . . *any physiological disorder or condition, cosmetic disfigurement, or anatomical loss affecting one or more of the following body systems: neurological, musculoskeletal, special sense organs, respiratory (including speech organs), cardiovascular, reproductive, digestive, genitourinary, hemic and lymphatic, skin, and endocrine; or any mental or psychological disorder such as mental retardation, organic brain syndrome, emotional or mental illness, and specific learning disabilities. (EEOC, 1991, p. I-26)*

Major life events include "caring for oneself, performing manual tasks, walking, seeing, hearing, speaking, breathing, learning, and working" (EEOC, 1991, p. I-27).

Congress passed the Americans with Disabilities Act (ADA) in 1990 to combat significant and continuous discrimination faced by those with disabilities. The act defined disability and required employers and others to provide reasonable accommodations to assist those with disabilities to attain and maintain employment. Reasonable accommodations might include changes in recruitment and application procedures, increasing the accessibility of a building or work area, providing

special equipment or interpreters, and restructuring a particular job. The ADA, coupled with other previous laws, was intended to guarantee the same civil rights to persons with disabilities as those enjoyed by the rest of the population. The reasons for these laws will become apparent in following sections.

Historic and Current Discrimination

Discrimination Based on Culture

That there are major difficulties experienced by multicultural groups is evident. From historic accounts of inhuman treatment of Native Americans, African Americans, and Asian Americans to current reports of police brutality of people of color populations, there is substantial evidence of systematic discrimination in our society.

Most multicultural groups in the United States have encountered some level of prejudice and discrimination in dealing with various societal institutions, including social service agencies. Europeans who colonized this country brought racism with them, which was evident in the wholesale genocide practiced on the indigenous Native American population. Although our government is predicated upon the primacy of dignity, freedom, equality, and human rights, our economy before the Civil War depended heavily upon slavery. The period between the Civil War and World War II saw many examples of racist behavior toward Native Americans, Asians, and Hispanics. Institutional racism within education was the law of the land until 1954, when the U.S. Supreme Court overturned supposedly separate-but-equal educational systems. Despite this ruling, de facto (actual) segregation of school systems still exists in hundreds of American school districts.

In the 1960s, minorities won expanded rights both to attend colleges and universities and to vote without harassment. Of course, these were rights that many white Americans had enjoyed for almost two centuries. Actually, they were rights enjoyed specifically (and only) by males until 1920, when women gained the right to vote. The right to vote was not extended to Native Americans until passage of the Indian Citizenship Act of 1924.

In the 1960s, 1970s, and 1980s, continued efforts were made to improve economic opportunities for people of color (Garvin & Cox, 1995). In the 1980s, a conservative, antigovernment series of political administrations systematically eliminated or reduced the role of the federal government in helping assure equality and economic justice to multicultural groups.

The picture for people of color at the beginning of the millennium remains problematic. African American families continue to be more likely to fall below the poverty level. Inner-city multicultural groups experience high levels of gang and drug-related violence. Medical and health problems affect these group members disproportionately. Economic disadvantage affects almost all people of color.

The level of disadvantage, combined with reduced federal and state social service programs and a corresponding increase in the poverty level, makes ignoring the link between governmental policy and economic deprivation difficult. Institutional racism remains a fact of life for a large portion of the multicultural population in the United States.

People of color must deal with experiences that many white families do not confront, such as educational and employment discrimination. In addition, most white families do not need to help their children understand and cope with racism and its negative effects on self-image.

Most multicultural groups have been victims of discrimination at the hands of most major social institutions in our society, including schools, the justice system, health care providers, even the social welfare system. Homma-True and colleagues (1993), after a thorough review of the mental health literature, found that major differences in diagnosis and treatment were made based on the race of the client. Patients of color were more likely to be given group rather than individual therapy and diagnosed with schizophrenia instead of less serious illnesses. Both medication and restraints were used with greater frequency, and people of color were more likely to be admitted involuntarily to mental health facilities. Similar findings of ethnic bias in diagnosing personality disorders were noted by Iwamasa, Larrabee, and Merrit (1995). Thus, bias can intrude even in the mental health arena. As a consequence, multicultural group members may be more likely to view such institutions with distrust and suspicion. Unfortunately, human services itself has too long focused on blaming-the-victim psychological change strategies. These strategies assume that the victims have brought upon themselves the problems they experience. For example, assuming that an unemployed father is simply lazy or chooses not to work is easier than understanding the role of racism and cyclical unemployment in a capitalist economic system. Thus, it is not unusual for multicultural groups to doubt whether human services have the skill or motivation to help solve basic institutional problems. Many problems of these clients are, in fact, intertwined with the behavior of oppressive institutions with which they interact.

Discrimination Based on Ability

As mentioned earlier, one of the primary reasons for the creation of the Americans with Disabilities Act was the pervasive and serious discrimination experienced by those with disabilities. This discrimination was evident from inaccessible housing, to denial of employment and educational opportunities, to a blatant lack of available transportation. Every major institution in society contributed in some way to limiting opportunity for people with disabilities. They were stereotyped as being unemployable, difficult to train, and in need of segregation from the rest of society. Reactions toward those with disabilities ranged from fear to pity. Some were avoided, and others were viewed as children, needing continued care. Most were simply considered incompetent. Others attributed the disability to a curse or gift from God. Only the creation of a series of laws opened up the possibility that persons with disabilities could lead normal, satisfying lives with dignity. Mackelprang and Salsgiver (1999) briefly describe these laws and the problems they were designed to combat.

The first major laws began with concern about soldiers who received disabilities in wartime. The National Defense Act of 1916 was created to help disabled soldiers find employment when they returned to civilian life. Four years later, the National Rehabilitation Act provided funds so that ordinary citizens could get job training and other forms of employment assistance, in addition to necessary prosthetics. It also shifted some of the cost for these services to the states.

In 1935, the Social Security Act provided public funds for blind persons and for children with disabilities. Subsequent changes to the law in 1956 expanded coverage to anyone with a disability. However, there were important restrictions on this coverage, resulting in many people not receiving assistance. The Supplemental Security Income program (SSI), enacted in 1974, guaranteed a basic income for people with disabilities. Federal funds were available to those who had medical disabilities, were unemployed, or were employed with very low wages. One of the ancillary benefits to SSI is that recipients qualify for Medicaid, which covers doctor, hospital, and other medical services.

The 1973 Rehabilitation Act expanded the rights and services available to those with disabilities. It ensured that most individuals with disabilities received priority services and required creation of an individual rehabilitation program. Perhaps equally important, it began a process of eliminating physical barriers in public buildings. Subsequent amendments to the act expanded the responsibilities of federal service providers to create affirmative action plans for those with disabilities and prohibited discrimination against persons with disabilities by any employer who contracts with the federal government.

In 1975, the Equal Education for All Handicapped Children Act was passed. The original act, plus later revisions, covered children between 3 and 21 years of age and mandated that education be provided in the least restrictive or most normal environment. The law also required that parents and the child play a major role in creating an individualized educational plan (IEP) for the child and advocated for services that would not stigmatize or discriminate against the child with disabilities.

Finally, in 1990 the Americans with Disabilities Act was passed. We have described this law earlier and its promise of expanded civil rights and opportunities for those with disabilities. However, the full impact of this and other laws has not been evidenced by greatly higher levels of employment among those with disabilities. There are many possible reasons for this, including the tendency for those doing the hiring to offer employment to those with whom they are comfortable, excluding the disabled (G. Nerrode, personal communication, May 1, 2000). Stoddard and colleagues (1998) found that while 77 percent of those with less severe disabilities were employed, those with severe disabilities had only a 26 percent rate of employment. By comparison, a person with no disability is employed 82 percent of the time. In all cases, women experienced lower employment rates than men regardless of disability status. The type of disability also makes a difference. Those with mental disabilities are half as likely to be employed as those with no disability.

Those who use a cane, crutches, or a walker are employed only 27 percent of the time. Those using a wheelchair experience even lower levels of employment (22 percent). Similar levels of employment hold for those who can't climb stairs, lift or carry 10 pounds, or walk three city blocks. Most disturbing, of those with a work-related disability, fewer than one-third are in the labor force.

Other factors also have a bearing on the employability of people with disabilities. For example, those with a college degree are three times as likely to be employed as those with less than a high school education (50 percent versus 16 percent). In contrast, an individual with no disabilities who lacks a high school diploma is employed 78 percent of the time,

a rate higher even than a college-educated person with a disability. While the correlation of age and employment rates for people without disabilities is quite high, the same is not true for those with disabilities. For people aged 55 to 64 who have a disability, the rate of employment drops to below 20 percent, versus 90 percent for those without such a disability.

The largest group of workers with disabilities are found in the "executive and administrative, machine operator, food preparation, and service and sales workers" categories, where about 25 percent are employed. This declines to less than one percent for the combined areas of computer programmers, librarians, counselors, pharmacists, lawyers, judges, physicians, dentists, and firefighters.

Clearly, the impact of the ADA has not been as strongly felt as is desirable. Those with disabilities still face obstacles to gainful employment, exacerbated by continued stereotyping and discrimination.

Barriers to Culturally Competent Human Services

Being an effective human services professional in a multicultural society requires that we be aware of the many barriers that impede our ability to function. For example, continued acceptance of the myth of the melting pot is a barrier. It uses an inappropriate and inadequate theory that often blames people of color for failing to "melt."

Another barrier is the assumption that all who come to our country will be overjoyed to be here. Some may be; others may be depressed or unhappy over leaving their homeland, loss of family members and loved ones, and the enormous burden of surviving in a strange land. Some may be anxious and fear the unknown. Expecting every new immigrant to be delighted is unrealistic.

A third barrier is the tendency to explain people's behavior by reference to their culture or disability. Certainly, many people of the same culture share life experiences. Yet this shared experience does not explain all or even most of a person's behavior. Instead, it ignores the enormous diversity that always exists within a given culture. All multicultural and disability groups are heterogenous. They are as different individually as any group.

Similarly, lumping all people of any one group together would be a mistake. For example, despite their enormous poverty and multiple problems as a group, most adult African Americans are employed, not receiving public assistance, and not involved in the criminal justice system.

A fourth barrier is an attempt to be color-blind. Cultural color blindness occurs when a person decides to "treat everybody alike" and pretends that culture and experience have no role in determining behavior. As with the third barrier, this is an extreme position and equally troublesome.

A fifth barrier is our tendency to assume that words mean the same thing to everyone. A client who talks of going home to her "man" may or may not be referring to her husband. Another client who says she "whips" her children may not be admitting child abuse. Language differences can be a source of confusion to human services professionals and other helpers.

A sixth barrier is assuming that clients think as you do. Two people can look at the same situation and come to totally different conclusions about what happened, who was at fault, and what should be done. Even eyewitnesses to events do not report similar enough accounts to be trusted in court. We tend to see life experiences in relation to our frame of reference. Expect that clients may think differently than you do. Take the case of a youngster sent to the principal because he was talking in class and got out of his seat. According to the teacher, his behavior was inappropriate to an academic setting and shows he was not paying attention. According to the child, he did not hear what the teacher said and, wanting to understand the assignment, got up to ask a friend in the next row.

A seventh barrier is expecting that clients will understand the human service professional's role. The chances are just as likely that some clients will make erroneous conclusions about you based on their experience with other human services practitioners they may have encountered. Clients may need to be told about confidentiality, what is expected of them, and what occurs in a counselor–client relationship. These explanations will be especially important with cultures that are hesitant to share personal information with non-family members. For example, in many Asian cultures, admitting a problem to someone outside the family is to lose face, which brings shame upon oneself and one's family and should be avoided.

An eighth barrier is insufficient self-awareness. By this statement we mean a lack of understanding of your own culture (including ethnic heritage, values, beliefs, expectations, and behavior). We may also have a lack of sensitivity to our own biases. All of us grow up exposed to a variety of beliefs about other groups and interpretations of what is "good" or "right." These beliefs are part of what makes us a product of our culture. They are also what often makes us ethnocentric. We may conclude that

things are "crazy," "odd," or "different" because they are not what we are used to. Thus, we tend to see life through a set of cultural sunglasses that color all we experience, personally and professionally.

A ninth barrier is the absence of a repertoire of effective, multicultural helping techniques. This barrier includes both those that are likely to be effective across various groups and those specific to a single group. Much of the remainder of this chapter will address such skills.

A tenth barrier is lack of knowledge of the culture and experiences of specific groups with whom you are likely to work. Practically speaking, the chances that you will become an expert in working with every cultural, ethnic, or disability group are unlikely. Rather, you are expected to take the additional time to learn about the cultural and life experiences of those unique groups who comprise your caseload or who live in your geographical area.

Integrating Cultural Competence in the Generalist Intervention Model

The various steps in the Generalist Intervention Model (GIM)—engagement through follow-up—are influenced by the worker's knowledge of diversity. Culturally competent practitioners will utilize their knowledge and skills differentially within each of the stages of the planned change process. In the sections that follow, we will identify issues, concerns, and topics that can influence worker behavior in the engagement, assessment, planning, implementation, evaluation, termination, and follow-up stages. These sections are intended to be only brief introductions to the influence of diversity on various steps of the helping process.

Engagement

Generalist practitioners must learn to approach clients from multicultural groups with a clear understanding of their own view of the world and how it differs from that of others (Chau, 1990). For example, individuals who have routinely experienced discrimination and oppression from people in authority may well approach the engagement process with trepidation, anger, and distrust. Workers should be prepared should these feelings be evident in the engagement phase. Additionally, recent immigrants unfamiliar with American norms and expectations may need to be approached differently. For example, common actions such as pointing your finger at an adult Hmong or crossing your arms when talking will both be perceived as insulting (Pitter, 1992). Language and cultural differences may require the sensitive use of interpreters.

The stigma associated with mental health problems may be a barrier in the engagement process and later necessitating a more indirect route to discussing sensitive family or individual problems (Matsuoka, 1990).

Taking a greater amount of time to develop the worker–client relationship when working with multicultural groups is common. Zuniga recommends the *platicando* or "informal and leisurely chatting that contributes to the warm atmosphere" (1992, p. 57).

The eye contact so dear to the hearts of most counselors may also be problematic. As we shall see later, some multicultural groups find maintaining eye contact uncomfortable, rude, or disrespectful. Thus, a recent immigrant from Nigeria may well avert his eyes as a sign of respect. The worker might interpret this action as deception without knowing the particular meaning eye contact holds for different groups. Even physical distance between worker and client may be an issue. Some groups, for example, may use a distance of less than 15 inches for conversation, while the norm for the worker may be two feet. Without knowing this differential use of space, the worker may find the proximity uncomfortable or even threatening (Weaver, 1992).

Assessment

Clients from multicultural groups often live in two cultures, the dominant one and the one associated with their ethnic or racial background (Norton, 1978), which poses a special challenge because the client must operate in these dual and possibly incongruent environments. That is, a behavior or action effective in one of these cultures may be ineffective or counterproductive in the other. The example of sharing one's meager food or resources with friends or relatives that opened this chapter is a case in point. The worker could not understand why anyone with such limited resources would make the problem worse by sharing with others.

Effective assessment requires recognizing client system strengths. Many groups have multiple strengths that may be overlooked by an insensitive worker or one who focuses on client problems rather than challenges. Consider such areas as spirituality, mutual support, respect for elders, and a willingness to share with others as strengths upon which to build. Fong and Peralta remind the worker that "cultural values are initial places to look for resources in

developing treatment plans and interventions" (1994, p. 6). Also look for resources outside the family as possible strengths. Churches and social organizations may be resources that are especially salient for some multicultural groups, especially African Americans, Hispanics, and Asian Americans.

Recognizing that different approaches to understanding and treating physical or emotional illness reflect group traditions and may enhance, and in some cases replace, typical health care interventions is also important. Workers must be open to this possibility.

Our ways of thinking about a client's situation can also affect our assessment. For example, if we think of a family as dysfunctional or multiproblem, are we really focusing on pathology and weakness?

Smith and Thrasher (1993) suggest using the term *overwhelmed,* which avoids blaming and a judgmental approach to helping. It also focuses attention on identifying the factors that overwhelm individuals and families.

Assessment is also concerned with the client's cultural or racial identity. The extent to which a client identifies with, accepts, and practices traditional values, norms, and beliefs can be an important variable to consider. For example, two Native American clients may have vastly different identification with their heritage. Assuming that the heritage is equally important to each of them would be a mistake. Assessment should explore the importance of the identity.

Many people from multicultural groups see themselves as "individuals within a collective." Their relationships with family members, community, their own cultural or racial history, and the larger world are critical to their sense of well-being. That sense of interdependence differs greatly from the typical Anglo American view of the individual. Without awareness of the importance of the larger picture, assessment decisions are likely to be in error (Comas-Diaz, 1996).

Assessing the responsiveness of agencies to the needs of multicultural groups is also important. Consider an agency where workers and administrators do not know the actual demographics of their own service area, lack linkages with agencies that serve multicultural groups, and are unconcerned about having a culturally and racially diverse staff. This agency is contributing to the oppression of multicultural groups. As such, it presents a logical target for change for the generalist practitioner.

Planning

In the previous example, the unresponsive agency might benefit from a plan that would focus increased attention on building relationships and developing resources with the community. Training of all personnel in order to create an agency characterized by culturally competent services is another logical goal.

Planning undertaken to confront community social problems can also be influenced by differences among multicultural groups. For example, North and Smith (1994) report on significant differences among white and nonwhite homeless populations. Homeless white men were more likely to suffer from alcohol problems, while nonwhite men reported histories of drug abuse that contributed to their being homeless. Despite equal levels of education and higher rates of employment for nonwhite homeless men, their total incomes were lower than whites. White women who were homeless experienced greater rates of interpersonal and intrapersonal difficulties, while their nonwhite counterparts suffered primarily from socioeconomic problems. As you can see, ending homelessness for each group will require planning for different strategies.

With micro-level interventions, cultural competence may involve knowing "when it is appropriate to reinforce the client's culturally patterned behavior or problem-solving method and when to encourage adoption of culturally different solutions" (Chau, 1990, p. 126). If the client's culturally sanctioned approach to resolving an issue appears to show some promise, the worker should encourage the client in its use. At the same time, the goal may be to help clients learn more mainstream behaviors that will surmount the obstacles they face (1990).

Another influence on planning is the decision to consider the family as the client instead of the individual when working with Asian clients. While Anglo Americans focus on the individual, the Asian culture typically places higher value on the family unit. Scannapieco and Jackson (1996) recommend a similar approach when working with African American families, where the extended family must be included in case plan development. Similarly, within both Hispanic and Asian families, including the elderly in the planning process is important. Their experience and perspectives are respected by family members and should be considered.

Implementation

Implementations that are focused on the individual or family must also be sensitive to the differences among and within multicultural groups. For example, the use of short stories, anecdotes, and analogies may be an effective means of approaching a topic

indirectly or symbolically. This approach has been suggested for both Hispanics and Asians to help the client system consider difficult-to-approach issues without feeling threatened (Unson, 1992; Zuniga, 1992). An example might be a client suffering from depression who is not taking her medication regularly. In discussion with the worker, the client admits she is ashamed and embarrassed about having to take drugs every day to cope with what she considers an emotional problem. She thinks she should be able to get over the depression if she just had enough willpower. Rather than reminding the client how important it is to take her medicine daily, the worker addresses the topic indirectly by drawing an analogy. She observes that the client's daughter takes medicine for her diabetes, a biochemical disorder caused by the body's inability to produce insulin. Depression, she explains, is also a biochemical illness requiring medicine to help the body function as it was designed. She comments that neither mother nor daughter can control biochemical problems through willpower.

Within Asian cultures, the worker will need to be very conscious of nonverbal communication that may have greater importance than spoken words. A professional helping relationship may slowly change to more of a mentor–mentee relationship as the implementation period continues, a difference the worker must consider as more appropriate (Unson, 1992). Rather than be considered the "expert," a role common at the start of a relationship, the worker will become more of a wise elder. This change in roles increases clients' sense of empowerment and reduces the distance between client and worker. Similarly, the worker may need to self-disclose more than usual, another step to reducing distance. Providing more suggestions and advice than is common is also recommended.

Interventions such as family preservation, some models of which have the practitioner as a partner and part of the family available at all times, would likely be considered inappropriate by many Asian families (Fong, 1993). A goal of empowering the family may well provoke conflicts with the "clan or larger community" (1993, p. 5). Nor will first-generation Asian males necessarily readily accept a female professional. First-generation Asians perceive the male as the authority figure and the family system as hierarchical. Human services professionals would not be perceived as partners either by male or female family members under these circumstances. The role is simply not supported by the culture. Thus, adaptations of the family preservation model clearly would be needed if this approach to implementation is selected.

Evaluation

There are at least two ways in which evaluation and research are influenced by diversity. First, the use we make of research findings appearing in our professional literature must be tempered by the realization that the results may not apply to multicultural groups. Generalist practitioners need to recognize that much of the research reported in the literature has limited generalizability. This limitation occurs in part because people from multicultural groups are underrepresented or nonexistent among the groups studied. Thus, the study results cannot necessarily be used as a basis for working with diverse clients without determining if the findings are culturally relevant. When examining studies reported in human services journals or at professional conferences, ask yourself if multicultural groups are represented in the research. This process will at least sensitize you to the potential limitations of some research.

The second influence of diversity is on the evaluation of your own practice and the research you undertake as a practitioner. To increase your cultural sensitivity, one of the most important recommendations is to involve the client directly in the evaluation process. Not only is this inclusion empowering, but it helps reduce client's feelings that they are being looked at under a microscope.

When deciding what evaluation approach is appropriate to use you also must consider whether or not the method must be adapted to multicultural groups. For example, asking questions in a face-to-face interview may be more effective than giving clients a questionnaire to complete (Marlow, 1993). If you are using instruments such as checklists, rapid assessment instruments, and similar items, determining whether or not these items have been validated with multicultural groups would be wise. Look the instrument over carefully to see if there is anything that might be inappropriate for diverse groups. Perhaps a questionnaire on family decision making lists only a mother and father as principal decision makers when the intended audience typically seeks the advice of the clan, extended family members, or others.

Similarly, instruments that were normed on Anglo Americans cannot be used with equal validity on other groups. What is typical for white college-educated males is not necessarily characteristic of women, nonwhites, or those with less education.

When using such devices as client satisfaction surveys, asking whether or not the ethnicity or race of the worker was significant to the client may be

helpful (Marlow, 1993), particularly when client and worker are from different groups. Asking the client to address how the worker might have been more helpful can allow the client freedom to address this issue. Contacting those who dropped out of the client–worker relationship to see if diversity issues played a role in their decision is also important.

Termination and Follow-Up

Diversity issues exist in the termination and follow-up stages as well as the other areas of the planned change process. For example, if racial issues were dealt with (as might happen in multicultural groups or in community interventions), taking time to discuss these topics during termination is important (Devore & Schlesinger, 1996). This process is especially true if the issues were difficult and emotionally charged.

Premature termination may occur when the worker is perceived as culturally incompetent or insensitive to clients from different ethnic or racial groups. This perception could occur because the worker has probed too far too fast or demonstrated lack of respect for the client. Offering clients the opportunity to come back at any time can leave the door open for a subsequent contact. It also communicates worker interest in the client's continued welfare. Periodic follow-up can also achieve the same end.

As you can see, diversity can and does influence each phase in GIM. Generalist practitioners must be alert to what impact a client's race, ethnicity, gender, or sexual orientation have on the helping process. This alertness is helpful as you seek to become a culturally competent human service worker.

 Practice Knowledge and Skills

The intent of this section is not to make you an expert on working with multicultural groups. Instead, you should begin to develop an understanding of the experiences of many group members. We also intend for you to learn specific skills that are generally effective with specific groups. The last portion of this section will focus on some principles that are useful across multiple groups.

Please remember that just because an individual is a member of one of these ethnic and racial groups does not mean that he or she adheres to all the values and customs described. For example, Chapter 10 discusses how people may become *acculturated*, that is, they adopt the "language, identity, behavior patterns, and preferences" characterizing members of the majority culture (Lum, 2000, p. 231). Clients with various ethnic heritages may embrace aspects of their traditional culture, or they may not. Similarly, they may adhere to traditional customs and values to varying degrees. Each individual is unique. Highlight 3.3, later in this chapter, discusses this issue further. The important thing is for you to be as knowledgeable as possible and sensitive to the possibility that these values and issues apply.

Native Americans

Intervening effectively with Native Americans requires understanding the unique history of this culture in North and South America. Unlike all the other groups who eventually populated these regions, Native Americans were here first. Their cultures ranged from highly sophisticated social systems (such as the Aztecs, Mayas, and Incas) to more simple organizations (such as Paiute). Most Native Americans were farmers and fishers living in villages and communities (Kitano, 1991). Though they numbered in the millions, they were no match for the military societies of Europe. Slowly, inexorably driven off their land, they were murdered and subjected to all manners of individual and institutional racism. At various times, exterminating, erasing, or otherwise ridding the continent of Native Americans was federal government policy. Military force was used to destroy tribal communities who refused to obey federal orders to move from their homeland. Tribal leaders were killed by white soldiers or by other Native Americans working for the U.S. Army. Using the melting pot myth, later efforts attempted to assimilate or acculturate Indians with the ultimate goal of destroying forever the culture of this group.

In the twentieth century, the federal government attempted to eliminate tribes by disposing of the reservations where they live. Massive efforts were undertaken to teach Native American youth the "white man's way." By removing children from their reservation homes and sending them to Bureau of Indian Affairs boarding schools, the federal government managed to destroy the family life of millions of Native Americans. In addition, they prevented many children from learning the traditional (and usually nonpunitive) child-rearing approaches used by Native Americans. Rather, the bureau's actions exposed them to the indifferent (and often brutal) discipline used at the boarding schools. Child abuse among Native Americans was relatively unknown until recently because corporal punishment (administering physical pain such as spanking) was rare. Boarding-school personnel used beatings, head shavings, and other indignities to punish Native American children for such crimes as speaking their native language, observing their religion, or running away from the boarding home. Many of the poor parenting skills noted among some Native American adults can be traced to these experiences.

Traditional cultural styles of Native Americans are significantly different from most European cultures. Knowing these differences is often important for human services. Applying culturally irrelevant or inappropriate interventions can be prevented with a basic knowledge of the culture of the client with whom we are working. Let us look at a few areas where Native American cultural values and approaches can influence human services effectiveness.

The Value of Time

Compared to Native American culture, white Americans are often said to be in a hurry (Devore & Schlesinger, 1996). Most of us maintain calendars to keep track of our busy schedules. We frequently violate speed limits as we hurry to get to our destinations. We talk of not wasting time or of ways to "save time," although no one has yet found a way to accumulate the time we have saved and use it later.

Traditional Native Americans do not share this near obsession with time. Instead, they have several values that supersede time—values like spending time with people or of not intruding on the life space of others. Practically speaking, this means that Native Americans are not married to the clock. Their approach to time is more flexible and relaxed. Consequently, they are less rigid when it comes to the starting time for meetings or being on time for appointments. For example, let's say you have an appointment at 10 A.M. with a Native American client. If a friend stops by to chat with your client just before your appointment, spending time with that friend is likely to take precedence over getting to the appointment on time.

Similarly, we frequently advocate that meetings start on time and that latecomers simply experience the consequences of their untimely arrival. Native Americans are much more likely to wait until all the important people are present, even if this means others must wait. The lack of a time focus is really part of a people-focused perspective on the world. Thus, expecting longer periods to develop relationships and to settle on mutually agreeable goals is advisable. Reaching those goals will also take longer. The idea of focusing on people instead of other issues is compatible with the values of the human services profession.

Native American Noninterference

We mentioned that Native Americans object to intruding in the lives of others. Native American noninterference could be considered a logical extension of the value of client self-determination. Within the culture, resenting workers who try to rush into the interview or rush into contacting is typical for Native Americans. Indian clients may need time to get to know (and trust) the worker and to become comfortable in the worker–client relationship (Good Tracks, 1973). This value also means that intrusive, aggressive styles of probing for information are likely to be ineffective. Participatory, self-directed relationships have greater value.

In group settings, the value of noninterference may manifest itself in other ways. Silence and lack of peer pressure are common. Peer pressure is just another way of intruding on others and is unacceptable. In task group situations, this value is apt to mean that decision making will emerge from consensus instead of majority rule. Group decisions are also more likely to take precedence over individual decisions. This means that the will of the group may overrule individual preferences of group members. Members thus defer to the decision of the group. When designing programs to benefit an entire community, maximum involvement of the people to be affected is important. Participatory decision making is critical.

Communication Patterns

We have mentioned the quietness of Native Americans. Indian communication usually is considered to be more nonverbal than in white culture. It is not a loud culture. Indian children who are quiet in school may be viewed as problems by teachers. Such teachers may be ignorant of the value Native American culture places on deference to authority and individual dignity (Baruth & Manning, 1991; Richardson, 1981).

Traditional Native Americans also do not self-disclose readily (Lewis & Ho, 1975), nor do they share information that might discredit their family. Family loyalty is important to Native Americans. Children are less likely to brag about their accomplishments, a behavior which would seem to place them above others. Conversely, not praising them in front of others is important. Praise that might be viewed positively by others may embarrass some Native Americans.

Fatalism

Other Indian values are also important to human services practice. For example, Native Americans show greater acceptance of fatalism (a trait they share with Hispanics). *Fatalism* is the attitude "that events are fixed in advance so that human beings are powerless to change them" (*Merriam-Webster's Collegiate Dictionary,* 1994, p. 423). The attitude that "what will be, will be" is anathema to professionals taught to believe that things in life can be changed. Taken to an extreme, Indians are sometimes criticized as "lazy." This criticism occurs when those ignorant of Native American culture misinterpret this more relaxed, laid-back lifestyle as being negative. Rather, such Native American behavior is rooted in their greater cultural acceptance of fatalism (Miller, 1982).

Sharing and Acquiring

A corollary is that many Native Americans do not possess the white value of acquisition for acquisition's sake. In Indian culture, sharing is more important than acquiring for oneself. This aspect often means that Native Americans will share their home, food, and resources with others though it places a strain on their own lives. If you think back to the case that opened this chapter, you will recall the upset human services worker wondering how the Black Bear family would take on responsibility for children of relatives when their own situation was so tenuous. Caring for and sharing with others, especially family, is more important than hoarding your own resources. One should realize that this value of sharing is not universal within Native American culture. For example, it is more important to the Sioux culture than in the Chippewa (Locke, 1973). However, the value of generosity tends to transcend tribal culture.

Voss and colleagues (1999) provide another lesson on the role of Native American sharing and the importance of understanding this culture. A Lakota child was being discharged from the hospital into the custody of his extended family. "The plan was for the child to live in a tent in the backyard. This was considered inadequate by state social services, who challenged the discharge plan, failing to recognize that it is not uncommon for Lakota children to share close space in the family or relative's home." It was also commonplace for many children from the extended family to "share a small space in the family dwelling or outbuildings or tents" during the summer. The practice "affirms the Lakota value of close kinship bonds and enjoyment of children" (p. 83).

Attending Skills

Attending skills may have to be modified when working with Native Americans. For example, we frequently exhibit the nonverbal behavior of leaning forward toward the client and maintaining eye contact in order to demonstrate our attentiveness. However, both behaviors are inappropriate. Leaning forward may be seen as intruding into the life space of another.

Likewise, Native American children who do not make eye contact with the teacher, or look away when the teacher looks at them, sometimes give the impression they are not paying attention. These children adopt such behavior because sustained eye contact is considered rude in Native American culture. As a human services professional, you will need to adjust your attending behavior to avoid violating these cultural taboos.

Helping Styles

Adapting one's helping style to the culture of the client is a challenge for the human services professional. Sometimes a portion of the approaches we normally use will work well. For example, techniques such as restatement, clarification, summarization, reflection, and empathy can be useful with Native American clients. Similarly, clients' confidence in you as the practitioner will increase to the extent that they believe in your ability, trust you, and know you understand their culture.

Dillard (1983) suggests that client-centered strategies are less likely to work with Native Americans, who may appear more passive. He believes that more directive approaches will be effective. Thus, considering using elements of both approaches may be appropriate. For example, the positive regard, honesty, authenticity, and sensitivity to feelings that characterize the client-centered approach might be used along with behavioral or cognitive-behavioral interventions. This combines the low-key, nonintrusive benefits of the first approach with the confidence-inspiring characteristics of the latter.

LaFromboise, Berman, and Sohi (1994) suggest that network therapy, a special Native American form of family therapy, may be helpful because it helps rebuild the family's support system. In network therapy, a relatively large group of family members, friends, neighbors, fellow employees, clergy, and other professionals are brought together to focus attention on a family (Barker, 1999). The goal is to strengthen the informal resources available to the individual, a more culturally acceptable means of helping.

One way of increasing client trust in you is through your involvement in other aspects of the client's life. Home visits, participation in tribal activities such as powwows (community social gatherings), and an evident appreciation for the culture are useful. Additionally, your office should contain some evidence of your interest in Native American life. This interest might include paintings, decorations, or books related to Native American culture.

A Cautionary Note

There are over 550 federally recognized American Indian tribes in the United States (Bureau of Indian Affairs, 2000). Though almost all have experienced varying degrees of institutionalized and individual racism and discrimination, their histories and tribal experiences are often quite different. The result is that individual clients may be different in perceptions, expectations, and behavior. You cannot expect to be an expert on every group. There is no shame in admitting ignorance of aspects of a culture or of a specific meaning or event in a client's life. A sensitivity to cultural influences and a willingness to learn about clients' experiences is essential to work with Native American and other cultures. See Highlight 3.2 for some on-line resources for professionals working with Native American clients.

Williams and Ellison (1996) suggest that considering Native Americans on a continuum of lifestyles ranging from traditional, marginal, middle class to Pan-Indian may be helpful. They suggest that traditionalists abide by traditional customs, are more likely to use natural healers for health care and value inclusion of the family in attempts to help.

Marginal Native Americans are in the middle between their traditional roots and the Anglo lifestyle, which is a stressful position because neither group may accept them. Middle-class Native Americans are much more likely to have adopted Anglo lifestyles, including using health care facilities and human services workers. They are likely to have more education, less contact with the reservation, fewer family members in their network, and previous experience with Anglo health care.

Pan-Indians have a multitribe perspective and adopt lifestyles that are in concert with traditional Native American values, though not those necessarily of a particular tribal group. They are in essence mixing a variety of Native American traditions and are less likely to use Anglo health services or mental health organizations. Recognizing that Native Americans may fall anywhere along this continuum, the generalist practitioner should not assume that

HIGHLIGHT 3.2

On-Line Resources

For the generalist practitioner practicing with Native Americans, there are several excellent on-line sources of information. These include:

- Indianz.com (http://www.indianz.com/) provides current news reports covering Native American issues in the United States.

- The Native American History Archive (http://www.ilt.columbia.edu/) provides a rich source of data on Native American history.
- WWW Virtual Library–American Indians (http://www.hanksville.org/NAresources/) offers the opportunity to search for a variety of resources on Native American history, culture, and other topics.

all members of this group share similar values, beliefs, and practices.

Hispanics/Latinos

Hispanics are one of the fastest-growing multicultural groups in the United States. Hispanic culture is often an amalgam of European, Indian, and African traditions and values. Even the term *Hispanic* covers such a wide group of nations as to be somewhat overbroad. For example, *Hispanic* covers people from 26 countries including Puerto Rico, Cuba, Mexico, and Central and South America (Castex, 1994; Lum, 2000). While the term *Hispanic* is used frequently, *Latino* is preferred by many others. *Chicano,* a term used on the West Coast, refers to Mexican-Americans and persons of Mexican lineage born in the United States. Note that *Latina* and *Chicana* are the feminine forms of Latino and Chicano, respectively.

Most of the groups covered by the term *Hispanic* came to the United States as immigrants. Yet many Mexican Americans can trace their lineage to ancestors who were residents of Texas, New Mexico, California, or Arizona when those territories were annexed by the United States. Consequently, they are not direct descendants of immigrants and share the same claim to birth rights as Native Americans. Like Native Americans, they also share a legacy of institutionalized racism and discrimination focused on genocide and acquisition of their territory (Lum, 2000). Institutional racism, you may recall, systematically produces unequal outcomes for multicultural groups. The history of the United States reflects a consistent devaluing of these groups. This pattern has implications for our current efforts to understand and work with all groups, including Hispanics.

Hispanic culture, like that of Native Americans, has vastly different values, beliefs, and practices

from Anglo culture. The term *Anglo* refers to U.S. citizens of non-Latin extraction. In the following sections, we will look at the impact some of these differences have on human services practice.

Family Centering

The typical Anglo value of individualism is at odds with the Hispanic family-centered cultural approach. The Hispanic family represents the one solid refuge from a difficult world (Bernal et al., 1983). The "family" *(familismo)* may really be a combination of both nuclear and extended relatives and other networks, such as friends and neighbors.

The family is central to Hispanic culture and is hierarchical in structure. That is, the father is the primary authority figure (Devore & Schlesinger, 1996). Children owe respect to the parents but especially to their father. Thus remaining in the home until they marry is not uncommon for children. This tradition occurs in part because children owe a debt to the family that they can never repay. Contrast this belief with the common Anglo idea that parents should do everything possible to help their children.

The closeness of the Hispanic family may be seen as problematic by those assessing the family using typical Anglo approaches. For example, the interdependence expected of, and seen among, family members may be viewed as enmeshment. Enmeshed families inhibit independent functioning of members through patterns of confused or unclear role boundaries. In other words, the family may be viewed as much too close. This type of family structure does not, however, mean that the Hispanics believe individualism is bad; instead, individualism must occur within the context of the family and traditional Hispanic values. Consequently, efforts to increase the independence (or reduce the dependency) of individual family members may be culturally inappropriate. As such, "*familismo* emphasizes interdependence over independence, affiliation over confrontation, and cooperation over competition" (Comas-Diaz, 1996, p. 158).

Parental Roles

Many Hispanic fathers appear somewhat aloof from the family, especially the children. Commonly, the father is less likely to express emotional support. The father's role is to pursue instrumental roles such as earning a living; thus he may appear more distant. He may not consult the mother in making decisions, yet he expects to be obeyed. The mother's role typically is to balance the father's (Baruth & Manning, 1991; Green, 1999). Mothers receive help in fulfilling this role from other members of the extended family. When intervening in Hispanic families, including other family members who play crucial roles in the family constellation may be necessary.

Similarly, even when the problem seems restricted to a single family member, encouraging family involvement whenever possible is often wise. Illness, for example, may be viewed as a family affair requiring family intervention. Even if the client does not mention family members, asking about them is appropriate. This interest shows an awareness of the importance of family members to the client. Sometimes, these casual questions will lead to disclosures of strengths or problem areas and can set the stage for further interventions. For example, asking about a daughter may elicit parental concern that she is becoming "too independent" of their control. Asking for further clarification from the parents will help the worker know whether the situation reflects normal parent–child tension associated with adolescent independence, potential delinquent behavior, or other problems needing help.

Communication Patterns

Like Native Americans, Hispanic communication patterns have a strong nonverbal tradition. Thus, the worker must be alert to facial expressions that often provide more clues to feelings than verbal comments. Verbal expressions of feelings are much less common than among white clients. Therefore, you should expect to spend more time in building a relationship and in assessing the situation than would normally be the case. That the client become comfortable with you and trust your skills is essential.

Interviews should typically begin with a period of small talk reflecting the informality valued by Hispanics. Jumping right in would be considered rude. Like Native Americans, Hispanics dislike being singled out and are apt to avoid competition. Hispanic culture emphasizes being personal and informal in contrast to the Anglo focus on efficiency and impersonality. Thus, Hispanics may appear passive and inappropriately nonaggressive when compared to the Anglo emphasis on competitiveness and quest for achievement.

Fatalism

As with Native Americans, fatalism plays a major role in the Hispanic outlook on the future. Consequently, Hispanics may disregard ideas that seem out of their control. Future-oriented approaches may be of less importance than concrete services offered right now. Thus, helping the family work on a current problem and demonstrating that you and they do have the ability to effect change may be more important. This approach might mean arranging temporary day care for an elderly family member with Alzheimer's disease, while postponing discussion of a son's future college degree. The parents may not believe that they have much control over the latter.

Bilingualism

Learning to speak Spanish clearly facilitates the efforts of a human services professional serving large numbers of Hispanic clients. Human services students with ability in language might seriously consider learning Spanish. The shortage of bilingual workers will continue to stymie efforts to serve large groups of Hispanic clients. For example, there are continual problems in getting Hispanics to use community mental health facilities. Bilingual human services could help confront this problem.

At the same time, the efforts of Hispanic children to learn two languages (English and Spanish) may be a source of stress for them. Learning Spanish at home and English at school may subtly communicate that their native language is not highly valued.

Intervention Styles

Being bilingual, however, will not help if the worker continues to use interventions that are appropriate primarily to Anglos. Fortunately, the usual approaches associated with good interpersonal interventions will be effective with many Hispanic clients. In other words, empathy, genuineness, warmth, and positive regard toward the client will be helpful. Hispanics value respect and dignity of the person. They may appear submissive when first seen because of their emphasis on not being rude. Attempting to teach skills such as assertiveness may be somewhat difficult, especially for Hispanic women, in view of the patriarchal nature of the culture. Teaching such women to be more assertive and recognize that others' needs do not always have to come first may be appropriate. Workers should remember, however, that encouraging assertiveness may place the client at odds with her own culture.

A more directive approach using fewer reflective techniques may be useful when combined with the characteristics described in the previous paragraph. For example, the worker may need to suggest specific actions that the client may wish to take to manage a particular problem. These suggestions can be done in such a way that the worker is seen as providing direct consultation or advice, which the client is free to follow. As always, giving clients advice carries some risk.

Using group and family interventions may also be appropriate because of the strong sense of connectedness in Hispanic families. Such approaches are often more effective with multicultural groups because of their focus on interdependence.

Castex (1994, p. 291) recommends four things that practitioners need to do when working with Hispanic clients. First, "ask where the client is from" and identify the client's nationality. Second, "ask if the client is a member of an ethnic group within that nationality." Third, "become familiar with the group history and the history of the group's migration." Finally, she recommends "identifying formal or informal providers of services directed toward members of this national group, such as religious and civic organizations, sports clubs, political organizations, and political officeholders."

A Cautionary Note

We have described how the term *Hispanic* applies to people whose heritage derives from any of several countries. Each of these countries has its own history, which influences how citizens experience the world. Knowing something about this history can help with individual clients. However, even immigrants from the same country are likely to have differences in expectations, social class, and life experiences. Each of these factors has implications for individual adjustment.

In addition, ethnicity is not immutable. People can select aspects or elements of their ethnicity

that they wish to observe. Despite the enormous influence culture has on people, none of us are automatically programmed to accept all the values and beliefs of our culture. We may choose to value certain aspects of our cultural heritage and de-emphasize others. Never assume that a Hispanic client (or any other client, for that matter) is controlled by cultural, ethnic, or racial experience. Human beings continue to confound those who would predict and control their behavior.

African Americans

Of all the other ethnic and racial groups that comprise the United States, only one, African Americans, came here as slaves. That background and an almost continuous history of maltreatment have combined to produce one of the saddest stories in the annals of the United States.

African Americans have been the victims of both institutional and individual racism in ways that have left almost indelible imprints on every man, woman, and child. By all the usual outcome measures (economic, educational, and occupational), African Americans have suffered at the hands of a predominantly white nation. African Americans have a substantially lower per capita income, despite their level of education. Almost 22 percent of African American families live in poverty, according to the U.S. Department of Commerce (2000). As a group they are much less likely to attain the educational qualifications needed for advancement in a technologically oriented society. Jobs that are open to them are more likely to be lower paying and offer less opportunity for advancement. They experience discrimination in employment, housing, health care, and education.

As a nation, we have had great difficulty confronting the multiple problems experienced by African Americans. Even well-intentioned programs that grew out of the 1960s War on Poverty (Job Corps, Head Start, VISTA) were seriously underfunded and opposed by those who benefited from the status quo. In recent decades, conservative political administrations have systematically dismantled programs benefiting the poor (African Americans included), producing dramatic results. Instead of having fewer people in poverty, a trend that began in the 1960s and continued into the 1970s, we now have more. We also have more homeless people and a larger proportion of untreated chronically mentally ill people (Ambrosino et al., 2001; Burt, 1992). This government indifference and neglect has disproportionately affected African Americans. Conservative attempts to gut affirmative action programs (programs designed by employers to encourage hiring of under-represented workers) have similarly hurt African Americans and other minorities.

Even our attempts to describe African Americans have been problematic. The term *colored people* gave way to *negro,* which was supplanted in turn by *black.* Although some would argue that the words we use are unimportant, words do convey a variety of messages. The term *black,* for instance, is simply a variant of *negro.* (*Negro* is from the Latin word *niger,* which means black.) Historically, the color black has been associated with ignorance, evil, and darkness. White is associated with light, goodness, and purity, all positive connotations. While the term *black* may have had value during the 1960s and 1970s (primarily through its association with Black Power), it still has significant limitations (Osborne et al., 1983). We have given up references to Asians as *yellow,* and it is rare that anyone speaks about the *red man.* Using terms that lack negative connotations and are consistent with the primary geographical origins of most African Americans (namely, Africa) makes more sense.

Communication Patterns

You may hear frequent references to the terms *Ebonics* or *Black English.* Often, these terms are an attempt to describe a pattern of word usage and sentence structure used by many African Americans. The connotation is often that Black English is a substandard variant of ordinary English. Actually, the language patterns of many African Americans follow a set of rules as complex and understandable as standard English (McMillen, 1997). Accepting this language and focusing our efforts on understanding African American clients is far more appropriate than to worry about whether or not the words they use are correct according to Anglo standards. If you do not understand what a word used by the client means, ask. This suggestion does not mean you must adopt language with which you are uncomfortable. To do so may come across as fake or insincere.

Proctor and Davis (1996) give a wonderful example of why pretending or assuming you understand what a client has said can be problematic:

> Client: *Like I was saying, Fred, I miss my main squeeze very much, even though I've got so many hammers after me.*

> Worker: *Well, Joe, it sounds like you're in good spirits. I am surprised in light of the fact that last week you were unhappy over your wife leaving you. Are you feeling better because of the woodworking you're doing?*

By not being familiar with some of the words, the worker does not understand that the client still misses his wife a great deal even though several women are interested in him. Asking would have been wiser. Fear of losing credibility should not stand in the way of achieving clarity.

More important than *how* African American clients communicate is *what* they communicate. Clients may be reluctant to reveal personal weaknesses because they do not know how the human services professional will react. Consequently, clients can appear suspicious of or reserved toward persons in positions of power or authority. A possible area to explore in assessment is how past interactions with other social systems have reinforced or extinguished certain behaviors. How have they influenced the person's self-esteem? For example, has the client experienced racism or discrimination that has left him or her feeling inferior or put down? Recognize that experiences with discrimination may lead to feelings of powerlessness and despair, manifest in nonverbal, resistive, or even hostile, defensive behavior. Sensitivity to the possible influence of these experiences may help you understand the communication patterns of African American clients.

Family Experiences

Religion plays an important role in the family lives of most African American and other people of color (Green, 1999). The church serves as a source of inspiration and support as well as a meeting place. African American churches have played an important part in the history of the civil rights movement. Thus, when working with African American families, assessing the significance of religious values and experiences for family members is important. Figuring out whether or not the church is a resource for the family is also important. For example, the church should be considered a "significant other" (e.g., like a family member, loved one, or otherwise important person) when determining family strengths and problems. As with Native Americans, attention should be paid to extended family members who may play an important role in family decisions.

Even single-parent households may have others who are playing one or more significant roles in the accomplishment of family tasks. These individuals could be related by blood, marriage, or friendship. Scannapieco and Jackson (1996) note that African American families have a rich tradition of kinship care in which members of the extended family provide temporary caregiving for children of relatives. When the possibility of placing a child outside the home is being considered, they recommend inclusion of all family members in the decision-making process. This method can be considered an effective step to preserving the African American family as well as empowering all family members. Understanding and using these resources can be helpful in the assessment and intervention stages (Devore & Schlesinger, 1996).

Helping Styles

We have discussed before the importance of showing respect for clients by using their formal names and titles. This advice remains salient for African American clients. Do not use nicknames, first names, or other signs of informality unless invited to do so. In other words, use Mr. or Ms. to convey respect. You might ask a client if she prefers "Mrs." or "Miss," and, if she does, use it. Although many consider them sexist terms, being referred to as she pleases is the client's right. This respect also will help ensure that the client knows you are seeking a relationship based on mutual respect and sharing of information, instead of the superior–inferior hierarchy that characterizes many professional–client relationships (such as doctor–patient or lawyer–client). We must communicate respect by recognizing and building upon client's strengths.

We have also discussed the importance of learning about the culture with which you will be working. For example, it may be wise to study African American literature and music to get a sense of how life experiences affect how the world is perceived. For example, many African American writers and poets paint a portrait in words of what it is like to be a person of color in a white society. Through their eyes you may become aware of events and behaviors that are perceived as negative (e.g., how celebrating Columbus's arrival is not perceived positively by many Native Americans). Similarly, reading African American newspapers is helpful. These typically reflect the interests and perspectives of group members and give additional insight into their world. As Proctor and Davis (1996) note, the clients may well wonder whether you can help them if you lack knowledge of their culture. Increasing your understanding of the culture can help raise their confidence in you.

In some situations, there may be value in acknowledging the differences in culture and experiences between you and your clients. This acknowledgment is especially true if these differences appear to be answered frankly. Most of us do not have to be hit with a brick to know it will hurt. Yet, some clients doubt whether you can understand their feelings if you have not gone through the same experience. Discussing these differences openly and honestly is likely to lead to a more productive relationship with your client.

Clients often expect those in power to be reluctant or hesitant to act on their behalf. With African Americans, there is genuine value in moving aggressively to confront the environmental obstacles with which they are struggling. Providing concrete services and connecting clients to these services through brokering are important. Avoid vague discussions about what might be done and concentrate on achievements that show your commitment to helping solve the client's problems. To the greatest extent possible, our efforts should be based on a goal of empowering clients. Empowerment is the "process of helping individuals, families, groups, and communities increase their personal, interpersonal, socioeconomic, and political strength and develop influence toward improving their circumstances" (Barker, 1999, p. 153). Thus, you need to be seen as a peer who helps people develop confidence in their ability to cause change in their lives. The counselor becomes a resource instead of an expert in this process.

Schiele (1996) has suggested that one emerging paradigm in human services practice is Afrocentricity. This model includes the cultural values of those of African descent that have significance for generalist practitioners. For example, human services professionals frequently use theories that focus on helping clients recognize that their thoughts are the "cause" of many of the specific feelings they are experiencing. These approaches are based on cognitive theory and are concerned with rational thought processes. If the client can just be taught to think more rationally, improvement in the form of fewer negative emotions, less depression, and greater satisfaction with life will result. Other interventions are concerned with helping the client get in touch with feelings, identify them, and work through troublesome emotions. The Afrocentric perspective does not consider either thoughts or feelings as occurring independently. Rather, they are coequal with neither being more important than the other. Rationality and emotionality are two sides of the same coin. As a consequence, practitioners who focus on feelings or thoughts as independent entities will likely be perceived as lacking understanding of the client. A concern with objectivity is also inconsistent with Afrocentricity. The client expects a worker to show positive feelings and avoid the professional aloofness that maintains a distance between helper and helpee.

We also need to assess if race or ethnicity is a factor within the institutional or organizational environment in which the client must operate. For example, some clients will blame themselves for situations that arise from subtle racism in work or school environments. While not all problems can be traced to macro system or environmental causes, the possibility should be considered whenever dealing with people of color. This consideration is especially true when the client is having trouble with other social systems such as being denied service, given the runaround, or otherwise mistreated.

Macro-Level Approaches to Intervention

Finally, we must look at our own agencies and environments to decide if they are sensitive and responsive to the situations of African Americans and other groups. Does our agency provide outreach services, or do we wait for multicultural clients to come to us? Do we recruit and hire people of color to work directly with clients or only for clerical and less powerful roles? Does the agency's environment reflect the cultural diversity of society? Do we contribute to clients' unhappiness with the system? Are we part of the problem or part of the solution?

A Cautionary Note

Remember that people's behaviors or problems cannot be explained solely by their culture or any other single factor. Be as cognizant of this idea with African American clients as you will be with other people of color.

Asian Americans and Pacific Islanders

Despite the fact that they have been called a "model minority," there is enormous variation within Asian culture (Fong & Mokuau, 1996). Among these groups are Japanese, Filipinos, Koreans, Burmese, Indonesians, Guamanians, Hmong, Samoans, South Vietnamese, and Thais, to name only a few. Contrary to popular belief, Asians and Pacific Islanders are not homogeneous. Each group has its own language, history, religion, and culture. The groups differ in terms of group cohesion, socioeconomic status, and level of education. For example, the level of education and socioeconomic status of Japanese Americans approaches that of the dominant white majority, while for Samoan Americans, both are lower.

In addition, we have both "between-group differences and within-group differences" (Wong et al.,

1983, p. 27). Wong and colleagues (1983) provide a list of possible factors capable of producing differences within a single group. These factors appear in Highlight 3.3.

As you can see from Highlight 3.3, many factors can affect Asian American or Pacific Islander clients and produce differences even within peoples from the same national background. Yet, similarities do exist. In particular, *filial piety* and respect for authority are common to all these groups. Filial piety means a devotion to and compliance with parental and familial authority, to the point of sacrificing individual desires and ambitions. Listening to and obeying parents is the duty of Asian children. Because of this respect for and obedience to the family, Asians generally seek to enhance the family name. This goal may be accomplished, for example, through occupational or academic success. On the other hand, they are apt to experience a sense of guilt or shame in seeking social services. They may believe that having personal or social problems reflects negatively on their family.

Another important concept among Asian Americans and Pacific Islanders is "losing face" (Fong & Peralta, 1994). Generally speaking, losing face is equated with being embarrassed, challenged, contradicted, or made to look bad in public. Using protocols such as treating those in authority with respect and seeking to involve these individuals in assessment, planning, and implementation are keys to helping clients maintain face.

Family Centering

Devotion to the family also means that clients are reluctant to discuss personal or psychological problems with nonfamily members. To do so is to bring shame on themselves and their families. The stigma of accepting service arises from the value placed on pride and dignity and the desire to keep difficulties within the home. There is an expectation that the family should take care of its own needs.

The father's role is "head of the family." Individual achievement of family members is encouraged when it brings recognition to the family (Phillips, 1996). Whenever possible, you should attempt to work through the father when planning interventions involving the family or other family members.

In addition, family experiences may be different depending upon whether we are working with people who have been in the United States for extended periods (50 or more years), are recent arrivals, or were born here. For example, recent and older immigrants may request specific services, such

HIGHLIGHT 3.3

Enhancing Cultural Competency: Understanding Within-Group Differences

Within-group differences include those factors that produce different expectations, experiences, aspirations, and reactions of immigrant groups of similar national origin. For example, any of these factors might help explain why two people of Vietnamese descent are so different culturally. While the emotions in various groups may differ little, the life experiences, sense of priorities, and intensity of reactions may vary dramatically. Wong and colleagues (1983); Philleo and Brisbane (1995); and Devore and Schlesinger (1996) have identified some of the factors that can produce within-group differences:

- migrational experiences (degree of difficulty, losses suffered, and so on);
- location of residence;

- generational status (the first generation frequently holds to traditional patterns more than subsequent generations);
- degree of assimilation/acculturation (some individuals and groups adapt more readily to a new culture, while others observe "the old ways");
- degree of fluency with one's native language;
- degree of fluency with English;
- extent of identification with one's country or region of origin;
- level and location of education (in one's former country or in the new one);
- age;
- composition and degree of intactness of one's family;
- level of integration into formal and informal networks (such as churches, clubs, family associations, and so on);
- religious/spiritual beliefs and values;
- financial resources; and
- whether both of one's parents are from the same nation.

as advocacy or brokering (Kuramoto et al., 1983). American-born Asians are more likely to accept counseling and interpersonal interventions. However, the experiences of refugees who left their homeland suffering enormously in the process will be quite different from other Asian immigrants. Services needed may vary as well.

Clients seen in family settings may appear uncaring or cold to outsiders. This apparent coldness is because Asian Americans and Pacific Islanders are less likely to show much feeling in interactions with their children, especially in the presence of strangers.

Communication Patterns

We have mentioned that many cultures employ nonverbal communication to a much greater extent than verbal communication. This fact is also true in Asian American cultures. Looks and gestures may convey more than words can ever tell. Therefore, you must be alert to this form of communication (Tamura & Lau, 1992). In addition, some gestures may be confusing to the novice. For example, a Japanese person may nod his head to show he is following your conversation. The uninitiated may notice this gesture and mistakenly conclude the client is in agreement.

Similar to Native Americans, confusing respect for authority with passiveness or refusal to express feelings is easy. Tactfully encouraging clients to self-disclose may help them become more comfortable with the expectations of the helping experience. For example, saying to a mother and father that "it must be very difficult to raise children to respect the old ways" acknowledges how such influences as peer pressure, drugs, or violence in neighborhood schools and urban gangs can undercut the best efforts of the parents.

Showing respect by learning the client's name is also important. For example, in Vietnamese, a person typically has a three-word name. The first word is the family name, the second is the middle name, and the third is a given name. Since formalities are observed, a stranger might mistakenly call Dinh Phuc Van, "Mr. Van." A close friend would call him "Van." If you recall, the practitioner in the vignette at the start of this chapter called the client "Dinh," as if it were an American first name. Not only did he use the wrong name as if he were on a first-name basis, but he did not use the "Mr.," which is a title of respect.

Attending Skills

Attending skills are just as important when working with Asian Americans and Pacific Islanders as with other groups. Like Native Americans, avoidance of eye contact is typical among some Asians. For example, the Vietnamese find eye contact more problematic than do whites. There is also a protocol to the introductions of many Asian Americans. For example, handshakes are generally a part of our lifestyle. We extend our hands to almost everyone. Within traditional Vietnamese culture, however, it is an insult for an adult male to shake the hand of, or touch, adult females. Similarly, avoiding being in a closed room with females over 12 years of age is important. You may remember that John Martin, the human services worker greeting the family of Dinh Phuc Van, shook Ms. Dinh's hand. The combination of failing to show respect by proper use of the man's name, failing to use the term "Mr.," and touching Ms. Dinh helped contribute to the premature end of this interview.

As newly arrived immigrants, the Vans are more likely to observe traditional customs, a point that the worker ignored. In time, the Vans may adopt such typical American customs as shaking hands in greeting and using first names. As with any such group, the degree of adaptation to the new culture will differ from one generation to another and over time within the same generation. Those who have been here for longer periods are more likely to adopt many of the same norms as native-born Americans. This adaptation is a pattern that has been observed for almost every ethnic group coming to the United States. Thus, the generalist practitioner would be wise to consider this factor when working with immigrants (Mokuau, 1990).

Intervention Skills

That clients have confidence in you is important. You should attempt to project a calm, dignified image and have a clear sense of where you are going with the relationship. If you look like you are floundering, clients will lose confidence in you. Thus, a more direct, goal-oriented, approach is often preferable. Counselors are expected to be directive, like other authority figures, including teachers. Similarly, you should strive to be reliable and dependable. Both are virtues in the Asian culture.

Self-disclosure may be useful to a degree if it helps engender trust in the worker. But, as always, the purpose of self-disclosure is to help the client, not address the counselor's needs. This suggestion means that disclosing some of your own experiences is appropriate when it relates directly to what clients are saying and when doing so will help show clients that you understand their experience. It should not be done simply because you feel like sharing information or because you want to talk about your experience.

Paraphrasing is a skill that probably should be used less than in most practice situations because it may seem unnatural to the client. That is, clients may perceive that you do not have confidence in (or that you doubt) what they have said.

Questioning should be used carefully and sparingly. Overwhelming clients or appearing to be bombarding them is easy. Questioning often gives the impression that when all the answers are provided, the worker will give the client a decision or recommendation. Sometimes, clients do not need a "solution" but a forum to talk about ideas and discover their own individual solution. Also, asking specific questions about topics such as illnesses or sexual behavior may be considered extremely rude or intrusive (Lum, 2000). When a client considers some problems private, asking about them may make the counselor appear pushy. Overcoming this hesitancy takes time and patience.

Speaking of time, some Asian American and Pacific Islander groups (for instance, the Vietnamese) have values about time similar to Native Americans. They view time as elastic, not static. Specific limited units of time are unimportant. They are often more patient and relaxed about time, and awareness of this value can make understanding some Vietnamese behavior and viewing it within a cultural context easier.

Community-based services are more likely to be accepted and used in the Asian American community, especially those located physically close to the population to be served. These agencies are more likely to develop close ties to the community, enhancing their utility to the clients.

Asian Americans and Pacific Islanders are more group- than self-oriented (Fong & Mokuau, 1996). Despite this fact, some group situations can be difficult for Asian Americans, especially if they must open up in front of strangers. In group situations, avoiding use of confrontative tactics with Asian American clients is important. Conflict is generally considered disharmonious. The loss of face that confrontation produces can undermine anything previously accomplished. Yet, assertiveness and considerable structure are appropriate, especially in the early phases of group interventions. Also in group situations, do not expect Asian Americans to compete with one another. Mutual aid and reciprocity are more valued than competition.

Individual approaches that are more useful with Asian Americans and Pacific Islanders include giving suggestions, warning clients about the consequences of particular courses of action, and adapting a more authoritative style (Diller, 1999). For example, with an Asian American client who is thinking about dropping out of college in midsemester, you might say: "Dropping out of school before the end of the semester is likely to affect your financial aid, your ability to remain in the dormitory, and your ability to take classes next semester." Clients need to be completely aware of possible consequences to make an informed decision about their options.

The value of cognitive approaches stems from the fact that Asian Americans and Pacific Islanders are often unwilling or unable to talk about their feelings. Cognitive approaches such as appeals to logic and clarifying the client's thinking may be acceptable alternatives to discussing feelings. Dillard (1983) even suggests appealing to shame and guilt, both of which are culturally relevant reasons for behaving in specific ways. Focusing on willpower and self-control approaches also fit in nicely with the Asian culture's belief system. For example, you might stress to the Asian American client previously described that she is the one who decides whether or not she achieves her goals and that she must make the decision to stay in school. This approach emphasizes the client's responsibility for her actions and her control over her future. Additionally, you may teach clients assertiveness skills, but you must do this carefully. A skill useful for navigating American society may be problematic in an Asian culture. For example, a traditional Asian American wife who suddenly becomes more assertive with her husband can provoke marital problems that did not previously exist.

Like many other cultures, Asian Americans and Pacific Islanders are more likely to recognize the value of indigenous healing approaches. The use of acupuncture, massage, natural medications, and herbs should not be discouraged simply because the worker does not recognize or use these treatments. Use of these approaches typically stems from cultural explanations of mental or physical problems. Problems are thought to be caused by the mystical (supernatural) or to be punishment for failing to abide by cultural norms. In some instances, the problem also may be attributed to bad luck (Devore & Schlesinger, 1996). Often, convincing the client both to use these natural approaches and to consult a physician is possible. You can thus assure the benefits of both cultures' wisdom.

Empowerment is a goal to which we should strive with all groups that have been historically exposed to or are presently experiencing discrimination and prejudice. However, as Fong (1993) has noted, this concept must be adapted with Asian Americans.

Clients who are trying to live between two cultures, often with conflicting values, may experience social or emotional problems. Coming to the United States was a major culture shock for many Southeast Asians. For example, problems with low self-respect may be common to groups that, after coming to America, have to accept welfare or low-status employment. They need help to understand and negotiate the systems that are causing or contributing to the problems.

Another way of showing respect for clients whose native language is other than English is through the skillful use of interpreters. However, children should never be used as translators for adults. Such juxtaposing of family roles causes embarrassment for both child and parent. When an interpreter is used, it should be another adult, preferably one already trusted by the client. You should address your questions to and look at the client, instead of talking to the interpreter. Some translated interviews look as if the client is invisible, because the worker talks only to the interpreter, which is a mistake.

Finally, focusing efforts on providing concrete services such as referrals, housing resources, and economic assistance in an atmosphere of respect for clients and their values is appropriate (Lum, 2000). Concrete services show the efficacy of the human services practitioner and the ability to help the client meet identified needs. They also, in turn, increase the client's confidence in the worker and can open the way to the client seeking help in additional areas.

A Cautionary Note

Clearly, there are both similarities and dissimilarities among the various cultural groups with which you may come in contact. Asian Americans and Pacific Islanders are an extremely diverse group. Wanting to adopt strategies that will work with all the groups subsumed under this title is logical. To do so would be likely to be a mistake. In a later section, we will look at some techniques that generally can be used with a wide range of Asian and other people of color. However, alert counselors must constantly guard against generalizations that do not apply to the particular clients with whom they are working.

People with Disabilities

As with people from different ethnic and cultural groups, people with disabilities share similarities and many differences. In this section we will identify some of the ways in which human services practitioners can become more effective in meeting this group's needs.

Language and Communication

Improving our ability to communicate with people with disabilities requires a rethinking of some of the language we habitually use. Often we speak without thinking about how others might construe its meaning. The language we use can perpetuate stereotypes and diminish the worth and dignity of those with whom we work. The Coalition (1994) provides some excellent guidelines on the use of language, as noted in Highlight 3.4.

Practice Roles

Human services practitioners can adopt a number of roles when working with various populations having disabilities. The following are suggestions for working with children in a school setting, people who have hearing impairments, and people with psychiatric disabilities.

School Settings. Pryor and colleagues (1996) identify a number of specific roles that school counselors can play in providing service to children with psychological or emotional disabilities. These include helping students without disabilities to understand and value human differences, consulting with teachers, and suggesting curriculum changes that address both emotional and social needs of children with disabilities.

People with Hearing Impairments. Desselle and Proctor (2000) point out that hearing impairments are such an invisible disability that it is easy for practitioners to ignore them. They point out that hearing aids often do not correct hearing in the same way that glasses improve vision. Unclear, fuzzy, or overly loud background noises may result in jumbled messages. Frustration with the device's limitations frequently results in a decision not to wear the hearing aid. Communicating with those having a hearing impairment requires greater patience. Recommendations include "face the person, maintain eye contact, speak

---

HIGHLIGHT 3.4

Talking about Disabilities— Some Dos and Don'ts

Do:

- Refer to a person's disability only when it is relevant to do so.
- Use the word "disability" instead of "handicapped."
- Refer to the person first and then the disability when needed (e.g., a woman with a cognitive disability rather than a mentally disabled woman). Remember the client is a person first and foremost and is not defined by the disability.
- Ask a person with a disability before trying to help him or her.
- Follow the walking or talking pace of the person with the disability.
- Assume that a person with disabilities has other strengths and abilities.
- When meeting a person with a visual impairment, introduce yourself and anyone else who is present.
- Continue to use terms such as *see, walk,* or *hear.* Avoiding these terms is awkward and overemphasizes the disability.

Don't:

- Use terms such as *crippled* or *defective* when referring to people.
- Refer to people with disabilities as "the disabled," "the mentally ill," "the blind."
- Employ terms that are unnecessarily derogatory such as *Mongoloid* or *spastic.*
- Use terms such as *invalid, victim of,* or *suffers from,* which are negative in application.
- Refer to the able-bodied population as "normal."
- Use terms such as *wheelchair bound* or *confined to a wheelchair.*
- Assume that people with a communication disorder, such as a speech impediment, hearing loss, or motor impairment, have cognitive disabilities as well.
- Suggest that those with disabilities are special, heroes, or in some way out of the ordinary because they cope with their disability.
- Use the term *handicapped* except to refer to parking places or accessible buildings.
- Lean on a wheelchair when talking; it is someone else's personal space.

slowly, pause between your words, and enunciate each word clearly" (p. 278). While a louder tone may be needed, it is not necessary to yell—think about how you feel when you're yelled at. Avoid speaking into someone's ear, as the absence of visual cues may inhibit your message. Avoid placing hands in front of your mouth or any other gesture that reduces the client's ability to see your face.

It is also important to find other ways of communicating when needed. Change your wording or rephrase a question if the client does not understand it. Use drawings or pictures as needed to convey topics where words would be confusing. Many human services workers have learned sign language to help them communicate with their clients who understand American Sign Language (ASL). Advocate for persons with a disability when they are not receiving appropriate services. Be aware of a variety of coping devices available for those with hearing disabilities. These include telephone devices for the deaf (TTD) and flashing light systems that operate when the doorbell is rung, an alarm clock goes off, a baby monitor picks up sound, or a smoke alarm rings. There are also closed-caption devices on television and similar devices at the movies to assist those with hearing deficits. Finally, hearing dogs are used in a manner similar to seeing-eye dogs. They alert owners to sounds such as telephones, doorbells, and smoke alarms.

Agencies can also become more sensitive to those with hearing impairments. Phone calls where the client asks for information to be repeated may be a sign of this disability. Carpeted floors tend to facilitate conversation, while solid surfaces provide acoustical problems. Adequate lighting can also ensure that the client can see the worker's face and more easily read lips or recognize other visual clues. In settings with large numbers of people with hearing disabilities (such as nursing homes), human services workers should be familiar with such things as proper placement of the hearing aid, battery replacement, and how to turn them on and off. Family members can also be helped to understand the problems experienced by the person with the impairment.

People with Psychiatric Disabilities. Mosher-Ashley and colleagues (1996) recommend that when working with clients having psychiatric disabilities, you should be alert to the potential for burnout among family caregivers. This means spending time talking to the caregivers to assess the need for support, respite care, or alternative placement. Helping caregivers learn to anticipate and manage behavioral problems common to chronic mental illness can

strengthen their capacity to continue in their role. Educate yourself about self-help organizations that exist solely to help those with mental disabilities. Most larger communities have one or more such groups. These organizations provide a sense of community as well as therapeutic value for the client. Many, such as the National Alliance for the Mentally Ill (NAMI), also serve as advocacy bodies for their members.

It is also important to encourage clients to stay on their medication, remain in therapy, continue with their group, and so on, and to give specific reasons for this. It is critical that the counselor remain upbeat and confident that clients can manage with their disabilities. You may be the only person who has faith in their ability to survive.

General Intervention Principles

Mackelprang and Salsgiver (1998) provide a set of general guidelines that will be helpful for human services intervention with people experiencing disabilities. The first principle is that human services workers should always assume people are "capable or potentially capable" (p. 241). It is part of our responsibility to help them use their capability or to develop it more fully. Though limited in one dimension, such as ability to hear, the client is able to think, write, and act. We should always recognize the other parts that comprise the whole individual.

The second principle is to refuse to accept interventions or approaches that target the problem as being the individual who in turn must be "fixed." Many of the problems experienced by those with disabilities are the result of stereotyping, prejudice, discrimination, and the outright refusal of individuals, agencies, organizations, communities, and others to make appropriate accommodations.

The third principle is that, at least at one level, intervention is a political activity that recognizes how access to societal rewards and benefits affects persons with disabilities. If societies had already taken all needed steps to provide reasonable accommodations, we would be likely to view those children with disabilities the same way we view our own children. That is, with the right combination of appropriate education, training, and opportunities, they will become adult members of society. On the other hand, if opportunities for our children are blocked or nonexistent and/or education and training are substandard, the chances increase that we will recognize our children as a social problem. Thus, disability is a "social construct" that must be viewed in the context of the society in which it exists.

The fourth principle is that disability has both a history and a culture. Persons with disabilities often share a history of "oppression, containment, and isolation" (Mackelprang & Salsgiver, 1998, p. 242). They also need to know the political process and how it has and can contribute to the well-being of those with disabilities.

Despite discrimination, there is also the possibility of joy to be found in disability. Most people with disabilities can and do lead satisfying lives. We contribute to this possibility when we recognize that having a disability is another characteristic—like ethnicity, gender, or sexual orientation—that helps make this multicultural society fascinating.

Finally, people with disabilities have the right to manage their own lives. They have the same right to accept or reject services as those without disabilities.

They also have the right to live as independently as possible with "the same rights and opportunities as persons without disabilities" (Mackelprang & Salsgiver, 1998, p. 243). Helping them achieve that is a primary role for the generalist practitioner.

Developing Culturally Competent Interventions

Culturally competent human services require skills in several areas: attending, assessment, and intervention. Highlight 3.5 provides several recommendations important in cross-cultural assessment.

Green (1999) discusses the attributes of a culturally responsive practitioner. She believes workers

---

HIGHLIGHT 3.5

Strategies for Cultural Competence

1. Consider clients first as individuals, then as members of a multicultural group, and finally as members of a specific group. This method avoids overgeneralizing.
2. Do not assume that ethnic identity tells you anything about a person's values or behavior. Within-culture differences are substantial, and two clients from the same culture may have vastly different life experiences.
3. Treat "facts" you have learned about cultural values and traits as hypotheses and subject them to testing with each new client.
4. Remember that multicultural groups are at least bicultural. That is, they all live in at least two cultures, their own and the majority culture. The percentage may be 90 to 10 in either direction, and the values systems may well be in conflict.
5. Allow clients to tell you which portions of their cultural history, values, and lifestyle are relevant to your work with them.
6. Identify strengths in the client's cultural orientation that you can build upon. Help the client identify areas that create social or psychological conflict related to biculturalism and work to reduce dissonance in those areas. Also, help the client adopt some Anglo behaviors in settings

where such behaviors are important. Like tools, they do not need to be used in every situation.
7. Be aware of your own attitude about cultural pluralism. Know whether you tend to promote assimilation into the dominant society or you stress the maintenance of traditional cultural beliefs and practices. Your own biases and perspectives are important and can affect your work with clients.
8. Engage your client actively in the process of learning what cultural content should be considered by asking clearly about the client's experiences, beliefs, and values.
9. Keep in mind that there are no substitutes for good clinical skills, empathy, caring, and a sense of humor.
10. Demonstrate interest in a client's traditions and customs.
11. Consult traditional healers and spiritual leaders.
12. Recall that respect and courtesy are always culturally appropriate.

Sources: E. E. Williams and F. Ellison (1996). "Culturally Informed Human Services Practice with American Indian Clients: Guidelines for Non-Indian Human Services," *Human Services, 41*(2). N. B. Miller (1982). "Human Services to Urban Indians," in J. W. Green (Ed.), *Cultural Awareness in the Human Services.* Englewood Cliffs, NJ: Prentice-Hall. E. K. Proctor and L. E. Davis (1996). "The Challenge of Racial Difference: Skills for Clinical Practice," in P. L. Ewalt, E. M. Freeman, S. A. Kirk, and D. L. Poole (Eds.), *Multicultural Issues in Human Services.* Washington, DC: NASW Press.

should think about clients in terms of both group strengths and limitations in addition to individual problems. In other words, you should be able to use knowledge about clients' racial or ethnic group in the assessment process (see Table 3.1). Simultaneously, you must remember that membership in a particular ethnic group does not automatically explain a person's behavior.

Other characteristics of a culturally responsive practitioner include recognizing one's own cultural limitations and appreciating cultural differences. Our own biases and anxieties when working with multicultural groups can become a problem. Anxiety or guilt can get in the way of being empathic. Moreover, we may tend to transfer our reactions to situations to clients assuming they will react, feel, and think as we do. A willingness and eagerness to learn about a client's culture will go a long way toward building better cross-cultural relationships.

Dillard (1983) has summarized his recommendations for effective cross-cultural practice, focusing largely on interpersonal dimensions and attending skills. These skills include:

1. Maintain awareness that nonverbal communication probably constitutes more of the communication in a counseling relationship with people of color than does the verbal component.
2. Recognize that eye contact can be a problem for many ethnic groups.
3. Use both open-ended and closed-ended questions. They are almost universally acceptable.
4. Remember that reflection of feelings works with many cultures but not with all (in many cultures, reaching for feelings should be used carefully and slowly).

5. Recall that paraphrasing generally is an acceptable technique in most cultures.
6. Utilize self-disclosure judiciously.
7. Give interpretations and advice in cultures expecting a directive helper.
8. Summarize from time to time.
9. Use confrontation appropriately and carefully with certain racial groups.
10. Remember that openness, authenticity, and genuineness are respected in all cultures.

Dillard (1983) concludes that using approaches that are not culturally sensitive is a form of ethnocentrism, a perpetuation of racism, and an imposition of one group's ideas on another.

Green (1999) argues that exploring how clients and their respective reference group see a particular problem is important. The way a person defines or views a problem is often affected by that person's culture. It is important to find out the views of important members of the client's family, including extended family members and nonmembers who have family status, such as godparents.

Whenever possible, we should focus on the specific problems for which the client sought help before getting into areas where the client has not yet seen a problem. For example, that a client is showing signs of serious problems in his marriage may be clear to us from an initial session. However, the client has sought help for problems with his oldest son. Thus, we should first focus our attention on this area.

As a corollary, you should use the client's definition of a successful intervention, not just your own. Sometimes, the client defines a problem as "solved" although the practitioner will recognize

Table 3.1 *A Brief Summary of Cross-Cultural Differences and Similarities*

	Family versus Individual Orientation	Respect for Elders	Concern with Shame and Loss of Face	Approach to Time	Fatalism	Importance of Spirituality/ Religion
African American	Family	High	No	Flexible	No	High
Asian American	Family	High	Yes	Depends on group	Some groups	High
Native American	Family	High	No	Flexible	Yes	High
Hispanic American	Family	High	Yes	Flexible	Yes	High
Anglo American	Individual	Low	No	Rigid	No	Low

additional areas where work could still be done. Self-determination is especially important in work with multicultural groups. Likewise, demonstrating respect for the client's worth and dignity will be effective in all cultures.

Openness to the use of indigenous (natural) helpers is also recommended by Green (1999). For example, many cultures value natural helpers (such as *curanderos,* medicine men) and other paraprofessionals. When clients have faith in the work of these auxiliary helpers, we should not discourage their utilization. Using both clients' cultural resources and those of their community are appropriate helping activities.

In some situations, there really is no easy or simple solution to be found. For example, clients have realistic problems (such as getting along on a public assistance budget). No amount of counseling will eliminate this problem. Providing empathy and helping clients find creative ways to stretch their budgets have their place but also their limits. Ultimately, political stances strongly supporting adequate resources for human services programs probably would be more helpful. Those stances include writing and calling your political representatives, lobbying for increased budgets, and working with professional associations and other organizations. In addition, human service workers must become active in the political process, which is the only way to ensure that elected officials at the school board, city council, legislature, Congress, governor's office, and White House are sensitive to diversity and the specific needs of multicultural groups.

Moreover, human services workers need to continue to focus efforts on political and social action to create changes that benefit those who have historically experienced discrimination. For example, health care should be available to all citizens and not be dependent solely on the beneficence of an employer. Recently, too many companies and businesses have hired part-time employees to avoid paying the health and other benefits available to full-time employees. Such policies affect multicultural groups and women adversely and disproportionately.

In addition, we need to encourage research that tests various approaches to understanding and intervening in problems experienced by various groups.

We should know which interventions work best with which groups and why. Our level of understanding in this area remains rudimentary at best.

InfoTrac College Edition

This chapter examined the concept of culturally competent human services practice. It included a review of diversity within the United States and an examination of the ways racism affects human services practice with people of color. The chapter identified a variety of culturally competent practice skills and assessment strategies while suggesting ways in which human services institutions can be more effective in delivering services to people of color. In addition, it reviewed some ways of providing effective service to those with disabilities. For additional information on related topics, please use the following search terms:
cultural competency
disabilities
ADA
Native Americans
Hispanics
Latinos
bilingual
African Americans
Asian Americans

On the Internet

Because of the very dynamic nature of the Web, URLs are subject to change. Therefore, be sure to check out the companion Website for this book at http://www.humanservices.wadsworth.com, where links will be updated periodically.
thearc.org
www.eeoc.gov
conbio.rice.edu
www.hanksville.org
www.aawc.com
www.unitedfarmworkers.com

CHAPTER 4
Gender-Sensitive Human Services Practice

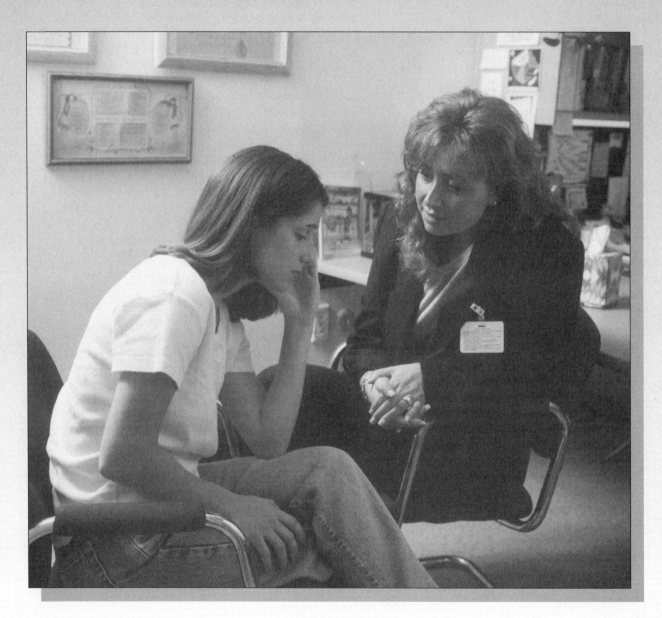

Ping, age 23, and her four young children are homeless, and all the shelters are filled. Married at age 17, she never worked outside of the home. She and her children had always been poor, her husband jumping from one low-paying job to another. Last month, her husband told her he was sick of her and all his responsibility and abruptly left. Ping has no money and desperately needs food and clothing for her family. She has no relatives or other personal support systems who could help her. Also, to remove herself from her homeless situation permanently, she needs job training with concurrent day care.

Abena, age 29, was raped 14 months ago and just discovered she has AIDS. Her health has deteriorated rapidly. She needs health care, including expensive drugs that could help her keep at least some of the more severe infections at bay. She had been a secretary, but her health problems no longer allow her to work. She has no health insurance, and her savings are completely depleted.

Danielle, age 15, has been on the streets for two years and is addicted to cocaine and alcohol. She ran away from home because her stepfather had been sexually abusing her since she was 11, and she could not stand it anymore. She needs both a home and an expensive rehabilitation program to survive.

Cheyenne, age 37, is violently assaulted by her spouse on a regular basis. The beatings are getting worse. She does not know how long she literally can live in her environment. She is only one of about 150 battered women identified in her small midwestern town. Counseling, day care, legal aid, and a place of respite for these women are desperately needed. However, a minimum of $23,000 is required to keep the shelter for them open another three months.

Ruth, age 57, has been divorced for 23 months. Her ex-husband, a businessman two years her senior, left her to run off with a 26-year-old woman. He got an expensive lawyer and manipulated most of their assets so that they were unavailable to her. She received half of the money from their house and $430 a month in alimony for two years. Their house was beautiful, but their equity in it was relatively small. As a result, Ruth now has almost no money left, and her alimony is about to stop. Her ex-husband has spent 35 years establishing a career for himself. He is well off. Ruth, however, has spent her life taking care of his home, entertaining his associates, and doing charity work for her community. She has no experience working outside of the home other than the minimum-wage job she has managed to get at a local frozen yogurt store. Her reserve of cash is almost gone. What she earns now will barely pay for her rent, let alone for her food, health care, and other needs. She has no idea what she will do.

 ## *Introduction*

All of the preceding situations involve women. All portray situations and conditions either unique to women or more likely to characterize women than men. The core issues for most of the examples are poverty and violence, two widespread problems that "directly or indirectly threaten the well-being of all women" (Jones, 1987, p. 880). This chapter explores the specific approaches to intervention with women and their special environmental circumstances. These circumstances are different from those that characterize the world of men. Specifically, this chapter will:

- demonstrate the importance of gender sensitivity;
- formulate a feminist perspective on micro, mezzo, and macro aspects of generalist practice;
- present a definition of feminism for practitioners;
- explore micro practice with women by describing common problems and proposing techniques for working with women;
- demonstrate how assertiveness training can be used to help women;
- recognize the importance of a feminist approach to macro practice;
- examine the issues of sexual assault, the physical abuse of women, and the feminization of poverty;
- propose micro, mezzo, and macro intervention approaches to correct them.

 ## *Gender Sensitivity*

As we begin to explore the special sphere of women, being familiar with a number of terms is important:

- *Sexism:* "Prejudice or discrimination based on sex, especially discrimination against women" that involves "behavior, conditions, or attitudes that foster stereotypes of social roles based on sex" (*Merriam Webster's Collegiate Dictionary*, 1994, p. 1073).
- *Gender role stereotypes:* Expectations about how people should behave based upon their gender. Female stereotypes include having "warmth," "expressiveness," "emotionality," and a "lack of competitiveness." Additionally, "a 'feminine' woman should be sexually attractive to men and, in turn, to be attracted to them" (Hyde & DeLamater, 2000, p. 361). Men, on the other hand, are supposed to have personality traits reflecting "aggressiveness, emotional toughness, independence, feelings of superiority, and decisiveness" (Strong & DeVault, 1997, p. 140).
- *Oppression:* "[T]he result of placing restrictions upon or discriminating against a designated group. People with lesser power, usually falling under some category of indistinguishable characteristics (for example, . . . gender), are denied rights, treated unfairly, or put down by a group holding greater power" (Kirst-Ashman, 2000, p. 12).

- *Sex discrimination:* Differential treatment of people based solely on their gender. Examples include paying males more than females for the same or comparable jobs or hiring only women for certain subordinate positions. "Sex discrimination is manifested in such activities as promoting men over equally capable women or paying male employees more than female employees for the same or comparable work" (Barker, 1999, p. 437).

Consider the following facts:

- Almost 60 percent of all women over age 16 work outside of the home (Renzetti & Curran, 1999). One-half of mothers with infants under one year old are employed outside of the home (Sapiro, 1999).
- White women earn less than 74 percent of what men earn (Rotella, 2001).
- For all races, women earn significantly less than men do at every educational level (U.S. Department of Commerce, 2000).
- Women are significantly more likely to be poor than men (Ruth, 1998; Stout & McPhail, 1998).
- Non-Asian women of color are significantly more likely to be poor than white women (Kirk & Okazawa-Rey, 2001; Renzetti & Curran, 1999; Stout & McPhail, 1998).
- Women are clustered in low-paying supportive occupations, such as clerical workers, teachers, and service workers, while men tend to assume higher-paying occupations such as managers, skilled blue collar workers, construction workers, and engineers (Amott & Matthei, 2001; Rotella, 2001; Thornborrow & Sheldon, 1995; U.S. Department of Commerce, 2000).
- "Even with a college education . . . and equivalent work experience and skills, women are far less likely than men to get to the top of their professions or corporations" (Kirk & Okazawa-Rey, 2001, p. 317).
- Every six minutes a woman reports being raped. Of every ten rapes, only one is reported. Twenty-five percent of women are raped sometime in their lives (Ruth, 1998).
- One out of every five "women involved in an intimate relationship with a man is beaten repeatedly by that man. Four women are killed by their boyfriends or husbands every day. Twenty-two to 35 percent of women who seek help in emergency rooms show signs of battering" (Ruth, 1998, p. 255).

 ## *Women and the Generalist Intervention Model*

We have established that professionals must be sensitive to and knowledgeable about various aspects of human diversity, including gender, to practice effectively. As a generalist practitioner, you will be called upon to work with women. Women are more likely than men to be poor. They are more likely to be primary caretakers of children and elderly people than men. Additionally, women are victimized by specific kinds of violence not suffered by men. This chapter will review a range of practice issues based on common circumstances facing women. Throughout the steps in the planned change process, understanding the world from a woman's perspective is critical. As we will see, she often experiences different options, strengths, and barriers than those encountered by men.

For example, consider Erline, age 25, a single mother with three children. Billy, her partner and father of her two youngest children, abruptly deserted her. As a construction worker with some specialized skills, he could get work almost anywhere and yet be hard for her to track down. They were not married. Hiring a lawyer, finding Billy, and getting him to furnish some child support would take much more money than Erline has ever seen. While they were together, Erline worked as a part-time checker at a local Superduper Saver Mart. Without Billy's financial support, Erline could not afford the rent and was evicted. She was forced to quit her job and take her children to a homeless shelter in a neighborhood renowned for its high crime levels. Erline had no close relatives or friends to whom she could turn. Billy had abused her regularly both physically and emotionally. He had forced her to cut off any friendships she did have.

LaTonya, the shelter's counselor, began the planned change process prescribed by the Generalist Intervention Model (GIM). During *engagement,* LaTonya found Erline to be shy and unassertive, different from most male clients with whom she worked. Erline had little confidence in her own abilities, including that of supporting her family financially. Erline had been raised to assume roles of mother and wife, not that of breadwinner, to which many men aspire. LaTonya gently encouraged Erline to share her concerns. She worked to establish an egalitarian relationship with Erline, a goal of feminist practice, where they would work together to help Erline and her family (Land, 1995; Van Den Bergh & Cooper, 1986). This role differs from the more formal historical and patriarchal perspective where a clinician with superior knowledge helps a client who assumes an inferior position (Chaplin, 1988).

During *assessment*, LaTonya emphasized the concept of empowerment for Erline. She worked with Erline to reframe her perception of herself and her position. According to traditional patriarchal standards, Erline felt she did not measure up. She had no economic resources, and she had failed in her relationship with Billy. Homeless men residing at the shelter rarely had children unless their wives were with them. Erline, on the other hand, was a responsible caregiver of her three children. LaTonya stressed the skills and parental competence that keeping a family together under such adverse circumstances required. LaTonya worked with Erline to identify her many other strengths, including intelligence, organization skills, job skills (Erline was dependable, responsible, and took employment very seriously), family commitment, and desire to improve her life circumstances.

Planning concentrated on consciousness raising, the process by which people examine their lives, increase awareness of issues affecting them, and begin thinking of ways to change their conditions. LaTonya helped Erline to "reconceptualize power," that is, view homelessness "not just [as] a personal problem but [understand] that female homelessness relates to gender, class, and racial oppression" (Johnson & Richards, 1995, p. 245).

LaTonya worked with Erline to identify and evaluate options available to her, including some she had never thought of before. LaTonya informed Erline that a nearby community college had a program to help women just like her get back into the labor force. First, interests and abilities were evaluated, and then training was provided for minimal cost. Grants and loans were available. Although a new concept to Erline, the thought of establishing a career for herself looked better and better as she made this a primary goal. A related goal was getting low-cost housing when she could afford it.

Another aspect of planning involved Erline's communication and assertiveness skills, dimensions often addressed in feminist counseling (Chaplin, 1988; Van Den Bergh & Cooper, 1986). Erline felt guilty for failing in her relationship. She felt the abuse Billy administered was her fault. LaTonya worked with Erline to stop blaming herself for everything, a common problem for women (Chaplin, 1988). Goals involved increasing assertiveness, enhancing communication skills, and evaluating personal potential.

During *implementation*, LaTonya and Erline discussed the logic and fairness of "the division between male and female behavioral traits such as the woman being the social and emotional caretaker and the man assuming the instrumental role" (Land, 1995, p. 10). Erline began to look more objectively at herself, her competence, and her options.

Erline also pursued her plan of getting vocational assessment and training. LaTonya helped Erline involve herself with a cooperative day care program sponsored by the shelter so she could attend school and later look for a job. LaTonya assisted Erline in getting her name on a waiting list for local low-cost housing.

Evaluation six months later indicated that Erline had made progress toward or achieved many of her goals. She had completed vocational testing and training and gotten a job as a receptionist at a health care facility. Although she would never be a millionaire, she managed to make enough to meet her family's needs. She found some temporary housing at a boarding house. Although inadequate, she knew it was only until she could get into a larger, better low-cost housing unit. She continued to participate in the shelter's cooperative day care program.

LaTonya *terminated* her involvement with Erline when the latter left the shelter. However, because of day care program involvement, LaTonya often briefly saw Erline.

 ## A Feminist Perspective on Micro, Mezzo, and Macro Aspects of Generalist Practice

Before we review specific intervention techniques for working with women, we need to set the stage. You must understand why working with women is different from working with men. A brief discussion of feminist practice will help to achieve this.

Feminism is a movement seeking legal, educational, social, and economic equality for women. Superficially, this definition may seem quite clear. However, in reality the issues are complicated (see Highlight 4.1).

Van Den Bergh and Cooper (1987) elaborate on the principles of feminist practice. They state that, in many ways, feminist practice conforms well with the principles and values of traditional human services practice. For example, both stress the importance of individuals' interactions with their surrounding environments and communities. Additionally, both

HIGHLIGHT 4.1

Are You a Feminist?

- Do you believe that women and men should have the same rights?
- Do you believe that women and men should be able to have the same access to jobs and social status?
- Do you believe that women and men should *not* be discriminated against or *denied* opportunities and choices on the basis of their gender?
- Do you believe that ideally people's attitudes and behavior should reflect the equal treatment of women and men?
- Do you think that many people need to become more educated about women's issues?

- Would you be willing to advocate on behalf of women (e.g., for poor women or women who have been raped)?
- Do you believe that both men and women have the right to their own individual differences (i.e., of course, differences that do not harm other people)?
- Do you think that our society is generally structured legally, socially, and economically by and for men instead of women? (This last question is probably the most difficult and perhaps the most painful to answer.)

If you've answered "yes" to all or most of these questions, according to our definition, which will be discussed later, there is a good chance that you are a feminist.

---

emphasize the significance of being concerned with "human dignity and the rights of self-determination" (Van Den Bergh & Cooper, 1986, p. 3).

A feminist perspective on micro practice with women targets women's inner feelings and access to personal power. For instance, "some research on self-reported personal worth or self-confidence has suggested that women tend to manifest lower general self-esteem than men" (Lott, 1994, p. 278).

Women also tend to be less aggressive than men; this fact is true essentially for all types of aggression, including both physical and verbal (Hyde & DeLamater, 2000; Masters, Johnson, & Kolodney, 1995). This lack of aggressiveness can also cause problems for women who do not appropriately stand up for their own rights. Self-esteem may be related to aggression in that women who do not value themselves may not feel capable of asserting themselves.

Later in the chapter, we will discuss the continuum of aggression, assertiveness, and passivity. We will also provide some intervention suggestions for helping women become more appropriately assertive.

A feminist perspective on mezzo practice focuses on women's relationships with others around them. This perspective involves both personal relationships and interactions in their work world. If women tend to have lower levels of self-esteem and aggression, how does this affect relationships? These situations again may involve having difficulty

in feeling good enough about themselves to be appropriately assertive.

The micro and mezzo levels of a feminist practice perspective are intimately intertwined. Classifying which aspect of working with women falls clearly within micro practice and which falls within mezzo practice is difficult. Likewise, the feminist macro practice perspective is intimately related to what occurs in women's personal, interpersonal, and work lives.

We have already presented some facts that reflect how women are oppressed. On the one hand, many women need to enhance their own self-esteem to better advocate for themselves. On the other hand, there are obvious impediments and hazards women must endure that have little or no impact on men's lives. For example, what structural barriers confront women in our society that lead them to earn significantly less than men? Why is there the likelihood that more than one in four women will be sexually assaulted at some time in their lives? How does this fact restrict women's behavior? Should they not go to the library at night to study because walking home is dangerous? How does it affect their ability to compete with men who do not have such fears and restrictions? In other words, feminists view our world as being one primarily built by and for men. The special needs of women frequently remain unmet.

A feminist perspective on macro practice then looks at the social policies and political structures that hamper women in leading free and productive lives. As a generalist practitioner, you need to be aware of oppression and willing to advocate for and sometimes fight on behalf of oppressed people (see Highlight 4.2). This chapter assumes a feminist perspective for generalist practice.

A Definition of Feminism for Practitioners

Feminism is a complex concept that is difficult to define concisely. It involves "the theory of the political, economic, and social equality of the sexes," in

---

 HIGHLIGHT 4.2

Principles of Feminist Counseling

Van Den Bergh and Cooper (1987) proposed seven principles of feminist intervention. These principles provide lenses with which to view women and their problems. They involve assumptions about the causes of many problems. Therefore, they are like molds with which professionals can shape their interventions. These principles provide clues and guidelines for how to proceed:

1. A client's problems should be viewed "within a sociopolitical framework" (Van Den Bergh & Cooper, 1987, p. 613). These problems are often rooted in a sexist social and political structure and cannot be considered simply personal or individual. Another way of making this statement is that for women, "personal is political" (1987, p. 613).

2. Clients need encouragement to free themselves from traditional gender role bonds. They need encouragement to make free choices and pursue the tasks and achievements they choose. Tasks and goals should not be limited to those allocated primarily to women. They should include those traditionally offered primarily to men.

3. Intervention should focus on the identification and enhancement of clients' strengths rather than on pathologies. Strengths provide a foundation upon which to build. Women need to be empowered so they "can increase their ability to control their environments to get what they need" (Van Den Bergh & Cooper, 1987, p. 613).

4. Women should be encouraged to develop "an independent identity that is not defined by one's relationship with others" (Van Den Bergh & Cooper, 1987, p. 613). In other words, women's identities should not be determined by whom they are married to or whom they are dating. Rather, their identity should be solidly based on their own strengths, achievement, and individuality.

5. Other women are considered valuable and important. In a society that devalues women in general, seeing other women as being insignificant is easy even for women (who, of course, are also part of that society). Feminist intervention urges clients to reevaluate their relationships with other women. This principle of feminist intervention emphasizes how valuable other women can be to clients. It is related to the concept of networking, or strengthening and seeking linkages between the client and relevant family members and friends. Other women can serve as effective resources in helping to achieve the client's goals. They can share their experiences and solutions they have found to similar problems. Additionally, they can provide nurturance and emotional support.

6. Feminist intervention emphasizes finding a balance between work and personal relationships. A corollary of this balance is that men and women are encouraged to share in both the nurturant aspects of their lives and in providing economic resources.

7. "Whenever possible, the personal power between . . . [practitioner] and client approaches equality. This [equality] means that feminist . . . [practitioners] do not view themselves as experts on clients' problems; rather, they act as catalysts for helping clients empower themselves. This reconceptualization of the . . . [practitioner–client] relationship is based on the feminist concern with eliminating dominant–submissive relationships" (Van Den Bergh & Cooper, 1987, p. 613).

Feminist intervention fits well with our generalist planned change model. It emphasizes focusing on clients' strengths and is oriented toward viewing the individual as a dynamic micro system interacting with the many mezzo and macro systems in her environment. Emphasizing the significance of the environment in which people live easily sets the stage for advocacy and macro practice change. You need to focus your attention on "the system" to find out what is wrong with it and then structure your interventions so that they work for positive change.

addition to "the organized activity on behalf of women's rights and interests" (*Merriam Webster's Collegiate Dictionary,* 1994, p. 428). Van Den Bergh and Cooper elaborate on the relationship of feminism to human services practice by emphasizing its "commitment to altering the process and manner in which private and public lives are organized and conducted" (1986, p. 1–2). They state that "basically, feminism is concerned with ending domination and resisting oppression" (1986, pp. 1–2).

Some people have extremely negative reactions to the word *feminism.* The emotional barriers they forge and the resulting resistance they foster make approaching the concept with them difficult. Others consider feminism a radical ideology that emphasizes separatism and fanaticism. In other words, they think feminism involves the philosophy adopted by women who spurn men, resent past inequities, and strive violently to overthrow male supremacists. Still others think of feminism as an outmoded tradition that is no longer relevant.

The definition of feminism presented here is designed to relate to basic concepts involving the daily lives of people like you (Kirst-Ashman, 1991). Many people have failed to develop a sensitivity to the sexist barriers surrounding them. For one thing, acknowledging such unfairness is painful. For another, it is easy to assume that "that's the way things are" simply because people have not thought about better ways of doing things.

For our purposes here, feminism is defined as the *philosophy of equality* between women and men that involves *both attitudes and actions,* that infiltrates virtually *all aspects of life,* that often necessitates providing *education and advocacy* on behalf of women, and that appreciates the existence of *individual differences* and personal accomplishments regardless of gender. There are five major components within this definition that relate directly to the core of professional human services practice.

The first component is equality. Equality does not mean that women are trying to shed their female identities and become clones of men. Nor does it mean that women should seek to adopt behaviors that are typically "masculine." Feminism does involve equal rights to opportunities and choices. It relates to women's and men's rights not to be discriminated against nor denied opportunities and choices on the basis of gender.

The second major component inherent in feminism is the fact that it embodies both attitudes and actions. Attitudes concern how we look at the world and perceive other people. Feminism involves viewing other people from a fair and objective perspective and avoiding stereotypes.

For example, consider a social services supervisor who firmly states she is a feminist. However, she ignores one of her male supervisees who consistently makes sexist comments about his female colleagues. The worker frequently tells sexist jokes about breast size. He also likes to tell his colleagues how women just get too emotionally involved with clients and cannot be objective enough to formulate effective intervention plans. This man's behavior is a form of sexual harassment. His supervisor is legally responsible to see that such obtrusive behavior does not occur in the work environment. The point is that although this supervisor may be a feminist in terms of attitude, she is not a feminist in terms of action. A feminist supervisor would confront her supervisee about his inappropriate, sexist remarks. Feminism involves acting on one's beliefs on behalf of gender equality.

The third critical component of feminism is the idea that it concerns all aspects of life. Equality does not only apply to an equal unhindered chance at getting a specific job or promotion. It also involves the right to have personal opinions about political issues and the right to make decisions within personal relationships. It entails a woman's right to make a decision about what to do on a Friday night date, as well as her right to choose whether or not to have a sexual encounter. Essentially, this step includes the acknowledgment that our social, legal, and political structure is oriented toward men, not women.

A fourth important aspect of feminism is the frequent need to provide education and advocacy on behalf of women. We have established that feminism involves values. Values provide the basis for decisions about how a person behaves. If a person sees things occurring that are contrary to her values, in this case to feminist values, actions may be necessary to help remedy the situation. Many times, people need information about women's issues. The male worker mentioned earlier who is sexually harassing female colleagues may need information about what sexual harassment is and how it negatively affects women. He may be ignorant of these effects. A feminist will share and provide information to others to initiate positive changes in their attitudes and behavior.

Sometimes, there will be a need for even greater effort, and advocacy may be called for. Advocacy is defending and actively representing others. One of its goals is empowerment of clients. This process often involves initiating change or going out of one's way to provide help. Feminism focuses on helping women achieve greater equality and opportunity. Feminist advocacy involves speaking out for others who need help. A natural part of advocacy is helping those in positions of lesser power and opportunity.

The fifth major concept involved in the definition of feminism is the appreciation of individual differences (Van Den Bergh, 1995). The feminist perspective lauds the concept of empowering women by emphasizing individual strengths and qualities. Feminism stresses freedom and the right to make choices about one's own life.

Micro Practice with Women: Common Problems

The issues women often bring to counseling situations are related to traditional gender roles and to the situations in which women often find themselves. This fact does not suggest that men never suffer from any of these needs but rather that women are more likely to have these needs because of their gender role socialization. These problems are clustered in two major categories, stressful life events and personal issues.

Stressful Life Events

Collier (1982) cites at least two groups of events that can be stressful to women and provides a number of examples. The first group involves happenings in women's personal lives, such as separation and divorce. For many women, the natural aging process can also cause undue stress. Accepting the inevitable fact that one will lose both youth and beauty can be difficult, especially in a society that particularly stresses their importance for women. Accepting the death of someone close can also be difficult. Finally, many women are forced to move from familiar surroundings to new, unknown environments due to a job change or out of economic necessity. Such changes and forced readjustments can be stressful.

The other group of events that can cause women substantial stress concerns work and financial status. Women may have low self-esteem and worry about the adequacy of their job performance. Or they may be overburdened with employment, home, and child care responsibilities. With or without jobs, women have a high likelihood of being poor and experiencing the resultant stresses and strains.

Finally, women may suffer from blatant sex discrimination at work. Collier describes a common scenario:

Because most women are taught to discriminate against themselves, they are often unaware that their low status and high frustration on the job is due to the pervasiveness of sex discrimination; they therefore tend to blame themselves as if for personal failings. Discrimination is not less blatant but just as pervasive and, if a woman does recognize its presence, she may become frustrated and collapse into unproductive anger, potentially stifling her own efforts. (1982, p. 51)

For instance, consider a woman who is hired at the same time as a man for identical jobs. Both have similar levels of education, experience, and skills. The woman, however, is hired at 80 percent of the man's salary. Women are unfairly socialized to blame themselves, however, and the woman in this example is likely to feel that there is something wrong with *her,* which results in her lower salary. She is likely to accept the situation as it stands (after all, it must be her fault), instead of fighting for what she rightly deserves.

Personal Issues

Collier describes eight problems that women frequently bring to counseling situations:

1. *Powerlessness.* Women who have been taught to be deferent and dependent often do not feel they can take control of their life. They feel no matter what they do, their taking control will not change anything. Lacking practice in being assertive and making decisions, they do not feel they have the potential to do so.

2. *Limited behavioral and emotional options.* Because of being herded down certain gender role–related paths, women do not often see the variety of alternatives that may be open to them. For instance, establishing a career for herself may not even occur to a divorced woman who has never worked outside the home. Or a battered woman may be so cowed by her perpetrator that she might not even think leaving him is an option.

3. *Anger.* Women often come to counseling harboring deep feelings of anger. They may be angry at the condescending treatment they have been receiving in their workplaces or in their homes. They may be angry that they are trying to be supermoms, superworkers, and superwives all at

the same time, and they just cannot do it. Or they may be angry that their perceived expectations of how they should be (gentle, nurturant, passive) are conflicting with how they really want to be. Instead of targeting the real cause of the anger, the woman often becomes angry at herself, which results in depression.

4. *Insufficient communication skills.* Women who come to counseling may not have the words to clearly express what they mean. Additionally, they may not feel that they have the right to say what they think. Opportunities to discriminate between nonassertion, aggression, and appropriate assertion may never have been available to them.

5. *Failure to nurture self.* Women who have devoted themselves to nurturing and caring for others may feel their own identity is lost. They may be searching for who they are and what they can do for themselves. They may have sacrificed so much for others that they no longer know what they as independent individuals need or want.

6. *Balancing independence with dependence to achieve interdependence.* Being dependent involves relying on someone else for support and probably being subordinate to that person. Being independent, on the other hand, entails being able to function well on your own without having to rely on anyone. Collier articulates a woman's dilemma:

   The normal woman finds it difficult to establish her autonomy. The feminine sex-role stereotype encourages her to create her existence not by doing but by accompanying others who do. Her role is to listen, to tend, to care, to understand, and to prohibit herself from expressing what she needs, wants, thinks, and feels at the expense of others. (1982, p. 69)

   One of your tasks as a human services professional focusing on a woman's inner emotional needs and development is to help her establish the difference between being too dependent and being completely independent (i.e., needing no one else for anything, including emotional support). The term for such a balance is *interdependence*, which involves feeling confident enough to function autonomously, yet acknowledging that you are a social entity whose interactions with other people are important to you.

7. *Lack of trust in self-direction.* If a woman has low self-esteem and little experience in independent action, that she will have difficulty trusting her own judgment for how to proceed is logical. Consider, for example, a professional woman in her early forties who has no children and is recently divorced. She is taking on herself the responsibility to build her house. It's a custom-built contemporary home with steeply descending areas of roof and bold lines. Whenever asked about the house, her statements seem to end with question marks. For instance, she might say, "It certainly is contemporary. I wonder if it's too drastic." Or, "I'm finishing the cabinets myself; I hope they're not too light-colored and the coating isn't too rough."

No one should criticize her. Building a home and making the hundreds of choices required ranging from what color the living room rug should be to where to place the electrical outlets is quite a task. Noting how "insecure" she appears, it would be easy to try to assure her that she has made an adequate choice. A counselor might slip into "nurturance mode" and say things like, "Why, it's beautiful; I'm sure you'll love it when it's done." A more helpful response would be, "I think you can trust your own decisions. You've given each one a lot of thought and done the best you can. That took talent and courage!" More than likely, a man would not react in the same insecure way that the woman has. But then traditional male stereotypes dictate that men are supposed to be decisive and never expose any sign of emotion or self-doubt.

Many times, your task as a professional will be to realistically bolster your female client's self-esteem. Additionally, you will often need to help her identify her alternatives, evaluate the pros and cons of each, and make a decision to the best of her ability.

8. *Old rules and expectations.* The old cliché "times change and so do people" comes to mind. In organizing our lives, most of us establish certain ways of doing things. We expect things to be a certain way and formulate rules for our behavior based on these expectations. Sometimes, however, we are forced to face major transitions. For instance, suddenly we face a divorce after six years of being a wife, mother, and homemaker who was not employed outside the home. Or other times, old rules and expectations no longer work well. For example, take the wife who gets a new job that requires her to travel around the country at least two weeks each month. This requirement forces major changes in her relationship with her husband. Although

they always "shared" tasks before, each spouse tended to undertake different household jobs. Now even taking out the garbage becomes an issue requiring new procedures and communication (Collier, 1982, pp. 57–77).

Helping Women in Micro Practice

We will address three major aspects of working with women on a one-to-one level: increasing empowerment, expanding the number and quality of options available to them, and establishing new rules and expectations for their behavior (Collier, 1982).

Empowering Women

As a practitioner, you can help a woman client regain her sense of power and control over her own life. Lott asserts that the

> . . . *personal traits that have clearly been shown to relate positively to measures of self-esteem or subjective well-being are the same for women as for men; and include assertiveness, independence, self-responsibility, and efficacy, characteristics typically included in the stereotype of masculinity* (1987, p. 277)

Enhancing Self-Esteem

Self-confidence and self-esteem are essential for empowerment. There are a number of tactics you can use to address this issue. First, you can help your client *explore* how she feels about herself. Ask her for positive and negative adjectives that she feels best describe her. Have her describe her strengths and weaknesses. Then help her to summarize how she perceives her self-esteem. Does she feel good about herself or does she criticize herself every chance she gets?

Second, you can give your client *feedback* about her responses. Is thinking of strengths difficult for her? You can share with her your perceptions about her strengths. Emphasizing strengths is illustrated throughout this text. Strengths may include virtually anything—personal qualities, being a hard worker, being motivated for change, being caring or articulate.

Third, help your client look more realistically at those areas where she is experiencing *guilt* (Chaplin, 1988). There is some tendency for women with low self-esteem to blame themselves for everything that is wrong. The battered woman typically blames herself of being battered. She had supper on the table one and a half minutes too late. Or perhaps your client blames herself for any unhappiness other

family members experience. She feels she could have been more supportive or should have anticipated the problem. You can help your client distinguish between the point at which her responsibility ends and other individuals' begins.

Fourth, you can help your client accept the fact that most aspects of life have both *positive* and *negative* sides. Categorizing themselves as essentially bad in comparison to other people who are essentially good is easy for people with low self-esteem. Looking realistically at themselves and the world around them is important for clients. A good approach is to view the world in terms of having both strengths and weaknesses, highs and lows, happinesses and sadnesses. Acknowledging the negatives does not mean you have to dwell on them. However, admitting to yourself that they exist can save a lot of energy trying to hide or fight them.

The other side of this strength/weakness coin is acknowledging, appreciating, and using strengths. You can help your clients appreciate the positive, while acknowledging the negative. For example, a single mother of five children may hate having to receive public assistance. Yet, a strength in this situation is that she is able to care for her children full-time. That is, it is a strength if the public assistance system doesn't force her to work outside the home.

The fifth thing you can do to enhance self-esteem is help clients target those areas in which they want to see *improvements*. You can assist them to pinpoint where they are exceptionally self-critical or on what aspect they want to work at feeling better about themselves. You can help them examine what qualities people with higher self-esteem have (Apgar & Callahan, 1980) and then help them work out how they might apply those characteristics to themselves.

Increasing Assertiveness

Professionals can teach women about assertiveness and how to develop assertiveness skills. They can provide practice situations and guide their female clients through more effective ways of handling difficult or uncomfortable situations. Assertiveness improves personal interactions, which in turn builds confidence.

Assertiveness involves verbal or nonverbal behavior that is straightforward but not offensive. Assertiveness involves taking into account both your own rights and the rights of others.

It sounds simple, but, for many people, appropriate assertiveness is difficult to master. For instance, consider the situation where you are patiently waiting in line at the grocery store. A man hurriedly steps in front of you, slams his six-pack of beer on the counter, and throws a $10 bill at the clerk. He is big, threatening, and obviously rude. Do you shyly allow him to continue because you will be glad to see him leave as soon as possible? Do you brashly step in front of him and shout, "You turkey, I was in line first!" Or do you calmly and straightforwardly say to the clerk, "Excuse me, I was in line first. Here are my groceries."

Many times, looking at a situation objectively and taking the feelings and needs of all concerned into account is difficult. It is often especially difficult for women who have been taught to be sensitive to others' needs, are frequently critical of themselves because of low self-esteem, and are not accustomed to assuming a strong leadership role.

Assertiveness involves specific skills that can be taught with assertiveness training. Here we will discuss in more depth the meaning of assertiveness and some concepts involved in assertiveness training.

The Meaning of Assertiveness.
Do you have trouble telling someone when you are annoyed? Do you hate arguments and avoid them at all cost? Do you feel uncomfortable asking people for favors even when you are in desperate situations? Do you feel that your views are not quite as important as the next person's? If you answer "yes" to any of these questions, you may be having difficulty being assertive enough.

Note that women are not the only people who sometimes have trouble with assertiveness. However, as we have discussed, traditional gender role stereotypes and expectations may make developing assertiveness skills harder for many women. Many female clients will have difficulty being appropriately assertive. They will come to you with problems involving poverty, jobs, domestic violence, relationships, or sexual assault. Many of them would benefit greatly by developing assertiveness skills to address their respective problematic situations.

Assertiveness can be perceived as the center of a continuum ranging from aggression to passivity. Alberti and Emmons describe typical behavior evident in each of these three styles:

In the nonassertive style, you are likely to hesitate, speak softly, look away, avoid the issue, agree regardless of your own feelings, not express opinions, value yourself "below" others, and hurt yourself to avoid any chance of hurting others. In the aggressive style, you typically answer before the other person is through talking, speak loudly and abusively, glare at the other person, speak "past" the issue (accusing, blaming, demeaning), vehemently expound your feelings and opinions, value yourself "above" others, and hurt others to avoid hurting yourself.

In the assertive style, you will answer spontaneously; speak with a conversational tone and volume, and look at the other person, speak to the issue, openly express your personal feelings and opinions (anger, love, disagreement, sorrow), value yourself equally to others, and hurt neither yourself nor others. (1975, p. 24)

Apgar and Callahan characterize the three styles respectively as the "martyr," the "persecutor," and the "balancer" (1980, pp. 43–44). A martyr is a nonassertive, passive person whose primary aim is to keep others happy. She will put aside her own needs and wants in deference to the wants of others because she does not think of herself as important.

The persecutor, on the other hand, thinks of only herself as being important. Other people do not really matter. The persecutor will insist upon getting her own way. She is aggressive. She "gets what she wants by dominating, manipulating, and humiliating others" (Apgar and Callahan, 1980, p. 43). Frequently, she is hostile in her interactions or ignores other people altogether.

The balancer does just that. She balances both her needs and the needs of others. Appropriate assertiveness involves consideration of both yourself and others.

Consider a situation where you are involved in a deep conversation with a good friend. Another mutual acquaintance walks up, rudely interrupts, and begins to talk about how he recently received the highest grade in the class on his last exam. The following illustrates possible responses:

- The unassertive martyr says and does nothing.
- The aggressive persecutor loudly screams, "Shut up, you lowlife dirtball! Can't you see we were talking? Go away."
- The assertive balancer calmly states, "Excuse me. You interrupted an important conversation. Maybe we can talk to you later."

Assertiveness Training.
Assertiveness training helps people distinguish among assertive, aggressive, and nonassertive responses. It gradually helps people to shape their behavior so that they become consciously more assertive. It helps them gain control of their emotions and their life. Alberti and Emmons

(1975) developed the following 13 steps to help establish assertive behavior:

1. Help your client scrutinize her own actions. How does she behave in situations requiring assertiveness? Does she tend to be nonassertive, assertive, or aggressive in most of her communications?

2. Ask your client to make a record of those situations where she feels she lacked assertiveness. How could she have behaved more effectively, either more assertively or less aggressively?

3. Help your client select and focus on some specific instance where she feels she could have been more assertive. Encourage her to visualize the specific details. What exactly did she say? How did she feel?

4. Help your client analyze how she reacted. Examine closely her verbal and nonverbal behavior. Alberti and Emmons cite the following seven aspects of behavior that are important to monitor during assertiveness training:

   a. *Eye contact.* Did your client look the person is the eye? Or were her eyes downcast? Did she find herself avoiding eye contact when she was uncomfortable?

   b. *Body posture.* Was she standing up straight or was she slouching? Was she sheepishly leaning away from the person? Was she holding her head high as she looked the person in the eye?

   c. *Gestures.* Were her hand gestures fitting for the situation? Did she feel at ease? Was she tapping her foot or cracking her knuckles?

   d. *Facial expressions.* Did she have a serious expression on her face? Was she smiling or giggling uncomfortably, thereby giving the impression that she was not really serious?

   e. *Voice tone, inflection, and volume.* Did she speak in a normal voice tone? Did she whisper timidly? Did she raise her voice to the point of stressful screeching? Did she sound as if she were whining?

   f. *Timing.* Making an appropriate assertive response right after a remark is made or an incident happens is best. Considering whether or not a particular situation really requires assertiveness is also important. At times, remaining silent and "letting it go" might be best. For example, telling a prospective employer that he has horrendously offensive breath during a job interview might not be best.

   g. *Content.* What she says in her assertive response is obviously important. Did she choose her words carefully? Did her response have the impact she wanted it to have? Why or why not? (Alberti & Emmons, 1975, pp. 31–32).

5. Help your client identify a role model and examine how that person handled a situation requiring assertiveness. What exactly happened during the incident? What words did the role model use that were particularly effective? What aspects of her nonverbal behavior helped to get her points across?

6. Assist your client in identifying a range of other new responses for situations where she lacks assertiveness. In the future, what other words could she use? What nonverbal behaviors might be more effective?

7. Ask your client to picture herself in the identified problematic situation. Having her close her eyes and concentrate often helps. Step by step, tell her to imagine how she could handle the situation more assertively.

8. Help your client practice the way she has envisioned herself being more assertive. Ask her to target a real-life situation that remains unresolved. For example, perhaps the person she lives with always leaves dirty socks lying around the living room or drinks all her soda and forgets to tell her when the refrigerator is empty. You can also help your client role play the situation. Role playing provides effective mechanisms for practicing responses before clients have to use them spontaneously in real life.

9. Once again, review her new assertive responses. Help her emphasize her strong points and try to remedy her flaws.

10. Continue practicing steps seven, eight, and nine until her newly developed assertive approach feels comfortable and natural to her.

11. Direct your client to try out her new assertiveness approach in a real-life situation.

12. Encourage your client to continue to expand her assertiveness repertoire until such behavior becomes part of her personal interactive style. She can review the earlier steps and try them out with an increasingly wider range of problematic situations.

13. Reinforce your client for her achievements in becoming more assertive. Changing long-standing patterns of behavior is not easy. Encourage her to focus on and revel in the good feelings she experiences as a result of her successes (see Highlight 4.3).

HIGHLIGHT 4.3

Each of Us Has Certain Assertive Rights

Part of becoming assertive involves clearly figuring out and believing that we are valuable and worthwhile people. Criticizing ourselves for our mistakes and imperfections is easy. Holding our feelings in because we are afraid that we will hurt someone else's feelings or that someone will reject us is also easy. Sometimes, feelings that are held in too long will burst out in an aggressive tirade. These situations apply to any of us, including our clients.

For example, let us say some close friends from a distant state come to visit with their 16-month-old baby, Robert. They obviously adore Robert. They also feel that Robert "has a mind of his own" and allow Robert to do more or less exactly what he wants. First, he plays with all your magazines and casually throws them all over the floor. You find this mildly annoying but do not get too upset because you rarely get to see your friends; and what harm can Robert do to magazines anyway? They then feed Robert some crackers and later some sticky candy. Robert smears the food all over himself, the furniture, and the rug. His parents do not seem to notice. You find this annoying but think that the furniture, the rug, and probably Robert can all be cleaned up later.

Robert then spies your prized collection of compact discs and heads directly for them. His mother calmly remarks, "Oh, look, Robert's found the compact discs. It's funny he hadn't noticed them before this." She smiles lovingly at him as he pulls the first one out of the case. This, you think, is too much, and try to calmly say, "Let's go into the kitchen and round up some lunch." Finally, back in the living room, Robert breaks a lamp. His parents say they're sorry. By this time all you're beginning to focus on is your anger. You muster up the stamina to say, "Oh, that's all right. It was an old lamp anyway." You retreat to the kitchen to take several deep breaths and regain control. You return to the living room with some drinks. Robert's father comes up to you and timidly says, "Well, Robert really ruined your picture." Earlier you had shown your friends a picture of your family given you by your grandmother. It was sentimentally invaluable to you and also irreplaceable.

The picture was the last straw. The room turns red. Your blood feels like it is boiling in your veins. You turn to your friends and say, "Get out! Get out! Take that devil-monster with you and never come back!"

This final cataclysm could have been avoided if early on in the process you had acknowledged that you, too, had rights.

The following are eight of your and your clients' assertive rights.

1. You have the right to express your ideas and opinions openly and honestly.
2. You have the right to be wrong. Everyone makes mistakes.
3. You have the right to direct and govern your own life. In other words, you have the right to be responsible for yourself.
4. You have the right to stand up for yourself without unwarranted anxiety and make choices that are good for you.
5. You have the right *not* to be liked by everyone (do you like *everyone* you know?)
6. You have the right, on the one hand, to make requests and, on the other hand, to refuse them without feeling guilty.
7. You have the right to ask for information if you need it.
8. Finally, you have the right to decide not to exercise your assertive rights. In other words, you can choose not to be assertive if you do not want to.

Source: Most of these rights have been adapted from those identified in L. Z. Bloom, K. Coburn, and J. Perlman, *The New Assertive Woman* (New York: Dell, 1976) and in K. Apgar and B. N. Callahan, *Four One-Day Workshops* (Boston: Resource Communications Inc. and Family Service Association of Greater Boston, 1980).

Other Positive Intervention Approaches for Women Clients

Earlier, we cited anger as one of the problems women often bring to a counseling situation. As a professional, you can encourage a woman to express her anger instead of holding it in. The real causes and targets of the anger can be identified. Once causes are recognized, you can "help the client learn to deal with anger directly through verbal and nonverbal communication styles, negotiation, confrontation, alliances and networks, compromise and resoluteness" (Collier, 1982, p. 277). You can help women to address the situations that cause their anger. If a woman is angry with her spouse, she can be taught how to express her feelings effectively so that whatever is happening to cause the anger can be changed.

Additionally, you can encourage a female client to take care of herself. The qualities that she likes about herself can be nurtured. A woman can learn that she has the right to time for herself to participate in activities she enjoys.

All of these suggestions, including those concerning enhancing self-esteem and increasing assertiveness, are related to each other. Each one strengthens the accomplishments of the others. Becoming more assertive enhances one's sense of control. An increased sense of control improves self-esteem. Greater self-esteem increases one's confidence in being assertive. The overall intent is to establish a confident, competent sense of self, which is every person's right.

Expanding Options. In addition to enhancing self-esteem, you can help women recognize the various alternatives available to them and evaluate the pros and cons of each. In other words, you can teach them how to make decisions and solve problems. Success at using such skills breeds more success. Once women have learned the process of making their own decisions and solving their own problems, they can apply these skills to more decisions and more problems. These alternatives can help to build their feelings of being in control.

Changing Rules and Expectations. Female clients often need to change not only how they view themselves and the world but also their expectations for what is appropriate, effective behavior, which includes both their own behavior and that of others. For instance, perhaps in the past a client felt she should be agreeable with and obedient to her spouse regardless of the issue. In view of her enhanced self-esteem and increased assertiveness, she no longer assumes this consistently deferent approach. Rather, she assertively shares her own feelings about issues and aims to get her own needs met in addition to those of her spouse. In other words, as part of the micro intervention process, clients will integrate what they have learned about themselves, and their values about how things "should" be will change.

Common Circumstances Facing Women

Understanding the special, internal dynamics of women at the micro level before proceeding to the mezzo and macro levels of intervention is important. Here we will arbitrarily examine three common circumstances facing women. They are sexual assault, domestic violence, and poverty.

For each, background information will first be provided so that you better understand the issue. Next, intervention strategies at the micro and mezzo levels will be proposed. Frequently, clearly separating out the micro level from the mezzo level of intervention is difficult because the personal and the interpersonal are so integrally related. Thus, we will discuss these strategies together. Finally, we will examine the macro aspects of each issue and propose macro methods of intervention (see Highlight 4.4).

Women as Survivors of Sexual Assault

During 1997 in the United States, there was one reported rape for every 275 women (Federal Bureau of Investigation, 1998). One study indicated that nearly 18 percent of all women in the United States "have been victims of rape or attempted rape" (AASECT, 1999, January, p. 7). The number of rapes reported to authorities thus "is a vast underestimate of the actual number of assaults committed each year" (Allgeier & Allgeier, 2000, p. 449). It is estimated that the number of reported rapes ranges from 8 to 16 percent of those actually committed (Crooks & Baur, 1999; Koss, 1988; National Victim Center, 1992). Hence, sexual assaults upon women are very common. How can this be? Why are women in our society so terribly vulnerable?

This section will examine the feminist perspective on sexual assault, typical reactions of rape survivors, and suggestions for counseling. Finally, a macro practice perspective on the problem will be explored.

First, we need to define our terms. The most intimate violation of a person's privacy and dignity is sexual assault. Sexual assaults involve any unwanted sexual contact where verbal or physical force is used. A commonly used legal definition of rape involves a sexual assault where penile penetration of the vagina occurs without mutual consent (Masters et al., 1995). Now we need to explore why sexual assault is such a major problem.

HIGHLIGHT 4.4

A Feminist Approach to Macro Practice

We have established that, in many ways, a feminist perspective corresponds well with the basic principles of generalist macro practice. Brandwein (1987) conceptualized at least four aspects of feminist macro practice and applies the feminist approach to policy making, community organization, and administration.

First, feminist macro practice values the process of how things are accomplished as much as the final result of the process. For example, policies, of course, are important. However, a feminist perspective emphasizes that how well a policy is implemented is just as important as what the policy says. Take an agency policy that states both men and women should be treated equally in terms of receiving annual raises in salary. The policy is clearly stated on the books. However, if women typically receive significantly fewer raises than men, then the policy is not working. Feminist macro practice then focuses in an ongoing manner on how well things are accomplished.

Second, feminist macro practice adopts a "win-win" rather than a "win-lose" philosophy (Brandwein, 1987, p. 889). Brandwein articulates that a feminist view of power "is not necessarily power over others, but self-empowerment" (1987, p. 889). In feminist macro practice, you do not have to crush the enemy. Rather, you work things out with those in disagreement. Power is not something available only in limited, finite quantities to be doled out to a select few. It can be shared, and compromises can be made. Feminist macro practice espouses a collaborative style of decision making in which a group of equals comes together and works toward a mutually satisfactory decision. There is no strict hierarchy where each participant has a quantifiable amount of power either more or less than every other participant.

A third principle of feminist macro practice emphasizes the importance of interpersonal relationships. A nonfeminist approach might emphasize forming relationships temporarily to complete some specified task. Feminist practice, on the other hand, values the establishment of relationships on an ongoing basis. The focus is not on the completion of any small or even large task. Rather, that all participants in the system continue working together productively is important.

The fourth principle is the high value placed on human diversity. Differences are applauded and appreciated rather than denied. All participants in a process are considered equal. There is no concept of one person being better than another for some reason.

So how do all these principles apply to the actual practice of generalist workers? First, the emphasis on diversity helps to sensitize feminist practitioners to the existence of inequality and oppression. Feminist practitioners then are more likely to turn to macro interventions to change the systems that cause the oppression.

Second, the high value placed on the process of how things are accomplished orients practitioners to focus on policy. Policies, of course, provide the rules for what you as a worker can and cannot do. Feminist practitioners are concerned with policies because policies control the ongoing process of how things are done.

The third application to macro practice involves community change organization. The feminist's concern with equality and collaborative decision making fits well with the idea of getting as many community people involved as possible. The emphasis on equality frames each participant's view as important.

A fourth application of feminist macro practice concerns administration. Feminists emphasize the value of employee input. Since employees are seen as significant participants, development of their skills is important. Attention is given "both to process and interpersonal relationships." This "would not be at the expense of accomplishing tasks, but would enhance the results" (Brandwein, 1987, p. 890).

The Feminist Perspective on Sexual Assault

The feminist perspective emphasizes that rape is the logical reaction of men who are socialized to dominate women. Rape is seen as a manifestation of men's need to aggressively maintain power over women. It has little to do with sexuality. Sexuality only provides a clear-cut means for exercising power. Rape is seen as a consequence of attitudes toward women that are intimately intertwined throughout the culture. The feminist perspective views rape as both a societal problem and an individual one.

Herman (1984) elaborates on this view. She points out that both aggressors and victims are brought up to believe that sexual aggression is natural. As a result, victims often blame themselves for the assault. The rationale is that they should have expected to be raped and should have been prepared or have done something to prevent it.

An analogous situation concerning self-blame is the example of a woman who has her purse snatched while shopping on a Saturday afternoon. If the self-blame concept were applied, it would follow that the woman would blame herself for the incident. She would chastise herself by saying it was her fault. She never should have taken her purse with her to shop in the first place. Maybe she should shop only by catalog from now on. Of course, taking that course of action would be absurd. The woman was not at fault. The one who should be held responsible was the purse snatcher, who broke the law.

Blaming oneself for being raped is equally inappropriate. The feminist view holds that society is wrong for socializing people to assume that male sexual aggression is natural. Socializing women to consider themselves weak and nurturant also contributes to the problem. Developing a victim mentality helps, that is, an expectation that for women to be victims is natural. The feminist perspective emphasizes that these attitudes need to be changed. Only then can rape as a social problem disappear.

The term *victim* implies weakness and powerlessness. From here on, therefore, we will use the term rape *survivor* instead. Survivor implies strength and is oriented toward the future. It coincides with the suggestions for counseling that emphasize helping rape survivors regain confidence and control of their lives.

Reactions to Rape

Burgess and Holmstrom (1974), studying the reactions of 92 rape survivors, found that women can experience serious psychological effects that can persist for a half-year or more following a rape. They call these emotional changes the *rape trauma syndrome,* "now considered to be a specific aspect of posttraumatic stress disorder" (Byington, 1995, p. 2139; Greenberg, Bruess, & Haffner, 2000; Hyde & DeLamater, 2000; Rathus, Nevid, & Fichner-Rathus, 2000).[1] The syndrome has two basic phases. The first is the acute phase, which involves the woman's emotional reactions immediately following the rape and up to several weeks thereafter. The second involves a long-term reorganization phase.

The Acute Phase. Immediately following a rape, the survivor usually reacts in one of two ways

(Masters et al., 1995). She may show her emotions by crying, expressing anger, or demonstrating fear. On the other hand, she may try to control these intense emotions and hide them from view. Emotions experienced during the acute phase range from humiliation and guilt to shock, anger, and desire for revenge (Lott, 1994). This now is considered a form of posttraumatic stress disorder (PTSD),

> . . . an official diagnosis that was originally developed to describe the long-term psychological distress suffered by war veterans . . . . Symptoms can include persistently experiencing the traumatic event (flashbacks, nightmares), . . . avoiding certain locations or activities [associated with the rape], and . . . sleep difficulties, difficulties concentrating [and] irritability. (Hyde & DeLamater, 2000, p. 448)

Additionally, during this phase women will often experience physical problems including difficulties related directly to the rape (Hyde & DeLamater, 2000). For instance, a woman may suffer irritation of the genitals or rectal bleeding from an anal rape. Physical problems also include stress-related discomforts such as headaches, stomach difficulties, or inability to sleep.

The two primary emotions experienced during the acute phase are fear and self-blame. Fear results from the violence of the experience. Many rape survivors report that during the attack they felt their life had come to an end. They had no control over what the attacker would do to them and were terrified. Such fear can linger. Oftentimes, survivors are afraid that rape can easily happen again. The second emotion, self-blame, results from society's tendency to blame the survivor instead of the perpetrator (i.e., the rapist) for the crime.

Women fail to report being raped for many reasons. Survivors whose bodies have been brutally violated often desperately want to forget that the horror ever happened. To report the rape means dwelling on the details and going over the event again and again in their minds. Other survivors fear retribution from the rapist. If they call public atten-

---

1. "Posttraumatic stress disorder (PTSD) is an official diagnosis that was originally developed to describe the long-term psychological distress suffered by war veterans, most of whom are men. Symptoms can include persistently experiencing the traumatic event (flashbacks, nightmares), . . . avoiding certain locations or activities [associated with the rape], and . . . sleep difficulties, difficulties concentrating [and] irritability" (Hyde & DeLamater, 2000, p. 448).

tion to him, he might do it again to punish them. No police officer will be available all of the time for protection. Other victims feel that people around them will think less of them because they have been raped. They may feel as if a part of themselves has been spoiled, a part that they would prefer to hide from other people. Rape is an ugly crisis that takes a great amount of courage to face.

An instructor describes her experience with a young female student that illustrates some of these points:

A student, age twenty-two, entered my office and sat down. She had a stern look on her face. She could have been there for any number of reasons. Perhaps she needed feedback on her research assignment or wanted me to double check that she had fulfilled all her requirements for her upcoming graduation. I asked her what she needed. Spontaneously, she began to cry almost uncontrollably. She said she had been at a party the past Saturday night (it was now Tuesday afternoon). The party was held at the home of a young lawyer who was a mutual friend of a group of her best friends. She described the party as being "typical," meaning a big crowd, lots of beer, some drugs, and loud music. She said that she found herself sitting on a bed with the young lawyer who lived in the apartment. (To me the scene resembled a common predating ritual where a couple meets and decides if there is some "spark" there.) Suddenly, he got up, closed the bedroom door, locked it, threw her down on the bed, and raped her. She was stunned. How could this be? He was a good friend of her friends. He was a lawyer!

So, we returned to the present. It turned out that her primary fear was that her friends would find out about the rape. We talked about how it was the rapist's fault, not her fault. We discussed how he had taken total control from her by virtue of a surprise attack. She never would have suspected that a lawyer would commit such a crime. I also commended her for surviving. In a crisis situation like that, a woman can have no idea what a perpetrator will do. He could kill her, for all she knew.

Finally, we discussed her friends. What true friends would condone such violence? She began to look at the experience more objectively. She began to get in touch with her intense anger at the lawyer for what he had done to her. She started to regain some of her sense of self-confidence. We also talked about pregnancy, but she felt the risk was minimal since she was taking birth control pills. Health issues such as sexually transmitted diseases also required attention. We spoke of the alternatives available to her. I called a local rape crisis center and made a referral that she said she

would follow up on. We talked about reporting the rapist. It was too late to prosecute successfully. However, she could report his name to the local authorities and said she wanted to do so. Finally, she said she was going to tell her friends about the whole experience. She felt they needed to know what this man was really like.

In summary, we could not erase the horror. The incident had happened. However, the young woman was able to begin dealing with her feelings and gaining control.

Techniques for helping rape survivors will be discussed more thoroughly in a later section of this chapter.

The Long-Term Reorganization Phase. The second stage of the rape trauma syndrome is the long-term reorganization and recovery phase; the emotional changes and reactions of this phase may linger on for years (Greenberg et al., 2000; Rathus et al., 2000). Reported reactions included fear of being alone, depression, sleeplessness, and, most frequently, an attitude of suspicion toward other people. Other long-term changes that sometimes occur include avoiding involvement with men and suffering various sexual dysfunctions such as lack of sexual desire, aversion to sexual contact, or difficulty in having orgasms (Masters et al., 1995).

Dealing with even the most negative feelings and getting on with their life is important for survivors of rape. In some ways, rape might be compared to accepting the death of a love one. The fact that either has occurred cannot be changed. Survivors must learn to cope. Life continues.

Counseling Survivors of Sexual Assaults

Three basic issues are involved in working with a woman who has survived a rape. First, she is most likely in a state of emotional upheaval. Her self-concept is probably seriously shaken. Various suggestions for helping a rape survivor in such a traumatic emotional state will be provided. Second, the rape survivor must decide whether or not to call the police and press charges. Third, the rape survivor must assess her medical status following the rape, including injuries, disease, or potential pregnancy.

Emotional Issues. Collier (1982) suggests that helping women who have been sexually assaulted involves three major stages. First, as a worker you need to provide the rape survivor with immediate warmth and support. The survivor must feel safe and free to talk. She needs to ventilate and acknowledge her feelings before she can begin to deal with them. To the greatest extent possible, help the survivor to know she is now in control of her situation. Do not pressure her to talk. Rather, encourage her to share her feelings, even the worst ones, with you.

Although talking freely is important to the survivor, that she not be grilled with intimate, detailed questions is also important. She will have enough of those to deal with if she chooses to report the assault to the police.

Frequently, the survivor will dwell on what she could or should have done. Emphasizing what she did *right* is helpful. After all, she is alive, safe, and not severely physically harmed. She managed to survive a terrifying and dangerous experience. Talking about how she reacted normally, as anyone else in her situation would most probably have reacted, is also helpful. This suggestion does not mean minimizing the incident; rather, one should talk objectively about how traumatizing and potentially dangerous the incident was. One other useful suggestion for dealing with a rape survivor is to help her place the blame where it belongs, namely on the rapist. He chose to rape her. It was not her doing.

The second stage of counseling, according to Collier (1982), involves eliciting support from others. This support may include that of professional resources such as a local rape crisis center as well as support from people who are emotionally close to the survivor. Sometimes, you will need to educate those close to the survivor. They must find out that what the survivor needs is warmth and support and to feel loved. Avoid questions that emphasize her feelings of self-blame, such as why she did not fight back or why she was wearing a low-cut blouse.

An instructor describes an anecdote illustrating the importance of educating people close to the survivor:

I was sitting in my office late one afternoon finishing up some extremely dull paperwork. The university halls were empty and desolate as they get in late afternoons. I suddenly heard a knock at my door and looked up. There stood an extremely tall, red-headed, handsome young man of about twenty-four or twenty-five. I knew at once that he did not look familiar. He then asked if I was so-and-so who had just been quoted in the university newspaper about some information on sexual assault. I replied that I was. Meanwhile, I thought to myself, "Now this guy could not have been raped . . . although you never know." I also became aware of how big he was and how alone I was.

At any rate, he sat down and told me his story. His girlfriend had recently shared with him how she had been brutally raped by one of their mutual acquaintances last year. He said he loved this young woman dearly and planned to marry her. However, he could not bear even to think about the horrible incident. He said she had been trying to talk to him about it because it still disturbed her, but each time she tried, he'd cut her off. His anger at the rapist was so overwhelming he feared he couldn't control it.

We sat for over two hours and discussed his situation and his options. We talked about the emotions survivors of sexual assault typically experience. What were the consequences of not allowing her to talk to him about the assault? Perhaps she would feel that he was blaming her for some part in the assault. Maybe she would feel dirty or permanently violated. Or, at the very least, he was probably communicating to her that she would be unable to talk to him about things such as this which were critically important to her.

On the other hand, what if he could acknowledge and gain control of his anger? What would he be communicating to her if he encouraged her to talk to him about something as painful as this? He came to realize that taking this route would probably communicate to her how much he loved her. She would see that he truly cared how she felt and was trying desperately to understand. It would also probably destroy any feelings she had that he felt she was damaged or to blame. Finally, it would communicate to the young woman that she would be able to share virtually anything with him, even something this difficult. He decided that he definitely needed to listen to his girlfriend and break through his own defenses and help her as much as he could.

The young man left my office with a number of handouts supplying information similar to that presented here. Although I never heard from him again, I sincerely hope that he was able to help his girlfriend work through the aftermath of that nightmarish experience. I also romantically like to think of them still living happily together.

Collier's (1982) third stage of counseling involves rebuilding the survivor's trust in herself, in the environment around her, and in her other personal relationships. Rape weakens a woman. It destroys her trust in herself and in others. During this stage of counseling, you need to focus on the survivor's objective evaluation of herself and her situation. You need to clarify and emphasize her strong points so that she may gain confidence in herself.

The survivor also needs to look objectively at her surrounding environment. She cannot remain cooped up in her apartment for the rest of her life.

She can take precautions against being raped but needs to continue living a normal life.

Finally, you can help the survivor assess her other personal relationships objectively. Just because she was violated by one aggressor, this event has nothing to do with the other people in her life. She needs to concentrate on the positive aspects of her other relationships. She must not allow the fear and terror she experienced during that one terrible incident to taint other interactions. She must clearly distinguish the rape and rapist from her other relationships.

A woman who has been raped may initially want to talk with another woman. However, talking to men, including those close to her, might also be important. That not all men are rapists is important for the survivor to realize. Sometimes there is a male partner, and his willingness to let the victim express her feelings, and, in return, offer support and empathy, is important (Masters et al., 1995).

Reporting to the Police.   The initial reaction to being raped might logically be to call the police and report the incident. However, many survivors choose not to follow through with this action. There are numerous reasons why people do not report the rape, including fear that the rapist will try to get revenge, fear of public embarrassment and derogation, an attitude that it will not matter anyway because most rapists get off free, and fear of the legal process (Masters et al., 1995). Taking a rape case to court is financially expensive and emotionally draining (Herman, 1984). Even then, few rapists are actually convicted (Byington, 1995).

Some positive changes are occurring in police investigation and legal handling of rape cases (Byington, 1995). Many police departments are trying to deal with rape survivors more sensitively. Some departments in larger cities have special teams trained specifically for dealing with survivors. In many states, information about the survivor's past sexual history is no longer permissible for use in court because it can serve to humiliate and discredit the survivor.

Some states have more progressive laws. Wisconsin,[2] for example, has established four degrees of sexual assault, in addition to forbidding the use of the survivor's past sexual conduct in court. According to Wisconsin law, the severity of the crime and the corresponding severity of punish-

ment is based on the amount of force used by the rapist and on the amount of harm done to the survivor. A wife is also able to prosecute her husband for sexual assault when he forces sexual relations upon her.

Despite the potential difficulties in reporting a rape, the fact remains that if the survivor does not report it, the rapist will not be held responsible for his actions. A rape survivor needs to think through her various alternatives and weigh the respective positive and negative consequences in order to come to this often difficult decision.

In the event that a survivor decides to report, she should not take a shower. Washing will remove vital evidence. However, survivors often feel defiled and dirty. Trying to cleanse themselves and forgetting that the incident ever occurred is a logical initial reaction. You need to emphasize to a client who has been raped that she should not wash, despite how much she would like to.

Reporting a rape should be done within 48 hours at the absolute most. The sooner the rape is reported and the evidence gathered, the better the chance of being able to get a conviction.

Medical Status of the Survivor.   In addition to emotional issues and the decision whether or not to report the incident, a third major issue, medical status, merits attention. At some point, the survivor needs to attend to the possibility of pregnancy. She should be asked about this issue at an appropriate time and in a gentle manner. She should be encouraged to seek medical help both for this possibility and to screen for sexually transmitted diseases, including HIV. The negative possibilities should not be emphasized, but the survivor needs to attend to these issues at some point. Of course, you should also urge the survivor to seek immediate medical care if she has any physical injury.

Macro Perspectives on Sexual Assault

We have been primarily discussing the micro and mezzo aspects of intervention with survivors of sexual assault. The micro aspects focus attention on woman's inner sense of self. The mezzo facets involve the survivor's relationships with others around her. The macro perspective on sexual assault is just as significant. It involves the way society perceives of rape survivors, how they are treated, and what services are available to them. Toomey (1987) describes and examines a number of macro perspectives on sexual assault. They include the significance of general societal responses and the evaluation of current services.

---

2. *See* Wisconsin Statutes §940.225.

General Societal Responses.   How society views rape survivors is important to what services are made available. Resources are generally scarce. Therefore, decisions must be made about what is important enough to expend them on and what is not. Herman articulates that:

> *In cases of rape, judges, juries, police, prosecutors, and the general public frequently attribute blame and responsibility to the victim for her own victimization. Unfortunately, these negative responses are often compounded by reactions from family and friends. Encounters with parents, relatives, friends, and spouses many times involve either anger at the victim for being foolish enough to get raped or expressions of embarrassment and shame that family members will suffer as a result of the attack. (1984, p. 37)*

If society and the general population consider rape to be a woman's own fault, they are less likely to support her with resources and services. One potential goal then of macro practice is to educate both the general public and those most likely to deal directly with rape survivors. This education might involve using your macro practice skills to disseminate information, set up educational task forces, or mobilize community groups.

One specific group needing education includes hospital staff in emergency rooms. They need to know how to deal with survivors emotionally, "while preserving evidence for criminal prosecution" (Toomey, 1987, p. 570).

Police and other legal staff involved in prosecution also need education. Initiatives have included "changing the attitudes of law enforcement officers, increasing the participation of female officers, and encouraging victim/witness support program in prosecutors' offices" (Toomey, 1987, p. 570).

"Rapist control" provides another legal approach to enhancing survivors' situations (Toomey, 1987, p. 571). This approach involves the extent to which perpetrators are reported, sought, charged, convicted, and imprisoned.

Women in the general population themselves also need education. They need to minimize their vulnerability, which means not only learning self-defense techniques and following suggestions to prevent sexual assault but also enhancing their self-concepts and gaining a greater sense of control.

Current Services.   Toomey summarizes the following trends in services for sexual assault survivors:

1. Continuance of 24-hour hot lines, as well as support and advocacy assistance.

2. Short-term counseling for victims in either individual or group situations.
3. Long-term work with victims (one year or more after the assault).
4. Couples and group work with victims and significant others.
5. Group work with families, especially around an assault situation within the family.
6. Special focus on adolescent victims.
7. Counseling for mothers of children who are victims.
8. Individual and group counseling with women who were victims of rape or incest in the past. (1987, p. 572)

Such services may or may not be available in the area in which you will work. Resources and services vary from one community to another. You may need to use your macro practice perspective to assess needs and advocate for service provision.

Jones proposes the following:

> *One way to assess the deficiencies in the programs and services for women of the traditional social agencies is to compare such programs to those of the many alternative agencies that have been founded in the past ten to fifteen years. Typically guided by feminist values, principles, and methods in their structure and operation, organizations such as rape crisis centers, shelters and programs for battered women and their children, nontraditional employment, training and educational programs, and women's counseling and health centers have provided services to individuals in addition to advocating for institutional and policy changes. [Professionals] should examine the work of these agencies to learn about the gaps in traditional services and successful methods for affecting positive changes in women's lives. (1987, p. 880)*

Additionally, in making determinations about service provision, addressing a number of questions is helpful (Toomey, 1987). How much effort can you afford to expend on macro practice efforts such as public education and advocacy and how much on direct service provision? Even if services are available, how effective are they? Can they be improved and, if so, in what ways? Are they accessible to all groups in the community or limited to only a privileged few?

Battered Women

Battered women is the second issue we will address from the micro, mezzo, and macro intervention perspectives. Terms associated with *wife beating* include *domestic violence, family violence, spouse abuse,* and *battered women.* Strong (1983) describes *battering* as a catch-all term that includes, but is not limited to, the practices of slapping, punching, knocking down, choking, kicking, hitting with objects, threatening with weapons, stabbing, and shooting. The battered-woman syndrome implies the systematic and repeated use of one or more of these practices against a woman by her husband or lover. Although we use the term *wife* throughout the next few sections, the principles involved apply to all women in intimate relationships characterized by battery regardless of marital status.

Some of the myths about battered women include the following:

1. Battered women are not really hurt that badly.
2. Beating and other abuses just happen; they are not a regular occurrence.
3. Women who stay in such homes must really enjoy the beatings they get; otherwise they would leave.
4. Wife-battering only occurs in lower-class families (Roberts, 1996).

A Profile of Battered Women

As many as half of all women will suffer from "violence at some time in their marriage" (Gibbs, 1998, p. 326). Past research emphasizes that the vast majority of spousal battery, perhaps 95 percent, has been done by men to women (Cultural Information Service, 1984; Davis, 1995; Dziegielewski, Resnick, & Krause, 1996; Kurz, 1993).

Some recent research indicates that men and women are equally likely to batter spouses (Renzetti & Curran, 1999; Straus, 1993). This latter perspective should be viewed cautiously for at least two reasons. First, there is no way to tell how much violence inflicted by women is done in their own self-defense when attacked (Lott, 1994; Renzetti & Curran, 1999; Straus, 1993). Second, women are much more likely to experience serious harm than men (Davis, 1995; Gibbs, 1998; Kurz, 1993; Lott, 1994; Renzetti & Curran, 1999). "Given the differences in size, strength, and resources between husbands and wives, some have questioned the appropriateness of labeling wives' abusive behavior toward their husbands 'battery'" (Renzetti & Curran, 1995, p. 238). Of all women treated in hospital emergency rooms, 22 to 35 percent are there to receive treatment for injuries incurred during domestic violence incidents (Davis, 1995; Dziegielewski et al., 1996; Gibbs, 1998; Randall, 1990). Battering women is so prevalent that women are more likely to be beaten in their own home than police officers are likely to be assaulted on the job (U.S. Department of Justice, 1994; U.S.

House of Representatives, 1988). Women "suffer more from domestic violence than from all other crimes combined" (AASECT 1994, p. 10; Renzetti & Curran, 1995).

Battered women do not like to be beaten (Renzetti & Curran, 1999). They may initially experience "shock, disbelief, and denial, followed by terror, then attempts to reestablish the level of safety previously believed to have existed, followed by depression with intermittent inner-directed rage and outbursts of anger" (Harway, 1993, p. 38). Women go to domestic-violence programs for help to stop the beatings and maintain their marriages (Norman & Mancuso, 1980). They do not enjoy the pain and suffering; but, for reasons that will be discussed later, they tolerate it.

The following sections will introduce a strengths perspective on battery, describe common characteristics of abusive husbands, explain the battering cycle, and explore why so many battered women opt to remain in abusive environments. Counseling strategies will be suggested to help a woman address her situation from the micro and mezzo perspectives. Finally, implications for macro practice intervention on the part of battered women will be discussed.

Survivors versus Victims: A Strengths Perspective

As with survivors of sexual assault, we will refer to people who have survived domestic violence as *survivors* instead of *victims*. Once again, instead of focusing on a woman's weakness, which the word *victim* implies, we will use the term *survivor* to emphasize her survival "strengths and efforts to leave" her abusive environment (McHugh, 1993, p. 61).

The Abusive Perpetrator

A series of traits tend to characterize men who abuse (Davis, 1995; Stout & McPhail, 1998; Strong & DeVault, 1997). They tend to have low self-esteem, to believe in the common myths about battering, and to firmly maintain traditional gender-role stereotypes. Additionally, men who batter are frequently emotionally immature and use domestic violence as a means of alleviating stress. An abusive man, in his personal insecurity, often becomes very jealous and possessive of his wife. Alcohol is frequently involved in violent incidents (Bennett, 1995; Davis, 1995; Renzetti & Curran, 1999). Some evidence suggests that men who batter have learned from their own parents to use aggressive behavior as a coping mechanism. For instance, a male child can learn abusive behavior by observing the behavior modeled by his own father. As an adult, the man learns he can gain satisfaction by battering as it gives him control over something in his life (Davis, 1995).

The Battering Cycle

Three basic phases tend to characterize battery in an intimate relationship (Davis, 1995; Lott, 1994; Walker, 1979a, 1979b). The first phase involves the building up of stress and tension. The wife tries to "make things OK" and avoid confrontations. There may be a few minor abusive incidents, but this phase is primarily characterized by the buildup of excessive tension.

The second phase in the battering cycle is the explosion. This point is where the tension breaks, the batterer loses control, and the battering occurs. Although this phase is the shortest of the three phases, it may last for a few hours to several days.

The third phase involves making up and being in love again. Because his tension has been released, the batterer now adamantly states that he is truly sorry for what he has done and swears he will never do it again. The battered woman relents and believes him. He is forgiven, and all seems well; that is, until the cycle of violence begins again.

Why Does She Stay?

Many people wonder why the battered woman remains in the home and in the relationship. There are many reasons why women stay in the battering environment (Davis, 1995; Forte et al., 1996; Papalia, Olds, & Feldman, 2001; Roberts, 1996; Walker, 1979a, 1979b). Approximately half of women who seek help from shelters and even those who initiate separation through the courts eventually return to their abusive home situations (Lott, 1994). The reasons they remain or return include economic dependence, lack of self-confidence, lack of power, fear of the abuser, adherence to traditional beliefs, guilt, fear of isolation, fear for their children, and love.

Economic Dependence. Many battered women are afraid to leave the perpetrator for economic reasons (Davis, 1995; Papalia et al., 2001; Roberts, 1996). Many are financially dependent on the abuser as the primary wage earner for both themselves and their children. Although battering women occurs at all socioeconomic levels, it is more likely to happen in families with fewer resources. Three economic factors related to increased wife abuse include poverty, underemployment and unemployment, and blue-collar employment status (Davis, 1995; Gelles & Cornell, 1990). When children are involved, there is the additional problem of who would care for them if their mother had to increase the amount of time she spent outside of the home in order to earn a living.

Lack of Self-Confidence. Domestic violence involves not only physical abuse but also sexual and psychological abuse (Burstow, 1992; Davis, 1995; Papalia et al., 2001). Psychological abuse may entail regular tirades by battering men who criticize and blast survivors with derogatory remarks. Bit by bit, such treatment eats away at the women's self-esteem and shrinks their self-confidence. Perpetrators tend to emphasize how their female partners could not possibly survive without them; and, after an extended period of time, these women start to believe them. In some ways, psychological abuse is similar to the brainwashing of prisoners of war (Davis, 1995).

Mustering the self-confidence to leave a painful situation and strike out for the unknown takes great initiative and courage. The unknown is frightening. If the domestic violence survivor remains in the home, at least she knows she has a place to stay.

Lack of Power. A battered woman views herself as having significantly less power in her relationship with the abuser than does a woman with a partner who is nonviolent (Forte et al., 1996). Battered women see their relationships as almost completely dominated by the perpetrator. Batterers' systematic regimen of intimidation, criticism, and violence places women in a vulnerable and difficult position.

However, one should note that even in the face of such adversity, indeed "daily surveillance and torture," these women utilize their strengths; Burstow explains:

> *They are not simply submitting, even where submission is key and even though submission is expectable and blameless. They are also making active and critical decisions about how to cope and survive on a moment-to-moment basis. They are deciding to hide certain things. They are deciding to duck. They are deciding not to duck. Each in her own way is resisting. Actively and passively, survivors resist violation, whether that resistance takes the form of numbing themselves so that they will not feel the pain, finding ways of avoiding the abuser's ire, or saying no. (1992, p. 153)*

Fear of the Abuser. Fearing brutal retaliation by the perpetrator if she leaves him is logical for a battered woman (Papalia et al., 2001). A person who has dealt with stress by physical brutality before might do so again when it is initiated by the stress of his female partner leaving him. The battered woman might even fear being murdered by an abandoned male partner.

One myth is that battered women stay in their relationship because they like being beaten, which is not true. For reasons discussed here, they tolerate their circumstances in order to survive.

Adherence to Traditional Beliefs. Because battered women tend to believe in traditional gender-role stereotypes, they often view their male partners as caretakers and providers. They tend to shun the alternatives of separation or divorce. Comprehending what they would do on their own is often difficult for them. A battered woman may believe that nurturing and maintaining her relationship with the abuser is her responsibility and blame herself for problems in that relationship (Harway, 1993; Renzetti & Curran, 1995; Stout & McPhail, 1998). A battered woman will typically report that terminating her relationship with the abuser would hurt her more because she has more to lose than he does (Forte et al., 1996).

Guilt. Many battered women feel that being abused is their own fault (Harway, 1993; Renzetti & Curran, 1995; Stout & McPhail, 1998). They tend to believe that men should be the dominant decision makers and leaders of the family and that women should be submissive and obedient. To some extent, this guilt may be due to their husbands telling them that they are to blame for causing trouble. Perhaps because of their low levels of self-esteem, being critical of themselves is easy for survivors. Their beliefs in traditional gender-role stereotypes may cause them to wonder how they have failed in their submissive, nurturant role of wife.

Fear of Isolation. Battered women often try to keep the facts of their battery a secret. They may feel and be isolated from friends and family by the time their battery reaches such crisis proportions. Frequently, the perpetrator strongly discourages his female partner's interactions with friends and family. He criticizes them. He makes communicating with them as difficult as possible for her. He gradually gets her to cut others off. Then he can have her all to himself. When the abuser becomes everything to the survivor, losing him means that she would be all alone.

Fear for Her Children. A battered woman usually fears for her children's safety. First, she might be worried about her ability to support them financially without her male partner. Second, she may firmly adhere to the traditional belief that children need a father. She may think that a father who abuses his wife is better than no father at all. Third, she may even fear losing the custody of her children. The abuser may threaten to take them away from her. She may have little knowledge of the complicated legal system and may believe that he can and will do it.

Love. Many battered women still love their abusive husbands. Many who seek help would prefer to remain in their relationships if the battering would stop. Walker (1979) cites one elderly woman's reactions to her husband's death. The woman, a university professor, had been married for 53 years to a man who battered her throughout their relationship. The woman states:

> We did everything together.... I loved him; you know, even when he was brutal and mean.... I'm sorry he's dead, although there were days when I wished he would die .... He was my best friend.... He beat me right up to the end.... It was a good life and I really do miss him.

Counseling Battered Women

Despite the difficulties in dealing with domestic violence, there are definite intervention strategies that can be undertaken. They involve police departments, shelters, and specific counseling approaches (Hutchins & Baxter, 1980).

The Police and Battered Women. Police officers often are the first outside means of intervention involved in episodes of domestic abuse (Hutchins & Baxter, 1980; Roberts, 1996). That this role is physically dangerous for them because of the high incidence of violence and injury has already been established. However, there is evidence that police departments are taking an increasingly active interest in addressing the issue of family violence (Hutchins & Baxter, 1980; Roberts, 1996). Because of the seriousness of the issue and the high potential for injury and fatality, they are acknowledging that something must be done. For example, training programs targeting domestic violence are being developed for police personnel (Roberts, 1996). One thrust of these programs is the development of specialized interpersonal skills for dealing with domestic violence. There is also a growing awareness that female officers may play a special beneficial role in the intervention process (Hutchins & Baxter, 1980).

Shelters for Battered Women. The most immediate need of a woman who has been seriously battered is a place to go. For this purpose, shelters have been developed around the country. This occurrence is relatively recent. The first American shelter for battered women, the Rainbow Retreat in Phoenix, Arizona, opened in 1973 (Hutchins & Baxter, 1980).

The one thing that all such programs have in common is the provision of a safe place where battered women can go to obtain temporary shelter. Beyond this commonality, Hutchins and Baxter (1980) conceptualize the range of philosophies adopted by shelters. On one end of the continuum are the more traditionally oriented agencies that emphasize the conventional values of keeping the family together and that orient themselves toward helping women resolve their problems with their mates, stopping the battering, and enabling these women to safely return home.

Neiding and Friedman (1984) describe a treatment program for couples oriented toward achieving similar goals. Because most battered women report that they would prefer to return home, the program focuses on situational and relationship variables and teaches both members of the couple such skills as "coping strategies, stress management, and relationship enhancement" (1984, p. 3).

On the other side of the philosophical continuum of battered-women shelters are those adopting a purely feminist perspective. For these:

[w]ife abuse is seen as a social problem, rooted in sexism and manifested in the suffering of countless individual women. The women are regarded as victims in need of immediate protection and long-term life change. Some of the shelters with this philosophy actively encourage permanent separation of the couple. (Hutchins & Baxter, 1980, p. 207)

Here the idea is that women need not be dependent on men, especially those who have been abusive to them. Rather, such abused women need to nurture confidence in themselves and develop their own alternatives.

Many shelters, however, adopt philosophies somewhere in between the purely traditional and the purely feminist. These shelters encourage women to think through their individual situations, evaluate their alternatives, and make their own decisions about what is best for them.

Counseling Strategies. The following are some basic suggestions, gathered from a range of sources, regarding how counselors can help battered women.

Offer Support. A battered woman has probably been weakened both physically and emotionally. She needs someone to empathize with her and express genuine concern. She needs some time to sit back, experience relief, and think.

Emphasize Strengths. The most important aspect of helping a battery survivor is to clarify and emphasize her strengths. She has been weakened and hurt both physically and psychologically. Cowger (1997) makes suggestions for emphasizing strengths during the assessment process:

1. *Believe the client.* A central concept in the strengths perspective is that clients are trustworthy and will tell the truth. A battery survivor may require assistance in looking at herself and her situation objectively, identifying alternatives she had not thought of before, and emphasizing strengths she does not yet appreciate. However, a client's perception of her reality is real. It should be taken seriously and addressed.

2. *Discover what the client wants.* This suggestion involves two facets, what the client expects you to do for her and how the client wants her situation improved. Does she want the perpetrator to enter a treatment program so she can go home again? Does she want to disappear with her children so that she can be safe? Is she still unclear about what she wants? You can help her articulate her concerns, identify possibilities, and evaluate her choices. You can also clarify to her what you can do to help. For example, you may be able to provide her with a safe place to stay but not put the perpetrator in jail. You can help her think through her alternatives but not make her decisions.

3. *Move the assessment toward personal and environmental strengths.* Help your client think about a wide range of strengths. Personal strengths may include the fact that she is bright, a terrific mother, a hard worker, or that she has established some excellent coping skills in the past. You might stress how well she communicates, has been able to protect her children under harrowing circumstances, has accomplished educational or training goals, or has developed exceptional organizational skills to hold her family together. Environmental strengths might include access to resources including finances, transportation, housing, family, friends, religious support, or available social services (Cowger, 1997, p. 64).

Review Alternatives. A battered woman may feel trapped and be so overwhelmed that many alternatives may not even have occurred to her. Her alternatives may include returning to the marriage, getting counseling for both herself and her husband, temporarily separating from her husband, establishing other means of financial support and independent living conditions for herself, finding good child care, or filing for divorce.

Furnish Information. Most victims probably do not have much information about how they can be helped. Information about available legal, medical, and social services may open up alternatives to better enable them to help themselves (Davis, 1995; Dziegielewski et al., 1996; Resnick, 1976).

Advocate. An advocate can seek out information for a survivor of domestic violence and provide her with encouragement. An advocate can also help the survivor get in touch with legal, medical, and social services resources and help the survivor find her way through bureaucratic processes. Advocacy involves expending extra energy, "going that extra mile," on the survivor's behalf.

Perhaps an even more critical aspect of advocacy involves changing legal macro systems. Duprey and colleagues explain:

Effective intervention requires some fundamental changes in current police and court practices. In many communities, advocates for battered women pushed for proarrest policies, a more aggressive approach to prosecution and sentences geared towards victim safety. Advocates promote civil processes that complemented the criminal court response and pushed for a coordination of civil and criminal approaches to ensure the maximum protection for victims. (1996, p. 10)

Resnick (1976) has developed a training manual for counselors of battered women. She makes some excellent and specific suggestions regarding, among others, the initial interview, the range of the victim's emotional reactions, and specific counseling techniques.

The Initial Interview. A battered woman will probably be filled with anxiety during her initial meeting with you as a counselor. She may be worried about what to say to you. Therefore, you should try to make the woman as comfortable as possible and emphasize that she does not have to talk about anything if she does not want to.

The battered woman may also anticipate that you will be judgmental and critical of her. Resnick emphasizes the importance of putting personal feelings aside and not pressuring the battered woman

into any particular course of action. This suggestion may be especially difficult when you have some strong personal feelings that the woman should leave the abusive situation. A basic principle is that what the woman will choose to do is her decision. In those cases where the battered woman chooses to return home, the counselor should help the woman clarify the reasons behind this decision.

Confidentiality may also be an issue for the battered woman. She may be especially fearful of the abuser finding out she is seeking help and of his possible retaliation. You need to assure her that no information will be given to anyone unless she wants it to. In the event that she does need a place to go, make her understand that the shelter is available.

The woman may show some embarrassment at being a "battered woman." The label may make her feel uncomfortable. Therefore, you should make efforts to dispel any embarrassment by emphasizing that she is not the perpetrator. The abuser is to blame for his own violent behavior. This problem has nothing to do with her character or with her intrinsic human value.

Emotional Reactions. Many battered women will display a range of emotional reactions, which include helplessness, fear, anger, guilt, embarrassment, and even doubts about their sanity. You need to encourage the battered woman to get all of these emotions out in the open because only then will she be able to deal with them. You now can help her look objectively at various aspects of her situation and help get control of her own life.

Specific Counseling Techniques. The foundation of good counseling is good listening ability (Resnick, 1976). The battered woman needs to know that she can talk freely to a human services professional and that what she says will have meaning.

A battered woman is often overwhelmed and confused. One of the most helpful things you can do is to help her sort through her various issues by using problem solving skills (Dziegielewski et al., 1996). She cannot do everything at once, but she can begin getting control of her life by addressing one issue at a time and making decisions step-by-step.

One other important counseling technique is helping the woman establish a "safety plan":

One portion of the plan must deal with the safety of the victim should she return to her abuser or come into contact with him under other circumstances. The plan should focus on how the victim can escape, where she can go, and who can help her. This should be laid out in terms of very specific behaviors, including such items as which phone she would use and where she could keep some clothes, an extra set of car keys, and the like. (Dziegielewski et al., 1996, p. 166)

In summary, battered women need to strengthen their self-esteem and define more objectively the alternatives available to them. They need a chance to vent their feelings and to have someone there to listen to them. They need to have a place of refuge until they can think through their situations and make plans of action for the future.

Suggestions for Macro Practice on Behalf of Battered Women

Most unfortunately, there is no national legislation that mandates that the rights of battered women be upheld and helpful services provided to them. The result is that states and localities have to orchestrate their own responses to the problem. Another result is inconsistency from area to area in terms of available services. In many areas, there are broad gaps of services. As a generalist practitioner, you may be employed in an area rich with related services. For example, most large cities have shelters and crisis hotlines for referrals. On the other hand, there may be a striking scarcity of resources in your area. In this latter case, you may choose to put your macro practice skills to work.

Research thus far has targeted strengthening the legal and criminal justice systems in order to curtail domestic violence (Fagan, Friedman, & Wexler, 1984; Saunders, 1995). In other words, areas where interventions and referrals are done in alliance with police help diminish the number of multiple battering complaints made to police departments. Star explains that "an active arrest policy and prosecution proved to be the most effective deterrent to further violence, especially in more severe cases" (1987, p. 473).

In view of this evidence, one avenue of macro intervention is to lobby actively for better legislation at the state and national levels. Strong national legislation that would require service provision to battered women and uphold their rights would be ideal.

Another aspect of macro practice is to advocate for the establishment of services within your community. Once again, informing the community of the need and organizing potentially interested community groups to help in the task is a possibility. Star articulates the need for "comprehensiveness, continuity, and coordination of services" among various human service agencies and other disciplines in order to combat domestic violence (1987, p. 474).

Star makes some additional suggestions for what you can do at the agency level. She states that:

... agencies can upgrade their professional staff's knowledge base and skills regarding the dynamics of and intervention in family violence through in-service training; establishing a legal aide position to keep staff apprised of court rulings and clients aware of their legal rights; offering support groups and family life education programs to clients; and maintaining positive relationships with community agencies to ensure timely and coordinated referrals. (1987, pp. 473–474)

Prevention of Violence Against Women

These past two sections have focused on describing violence against women and how to help women who have survived it. Ideally, the more effective approach to dealing with such violence is to prevent it in the first place. Kirk and Okazawa-Rey (2001) assert that truly wiping out violence against women would take a major "political movement" (p. 227). Such an endeavor would involve at least three thrusts.

First, people must be educated regarding the dynamics of violence against women and the stereotypes and assumptions supporting it. Children should be educated early on regarding these issues and seriously discouraged from manifesting violent behavior. Similarly, "public information and awareness" should be fostered and funded; such efforts might include "public service announcements, bumperstickers, and ads on billboards, buses, and TV" (Kirk & Okazawa-Rey, 2001, p. 228).

Second, policy and legislation should be developed to protect potential victims and provide consequences to perpetrators. In cases of domestic violence, perpetrators should be prohibited from establishing contact with victims and their children. An example of positive legislation, "the Violence Against Women Act, adopted in 1994, provides for tougher law enforcement, funding for shelters, a national domestic violence hotline, and educating judges and court personnel, as well as young people, about domestic violence" (Papalia et al., 2001, p. 543).

Sexual assault laws should be consistently developed in all states that focus on consequences for the harm done to victims and the amount of force used. This contrasts sharply with prior legislation that focused on victims' past sexual histories and the amount of resistance used against attackers.

The Feminization of Poverty

The term *feminization of poverty* has been coined to reflect the fact that women as a group are more likely to be poor than are men (Rotella, 1998). We have already established that most women, even those with very young children, work outside of the home (Renzetti & Curran, 1999; Sapiro, 1999). Women earn less than 75 percent of what men earn (Rotella, 1998). Women are significantly more likely than men to be poor within their lifetimes (Ruth, 1998; Stout & McPhail, 1998). Female-headed families are especially at risk of poverty (Stout & McPhail, 1998). Women of color suffer even greater risks than white women (Renzetti & Curran, 1999; Stout & McPhail, 1998). Highlight 4.5 provides some additional supportive facts.

Women are clustered in low-paying supportive occupations. Over 70 percent of women are employed in occupations made up of more than 80 percent women; these include nurses and health technicians, elementary and secondary school teachers, sales clerks, clerical workers, apparel and textile workers, and service workers (including waitresses, maids, and dental assistants) (Thornborrow & Sheldon, 1995; U.S. Department of Labor, 1991). Men, on the other hand, tend to work in such better-paying occupations as physicians, managers, engineers, lawyers, and construction workers.

Perhaps an even more striking finding is that for most of these job categories (including those that are viewed as being feminine and those viewed as being masculine) women will earn less than men in the same job category doing the same work. For example, the percentages of women's earnings compared to men's are reflected in the following job categories: 80 percent for computer programmers; 73 percent for bookkeepers; 76 percent for cooks; 61 percent for office managers; and 68 percent for salespersons (Lott, 1994; U.S. Department of Labor, 1991). Other studies have found similar gender differences in salary for physicians, engineers, accountants, and lawyers (*U.S. News & World Report,* 1996).

Micro and Mezzo Perspectives on Women and Poverty

People living in poverty are subject to a number of stereotyped, judgmental, negative perceptions by

---

HIGHLIGHT 4.5

Women of Color Are "Doubly Disadvantaged"[a]

- Families maintained by women comprise 13.7 percent of all white families, 45.9 percent of all African American families, and 23.9 percent of all Hispanic families (Rotella, 1998).
- "Over half of persons living in families maintained by black and Hispanic women are poor compared with 31.8 percent of persons in families maintained by white women" (Rotella, 1998, p. 357). This statistic compares with 6.76 percent of all white families where both spouses are present who live below the poverty line (1998, p. 357).
- The proportion of families who have children under 18, live below the poverty line, and are maintained by women is 45.7 percent for all white families, 63.2 percent for African American families, and 68.3 percent for Hispanic families. This statistic compares with 9.9 percent of all white families with both spouses present that have children under 18 and live below the poverty line (Rotella, 1998).
- Unemployment rates for white men and women are 3.8 percent and 4.4 percent respectively; unemployment rates for African American workers are more than double, and rates for Hispanics are more than 50 percent higher than those of whites (Renzetti & Curran, 1999).
- Median weekly earnings are $595 for white males, $444 for white females, $375 for African American females, and $318 for Hispanic females (Renzetti & Curran, 1999).
- Both African American and Hispanic families have experienced a "drop in income relative to white families, while experiencing a large increase in female heads-of-household" (Strand, 1995, p. 2158).

---

a. This term is taken from A. H. Stromberg and S. Harkess (Eds.), "The Doubly Disadvantaged: Women of Color in the U.S. Labor Force," in *Women Working,* 2nd ed. (Mountain View, CA: Mayfield, 1988), pp. 61–80.

much of the public at large. Collier (1982) speaks of how we foster an independent anyone-can-be-president image in this country. This image conflicts with the fact that permanently poor people exist here. Why are these people poor in a nation where, theoretically, anyone can become rich? She continues:

> We see them as not only poor but also immoral, as associated with crime, violence, alcohol and drug addiction, prostitution, and (the worst sin of all) lack of willpower. . . . Our judgments about the lower class tend to be more moralistic than sensible. If we see a prostitute, we see an immoral woman rather than one who lacks job skills and wants money. . . . We assume that people are poor because they do not want to be otherwise, though the reality is the opposite. (1982, pp. 229–231)

Contrast the situation of the middle class with that of the lower class. How does education in the inner cities compare with that in the much-richer suburbs? How well are lower-class people prepared educationally to compete for college entrance, vocational training programs, or jobs, compared with middle-class people? In terms of prioritizing need, where will a poor, single mother find enough additional money to pay for day care for her children, transportation to and from work, and appropriate clothing to get and keep a job? Her main concern is to keep her family solvent from day to day with enough food and shelter to live. The point is that the same options are simply not available to poor people that are to middle- and upper-class people (Collier, 1982).

For example, one professional describes her experience:

> I will never forget a client who taught me about the futility encompassing poverty. She was a fifteen-year-old female client named Marcia. Her mother had never been married and had given birth to Marcia when she was just sixteen.
>
> Marcia attended a day treatment facility where she received special education and therapy, yet still returned to her home each evening. She had a lengthy history of self-abuse including drug abuse, truancy, running away, and promiscuity (it is interesting how this latter term is not used to characterize boys). Marcia was assigned to my caseload for counseling.
>
> Marcia was obviously bright. She grasped ideas quickly and articulated her thoughts well. At times, she showed interest in areas such as photography and nature, which contrasted starkly with what was available in her home environment. Although she was still behind in school, she was making significant strides and demonstrated excellent potential for being a good student.
>
> At one point, I asked Marcia if she had ever considered going to college. She looked at me as if I had just developed hundreds of huge purple spots all over my body. "Where would somebody like me ever get the money to go to college? Are you nuts?" she asked.
>
> The interesting thing was that I could not think of a rational response. "Yep," I thought to myself, "where would she get the money?" She would not get it from a scholarship because she essentially had no grade point at her special therapeutic school. Her mother and everyone else she knew except for staff at the treatment center were devastatingly poor.
>
> Working her way through college would be difficult because any job she would be able to get would barely cover the cost of food, clothing, and rent. Worse yet, where would she get the confidence to go on to college, assuming that she could even obtain her high school equivalency through our program? Where would she find out how to apply to schools? Where would she learn how to act and how to study? She was used to the streets and special treatment programs. Nobody she knew at home ever went to college. In fact, few even completed high school. There was no one to serve as a model or to encourage her. My involvement with her would only last a few months. Then what?
>
> The hurdles this young woman would have to overcome were awesome. Her realistic alternatives were severely limited. I certainly had no magic answers.
>
> Several years later, long after I left my job, I ran into another staff member. We began talking about old times and Marcia's name came up. I found out she had gotten pregnant when she was seventeen, quit school, and lived with a series of men after that.

Marcia's environment was restrictive. Her resources were limited, and she simply was not prepared to compete in a middle-class world. That is why when we talk about women and poverty, we will emphasize the macro approaches for change. The "system" as it exists provides her with few, restricted options and it, rather than Marcia, needs to be changed.

Of course, some individuals can fight against amazing odds and eventually get a good job or receive vocational training or even a college degree. But the chances of success for the vast majority of these individuals are slim.

At the micro and mezzo levels of intervention, you can essentially do five things to enhance your client's strengths. First, you can work to increase your client's self-confidence. Second, you can help your client to define and evaluate the realistic opportunities available to her. Third, you can educate her regarding the resources that are available and help her get involved with them. Fourth, you can do "outreach" to clients yourself (Collier, 1982). This method involves going out into the community and your client's homes, asking questions, educating them about how to deal with the system, and going far beyond your call of duty in helping them to do so. Finally, you can teach and encourage each client to work with the system to her advantage (1982).

Macro Perspectives on Women and Poverty

You already know a little about macro practice. You know making even minor changes in bureaucratic systems can be difficult. However, this issue is so crucial that evaluating the possibility of macro changes whenever you can is important as a generalist practitioner. We will discuss three potential approaches: reforming society's ideas about women's life experiences involving employment and family responsibilities, bettering conditions and resources in the workplace, and improving legislation providing for equality. The first two are closely related to changes in legislation, as incentives for such changes are essential.

Reforming Society's Perspective

Gottlieb describes the difficulty we face in trying to change a system that places women "in a disadvantageous power position" that "results in serious social, economic, and political consequences for women as a group" (1987, p. 562). She states that:

> . . . long-standing systems of belief are difficult to change, and entrenched power resists dislodging. Although affirmative action and antidiscrimination laws and policies have had an impact, they have not replaced the tenaciously held view of men and women. The restrictive role society imposes on women and the power differential between men and women continue to foster a range of discriminatory practices. (1987, p. 568)

Although this situation is depressing, it cannot be ignored. Being aware of this oppression so that you can work to educate others and effect change is a generalist practitioner's responsibility.

Society's perspective on women's family and work responsibilities is an enormous problem. On the one hand, society has traditionally viewed a woman in terms of her family role, and she is considered the nurturant, giving maintainer of the home whose primary responsibility is to keep her family healthy and together (Lott, 1994).

Women who are married have poor odds of being able to fulfill this primary role without assuming economic responsibility for their family. Almost one in two marriages ends in divorce (Johnson & Wahl, 1995). Women suffer an instant 73 percent drop in their standard of living following a divorce, whereas a divorced man enjoys an average increase of 42 percent (Renzetti & Curran, 1999; Ruth, 1998; Weitzman, 1985).

Thirty-seven percent of female-headed families are in poverty compared to 12 percent for two-parent families (U.S. Bureau of the Census, 1998). Upon further examination racial differences also emerge. About 21 percent of all white households headed by single mothers live in poverty, whereas over 57 percent of such African American and almost 31 percent of Hispanic families do. As a result, children living in single-parent families headed by women, especially women of color, experience greater risk of poverty. All three of these variables—race, single-parenthood, and female family head—increase risk. It is a significant problem. A multitude of women have primary responsibility both for their family's caretaking and for its economic support.

In the past, many poor women and their children received public assistance, although no state provided enough assistance to bring families above the poverty level. In August 1996, Congress abolished the former cash assistance program called Aid to Families with Dependent Children (AFDC) and passed what is known as the Personal Responsibility Act (PRA). This replaced AFDC with a new program, Temporary Assistance to Needy Families (TANF). The new law "weakens the principle of entitlement, the linchpin of the welfare state in the United States. The transformation threatens to bring much harm to poor and working class people, especially women and children" (Abramovitz, 1997, p. 311).

AFDC entitled people in need to receive financial aid. The PRA abruptly terminated the government's responsibility to provide assistance to these people. Instead, the PRA both limits the amount of federal aid provided to states and "shifts the federal role from one of assistance to one of punishment" (Abramovitz, 1997, p. 312). Abramovitz explains that "TANF either obligates or permits the states to restrict eligibility for benefits based on the number of years a person has been on welfare (time limits), his or her participation in a work program (work requirements), his or her citizen status and childbearing decisions, and any existing convictions for a drug felony" (1997, p. 312). She continues that instead of shielding people from abject poverty and crisis, "the new federal welfare policy will regulate the behavior of the poor even more than before" (1997, p. 312).

Pierce elaborates upon the problems in society's philosophy regarding women, work, and public assistance:

1. The obsession with "put them to work" results in women taking jobs with income or benefits (particularly health insurance) that are insufficient for their families' needs.
2. Training available . . . has too often been for traditionally female jobs (e.g., cafeteria worker) that pay poverty-level wages. Such "opportunities" thus reinforce the occupational segregation and ghettoization of women and the poverty that results.
3. Even in training programs, often no provision is made for child care. (1989, p. 502)

Society is telling women that they must assume responsibility for their children, both as primary caretakers and as economic providers, but it does not provide the minimal essential resources to do so. Even women who pursue such job "opportunities" often cannot afford to continue because of day care unavailability, lack of health insurance, or because such jobs are in "marginal, unstable industries" (Pierce, 1989, p. 502).

The link between women's family responsibilities, poverty, and their access to adequate working opportunities is becoming clearer. If we expect women to both care for their families and support themselves, more resources must be provided. Women need to have greater accessibility to adequate jobs. Their work environment needs to be more supportive, and supplementary resources for their children must be made more available. The final sections of this chapter address these issues.

Improving Conditions in the Workplace

As a generalist practitioner, you need to be aware of intimidating conditions for women in the workplace so that you may use your macro skills to alleviate them. Lott (1987, 1994) cites at least six conditions that make performing effectively in the workplace particularly difficult for women. The first involves the numerous family responsibilities and

the many roles women are expected to perform in their work and personal worlds. Additionally, employed women who are in relationships with men still maintain primary responsibility for most of the in-home work. Consider the following facts:

- Women employed outside of the home assume as much responsibility for household tasks as those who work as full-time homemakers (Hammond & Mahoney, 1983; Lott, 1994; Pyke & Kahill, 1983; Radloff, 1975).
- Women spend significantly more time and expend significantly more energy caring for their homes and children than men do; women are also much more likely than men to accommodate themselves to what other family members need and want (Lott, 1994; Renzetti & Curran, 1999). For example, women are much more likely than men to use their employment sick days to stay home and take care of sick children or attend to other matters involving their children (Englander-Golden & Barton, 1983), despite the fact that both men and women took similar total amounts of sick leave.
- Women employed full-time do significantly more housework than their husbands who are also employed full-time (Renzetti & Curran, 1999; Sapiro, 1999).

What can a generalist practitioner do about these problems? You can work to influence employers to provide assistance to working women. Four strategies are possible. First, child care could be provided (Harkess, 1988). It could be considered one of a series of possible benefits from which employees might choose. For instance, if one spouse has medical coverage at her full-time job, the other might opt for child care at his full-time job instead of duplicating health care coverage.

A second thing you can advocate for employers to do is to offer flexible working hours (Harkess, 1988). The strictly enforced nine-to-five working day is not carved in stone. Arranging for alternative day care or being home when the children arrive from school may be easier if a parent is allowed to work from 7 A.M. to 3 P.M. instead.

A third suggestion for employers is to provide better part-time work for women (Harkess, 1988). Wages and benefits should both be proportional to those provided full-time workers.

The final suggestion for employers is to provide adequate mandatory parental child-care leaves (Lott, 1994) at full or partial salary. Return to the same job should be guaranteed, and a woman's seniority should not be sacrificed because of her leave.

In addition to multiple roles, a second condition confronting women in the workplace is one we've already established. Namely, jobs are segregated by gender. Attending to this issue involves encouraging women to pursue fields and careers traditionally sought primarily by men. Examples include math, science, engineering, and skilled trades such as carpentry. Similarly, it means encouraging men to seek jobs traditionally held by women, such as child care work, teaching, and nursing. Employers can be pressured to recruit women into nontraditional fields more actively (Harkess, 1988).

A third problem women encounter in the workplace involves a lack of positive female role models holding powerful positions. Although "some women have, in recent years, moved into important decision-making positions, recognition of this has been slow and hampered by continued portrayal of stereotypes in media advertisements" (Lott, 1987, p. 223). When you watch television, read the newspaper, or browse through your favorite magazine, watch for how women are portrayed in comparison to men. Who is portrayed as strong, and who is meek? How much emphasis is placed on women's beauty? Who is pictured concerning topics such as governmental leadership and high finance? These images convey subtle and not-so-subtle information about how men and women are supposed to be.

In effect, few women have been promoted to powerful, highly visible positions. For example, after the fall 2002 elections, only 63 of the 440 members of the House of Representatives and 13 of the 100 U.S. Senators are women. Ruth (1998) notes that:

No woman has ever been president. Only very recently have women occupied top-level cabinet positions, and proportionally very few American women have had major power in national or international affairs. (p. 344)

What can you do to remedy this problem? For one thing, be sensitive to the composition of any particular group. Is there gender balance? If women are lacking, encourage their inclusion. Evaluate political candidates concerning their views on women and women's issues. Strongly support female candidates whose views coincide with yours. Educate other people to become more gender sensitive. When you see things in the media that you find gender insensitive or offensive, write and complain. Encourage and support women to assume important positions. If you are a woman, consider aiming for important positions yourself.

A fourth barrier to women in the workplace concerns salary discrimination. We have already indicated that women earn less than 75 cents for every dollar earned by men. Several factors contribute to this problem. For one thing, women are significantly more likely to experience a work interruption because of having children, or, perhaps, caring for aging parents (Kirk & Okazawa-Rey, 2001).

A second factor contributing to the wage differential involves occupational discrimination by sex. We have discussed how women tend to be clustered in a few occupations with relatively low pay. Like the other impediments to women in the workplace, the salary problem is not easy to solve. However, once inequities are identified, you can fight to have them obliterated. You can use your macro skills to apply pressure for change. In some instances, conflict in terms of legal action may be necessary.

A fifth factor contributing to a problematic work environment involves discrimination in benefits and job loss. This problem may be due to a woman finding "that her request for maternity leave is reacted to negatively by her employer, that she is without a pension after years in the work force, or that she is among the first to lose her job during slow periods in the economy" (Lott, 1987, p. 226). Elaborating on the extensive research in support of such inequities is beyond the scope of this text. Nevertheless, as a generalist practitioner you must be aware of such potential discrimination and combat it where it exists.

Establishing labor unions is one method to confront and change inequitable practices (Harkess, 1988; Lott, 1994). A strong union with numerous members can exert substantial pressure on an employer. Women must have significant clout within a union's membership for it to work on their behalf. A variety of macro skills for organizing could be useful here.

A sixth factor working against employed women on their jobs is sexual harassment. Sexual harassment involves unwelcome sexual advances, requests for sexual favors, and other verbal or physical conduct of a sexual nature where the following results. First, submission to such conduct is required as a condition of employment or education. Second, submission to such conduct is used as a basis for decisions that affect an individual's employment or academic achievement. Third, such conduct results in a hostile, intimidating, or anxiety-producing work or educational environment.[3]

Sexual harassment includes not only sexual solicitations and physical attacks but also any type of behavior that makes a work setting uncomfortable, unproductive, or hostile. Harassment also includes gender-biased remarks, crude sexist jokes, and unfair treatment on the basis of gender.

An accurate, specific profile of when, where, how, and to whom sexual harassment occurs does not exist. However, it is quite prevalent in a variety of settings (Lott, 1994; Renzetti & Curran, 1999; Stout & McPhail, 1998; U.S. Merit Systems Protection Board, 1981). To gain some insight on how to combat sexual harassment, see Highlight 4.6.

Improving Legislation for Equality

Chapter 13 will discuss specific skills for influencing decision makers. Those same skills apply here regarding the improvement of proequality legislation. We will, therefore, discuss three of the issues that demand legislative attention: pressing for antidiscrimination legislation and initiating lawsuits when unfairness surface (Lott, 1994); bolstering affirmative action activities (Gottlieb, 1987); and actively supporting the comparable worth movement (Gottlieb, 1995; Lott, 1994).

Antidiscrimination Legislation. A number of bills have been passed since 1963 that prohibit discrimination on the basis of gender (e.g., the Equal Pay Act of 1963 and Title VII of the Civil Rights Act of 1964). Thus, some legislative progress has been made. For example, Freeman explains that "laws have been passed in most states prohibiting sex discrimination in employment, housing, and credit and in some states prohibiting discrimination in insurance, education, and public accommodations" (1995, p. 394).

Yet looming problems and issues still remain. Lott (1994) identifies a primary problem with implementing much of the legislation by stating, "Machinery exists to counter sex discrimination in employment. Unfortunately, this machinery has

proven cumbersome; time-consuming; painfully slow; and a drain on the energy, financial resources, and self-confidence of those who bring forth individual complaints" (1994, p. 263). There is indication that class action suits have exerted more pressure with greater success than those initiated by individuals (1994). For example, a class action suit against *The New York Times* significantly increased the proportion of women reporters and photographers in addition to opening up opportunities for women to become editors and managers (1994).

Pollard maintains that "equity in pay and employment benefits still remain key concerns of women" (1995, p. 501). Freeman states that "it is practically a truism that male-dominated jobs pay more than female-dominated jobs, regardless of that job's content, location, or working conditions" (1995, p. 392). Ruth asserts that "one of the most important debates about women and employment concerns the rules governing benefits for pregnant women" (1998, p. 409). This involves employers avoiding hiring women because they fear potential pregnancy, not providing women with paid pregnancy leaves, and even firing or laying off pregnant women. One should note that the Family and Medical Leave Act of 1993 provides working pregnant women with some relief. This law applies "to employers with at least fifty workers" and "allows employees of either sex up to twelve weeks of unpaid leave for disability, the birth or adoption of a child, or illness of a family member" (1998, p. 410). The downside is that the leave is unpaid and that the law only applies to large organizations.

Legislative progress can be made on women's behalf. Generalist practitioners can be vigilant in their pursuit of gender-fair policies and positive legislative change. Affirmative action and comparable worth policies discussed briefly in the next section provide examples of legislative issues to address.

Affirmative Action. Affirmative action involves "positive steps taken by an organization to remedy imbalances regarding people of color and women in employment, promotions, and other opportunities" (Barker, 1999, p. 12). You can use affirmative action to pursue three positive thrusts on the behalf of women (Gottlieb, 1987). First, affirmative action can be used to monitor the proportion of women in any particular job category. Employment of women in a specific agency or organization should approach that proportion. For example, if 14 percent of all skilled bricklayers in the country are women, then logically about 14 percent of the bricklayers employed by a given construction company should be women.

---

3. The definition of *sexual harassment* is taken from Resolution #2384 of the Board of Regents of the University of Wisconsin System dated May 8, 1981. The Equal Employment Opportunity Commission has published a similar definition of *sexual harassment* in "Guidelines on Discrimination Because of Sex, Title VII, Sec. 703," *Federal Register* 45 (April 11, 1980), as have S. M. Shaw and J. Lee in *Women's Voices, Feminist Visions* (Mountain View, CA: Mayfield, 2001).

HIGHLIGHT 4.6

Confronting Sexual Harassment

Victims of sexual harassment have several routes available to them. Each has its own positive and negative consequences. Alternatives include ignoring the harassing behavior, avoiding the harasser, or confronting the harasser and asking him to stop (Martin, 1995). One study (U.S. Merit Systems Protection Board [MSPB], 1981) found that ignoring the behavior had virtually no effect. Asking the harasser to stop, however, effectively terminated the harassment in half of the cases.

Avoiding the harasser is another option. A severe shortcoming of this approach is that the victim is the one who must expend the effort in avoidance behavior. The ultimate avoidance is actually quitting the job or dropping the class in order to avoid contact with a sexual harasser. This route is the least fair (and potentially most damaging) alternative for the victim.

There are, however, several other suggestions to help victims confront sexual harassment. In many cases using these strategies will stop harassment. First, a victim needs to know her or his rights. A call to the Equal Employment Opportunity Commission (EEOC), the federal agency designated to address the issue of sexual harassment, can be helpful. Many women can obtain necessary information about their rights and the appropriate procedures to follow for filing a formal complaint.

Sexual harassment is illegal at the national level. Many states also have laws that specify what can be done to combat it and often have agencies or offices that victims may call for help and information. For example, Wisconsin has the Wisconsin Equal Rights Division to address such issues. Additionally, organizations and agencies have specific policies against sexual harassment. Filing a formal complaint through established procedures is often a option.

Most victims, however, choose not to pursue the formal complaint route because they fear reprisal or retaliation (Martin, 1984; Sapiro, 1999; MSPB, 1981). Others do not want to be labeled "troublemakers." Still others choose not to expend the time and effort necessary to carry out a formal process. Most victims simply want the harassment to end so that they can do their work peacefully and productively.

In addition to knowing your rights, the following suggestions can be applied to most situations where sexual harassment is occurring:

1. *Confront your harasser.* Tell the harasser which specific behaviors are unwanted and unacceptable. If you feel you cannot handle a direct confrontation, write the harasser a letter. Criticizing the harasser's behavior rather than the harasser as a person is helpful. The intent is to stop the harassment and maintain a pleasant, productive work environment. There is also the chance that the harasser was not aware that his or her behavior was offensive. In these cases, giving specific feedback is frequently effective.

2. *Be assertive.* When giving the harasser feedback, look him or her directly in the eye and assume an assertive stance. Do not smile or giggle even though you may be uncomfortable. Stand up straight, adopt a serious expression, and calmly state, "Please stop touching me by putting your arms around me and rubbing my neck. I don't like it." This situation is serious, and you need to get your point across.

3. *Document your situation.* Record every incident that occurs. Note when, where, who, what was said or done, what you were wearing, and any available witnesses. Be as accurate as possible. Documentation does not have to be elaborate or fancy. Simple handwritten notes including the facts will suffice. Keeping copies of your notes in another location is also a good idea.

4. *Talk to other people about the problem.* Get support from friends and colleagues. Sexual harassment often erodes self-confidence. Victims do not feel they are in control of the situation. Emotional support from others can bolster self-confidence and give victims the strength needed to confront sexual harassment. Frequently, sharing these problems with others will also allow victims to discover they are not alone. Corroboration with other victims will not only provide emotional support, but it will also strengthen a formal complaint if that option needs to be taken sometime in the future.

5. *Get witnesses.* Look around when the sexual harassment is occurring and note who else can observe it. Talk to these people and solicit their support. Try to make arrangements for others to be around you when you anticipate that sexual harassment is likely to occur.

A second manner in which affirmative action can be used involves "identifying areas in which women are poorly represented, setting goals for improvement, and monitoring those goals" (Gottlieb, 1987, p. 565). Affirmative action provides a rationale and mechanism for addressing these inequities.

The third way in which affirmative action can be helpful involves wiping out discriminatory policies and practices. For example, advertising a job position for a counselor who must be a male violates affirmative action principles.

Comparable Worth.   We have established several facts. First, most women work outside of the home. Second, women tend to be clustered in relatively low-paying occupations. Third, women have significantly less political power in terms of the actual number of political offices they hold.

The principle of comparable worth may be defined as "calling for equal pay for males and females doing work requiring comparable skill, effort, and responsibility under similar working conditions" (Bellak, 1984, p. 75). Comparable worth does not refer to jobs that are identical but rather that are similar or comparable (Gottlieb, 1995). For example, a male janitor might receive a substantially higher salary than a female secretary, even though both jobs might require similar *levels,* not types, of training and experience.

Twenty states have adjusted women's salaries "to correct sex bias," seven states have implemented a pay-equity plan, and twenty-two additional states are investigating possible gender discrimination in salaries (Gottlieb, 1995, p. 2523). Currently, only state governments, not private businesses and corporations, have attempted to address the issue.

Comparable worth is being used as a basis for an increasing number of pay-discrimination suits. As a generalist practitioner, you can support the concept and work on its behalf.

There are two basic suggestions for how the doctrine of comparable worth might be attained. First, a system of "job evaluation" must be developed. Job evaluation would involve evaluating each job in an organization on the basis of "skill requirements, effort, responsibility, and working conditions" (Schwab, 1984, p. 86). A system would have to be

worked out whereby these job aspects could be analyzed, compared, and rated on a certain scale. The end result would be comparable job classifications with *comparable* salaries.

The second recommendation for implementing the doctrine of comparable worth would be to establish legislation to mandate compliance. Laws are needed that require both governmental and private business organizations to abide by comparable worth. These laws would require the development of job evaluation systems. They would also necessitate careful monitoring of organizations to make certain that the organizations comply with or obey the rules.

 InfoTrac College Edition

This chapter discussed the importance of gender sensitivity and understanding a feminist perspective on human services practice. Also covered were concepts of sexism, feminization of poverty, and assertiveness training for women. For further information on these and related areas, enter the following search terms:

feminist
feminist theory
sexual assault
women and poverty
assertiveness training

 On the Internet

Because of the very dynamic nature of the Web, URLs are subject to change. Therefore, be sure to check out the companion Website for this book at http://www.humanservices.wadsworth.com, where links will be updated periodically.
now.org
www.polaris.net/~ratliff/emily/women.html
www.domesticviolence.org
www.wwwomen.com
www.ssc.wisc.edu/irp
cpmcnet.columbia.edu/dept/nccp

PART TWO

The Steps of Planned Change

CHAPTER 5

Engagement and Assessment in Generalist Practice

CHAPTER 6

Planning in Generalist Practice

CHAPTER 7

Implementation Applications

CHAPTER 8

Evaluation and Termination in Generalist Practice

CHAPTER 5

Engagement and Assessment in Generalist Practice

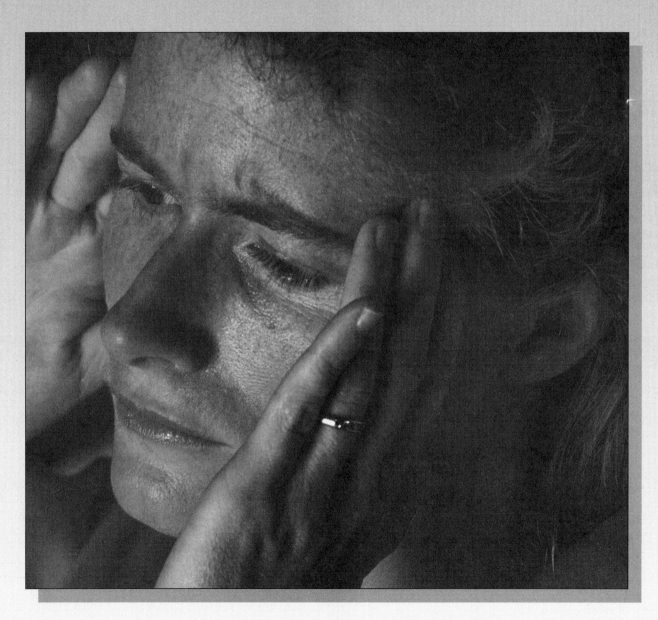

Jae Black, a protective services worker called in to assess a reported case of child abuse, looked around the room. An emaciated child, age 3 or 4, squatted in the corner. Her long, dark hair was snarled and greasy. Whimpering, she hid her eyes with her hands. Her skin was mottled with dirt and what appeared to be purplish bruises. The floor and walls were barren and smeared with dirt. Tattered drapes fluttered at the open windows. The autumn air was nippy with early morning frost. The archaic radiator in the corner emitted no heat.

An anonymous neighbor had called in and reported that the girl's mother was a "coke freak" who frequently left the little girl home alone. In her brief, initial assessment of the situation, Jae noted the girl's apparent neglect (the apparent lack of appropriate physical care, food, and heat) in addition to potential abuse (the bruises from some unidentified cause).

A number of thoughts went through Jae's mind. They included the procedures for reporting this situation and removing the little girl from the premises. How was the little girl feeling inside? What emotional and physical damage had already been done to her? Jae approached the tiny body slowly and spoke in a calm, soothing tone, trying to assure the child that everything would be OK.

Other thoughts swept through Jae's consciousness. Where was the mother? In what condition was she? How could she be contacted? What would the mother's chances be in a drug rehabilitation program, if drug abuse were indeed one of the woman's problems? Were there relatives available who could help?

If there was no one else, how fast could Jae place the little girl in temporary foster care? What kind of care was available? Sometimes, good foster placements were hard to find. What effects would placement have on the little girl?

Child abuse and neglect were massive problems in the large city where Jae worked. Jae's and her colleagues' caseloads were large. Treatment services were too limited.

Jae decided that something needed to be done. She herself knew of dozens of cases similar to this one. The needs of these children had to be publicized. The community needed to do more about this increasingly serious problem. Jae decided to talk to her supervisor as soon as she returned to the agency. Her supervisor just might be receptive to setting up an agency task group to work on the problem. Maybe, if these children's needs could be more obviously identified, people in the community would respond positively to supporting more services. Perhaps then, the community and city leaders would listen and devote more resources to this problem. Even members of her church might respond to her pleas. She decided she would bring the topic up at the next church meeting.

Jae was committed. First, she must attend this small child's immediate needs. But the problem was much larger than this little girl. The entire community should be forced to confront the problem and the issues. Next, she would set out to assess the problem on a macro basis. How extensive were child abuse and neglect? What services were already in place to combat the problem and provide intervention for the children and their families? How effective were these services? Were there other resources in the community that could be called upon for help?

 ## *Introduction*

Engagement and assessment are the first two steps in the planned change process. Each is critically important to the eventual outcome of the helping relationship between the generalist practitioner and the client system. Engagement is concerned with the process of establishing the client–worker relationship upon which subsequent steps depend. Assessment considers the process of gathering and organizing data and information in order to arrive at an accurate picture of the person-in-environment situation. This chapter will discuss engagement and assessment considering potential micro, mezzo, and macro dimensions of each. However, because this text emphasizes micro skills in generalist practice, they will be the primary focus of this chapter. Specifically, this chapter will:

- identify the activities and skills needed for engagement;
- identify the major goals inherent in any assessment preceding intervention;
- discuss a variety of micro assessment issues, including defining problems, types of problems, the importance of identifying various client strengths, and locating sources of assessment information;

- explain several commonly used micro assessment mechanisms, including the *Diagnostic and Statistical Manual (DSM),* the Rathus Assertiveness Schedule (RAS), and an alcoholism test;
- propose means for deciding to work with families and review a variety of areas critical to the assessment of families;
- describe the use of home visits as an assessment mechanism;
- discuss assessment from a mezzo practice perspective focusing on groups;
- appraise the value of home visits, provide some suggestions to maximize their effectiveness, and describe suggestions for your own safety;
- discuss aspects of assessing both task and treatment groups, including appraising potential sponsorship and targeting potential membership;
- describe how to do a community needs assessment from a variety of approaches; and
- formulate and demonstrate the steps necessary in analyzing a community or neighborhood.

 ## Engagement

Engagement, the first step in the planned change process, focuses on establishing a professional relationship between the worker and the client system. Professional worker–client relationships are characterized by a clear purpose, a commitment to meeting client needs, ethical standards of practice, and worker emphasis on communicating warmth, genuineness, and empathy. Engagement is the point where the worker and client first meet and begin to identify client needs. It is also where the empowerment process begins.

Engagement begins with the first contact between worker and client. Sometimes, this contact is referred to as "intake." This initial contact may be over the phone or in person, but either way it sets the stage for each of the following steps in the planned change process. Engagement occurs whether the client willingly initiates the contact or is required to meet with the worker. Involuntary contact with the worker may come about in situations such as those involving child abuse/neglect investigations or probation and parole work. In either case, the generalist practitioner must understand the common activities and actions needed to successfully complete the engagement phase. These activities include:

- greeting clients in such a way as to encourage them to talk with you;

- demonstrating effective attending skills that communicate your interest in the client's situation;
- discussing agency services and client expectations;
- deciding whether the agency and worker can be of assistance;
- offering agency and worker services to the client;
- orienting the client to the helping relationship; and
- completing any required paperwork.

Greeting the Client

Greeting the client is a relatively simple step. You might say, "Ms. Bowen, I'm Annie Nervosa, the counselor here at The Elms Center" (of course, you would not make this statement if the client was named Smith and your name was Jones). Offer your hand to the client and offer her a seat. You might follow this offer with a question, "Would you prefer to be called Ms. Bowen or Jane? You may call me Annie." Be careful to use clients' full names rather than automatically assuming they want to be addressed informally. By using the more formal form of address you indicate respect for the client, a critical element when working with individuals or groups that have experienced discrimination and adverse treatment from others.

If you do not know the reason for the client's visit, follow your introduction with a comment such as, "I understand you wanted to talk with me about something." This statement then opens the discussion allowing the client to elaborate on the reason for the interview. If you do know the reason for the initial contact, mention it up front. For example, "I asked to see you because your son Frank came to school today with bruises all over his legs and buttocks." Or you might say, "In your phone call you said you wanted to discuss problems you're having with your mother." You will note that each of these responses was in the form of a statement to which the client could respond. You could also solicit the same information by asking the client directly, "What brings you to our agency today?" Or, "How can I help?" Either way, the emphasis is on encouraging the client to talk with you.

Demonstrating Effective Attending Skills

Effective attending skills enable the worker to understand precisely what the client is saying, including both verbal and nonverbal communications. Attending skills have as their goal enhanced understanding between worker and client. Listening carefully is one attending skill. A common problem in novices is the tendency to be thinking about their next question rather than listening attentively to the client. Listening skills are learned. They require practice, focusing on both the client's words and meanings. For example, a worker might say, "Jean, you talked about Scotty's cutting class as a problem, but you also smiled as you talked." Jean then responds, "Well, I was just thinking that he reminds me so much of me at his age. I hated school and usually hung out with my friends." By pointing out a discrepancy between the client's verbal and non-verbal communication, the worker is demonstrating interest in the client's situation as well as evidencing effective attending skills.

Other attending skills include such things as making eye contact with the client, leaning forward to communicate interest, and nodding or otherwise encouraging the client to continue. Of course, there is always the potential for attending behaviors to cause problems. For example, direct eye contact is considered rude by some cultures (Hull, 1982), and nodding may confuse clients into thinking you are agreeing with what they are saying. The key is always to pay attention to see whether your responses and actions are facilitating or discouraging the client's communications.

Attending skills also allow focusing on both client thoughts and feelings. Sometimes, clients are unclear about what they are thinking and feeling. A worker may say something like, "You sound really angry about Hansel's behavior," and the client might respond with, "I think it's just terrible the way he acts." By listening carefully to what emotions are expressed or evident, the worker can help the client recognize these as well. Clients may even need help understanding the difference between what they are thinking and what feelings accompany those thoughts. The ultimate goal of this exchange is to communicate to clients your interest in them and your willingness to explore both feelings and thoughts.

Questions used during this phase should be open ended, designed to offer clients an opportunity to discuss and expand upon their thoughts and feelings. Ask, "How did that make you feel?" rather than, "Did that make you mad?" Try, "Describe what that was like," instead of, "That sounds awful." Let the client articulate the problem. Use closed-ended questions to gather data such as birth dates, ages, and addresses or when trying to pin down exactly what the client wants.

Use silence as necessary to allow the client time to think about your questions or comments. While uncomfortable at first, silence can be useful to help clients consider their thoughts and feelings without the worker needing to fish for these items.

Take notes of information you are unlikely to remember but always discuss this with the client. You might state, "I'd like to take a few notes while we talk. What you're telling me is important, and I want to be sure I get the key ideas down. Will that be OK?" Do not let the note taking distract you or the client from the main task.

Discussing Agency Services and Client Expectations

Sometimes, clients come to the worker with totally unrealistic ideas about what the agency or practitioner can or will do. Part of the purpose of the engagement phase is to help the client assess whether the worker and agency can help. The worker should describe as accurately as possible the services offered by the agency, any costs involved, and the possible length of such services. If the agency's services do not match client needs, helping the client find an appropriate agency or organization that can help is your responsibility. Making a referral may be the best outcome of an engagement phase when your agency cannot help.

If you are asked a question about the agency you cannot answer, tell the client you do not know. Admitting ignorance is good role modeling. You can always get the information later. After all, you want to empower the client, and learning that the worker is just as capable of lapses in memory or knowledge can sometimes help.

Deciding If the Agency and Worker Can Help

Your responsibility is to accurately convey the nature and extent of help available. Only when they are informed about what is available can clients' choices be exercised. Having a choice is critical to empowerment. Sometimes, the agency offers services that are related but not directly concerned with the client's problem. Perhaps you can advocate for change within your own agency to see that a given service is provided, which is especially important if a number of clients all need a service that is not currently available. You should answer clients' questions or get them the information they need. If the agency cannot be of service, offering to make a referral is appropriate. Again, the choice is up to the client. A client should never be in the situation of thinking a service is available only to find out later that it was not. The provision of correct information is key to this part of the engagement process.

Offering Agency and Worker Services to the Client

Once clients are well informed about the services available, they must decide if a continued relationship with you or your agency is desirable. Clients must feel free to make that decision without the worker's interference. There are clear exceptions to this rule, however. Involuntary clients may not have much freedom to reject an agency's services. A convicted child molester may be required to undergo treatment. An abusive husband may be ordered to participate in anger management sessions by a court or probation agency. In these situations, maximizing client freedom and sense of empowerment is still desirable. While choice may be reduced to selecting the night of the week when sessions will be attended, having some choice is still preferable to no choice at all.

Orienting the Client to the Helping Process

If the engagement process is handled appropriately, the early stages of it should model the helping process. A willing and active listener coupled with a committed client should be a given. Sometimes, additional clarification is needed. A worker might ask a client, "Do you have any questions about what will go on during these group meetings?" The client can then respond by asking for information. If clients mistakenly assume that the worker will ask questions to better understand their problem and then will give them a magic answer, they will be disappointed and angry to discover how the helping process really works. If, on the other hand, the worker clearly indicates that the practitioner and client will share their respective expertise about the problem, this process makes a good beginning. After all, clients are already experts on their own difficulties as well as what resources they have employed. Part of the function of the helping relationship is to explore, locate, or build additional resources and to help the client draw upon these for problem resolution.

The clients will also need to know the rules and conditions under which help is given. Laws, policies, and professional ethical standards may need to be discussed so that clients know their rights. Workers should never promise complete confidentiality unless the laws of the state and agency policy provide for it. Usually, clients should know that their communications with the worker may be shared with a supervisor, law enforcement agency, insurance company, or others as needed.

Finally, workers should negotiate with clients such matters as frequency of sessions, as well as time and place of meetings. They should also discuss the total number of sessions.

Completing Required Paperwork

All agencies have paperwork. Sometimes, the generalist practitioner seems to be buried in paper. Clients may need to sign contracts, insurance forms, release of information forms, and other documents needed for service. The worker should help in this process by explaining the forms, answering any questions, and indicating the degree of confidentiality in which these documents will be held. Agency records may be subpoenaed, and all such forms in the record will be available for others to see; clients should know this fact. At the same time, the chances of being subpoenaed are relatively rare with any particular case. Clients should be aware of this rarity as well.

The previous steps are generally common to all engagement processes no matter where they occur. The diverse nature of generalist practice, however, can affect where this engagement process actually occurs. While the face-to-face meeting between worker and client located in an office setting is common, it is certainly not the only place where engagement may occur. Sometimes the first step in engagement happens over the phone when a client solicits help. Crisis phone services, for example, can be provided without face-to-face contact. Similarly, the initial client contact with a worker may involve a lengthy phone conversation where some elements of the engagement process are completed telephonically.

Additionally, many engagement processes occur in the client's home during home visits. Here the courtesy and respect shown in the office are compounded because the meeting place is the client's home, no matter how poorly kept or sparsely furnished. Asking permission to sit and commenting positively about such things as family pictures, drawings, and other child-produced artwork is good practice. There is generally a good deal less privacy in the home than in the office, which you should anticipate. If concentrating is impossible because, for example, of a loud TV, you may ask to have the volume lowered so that you can better hear the client. Remember, the situation you are in may be an accurate reflection of everyday life in this household; use this information as part of the assessment process.

Finally, some interviews may occur in other settings. For example, you may interview an AIDS patient in a hospice or hospital or an elderly client in a nursing home. You might conduct the engagement process in a school, prison, or other institutional facility. It could occur on a downtown street or in a community center. The engagement process may be begun, conducted, and completed in any number of nonoffice or nonhome locations.

Assessment

Assessment is the second step in the planned change process. It involves understanding a problem, learning its causes, and identifying what can be done to improve the situation. The generalist practitioner evaluates problem situations within an environmental perspective (see Highlight 5.1). A problem involves not only individuals and families but also the larger communities and systems in which these people live. From the onset of the planned change process, generalist practitioners focus on problems and issues from macro to micro perspectives.

People are dramatically affected by the individuals, groups, and organizations around them. A young child may be devastated by a sharp scolding from a parent. The presence or lack of friends and social supports within an office environment may affect whether people love or hate their jobs. Which president is elected may affect the amount of taxes an individual is required to pay, the types of freedom a person can enjoy, and the absolute quality of life itself.

Assessment can be considered from at least four perspectives (Rauch, 1993). First, we can assess individuals and families by focusing on the transactions between and among clients, family members, friends, and other systems in the immediate environment. We can look at the actual functioning of a family, its strengths, culture, and customs.

Second, focusing on functioning at different points in the life cycle is also possible. For example, the challenges of childhood and adolescence present different potential problems than does adulthood or the aging process. Yet each stage in the human life cycle involves tasks, stresses, strengths, and resources that can be the focus of assessment.

HIGHLIGHT 5.1

The Difference between Diagnosis and Assessment

Assessment differs from diagnosis in at least four major ways. First, the environmental surroundings of the client, which include the mezzo and macro aspects of the client's situation, are considered as important as the micro aspects when trying to understand any problem situation.

Second, because problems may exist outside of the client, the outside systems can become targets of change. In other words, organizational policies or public laws may be the source of the problem. Thus, practitioners often focus their efforts on changing these laws rather than trying to "cure" clients.

The third major difference between diagnosis and assessment involves the client's involvement in the planned change process. Using the medical model, a client is diagnosed as having a problem. Then a practitioner provides some kind of therapy and thus expends some effort. However, the client is the target of change, rather than a partner in the change process. Assessment in generalist practice emphasizes that practitioners work *with*, not *on*, clients. The practitioner and client work together in the change process. Both work to assess the problems, not only in an individual client's life but also those systemic problems outside of the client. Thus, both can work together to make changes and solve the problem.

The fourth primary difference between diagnosis and assessment concerns the approach to clients' strengths. Diagnosis focuses on pathology. What are the problems? What's wrong with the individual client? Assessment, on the other hand, targets not only the client's problems but also the client's strengths. Emphasizing strengths allows the practitioner both to tap "clients' potentials for growth" and to "help in enhancing their self-esteem" (Hepworth et al., 1997, pp. 197–198).

Third, specific problems can be the focus of our assessment. These problems include disorders such as depression, substance abuse, and behavioral problems. Different approaches and, perhaps, instruments are available to assist in assessing these areas. This chapter will describe one such instrument used with clients suffering from alcoholism.

Fourth, the techniques and assessment methods used by practitioners run the gamut from micro to mezzo to macro situations. Some assessment approaches require graduate education and are less appropriate for generalist practitioners. Of course, ethnic, racial, and cultural factors may play a role in assessment. For example, a worker may assume that a client or family will display a particular pattern of behavior because of ethnic background and allegiance. This assumption could lead to an inaccurate assessment. The fact that a client, family, or other group being assessed belongs to a particular racial group must be considered as an additional variable in assessment just as age and gender.

How to Approach Assessment

Accurate assessment of the person, problem, and situation is well documented as an important step in the helping process (Baer, 1979; Richmond, 1917). Information about the problem or situation needs to be gathered, analyzed, and interpreted. Such situations may involve parents who have difficulty controlling the behavior of their children or families not receiving the public assistance they desperately need. Regardless of the type of situation, careful thought is necessary in order to make effective decisions about how to proceed.

Assessment in generalist practice should always involve four considerations. These include micro, mezzo, and macro dimensions of a client situation, in addition to aspects of human diversity. This chapter will focus primarily on the first three.

Each dimension requires a focus on two broad categories of information. The first involves clients' problems and needs. The second entails clients' strengths. Figure 5.1, originally proposed in Chapter 1 (The Generalist Intervention Model), illustrates this approach.

Before describing specific assessment techniques, five major points need to be made. First, *involvement of the client is absolutely essential.* To formulate in your own mind what you think the client's problems really are is tempting; however, these formulations may differ radically from what the client sees as the problems. For example, you might determine that the client has

an alcohol addiction problem. The client, however, may feel that the real problem is abject poverty. To him, drinking provides an escape from reality. Thus, part of the art of professional intervention is to view any problem from a variety of perspectives and to develop a mutually agreed upon plan.

A second major point is that *assessment always involves making judgments* (Johnson, 1998). Life would probably be easier if there were a recipe book for problem solutions—you could look up some designated problem and follow a clearly specified, step-by-step process to reach a solution. However, we know that people, their lives, and their situations are complicated. Each configuration of strengths, weaknesses, and issues is different. You need to make decisions regarding what is relevant and what is not. This decision making involves isolating certain aspects of a problem for assessment and intervention. It also involves prioritizing what you feel is important to pursue. On the one hand, this process is not always easy.

The third significant point to be made about assessment involves *strengths.* We have already established that highlighting strengths is one of the striking ways assessment differs from diagnosis. You have clients because they have problems. However, one cannot emphasize enough how attending to strengths is as important, perhaps even more important, than attending to problems. Strengths provide you with an already available means of finding solutions.

A fourth important point about assessment is that a *single, clear definition of the problem may not exist.* Later we will explore the complexity and variety of problems clients face. Doing the best you can to identify, define, and prioritize problems is up to you. Frequently, it is not an easy task. Problems can be vague and multifaceted. Even problems are not perfect.

A fifth major point is that *assessment is a continuous activity.* Because problems, strengths, and issues can be vague, and aspects of any situation can change over time, practitioners must be vigilant. They must be ever watchful, regularly fine-tuning, modifying, even making major changes in their plans and interventions. They must continue to make judgments about what might be the most effective plan and intervention approach as time goes on. In other words, as a generalist practitioner, you may need to focus on and assess different aspects of a client's situation as your work with that client progresses.

Figure 5.2 illustrates assessment as an ongoing process. Arrows below each of the other planned change steps lead back to the assessment phase.

Figure 5.1   *Assessment in the Generalist Intervention Model (GIM)*

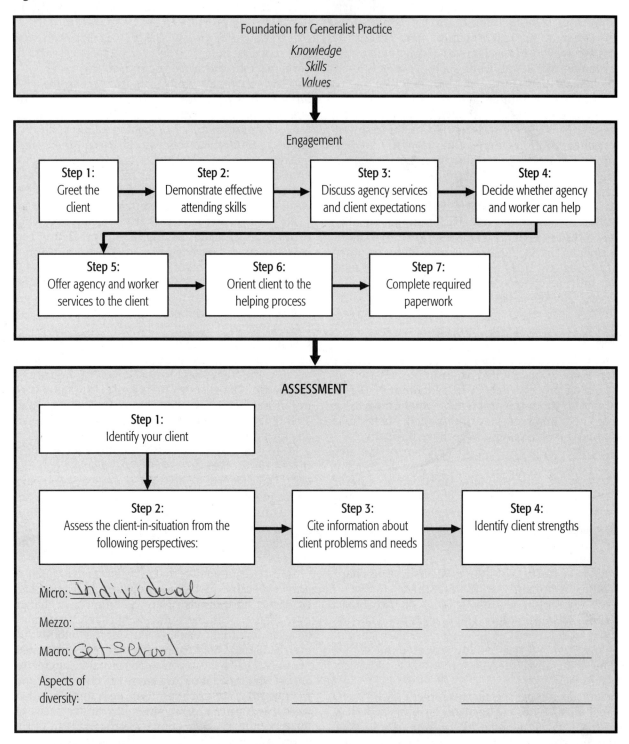

A single, pregnant teenager provides one example of the importance of assessment as an ongoing process. When the young woman initially discovers her unplanned pregnancy, you may need to help her evaluate her various alternatives (abortion, adoption, or keeping the baby). If her decision is to have and keep the baby, your focus of attention changes. You would then likely decide to assess her current

Figure 5.2   *Assessment in Planned Change Is an Ongoing Process*

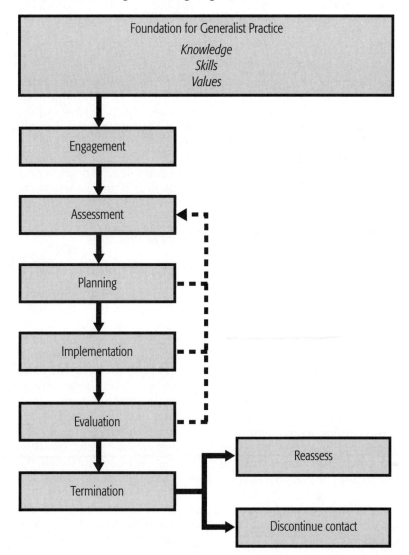

environment. From a micro perspective, this assessment would include health and nutritional status. You might also assess her family relationships and support systems. If needed, you might refer her to a support group of other single, pregnant teenagers, a mezzo intervention. Finally, from a macro perspective, you might assess the programs and services available to her and other young women in similar circumstances. You may determine that they can function as strengths for her. You then would try to involve her with the appropriate services and resources. On the other hand, if you found resources lacking, you might turn your attention to assessing and improving these resources.

Goals of Assessment

During any assessment, the generalist practitioner should aim to accomplish several goals. First is a clear understanding of the need, problem, or situation that will be the focus of work with the client system. For example, is the problem drug dependency, drug dealing, child abuse, marital interaction, truancy, or lack of resources? How the worker frames the problem provides direction for intervention.

Second, it is critical to recognize the strengths, assets, skills, and abilities that clients bring to the client–worker relationship. These may include persistence, spiritual resources, motivation, intelligence, and commitment to others, as well as a close experience dealing with the problem at hand, among others.

Third, it is important to formulate a clear description of the client system. This is true whether the client system is an individual, family, support group, social services agency, or a community. On whose behalf is the worker intervening? Does the delinquent child, parents, or the entire family compose the client system? Is the worker trying to get resources for a single family or an entire community?

Fourth, the generalist practitioner needs to understand the client system's interactions with other systems. For example, is the client system isolated or estranged from friends or family members? Is the client system connected to any support networks? Has the system, in another case a community, been deprived of adequate county, state, and social service support and resources?

Fifth, a practitioner must identify any missing information important for better understanding the situation. Missing information could range from psychological tests results, medical examination details, opinions or positions of significant others, data available from community agencies, to any other data that will help complete the assessment. The types of missing information sought will probably depend on whether the client system is an individual, family, group, organization, or community.

Finally, it is critical to put all of the information together. We assess client situations in order to formulate intervention plans. In turn, plans provide guidelines to solve client problems. This process involves making a number of judgments. The practitioner must prioritize different aspects of the situation. Likewise, the practitioner must decide whether intervention is best approached from a micro, mezzo, or macro perspective or some combination of these three.

Assessment from a Micro Practice Perspective

This section will focus on assessment of individual client systems. First, how to define the problem will be described. A classification of common problem areas will then be identified, and a number of areas targeting potential client strengths will be recognized. Finally, a variety of assessment instruments for assessing individual characteristics will be discussed.

Defining Problems and Issues

Johnson (1998) suggests that defining a problem takes three steps. First, the worker must recognize the client's unmet needs. What does the client lack that is causing a problem? Second, the worker must identify the "blocks to need fulfillment" (1998, p. 267). What is it about the client and the client's situation that prevents the client's needs from being fulfilled? Third, the worker must determine the "strengths, limitations, motivation for change, and resistance to change that are applicable to the persons and systems involved" (p. 267). How can the problem be described so that the worker has direction for proceeding with planning and intervention? It is often helpful to look at the problem in terms of what needs are lacking. One example is a homeless client needing shelter. The problem is homelessness or lack of shelter, and one intervention goal is finding some kind of shelter.

Types of Problems

Being aware of the types of problems clients typically have is important for generalist practitioners. As a worker, you need to know what to look for and what areas to assess. Here, we will look at ten categories of problems commonly confronting clients (Northen, 1982, 1987; Reid, 1978; Reid & Epstein, 1972).

One should note that micro, mezzo, and macro aspects of practice are frequently intertwined. Therefore, identifying any particular category of problems with only one of these practice perspectives is not possible. For example, take a person addicted to cocaine. From the micro perspective, a worker would focus on the personal habits and impacts on the individual. The mezzo perspective, on the other hand, would accentuate the addicted client's interactions with the people close to him. Additionally, it would address the impact his addiction was having on these people. Finally, a macro perspective would direct attention to the major social problems in society that foster cocaine addiction, the ease with which cocaine can be purchased, and the treatment services available to the client.

Similarly, Raber (1996) has identified the impact that job loss has on one's mental health and relationships within families. These job losses often result from corporate downsizing or attempts by companies to wring increased profits from their operations. While shifting a manufacturing plant from the United States to another country might make financial sense for the company, it can have devastating impacts on the individual, family, and community. In both assessment and planning stages, the generalist practitioner must be acutely aware of how global or national trends at the macro level significantly affect the micro and mezzo levels.

Interpersonal Conflict.   The first category of problems involves "interpersonal conflict" (Reid & Epstein, 1972, p. 42). These problems involve individuals having difficulty relating to each other. A delinquent teenager may be unable to form friendships with peers. An elderly woman in a nursing home may refuse to cooperate with staff attempting to meet her increasingly serious health care needs. An adult with a developmental disability may get into frequent fights with his peers at a sheltered workshop because of poor social and communication skills. Or a married couple may be in almost constant verbal conflict.

Interpersonal conflicts may involve both communication and behavior. Problems may exist regarding how information is conveyed and received between two people. Likewise, problems may center on how people treat or act toward each other.

Dissatisfaction in Social Relations.   Even when no overt conflict exists, people may identify "dissatisfaction in social relations" as a primary problem (Reid & Epstein, 1972, p. 43). One may feel unable to get as close to others as she would like. Another may feel that lack of assertiveness prevents his needs from being met. Still another might feel unable to divorce himself from the guilt that he feels his mother imposes on him.

Problems with Formal Organizations.   "Problems with formal organizations" are frequently cited by clients (Reid & Epstein, 1972, p. 44). Clients may not feel they are getting the resources they need. A Social Security check may be received late or be for an amount less than anticipated. Adequate health care services for pregnant teens may be unavailable. A client may feel that she is being treated rudely or abruptly when signing in to see her caseworker. Or the client may feel that she has been made to wait an inordinately long period of time to see a counselor.

Difficulties in Role Performance.   Sometimes, clients will have "difficulties in role performance" (Reid & Epstein, 1972, p. 45). A role is a culturally expected behavior pattern that characterizes people having a particular position and status in society.

Most problems in role performance involve "family roles, usually roles of spouse or parent, although roles of student, employee, and patient also receive considerable emphasis" (Reid & Epstein, 1972, p. 45). A difficulty in role performance can best be distinguished from interpersonal conflict by the fact that role performance is more one sided. An example is a

father who is physically abusing his 5-year-old daughter because "she just won't behave." He is having difficulty fulfilling his role as parent. One intervention tactic would be to train him in more appropriate and effective child management techniques. He, not the daughter, would be the target of intervention.

Problems of Social Transition.   Sometimes, clients will have problems making "social transitions" (Reid & Epstein, 1972, p. 46). In other words, they will experience difficulty dealing with some major change in their lives. Such changes may include divorce, having a baby, moving to a new locale, or coping with any change. Any of these may involve serious emotional upset and disruptions in clients' coping abilities.

Psychological and Behavioral Problems.   Clients may experience "psychological or behavioral problems" (Northen, 1987, p. 173; Reid, 1978). These involve a broad gamut of emotional upheavals and inappropriate, self-defeating, criminal, or uncontrollable behavior. A client may be seriously clinically depressed or struggling with anorexia nervosa, a serious and potentially life-threatening eating disorder. Or a client may have uncontrollable *agoraphobia,* "anxiety about being in places or situations from which escape might be difficult (or embarrassing)" (APA, 2000, p. 433). People with severe cases of the latter may feel trapped in their own homes, yet terrified of leaving.

Many conditions affect both psychological state and behavior. Depressed people often isolate themselves emotionally and physically from others. Anorexics allow food, or the lack of it, to become the focus of their whole lives and behave accordingly. Agoraphobics experience both psychological terror and severely restricted behavior.

Inadequate Resources.   The problem of "inadequate resources" may reflect a number of deprivations of basic needs (Reid & Epstein, 1972, p. 48). Many times, this problem is related to poverty. Without enough money, you may not be able to buy sufficient food, visit a physician, or pay rent.

Inadequate resources may also refer to a lack of resources or services available to the client. For example, a Native American community may have no health services available to them within a realistic distance, or the existing resources may not cover the need. Consider a family of six that needs a minimum of $450 each month to provide adequate nutrition. They receive only $200 in public assistance and food stamps. Thus, their need is not being met, and they are subject to inadequate resources.

Problems in Decision Making. Sometimes clients will find themselves in emotional dilemmas in which they experience serious difficulties in making important decisions (Northen, 1987; Reid, 1978). They may come upon life crises that create emotional turmoil and for which they see no positive solution. When under such duress, losing objectivity is easy. Emotional crises can blind people to their rational choices. Such emotion-laden decisions include an infinite number of scenarios: whether or not to have the baby in an unwanted pregnancy; whether or not to follow through on the divorce if the husband is unfaithful but the wife still loves him; whether to place a person recently paralyzed in a car accident in his own home, a group home, or some other residential setting.

In any of these instances, generalist practitioners can help clients immobilized by emotion to identify the various alternatives available. Because of their training, likewise, workers can assist clients in evaluating the pros and cons of each realistic alternative and come to decisions.

Cultural Conflicts. "Cultural conflicts" provide a final category of problems typically encountered by clients (Northen, 1987, p. 173). Sometimes they involve discrimination and oppression by majority groups. For instance, urban African American students may be denied access to similar educational benefits available to white suburban students. At other times, these conflicts concern difficulties in relating to and becoming acclimated into the larger society. For instance, consider the Hmong people who emigrated to the United States and Canada from Southeast Asia after the Vietnam War. They had to learn a new language and customs while still striving to maintain their own values and cultural integrity.

Prioritizing Problems. When working with actual clients, the number of potential problems may seem overwhelming. However, there are approaches for prioritizing which problem to work on first, second, and so on. Such prioritizing is part of the planning phase in the planned change process and thus will be discussed in the next chapter.

Some Final Notes. These categories of problems are intended to provide ideas about what aspects of clients' lives require assessment. They are not necessarily distinct from one another. An example is a two-parent family where the father is sexually abusing his two adolescent daughters. This situation involves at least the following: difficulties in role performance, dissatisfaction in social relationships, and psychological/behavior problems.

Empowerment: Identifying Clients' Strengths

Jones and Biesecker (1980) and Cowger (1994) emphasize the importance of identifying strengths in the assessment process. Strengths can include anything the client is good at, all those people in a client's life who can provide assistance, and any other identifiable resource. Strengths can be divided into the following seven categories:

1. family and friends (Jones & Biesecker, 1980);
2. education and employment background;
3. problem-solving and decision-making skills;
4. personal qualities and characteristics;
5. physical and financial resources;
6. attitudes and perspectives; and
7. miscellaneous other strengths.

Family and Friends. Does the client have family and friends, or both, available to provide support and resources? How motivated are they to help the client? Is their help potentially significant to assisting the client deal with the situation at hand?

For instance, take Blake, a 9-year-old child with developmental disabilities living with his single, alcohol-addicted mother, Stephanie. Stephanie has been accused of neglecting Blake on four occasions. She has previously been told that unless she undergoes inpatient treatment for her addiction, Blake will be removed from her home. The court warns her that the removal may be permanent. Stephanie states that she loves Blake dearly and does not want to lose him. She just cannot stop her addiction on her own. She is finally willing to seek help.

The problem involves who will care for Blake while Stephanie is in treatment. Good foster homes, especially those equipped to care for children with special needs, are hard to find. Stephanie's worker explores potential support systems with Stephanie. The worker discovers that Stephanie's mother lives in the same city and has expressed willingness to care for Blake, even on a permanent basis. Additionally, Stephanie's sister Sabrina lives within several blocks of Stephanie's home. Both sister and mother are terribly concerned about Stephanie's addiction and have urged her to seek treatment many times. Although Sabrina has three children of her own in addition to a full-time job, she is willing to assist their mother in Blake's care. Both Sabrina and her mother can now serve as significant resources. In addition to taking care of Blake, they can be used as sources of significant emotional support as Stephanie seeks help.

Education and Employment Background. This information is especially significant in cases where unemployment or financial need is a major problem. Does the client have educational prerequisites, skills, or work experience that would qualify him or her for a job with better compensation? Can skills formerly used in one setting now be applied in a different setting?

Mavis, age 54, provides an example. Her husband Bubba died suddenly in a car crash. She was not only emotionally distraught but also in serious financial turmoil. Bubba had handled the finances (at least she had thought he had) throughout their 21-year marriage. Upon his death, she abruptly discovered that they were deep in debt, having lived way beyond their means for years. She suddenly needs to find a job, and fast.

Mavis has not worked full-time since she married Bubba. However, she did have a college degree in biology. For the past three years, she had been working for a small, local hardware store. Her job was to do the ordering and keep the accounts. She had discovered that she was exceptionally good at such activities. In fact, she had revamped the store's entire accounting system. She also found she had a knack for working with computers. Such assessment of Mavis's life experience thus established strengths including organization skills, dependability, and computer skills. These, in addition to her college degree and her mature, well-developed social skills, made her an attractive job candidate for a number of positions.

She initially found a job as an administrative assistant for a firm assisting companies in computer system installation. Although this was an entry-level job with relatively low pay, she soon worked her way up. Eventually, she became a consultant to companies all over the country.

The point here is that many times, people have skills and qualities that can be applied to jobs even when clients have never formally held those specific jobs. As the worker, you need to investigate specific qualities they have developed. Many times, people will be surprised that they do have valuable assets. You can help them clarify their strengths and the value of such strengths. Resulting enhanced self-esteem can help make clients stronger and better able to pursue their goals.

Problem Solving and Decision-Making Skills. The extent to which clients have experience solving difficult problems in the past can also be useful. What means have they used to remedy similar situations before? Can this approach be used again? Assessing their handling of previous problems can provide significant clues regarding how they can proceed once again.

Personal Qualities and Characteristics. Many strengths fall within the personal realm. For instance, is the client articulate and pleasant? Intelligent? A good listener? Does the client keep appointments dependably and punctually?

Labeling and emphasizing positive qualities can educate the client about him- or herself and build self-confidence. Additionally, this information can provide clues about ways to proceed in the planned change process. For instance, will he be able to approach the landlord in a rational manner and request necessary repairs? Will she check back at the unemployment office regularly in search of work? Will his pleasant, caring manner toward others enhance his ability to make friends (despite his lack of self-esteem)? Is she well-respected in her neighborhood and able to assume leadership responsibility?

Physical strengths can also be pertinent. For example, is she strong enough to accomplish a job requiring some degree of physical strength? Is the client attractive in appearance?

Health is also an important asset. Even for those with some physical disability, defining and emphasizing what people *can* do, instead of dwelling on what they *cannot* do, is important.

Physical and Financial Resources. Because clients most frequently stress their problems to practitioners, overlooking strengths is easy. Does the client currently reside in adequate housing? What kinds of property does the client own? Does he own a car or other vehicle? Are there any savings upon which to rely? Does she have a source from which she could borrow money, should the need arise? These things can provide a sense of security and continuity.

Attitudes and Perspectives. Does the client appear motivated to work on solving the problem? Does she seem willing to talk and work with you? Motivation and positive attitudes toward change are critically valuable assets.

Some clients maintain strong values, which sustain them during difficult times or motivate them to make changes. For instance, an extremely religious client may rely on her beliefs, minister, and fellow parishioners to help her cope with the death of her father. These avenues can provide her with strength. Likewise, parents who maintain a strong belief in the value of education can provide substantial support for a teenage son contemplating dropping out of school to join a neighborhood gang.

Clients may have spiritual beliefs that govern how they perceive negative experiences, sickness, or bad luck. They may have perspectives on what is right and wrong, responsibility for caring for oneself or others, or a basic philosophy about life in general. The spiritual dimensions of clients' lives have been too frequently ignored by human services workers and other practitioners (Sermabeikian, 1994). Asking questions about these areas is just as appropriate for the generalist practitioner as seeking information about ethnic identity, client feelings, and physical or mental health. Each is an important facet of understanding the client within the environment.

Miscellaneous Other Strengths. We know each individual is unique. Thus, there are innumerable possibilities regarding strengths that may neither occur to you nor be readily apparent. Listening carefully to what clients indicate is important to them is invaluable. Sometimes strengths appear or develop during the course of the assessment and even during the intervention process.

For example, take Abe, age 15. He was in a special education and treatment program because of violently uncontrollable physical attacks on peers and some minor delinquent acts. He had been seriously physically abused by a stepfather as a child. Thus, he was trying to cope with the awesome rage he felt within.

Abe moved in with his biological father upon entrance into the special program at age 13. Major therapeutic goals involved getting in touch with his feelings and in control of his temper. He became involved with Junior Achievement. There he made friends, gained confidence, and developed innovative projects. One of his other strengths was that he was exceptionally bright. By age 17, Abe returned to regular public school and later successfully graduated.

Other strengths may involve athletic ability, musical talent, acting ability, or special interests. Interests may range from collecting old beer cans to counted cross-stitch to deer hunting. Any of these may provide potential sources of satisfaction, motivation, and enhanced self-esteem.

Which Problem Should You Work On?

Many of your clients will have multiple problems on multiple levels. In view of the numerous categories of problems, how will you choose which to work on? The first thing to do is to ascertain that the problems to be considered fulfill three criteria (Northen, 1987). First, the client must recognize that the problem exists. Second, the problem should be clearly defined in understandable terms. Third, you and the client should realistically be able to do something to remedy the problem.

Reid and Epstein (1972) make several suggestions concerning how to decide which problem will be worked on (i.e., which problem will be the "target problem"). After exploring with the client the range of problems of most concern, each problem is defined in "explicit behavioral terms" (1972, p. 58). In other words, the precise nature of the problem should be clear in your mind. Additionally, the problem statement should include descriptions of behaviors that will later allow you to measure your progress and determine when you succeed in solving the problem.

Frequently, clients have such complex problems or so many problems that they are overwhelmed. Everything seems to be wrong. A helpful approach for the generalist is to use the skill of partialization. Partialization is breaking down a problem or a series of problems into manageable parts. The client who says his life is a mess is really describing an overall feeling he has about himself and his situation. Unfortunately, this statement does not help you much in your assessment. Knowing what specific areas of his life are going poorly is more important. Only then can you begin to gather important clues about what strengths and resources are needed to bring about a change. Thus, you might ask the client to tell you the three major areas where he feels things are not going well. You may discover that these also must be partialized into problems you can both understand and manage. Teaching clients how to use partialization as a general method for attacking their own problems can help them later when they are no longer receiving services (see Highlight 5.2).

Finally, problems should be ordered in terms of their priority to the client. For example, a client may be concerned with the following problems in order of priority: paying the rent, her husband's drinking, her child's truancy, and an overweight condition that is resulting in a number of health problems. Paying the rent is probably the problem you should address first.

HIGHLIGHT 5.2

Examples of Questions You Can Ask during Assessment

The following are examples of the types of questions you can ask as you assess the client and his or her situation (Hepworth et al., 1997). Of course, each situation is unique. These questions are simply examples.

- "What do you feel are your major problems at this time?"
- "How would you rate these problems in terms of their severity?"
- "How are others involved in the problem?"
- "Have you been involved with other agencies or received services before? If so, what were they?"
- "How do you think this particular problem affects you?"
- "In what situations is the problem most likely to take place?"

- "How often does the problem occur?"
- "How long does the problem usually last?"
- "How do you usually react when the problem occurs?"
- "How have you tried to solve the problem in the past?"
- "Has anything you've tried been at all helpful? If so, what?"
- "What do you think you need to solve the problem?"
- "What are your strengths (e.g., you work hard, you have a good supportive family, or you're easy to get along with)?"
- "Do you think any of these strengths can help to solve the problem?"
- "What kind of help or resources do you feel you need (e.g., financial, health care, legal, etc.)?"
- "What are you willing to do to solve the problem?"
- "What things about your situation are preventing you from solving the problem?"

Ordering priorities is not as easy as it sounds. Frequently you will rank the client's problems differently than the client will. In these cases, exploring the problems with the client is up to you. You will need to establish a list of priorities satisfactory to you both. Once again, this process involves both good communication skills and making judgments.

Gathering Information: Sources of Assessment Data

There are at least seven basic "sources of information" about your clients (Hepworth et al., 1997, p. 199). First, many agencies require clients to fill out forms to provide information. Client self-assessments can be mailed to the client prior to a scheduled appointment or completed in the office. Clients can provide such details as: childhood and current relationships with one's own parents, siblings, and peers; parenting expectations and behaviors; employment information; current family relationships with one's spouse, significant other, and children; sexual history information; and financial or legal data. The worker can then review the information and obtain greater detail than that which might be solicited during a standard interview.

Second, of course, you can obtain much information from clients' responses to questions during your interview. The third means of gleaning information can also occur during the interview. Observe the client's nonverbal behavior. Is the client fidgeting? Does she avoid eye contact when approaching certain topics? Do his nonverbal and verbal behavior coincide?

Fourth, if you have the opportunity, you can observe the client's interactions with other people. Observing interaction with other family members can provide you with useful insights about the client.

Fifth, information is sometimes available from outside sources. These sources can include the client's family and friends, along with any professionals having knowledge of the client or situation. Referral sources may also be able to provide information, as will reports from other agencies that have worked with the client. With the client's permission, data from physicians, psychologists, psychiatrists, and other counselors should be sought whenever available.

Sixth, sometimes the client has gone through psychological and other testing. If so, what information does this provide about the client's emotional state and behavior? Later on in this chapter, we will discuss specific instruments, including the Rathus Assertiveness Scale (RAS) and an alcoholism test.

Finally, your seventh source of information is based on your own interactions with the client. Does the client react with hostility to your questions? Does he appear extremely needy or dependent? Is she speaking irrationally? Here, your own "gut reactions" may be useful. If you have certain types of reactions to or impressions of the client, the chances are likely that other people will have similar responses.

Assessment Instruments

Multitudes of assessment instruments are available to evaluate various aspects of clients' lives. Mental health, suicide potential, assertiveness, self-esteem, a child's need of protection from abuse, interaction between spouses, and availability of resources are among the many variables frequently assessed by generalist practitioners. Of course, the worker's field of practice will dictate which variables are most important to evaluate. For instance, a protective services worker must make assessments regarding the extent to which children are in danger of abuse. Likewise, a worker in public assistance must primarily assess the extent to which a client has access to financial resources.

Three assessment instruments have been selected for discussion here. They reflect the varied types of approaches to assessment available today and include some likely to be used in practice. The specific assessment approaches addressed here include the *Diagnostic and Statistical Manual,* the Rathus Assertiveness Schedule, and an alcoholism test.

Diagnostic and Statistical Manual (DSM)

The *Diagnostic and Statistical Manual (DSM)* represents the American Psychiatric Association's (APA) official classification of mental disorders. Each disorder is labeled with a numerical code and criteria for distinguishing among various mental disorders. Mental disorders (another term for mental illness) involve "impaired psychosocial or cognitive functioning due to disturbances in any one or more of the following processes: biological, chemical, physiological, genetic, psychological, or social" (Barker, 1999, p. 299). APA originally published the manual in 1980 and periodically revises it to reflect new research and information.

As a generalist practitioner you will not practice "therapy" in a private office with comfortable couches. Rather, you will intervene with clients *and*

the multiple systems with which they are involved. You will probably not be called upon to make a formal assessment using the *DSM*. In other words, you will not have to figure out the specific numerical code that best reflects a client's mental status. However, you will be expected to work both with clients who have been diagnosed and with the system of other professionals working with those clients.

Mental health professionals use the *DSM* to assess individuals by concentrating on five major dimensions or axes (American Psychiatric Association, 2000). The use of these axes helps practitioners look at multiple aspects of functioning and avoid missing important factors that may be contributing to the client's problem.

The first axis involves *clinical disorders* and conditions not directly attributable to a mental disorder but for which people seek help. These disorders include mood (such as bipolar or depressive disorders) and anxiety disorders (such as obsessive-compulsive and posttraumatic stress disorders). The second part of axis one covers such things as borderline intellectual functioning, academic or marital problems, and parent–child difficulties, among others (American Psychiatric Association, 2000).

The *DSM's* second axis involves *personality disorders* such as paranoid disorders, antisocial personality, borderline personality disorders, and mental retardation. The third axis concentrates on any *physical conditions* that may influence the person's emotional health. These include infections, AIDS, diabetes, diseases of the nervous system, and several others.

The fourth axis covers environmental and psychosocial problems affecting the mental disorder. These problems include any number of individual or family crises, stressors, loss of significant others, or loss of a job. Positive stressors can also play a role. These psychosocial or environmental problems may contribute to, or result from, the mental disorder.

Axis five is a global assessment using the clinician's judgment of the client's overall level of functioning. It generally describes the individual at the time of the assessment or may be used to identify how the person functioned in the immediate past. A numerical rating of 1 to 100 is used in conjunction with the time period. For example, a client's highest level of functioning may be related as 85 at the time of assessment.

Together, these assessment dimensions can depict a relatively clear picture of an individual's behavior, life functioning, and emotional status. The *DSM* emphasizes characteristics of the various mental disorders without specifying causes; this process allows professionals to maintain their own theories regarding why such mental illnesses occur.

The *DSM* is useful for at least four reasons (Williams, 1987). First, it provides a means for a variety of professionals (e.g., nurses, counselors, psychiatrists, psychologists, and human service workers) to communicate with each other about specific mental, emotional, and behavioral problems. Giving a client's problem a diagnosis makes it easier for each professional to know what others are talking about when they discuss that problem.

A second benefit of the *DSM* is its helpfulness in evaluating and treating clients with mental disorders. The manual focuses more on descriptions of the symptoms and behaviors of a particular disorder rather than on what causes that disorder. Therefore, defining the specific problem that requires intervention helps.

A third benefit is the manual's utility in teaching about mental disorders. Classifying a disorder by describing its symptoms enhances our understanding of that disorder.

Finally, the *DSM* provides better opportunities to do research on mental disorders. For instance, it enables researchers to place people receiving treatment into specific categories. They can then investigate whether certain treatments or interventions are effective with specific disorders.

Generalist practitioners, however, should be wary of at least three factors when using the *DSM*. First, it only describes particular conditions. It does not provide intervention strategies and is only an assessment mechanism upon which specific interventions can be built.

Second, there can be some tendency to focus on the individual pathology or "mental illness" instead of on a client's interaction with the environment. The manual does use the term "client" instead of "patient." Earlier in the chapter, we discussed the difference between "diagnosis," a medical term focusing on individual pathology, and "assessment," which in generalist practice also stresses the environment's impact upon the client. Additionally, the manual uses the terms "clinician" and "mental health professional" instead of "physician" and "psychiatrist" (Williams, 1995, p. 738). Still, the manual targets individuals. There may be some tendency to "cure" the individual, rather than intervene in the systems intimately intertwined with the client. People using the manual as a formal assessment tool are primarily psychiatrists, psychologists,

and other human service practitioners. The psychiatric tradition is rooted in the medical model. Thus, generalist practitioners must be cautious to maintain their orientation toward the environment and its profound impact on clients.

A third reason for wariness when using the *DSM* concerns imperfections in its categories. Professional discretion is involved in assigning diagnoses to individual clients. Individuals and their behaviors are complex and difficult to place in neat, compact categories. Questions can also be raised regarding the potential hazards of labeling people. How might such labels affect and bias expectations? Labels tend to interfere with the notion that each individual is unique, having a unique combination of strengths and weaknesses. Labels also can stigmatize clients, affecting their self-perceptions and the perceptions of others.

Assessing Assertiveness. Assertiveness involves being able to state your thoughts, wants, and feelings straightforwardly and effectively. It concerns the ability to establish an appropriate stance between being too aggressive and too timid. Aggressiveness in this context implies taking only your needs into account. Essentially, you ignore the needs and rights of others. Timidity, on the other hand, concerns placing the needs and wishes of others far before your own. Assertiveness, then, means striking a balance. The implication is that you take both your needs and the needs of others into account. You then try to make some objective judgment about what behavior, response, or plan of action is fair to you both.

The Rathus Assertiveness Schedule (RAS) is an instrument composed of 30 items that measure an individual's assertiveness. It can be a useful tool to gauge clients' ability to determine how well they can speak on their own behalf assertively without aggression (see Figure 5.3).

Assessing Alcohol and Other Drug Abuse. Drug abuse involves improper use of some chemical substance in a manner that is harmful physically, mentally, or emotionally. Alcohol abuse, of course, is a form of drug abuse. It can be detrimental to the user and to others. The National Institute on Alcohol Abuse and Alcoholism (2000) reports that "alcohol-related problems include economic losses resulting from time off work owing to alcohol-related illness and injury, disruption of family and social relationships, emotional problems, impact on perceived

Figure 5.3   *The Rathus Assertiveness Schedule (RAS)*

Directions: Indicate how characteristic or descriptive each of the following statements is of you by using the code given below:

+3   Very characteristic of me, extremely descriptive
+2   Rather characteristic of me, quite descriptive
+1   Somewhat characteristic, slightly descriptive
–1   Somewhat uncharacteristic of me, slightly nondescriptive
–2   Rather uncharacteristic of me, quite nondescriptive
–3   Very uncharacteristic of me, extremely nondescriptive

___   1.   Most people seem to be more aggressive and assertive than I am.
___   2.   I have hesitated to make or accept dates because of "shyness."
___   3.   When the food served at a restaurant is not done to my satisfaction, I complain about it to the waiter or waitress.
___   4.   I am careful to avoid hurting other people's feelings, even when I have been injured.
___   5.   If a salesman has gone to considerable trouble to show me merchandise which is not quite suitable, I have a difficult time saying "no."
___   6.   When I am asked to do something, I insist upon knowing why.
___   7.   There are times when I look for a good and vigorous argument.
___   8.   I strive to get ahead as well as most people in my position.
___   9.   To be honest, people often take advantage of me.
___   10.   I enjoy starting conversations with new acquaintances and strangers.
___   11.   I often don't know what to say to attractive persons of the opposite sex.
___   12.   I will hesitate to make phone calls to business establishments and institutions.
___   13.   I would rather apply for a job or for admission to a college by writing letters than by going through with personal interviews.
___   14.   I find it embarrassing to return merchandise.
___   15.   If a close and respected relative were annoying me, I would smother my feelings rather than express my annoyance.
___   16.   I have avoided asking questions for fear of sounding stupid.
___   17.   During an argument I am sometimes afraid that I will get so upset that I will shake all over.
___   18.   If a famed and respected lecturer makes a statement which I think is incorrect, I will have the audience hear my point of view.
___   19.   I avoid arguing over prices with clerks and salesmen.
___   20.   When I have done something important or worthwhile, I manage to let others know about it.
___   21.   I am open and frank about my feelings.
___   22.   If someone has been spreading false and bad stories about me, I see him (her) as soon as possible to "have a talk" about it.
___   23.   I often have a hard time saying "no."
___   24.   I tend to bottle up my emotions rather than make a scene.
___   25.   I complain about poor service in a restaurant or elsewhere.
___   26.   When I am given a complaint, I sometimes just don't know what to say.
___   27.   If a couple near me in a theater or at a lecture were conversing rather loudly, I would ask them to be quiet or to take their conversation elsewhere.
___   28.   Anyone attempting to push ahead of me in a line is in for a good battle.
___   29.   I am quick to express my opinion.
___   30.   There are times when I just can't say anything.

To score:
1. Take the RAS.
2. Change the sign from positive (+) to negative (–) or negative (–) to positive (+) for your answers to the following questions: 2, 4, 5, 9, 11, 12, 13, 14, 15, 16, 17, 19, 23, 24, 26, 30.
3. Add up your total.
   a. A score of –90 to –20 means you're generally unassertive and probably too much so. The lower your score, the less assertive you are.
   b. A score of –20 to +60 indicates that you're within the realm of being appropriately assertive much of the time.
   c. A score of +60 to +90 means you're very assertive or possibly aggressive. This is a warning category.

| –90 | –20 | +60 | +90 |

Source: D. B. Hull and J. H. Hull, "Rathus Assertiveness Schedule: Normative and Factor-Analytic Data." *Behavior Therapy,* 9(1978), p. 673. Copyright © 1978 by the Association for Advancement of Behavior Therapy. Reprinted by permission of the publisher and the author.

health, violence and aggression, and legal problems" (p. 10). Alcoholism is associated with increased risk for many health problems including stroke, hypertension, certain cancers, and mental disorders.

Because of the prevalence of alcohol and other drug abuse, assessing the extent to which it is a problem for a client is important for a generalist practitioner. There are numerous assessment instruments available. One is illustrated in Figure 5.4.

Family Assessment

Family membership is intimate. Family members share tasks and responsibilities that contribute to

Figure 5.4   *An Alcoholism Test*

Respond as truthfully as you can to the questions posed below about how you use and need alcohol. (Although this test relates to alcohol use, many of the questions could also apply to other drug use).

1. Do you ever drink to escape from your problems (for example, disappointment, stress, or aggravation with someone close to you)?
   Yes _____   No _____
2. Have you ever tried to cut down or stop your use of alcohol and failed?
   Yes _____   No _____
3. Have you ever suffered memory loss while drinking even though you did not pass out?
   Yes _____   No _____
4. Do you start drinking before going to parties or drink significantly more than your friends while there?
   Yes _____   No _____
5. Do you ever feel guilty about drinking?
   Yes _____   No _____
6. Did your behavior while drinking ever embarrass you the day after?
   Yes _____   No _____
7. Are you compelled to continue drinking even after friends or family members say they think you've had enough?
   Yes _____   No _____
8. Have you ever switched from one form or brand of alcohol or changed your pattern of use in order to increase control of your drinking?
   Yes _____   No _____
9. Has your drinking ever caused problems with friends or family?
   Yes _____   No _____
10. Do you find you need to have a drink in the morning in order to get going?
    Yes _____   No _____
11. Do you look up to people who can really "hold their liquor"?
    Yes _____   No _____
12. Do you prefer to drink alone?
    Yes _____   No _____
13. Do you feel like you "have to have a drink" more often than you used to?
    Yes _____   No _____
14. Have you missed days at work or school because of hangovers or other effects from drinking?
    Yes _____   No _____
15. Do you think your drinking has caused problems during the past months?
    Yes _____   No _____
16. Are "blackouts" (i.e., periods of time while drinking that are marked by memory lapses) occurring more frequently?
    Yes _____   No _____
17. Do you conceal alcohol so others won't know you have it?
    Yes _____   No _____
18. Do you ever feel your life would improve if you stopped drinking?
    Yes _____   No _____

The more questions you answered yes, the more likely you are to have a problem with alcohol.

Source: This test incorporates the intent of questions posed by a pamphlet *A Message to Teenagers . . . How to Tell When Drinking Is Becoming a Problem* (New York: A. A. World Services, Inc., 1988); a handout entitled *Who Has a Problem?* (Madison, WI: AAA Wisconsin Division Safety Department, undated); and the book *Treating Alcoholism: An Alcoholics Anonymous Approach* by N. K. Denzin (Newbury Park, CA: Sage, 1987).

the maintenance of the family's identity and functioning. On one hand, families are made up of unique individuals. On the other, each individual family member is a subsystem of the larger family system. Therefore, anything affecting an individual member also has repercussions for the entire family and all its members.

Because of their unique qualities involving identity and intimacy, families are considered special types of groups. In one respect, families, as groups, are part of mezzo practice. In another, the importance of the family to individual clients often places family intervention within the realm of micro practice. For our purposes, we will consider work with families to lie somewhere on a continuum between micro and mezzo practice.

Choosing to Work with Families

Working with the family system is one of many intervention alternatives in the planned change process. A worker may choose during assessment (step 2 of the Generalist Intervention Model) to plan (step 3) and implement the plan (step 4) to address the family as the primary target of attention. Additional options, of course, involve the assessment of other micro and mezzo aspects of potential intervention in addition to macro dimensions. This assessment may lead you to the question of when a generalist practitioner should choose to work with a family and when with either the individual alone or with some other external system.

There is no easy answer to this question. However, there are some variables to take into account when making an assessment and planning an intervention. First, you need to ask yourself to what extent the problem affects other family members. Second, do you have the time and resources to work with other family members? Third, in terms of prioritizing problems, are those aspects of the problem involving other family members among the most critical to be addressed? Finally, to what extent do you think family intervention is likely to be successful?

Family Assessment Skills

We have established that the family is a special type of system. It has momentous significance concerning individual members' physical and emotional well-being. Assessing families also poses challenges for the generalist practitioner. It is not unusual for family members to have different ideas about the nature, source, and extent of the problems they are experiencing. These differences are to be expected because each member experiences his or her familial environment differently. From these contrasting views you develop a real understanding of what being a member of that family is like, for example, that family members see one member as the primary "problem" or that individual members feel excluded from the family is common. Your task is to ensure that all perspectives are valued and that each member feels you are interested in his or her views. Because you have several family members, there are several more sets of strengths to consider. These include individual strengths as well as strengths that characterize the entire family. Working with the entire family, however constituted, requires you to communicate with all members, while avoiding the perception that you are "siding" with any individual or dyad in the family. Remember that you are assessing the individual family members and the interactions among and between them. Of course, family assessments also run the risk of producing more data than you can handle, but this overabundance is inherent in the task.

Family Communication. Family communication involves how well each family member conveys feelings and ideas to the other members. To what extent does each sender's *intent* match the *impact* on the receiver? The effectiveness of a family's internal communication is important not only for assessment purposes but also for planning and undertaking the intervention. Improving communication is frequently a core goal when working with families.

Family Structure. Family structure involves the organization of relationships and patterns of interaction within the family. Assessment of five dimensions of family structure is especially relevant. First, the family is *functioning as a system* that is intact with appropriate boundaries and subsystems. The second dimension involves *family norms*, the rules that specify the behavior within the family group. Third, there are *family roles* that concern both the status differential and behavioral expectations the family has for each of its members. The fourth dimension involves the appropriate *balance of power* within the family and among its members. Finally, *intergenerational aspects* and the impact of family history upon current family functioning are vital.

Life-Cycle Adjustments. Assessment of how the family adapts to various predictable phases of its life cycle is important. Births, deaths, marriages, and grown children's departures are examples that call upon the family's coping abilities.

Impacts of the Social Environment. How good is the family's *fit* with its social environment? Does it have adequate social supports, or is it isolated? Is the family receiving satisfactory resources to survive and thrive? How well integrated is the family with its surrounding community? These and related questions are critical for assessing family functioning and planning interventions.

Family Relationships

Assessing family relationships involves understanding the entire family system. The amount of data involved in family assessments requires the use of some method for sorting out and organizing the information. Moreover, the family must be involved in this assessment and understand the potential meanings of the information. Two useful tools for gathering and helping families understand that data are the eco-map and genogram (Hartman, 1978). The eco-map provides a graphic representation of the family's ecological system. It depicts family membership and relationships and can help individuals and families recognize their own strengths and areas of weakness. Because eco-maps and genograms convey a view of the family at a particular point in time, they can also be used to monitor or evaluate changes over time. The breadth of systems reflected in the eco-map assists clients to visualize their situation from a different point of view, to suggest areas where change is needed or where resources appear to be absent and to highlight areas of support within the larger environment.

Constructing an eco-map begins with a large circle at the center of a piece of paper. In that circle we place the individual members of a family. Males are identified by boxes and females by circles. Around the outside of the center circle are a series of other smaller circles representing other systems with which the family interacts. These systems might include extended family members, friends, schools, law enforcement, social welfare agencies, church, employment, and health systems. Once each significant system is entered, relationships among the various systems are depicted by a series of lines. For example, a straight solid line ————— is used for strong relationships. Weak or insignificant relationships are shown as a series of dashes - - - - -. Relationships characterized as stressful or strained are indicated by a zigzag line. Arrows along the lines indicate the direction in which energy or resources flow. Figure 5.5 shows the Ruth family eco-map. Several things are evident from this diagram. For example, the Ruth family has four children, two

boys and two girls, and the Ruths themselves are middle aged.

Anita is involved in a group for first-time criminal offenders after an arrest for shoplifting last year. She says she enjoys the group, which is the family's only involvement in the criminal justice system. Anita has an IQ of 75 and works around the farm helping her dad.

Mario, currently in graduate school, is a member of a gay and lesbian student organization on campus. He "came out" to his parents last year when the family was in crisis over Anita's arrest. His relationship with his dad is strained because of his sexual orientation. He does not have a partner at this time.

Mark is trying to make a living as a professional bowler. Sports are the only thing he is interested in, and he has tried his hand at baseball, football, and basketball. He hates farming, which affects his relationship with his father.

Tia just graduated from college with a degree in criminal justice. She has applied to be a police officer and is living with her parents in the meantime. Like the rest of her siblings, Tia is single.

Jan, like the rest of the family, is very much involved in the church, which provides a good deal of support. Even though she does not work outside of the home, she serves on several committees and participates in most church functions. She has a very stressful relationship with her father, as does the rest of the family. Her father engaged in sexual abuse with his daughters and now is experiencing Alzheimer's disease. He lives alone and probably will need a nursing home soon. Neither Jan nor her sister is interested in trying to help their dad. Their mother is deceased.

Jed is a farmer by occupation, but the family farming business has lost ground to agribusinesses. Jed does not own enough land to make his farm profitable and figures he will eventually be forced to sell it. His single hobby is playing in a 1960s-style rock band with a few of his school-days friends. Unfortunately, his hearing has been damaged from years of working around loud farm machinery. Now he finds himself increasingly limited as a musician because he cannot hear some of the music the band plays, and, because of his disability, he joins the band infrequently. Jed refuses to be tested for a hearing aid, claiming "they're for old folks." Jed's parents are very much involved in the family, providing emotional ties and financial help. They sold the family farm to Jed and still feel a great deal of attachment to the land.

Obviously, there are a number of relationship and resource problems facing this family. The father's

Figure 5.5 *Eco-Map*

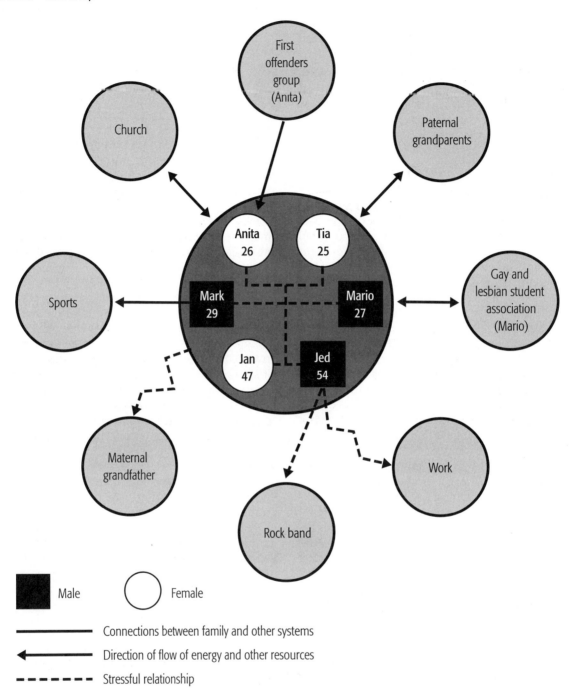

reluctance to get a hearing aid is undermining one of his most important sources of support. His relationship with his two sons is problematic at this time, and he feels a great deal of stress over his failure to maintain the family farm. Jan does not work outside the home, and Jed worries about what changes will occur with Jan and Anita when the family has to leave the farm. An eco-map can be helpful in displaying to families and individuals how their connections and resources actually look. It can also help remind them of the things that are or were truly important in their lives. Arrows showing a general flow of energy away from the family can help in understanding why they lack the emotional resources to deal with new crises. Changes in the eco-map over time can be used to help a family recognize the progress they are making. Whenever possible, clients should be involved in creating the eco-map, because they can help the counselor organize information for an assessment.

A genogram is another useful tool for family assessment because it provides a means of depicting a family from one generation to the next. More specifically, it presents a chronological picture of the family, noting important events, additions and losses to the family, communication and relationship patterns, and occupational or work connections. Generally, a genogram denotes three or more generations in a family. Like an eco-map, genograms are best constructed by the counselor and family members working together. Also like eco-maps, genograms use boxes for males and circles for females. Triangles are used in the event that the sex of a person is not known. Marriage is shown as a line connecting male and female, usually with the wedding date noted. Divorces are evident by a line bisecting the marital line with the date shown. Children are listed in chronological order from left to right. Deaths are noted by an "X" through the box, circle, or triangle, again with the date indicated. A dotted line is usually drawn around family members living in the same household. Figure 5.6 shows a genogram of the Johnson family over two generations. Deaths of Jamal senior and granddaughter Meg are shown.

Marriages and, in the case of Jamal and Gwen, a divorce are evident. The pattern of giving children family names is also noticeable. From the dotted line we can see that Jared, Sheree, and Gwen are now living together in the same household. Like a family tree, a genogram can be used to record important connections between and among family members and generations. A pattern of divorces may be evident from one generation to the next as well as traditions having to do with family size.

Because the information needed to construct the genogram must come from family members, the absence of information can pinpoint cut-offs between relatives. Additional information about the cause of family members' deaths may identify risk factors. Of course, a genogram can serve as a written record for all family members and may provide useful information for children to be placed for adoption (Hartman, 1978). Both the genogram and eco-map are useful tools for working with families and individuals.

Home Visits

Home visits involve calling upon clients in their own homes in order to provide some type of professional service. This content is included here because of the significance home visits can have in assessing a family's environment (or an individual's, for that matter). Striking information can be gained during a

Figure 5.6   *Genogram*

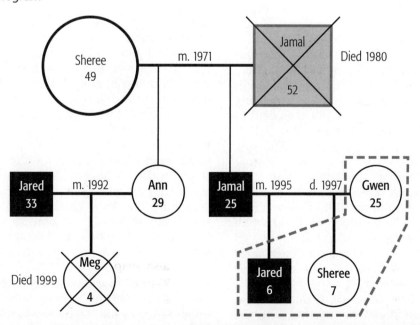

home visit that is simply not available in the more sterile, agency interview situation.

One should note, however, that there are other reasons for making home visits than to do assessments. Barker (1999) cites a number of them. First, the clients may be physically disabled. Leaving their own homes may be extremely difficult or impossible for them. Second, some workers make home visits "because they believe the helping process can be more effective and efficient if conducted in an environment familiar to the client." Finally, some home visits are made "because the worker seeks to mobilize a neighborhood or county toward a social cause" (Barker, 1995, p. 170). In the latter case, workers need to get involved in the community in order to gain community members' trust and commitment.

Workers' Reactions. One aspect of home visits that can be difficult for workers is the shocking nature of what people must endure as a result of their impoverished environments or their state of physical or mental health. Many human services workers come from middle-class background where there is a certain level of learned expectations regarding cleanliness and household organization. Of course, clients vary drastically regarding their values, just as any group of people vary. However, generalist practitioners address and deal with the very worst of people's problems. Thus, there are times when workers must be prepared to look beyond extreme circumstances, remain objective, and try to see things from the client's point of view.

For instance, during her internship, one student confided in her faculty advisor about a serious problem she was having with one of her clients. Her placement involved providing supportive services to a caseload of elderly clients so that they might remain living in their own homes. The student would regularly visit clients and help them get groceries, pay their bills, see friends, visit physicians when needed, and complete other daily living tasks. The student described this particular client as living in an old trailer house cluttered with cast-off clothing, broken furniture, and garbage. The sink was piled high with dishes filled with rotting remnants of food. Although the student found the environmental situation difficult to visit, this was not the major problem. She stated that she was horrified at how cockroaches seemed to be crawling everywhere throughout the trailer. She continued that the very last straw was seeing a cockroach crawl out of her client's ear, up the side of the woman's face, and across her forehead.

The faculty advisor acknowledged that this was an extremely difficult situation. Together with the student's field supervisor, the student and advisor planned an evaluation of the client and her living conditions. Frequently, such evaluations were done at the field placement agency. Together with the client, living conditions were assessed and decisions made. Some alternatives for this particular situation included providing the client with additional homemaker services, involving a visiting nurse to assess health conditions, considering removing the client from the trailer, and arranging for alternative living conditions. One of the things discovered was that the elderly woman's intellectual functioning appeared to be deteriorating. This deterioration was magnified by her almost total isolation, except for the visits by people providing her with supportive services.

Scheduling Home Visits. Home visits should be at a time as convenient as possible for family members. Oftentimes, this convenience is not during typical nine-to-five office hours. Evenings or even weekends might be the only time family members are home. In such cases, a job with flexible scheduling is helpful. Otherwise, you must work overtime or accept the fact that some home visits are impossible to make within your job specifications.

Home visits can be scheduled by phone. During the initial conversation, you should identify who you are and clearly state the purpose of the visit. For instance, you would like to talk about the Hamptons' son's progress in school.

Some clients will not have phones, which makes arranging for a visit more difficult. In this case, one possibility is to write the family and schedule a time that you anticipate to be most convenient for them. Simply notify them that since you cannot contact them by phone, you would like to meet with them at a specific time and date in their home. You might then ask them to notify you if that time is bad for them. You also might ask them to suggest another time that they feel is better.

Sometimes, this suggestion will not work. For example, a practitioner attempts to visit a family four times without success. Each time, he notifies them by mail as suggested earlier. Each time, he stops by their house and rings the doorbell to no avail. They are either not at home or are simply not answering the door. The bottom line is that they simply did not want to see him, for whatever reason. On this occasion, he has to accept the fact that he will be unable to make this particular visit.

Taking Care of Your Own Safety. Considering your safety when visiting various areas and neighborhoods is important. Some areas are simply rougher than others. You must weigh the extent to which you need or are required to make a home visit against the potential danger in which it will place you. For instance, a home visit in a gang-ridden, urban neighborhood at night is a bad idea.

You should also be aware of areas with high crime rates and take as many precautions as possible. Be aware of where you are and who is around you. If racial tensions are high and you are of a minority race in that neighborhood, being aware of this fact is especially important.

This warning is not meant to scare you. Neighborhoods, as we know, vary regarding these safety issues. Being aware of facts and making rational decisions is vital. Highlight 5.3 identifies a number of safety tips.

HIGHLIGHT 5.3

Be Alert, Streetwise, and Safe

You can do a great deal to reduce your risk of becoming a crime victim. The most effective weapons against crime are *common sense, alertness,* and *involvement.* Armed with these, you can protect yourself by reducing the opportunity for muggers, purse snatchers, and other street criminals to strike.

Elementary Street Sense

- Wherever you are, be alert to what is going on around you. Do not get distracted or daydream. Look to see who is ahead of, beside, and behind you.
- Communicate visually that you are a calm, confident individual. Stand tall with your head erect and walk purposefully. Make quick eye contact with the people around you, so that you give the impression of awareness.
- Always trust your instincts. If you feel uncomfortable in a place or situation, leave as soon as possible.
- Do not drop your guard because you feel that you are in a familiar area. Crime knows no boundaries.

Walking Smart

- Plan the safest route to your destination and *use it.* On the sidewalk, use the part farthest away from shrubs, doorways, and alleys, where people can hide.
- Walk with a companion whenever possible. There is safety in numbers.
- Learn the neighborhood. A few minutes to notice what stores are open, the type of street lighting, and the locations of telephones may be important if you need help later.
- If carrying a purse, hold it close to your body or wear it under your coat. Keep a firm grip on it, and don't let it hang loosely by its straps. Carry wallets in an inside coat or front trouser pocket.

- Do not overburden yourself with books, backpacks, or packages. Wear shoes or clothing that don't restrict your movements. Notice how many women executives wearing 500-dollar suits walk the city streets in designer sneakers. Three-inch-high heels would make them easy prey for attacks.
- Have your key in your hand when entering your residence or car. This allows quick access and also provides a weapon if you are attacked. Remember to look into the back seat before getting into your car to make sure nobody is hiding there.
- Avoid carrying large amounts of money and do not wear expensive jewelry or clothing when going on home visits. Thieves give in easily to temptation.
- Consider buying and carrying a shriek alarm.
- Leave all headphones at home. You need to use all your senses. Headphones eliminate sounds that would alert you to danger.
- Do not give money to people who ask for it on the street. Your "loose change" is not really going to help their situation.
- Familiarize yourself with the emergency buttons of the elevators you ride frequently. Always stand near the controls.
- Look inside the elevator before you get on board to make sure nobody is hiding inside.
- Get off the elevator if someone suspicious enters. If you are uneasy about someone who is waiting with you for the elevator, pretend that you have forgotten something and do not get on the elevator with the person. Listen to your gut reactions and intuition about what and who is around you.
- If you are attacked while in the elevator, hit the alarm button and as many floor buttons as possible.

Defensive Driving

- Always lock your car doors, even when driving. Do not put your purse or other valuables on the seat next to you. Thieves have broken windows, even while a car is waiting at a stoplight, to reach inside and steal. Keep your windows rolled up whenever possible.

- Keep your car in good running condition and always have enough gas to get where you are going and back again. If you do have car trouble, raise the hood and sit in the locked car. If someone offers to help, always stay in the car.
- Park in well-lighted areas that will still be well lit when you return to your car. If you expect to return to your car after dark, park near or under a light.

Tips for Buses

- Use well-lighted and busy bus stops. Stand with other people whenever possible.
- Sit near the front, close to the driver. Do not fall asleep.
- Tell anyone who is harassing you, firmly and loudly, "Leave me alone!" Persistent persons should be reported to the driver.
- Be alert to who gets off the bus with you. If you feel uneasy, walk directly to a place where there are other people.

If You Are Threatened

- Remain calm—try not to panic or show any signs of confusion.

- Do not resist if the attacker is armed or is only after your valuables. You do not want to escalate a property crime into a violent confrontation.
- If resistence is an option, do not get scared. Get mad! Shout "No!" "Stop!" "Fire!" "Call the police!" loudly and forcefully. Try to incapacitate or distract your assailant long enough to escape. A jab to the throat or eyes or even a swift kick to the knees or groin may give you a few minutes to get away or attract attention for help.
- After the attack, call the police *immediately*. Identify yourself and your location. During the attack, make a conscious effort to get a good look at the assailant: facial features, type of clothing/shoes, height and weight, race and sex, or anything distinctive (e.g., a large nose or obvious scars). If a vehicle is involved, try to get the license number.
- *Remember* that any crime is a traumatic experience, even if you are not hurt. Turn to others for help and support. Tell your field supervisor and faculty liaison. Allow others to help you get in touch with such supportive services as a victim assistance program.

Source: This material has been adapted from the pamphlet *How to Be "Streetwise"—and Safe,* published by the Marquette University Public Safety Department. Reprinted by permission of the Marquette University Public Safety Department, 1212 W. Wisconsin Ave., Milwaukee, WI 53233.

Assessment in Mezzo Practice: Assessing Groups

In the assessment process, a generalist practitioner identifies a need and then may determine that this need can best be met through formulating and working with a group of individuals. Needs involve virtually any issue. A category of clients may have some kind of treatment need because of problems they have (e.g., alcohol addiction, incest, or lack of assertiveness). There may be a need to structure a group within an agency to work on revising policies. Or there may be a need to formulate a group for lobbying a state legislature to change an excessively restrictive public assistance policy.

Assessment in groups is an ongoing process carried out prior to the group's formation, throughout intervention, and after completion of the group (Toseland & Rivas, 1998). As we know, assessment and evaluation are two sides of the same coin. During the initial assessment phase, problems,

strengths, and needs must be clearly established so that progress may later be evaluated. Regardless of the type of group, two dimensions must be the first focus of attention: potential sponsorship and potential membership.

Potential Sponsorship

Almost all practitioners function under position descriptions, summaries of the duties and responsibilities inherent in the particular worker's job. Working with groups may or may not fit with the worker's primary job responsibilities. The extent to which the job description incorporates working with groups has a direct impact on the ease with which a worker can run groups.

Consider the worker responsible for multitudinous duties, none of which directly correlates with formulating groups. Work with groups may be difficult or impossible for that worker to do. She may have no time flexibility in view of her other duties.

Likewise, the agency may see working with groups as an activity of relatively low priority. On the other hand, a job description that includes the responsibility of teaching parenting skills to individuals and *groups,* thereby includes group work as a natural part of the worker's expected activities.

The agency's sponsorship or support of group work is very important (Shulman, 1999). Before beginning work with groups, a worker must assess the extent to which this support exists. Toseland and Rivas explain, "Treatment groups rely on agency administrators and staff for sanctions, financial support, member referrals, and physical facilities for the group. Similarly, task groups are intrinsically linked to the functioning of their sponsoring agencies and must continually refer to the agency's mission, bylaws, and policies for clarification of their task, charge, and mandate" (1998, p. 149).

Treatment groups may be incorporated into the goals of agencies geared to working with some category of clients' problems. Running such groups may then be part of the worker's normal routine. On the other hand, the agency administration may be oriented toward working with *individuals.* Strong resistence on the part of the administration makes the formulation of groups very difficult and sometimes impossible. When you consider forming a treatment group, assessing your agency's support of such an endeavor is crucial. If support is seriously lacking, you should ask yourself if the time and effort it will take are worth the exertion.

Assessment regarding agency support of task groups is also important. If you determine that a task group is needed to accomplish a purpose or fulfill some need, you must first assess how open the agency is to evaluating issues and implementing changes in policy and practice. A number of questions may be appropriate: Do agency decision makers typically react positively to innovative suggestions? Which decision makers might be most likely to provide support for a task group? What kinds of information would be helpful to them? Are the chances of successfully formulating a task group worth the effort of persuading the administration to support it? In summary, the practitioner must assess the potential agency support, how that support might best be mustered, and, in the end, whether the endeavor is worth the effort.

Who Should Be Members of the Group?

Assessing agency support should be done early in the assessment process. Another early step concerns figuring out who the group members should be. This decision involves clearly defining the proposed group's purpose and addressing a number of questions: What characteristics should group members have? How will their needs be met by the group's purpose? How motivated will they be?

Toseland and Rivas (1998) suggest that the practitioner collect information about potential group members including problems, needs, and strengths. Information can be gathered through interviewing, consultation with colleagues about the problem or issue, and reading any available information and documentation about the issue (e.g., see Highlight 5.4).

Selection Criteria for Treatment Group Membership. Unfortunately, there appears to be no clear-cut recipe for perfect group membership. Most groups are formed and run while dealing with limited resources, infinite variation of individual characteristics, and agency or job constrictions. A precise formula involving exacting measurements is unrealistic and virtually impossible. However, there are a number of commonsense principles that can help to determine group composition. These include motivation, group purpose, common communication skills, and a generalized assessment of the potential advantages and disadvantages of the group.

Motivation. One of the most critical variables in including a particular member in a group is motivation. Little can be accomplished with individuals who are not committed to the group and not willing to work on behalf of themselves and the group.

However, oftentimes generalist practitioners will be in the situation of running treatment groups where members are wary or simply involuntary. For example, consider groups run in residential treatment centers or group homes for children with behavioral and emotional problems. Or consider a deferred prosecution group where first-time offenders are given the choice of paying a large fine, going to jail for a while, or participating in a group (such a group would focus on increasing self-awareness, understanding one's motivation for committing the crime, and designing ways to avoid committing crimes in the future).

Making an accurate assessment of a client's motivation for participating in a group is important. Often, this assessment involves more than the decision of whether a member will or will not become a member of a group. It will also involve the extent to which the worker needs to work on enhancing the motivational level of an individual or that of the entire group.

HIGHLIGHT 5.4

Sociograms

A common technique for assessing children's interaction is referred to as *sociometry* (Rose, 1981). This assessment involves asking children questions about their relationships and feelings toward other people. After information is gathered, the relationships can be illustrated on a diagram called a *sociogram*. Sociograms can be extremely useful for assessing children's interactional patterns, such as for those who have low self-esteem and difficulty relating to peers.

A sociogram can be a "sensitive instrument for demonstrating change of behavior in children" after treatment (Rose, 1981, p. 33).

Children in a group might be asked such questions as which three peers do they like the best, which three do they like the least, whom do they most admire, whom would they like to sit next to, and whom are they most afraid of. Each child can be represented by a circle. Arrows can then be drawn to the people they indicate in answer to each question.

A sociogram of a special education class is depicted below. A sociogram can be created to illustrate the results of each question asked. Our example plots out two questions. Sociogram A reflects students' feelings about whom they thought was the strongest leader in

the group. Sociogram B illustrates which peer they most liked in the group.

Sociogram A clearly illustrates that Toby was thought to be the strongest leader in the group. He is bright, energetic, and very "street smart." However, Sociogram B clearly illustrates he is not the most popular or best liked in the group. Both Tom and Gertie shine there. They are more mature than the other group members. They are assertive and fairly self-confident, yet they do not impose their will on the others. They are among the brightest in the group. Toby, on the other hand, is more feared than respected in the group. The others admire his apparent sophistication, yet they do not trust him. He does not let anyone get close to him emotionally or even spatially.

Vince's opinions differ radically from the other group members. Vince stays by himself most of the time. He loves to wander off whenever he can sneak away. He sees Dean as being both a strong and likable leader. Dean is a very active, verbal person who is always in the center of activity. He has some trouble controlling his behavior and tends to provoke the other students. Perhaps Vince admires Dean's involvement.

These two sociograms are examples of how a group's interaction can be assessed and visually pictured. Although they only begin to portray some of the complexities of the group's interaction, they do provide some interesting clues upon which later interventions can be planned.

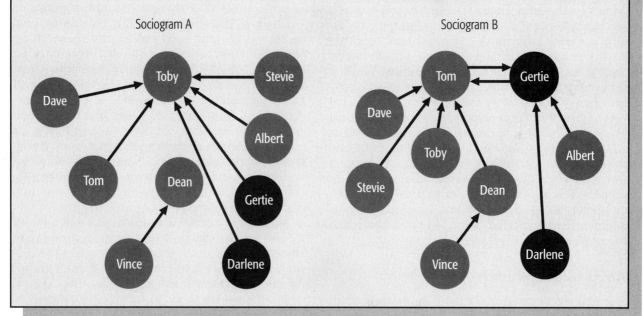

Group Purpose.   That people are assessed and selected for membership in a particular treatment group for some clearly specified reason makes sense. Examples include a group to work on marital issues, a social skills improvement group, a child management group, or a support group for children with parents placed in a nursing home. The important thing is that group members are there to work together on some common problem or issue.

Common Communication Skills.   Group treatment is based on communication. Whatever is accomplished in a group is done through this medium. Therefore, group members must be able to communicate effectively with each other, which implies that group members should have a similar ability to use language and express themselves. The important thing is for you to determine that group members will be able to communicate ideas and feelings to each other adequately.

Group Advantages versus Disadvantages.   For each group member there are frequently benefits and limitations to participating in a given group. If the advantages exceed the less appealing aspects of the group, the member is more likely to be motivated to join and continue in a group. Rewards might include the potential for seeing improvement in a problem, decreased emotional pain, enjoyment of other group members, or an increase in self-confidence. Disadvantages, on the other hand, might include the time and effort it takes to participate, dislike of or lack of communication with other group members, or resentment about feeling forced to participate.

Toseland and Rivas (1998) suggest some approaches for dealing with resistence on the part of group members. These include acknowledging the coercion members feel about being forced to participate, encouraging maximum self-determination within the prescribed limits, and reminding members that they can choose not to participate. The latter decision carries consequences for those mandated by the court or other agencies to attend, but the final decision always rests with the client.

Gathering Information about Potential Treatment Group Members.   For treatment groups there are at least three primary assessment mechanisms. First, interviews with potential group members prior to beginning the group are helpful. Assessment regarding the clients' problems, communication skills, social interaction skills, prior experience with groups, attitudes toward such a group, and motivation to participate can all be assessed.

A second mechanism involves the use of self-assessments. There are many such highly developed and widely used instruments available. The appropriate instrument would be chosen, of course, in view of the problem to be addressed. For example, earlier in this chapter in a section on assessment in micro practice, several such instruments were mentioned, including the Rathus Assertiveness Schedule. Traditional psychological testing is another possible means of providing useful information about potential group members.

Third, those who referred a client to the group may also be able to provide useful information. The client should give permission prior to the worker soliciting information from collateral contacts, although with some mandated group participants, the client's degree of freedom in this regard may be limited.

Selection Criteria for Task Group Membership.   Selection criteria for task groups are similar to those for treatment groups. Toseland and Rivas (1998) suggest a number of variables to consider, including the individual's interests and areas of expertise, homogeneity versus heterogeneity of group members, potential group members' prestige in the community, their relationship with the sponsoring agency, and their diversity and demographic characteristics.

Individual Interests.   Assessing the extent to which a potential member is genuinely interested in the group and the group's task is essential for a group leader. This interest is directly related to motivation—a motivated individual is more likely to cooperate and work in the group. In assessing potential motivation, a worker might ask him- or herself a number of questions. For instance, what interest has the individual expressed in this or similar tasks before? How important will the potential member view the tasks? What direct or indirect benefits might the individual get out of the group (e.g., increased status, enjoyable or profitable interpersonal contacts, or greater visibility)?

Expertise.   Task groups often need a range of competencies or expertise to accomplish their goals. For instance, a task group aimed at establishing a rape crisis center could benefit by inclusion of a physician concerning the medical implications, a police officer regarding legal aspects, and representatives from local women's groups regarding advocacy.

Homogeneity versus Heterogeneity. There are no clear guidelines regarding the extent to which a group should be homogeneous (composed of people with similar characteristics) or heterogeneous (consisting of people with dissimilar characteristics). On the one hand, group members need to be homogeneous enough to communicate and work with each other. On the other, members must be dissimilar enough to provide the necessary range of skills and ideas. The group leader needs to attend to these issues, weigh the pros and cons of various alternatives, and make final decisions regarding what is potentially best for the group and its purpose.

Prestige in the Community. Many times, depending on the group's purpose, gaining outside public support in order to accomplish a task is important. This support can involve inviting important or well-respected community members to join the group. An example involves a task group aimed at developing a stronger sex-education program in a school district. Appropriate members might include experts in sexuality education, local religious leaders, lawyers, physicians, and business people. Sometimes, this task is controversial. Recruiting religious leaders might lend increased public trust to the group.

Likewise, involving respected professionals leads to enhanced credibility. Finally, tapping local businesses for membership can sometimes gain financial assistance.

Relationship with the Sponsoring Agency. Some task groups are formed within an agency. For example, a task group for updating staff policies might best be composed of an agency's own staff members. However, other task groups might be more effective if they involve a cross section of agency and community members.

For instance, consider a task group whose purpose is to reestablish funding of a special treatment program for adolescents with behavioral and emotional problems. The urban county that had previously supported the development and maintenance of the program slashed the program from its budget during a financial crisis. The most effective task group in this case might include agency personnel who had been providing the service, parents of children whose treatment had been cut off, and any other professional, religious, and business community leaders who support the program.

Diversity and Demographic Characteristics. At least three demographic variables are often important

when assembling a task group: age, gender balance within the group, and "sociocultural factors" (Toseland & Rivas, 1998, p. 158).

The worker, of course, needs to use common sense regarding the extent to which such demographic characteristics are important. Sometimes potential members with diverse characteristics will not be available. Other times, such members will not want to join the group.

However, attending to both gender and ethnic/racial/cultural balance within a group is generally important for the worker. Task groups aimed at providing services to women should have adequate representation of women. Likewise, task groups working on an issue involving some ethnic, racial, or cultural group should have adequate representation from the relevant group or groups in their membership. What "adequate" means is at the discretion of the worker's professional judgment.

Gender and sociocultural balance is especially important because of traditional oppressive power imbalances. Members of oppressed groups must be involved in and in control of decisions that affect them.

Recruiting Task Group Members. Another crucial step involves the recruitment process for potential members (Toseland & Rivas, 1998). Task group members can be targeted using the variables described earlier. The worker can personally invite the individual to become a member of the group via a meeting, phone call, or letter. Additionally, the worker can publicize the need for members with certain areas of expertise or interests through fliers, notices in newsletters and newspapers, word of mouth, and even announcements in the radio and television media.

Ongoing Group Assessment. We have established that assessment in groups is an ongoing process. A practitioner is responsible for monitoring the ongoing group climate. One especially relevant area for assessment involves "communication and interaction patterns" (Toseland & Rivas, 1998, p. 215). The practitioner's responsibility as group leader is to monitor the openness of communication and the appropriateness of interactions. This responsibility involves encouraging participation of all group members yet not allowing domination. It also concerns establishing and maintaining group structure so that progress can continuously be made toward accomplishing group goals.

Ongoing Assessment in Treatment Groups. A number of ongoing assessment mechanisms have been developed for treatment groups (Toseland & Rivas, 1998). First, the individual self-rating questionnaires previously mentioned can be administered periodically to monitor progress in specific areas.

Second, clients may keep diaries or logs of daily events concerning the problems addressed in treatment. This approach helps clients focus on their problems and their progress toward solving them.

A third assessment mechanism involves charting the clients' improvement, which is discussed more thoroughly in Chapter 8. Simple charting might involve noting on a chart whenever a specified behavior occurs. For example, a client involved in an assertiveness training group might note on a chart each time she musters up enough confidence to contact another person by phone outside of the group.

Role playing within the group provides a fourth assessment mechanism. The group leader can ask group members to practice what they have learned in the group. The worker may then observe their progress, share perceptions with the clients, and provide suggestions for improvement. After role playing, the worker can also solicit feedback from other group members. This information can be useful to both the role players and the individuals assessing them and articulating their feedback.

Finally, the worker can bring in outside observers to assess treatment groups. Observers can be used either in the group or to report clients' observed progress outside the group. An outsider observing the group, for instance, can note how frequently each group member speaks and for how long.

Another example concerns assessment feedback outside of a socialization group for children. The worker might contact the children's teachers to determine the extent to which they apply what they learn in the group to outside situations.

There are always ethical, reliability, and validity issues to consider when contemplating the use of outside sources of information. To the extent to which they are capable, clients have the right to determine whether you may contact others outside of the group. Clients should be fully informed about the involvement of family members, teachers, and others who will be asked to monitor their behaviors. Clients may be asked to suggest possible outside monitors in keeping with their right to self-determination. The information source must also be capable of providing a valid assessment of the client. People with their own biases or axes to grind may not provide accurate or consistent information.

Assessment in Macro Practice

Micro practice, mezzo practice, and macro practice are all intimately intertwined. Any practice, of course, involves working with other people, necessitating the mastery of micro skills. Macro practice does not involve a focus on individuals or even on groups of individuals. Rather, macro practice focuses on making positive changes that affect large numbers of people. To implement these changes, generalist practitioners must work together with other individuals and groups. Thus, macro practice is both based upon and highly interactive with the other two practice modes. The remainder of this chapter will focus on one example of macro system assessment, namely the assessment of a community's needs.

Assessment of Community Needs

Human service workers often need to confront the environment in which they work. Necessary services may be unavailable. Public bureaucracies may be unresponsive to clients' needs. Archaic policies may significantly interfere with clients' lives.

Thus, the generalist practitioner may need to work to make changes within the community in which clients live. Focusing on community change instead of trying to change the client or something about how the client lives is difficult at first for many students. Nonetheless, combating inequities in the system can be a productive way to initiate changes for large groups of people.

Community needs assessment entails evaluation of "problems, existing resources, potential solutions, and obstacles to problem solving . . . The purpose of needs assessments is to document needs and establish priorities for service" (Barker, 1999, p. 323). Essentially, then, a community needs assessment does just what the name implies—it involves assessment of a community's needs. Northwood (1964) makes an interesting distinction between the concepts of *need* and of *problem:* "A need usually refers to a lack of something, which lack contributes to the discomfort of members of the group. A problem usually refers to the presence of something, which presence contributes to the discomfort of members of the group" (1964, p. 202). In other words, needs involve what is missing, while problems concern negative happenings already in existence.

There is no one best approach to community needs assessment. Each situation and approach is unique. However, there are at least four general variables to take into account when considering a needs assessment—"information . . . resources available

... state of program development ... and community attitudes" (Siegel, Attkisson, & Carson, 1987, p. 72).

Information. Before attempting a needs assessment, knowing what kind of information you are seeking is important. If you are working for a local agency, what information would be most relevant in terms of what that agency will be able to do? What are the best ways of obtaining the most accurate information? How difficult will the information be to obtain?

Resources Available. A second variable to consider involves resources. On the one hand, you will need enough support and financial backing to conduct the assessment. On the other, how desperate is the community to have its needs met? In other words, are the needs extremely grave and meriting immediate attention? Will the potential reward of the assessment merit the time and expense it will take to conduct it?

State of Program Development. Consideration of the current state of the community's resource system is also important. Are there other existing resources in the community that could potentially meet the community's needs at lesser costs? Would a needs assessment provide information useful for changing or improving the current state of the resource provision system?

Community Attitudes. Finally, community attitudes are important to consider prior to conducting a needs assessment. Will relevant community members be willing to provide information and participate in the assessment process? Does the community have the potential to respond positively to the implications of such an assessment? Will you find support in the community to carry out the assessment and implement recommendations? Or will you encounter massive resistance?

An Example of a Community Assessment

In order to work with people in a community and understand their needs, being familiar with the culture, values, priorities, issues, and problems characterizing the community is important. Warren and Warren (1984) propose one process for analyzing a community or neighborhood, which includes the assessment of needs. Their step-by-step assessment guide can be used "to capture the distinctive interwoven helping patterns—the networks crisscrossing the neighborhood fabric" that make each neighborhood or community unique (1984, p. 27). First, a five-step process of performing a needs assessment will be explained. A format for gathering information is provided in Highlight 5.5.

Step 1: Exploring the Nature of the Neighborhood. The first step in the investigatory process involves finding out how people in the neighborhood function. Before you *do* anything, you need enough background information to know *what* you are doing. How do people in the neighborhood or community solve their problems? What workable resources are available? Answers to these questions begin to provide you with information about the community's strengths and weaknesses. They can also help you determine the community's needs.

Local centers of government are good places to get information during this phase of your community assessment. A city hall, local courthouse, branch of social services, the chamber of commerce, and even a library all have useful information. There might be pamphlets available about the community. Or notices about community events and services might be posted to inform the public (and you) about what generally goes on within the community.

Getting maps can be tremendously helpful because they can increase your confidence and agility in getting around the community. Maps also can give you information about how the community you are assessing fits in with surrounding communities or neighborhoods.

Telephone books also provide useful information. Not only can you find out where government offices are but you can also find and explore the types of businesses in the community, the health care services available, and such other resources as churches and activity centers.

Newspapers provide a lot of information. Advertisements reflect what businesses are available and what appears to be significant in the local culture. News items reflect what the community feels is important. For instance, consider the fact that local cow prices are regularly posted on the front page of the small rural paper, the *Benjamin Key*. These postings imply that many community residents are rural farmers interested in this type of news.

Even if your job is oriented more toward micro and mezzo levels of social work practice, getting to know your clients' community is significant. Getting information and thinking about a community can prepare you much more effectively for working with its people.

HIGHLIGHT 5.5

A Format for Analyzing a Community or Neighborhood

The following is a prescribed format for analyzing a community. It addresses community characteristics and community life. Additionally, it assesses the public welfare and social service system available in the community. Suggestions for assessing a community have already been provided. Now we will provide a format for the specific types of questions to ask and how to organize that information.

The questions asked in the various sections are not exhaustive nor all of equal importance. They are suggested as beginnings in a search for change. Some of them may not be useful or may not fit your particular local government. However, most can be adapted. Some may uncover issues that require more careful study than this format allows.

One other thing to remember is that a community is not an isolated entity. Rather, it is part of a much larger social, legal, and political system. What is decided at the national, state, and even county levels can impact upon a community's functioning. The following format directs attention only to the community itself. It will at least, however, give you a jumping-off point for beginning to understand your community.

A. COMMUNITY CHARACTERISTICS

1. **Ethnic/Racial Configuration**
   a. What are the major population characteristics (e.g., what percentage is white, African American, Asian American, American Indian, or Hispanic)?
   b. What are the principal ethnic and religious groups?
   c. What is the age composition?
   d. How do the population characteristics compare to state and national demographics?

2. **Economic Factors**
   a. What are the principal economic characteristics of the community?
   b. How are most of the people employed?
   c. What are the major industries?
   d. What other sources of wealth are there?
   e. Have there been recent changes in the economic life of the community (e.g., industries moving in or out of the area or major expansions or cut-backs)?

3. **Unemployment**
   a. How does the unemployment rate compare with state and national rates?
   b. What variables tend to characterize the unemployed population (e.g., is it largely African American, Hispanic, female, or within the 18- to 22-year-old age range)?
   c. Have there been recent changes in this unemployment rate?
   d. If so, to what can these changes be attributed?
   e. Are there sections of the community where the rate is appreciably higher than the average?

4. **Income Levels**
   a. How does the median or per capita income compare to state and national averages?
   b. Is the average skewed because of large numbers of wealthy people?
   c. Are there large numbers of poor people in the community?

5. **Housing Patterns**
   a. What are the housing patterns within the community?
   b. What percentage of residential property is high, moderate, or low cost?
   c. What is the condition of the community's housing (e.g., mostly new, well-kept and maintained, or deteriorating)?
   d. What pattern characterizes the range of rents in the community?
   e. How available is moderate and low-cost housing?
   f. Is the community dependent on a large metropolitan area for employment or housing?

B. COMMUNITY LIFE

1. **Communication and Interaction**
   a. How many newspapers are there?
   b. If there is more than one, are they independently owned?
   c. How many radio and television stations are there?
   d. Are radio and/or television stations owned by newspapers?
   e. Is community news carried on a regular basis in a metropolitan newspaper?
   f. What are the principal out-of-town media influences?

g. How does one learn about local governmental activities, hearings, meetings, or cultural activities?

2. Social Services

a. What private social service agencies exist in the community?

b. Are there specific organized groups aimed at improving social services within the community?

c. What types of fund-raising exist in the community and why?

3. Civic and Service Organizations

a. What are principal community-wide civic and service organizations?

b. Are there fraternal groups?

c. Which labor and business organizations operate in the community?

d. Are there cultural groups?

e. Do such groups work together on community-wide problems?

f. Are such coalitions ad hoc groups or groups of longer standing?

g. Which groups are more likely to be aligned and on what kinds of issues?

h. Are there neighborhood groups?

i. If so, around what are they organized—cultural, school, political, or other interests?

C. AVAILABLE SOCIAL SERVICES

1. Administration

a. What governmental agencies are involved in operating the public welfare/social services in the community?

b. What employees are engaged in public welfare/social service activities?

c. How are these employees selected?

d. What qualifications are required?

2. Interagency Cooperation

a. What cooperative programs, if any, exist among public welfare agencies and the juvenile court, probation officers, school, day care centers, nursing homes, public health services, and other agencies?

b. What cooperation, if any, exists between public and private social service agencies?

c. Is there regular exchange of information?

d. Is there any joint planning going on?

3. Noninstitutional Care

a. What agency or agencies administer services for abandoned children?

b. Are foster homes used?

c. What is the rate of pay to foster homes?

d. How are such foster homes chosen?

e. How are such homes supervised?

f. What money is available for people in need?

g. What general assistance is available?

h. What is the average amount available for each person?

i. What is the caseload per worker for income maintenance and social service workers?

j. Are there efforts being made to help parents find jobs?

k. If so, what kind of efforts?

l. Are there adequate day care services?

m. Is there an adoption service?

4. Other Public Assistance Programs

a. What other assistance programs exist (e.g., temporary assistance, special and corrective needs, exceptional needs such as bus fares and help during emergencies, temporary housing, employment services, legal services, or others)?

b. What money is available for such assistance?

c. From what sources is it available?

d. How do individuals apply for such assistance?

e. How is information about such special assistance made available to the people?

D. SUMMARY

a. In one to two paragraphs, summarize your major perceptions about this community.

Source: Most of this format for analyzing a community or neighborhood was adapted from *Know Your Community* (1972), published by the League of Women Voters of the United States. Reprinted by permission of the League of Women Voters of the United States, Washington, DC.

Step 2: Getting to Know the Area and Its Residents. Getting a general impression of the community is probably the most useful thing to do at this point. Drive around the area and pay attention to what it is like. What are the buildings like? Are they well kept or in disrepair? Do some buildings look abandoned? Where do people seem to congregate? What businesses characterize the community? What are your general impressions of the community as a whole?

As you continue to explore, establish the community's boundaries in your own mind. What areas in the community will be your chief concern? Are there geographical boundaries that characterize the community? For instance, is there a main street on which community members focus their attention? Or do rivers, valleys, or industrial sections cut the community in half or in sections?

Step 3: Identify the Community's Strengths.
We have already established that assessing strengths is just as important as evaluating problems or needs. Healthy businesses, homes kept in good repair, social clubs and organizations (e.g., Boy Scouts, bowling teams, or the Polish Nationalist Society), churches, and even friendly interaction with community residents all contribute to the community's strengths.

Step 4: Talk to People in the Community.
Identifying major community figures is critical. Talking with these people can give you substantial insight into the fabric and values of the community.

Warren and Warren emphasize that the elementary school principal is "a MUST" (1984, p. 32). The person in this position is in regular contact with the core of community residents. The principal must work integrally with community families and understand their issues. You can obtain information about the economic situation, types of recreation people generally enjoy, religious affiliations, racial tensions, and other concerns.

Other individuals to contact include a range of community leaders. You should not try to contact every leader. Rather identify those whom you feel might have information most relevant for your needs. These might include local ministers and priests, such public officials as city or county council members, the town board chairperson or the mayor, presidents of clubs and organizations (for instance, the Kiwanis club or the Parent/Teacher Association), the heads of the homeowners' associations or Neighborhood Watch groups, prominent business people, and other human service practitioners in the area.

Sometimes, there are extremely vocal community members whom others feel complain all the time. Talking to these people can be useful in targeting some of the community's hot spots. Oftentimes, these people are relatively easy to talk to because they want to have their gripes heard.

Obtaining information about a broad cross section of the community is important. This information includes the range of age groups represented in the community. As we know, people's concerns vary according to their life's developmental stage. Additionally, finding out about all the primary ethnic and racial groups within the community is critical. You need to know about values and customs. You also need to know about conflicts between groups in order to examine how the community really functions.

Interviewing Persons in the Community. Warren and Warren (1984) make at least seven specific suggestions for things to say during your interviews with key community people. First, take time for "chit chat" (1984, p. 34). The generalist practitioner utilizes micro practice skills even when pursuing a macro practice objective. In other words, establishing rapport with any new person you're interviewing is important. Warm, friendly, informal small talk about the weather, the place you are meeting, or the neighborhood itself is usually appropriate.

A second suggestion is to provide your interviewee with a clear definition of your purpose. Why are you there? Why should he or she take the time to talk to you? Your purpose might be to familiarize yourself with the clients' community life because you have started a new job and will be working with them. Likewise, it might be that you are interested in initiating some new services within the community and would like to find out how to begin.

The third interviewing suggestion involves clearly explaining to your interviewee what community of people or neighborhood you are interested in. Is it a public school district (especially, if you are talking to a school principal)? Or, is it a geographical neighborhood delineated by specific streets? Or is it an entire town? Regardless, avoiding misunderstandings and inaccuracies is important for you and your interviewee.

A fourth suggestion for interviewing involves getting "leads" from your interviewee (Warren & Warren, 1984, p. 34). Who might better be aware of other people most involved in and knowledgeable about the community than those who are already integrally involved with that community? Get names, telephone numbers, and addresses, if available. Make decisions about who might be most helpful to you and follow through on contacting them.

The fifth suggestion involves the art of interviewing. Your micro practice skills will come in handy here. You want your interviewees to feel comfortable with you, open up to you, and share what they know about the community. Your intent is to find out information about a community, not to fill in blanks on an established questionnaire. Therefore, you want to give your interviewee opportunities to talk and raise new topics. Providing some relevant information about yourself can enhance the interviewees' comfort with the interview. It can also convey to the interviewees that such initiation of their own thoughts, ideas, and other topics is appropriate.

A sixth suggestion for interviewing concerns getting specific information you need. You might "propose a hypothetical situation" (Warren & Warren, 1984, p. 35). For example, you might ask, "What if I contacted the person you suggested? Do you think she would be willing to take time and give me some information?" In another case, you might say, "I'm thinking about plans for the future. What if I initiated the program we were talking about? How cooperative do you think the community would be?"

The seventh suggestion involves closure of the interview. Becoming goal oriented and pressing methodically for the information you need is easy. However, encouraging your interviewee to share feelings about the information already given or about the interview itself is also important. You might simply ask if there is anything the person would like to add. In other words, make sure the interviewee has the opportunity to share opinions and to conclude the interview.

Step 5: Gather Other Information.   Sometimes, the information you will need is not available locally. For example, what if you are interested in gathering comparative information about other communities or about programs that have been tried elsewhere that might work in your community? Much of this information can be found in databases, public libraries, and other venues. One easy way to gather this information is through the Internet. Potential information sources include the Welfare Information Network (WIN), which provides access to more than 400 organizations and over 16,000 electronic sources. The WIN gathers information regularly on other Websites and provides data on policy issues, new state and local social programs, caseloads, characteristics of clients, and program designs. It also has available material on managing programs, assessment, and information on potential grants. Such information is helpful for macro assessment and also assists in planning, a topic addressed more thoroughly in the next chapter. The Network's online address is http://www.welfareinfo.org.

Another ready source with over 5000 pages of relevant information is The Community Tool Box at http://ctb.ukans.edu. This site contains information on topics such as community organization and change, developing a community leadership corps, and increasing access for people with disabilities.

Over time, you will learn to use these resources and to locate links to other sources that will expand your skills at assessment, planning, intervention, and evaluation.

Assessment, Client Empowerment, and Strengths

It is sometimes easy to focus on gathering information for an assessment and lose sight of the purpose of this step in the planned change process. The information we gain is attained for the sole purpose of our collaborative work to help client systems resolve problems, expand their capacities, and use available resources more effectively. Assessment that focuses solely on the shortcomings of clients ignores their strengths and ability to participate fully in the change process. Client systems have a right and an obligation to be active partners in the change process. Similarly, we must continue to expect as much from our clients as from ourselves. We empower clients when we help them develop the ability to solve their own crises. Whether the client system is an individual, family, group, organization, or community, it is essential that we use the assessment process to recognize and build on client strengths and empower them to participate actively in the change effort.

Info Trac College Edition

This chapter discussed critical activities and skills needed for engagement as well as the goals involved in assessment in generalist practice. It reviewed steps in the engagement and assessment process while looking at some commonly used micro assessment mechanisms. Family and group assessment were also covered. Finally, the chapter considered assessment approaches appropriate for neighborhoods and communities. For more information on some of these topics, please use the following search terms:

eye contact
strengths
interpersonal conflict
role performance
psychological problems
behavioral problems
empowerment
spirituality
self-assessments
assessment instruments

DSM
family assessment
home visits

On the Internet

Because of the very dynamic nature of the Web, URLs are subject to change. Therefore, be sure to check out the companion Website for this book at http://www.humanservices.wadsworth.com, where links will be updated periodically.

newfederalism.urban.org
www.smartdraw.com
www.vcu.edu
wchd.neobright.net

CHAPTER 6
Planning in Generalist Practice

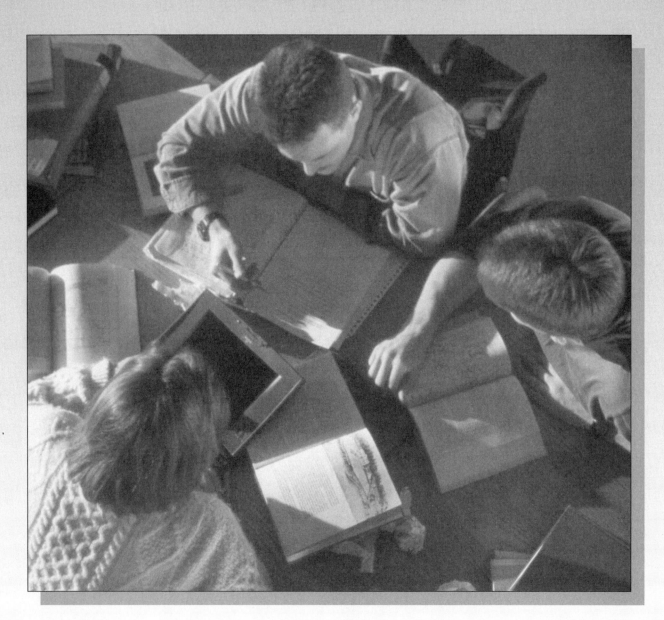

How would you plan to work with this family?

Reggie, age 6, has cerebral palsy, a "disability resulting from damage to the brain before, during, or shortly after birth," resulting in "muscular incoordination and speech disturbances" (*Merriam Webster's Collegiate Dictionary*, 1994). Reggie cannot walk and has difficulty controlling his hands. He lives with both parents and three sisters. His family is poor, despite the fact that his father works two minimum-wage jobs. His mother is unable to work outside of the home because of the extensive care her children, especially Reggie, need.

Here is one way to plan what to do:

1. *Work closely with Reggie and his parents.* They must believe in and be committed to the plan for it to succeed.
2. *Prioritize the problems.* Together with Reggie's parents, you determine that Reggie's physical disability is the top priority. Other prioritized problems and needs include respectively: inadequate finances; father's low skill level; mother's inability to work outside the home; the need for day care; and poor housing.
3. *Translate the problems into needs.* Work with the top priority problem first, Reggie's disability. Reggie needs a thorough evaluation to determine the extent of his disability. Depending on the findings, he may need such services as physical therapy, speech therapy, occupational therapy, or special education.
4. *Evaluate the level of the intervention (micro, mezzo, or macro).* Will you initially plan to pursue a micro, mezzo, or macro approach to intervention? At this point, you select a micro intervention. You know that evaluation and therapeutic services are available. You also know that Reggie's family will qualify for financial aid to receive these services because of its

low income level. Thus, you determine you do not need to address problems in agency policies or the social services system's delivery of services (some potential macro approaches). Reggie and his needs become the focus of attention right now. Mezzo intervention such as family counseling or support groups might be future options, but you determine they are inappropriate at this point.

5. *Establish goals.* You and the family decide that your goal will be to have Reggie's capabilities thoroughly evaluated so that you will know what services he needs.

6. *Specify objectives.* You will schedule an evaluation through your agency.

7. *Formalize a contract.* You and Reggie's parents establish a verbal contract. You will set up the evaluation process within the next week and contact the family about the details. They are committed to bringing Reggie in as soon as the evaluation can be scheduled.

 ## Introduction

Reggie and his family portray one way that, as a generalist practitioner, you might formulate a plan for intervention. This chapter will concentrate on eight basic steps that form the core of planning in the generalist intervention model. Planning involves establishing goals, specifying how such goals will be achieved, and selecting the most appropriate courses of action.

In the planned change process, planning immediately follows assessment and precedes the actual intervention. Your plan is based on your assessment of the client's situation, strengths, problems, and needs. Subsequently, your plan serves to guide how you proceed to help your client.

Specifically, this chapter will:

- examine the eight-step planning process;
- demonstrate how each of these steps can be applied in generalist practice;
- employ a generalist perspective that integrates a micro, mezzo, and macro approach to human service practice;

- discuss how goals and objectives are established and demonstrate the importance of specificity;
- describe how to formulate contracts using various formats;
- discuss special aspects of planning involved in mezzo practice;
- examine program development and relate it to planning in macro practice.

 ## Steps in the Planning Process

The eight steps in the planning process are working with your client(s), prioritizing problems, translating problems into needs, evaluating the level of intervention (micro, mezzo, or macro), establishing goals, specifying objectives, setting action steps, and formulating a contract. These steps are illustrated in Figure 6.1.

Step 1: Work with Your Client(s)

The importance of involving the client in every part of the intervention process cannot be overemphasized.

Figure 6.1   *Planning in the Generalist Intervention Model*

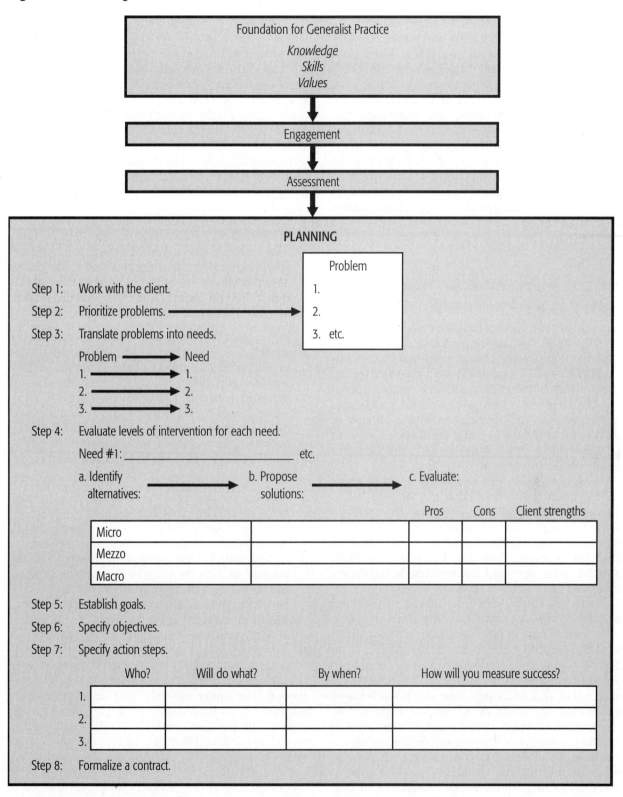

Jones and Biesecker stress, "Clients should participate in the assessment and development of Goal Plans as much as possible. Plan *with* the person, not *at* or *for* him or her" (1980, p. 7). This suggestion is pretty straightforward. However, saying this is easier than doing it. Especially with busy caseloads and numerous distractions, pressuring clients to accept the plans *you* would like them to make without soliciting adequate input from them is easy. Talking with clients and clarifying their needs and wishes takes time. Be courteous to your clients and demonstrate that you are interested in what they have to say. If clients do not feel that they are included and, indeed, *own* the plan themselves, they will probably not be motivated to cooperate. Remember, empowering clients means enhancing their right to self-determination.

Step 2: Prioritize Problems—Which Problem Should You Work on First?

Many clients will have multiple problems on multiple levels. In the last chapter, we defined nine categories of problems: interpersonal conflict, dissatisfaction in social relations, problems with formal organizations, difficulties in role performance, problems in social transition, psychological and behavioral problems, inadequate resources, problems in decision making, and cultural conflicts. In view of the numerous kinds of problems, how can you choose which one to work on?

The first thing to do is to focus on only those problems that fulfill three criteria (Northen, 1987). First, the client must recognize that the problem exists. You may or may not agree with your client about where the problem stands in a prioritized list of all the problems involved. However, the client should at least agree that the problem is significant enough to merit both of your attention.

Clients who deny problems or fail to see their importance will not want to waste time on them. For instance, a client who denies his alcohol addiction will probably refuse to discuss the subject in an interview with you. However, you may be able to identify related problems, such as child abuse (while drinking) or lack of money (due to job loss because of the drinking), which are significant to the client.

A second criterion for addressing a problem is that the problem should be clearly defined in understandable terms. You and your client both need to know exactly what you are talking about in order to find a satisfactory solution. The importance of clarity and specificity in goal setting is an ongoing theme throughout this chapter.

A third criterion is that it be realistically possible that you and your client will be able to do something about the problem. Fixating on hopeless problems is a waste of time for you and your client. For example, dwelling on the problem of a spouse who left home three years ago and has not been heard from since is probably useless. Discussing problematic aspects of your client's situation as it stands right now might better merit your time. For instance, she might currently be very concerned about child care, finances, and housing.

Reid and Epstein (1972) make several suggestions regarding how to decide which problem to work on (the "target problem"):

1. *Identify with the client the range of problems that are most significant to the client.* This list may be long or short. The important thing is to explore with clients all of their concerns. You will probably perceive some of the problems as being much less significant than others. Include them anyway, because you will address them later.

2. *Restate each problem using "explicit behavioral terms"* (p. 58). In other words, the precise nature of the problem should be clear in your mind. Additionally, the problem statement should include descriptions of behaviors that will later allow you to measure your progress and determine when you have succeeded in solving the problem. We will discuss the importance of behavioral specificity in more depth later in the chapter.

3. *Prioritize the problems in order of their importance to the client.* This prioritization alerts you to which problem you should address first, second, and so on. For example, a client may be concerned with the following problems in order of priority: paying the rent, her husband's drinking, her child's truancy, and her overweight condition, which is resulting in a number of health problems. Paying the rent, then, is probably the problem you should address first.

Once again, this process is not as easy as it sounds. Frequently, how you rank the client's problems will be quite different than how your client ranks them. In such cases, it is up to you to further explore the problems with clients. You will need to establish a list of priorities satisfactory to both of you. Once again, this process involves both good communication skills and making judgments. Reid relates a typical scenario when practitioner and client are not in complete agreement regarding problem priority:

The focus is on what the client wants and not on what the practitioner thinks the client may need. The practitioner may point out, however, potential difficulties the client has not acknowledged or the consequences that may result if these difficulties are allowed to go unaddressed. In other words, the target problem is not necessarily defined by what clients say they want initially, but rather by what they want after a process of deliberation to which the practitioner contributes his or her own knowledge and point of view. As a result, clients may alter their conception of their problem or . . . may realize they do have difficulties they may wish to work on. (Reid, 1987, p. 758)

4. *Establish an initial agreement with the client regarding the problem you will attend to first.* This problem needs to be one in which the client is interested. It should be one that you determine can be solved, even if it is not the very first one on your list. For instance, take a client who states the problem most critical to her is finding a job. She indicates her second most critical problem is that her landlord has turned off her heat in the middle of an icy winter. After exploring the matter, you determine that finding her a job is a more complicated task than it initially might seem. Your client is unskilled, has no high school diploma, and is responsible for several small children. Issues such as job training, transportation, and day care will require more effort to resolve.

   However, you see the heat (or lack thereof) problem as being more amenable to intervention than the unemployment problem. For one thing, for landlords to turn the heat off in apartment rentals in your state during winter is illegal. Therefore, calls to the landlord and, perhaps, the appropriate authorities have a good potential for resolving this problem. You can help your client explore potential solutions for both problems. Hopefully, you can come to an agreement to work on a problem that you feel can be solved in a relatively short period of time. Sometimes you determine with the client that more than one problem can be addressed at the same time. For instance, consider the client mentioned previously. Her third problem might be that she does not have enough money to feed her children. You think she qualifies for assistance that she currently is not receiving. You can proceed to investigate the possibility of getting her these resources at approximately the same time you are working on the heat problem.

Step 3: Translate Problems into Needs

Problems, of course, involve any source of perplexity or distress. Many times they are initiated by lack of resources. Clients will come to you because they have problems they need to solve. Helping them accomplish that is your job.

Needs, on the other hand, are "physical, psychological, economic, cultural, and social requirements for survival, well-being, and fulfillment" (Barker, 1999, p. 333). To figure out what to do, you must translate your clients' problems into their needs.

Take, for instance, the lack of adequate resources—not having enough money. Dwelling on the problem does not help you figure out what to do about it. However, if you translate the problem into what the client *needs to solve it,* you can formulate ideas about what to do. The problem of lack of money means that the client *needs* better access to resources. The next logical step, then, is to ask yourself the question, "Where might such resources be acquired?" Possible sources include public assistance, food stamps, paid employment, and charitable organizations, among many other resources. These ideas orient your thinking to possible goals for the client and strategies for achieving these goals. For example, you might then discuss with your client the possibility of applying for assistance or seeking job training. Figure 6.2 illustrates a variety of identified problems and their translation into related needs.

Problems, needs, and goals are all interrelated. Your goal will be to satisfy the need causing the problem. Simply translating problems into needs orients you toward establishing goals. It turns your thoughts from focusing on what is wrong to concentrating on how what is wrong can be remedied. Your major goal is usually to satisfy your client's needs.

Step 4: Evaluate Levels of Intervention— Selecting a Strategy

Together with your client, you need to identify and assess various strategies for achieving the major goals related to the specified problems. A "strategy is an overall approach to change in the situation" (Johnson, 1998, p. 300). In other words, your strategy is the route you and your clients will take to meet their needs. You can develop a strategy by doing the following:

1. Focus on the need you have selected with your client to work on first.

Figure 6.2 *Examples of Related Needs Translated from Identified Problems*

Identified Problems	Related Needs
Alcohol addiction	Ongoing sobriety
Child abuse	Stop abuse, emotional control, child-management techniques
Unemployment	Employment
Homelessness	Place to live
Depression	Treatment for relief of depression
Grief at death of loved one	Grief management
Misbehavior of children	Improved parental control of children, child-management techniques
Poor performance in school	Improved school performance, motivation, family stability
Compulsive stealing	Treatment for compulsivity, access to adequate resources
Alzheimer's disease and loss of control	Placement in supportive setting

2. Review the need and consider identifying micro, mezzo, and macro alternative strategies to arrive at a solution.
3. Emphasize your client's strengths when establishing strategies.
4. Evaluate the pros and cons of each strategy you have considered with your client.
5. Select and pursue the strategy that appears to be most efficient and effective.

First, you and your client need to identify and review potential strategies that may involve micro, mezzo, or macro aspects of practice. You want to decide what your "unit of attention" will be; the unit of attention is "the system being focused upon" as a target of change (Johnson, 1998, p. 299). You should not just focus on the micro aspects of the client's problem situation, namely what you and your client can do yourselves on your client's behalf. Perhaps your client's family needs to become involved. This inclusion, of course, involves a mezzo approach to intervention. Or perhaps your client could benefit from a treatment or self-help group. For instance, a client with a gambling addiction might benefit from involvement in Gamblers Anonymous, a national self-help organization (similar to Alcoholics Anonymous) for people with gambling problems.

Instead of micro or mezzo approaches, strategies involving macro skills might provide the most appropriate route for solving a particular problem. For instance, take a Hispanic client, Jose Quervo, whose young children have not been allowed to enter a neighborhood school, despite the fact that the family has lived in that school's district for over a year. You feel that this is blatant discrimination on the basis of culture and race. You might advocate with the school system on your client's behalf. Or you might determine that educating school board members about the problem and collaborating with them to change policies might be more effective. You might even decide that legal confrontation is necessary to change the school system's policies.

In some cases, more than one strategy may be needed to attain a particular goal. In the case of the Quervo family, you and Mr. Quervo might conclude that he and his spouse could benefit from English lessons. They speak just enough English "to get along." They indicated that they had difficulty expressing themselves adequately. Lessons could provide them with an enhanced ability to negotiate the difficult school system themselves. Note that this tactic would add a micro strategy (namely, the clients learning English) to the macro strategy already discussed (i.e., changing the school system's policy), although both are directed at the same goal. The goal, of course, is for the Quervo children to attain education.

There will probably be many potential strategies possible to achieve any particular goal. Use your professional judgment, expertise, and creativity to formulate the best strategy.

Sometimes brainstorming with clients helps generate ideas. Brainstorming is "the creative process of mutually focusing efforts on generating a broad range of possible options from which clients can choose" (Hepworth et al., 1997, p. 374). However, one should note that practitioners probably provide most of the resource information and technical help; clients would not need your help in the first place if they had all the answers.

Strengths

Emphasizing and incorporating client strengths when establishing strategies is useful in several ways. First, strengths provide blocks upon which to build intervention plans. Instead of focusing on problems, needs, and deficits, strengths provide you with something positive to empower clients. Second, emphasizing clients' strengths allows you to give your clients positive feedback. You can talk about their strengths with them and build up their confidence. Emphasizing strengths can be used to convey your respect to clients. Third, incorporating clients' strengths into strategies allows you to work with and think about something concrete. To nonprofessionals, the intervention process (along with the professional jargon and fancy words involved) can appear vague and confusing. Highlight 6.1 elaborates upon strength areas you can explore with clients.

The following example illustrates how strengths can be incorporated into planned strategies. Harley is a homeless Vietnam veteran with posttraumatic stress disorder. This disorder involves anxiety following a frightening or stressful event such as military combat, rape, or a natural disaster. Symptoms include recurring dreams, loss of sleep and concentration, and loss of feelings. Harley manifests virtually all of these symptoms. He has not held down a job or even lived in the same residence for more than a month since the war ended. He has serious problems.

As a human services professional, how can you help Harley? First, translate his problems into needs. He needs therapy to deal with his stress disorder, emotional support from family and/or friends, a place to live, and a job. Because his disorder affects virtually every aspect of his life, you may easily be overwhelmed by his situation. However, elaborating upon his strengths provides inklings about what to do.

 HIGHLIGHT 6.1

Potential Areas of Clients' Strengths

Jones and Biesecker (1980, pp. 48–49) cite the following nine categories you might explore with clients to identify and elaborate upon their strengths. Under each category is a series of questions. These are the types of questions you might consider asking your own clients:

1. *Special interests and activities.* Do you have special interests on which you would like to spend time? What skills and talents do you feel you have? Do you belong to any organizations or groups? If not, have you in the past? What types of activities do you participate in that make you feel good?
2. *Family and friends.* With which family members are you particularly close? Whom can you call on for support? Whom do you feel comfortable enough with to confide in? Do you have any close friends? Are you friends with any of your neighbors?
3. *Religion and values.* Is religion important and meaningful to you? If so, with what creed or denomination are you involved? Do you have a minister or priest you feel comfortable in going to for support or guidance? What values in life are especially

important to you? Honesty? Being close to others? Supporting your children? Being dependable?

4. *Occupation and education.* What educational level have you achieved? What work experience and marketable skills do you have?
5. *Reaction to professional services.* What, if any, human services have you been involved with that you found helpful? How have you benefited from these services? Were there any particular professionals whom you especially liked or found exceptionally helpful?
6. *Emotional and mental health.* What things make you the happiest? During what times do you feel the strongest and most capable? What types of events or happenings help improve your mood? How do you usually go about making decisions or solving your problems?
7. *Physical condition.* What kinds of physical activities do you like most? What kinds of physical activity make you feel good? Which aspects of your health are especially good?
8. *Support system.* Where does most of your income come from? Do you have other assets you can rely on in needy times? Whom can you depend on to help you when you need it?
9. *Other.* What strengths do you have other than the ones we have already covered?

Harley's strengths include: his status as a veteran (allowing him free access to Veterans' Administration [VA] hospitals and facilities), good physical health, a high school diploma, and an extremely supportive and concerned family. To figure out strategies to meet his needs (your ultimate goal), take his strengths and resources into consideration.

First, Harley can be referred to the VA hospital for evaluation and therapy. The VA also has a program that provides temporary housing for veterans suffering from similar disorders. His family can be involved in his treatment to provide support in his continuation of it. His good physical health and high school diploma indicate that he is qualified for a number of blue-collar, physically oriented jobs. A related strength, we find out, is that when he was able to get and hold a job for a few weeks, it was usually in construction. He indicates that this kind of work is what he most enjoys when he is in better control of his disorder. Thus, perhaps a long-term goal is to involve him in this kind of work when he is ready.

Pros and Cons

In the process of planning strategies, you need to evaluate the pros and cons of each. You and your client will not be able to do everything at once. You will probably need to determine what the most efficient and potentially effective strategies would be. Remember the Quervo family. Major problems included enrolling their children in school and poor English-speaking skills. Consider the pros and cons of two of the possible strategies identified, as discussed below.

Macro Strategy 1. Advocate with the school system on behalf of your clients.

Pros

- The school system cannot legally deny children access on the basis of language or race, so the legal system is on the family's side. The system, therefore, might respond to additional pressure from the worker.
- The worker knows the school's vice principal and two school board members. The school board, of course, has the greatest authority over what goes on in the school system. The worker feels there is good potential here to exercise influence in order to change the school's prior decision and overall policy.

Cons

- The school's principal and a number of other school board members are renowned for their conservative approach to changing policy. Thus, they might balk at additional pressure.
- Advocacy takes a lot of time. The worker's caseload is large, and there are numerous crises to attend to.
- The advocacy process is vague. The worker would need to sit down and develop a well-specified plan for whom to contact and how.
- The children might not be accepted into school for an inordinate period of time. Thus, their education could be seriously impeded.

Micro Strategy 2. Enroll parents in English classes so they may better advocate for themselves.

Pros

- This would enhance the Quervos' empowerment, ability to communicate, and prowess to fight for their own rights.
- The difficulties they experienced in dealing with a primarily English-speaking community would be decreased.

Cons

- No low-cost English classes are readily available in their area.
- Such classes are time consuming and require high motivation to continue with them over a substantial period of time.
- Although such education may be of some use to the Quervos in the long run, its usefulness in the current problem is questionable.
- There is some debate, especially in certain areas of the country with large Hispanic populations, whether English must be the primary language. Is it fair or right to force English upon people already adept in Spanish?

The pros and cons noted in the above two examples of strategies are arbitrary. That is, there are many other approaches for you to consider. However, these examples are intended to convey the idea of what identifying, struggling with, and finally deciding on an actual course of action in real practice situations are like.

Step 5: Establish Goals

Hepworth and colleagues (1997) cite five basic purposes for establishing goals. First, specifying goals guarantees that worker and clients concur regarding what they want to pursue. Second, goals "provide direction and continuity in the helping process and prevent needless wandering" (p. 344). Third, goals aid in the identification, formulation, and evaluation of relevant strategies to proceed with the intervention. Fourth, they help practitioners observe and appraise the progress being made in the intervention. Finally, goals "serve as outcome criteria in evaluating the effectiveness of specific interventions and of the helping process" (p. 344).

In summary, goals are established to clarify the purpose of an intervention. A clearly stated goal allows you to determine whether your intervention has been successful. Goals are necessary whether your intervention strategy involves micro, mezzo, or macro practice. In micro practice, goals guide your work with individual clients. Mezzo practice intervention may require goals involving each individual member and the entire group as a whole. Finally, in macro practice, a generalist practitioner might use goal-setting to help a community or organization target what it wants to accomplish and how it will go about doing this.

Human services professionals set goals to help a client system identify and specify what it wants to achieve within the worker/client relationship. Worker and client must be moving in the same direction. They must clearly understand what they are trying to accomplish. Examples of goals include:

- Get landlord to fix leaking plumbing.
- Improve parents' child behavior management skills.
- Participate in support group for spouses of alcoholics for six months.
- Change agency policy to include home visits for work with families.
- Develop program for rural homeless children.

Thus, your goal is a broad statement of what you and your clients want to achieve.

Step 6: Specify Objectives

Goals are usually so broadly stated that identifying how they will be achieved is virtually impossible. For instance, take the goal "get landlord to fix leaking plumbing." The goal statement gives no indication of how the goal can be accomplished. Will the client picket the landlord's office to demand attention? Will you call the Health Department to complain and demand that the landlord comply with housing

codes to maintain plumbing in good working condition? Will the landlord suddenly see the error of his ways and get the pipes fixed?

Both you and your client know what needs to get done. The client needs plumbing that works adequately. The next step, then, is to break that goal down into smaller objectives.

Objectives are behaviorally specific regarding what is to be achieved and how success will be measured. For example, take the goal "get client a job paying at least $300 a week." To attain this goal, you and the client need to set objectives to help move her toward this end. If she has not completed high school, an objective might be to gain a high school equivalency certificate. A second objective might be to then complete six months of job-skill training at a technical school.

Objectives can be further broken down. For example, the client would need to apply for admission to the job-skill program and seek financial aid to pay for her schooling. Each is a step on the way to the objective of completing the job training program and the goal of a job paying at least $300 per week. Recall that goals and objectives exist to keep you and your client on track.

Objectives Should Be Measurable

How will you know whether the goal has been achieved? For example, take an impoverished, single parent client with three small children. Her *problem* is poverty. She *needs* money. Her *goal* is to get enough financial assistance to supply her family with food, shelter, and clothing. You and your client establish three specific *objectives* for helping her solve her problem. They include obtaining financial help from the local welfare office, becoming involved in a housing program,[1] and receiving food stamps.[2] Have your objectives been met when she

---

1. *Housing programs* are "publicly funded and monitored programs designed to provide suitable homes, especially for those unable to find or pay for homes themselves. In the United States most of these programs are administered by the Department of Housing and Urban Development (DHUD). These programs include low-rent public housing, rent-subsidies, home ownership assistance" among others (Barker, 1999, p. 222).
2. "The food stamp program, which was created to supplement the food-buying power of low-income people, is the nation's response to its hunger problem. Monthly benefits in the form of coupons used to purchase food are entirely federally financed. . . . Eligibility for the program is restricted to households that meet income, resource, and work requirements prescribed by law" (Wells, 1987, p. 628).

begins receiving financial assistance and food stamps but remains on a long waiting list for housing assistance? Or have your objectives been met when she receives $237 a month in financial assistance, $90 a month in food stamps, and $100 in rent subsidy, even if this total amount is inadequate for her to survive?

Instead, you could specify a more measurable objective. For example, you could establish the maximum amount she could possibly receive for each of these sources. If the $427 is the maximum she is allowed to receive under current guidelines and you have specified that as your objective, then you have succeeded in reaching it. You may need to set another objective to gain additional resources so that she can feed and house her children adequately.

Specifying goals and objectives, in addition to measuring their success, will be addressed more thoroughly later in the chapter. For example, setting objectives in micro practice involves determination of the specific performance required (what is the basic objective you're trying to achieve?), the conditions under which this objective can be accomplished, and the standards by which its success can be measured. We will also address goals and objectives within the contexts of micro, mezzo, and macro practice. Emphasis will be placed on the importance of establishing clear, specific, and measurable statements regardless of your practice area.

Sometimes Goals and Objectives Are Confusing

Sometimes the two terms become confusing because many people use goals and objectives synonymously. For our purposes, an objective should *always* be clear, specific, and measurable. A goal is often too complex to be measurable. Goals should still be stated as specifically as possible. Simple goals should be stated as if they were objectives. From here on, we will refer to objectives instead of goals in order to emphasize the importance of specificity.

Setting Objectives in Micro Practice

Many of the principles that apply to micro practice (e.g., the importance of being specific) apply to macro practice as well. In this section of the chapter, we will examine objectives within the context of work with individual clients. However, our emphasis on how objectives should be stated will apply to mezzo and macro practice as well.

Throughout this discussion, we will be referring to objectives. However, remember that the principle of being clear and specific applies to both objectives and goals.

Establishing Objectives. Establish specific objectives with your clients. What does this statement mean? For one thing, the objective should indicate exactly how it can be met. It should be easy to tell when you have achieved your objective and when you have not. Consider the following:

- *Objective: The client will become happier.* How happy does the client have to be in order to have achieved this objective? Should he get very happy, or is just a little happy enough? Are we talking about one smile a day? Or can the client be happy without smiling? What does "happy" mean anyway?

There is obviously a broad range of subjective interpretations possible concerning this objective. It is not a good objective. The point about being specific is that you should have to expend as little thought and effort as possible to determine whether the objective has been met.

- *Objective: The client's daughter (Sophia) will behave better.* Does this statement mean that Sophia, age 6, will stop pinching her infant brother (which she does frequently throughout the day) and stop spitting at her mother when being reprimanded? Is the objective met if Sophia pinches her brother only ten times during the day instead of her usual two dozen? What if she stops pinching but continues to spit? Has the objective been met? Is she behaving better enough?

Once again, interpreting the objective is difficult. Like the first example mentioned, this objective is subject to a range of interpretation. You would be put in the uncomfortable position of struggling to interpret whether you arbitrarily thought the objective had been met.

- *Objective: The client (Mindy) will improve her communication skills.* This time, the client is an 18-year-old woman with developmental disabilities. Although Mindy reads at a fourth-grade level, she is shy and rarely speaks to anyone. Will this objective be met if she speaks more frequently to her parents? How much more frequently? Is two times a day enough? What if she only says one word each time? Or, should she speak to her parents two times each day for at least five minutes each time for the objective to be met? Should Mindy also be more adept at speaking to strangers she meets before the objective is met?

What about the *listening* part of her ability to communicate? Must her capacity to listen and understand be improved before this objective is met? Does this objective involve her ability to carry on a full and meaningful conversation?

Once again establishing what is really meant by this objective is difficult. You would have to make a subjective decision regarding whether you were successful at meeting the objective or whether you needed to continue striving to achieve it.

What are your thoughts right now? Do you think we are being much too particular and absurd? The intent of these examples is not to frustrate or annoy you. In practice, you will be responsible for both formulating and achieving goals and objectives. You will be accountable to your client, your supervisor, and your agency for achieving your intervention goals and objectives. Therefore, being able to cite clear, concrete, readily understandable objectives is to your advantage. For any of the three objectives mentioned earlier, questions could easily be raised about whether you were achieving them or not. A clearly defined, specific objective helps us evaluate exactly what has been achieved.

Specifying objectives in the planning process is helpful. Ideal objectives are observable actions that are possible to measure in order to monitor progress. Our clients, supervisors, and colleagues should have a graphic, coherent picture in their minds of exactly what we mean.

Objectives then should meet three criteria: objectivity, clarity, and completeness (Hawkins & Dobes, 1975; Kazdin, 1989). Unbiased *objectivity* involves "observable characteristics or environmental events" (Kazdin, 1989, p. 54). In other words, objectives should refer to something that can be seen and measured. For example, take one of our earlier "bad objective" examples regarding improving communication skills for Mindy, the young adult with developmental disabilities. In this case, what exactly should be improved? Should she be expected to speak in complete sentences and use correct grammar? Should she be expected to initiate conversations and ask questions in order to achieve "improved" communication skills? The objectives leading up to the goal should specify exactly *what* behavior and *how much* of that behavior Mindy would need to learn in order to achieve the goal. In other words, improved communication would have to be carefully defined.

The second criterion for a good objective is clarity. *Clarity* means that a goal or objective is so "unambiguous that it can be read, repeated, and paraphrased by others" (Kazdin, 1989, p. 55). Regardless of who is doing the evaluating, all observers should see the same thing and be in agreement. In Mindy's case, anyone knowing what the objective is and observing Mindy's communication behavior should be able to determine whether the objective has been met or not.

Completeness, the last criterion, means that enough information should be given about how the objective can be attained. Once more, consider Mindy. The objective should specify the circumstances under which her communication should be improved. Should it involve interactions only with her parents and loved ones? Or should it involve communication and interaction with others? Would it suffice to improve her communication with clerks at stores she visits? Or would she also need to initiate communication with complete strangers in order to achieve the objective?

Ideal Objectives Can Be Measured.   We have established that one of the major purposes of formulating objectives is to provide a means for measuring whether they have been attained or not. The point of having an objective is to reach it and know that you have done so. Three required components in a clear, well-written objective are "performance," "conditions," and "standard or level of performance" (Thompson, 1977, p. 49). Much work has been done in the area of educational achievement and behavioral child management especially as applied within family or school settings (DeRisi & Butz, 1975; Jones & Biesecker, 1980; Thompson, 1977). Therefore, our discussion here will relate examples involving children's learning and behavior.

Performance, the first component of a well-written objective, involves what the client, worker, or other individual involved is to perform in order to attain the objective. The performance component in the context of changing a child's behavior illustrates exactly what you expect the child to do. What specific activity or behavior is involved in achieving the objective? Examples include, "unties and ties shoelace," "counts to 20," "recites letters of the alphabet," or "washes dishes" (Thompson, 1977, p. 49).

The second component of a clear objective involves the conditions or circumstances under which the behaviors involved in achieving the objective are performed. What materials does the child need in order to finish the activity and subsequently achieve the objective? Must the child perform the activity alone, or can someone help her? Is there a limited time frame within which she must complete the task? Examples of conditions include "given shoes with shoelaces," "within two minutes," "without prompting," or "for his parents in their kitchen after supper."

The standard of performance involves how well, how soon, or how often the performance, activity, or behavior should be done. Does the activity have to be done perfectly? Must it be done every single day? Is the objective still achieved if the child misses one day a week or mixes up two letters of the alphabet?

Highlight 6.2 applies this three-component basis for setting good objectives to situations typically found in human services. The importance of

---

HIGHLIGHT 6.2

Using the Concepts of Performance, Conditions, and Standards to Establish Goals and Objectives with Clients

For each of the following scenarios, a client will be described briefly. Subsequently, an arbitrary objective using the performance/conditions/standards formula will be presented. These scenarios illustrate an extension of the who-should-do-what-by-when formula for delegating responsibility and specifying objectives. For each scenario, the client is *who*. Likewise, the performance, conditions, and standards specify the *what* and by *when*.

Early, age 83, resides in a large nursing home. He has arthritis, is gradually losing the use of his hands, and is slowly failing. The *objective* for this client is:

- *Performance:* Early will enhance and maintain eye-hand coordination
- *Conditions:* by participating in a crafts activity hour offered four times each week
- *Standards:* and attending them three out of four times each week (75 percent).

Mortitia, age 24, has been reported for physically abusing her two small children when they do not obey her demands. The *objective* for this client is:

- *Performance:* Mortitia will learn parent-effectiveness skills
- *Conditions:* by attending Parent Effectiveness Training Classes every Thursday evening at the local YMCA
- *Standards:* and attending all six training sessions (100 percent of the time).

Jonas, age 15, is labeled by his parents as uncontrollable. He has been arrested for selling drugs twice, is frequently involved in gang-related fights, and often gets home after his curfew. The *objective* for this client is:

- *Performance:* Jonas will arrive home by his curfew
- *Conditions:* at 9 P.M. on weeknights and 11 P.M. on weekends

- *Standards:* 13 out of 14 nights every two weeks (93 percent of the time).

Ivory, age 21, has three small children and works a full-time first-shift job at a bakery. Ivy's own mother, who has been caring for Ivy's children, has recently become ill and can no longer babysit. Ivory does not want to lose her job. The *objective* for this client is:

- *Performance:* Ivory will arrange for day care for her three children
- *Conditions:* by calling five day care agencies to determine cost and her children's eligibility
- *Standards:* and reporting her findings to her counselor by next Thursday.

Britany, a 26-year-old adult with developmental disabilities, lives in a group home with other adults of similar ability levels. She moved in after the death of her mother, with whom she had lived her entire life. The *objective* for this client is:

- *Performance:* Britany will complete specified daily living tasks
- *Conditions:* and check off completed tasks on the clipboard holding her daily log of activities (e.g., making her bed, getting to work at the sheltered workshop on time, vacuuming the living room)
- *Standards:* and complete 80 percent of all her required tasks each day.

Commentary

These are clear goals and their attainment is easily measured. If Britany, for example, only completes 78 percent of her required tasks, she has not met her objective. Likewise, if Jonas misses his curfew two times in two weeks, he has not accomplished his objective.

Clearly specifying how objectives will be evaluated will save you many headaches in the long run. Specifying and agreeing upon goal expectations in advance will help you avoid potential arguments, having to make judgments about excuses, and even being the target of manipulation.

specificity continues to be a major theme (see Highlight 6.3).

Step 7: Specify Action Steps

Establishing objectives also requires specifying the action steps that are necessary in order to achieve those objectives. In order to achieve them, involved individuals will need to get things done. The basic formula for delegating responsibility is to specify *who* will do *what* by *when*. "Who" is the individual specified for accomplishing a task. "What" involves the tasks the individual has to complete in order to

achieve the goal. Finally, "by when" sets a time limit so that the task is not lost in some endless eternity.

The following are examples of action steps:

- Ms. M (*who*) will call her mother about helping care for the children (*what*) by 3 P.M. next Monday (*when*).
- I (*who*) will contact my supervisor and establish a location for the group to meet (*what*) by Wednesday, November 23 (*when*).
- Mr. S. (*who*) will survey the agency's clientele to determine their primary needs and be ready to

---

 HIGHLIGHT 6.3

Clarifying Vague Goals and Objectives

Below is a case of a client with multiple problems. Following the scenario, there are a series of vague statements that could be incorporated as possible objectives for the client portrayed. The words and phrases used in the vague goal statements are taken from Jones and Biesecker (1980, p. 28). Unfortunately, these phrases are sometimes embodied in the goals proposed in real case records and reports.

For each vague goal statement:

1. Explain why the goal is vague. For example, which specific words are vague? How might their meanings be misinterpreted or interpreted in many different ways by different people?
2. Reformulate these objectives by using specific terminology and incorporating the performance/conditions/standards format illustrated in Highlight 6.2.

Sarah, age 24, has paraplegia. She broke her back in a car accident when she was 16. Afterward, she became clinically depressed, withdrawing from family and friends, and has isolated herself in her apartment for the past three years. She dresses slovenly, is generally lethargic, and remains unmotivated to get training for employment or improve her social life. The low-rent apartment building in which she lives is being torn down. Sarah is panic-stricken, hostile to human service professionals and family members trying to help her, and does not know what she will do.

Respond to the following potential goals for Sarah and answer the two questions posed above for each.

The first statement is followed by an example of how you might respond to the remaining goal statements.

- *Vague statement of objective (Example):* Improve family relationships. *Reason for vagueness: Improve* is a vague term. How can you measure relationship improvement? How can you tell when the goal is achieved? Which family relationships are being targeted? Those with parents? Siblings? Grandparents? What aspects of the relationships should change? What does "relationship" mean?
- *Improved restatement of an objective (performance, conditions, standards):* Sarah will call her mother on the telephone and speak to her for at least five minutes three days each week.

Now, do the same thing for the following vague goal statements:

Vague Objective Statement	Reasons for Vagueness	Improved Restatement: Performance/ Conditions/ Standards
1. Promote emotional well-being:		
2. Increase self-awareness:		
3. Find adequate housing:		
4. Facilitate adequate functioning:		
5. Accept physical disability:		
6. Dress appropriately:		
7. Increase motivation:		
8. Show interest:		
9. Respond appropriately:		
10. Improve self-concept:		
11. Develop a relationship:		
12. Decrease hostile attitude:		

make a report (*what*) by the February staff meeting (*when*).

You might be asking yourself, "Why is it so important to be so precise?" The answer is that if you are not explicit regarding who has the responsibility for accomplishing the task, it is likely that the task will not get done.

As a student you are probably very busy. You are not likely to have much time to do anything but the required coursework. Doing a lot of in-depth reading on topics that interest you would be nice. However, you probably assign these interests a relatively low priority. You do what you *have* to do first. It is the same for generalist practitioners. As a human service professional, you will likely have many clients and will constantly strive to prioritize what needs to get done first. If completing a task by a certain deadline is not your specifically identified responsibility, putting it off . . . and off . . . and off is easy. Such tasks rarely, if ever, get done.

For example, you are at a staff meeting where you are discussing the progress of a client of yours with a developmental disability. Other professionals at the meeting include your supervisor, a psychologist, a vocational counselor, a physician, a speech therapist, an occupational therapist, and a physical therapist. The purpose of the meeting is for each professional to report what progress has been made with this client to formulate plans and goals for the future. One of the goals established by the group is to "make a referral to another agency for intensive vocational testing." Such testing would determine your client's specific skills, abilities, and job interests. However, the task of making the referral has not been clearly specified and assigned.

Two months later, the same group meets again to reevaluate this client's progress. Your supervisor, who is leading the staff meeting, asks for a report on the vocational testing results. You gaze at the psychologist with a blank expression on your face. The psychologist looks at you. The occupational therapist looks at the vocational counselor. The vocational counselor looks at the psychologist. And so it goes. Each staff member assumed that some other staff member would make the referral. All were terribly busy with their own job responsibilities and had no time to do anything they did not absolutely have to do. As a result, no one "naturally" assumed responsibility for completing the task. Thus, the task did not get done. The client had lost two months of precious (and expensive) time. One should note that the phrase "get done" sounds as if the task will magically do itself without any human intervention. In other words, this phrase is one to carefully scrutinize and probably avoid.

Step 8: Formalize a Contract

Thus far, we have established seven steps in the planning phase of the planned change process: work with your client, prioritize problems, translate problems into needs, evaluate levels of intervention (micro, mezzo, and macro), establish goals, specify objectives, and specify action steps. The eighth and final step of the planning phase is to establish an intervention contract.

A contract is an agreement between a client and worker about what will occur in the intervention process. It can include goals, objectives, action steps, time frames, and responsibilities of people involved.

This definition can be broken down into four major components:

1. A contract specifies what will occur during the intervention process.
2. A contract is established by a worker and client making an agreement together.
3. A contract generally contains four types of information: goals, methods, timetables, and mutual obligations.
4. A contract's format can be written, oral, or implied.

The Purpose of a Contract

A contract represents the culmination of the planning step in the planned change process. It clarifies and summarizes exactly who is responsible for completing which tasks. Halley and colleagues describe the usefulness of contracts:

> . . . *contracts are one way to ensure the consumer's rights, to free the consumer, and to increase consumer control in developing and implementing the plan. Such contracts are not legal documents; rather, they are a way to involve interested persons and to identify each person's roles in the achievement of the desired outcomes. Contracts help to document who does what and when. Thus, contracts explain to the consumer what the worker and the agency will do, clarify what is expected of the consumer and significant others and provide a basis for tracking progress. (1998, p. 363)*

Contracts identify expectations and help avoid potential misunderstandings. The plan should be very clear to everyone involved.

Contracts can be used in any arena of practice. In micro practice, they can summarize specific responsibilities of client, worker, agency, and any involved others. In mezzo practice, contracts can specify individual and group goals and tasks. In macro practice, contracts can formalize any number of agreed-upon plans. A contract can, for instance, specify individual responsibilities of task group members advocating for a policy change concerning HIV-positive clients. This group's intent is to lobby for a change in state law that will prohibit insurance companies from canceling the policies of persons diagnosed as HIV-positive.

Another example of a contract in macro practice is the *purchase of service agreement* which is a:

> . . . *fiscal arrangement or contract between two or more organizations. One organization agrees in advance to pay a specified amount to the other for providing a predetermined number of services within a specified time period. Purchaser organizations are thus able to extend services to their clientele, and provider agencies can increase their budgets, extend their services, and in some cases increase their profits.* (Barker, 1999, p. 392)

A more specific example of a purchase of service contract is a rural county social services agency with children in foster care needing speech therapy services. The county was too small and had too few children needing such therapy to hire its own speech therapist. The county officials decided to purchase the needed speech therapy services from a private agency, Catholic Social Services (CSS). CSS was a statewide agency hiring a number of speech therapists to travel around the state and supply part-time speech therapy services to a number of counties in similar circumstances (i.e., needing speech therapy services for only a few clients).

Make Contracts with Clients

A contract summarizes what you and your client system agree to do during the intervention process. The emphasis is on the word *agree*. We continue to stress involving clients during every phase of the intervention process. The extensive involvement of clients in the development of intervention contracts is simply an extension of this theme.

The contract is not a legal contract as such. It has little to do with the contracts disputed in courts of law. It articulates a commitment valid only within the practitioner–client relationship. On the other hand, an intervention contract is flexible and subject to change by agreement between the worker and the client as new information or directions are identified.

There are several advantages to client involvement in establishing contracts. First, contracts can help motivate clients to work on their problems, because they were active in establishing their own goals, objectives, and action steps. Second, client empowerment is enhanced as clients learn they can take charge and be major participants in the change effort. Third, clients who are "disorganized or forgetful" will benefit from a contract that reminds them of their agreements and responsibilities (Johnson, 1998, p. 316). Finally, contracts provide a record of goals and plans that can assist in monitoring and evaluating the planned change effort.

That clients understand everything incorporated into a contract is important. All the contract's terms and words should be clear to them.

Culturally Competent Contracting

The very nature of contracting presupposes willing agreement between two or more parties—a client and a counselor. However, as Devore and Schlesinger (1996) point out, contracting is sometimes problematic for people from different cultures. For example, contracting itself may be confusing to clients whose native language is not English. In addition, those whose experiences with human service agencies have been negative or hurtful are likely to be guarded and uncomfortable. Their willingness to enter into an agreement may be affected by this discomfort. Perceived or real power differentials between historically oppressed people of color and human services professionals can also produce unwillingness to enter into a contract. As Longres (1991) notes, changing stratification systems that result in high- and low-status people is an essential role for human service professionals. The human services value of self-determination is an important variable in culturally competent practice because clients must be confident that their choices have precedence in deciding whether and what to agree to (Ewalt & Mokuau, 1996). Only when the client fully trusts the worker is a contract going to be agreed to and progress made in a cross-cultural relationship (Lee, 1999).

The Format of a Contract

Contracts can be established in three different ways. First, they can be written and signed. Examples of this type will be given later. Second, they can involve a verbal agreement between client, worker, and any others involved. Third, they may be implicit or assumed.

The Written Contract. The written contract is the most formal type. It clearly and visually reflects what client, workers, and anyone involved have agreed upon. It should state specific objectives and follow the who-will-do-what-by-when format discussed earlier.

A primary advantage of a written contract is that it becomes a clear, virtually indisputable record. There can be no distortions of what earlier agreements involved. It can be reviewed by the worker and client at any time to refresh memories about what they agreed upon.

Another advantage is that participants sign the contract. A signature illustrates commitment and makes later questioning of who agreed to do what by when difficult.

Written contracts, however, have two disadvantages. First, they take time to draw up (Sheafor et al., 1997). A practitioner may be rushed, extremely busy, late, or overwhelmed. Second, some legal questions can be raised (Epstein, 1980). How binding would any particular contract be if brought before a court? Would a worker who fails to complete responsibilities recorded in a contract be liable?

Sheafor and colleagues (1997) reflect on how to respond to some other extenuating circumstances:

It may be necessary to prepare the contract in the client's first language (e.g., Spanish) if he or she has poor understanding of English. In cases where the client cannot read, the worker should consider recording the agreement on a cassette tape, in addition to preparing a written statement. (1997, p. 429)

Finally, a copy of the written contract should always be placed in the client's file. It should be easily accessible at any time during the intervention process.

The Oral Contract. Oral contracts specify essentially the same thing as written contracts, although orally—the intent is to clearly identify all objectives and responsibilities in the planning process. Oral contracts should be just as clear as written contracts.

There are two advantages to an oral contract. First, it can be made swiftly and in a relatively easy fashion. Second, it can be a "help" when working with a "resistant or distrustful client" who refuses to sign a written document (Johnson, 1998, p. 316). You can solicit agreement from such a client without trying to force a signature.

The client's record should still indicate that the oral contract was made along with a brief summary of what was involved; this summary should include "who participated in the decision making, what decisions were made, [and] what alternatives were considered and why they were rejected" (Kagle, 1991, p. 39).

The major disadvantage of an oral contract is that forgetting the details of an agreement is easy unless they are written down. Jotting down informal notes to themselves so that they can remember exactly what transpired might be helpful for human services professionals.

Implicit Contracts. Implicit contracts are agreements that are implied or assumed but not actually articulated. Be wary about using them. It is easy to make two assumptions that can be false. First, you can mistakenly assume that your client has agreed when he or she really has not. Second, you can assume that your client understands all the conditions and responsibilities of your perceived implicit contract when he or she does not.

In groups where interpersonal processes can be complex, there may be numerous assumed agreements. These might concern how individuals will perform and behave inside and outside of the group. There may be too many, and they may be too subtle to label openly. Assumed agreements essentially compose an implicit contract. For instance, an implicit contract within a treatment group for alcoholic adults might be a prohibition of encouraging other group members to drink. Another term of the implicit contract for this group might be to behave in a socially appropriate manner. Thus, fingers should be kept out of noses, ears, and other orifices, and members should not swear at each other.

What to Include in Intervention Contracts

At the least, intervention contracts should include identifying information about the client and specified objectives and signatures of client and worker. Each type of information merits further discussion. Figure 6.3 depicts an example of an intervention contract.

Identifying Information. An intervention contract must always contain information that identifies the client. Included would be the client's name and perhaps a case number. Other times, there is a brief description of the problem included, as is illustrated in Figure 6.3. This description can help quickly orient a worker, who deals with many cases and many problems, to a particular case.

Contracts involving groups may include all members' names. The type of group may also be used as identifying information.

In contracts with other agencies, sometimes their names are specified as well. At other times, the contract will be identified by a project name.

Figure 6.3 *An Example of a Written Contract Format*

Contract for Intervention Plan

Client Name: _____

1. Description of the Problem: _____

   _____

   _____

2. Primary Goals: _____

   _____

   _____

3. We, the undersigned, agree to the objectives in the following plan:

   A. _____

   B. _____

   C. _____

   D. _____

   E. _____

_____   _____
(Signature of Client)   (Signature of Counselor)

_____   _____
(Date)   (Date)

Specified Objectives and Action Steps. The core of any intervention contract involves specification of objectives. Our previous discussion concerning the writing of objectives applies directly to writing them into contracts. They should be clear and easily understood by anyone reading them. They should indicate action steps, that is, who will do what by when, and they should be measurable.

Signatures. All written contracts should be signed. These signatures demonstrate that the participants are well informed about the plan, its objectives, and each participant's responsibilities. Additionally, a signature indicates commitment to the plan.

Contracts used in mezzo and macro practice may need room for a number of different signatures. All participants in the intervention plan should have a place to sign.

Dates. Finally, all intervention contracts should include the date the agreement was made. This date, which can usually be found directly underneath the participants' signatures, indicates the contract's currency. An old date might indicate that the contract's contents need to be reviewed.

Formats Vary. In reality, contract formats vary radically. For example, Kagle illustrates a contract called a "service agreement" with the following four components: "(1) Purpose(s) or goal(s) of service; (2) plan of service; (3) (client name) agrees to undertake the following responsibilities; (4) on behalf of the agency, (worker name) agrees to undertake the following responsibilities" (1991, p. 138).

Additionally, instructions for filling out the service agreement are included. Dates are also recorded a bit differently than those illustrated in Figure 6.3.

They indicate the time that the contract covers—the date it was signed and the date it should be completed. The contract then ends with signature lines for both client and worker.

You should be prepared to find such different contract formats. Formats may depend on the agency's mission, client needs, and contract purpose. Regardless of the format your agency uses, the principles applying to writing good objectives still apply. Who is responsible for what tasks should be clear. Task completion dates should be specified. Finally, objectives should be measurable, so no question exists about whether or not they have been accomplished.

Contracts Often Change Over Time.   Contracts continue to change over time. Objectives are reached, new objectives are established, clients' situations change, and intervention plans must be adjusted to meet these changes. You should indicate such changes and the dates they were made either on the old contract or on a revised one.

Figure 6.4 illustrates a series of three monthly contracts used for residents in a halfway house for people recovering from alcohol and other types of drug abuse. Because the clients reside there, they receive daily supervision in addition to professional counseling. The goal is to help integrate them back

Figure 6.4   *An Example of Progressively Changing Contracts*

CEPHAS HALFWAY HOUSE
Lutheran Social Services

First Month Contract

In addition to following the House Rules, I, _____ , agree to the following

terms in order to keep my residency at Cephas Halfway House.

I will look for employment in the Waukesha area every day until I find a job.

When I become employed, I will open a savings account and try to save at least one hundred

dollars ($100).

Once this is done, I will approach my counselor to negotiate a second month contract, which will

include goals that my agent and counselor want.

1. Weekly counseling sessions _____

2. _____   6. _____

3. _____   7. _____

4. _____   8. _____

5. _____   9. _____

_____   _____
(Staff)   (Date)

(Resident) _____

Source: This material has been adapted from contracts used by Cephas Halfway House, Waukesha, WI. Used with permission of Lutheran Social Services of Wisconsin and Upper Michigan, Inc., W226 N55A Eastmound Dr., Waukesha, WI 53186.

into the community. Thus, the contracts focus on gaining employment and saving money.

Several differences are reflected in the three contracts. Some content changes as the months progress. Note six elements about the "First Month Contract." First, the contract starts with a basic commitment to follow the house rules. Second, it structures a statement committing the client to actively seek employment in a specified geographical area. Third, the contract requires that the client strive to put the specific amount of at least $100 in savings. Fourth, it structures the fact that a new contract will be established within one month. Fifth, it specifies that weekly counseling sessions are required. Sixth, blank spaces two through nine are left for the specification of individualized objectives.

Now view the "Second Month Contract" depicted in Figure 6.4. This contract is much less structured. The idea is that clients are gradually encouraged to

make more decisions and accept greater responsibility for themselves. This contract omits the item about commitment to house rules. It allows the client to specify how much will be put into savings. Note that putting money into savings is still required. The contract assumes the client has already gotten a job. Likewise, weekly counseling sessions are still required. Additionally, blank spaces two through five are provided for establishing individualized objectives.

Finally, consider the "Third Month Contract." Once again, the client is required to place a set amount into savings but is again permitted to determine that amount. Next, a new goal is added, namely to work actively on the transition from a supervised living environment to living independently within the community. The contract then requires that the client continue evaluating individual goals and working with the counselor to develop new goals. This contract requires that the client

Figure 6.4 *An Example of Progressively Changing Contracts (continued)*

CEPHAS HALFWAY HOUSE
Lutheran Social Services

Second Month Contract

I, _____ , will agree to increase my savings account to _____

by the end of my second month. If there is any restitution, I will sit down with my agent and work

out some arrangement and make out a schedule of payment in addition to the above.

My goals for the second month are as follows:

1. Weekly counseling sessions _____

2. _____

3. _____

4. _____

5. _____

_____   _____

(Staff)   (Date)

_____

(Resident)

attend group meetings instead of individual "weekly counseling sessions." Places for individualized objectives remain.

This series of contracts provides a good example of how objectives and the contracts that reflect them can change. The contracts go from making specific requirements to enhancing the client's independent decision-making capacity. Obviously some of the objectives are highly structured—that clients must abide by some rules in order to continue in the program is the nature of this treatment program. The agency has found this structure to be the most effective means of treatment. Client participation in the treatment contract is encouraged as much as possible within this setting.

 ## Planning in Mezzo Practice

Parts of the planning process for working with groups have been discussed in Chapter 5. Namely, formulating group membership depends on a number of variables, including motivation of potential group members, group purpose, members' ability to communicate with each other, group size, group structure, and group duration.

The six-step planning process described in this section can be similarly applied to planning when working with groups. Of course, variations do exist because of the increased complexity when more than one client is involved.

Figure 6.4   *An Example of Progressively Changing Contracts (continued)*

CEPHAS HALFWAY HOUSE
Lutheran Social Services

Third Month Contract

I, _____ , agree to increase my savings account to _____ . In

addition to this, I will work closely with my counselor in preparing for the transition from Cephas

Halfway House to community living. Goal achievements will be looked at closely. I will continue to

work on my goals previously set, in addition to what my counselor and I agree on in this third

month. I will continue to attend my group meeting.

My goals for the third month are as follows:

1. _____

2 _____

3. _____

4. _____

5. _____

_____   _____
(Staff)   (Date)

_____
(Resident)

The Complexity of Setting Objectives in Mezzo Practice

As we know, a *client system* can be an individual, group, or large organization. Your *client* is the individual or group you are helping. Working with families and other groups becomes more complicated than working with single individuals, because you need to take all group members' needs into consideration. Nonetheless, the bottom line is to *work with the client or clients*. With task groups, treatment groups, and families, you need to make certain that each and every member is involved in the planning and goal-setting process.

Toseland and Rivas (1998) establish six points about formulating goals and objectives in groups.

Clarifying Goals and Objectives

First, discussing and clarifying their goals and objectives takes substantially more time for members in groups. Much depends on the diversity of membership and the individuals' level of motivation. Even group members whose views diverge most strongly from the majority of other members must be satisfactorily integrated into the goal-setting process. Likewise, the least motivated group members must also be included for the group to succeed at its goals and objectives.

Input from Both Worker and Clients

Both the clients and the worker can propose, devise, and refine group goals and objectives. To be effective, the goal-setting process must meet the worker's needs as well as those of the group (Toseland & Rivas, 1998, pp. 190–191).

Workers' Perspective

Practitioners often propose goals and objectives reflecting their unique perspective:

> As members of social service organizations, workers are aware of the aims and the limitations of the services they provide. . . . Workers' formulations of goals reflect what they believe can be accomplished with the support, resources, and limitations within which the group operates. (Toseland & Rivas, 1998, p. 191)

In treatment groups, practitioners:

> . . . often have an opportunity to meet each member during the planning stage. Potential members are selected, in part, because of their compatibility with the purposes and goals developed for the group. Workers make preliminary assessments of members' needs and capacities, and of the tasks that face each group member. Goals are formulated on the basis of the assessment process. (Toseland & Rivas, 1998, p. 191).

Likewise, in task groups, a practitioner can make assessments of the strengths, weaknesses, and areas of expertise demonstrated by individual group members. The practitioner can then help members develop goals and objectives that maximize their individual strengths. For instance, take a group whose task is to evaluate an agency's personnel policies and make recommendations for change to the upper-level administration. One member might be well oriented to minute detail and accuracy. That member might be the one to pursue the objective of evaluating the current agency policy manual for inconsistencies, which would help prepare for the primary goal of overhauling the entire policy manual.

You would not want such a task assigned to a group member who has little tolerance for detail. Accuracy, sometimes tedious accuracy, is necessary to complete this task adequately. The latter member, however, although poor in attending to detail, might be especially adept at developing new ideas and alternatives. This member's objective might be to survey personnel to develop a list of existing problems and suggested changes for the manual. Both members' individual strengths would then be put to their most effective use.

Group Members' Perspective

Individual group members establish goals and objectives on the basis of "their own perspective on the particular concerns, problems, and issues that affect them and their fellow group members" (Toseland & Rivas, 1998, p. 191).

When a group meets for the first time, members tend to formulate their goals based on five major variables. First, individual members' proposed goals and objectives are based on their evaluation of their own wants, lacks, and needs. What is the goal/objective that each member wants from the group? What does each member want the group to accomplish?

The second variable involves how effective each member has been in accomplishing such goals in the past. How likely is future success based on past experiences? How likely is failure?

The third variable involves other pressures and demands influencing group members. How much time and energy can each member afford to devote to the group and its goals in view of other social and professional responsibilities?

The fourth variable concerns what each member feels capable of accomplishing. What skills, abilities, or competencies does the member bring to the group? What does the member feel capable and incapable of doing?

Finally, the fifth variable involves the member's prior involvement with the agency promoting the group and that member's faith in the agency's ability to accomplish goals effectively. Have past experiences been positive or negative? Does this member join the group with an optimistic, pessimistic, or neutral attitude?

Variations in Goals

Groups vary in the degree to which they are capable of developing shared group goals and objectives. Sometimes, individual goals vary to such an extreme that it is difficult to find common ground. Other times, group members have obviously similar needs that can lead to the establishment of common goals.

Consider, for example, a treatment group of agoraphobics (people who have extreme and irrational fears of open or crowded places). They often strive to avoid any location where they may feel uncomfortable. Extreme cases may feel safe and at ease only in their own homes. People subjected to such a desperate condition usually find their daily activities and lives seriously curtailed. Such individuals would probably be highly motivated to establish goals oriented to coping with and ridding themselves of this oppressive state.

In groups where members have unrelated needs and distinctly different perspectives, it will probably be much more difficult to work together and establish common goals. An example is a task group trying to establish a neighborhood recreational center. It is composed of members from a wide cross section of the community. If one member joined the group primarily to create a job for himself, another to find potential dates, and still another to provide a centralized hub of activity for neighborhood adolescents, the group might find it extremely difficult to agree upon its goals.

Categories of Goals

Group goals and objectives can be classified into three major categories (Toseland & Rivas, 1998). First, there are goals that involve nourishing the group and keeping it going. These are "group-centered goals" (p. 192). Such a goal might be to enhance group members' ability to express their ideas and work out compromises. The second category of goals is made up of

the "common group goals" referred to earlier (p. 192). These involve a goal arrived at and shared by all group members. For instance, members of a task group might aim to decrease community taxes. A third type of goal is the "individual goal," which is where the individual member works to attain some specific goal for himself.

An example of the individual goal involves an eating disorders self-help (treatment) group. Eating disorders encompass a variety of psychological and physical problems involving eating behavior. One disorder, anorexia nervosa, is a condition where people, usually young women, experience a severe fear of gaining weight. This fear leads to extreme weight loss and sometimes starvation. A group member with this condition might formulate individual goals and objectives concerning her personal eating patterns. Additionally, she might establish a goal for a specific amount of weight gain. A young woman who is five-foot-eleven and 83 pounds might establish a weight goal for herself of 125 pounds.

Contracts in Mezzo Practice

Toseland and Rivas (1998) identify five potential types of contracts involving groups. First, there may be a contract between the sponsoring agency and the group itself. This might cover what types of facilities will be provided and include group responsibilities regarding the facilities. A second contract, as would be expected, is between the worker and the group. This type of contract usually covers such things as group procedures and goals. A third contract might exist between the group and an individual group member. A fourth contract could be developed between the worker and a group member. Finally, two or more members of the group might enter into an agreement. The last three types of contracts are more likely to focus on "individual treatment goals or individual task assignments" (p. 193).

 ## Planning in Macro Practice

Planning in macro practice follows the same basic steps as planning in micro and mezzo practice. As will be shown in Chapter 13, there are many avenues with which to practice on the macro level, such as social reform, social action, cause advocacy, and case advocacy. Likewise, there are many ways to change or initiate policies, programs, and organizations. Focusing more heavily on the micro and mezzo aspects of practice is easy for a beginning professional. Working with people and helping them solve their individual problems is fascinating. Each person and problem is unique.

In order to demonstrate the significance and relevance of macro planning, we will provide one specific example here, namely that of program development. Program development involves establishing a different or new service to clients. Sometimes, new programs are developed within existing agencies. At other times, they require starting up a whole new agency. Programs can entail virtually any type of service provision. Services can range from providing mental health counseling for veterans to residential treatment for delinquent adolescents to nursing home facilities for the elderly.

The chances that you will be part of some program's development is likely; that you will be in a position to initiate some program yourself is also quite possible.

An Approach to Program Planning

Hasenfeld (1987) proposes a number of specific procedures to follow in the program development process:

1. Articulate the problem and translate it into what clients need.
2. Marshal support for program development.
3. Allocate "responsibilities to a board or advisory council" (p. 456).
4. Describe the purpose (or overall goal) of the proposed program.
5. Formulate clear subgoals or objectives.
6. Implement a "feasibility study" (p. 458).
7. Solicit the financial resources you need to initiate the program.
8. Describe how the program will provide services.
9. Get the program going.
10. Establish how services will be effectively provided on an ongoing basis.

These procedures comply with our basic planning steps in the planned change process. The following discussion describes each of these procedures and integrates them within the planning model (see Figure 6.1 on page 169).

Work with the Client

Working with the client system means that you need to work closely with those people who will be receiv-

ing the service. In macro practice, it also entails working with other professionals, organizations, and agencies that can help you with your intervention. They can provide you with information about individual clients' needs and assist in the actual intervention process. Working with the client system means that you remain open to feedback and remain responsive to the needs of others in the process.

Prioritize Problems

That problems have already been identified during the assessment phase of the planned change process has been assumed here. You are proceeding to develop a program. You are doing so because you have identified some specific problems. For example, there are no shelters for homeless people in your area, or poor people are not getting access to the health care they need. Your intent is to identify the order in which you will address your specified problems. Your proposed program will take shape according to what problems you determine are most important to solve.

For instance, consider the problem of poor people not getting adequate access to health care. How you define and prioritize problems will have a significant impact on how your program will eventually work and what services it will provide. You might decide that the most significant problem is that there is no health delivery service in the targeted area. People are not getting health care because there is none. In this case, you may begin initiating an entire health program with facilities to be set up in the area where the care is needed. Highlight 6.4 provides an example of objectives.

On the other hand, you might decide that the primary problem is not that health care is unavailable. Rather, the problem is that poor people have neither money nor health insurance to pay for the health care provided in the community. In this situation, you might try to establish a program to provide poor people with funding for health care. Or you could determine that funding is already potentially available. What is needed is a program to educate needy people regarding what is available and to assist them in applying for the funding.

Translate Problems into Needs

We have discussed how translating the problem into a need helps give direction on fulfilling that need. It orients you away from focusing on what is wrong to what can be done to solve the problem(s).

HIGHLIGHT 6.4

Planning a Health Clinic

Census data from Phoenix Township painted a bleak health care picture. Over one-fourth of the 13,000 residents lacked affordable health care. Many lacked medical insurance but did not qualify for Medicaid or other governmental health care programs. A committee composed of health care professionals, human services practitioners, and community residents develops a plan to address this problem. The goal of improving health care services for low-income Phoenix residents has several objectives:

1. The chair of the committee will make a formal request to the school board to donate space in the township high school for a free clinic. This request will be completed by June 1.

2. All committee members will solicit donations from area businesses and individuals to pay for the part-time medical staff that will staff the clinic. A total of $25,000 must be raised by August 15 to augment a pledge of $25,000 made by Phoenix Memorial Hospital.

3. The clinic will open its doors September 1 and will be staffed nine hours per week by a nurse practitioner and two hours a week with a doctor. Initial staff will be drawn from committee members.

The committee establishes a number of other objectives. These objectives cover such areas as advertising the free clinic, soliciting referrals of low-income clients, evaluating the success of the clinic, and several others. As you can imagine, the success of this kind of macro-level undertaking requires careful attention to who will do what by when.

This process is equivalent to Hasenfeld's (1987) first procedure for establishing a new program or service. Namely, articulate the problem and translate it into what clients need. You have already established and prioritized problems. Now you need to translate them into needs that can be documented and clearly understood.

Hasenfeld continues with five steps for clarifying and substantiating an unmet need:

1. Get data and information to clarify exactly what the need is. Substantiating data can also be used to prove that the need is great enough to merit intervention. You can obtain facts from statistical reports kept by public agencies. Census data is often helpful. Public and private agencies often keep information on the requests for service they can't meet. Research studies also sometimes document needs. Be creative. Think about what kinds of facts would be helpful to prove the need. Who else might be interested in the problem and need? Might other interested parties make documentation available?

   For instance, take the problem of many community teenagers being heavily involved in drugs. You determine that they need the establishment of a drug treatment program within the community. Where could you find facts and statistics to establish this need? One source might be police statistics. How many drug-related arrests have been made? Can the lack of treatment programs and referral sources be documented from their records? Another source might be local schools. What records are available regarding drug problems and seizures? Are research reports available, addressing similar adolescent populations, that can support the need for drug rehabilitation programs in general?

2. A second step is to recognize and specify what other agencies or programs in the community are already addressing the identified need. If the need is already being met somewhere else, why go through the effort needed to start a new program? Continue with our adolescent drug problem example. If a local hospital is already offering a program to address the treatment and rehabilitation need, further program development may not be necessary. Rather, your intervention approach might then be to educate teens and parents about the problem and program, in addition to facilitating their access to the already-existing program. On the other hand, establishing that no relevant programs exist only strengthens your position that a program is needed.

3. Talk to other professionals involved with clients. Find out how they perceive the problem and need. This can enhance your understanding of what is involved and give you ideas on how to proceed.

4. The fourth step emphasizes involving clients. Talk to community residents and find out how they perceive the problem and need. For example, parent–teacher associations, church groups, and community businesspeople and professionals might provide further insight and support for your plans.

5. Consider doing a more formal needs assessment. This technique will be addressed in Chapter 13. Such studies can document specific needs in a convincing manner. (Hasenfeld, 1987, pp. 454–455).

Evaluate the Levels of Intervention

Here, we have already chosen the macro approach as the target strategy in this discussion. The intent of Hasenfeld's program development formulation is to illustrate one type of macro practice planning.

Establish Goals and Specify Objectives and Action Steps

The goal in program development, of course, is to define and develop a new program. Hasenfeld's steps two through ten describe objectives to pursue in order to achieve this goal. Step one concerns determining that the need exists in the first place.

Step two concerns marshaling support for program development. Initiating and establishing a new program or service completely by yourself is difficult, if not impossible. You need support from a variety of other sources. One especially useful means of soliciting a steady source of support is to establish an "action group." Such a group "then gathers resources and influence, actively representing the new program's objectives, and fights for its support in the community" (Hasenfeld, 1987, p. 455). Additionally,

> . . . such a group can help you identify and articulate the primary goals for the proposed program, specify the client systems to receive services, target potential financial resources for the program, and share information about the program and its goals with other groups, agencies, and organizations within the community (such as city council, county government, mental health board, United Fund). (p. 456)

The committee referred to in Highlight 6.4 is one example of an action group. Action group members should be chosen very carefully. Chapter 3 examined task groups and their membership. You will want motivated individuals who are seriously interested in the proposed program. Additionally, you might solicit support by including influential community professionals, religious leaders, and businesspeople. They can provide you with credibility. Their views are generally listened to.

Finally, you might select action group members for their specific areas of expertise. For example, a certified alcohol and other drug abuse counselor could provide valuable input regarding how a drug rehabilitation program needs to be structured. Likewise, a lawyer whose practice targets juveniles or a police officer could contribute relevant information regarding the legal aspects of working with juvenile drug abusers.

From members of this action group, you might establish a more formalized "board of directors, . . . advisory council, or . . . an internal task force within an existing agency" (Hasenfeld, 1987, p. 457). A board of directors is "a group of people empowered to establish an organization's objectives and policies and to oversee the activities of the personnel responsible for day-to-day implementation of those policies. The boards of social agencies often comprise volunteers who are influential in the community and reflect the views prevalent in the community" (Barker, 1999, p. 50). In other words, such a formalized group can lend support, credibility, and community influence.

Hasenfeld's step three entails allocating responsibilities to a board or advisory council. The who-should-do-what-by-when formula clearly applies here. Board tasks can include "general direction and control of the agency—policy development, short- and long-term planning . . . , hiring competent administrative staff . . . , facilitating access to necessary resources . . . , public relations, [and] evaluation [for] accountability" (Gelman, 1987, p. 207).

Step four concerns describing the purpose (or overall goal) of the proposed program. A program's mission involves three facets. First, unmet needs must be clearly defined and documented. Second, the clientele receiving the services must be clearly identified. Third, the services to be provided by the program must be plainly delineated. In other words, the purpose of the program should be well articulated so that everyone involved understands the program's structure and intentions.

Step five involves formulating clear objectives. As we have established, objectives must be very clear. This rule applies to micro, mezzo, and macro practice. Earlier, we discussed behavioral specificity within the context of micro practice. Objectives in macro practice should be just as clear and measurable as in any other type of intervention. Specifying the performance expected, the conditions under which that performance is to occur, and the standards by which success is measured in macro practice corresponds to doing the same thing in micro practice.

For example, return to the illustration of developing a program for adolescent drug abusers. A program objective might be to provide a six-week inpatient treatment program (performance) for all identified drug-abusing teens within a geographic area (conditions) with at least 90 percent of clients remaining drug-free for six months after leaving the program (standards). Inpatient programs are those that require clients in treatment to live right in the facility both day and night.

Such an objective would also require a variety of action steps in order to be completed. What steps would need to be followed to develop this program? *Who* would need to do *what* by *when?* Macro practice, of course, involves more individuals and groups, agencies, policies, and organizations, than does micro practice. Therefore, you might expect to have more action steps when working on the macro level than when working with a single individual. These might involve any number of individuals and groups before goals can be accomplished.

Step six of program development entails implementing a feasibility study. This implementation is "a systematic assessment of the resources needed to accomplish a specified objective and concurrent evaluation of an organization's existing and anticipated capabilities for providing those resources" (Barker, 1999, p. 171). In other words, you need to explore how realistic developing the program is. How much will staffing and facilities cost? What kind of backing can you expect from the community housing the program and from other community agencies?

Additionally, what other types of resources might be available? Hasenfeld (1987) suggests five potential sources: grants, assistance from local government, private donations by individuals and agencies, services and goods donated by other agencies, and the use of volunteers.

One especially beneficial resource for many agencies is the United Way. This agency is a national union of local organizations that coordinates fundraising and distribution of those funds to designated social service agencies at the community level.

The main point is that you need to determine that you have enough resources to continue with your program development plan. If you cannot possibly afford to implement the program, you might as well halt the process at that point.

Soliciting the financial resources you need to initiate the program is step seven. Earlier, your feasibility study identified possible funding sources. This step involves actually *getting* the necessary funding to start the program. You need to transform the *potential* funding sources into *actual* funding sources. You need to work with these resources and convince the people controlling them that your proposed program does indeed merit their attention, support, and money. Additionally, you may want to instigate some fundraising efforts, a macro technique mentioned in Chapter 13.

Step eight concerns describing how the program will provide services. How will the program actually work? For instance, what type of treatment techniques will the drug rehabilitation counselors be expected to use? What kind of training do they require in order to do their jobs well? Will there be an outpatient program in addition to inpatient? In outpatient treatment programs, clients receive health care by visiting the clinic or facility, not by staying overnight or receiving more extended ongoing care. How will the inpatient units be run? What types of treatment programs will clients have (e.g., group counseling, individual counseling, or job-seeking assistance)?

Specifying the details that describe how the program will be run is important. What specific services will the program deliver to clients? Exactly how will the program reach its specified objectives?

Actually getting the program going is step nine. Staff with the necessary credentials need to be hired and scheduled. These staff need to fully understand how the program is structured and run. All procedures should be stated as clearly as possible.

Sometimes, a trial run is helpful. Trying out the program with a few clients instead of having the program start out at full capacity can identify flaws. Such flaws can be addressed and remedied more easily when programs first begin. Precedents (i.e., established ways of doing things that guide how those things are done in the future) have not yet been set. Getting the new program to respond to needed changes is important.

Step ten in program development concerns establishing how services will be provided on an ongoing basis. *How* services are delivered to clients is just as important as *what* services are delivered. Clients should be able to depend on any service being provided in a timely, predictable fashion. Appointments should be scheduled and meetings held according to clearly defined procedures. Staff should have straightforward, accurate job descriptions. They should all know exactly what tasks they are responsible for. Finally, billing should be organized and predictable.

Formalize a Contract

Contracts can be useful in program development on a variety of levels. They might be used to solidify the agreements made in action groups or by a board of directors.

The purchase-of-service contracts described earlier might be established with other agencies to provide services your program cannot. For instance, your agency might contract with another agency to provide vocational rehabilitation counseling. Your program might even employ contracts with food suppliers and professional laundry facilities in order to take care of inpatient clients' daily needs.

 ## InfoTrac College Edition

This chapter examined eight steps in the planning process and their applicability to generalist practice. A discussion of goals, objectives, and action steps focused on the importance of specificity. The use of contracts was also considered along with issues related to planning in mezzo and macro practice. For more information on related topics, please use the following search terms:

problem families
group counseling
group work
human services for the mentally handicapped

 ## On the Internet

Because of the very dynamic nature of the Web, URLs are subject to change. Therefore, be sure to check out the companion Website for this book at http://www.humanservices.wadsworth.com, where links will be updated periodically.
ub-counseling.buffalo.edu
www.neighborhoodsonline.net/index.html

CHAPTER 7
Implementation Applications

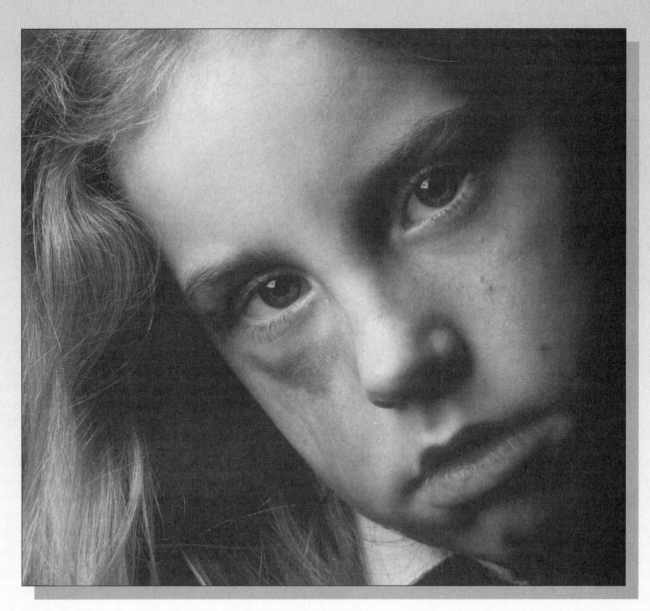

"Two Children Found Locked in Tiny Room Filled with Animal Feces"

"Elderly Hit Hard by Flu Epidemic: Health Care Lacking"

"Economy Slumps, Suicide Crisis Line Buzzing"

"Drunken Man Runs Down Two Teens, Kills Both"

"Managed Care Denies Child Operation"

Any of these headlines might be found in your local evening newspaper. They are included here because they refer to issues that often involve the implementation of human services intervention. These issues are child maltreatment, empowerment of the elderly, crisis intervention, alcohol and other substance abuse, and managed care.

Figure 7.1   *Implementation in the Generalist Intervention Model*

 ## Introduction

Implementation in generalist practice deals with carrying out the intervention plan after initial engagement, assessment, and planning. It is the actual *doing* of human services. Figure 7.1 illustrates this process, which involves following, monitoring progress, revising as necessary, and completing the established plan. We have established that intervention is the use of "thoughtful and planned efforts to bring about a specific change" (Sheafor et al., 2000). It encompasses many of the actions that human services workers employ to address client and social problems. Thus, depending on the issues and client groups involved, special knowledge, skills, and techniques are useful when implementing an intervention plan. This chapter investigates several approaches generalist practitioners commonly use to address problems in designated practice areas.

These areas are chosen for inclusion to reflect a broad range of practice issues and scenarios. They include child maltreatment, empowerment of the elderly, crisis intervention, alcohol and other drug abuse (AODA), and dilemmas posed by managed care.

This chapter will:

- describe child maltreatment and explain how the Generalist Intervention Model (GIM) can be applied;
- review risk assessment in child maltreatment;
- introduce applications of mezzo and macro practice to child maltreatment;
- discuss empowering practice with the elderly;
- explain the major concepts in crisis intervention;
- examine a model of crisis intervention that coincides with the planned change process, identify specific techniques involved, and apply the model to a case situation;

- recognize the significance of crisis intervention at the mezzo and macro levels in addition to the micro level;
- review terms commonly used in interventions involving alcohol and other substance abuse;
- describe typical characteristics of alcoholics and their families;
- discuss the generalist practitioner's role in implementing planned change with abusers and their families;
- identify a number of techniques effective in alcohol abuse counseling;
- recognize a number of potential referral sources for clients who abuse alcohol or other mind-altering substances;
- relate mezzo and macro aspects of the implementation process with alcohol and other substance abusing clients;

- discuss managed care, describe its impact as a macro context for implementation in generalist practice, and identify several potential ethical dilemmas.

Child Maltreatment and Protective Services

Child abuse and neglect is an area of practice many human services professionals are likely to enter. Even workers addressing other issues and serving other populations must have a sound knowledge and skill base to assess maltreatment's occurrence and make appropriate referrals. See Highlight 7.1 for a profile of child maltreatment.

HIGHLIGHT 7.1

A Profile of Child Maltreatment

There are a number of ways that children can be abused or neglected. The umbrella term that may be used to include all of them is *child maltreatment* (Kadushin & Martin, 1988, p. 226). Maltreatment includes "physical abuse, inadequate care and nourishment, deprivation of adequate medical care, insufficient encouragement to attend school consistently, exploitation by being forced to work too hard or too long, exposure to unwholesome or demoralizing circumstances," sexual abuse, and emotional abuse and neglect (Kadushin & Martin, 1988, p. 226; Wells, 1995). Definitions used by legal and social service agencies vary from state to state. Usually, however, all can be clustered under two headings: child abuse (both physical and sexual) and child neglect.

Child maltreatment is a critical issue for human services professionals to understand. You need to know the clues that signify maltreatment. Even if you do not work in protective services, you need an understanding of child maltreatment in order to assess the possibility of occurrence in any families you work with. You can then make appropriate referrals to resources that can help.

Definitions and Indicators

Kadushin and Martin define *physical abuse* as "beating a child to the point at which the child sustains some

physical damage" (1988, p. 288). However, they conclude that in reality, there is often a fine line between physical abuse and parental discipline.

Definitions of physical abuse vary from one place to another (Brissett-Chapman, 1995; Wells, 1995). Some definitions focus on whether or not the alleged abuser's purpose is to harm the child. Others ignore the intent and emphasize the potential or actual harm done to the child.

Both physical and behavioral indicators provide clues that a child is being physically abused. Physical indicators can be broken down into six basic categories (Beeler, Rycus, & Hughes, 1990; Crosson-Tower, 1999; Kemp, 1998):

1. *Bruises.* Bruises on any infant should be suspect. Infants are not yet mobile; therefore, the chances that they can bruise themselves are not likely. Bruises in unusual places or forming unusual patterns may indicate physical abuse. Bruises in a recognizable shape, such as a hand mark or a belt mark, should be noted. Finally, bruises displaying a variety of colors may portray abuse, suggesting that a series of bruises have been received over time. Bruises usually progress from an initial bright red to blue to blackish-purple within the first day; they become shaded with a dark green color after four to six days and finally turn pale green or yellow after five to ten days have passed (Davis, 1982).
2. *Lacerations.* Cuts, scrapes, or scratches, especially if they occur frequently or their origin is poorly

(continued)

explained, may indicate physical abuse. Lacerations on the face and genitalia should be noted. Bite marks may also indicate abuse.

3. *Fractures.* Bone fractures and other skeletal injuries may indicate abuse. Strangely twisted fractures and multiple fractures are especially telltale signs. Infants' fractures may be the result of abuse. Additional indicators are joint dislocations and injuries where the periosteum, the thin membrane covering the bone, is detached.

4. *Burns.* Burns, especially ones that take odd forms or are in patterns, may indicate abuse. Children have been burned by cigarettes and ropes (from being tied up and confined). Burns on normally inaccessible portions of the body, such as the stomach, genitals, or soles of the feet, are abuse clues. Patterned burns suggest that the child has been burned with some hot utensil. Sacklike burns result when a hand or foot has been submerged in a hot liquid (Davis, 1982). A doughnut-shaped burn will occur on the buttocks if a child has been immersed in very hot water. The center unburned area occurs when the child's skin touched the bottom of the receptacle holding the water (Schmitt, 1980).

5. *Head injuries.* Head injuries that can indicate abuse include skull fractures, loss of hair due to vigorous pulling, and subdural hematomas (i.e., blood that has collected beneath the outer covering of the brain after strenuous shaking or hitting has occurred). Black eyes should be suspect. Retinas may detach or hemorrhage if a child is shaken vigorously.

6. *Internal injuries.* Children have received injuries to their spleen, kidneys, and intestines due to hitting and kicking. The vena cava, the large vein by which blood is brought from the lower extremities to the heart, may be ruptured. Peritonitis, where the lining of the abdominal cavity becomes inflamed, can be another indicator of abuse.

In summary, some of the major questions to ask yourself if you think a child may have been physically abused are:

- Does this child get hurt too often for someone his or her age?
- Does the child have multiple injuries?
- Do the injuries occur in patterns, assume recognizable shapes, or look like some of the injuries described here?

- Are the injuries such that they do not seem possible for a child at that stage of development?
- Do the explanations given for the injuries make sense? (Downs, Costin, & McFadden, 1996)

If something does not seem right or logical to you, it may require further investigation. It might be called a "gut reaction" but if a little voice in the back of your mind is saying, "Oh-oh, that certainly is odd," pay attention. It might be a clue to abuse.

In addition to physical indicators, behavioral indicators provide another major dimension of clues to physical abuse. A physically abused child tends to adopt behavioral extremes. Virtually all children display these extreme behaviors at one time or another. However, the frequency and severity of these behaviors in abused children are clearly notable. Four categories of behavioral indicators have been established:

1. Some children display extremely passive, accommodating, submissive behaviors aimed at preserving a low profile and avoiding potential conflict with parents that might lead to abuse (Beeler et al., 1990; Crosson-Tower, 1999; LeVine & Sallee, 1999). Abused children can learn to be exceptionally calm and docile in order to avoid any possible conflict with the abusive parents. If they are invisible, the parent may not be provoked. Many times abused children will even avoid playing because it draws too much attention to themselves. Martin and Beezley (1976) call this behavioral pattern *hypervigilance.*

2. Abused children may exhibit notably aggressive behaviors and marked overt hostility toward others, caused by rage and frustration at not getting needs met (Crosson-Tower, 1999; LeVine & Sallee, 1999). Other physically abused children assume an opposite approach to the overly passive manner identified earlier. These children are so desperately in need of attention that they will try almost anything to get it. Even if they can provoke only negative attention from their parents, their aggressive behavior is reinforced.

3. Still others show role-reversal behavior, where the child assumes a parenting role in relationship with parents or extremely dependent behavior in response to emotional needs (Beeler et al., 1990). Some physically abused children form behavioral patterns in reaction to their parents' own needs. For instance, parents who are seriously immature and in need of nurturance themselves may elicit overly mature, responsible, almost adultlike behavior from

their children. These parents expect their children to assume the parental role and the children may act like little adults. On the other hand, some abusive parents will desperately need to keep their children dependent and to feel themselves in control. Children of these parents will behave in ways appropriate for children much younger (Crosson-Tower, 1999). They will cling to their parents and often display babyish behavior.

4. Developmental lags are seen in some abused children (Beeler et al., 1990; Crosson-Tower, 1999; Kemp, 1998). Because abused children are forced to direct their attention and energy toward coping with their abusive situation, they will frequently show developmental delays. These may appear in the form of language delays, poorly developed social skills for their age level, or lags in motor development.

Child neglect is "the failure of the child's parent or caretaker, who has the material resources to do so, to provide minimally adequate care in the areas of health, nutrition, shelter, education, supervision, affection, or attention" (Wolock & Horowitz, 1984, p. 15). The following are eight general indicators of child neglect (Crosson-Tower, 1999; Zuravin & Taylor, 1987):

1. *Physical health care.* Illnesses are not attended to, or proper dental care is not maintained.
2. *Mental health care.* Children's mental health problems are either ignored or left unattended.
3. *Supervision.* Children are often or almost always left alone without adequate supervision. Examples of incidents reflective of this situation include when very young children or infants are left unattended. Another common situation is when very young children are left in the supervision of other children who themselves are too young to assume such responsibility. A third common situation occurs when unsupervised children get involved in activities in which they may harm themselves. For example, we periodically read in the newspaper how a young, unsupervised child plays with matches, starts a fire, burns down the house or apartment building, and usually dies in the fire. A fourth example involves children who don't receive adequate supervision to get them to school on time or at all.
4. *Substitute child care.* The most blatant form of neglect is abandonment, where parents leave children alone and unattended. A related scenario involves parents who fail to return when they're supposed to, thereby leaving designated care

providers in the lurch, not knowing what to do with the children.
5. *Housing hazards.* Housing may have inadequate heat, ventilation, or safety features. Dangerous substances such as drugs or weapons may be left in children's easy reach. Electrical fixtures may not be up to code and therefore dangerous.
6. *Household sanitation.* Food may be spoiled. The home may be filled with garbage or excrement. Plumbing might not work or be backed up.
7. *Personal hygiene.* Children's clothing may be ripped, filthy, and threadbare. Their hair might be unkempt and dirty. They themselves might be unbathed and odorous.
8. *Nutrition.* Children who frequently complain that they're hungry and searching for food may be victims of neglect. Children receiving food that provides them with inadequate nutrition may be neglected. Significant delays in development resulting from malnutrition may also be a clue to neglect.

Emotional neglect is "passive or passive/aggressive[a] inattention to the child's emotional needs, nurturing, or emotional well-being" (Brassard, Germaine, & Hart, 1987, p. 267). This neglect includes "parents who overlook their infants' cues and signals, particularly the children's cries and pleas for warmth and comfort" (Erickson & Egeland, 1996, p. 7). Neglectful parents may be extremely insensitive and unresponsive to their children's emotional needs and have little involvement with their children (1996, p. 7).

Sexual abuse is "forced, tricked, or manipulated contact with a child by an older person (generally five or more years older) that has the purpose of the sexual gratification of the older person" (Conte, 1995, p. 402). *Incest,* a form of sexual abuse, is "sexual intercourse between people too closely related to legally marry (usually interpreted to mean father–daughter, mother–son, or brother–sister)" (Strong & DeVault, 1997). Three categories of symptoms indicate that sexual abuse may be occurring—physical problems, emotional indicators, and increased or inappropriate sexual behavior (Berliner, 1995; Strong & DeVault, 1997).

(continued)

---

a. *Passive-aggressive behavior* is the use of covert, unobtrusive, or ambiguous actions to resist and undermine goals and activities. For example, an emotionally neglectful parent might nod his head, pretending concern, in response to his child who has fallen and badly scraped her knee and then walk away, ignoring her.

A variety of physical problems are indications of sexual abuse. For instance, a small child may become infected with a sexually transmitted disease. There may be pain, bleeding, or bruises in genital or anal areas. Pregnancy is still another indicator, especially if it occurs when a child is of an unusually young age to have sexual intercourse.

Emotional indicators provide the second category of symptoms. They include depression, anxiety, low self-esteem, and thoughts of suicide (Berliner, 1995; Berliner & Elliott, 1996; Strong & DeVault, 1997).

The third category of sexual abuse symptoms involves increased or inappropriate sexual behavior. Sexually abused children "tend to have more sexual behavior and engage in sexual behavior imitative of adult sexual activity" (Berliner, 1995; Berliner & Elliott, 1996, p. 56; Friedrich et al., 1992). For example, one 8-year-old child's teacher expressed concern when she had to stop the child several times from mimicking sexual intercourse with another child (the term this teacher used was "humping") on the playground. Sexually abused children may also "exhibit compulsive sex play or masturbation and show an inappropriate amount of sexual knowledge" (Carroll & Wolpe, 1996, p. 593). Another teacher was alerted when one of her fifth-grade female students handed in 18 poems. The assignment had required only one. Each of the poems was saturated with sexual images and terminology.

Incidence of Child Maltreatment

The actual number of child maltreatment cases is difficult to determine. Specific definitions for who can and cannot be included in specific categories vary dramatically. One thing, however, is certain: Any figures that are reported reflect a minimal number of actual cases. All indications are that vast numbers of cases remain unreported.

Nearly 2.9 million cases of child maltreatment were reported in one year; about one-third of them were confirmed after protective service investigation (Downs et al., 1996). Of these, 49 percent were for neglect, 23 percent for physical abuse, and 14 percent for sexual abuse. The remaining cases (in order of frequency) fall under the categories of "other," emotional maltreatment, medical neglect, and "unknown."

A Profile of Victims

Brissett-Chapman (1995) summarizes characteristics of victims. The median age is 7, with 7.6 percent of

reported cases being under a year old. Approximately 53 percent are girls and 46 percent boys. About 55 percent of the children are white, 26 percent African American, and 9 percent Hispanic (although the number of Hispanic cases is probably underestimated because the category was not always included in the reporting process).

Other factors increasing risk of abuse include unplanned pregnancy, an extremely difficult pregnancy or birth, and physical abnormalities, any of which might cause parental resentment toward the child (Downs et al., 1996). Abused children tend to have more difficulties than those who are nonabused, including behavior problems, disobedience, school failure, and social difficulties (1996). However, knowing whether these problems helped trigger the abuse or resulted from the abuse is hard to tell.

Characteristics of Perpetrators

Perpetrators of physical child abuse tend to have problems in seven major areas (U.S. Department of Health, Education, and Welfare, 1979). Although no one person may have all eight problems, most abusers will be characterized by at least some of them.

First, they themselves most likely have serious needs for support and nurturance that remain unfulfilled from their own childhood (Crosson-Tower, 1999; Kolko, 1996). A basic quality characterizing abusers is low self-esteem. Because they have never had their own needs met, they are unable to meet the needs of their children. They often invite rejection and hostility because they have little confidence in their own abilities. They do not know how to reach out for support. They often feel they are undeserving but still have desperate needs for human support. Many perpetrators have been abused as children themselves.

A second problem characterizing abusers involves social isolation (Crosson-Tower, 1999). Their own self-confidence is low. They feel as though no one will like them anyway, so they isolate themselves. They reject attention, even though they really need others for emotional support. They fear rejection, so they do not even try to reach out to others. As a result, when normal everyday stresses build up, they have no one to talk to and help them cope.

Inability to take care of a child adequately because of their own emotional needs is a third problem characterizing abusive parents (Crosson-Tower, 1999; Kolko,

1996). We have already mentioned how abused children may display a role reversal with their abusive parents or become extremely dependent on their parents. This role reversal is the other side of that coin. Some parents look for parental support from their children. Others feel the need to control their children and keep them dependent. Sometimes the parent views the child as an extension of him- or herself. Parents see themselves as being bad, and so their children are also bad and deserving of punishment. Children with physical or mental disabilities are at risk because of the additional resentment they may elicit (Brissett-Chapman, 1995).

A related problem is the fourth characterizing abusive people—they do not know how to raise their children in a nurturing family environment (Kolko, 1996). Their own family of origin environment may have been hostile and abusive. They may never have observed nurturing behavior on the part of their own parents and caretakers. Their expectations for what constitutes appropriate behavior at the various developmental levels may be lacking. For instance, demands upon the child for behavioral submission and even perfection may be highly inappropriate.

The fifth problem involves the marital relationship (Costin, Bell, and Downs, 1991). Low self-esteem may also have an impact on the marital subsystem. Abusers may not know how to get their needs met. They may let their disappointments and anger build up because they do not know how to appropriately express their feelings. They may feel isolated and alone even within the marriage. Children may become easy targets for parents to communicate with each other. Children may provide a conduit for the expression of violence and anger actually directed at a spouse.

The sixth problem often facing abusers is that of extreme external stress and life crises (Crosson-Tower, 1999; Kolko, 1996). Some child abuse is related to lower socioeconomic status and single parenthood (Brissett-Chapman, 1995). Poverty causes stress, as can the lack of a partner to provide emotional support. Additional life crises such as losing a job, illness, a marital dispute, or even a child's behavior problem may push people over the brink of where they can control themselves and cope. They may take out their stress on the easiest, most available targets, namely, their children.

A seventh factor contributing to child maltreatment is alcohol and other substance abuse (Brissett-Chapman, 1995; Costin et al., 1991). Drugs may lower parents' self-control and inhibitions, allowing them to become easily angry or violent. Drugs may demand parents' attention and detract from their interest in providing care for their children.

Parents who neglect their children appear to have characteristics similar to physically abusive parents, although poverty is also "highly correlated with neglect" (Lindsey, 1994; Mather & Lager, 2000, p. 102). A typical neglectful parent is "an isolated individual who has difficulty forming relationships or carrying on the routine tasks of everyday life. Burdened with the anger and sadness over unmet childhood needs, this parent finds it impossible to consistently recognize and meet the needs of her or his children" (Tower, 1989, p. 91). This description, in some ways, resembles the description of the physically abusive parent. However, an abuser lashes out, whereas a neglectful parent tends to withdraw and fails to provide adequately for children.

No clear-cut description characterizes people who sexually abuse children "other than that most are male and are known to the victim" (Crooks & Baur, 1999, p. 591; Gibbons & Vincent, 1994; Guidry, 1995). There is some evidence that they tend to be "shy, lonely, poorly informed about sexuality, and very moralistic or religious" (Bauman, Kasper, & Alford, 1984; Crooks & Baur, 1999, p. 591). They "are likely to have poor interpersonal and sexual relations with other adults, and may feel socially inadequate and inferior" (Crooks & Baur, 1999, p. 591; McKibben, Proulz, & Lusignan, 1994; Minor & Dwyer, 1997). Other possible characteristics involve "[a]lcoholism, severe marital problems, sexual difficulties, and poor emotional adjustment" (Crooks & Baur, 1999; Johnston, 1987; McKibben et al., 1994).

What would you, as a protective services worker, do when you received a report that child maltreatment might be occurring? Child protective services (CPS) are those involving assessment and interventions by human services workers and others in situations where children are deemed at risk of maltreatment. Protective services workers usually are employed by public departments of social services or law enforcement agencies and courts addressing the problem. The workers' major aim is to explore whether or not abuse is occurring, assess both strengths and risks involved in the family situation, make plans to ensure safety and minimize future risks, and implement plans to maintain healthier family functioning.

Family Preservation Philosophy

Philosophy involves the concepts and principles about how the world should, or actually does, function. Philosophy provides values and guidelines for what is considered important, which enables it to be used as a tool of intervention to help guide the intervention process. It emphasizes the aspects of a problem situation and the helping process that should be the focus of attention. Child maltreatment provides an example. A philosophy based on the medical model would orient your focus on the pathology of the child abuser. The medical model emphasizes how illnesses (or problems) should be cured (or solved). The focus is on "fixing" the individual. In the case of child abuse, then, intervention or treatment would be directed at the abuser.

A philosophy based on family systems, on the other hand, would emphasize the importance of the entire family's interaction with each other and the environment. Such a philosophy would guide intervention to involve all family members. It would not limit the intervention to the abuser alone.

One trend in protective services involves home-based services and an intensive family preservation philosophy and approach. This approach refers to "providing services to vulnerable families in order to prevent out-of-home-placement of children" (Maluccio, 1990, p. 18; Wells, 1995). A family preservation philosophy also involves concepts and principles about what's important for intervention in cases of child maltreatment. These concepts and principles provide guidelines for how practitioners should proceed with intervention (Chapter 11 discusses family preservation more extensively).

A significant principle concerns the importance of children remaining with their own families if at all possible. People are considered capable of changing if they have help, and family preservation emphasizes the importance of positive intervention when crises occur, so that children need not be placed out of their own homes.

Holder and Corey (1991) describe a philosophical perspective on family preservation that emphasizes eight points. First, the problem is seen as a social issue. Child maltreatment occurs within the family not because one or two parents intentionally decide to be mean to their children but rather because of external stresses and pressures upon parents. The focus is on the environment and parents' interactions with that environment. Child maltreatment is more the fault of a difficult and nonsupportive environment than the intentional deeds of particular parents. A second principle holds that condemning

and punishing parents who maltreat their children does no good. Assuming that parents will change their behavior if they are chastised is unrealistic. Rather, the cause of the problem lies in pressures coming to bear upon parents from the outside environment. Thus, these pressures should be the focus of intervention.

A third philosophical perspective is that intervention should not interfere with the family's dynamics and ongoing activity any more than is absolutely necessary. The family should be helped to improve its functioning on a day-to-day basis together. Neither abused children nor an abusive parent should be plucked out of the home. Rather, the home environment should be healed and strengthened so that all family members may flourish within it.

The fourth principle indicates that workers should concentrate only on working constructively with the families "to ensure a partnership role" (LeVine & Sallee, 1999, p. 366). "Helpfulness" is the key word (Holder & Corey, 1991, p. 2). Practitioners should *help* parents become stronger and more effective.

The fifth principle is that workers can help maltreating families by coordinating their intervention efforts with those of other professionals (Mather & Lager, 2000). One way of doing this coordination is through case management (the coordination of the work of all the professionals participating in the intervention). Chapter 15 addresses this activity in more depth. You, then, as the worker, do not have to do everything for the family yourself. Instead, you can be most useful by overseeing and integrating the work of others.

This philosophy is positive. The sixth principle dictates that the majority of maltreating child caretakers can improve their conduct with support and assistance. This view is different from approaching a difficult, abusive situation that you feel is hopeless. Instead, you review alternatives for helping the family until you find some that work. LeVine & Sallee (2000) explain that "[r]espect is shown for each family's strengths, potential, natural striving toward growth, and capacity for change. Each family is individualized, and its unique strengths and capacities are identified" (p. 366) and emphasized in the change process.

A seventh principle offers the guidance that keeping maltreated children within their own families, if at all possible, is best (LeVine & Sallee, 2000). This principle relates to the idea that risk can be minimized and the children's safety maximized if internal and external pressures can be controlled and parents are taught coping strengths.

The final guiding principle is that clients should always be integrally involved in the intervention

(Crosson-Tower, 1999; LeVine & Sallee, 2000). As workers, we do not go into their homes and prescribe what they should do. This approach does not work. If you remember, this approach coincides with our consistent emphasis in generalist practice on client involvement.

The Generalist Intervention Model: Engagement

As with other aspects of human services, protective service workers follow the planned change process proposed by the Generalist Intervention Model (GIM). Engagement is especially critical in child maltreatment cases. When a protective service worker abruptly appears on a family's doorstep, feelings of "anxiety, discomfort, guilt, shame, defensiveness, as well as anger, resentment, resistance, and opposition" are likely aroused (Kadushin & Martin, 1988, p. 254). Defusing these negative reactions as much as possible is then up to the worker. The worker should "respond to the emotional needs of the child and family" (Brisset-Chapman, 1995, p. 361).

There are a number of suggestions for how to proceed (Kadushin & Martin, 1988). First, the worker should have a forthright and candid approach, making "a clear statement" on the agency's behalf "that it has learned that the child is in potential danger and that, representing the community, it would like to enlist the aid of the parents in determining what is happening" (1988, p. 253). The worker should emphasize that the process is a joint process where both worker and family are trying to address and resolve the problem. The worker should assume an approach of helper rather than authoritative investigator. The worker should reflect the agency's concern for the well-being of the entire family.

The Generalist Intervention Model: Assessment

At least two tasks are essential during initial family assessment (Brissett-Chapman, 1995). First, the worker should "interview and observe the child and family for indicators of mental health or clinical problems that suggest child maltreatment" (1995, p. 360).

Family Assessment: Interviewing the Child

There are several suggestions regarding talking to the child during both the engagement and assessment stages. First, you should be aware of how a child's perception might differ from that of adults in at least three dimensions (Crosson-Tower, 1999).

Note that these differences may vary according to the child's developmental level and even from one child to another of the same age (Crosson-Tower, 1999; LeVine & Sallee, 2000; Sheafor et al., 2000). To begin with, children often use metaphors or stories representing what they want to say instead of using literal facts as adults do. Therefore, it's necessary for you to listen carefully in order to comprehend on many levels what the child means to say. Another difference between children and adults is perception of time. Specific numbers of days or weeks may have little meaning to children. However, referring to "milestones" such as "the time you got up" or "how long before Christmas" may provide better ways for the child to communicate about time (Crosson-Tower, 1999, p. 232). A third difference between children and adults is how a child's attention span is usually much more limited. Therefore, using activities such as role playing, play therapy,[1] or drawing may help a child attend longer and convey more information (Sheafor et al., 2000; Thompson & Rudolph, 2000).

A second suggestion for interviewing children is to pay special attention to the interview setting (Crosson-Tower, 1999, Sheafor et al., 2000). Children are not accustomed to being interviewed nor to being the center of adult attention during an interview's structured format. Selecting a familiar room where they feel comfortable, or at least someplace where there is some privacy, is helpful (Sheafor et al., 2000).

A third suggestion is to be especially sensitive to the child's emotional perspective in view of the turbulent context of abuse. Thompson and Rudolph (2000) explain:

> Abused children are not easy clients. They have learned not to trust themselves, other people, or their environment. The world and the people in it are inconsistent and hurt them. Withdrawal from this painful world is safer than chancing relationships. Building friendship and trust may be difficult. (p. 438)

Introducing yourself and informing the child about the purpose of the interview and your own role is the fourth suggestion (Crosson-Tower, 1999; Sheafor et al.,

---

1. Play therapy is a type of psychotherapy where the worker or other professional uses play, a natural means by which children express themselves, to facilitate communication (Thompson & Rudolph, 2000). The child can use toys such as dolls to act out situations, address conflicts, and express emotions that are difficult to talk about (Barker, 1999).

2000). This must be done carefully, however, so as not to frighten the child or imply blame. After introducing yourself, you might say something like "My job is to help children who are having problems at home" (Sheafor et al., 2000, p. 487). To enhance your own credibility you then might say, "I've talked to many boys and girls who had this kind of problem" (Crosson-Tower, 1999, p. 234). Knowing more about why he or she is there may help to alleviate some of the child's anxiety. Please note that there is no formula for the perfect way to communicate with a child about maltreatment. It requires sensitivity and focused attention to respond to a child's unique emotional and developmental levels and perspectives about his or her family situation.

A fifth suggestion for interviewing a child is to use some initial small talk about the child's favorite toys, television shows, or what the child is wearing. This can soften the rigidity of the interview situation and enhance the engagement process (Sheafor et al., 2000).

Helping a child anticipate what will happen in the future is the sixth suggestion; there are several ways to accomplish this (Crosson-Tower, 1999). You might initiate the process by asking what the child "expects or wants to happen" (Crosson-Tower, 1999, p. 237). It is important that the child know that his or her desires may have little or nothing to do with what may actually occur. It should be clear that many variables are involved, and the child should not "be left feeling to blame for the outcome" (Crosson-Tower, 1999, p. 237). To the extent possible, give details about the future process. If you will be interviewing the child again or meeting with the parents, you might say so. If a court appearance is ensuing, you might fill in some details about how the courtroom looks and what it's like to be part of the court process. The unknown is often scary, even for adults. The more a child knows about what to expect in the future, the more secure and less scared the child will probably be.

Family Assessment: Understanding the Family

In addition to soliciting information from the child, obtaining an accurate understanding of the family's circumstances is important (Crosson-Tower, 1999; LeVine & Sallee, 2000). Questions should focus on the forces of risk discussed below.

Details such as times, dates, and specific incidents can help the worker to discuss with the family why the worker, his or her agency, and the family should be concerned about the issues. For example, the parents arrived home at 1:30 A.M. on Sunday, October 25, and were very intoxicated. Their three children—2, 5, and 8 years old—had been alone the entire evening. When the parents arrived, the 2-year-old woke up and started to cry. The father screamed at her to "shut up," slapping her twice across the face. A worker can use these details to discuss with the parents such issues as potential problems when children are unsupervised, loss of personal control after drinking, how to establish control of children's behavior, and maximizing children's well-being.

Risk Assessment

The second task during initial assessment is to determine the degree of risk and the need to further involve the family with social services or law enforcement (Brissett-Chapman, 1995). Risk assessment has become an important process in deciding how likely the chances are that child maltreatment will occur in the family environment (Brissett-Chapman, 1995; Costin et al., 1991; Crosson-Tower, 1999; Downs et al., 1996; Holder & Corey, 1991). A number of structured risk assessment models have been developed that predict future child maltreatment incidents (Brissett-Chapman, 1995; Costin et al., 1991). Risk assessment is future oriented in that "it attempts to establish the likelihood, or an educated prediction based on a careful examination of the data [, and] that the child will be maltreated at another time" (Costin et al., 1991).

Holder and Cory (1991) maintain that risk assessment has two prmary purposes. One is to maximize children's safety within their environment. The other is to work to change and control those forces that act to increase risk within their environment. A child has greater safety when stresses impinging on the family are minimized and family members have been strengthened to better ward off future stresses.

We have established that risk involves the likelihood that a child will be maltreated. Assessing how much at risk a child is for potential maltreatment is the protective services worker's responsibility. There are five forces that can either contribute to or diminish risk in a home: "maltreatment force," "child force," "parent force," "family force," and "intervention force" (Holder & Corey, 1991, p. 23).

Maltreatment Force. Maltreatment force involves the type and severity of maltreatment that are occuring in the home (Brissett-Chapman, 1995; Costin et al., 1991; Crosson-Tower, 1999; Downs et al., 1996). Are children being neglected, burned, beaten, or sexually molested? It also focuses on the conditions under which maltreatment usually occurs. Is the abusive parent drunk, depressed, or explosive? Does the maltreatment occur randomly or only in times of crisis?

Child Force. Child force involves the maltreated child's personal characteristics (Brissett-Chapman, 1995; Costin et al., 1991; Crosson-Tower, 1999; Downs et al., 1996). Is the child extremely withdrawn, brashly aggressive, or very slow to respond? This force also involves the extent to which you, as the worker, perceive the child as being susceptible to maltreatment. For instance, very young children and physically disabled children are exceptionally vulnerable.

Parent Force. Parent force entails the characteristics of the parents in the family (Brissett-Chapman, 1995; Costin et al., 1991; Crosson-Tower, 1999; Downs et al., 1996). How do they feel about themselves? Do they feel guilty after maltreatment occurs? How do they cope with external stresses?

A second aspect of parent force is the parents' child management skills. To what extent do the parents rely on physical punishment to control their children? How do they interact with the children? How responsive are they to the children's wants and demands?

The third facet of parent force concerns the parents' own upbringing and past experiences. How were they treated by their own parents? Do they have a prison record or other convictions? Do they have health difficulties? The final component of parent force is the interactional patterns of the parents with others.

How do they communicate with other people? Do they have friends or neighbors with whom they associate? To what extent are they isolated from others?

Family Force. Family force concerns three elements. First, what demographic variables characterize the family? Are there one or both parents involved? How many children are there? Is the family a blended stepfamily? What levels of education, job training, and work experience do the parents have? What is their income level? Is unemployment a problem? What are their housing conditions?

The second facet of family force involves how the family can "function, interact, and communicate" (Crosson-Tower, 1999; Holder & Corey, 1991, p. 30). If parents are married, how do they get along? How

do they talk to each other? How would you describe their lifestyle? Are they prone to crises?

The third facet of family force is the overall support and nurturance the family receives from the surrounding social environment (Crosson-Tower, 1999). What relationships does the family have with extended family members? Do they have access to adequate transportation? Are they socially isolated?

Intervention Force. The fifth force that workers assess in risk management involves the intervention force. This force concerns your anticipation of how the family will react to intervention. Will the family members be angry, afraid, or wary? Intervention force also entails the outside pressures upon the family that might hinder the intervention process with the family. How large and manageable is your caseload? How frequently can you see the family? Are you readily available to them?

Assessing the Forces of Risk. Various structured risk assessment instruments are available to assist workers in risk determination; however, explaining them in detail is beyond the scope of this text. Brissett-Chapman expresses hope

> . . . that such structured risk-assessment models will increase the consistency, timeliness, appropriateness, and quality of decisions and the documentation of cases presented in court, as well as workers' accountability for the actions they take. (1995, p. 361)

The idea behind risk-assessment systems is that maltreating families lie somewhere along a risk continuum. The more pressures a family faces and the less external support it has, the greater the child maltreatment risk. Through intervention, the family is strengthened and supported while maltreatment risk to children decreases. Eventually, the worker can make the determination that the family has achieved its goals and is strong enough to cope with external social stresses. Thus, when the maltreatment risk is significantly decreased, the case will be closed.

The Generalist Intervention Model: Planning

As with any type of planning in generalist practice, objectives are specified, responsibilities assigned, and the who-will-do-what-by-when process is clearly established. Means of evaluating objectives are also determined. There are at least eight dimensions upon which goals are frequently based for families in risk management. They include:

1. *Self-sufficiency.* Parents and families frequently must enhance their ability to function independently. This dimension has to do with families being better able to fend for themselves and satisfy their own needs. Specific objectives often involve increasing self-esteem and confidence.

2. *Communications skills.* Goals focusing on improved communication skills among family members are common. Members may be encouraged to identify and express their feelings openly and honestly. Listening skills can be enhanced. Family members' ability to understand others' points of view can be improved.

3. *Parenting knowledge.* Parents may not know how to handle and control children. They may have been brought up in emotionally deprived environments themselves, and they may resort to force for controlling children's behavior because they have never been taught any other behavior management techniques. They can be taught not only to control, but to play with and enjoy their children.

   Additionally, parents may need knowledge about normal development. They need to know what is normal behavior at each age level. Appropriate expectations may reduce the frustrations parents feel when children do not behave the way parents think they *should.*

4. *Stress management.* Parents can be taught to better manage their stress levels. They can be taught to release their feelings more appropriately, instead of allowing emotional pressure to build up and explode. Learning such specific stress management techniques as relaxation approaches can also help them cope with stress.

5. *Impulse control.* Many parents in families at risk have poor impulse control. They are under tremendous stress. They often need to learn how to direct their energies in more fruitful ways than violently lashing out at their children.

6. *Problem-solving skills.* Parents in high-risk families may be so frustrated and stressed that they feel they have little control over their lives and behavior. They can be taught how to analyze problems, translate these problems into needs, establish potential alternatives to meeting these needs, evaluate the pros and cons of alterna-

tives, and, finally, select and pursue their most promising options.

7. *Interactive nurturing.* Many times, family members need to be taught how to both express their positive feelings and accept affection. They can be taught how to empathize with each other, verbalize their feelings, and reinforce their support and caring for each other.

8. *Resource enhancement.* A primary means of increasing the strength of families at risk is to increase their resources. Adequate employment, income, housing, food, and clothing all contribute to a family's well-being (Holder & Corey, 1991, Appendix N, pp. 1–30).

The Generalist Intervention Model: Implementation

The implementation approaches specified in the plan are carried out during this service provision step. This step includes tasks for the CPS worker, the client family, and other professionals involved in the case. Other professionals may include those from medical, mental health, educational, and legal agencies (Costin et al., 1991; Crosson-Tower, 1999). Services may include homemaker services, parent-aides, visiting nurses, special school programs, day care, emergency shelter and foster care, parent education programs, job-seeking and employment services, crisis nurseries and respite care to provide parents with breaks from child care, adequate housing, financial assistance, and transportation to and from programs. Any services that fortify a family's strengths may be part of the treatment implementation. The chances that you, as a CPS worker, may function primarily as a case manager—the one who coordinates a range of services during this part of the intervention—are quite possible.

The Generalist Intervention Model: Evaluation and Termination

During the evaluation step, progress is documented, goals and objectives are reviewed, and intervention plans are amended to meet the current risk situation. Hopefully, the service provision during the intervention process has significantly decreased risk, increased safety, and generally strengthened the family unit.

A case is terminated when risk is no longer present or has been significantly decreased so that the children are adequately safe. Goals and objectives that have been attained are specified and documented. A final risk assessment is likely to be concluded and recorded.

Child Maltreatment and Mezzo Practice

As work addressing child maltreatment inherently focuses on the family, mezzo practice is integrally involved. Other aspects of mezzo practice might include linking abusive parents with support or child behavior management groups. Support groups for survivors, both as children and adults, are other possibilities.

Child Maltreatment and Macro Practice

There are numerous recommendations for changes in policy and practice at the macro level concerning the welfare of maltreated children. A current trend is the focusing of resources in finding and reporting cases, thereby draining financial support from other aspects of treatment (Wells, 1995). Brissett-Chapman calls for a "continuum approach" to

addressing child maltreatment including prevention, reporting, and treatment (1995, p. 364). Human services professionals must actively advocate for resources and positive change in these directions (for an idea of how these skills can be applied to the elderly, see Highlight 7.2) (Wells, 1995).

Schene (1996) calls for macro improvements in at least five areas. First, instead of emphasizing the reporting of child maltreatment, we should focus on providing services aimed at prevention. Second, a more supportive system geared toward improving resources and services for families in general is essential to maintain family strengths. Third, more resources should be directed at treatment instead of case finding. Fourth, we should focus on treatment outcomes and improvement rather than on treatment process. Fifth, more community and neighborhood supports should be located and developed.

HIGHLIGHT 7.2

Generalist Practice, Empowerment, and the Elderly

Working with special populations and at-risk populations often requires special skills. We have talked about working on behalf of children when addressing child maltreatment. Now we will focus on later lifespan issues and practice techniques for working with the elderly. Zuniga describes practice with the elderly as "complex and demanding, given the range of needs of this population, the various subgroups of at-risk elderly people, and the multiple roles" that must be employed to respond to client needs (1995, p. 173). She adds that demographic trends indicate that practitioners will be working with increasing numbers of older people.

Cox and Parsons emphasize that an empowerment orientation to practice "can assist older people to utilize their strengths, abilities, and competencies in order to mobilize their resources toward problem solving and ultimately toward empowerment" (1994, p. 19). They emphasize that empowerment rests on principles including clients' integral involvement in the problem definition and planned change process, emphasizing and using clients' strengths, teaching needed skills, using support networks and collective action, and linking with necessary resources.

Elderly people often must deal with decreased power on several levels. First, physical health tends to decline as

people age (Dunkle & Norgard, 1995; Zuniga, 1995). The elderly must rely increasingly on supportive help to survive. Second, although elderly people generally maintain good mental health (Dunkle & Norgard, 1995), many experience "a modest impairment of short-term memory, a decrease in speed of learning, a slowing of reaction time, and some degree of mild forgetfulness" (Cox & Parsons, 1994, p. 23). Third, they often experience loss of support systems as their peers' health declines. Fourth, retirement may require adaptation on the elderly's part, requiring them to learn new ways for spending time (Zuniga, 1995). They may also experience feelings of uselessness when no longer employed. Fifth, the elderly may encounter age discrimination by younger people based on prejudicial stereotypes such as emphasis on physical, mental, and economic weakness.

Zuniga (1995) emphasizes four concepts essential in empowering elderly people: adaptation, competence, relatedness, and autonomy. First, workers should focus on *adaptation* to new experiences, issues, and even losses. An empowering approach emphasizes how people use their strengths to survive, adapt to new experiences, and learn to appreciate the positive aspects of these new experiences. A second concept is *competence*. Workers can help elderly people focus on and emphasize what they *can* do instead of what they *cannot* do. Each individual should appreciate his or her own level of competence. *Relatedness,* the third concept, involves the sense of belonging and relating to

(continued)

other people. Hence, practitioners should work to strengthen elderly people's relationships with others, including friends, family members, and professional caregivers (such as visiting nurses or physical therapists). Support, activity, and educational groups are other options. *Autonomy,* the fourth concept, involves helping people live as independently as possible:

> *Adaptation for elderly people often is related directly to having to adjust to being less physically able, feeling weak because of an illness, having to rely on medication for the rest of their life, or having to rely on strangers for daily living needs. Thus, it appears that at every juncture, an elderly person's ability to maintain independence is threatened. Helping elderly clients accept their limitations while negotiating ways to support other areas of autonomy is a core practice need in working with this population. (Zuniga, 1995, p. 175)*

Toseland (1995) suggests five strategies for workers to increase their sensitivity to elderly people and thus enhance their effectiveness. First, practitioners should identify and face any preconceived notions and stereotypes they might harbor about the elderly. These judgments must be identified before they can be eliminated or changed. Second, workers should appreciate the different life situations experienced by people from different age groups within the elderly population. For example, women seeking work in the 1930s will have experienced very different conditions than those employed in the 1940s (1995). Women in the 1930s probably had a very difficult time finding jobs during the Great Depression when unemployment was skyrocketing. However, women in the 1940s likely had a pick of many jobs when men were fighting World War II and industry was begging women to come to work.

The third strategy for increasing sensitivity toward elderly people involves understanding that they are individuals with unique characteristics, experiences, and personalities just like anybody else. Consider one woman, Florence, 84 years old, whose life was filled with difficulties including a decade of tuberculosis; her husband's abrupt death by heart attack at age 51 as he slept beside her; her caretaking responsibilities for her own aging, mentally ill mother for 15 years; and having to pinch pennies her entire life. Nonetheless, Florence remained cheerful, optimistic, and interested in the world around her throughout her life. One of her nieces took her to China, Disney World, New Orleans, and Europe after she turned 78 (not all in one trip, of course).

Contrast Florence with Carolle—also 84—Florence's maid of honor 65 years earlier. Carolle had a long, good life with a husband who adored her. He cooked and cleaned for her in addition to holding a lucrative engineering job. He died when she was 78. At that time Carolle remained financially stable. Carolle began experiencing health problems including hearing loss and diabetes at age 80. Complications from the diabetes forced her to enter a nursing home at age 83. Carolle's personality had always been persnickety. She demanded that she get her own way and usually got it, thanks to her devoted spouse. She was never interested in the world around her, despite the many innovations developed during her lifetime (television, a moon walk, personal computers, and so on). She was always a complainer; everything was always wrong.

Florence visited Carolle faithfully every Sunday for years and endured her endless whining and complaining. There could not be two more different people.

A fourth strategy for increasing sensitivity to elderly people involves learning about how both gender and cultural background influence the aging experience. Both "older women and older people of color are at a higher risk of being unhealthy, poor, alone, and inadequately housed" (Toseland, 1995, p. 154). Long-term experiences with discrimination can affect attitudes and expectations. Worker sensitivity to cultural differences in terms of communication, family relationship, and gender roles is critical (Chapter 3 discussed a range of cultural and ethnic differences more thoroughly).

The fifth suggestion for increasing sensitivity to the elderly concerns understanding the developmental aspects of later life such as people's physical, mental, living, and socioeconomic conditions.

Empowerment in Micro Practice with the Elderly

Cox and Parsons (1994) suggest six specific empowerment strategies for micro practice with elderly people:

1. Listen carefully to what clients are saying and work to understand what they mean. Cox and Parsons explain that "engaging and drawing out the emotions of elderly clients and helping them frame their situations in view of past experiences and events are effective listening techniques" (1994, p. 112).

2. Help clients identify their coping skills and their abilities to implement planned change. Encouraging clients to talk about what is important to them, including their significant life experiences, is helpful. Explore how they have coped with their difficulties in the past.

3. Show clients videotapes of other elderly people talking about how they have learned to cope with similar issues. As with support group involvement, these sessions may help clients understand that they are not isolated and alone in their concerns.

4. Share newspaper articles, stories, or other informative materials with clients, especially those about elderly people who have initiated service activities and political action. The Gray Panthers, an advocacy organization for the social and economic needs of the elderly, is a good example of how people can work together for legislative and political change.

5. Connect clients with other older people to provide "mutual support and education" (Cox & Parsons, 1994, p. 112). Groups might include those experiencing similar life issues "such as retirement, illnesses such as Alzheimer's disease, and chronic health or mental health conditions; and families of older people who have a terminal illness" (Bellos & Ruffolo, 1995, p. 171).

6. Encourage clients to help others. For example, one social services agency organized a number of elderly clients and helped them assess their special competencies. They were then organized as volunteers to help each other. Those who could drive would transport others who could not for grocery shopping and medical appointments. People with good eyesight volunteered to read to those who could not see as well. People with exceptional organizational skills volunteered to organize and oversee the volunteer activities. Many people put their strengths to use and became productive members of the community.

Empowerment in Mezzo Practice with the Elderly

We have already mentioned the use of various support groups to help elderly people. Family relationships should be nurtured and strengthened. Self-help groups for people providing care to the elderly, especially those requiring much support, can help invigorate these caregivers and indirectly support elderly clients (Biegel, Shore, & Gordon, 1984). Respite care, which involves the temporary relief and assumption of responsibilities by someone else, can also be provided to family members caring for elderly relatives (Bellos & Ruffolo, 1995).

Empowerment in Macro Practice with the Elderly

Generalist practitioners can become politically involved in "protecting older people's autonomy, providing choices for care for older people and their families, and increasing the accessibility of services that are culturally competent for all groups of older people" (Bellos & Ruffolo, 1995, p. 169). Keeping a careful eye on proposed legislation addressing older people's health care and social service needs is critical (Cox & Parsons, 1994). For example, increasing the age at which older people can first begin receiving Social Security benefits has significant impact on elderly people's financial standing. Likewise, monitoring the availability of adequate health care for elderly people is paramount. Legislative advocacy can effectively help establish an adequate quality of life for many elderly people.

Working to improve and develop community services for the elderly provides other important macro practice possibilities. For example, community-based adult day care services can be developed (Bellos & Ruffolo, 1995). Day care programs can provide a wide range of "health, social, and related support services" including "individual and family counseling, group work services, outreach and broker services, supportive services, and care planning services" to a community's elderly residents (1995, p. 170).

Another example of a community-based program is one directed at educating community clergy to enhance linkages "between organized and informal support systems" (Biegel et al., 1984, p. 99). A university school of social welfare provided training with the following goals: "to impart a foundation of knowledge of the aging process, to examine the specific needs and contributions of aged individuals, to impart knowledge of community resources available for the aged individuals, and to increase participants' awareness of creative ways to minister to the aged" (1984, p. 99).

Crisis Intervention

Crisis intervention is a brief and time-limited therapeutic intervention where a human service professional or other mental health professional helps a client system in crisis recognize the precipitating problem and identify potential coping methods (Roberts, 2000). In other words, crisis intervention helps people learn to cope with or adjust to extreme external pressures. Kanel (1999) defines a crisis as a situation where:

(1) a precipitating event occurs; (2) the perception of this event leads to subjective distress; and (3) usual coping methods fail, leading the person experiencing the event to function psychologically, emotionally, or behaviorally at a lower level than before the precipitating event occurred. (p. 1)

Human services professionals use the term *crisis* in two ways (Barker, 1999). First, it can take the form of internal emotional distress on the part of an individual or family experiencing such incidents as the death of a loved one, job loss, or unwanted pregnancy. Second, it may be a social event in the macro environment causing disaster and major disruption of life for a large number of people (for example, a major earthquake, flood, drought, or bombing attack).

Virtually any upsetting event can evoke a crisis. These include family and other interpersonal difficulties, financial problems, physical illnesses, accidents, problems related to age (such as those common in adolescence or old age), substance abuse, sexual assault, and involvement in the legal system (Dixon, 1987; Kanel, 1999; Roberts, 2000).

The Crisis Process

Golan (1987) relates how crises typically progress. First, an individual is exposed to a heavy amount of stress over some period of time. Second, this stress acts to make the person exceptionally vulnerable to intimidation and assaults from outside (1987, p. 364). The usual emotional protection from worrisome and painful incidents is weaker than usual. The third aspect is some "precipitating factor" that acts as "a turning point to push the individual into a state of active crisis, marked by disequilibrium, disorganization, and immobility" (1987, p. 364). As the crisis continues, the individual perceives the precipitating factor and other stressors to which he or she is being exposed as increasingly serious threats.

Finally, the person experiences surging anxiety and such accompanying troublesome emotions as depression or grief.

At this point, the individual will probably be most receptive to help. Normal defense mechanisms have been weakened. As people become more anxious and emotional, they typically become less objective and logical. Crises breed desperation which fosters panic and immobility. People in crisis can easily become frozen in their tracks. Your job is to get them moving again.

Crisis can happen to individuals, families, groups, communities, and organizations; however, regardless of level, the essential process of crisis buildup remains the same.

Major Concepts in Crisis Intervention

There are many frameworks for crisis intervention. However, virtually all of them have the following themes in common:

1. *The primary goal of crisis intervention is to help the client return at least to the precrisis level of functioning* (Dixon, 1987; Ell, 1995; Golan, 1987; Okun, 1997).

We have described the crisis process. A person is under a large amount of stress for some period of time. Subsequently, another upsetting event or series of events occurs. The person becomes emotionally shaken, usually loses an objective sense of self-direction, and becomes unable to proceed. Crisis intervention involves helping people in crisis return to the level of functioning they were at prior to the precipitating event. This means that crisis intervention goals are very specific and deal only with issues directly related to the crisis situation.

An example is a situation in which you, as the practitioner, receive a call from a client threatening suicide. Your primary goal would be to help that person return to her level of functioning prior to having suicidal thoughts and feelings. Crisis intervention would not seek to achieve more complicated, long-term goals. For example, you would not try to help the person to become more popular or improve her personality. These goals might be worked on in a longer-term counseling format.

This type of intervention does not mean that you should tell your clients to get worse again if they enhance their level of functioning above its precrisis level. If clients make greater improvements, that is wonderful. Your maximum goals with clients would be some improvement above their precrisis level of functioning. Goals in crisis intervention should be realistic and focus primarily on the individual's ability to cope with the *crisis*.

2. *Crisis intervention is relatively short term* (Ell, 1995; Okun, 1997; Parsons & Wicks, 1994).

Because the intent is to return the client to the precrisis level of functioning, crisis intervention progresses quickly. In the past, a crisis was typically believed to last from six to eight weeks (Halley et al., 1998; Parad & Parad, 1990). However, crises are now thought to last "considerably longer . . . depending on the nature of the precipitating event and the life circumstances of the individual or family" (Ell, 1995, p. 661). Your length of involvement will usually be shorter than your interventions in noncrisis situations. If, for example, you are working in a hospital emergency room, your contact would likely be for less than one day (Wicks & Parsons, 1984). In other settings, such as a mental health center, your length of intervention might last from four to six weeks (Kanel, 1999). Regardless, crisis-intervention contacts are significantly shorter than most other client relationships in practice.

3. *"Specific, current, observable difficulties are the target"* of the intervention (Parsons & Wicks, 1994, p. 102).

Crisis intervention focuses purely on the crisis and those aspects of the client's life directly related to the crisis. Therefore, crisis intervention does little delving into clients' pasts. Only information about the past directly relevant to the crisis is gathered. You cannot afford to waste time on anything but resolving the immediate crisis.

4. *Crisis intervention strategies generally work better than other approaches when dealing with crises* (Aguilar & Messick, 1974; Ell, 1995; Parad & Parad, 1990).

Crisis intervention is a well-defined, viable approach that is indeed the best approach to crisis situations. Crises are by nature severe. Their resolution merits the top priority in intervention. Other related stresses and problems can be dealt with later using other methods.

5. *The practitioner in crisis intervention "assumes a more active role" which is often more directive than* *that assumed in other approaches to generalist practice* (Aguilar & Messick, 1974, p. 15; Halley et al., 1998; Okun, 1997).

Throughout this text, we emphasize the importance of client involvement. Integral client participation throughout the planned change process is essential. Clients should also be as involved as possible in the crisis-intervention process. However, the key phrase here is *as possible.* You might have to expend more pressure to get the client moving from his or her emotionally frozen position. With crises, you usually do not have the luxury of relaxed discussion time. Consider a bewildered, homeless client living with her family in her car when the wind chill factor is hitting 25 degrees below zero. You probably will not have time to discuss all possible options available in a leisurely fashion. Rather, you may need to strongly encourage her to take some direction you specify in order to keep her family from freezing.

Steps in Crisis Intervention

The following explores a clearly defined four-step crisis intervention model that coincides with the planned change process in generalist practice (Aguilar & Messick, 1974).

Step 1: Assessment

The first step in crisis intervention is assessment. Engagement is assumed to be a part of this first step. The art in crisis intervention is to focus on the specific precipitating event that brought the client to you. Only clearly related aspects of the client's situation should be addressed. At least five specific areas of questioning should be pursued (Aguilar & Messick, 1974).

First, you must determine why the person called you or came in to see you on that particular day (Halley et al., 1998; Roberts, 2000). What precipitating event has occurred? The crisis usually occurs less than two weeks before a client seeks professional help. Often, the precipitating event has occurred within the prior 24 hours. For instance, one client was just told he has brain cancer, or another client just discovered that her husband is having an affair.

A typical first question to the client is something like, "What brings you in to see me today?" or "What has happened to make you so upset?" The intent is to identify and specify as soon as possible what the crisis is.

A second line of questioning should involve how your client views the crisis situation and precipitating event (Roberts, 2000). How does he or she feel about the event? What impact does the client think it will have on his or her life now and in the future? You might ask yourself how objective your client appears to be about the situation.

The third relevant line of questioning involves whether your client has access to support from others (Halley et al., 1998). Is there anyone the client can talk to? Whom does he or she feel comfortable asking for help? The general guiding principle is "the more people helping the person the better" (Aguilar & Messick, 1974, p. 58). Crises are stressful, and you must act fast. The more support you can muster to help your client return to the precrisis level of functioning, the better.

The fourth area of information to pursue is your client's history in solving similar problems (Halley et al., 1998; Okun, 1997; Roberts, 2000). Has the client ever experienced this crisis before? If so, how did it get resolved? How does your client usually cope with stressful events in general? Can any of these coping skills be applied to the current situation?

A final and very critical area of information to solicit involves the extent to which your client is either "suicidal or homicidal" (Aguilar & Messick, 1974, p. 59; Halley et al., 1998; Roberts, 2000). If you determine that your client is seriously considering violently harming him- or herself or others, you may need to take more drastic steps. For example, immediate hospitalization or referral to a treatment program might be necessary.

Step 2: Planning

During this step, you must evaluate the extent to which the crisis has interfered with your client's ability to function. Which daily activities will the client be able to resume? Will he or she be able to return to a job, homemaking, parenting, education, or other activities? Additionally, how are others close to your client reacting to the crisis? Is your client receiving any support from them?

The second primary aspect of planning is to review potential alternatives, evaluate the pros and cons, and determine the course of action to pursue. Reviewing strategies that have worked in the past and deciding whether they might not be useful again is important during this phase.

Step 3: Implementation

Any of a variety of helping techniques can be used in crisis intervention. For example, workers addressing crisis situations vary in terms of the training they have had and in their practice settings. Regardless of background and setting, good interviewing and relationship-building skills are especially important. The crisis demands that you and your client move forward in a hurry. Aguilera and Messick (1974) make the following four suggestions for what to address during the implementation phase of the process:

1. Help the client look at the crisis situation more objectively (Halley et al., 1998; Roberts, 2000). People in crisis are in turmoil. When you are in emotional turmoil, it is difficult to think clearly and objectively. The worker's task is to help clients assess their situation rationally and begin to cut through the cloud of emotion that biases their rational thinking. Are they blowing the crisis and its related issues out of proportion? Are they failing to take into account other positive aspects of their lives? You can help clients evaluate their strengths and weaknesses more objectively and begin moving toward crisis resolution.

2. Help the client express hidden feelings (Roberts, 2000). Stress frequently results in anxiety and strong negative feelings. People trying to cope with stress will often desperately try to control these feelings, to hold them inside. They may fear the pain associated with anxiety, worry, grief, disappointment, and sadness. All such restrictive retention of feeling does is immobilize people. Before they can deal with their feelings and make logical choices regarding how to proceed, clients need to acknowledge that these feelings exist. Part of your role in crisis intervention is to help clients explore their emotional state. What blockages are preventing them from returning to their precrisis level of functioning? What feelings are making them "stuck"?

3. Use past coping methods in resolving the crisis (Greene et al., 2000; Halley et al., 1998; Okun, 1997; Roberts, 2000). During assessment you should already have identified what mechanisms the client has used to cope with similar crises and issues in the past. Can these be applied to the current crisis? Additionally, what new methods of coping might you suggest your client try? Perhaps, in his or her emotional turmoil, the client is having difficulty seeing what alternatives exist.

After the problem and precipitating factor for the crisis are clearly defined for the client, you can suggest potential alternatives to solve the problem. Part of the implementation process is to enable the client to make changes. Because crisis intervention is more directive than many other forms of intervention, "specific directions may be given as to what should be tried as tentative solutions" (Aguilar & Messick, 1974, p. 59). If you are in the position of meeting with the client again, you can later evaluate progress made and the effectiveness of the attempted alternatives. If the alternatives did not work, you can help your client to identify and assess the potential of new ones.

4. Reestablish old or develop new social support systems (Aguilera & Messick, 1974; Halley et al., 1998). Such systems may include "family, friends, neighbors, church, organizations, work [and] recreation" (Halley et al., 1998, p. 447). If the crisis involved a loss such as a death or divorce, you can help the client identify people who can help them through the crisis. Likewise, you can help clients call upon those people closest to them in such crises such as job loss or major health problems.

People in crisis need as much social support and nurturance as possible. Identify and use the support that is already there. If such support is scanty or nonexistent, help the client develop new relationships. During the crisis intervention process you may choose to pursue any or all of these four options. There may be crisis cases where none readily apply. Regarding the best way to proceed is up to your professional judgment.

Step 4: Anticipatory Planning

Anticipatory planning helps clients prepare for future crises (Aguilar & Messick; 1974; Halley et al., 1998). The final phase in crisis intervention focuses on articulating and summarizing what clients have learned during the crisis intervention process. What means have they developed to cope with stress? What have they learned from working through this crisis situation that they may use in future stressful times? One task of the worker is to help clients clearly identify and articulate coping behaviors so that these skills are more readily available when needed next.

In essence, the anticipatory planning phase of crisis intervention includes the evaluation and termination steps of the planned change process. Because of the fast-moving nature of crisis intervention, these phases are accomplished quickly. Often they are melded together. For instance, the summarizing involved in anticipatory planning incorporates evaluation, as only effective coping mechanisms are included. Termination promptly follows.

Highlight 7.3 applies the crisis intervention process to a case example.

HIGHLIGHT 7.3

An Example of Crisis Intervention in Micro Practice

Mindy's husband, Mork Murphy, was killed abruptly in a car accident two weeks earlier. Mindy, age 36, and Mork, age 39, had been married for 17 years. They had two children: Mordred, age 17, and Matissel, age 14.

Mindy was distraught with grief. She did not know what to do next. She had lived with Mork for almost half her life and just assumed he would always be there for her. They had had their ups and downs, but generally she felt it had been a steady, fairly happy marriage (that was, of course, except for his one extramarital fling 15 years earlier). But even the fling had become ancient history to Mindy.

Mork had been the family's primary breadwinner. He was an accountant who earned $46,743.67 a year.

Mindy had almost always worked outside of the home. However, it had consisted of doing nearly minimum-wage jobs on a part-time basis. They owned their mid-sized home in a suburb of Milwaukee. Rather, they owned about $14,000 in equity and made $1100 monthly payments.

Mindy had spent the past two weeks coping with the immediate crisis commonly caused by sudden tragic deaths. She had had funeral arrangements to make, in addition to a multitude of insurance and legal issues to settle. This moment was the first time she really had time for the momentous impact of the event to hit her. What would she do now? She was lonely. She was acutely grief stricken. She was worried about her two children, both of whom were also seriously affected by their father's abrupt death. She could not afford to maintain the style of life the family had become accustomed to. She panicked. She also had the wherewithal

(continued)

to seek help. She called the crisis-intervention unit of the local community mental-health center.[a] The intake unit set up an appointment for her with Lamont Cranston, a crisis counselor.[b]

Step 1: Assessment

Mindy met with Lamont early the next day. After cordial introductions, Lamont asked what brought her in to see him. She explained her situation to him.

They began the assessment process. Lamont's intent was to crystalize the *problems affecting Mindy* and *how she felt* about them. After some discussion, they established the following list of prioritized problems: an immediate financial crisis, her extreme level of grief, worry about her children, worry about her future (specifically, her living arrangements), and her loneliness.

Lamont continued by gently asking Mindy about her friends and family. He was investigating her *current access to support* from others. Had people generally been supportive to her during this time of great need? Were there any friends or family members in particular to whom she could turn for help? Were she and her sons able to provide each other with support?

Lamont empathized with Mindy concerning the depth of her grief. He emphasized that having an intimate partner of so many years plucked from her so hastily was indeed difficult. Searching for her innermost feelings, he indicated how losing her husband might be the most difficult loss she had ever had to deal with. Mindy responded that it was. Only the death of her own mother five years ago reminded her of how she felt today. Lamont then asked in a soft and warm manner how she had managed through the difficult times of coping with grief for her mother. He was seeking to *identify coping mechanisms Mindy had used in the past.* Mindy responded that her sister and one special old friend had both been exceptionally helpful to her at that time. She continued that she had not had much time to talk with either of them during the past two weeks.

___

a. A community mental health center is a local agency receiving some federal funding that offers various psychiatric and social services to community residents (Barker, 1999). These include inpatient and outpatient services, counseling, emergency services such as crisis lines, and programs for people addressing a range of issues across the lifespan such as substance abuse, child behavior management, or coping with Alzheimer's disease.
b. Note that items in italics reflect application of the substeps involved in the crisis intervention process.

Finally, Lamont asked gently, yet straightforwardly, if Mindy was having any destructive thoughts about herself or others. He explained how easy it is for some people to turn their grief and anger at what had happened toward themselves or others close to them. Mindy indicated that she had not had such thoughts. Lamont at this time, of course, was *evaluating the extent to which Mindy might be suicidal or homicidal.*

Step 2: Planning

Lamont *evaluated the extent to which the crisis interfered with the client's ability to function.* He determined that although this crisis situation had temporarily immobilized Mindy, she probably had the potential to carry on with her life if she was given adequate direction. Prior to her husband's death, Mindy had held her regular, although low-paying, receptionist position for the past four years. She reported having no major difficulties with her children other than what she termed "typical parent–adolescent spats." She was regularly involved with her own extended family members, many of whom lived in nearby areas. Thus, Mindy had a number of strengths upon which to base her plans.

Lamont and Mindy *discussed alternative solutions* to some of her problems at this time. Her primary problem was that of financial crisis. He referred her to a financial planner right within his agency. The planner could help her determine the minimum amount of money she needed in order to live, review her total assets (e.g., current income, house equity, savings, insurance payments, and cash), and identify what alternatives she could pursue about her housing situation. Later on, Mindy might pursue with him the possibility of job training and financial resources to assist in solving her financial problems.

Mindy's second major problem involved her grief. Lamont referred her to a self-help group for survivors of the death of a loved one (held at another social services agency). He cited the specific time and place the group met. If they chose, her sons could also attend. Mindy indicated that she would pursue this idea.

Mindy's other problems involved worry about her future in general and her living arrangements in particular. Both of these were directly related to her financial decisions. Lamont urged her to put off consideration of the two former problems until she had time to establish clearly the state of her financial affairs. Then she could review the options available to her.

They articulated specific objectives regarding who Mindy was to call by specified dates. Finally, they set up another appointment to meet one week from that day.

Step 3: Implementation

Altogether, Mindy met with Lamont four times over four weeks. She indicated that her meetings with the financial planner were going well. After including her husband's life insurance benefits, her assets were greater than she had anticipated. The planner was helping her develop short-term and long-term goals regarding living arrangements and employment.

Mindy and Lamont talked about other realistic alternatives available to her. He helped her to start working through the emotional turmoil that was immobilizing her. She remained very sad. However, she began to understand that she would persevere through this very difficult time in her life. Lamont's intent was to help her *gain a more realistic, objective perspective on her life* so that she could go on.

Additionally, during their meetings, Lamont encouraged Mindy to stop desperately trying to *contain her hidden feelings and emotions* so that she could begin to deal with them and recover. Sometimes, she cried sorrowfully. Lamont encouraged this as a natural expression of her grief.

Together, they continued to *explore and use coping mechanisms.* Lamont encouraged her to frequently contact her sister and her close friend, both of whom were so comforting to her after her mother's death. Additionally, Mindy and her sons did attend the self-help group Lamont had suggested, which she said was beneficial to her. She indicated that she was motivated to continue for the next few weeks and possibly even months.

In her discussion with Lamont, Mindy recognized that she had much respect for the minister of her church. Although she had never discussed such personal matters with him before, she went to talk to him about her grief. Afterward, she told Lamont that her pain was still raging. However, her minister had helped her gain some peace.

In terms of *reestablishing her social support network,* Mindy was not ready to entertain other people or enjoy herself regardless of the circumstance. However, she was able to return to work. She continued to attend her sons' sporting events, as both boys were actively involved in school sports. She spoke with her sister and good friend regularly.

Step 4: Anticipatory Planning

During Mindy's final session with Lamont, they *summarized together the progress she had made* in so short a time. She was coping with her financial crisis by obtaining help from an expert. She and her sons discovered that self-help groups can be beneficial. Additionally, Mindy worked on maintaining open communication with her sons so that they might support each other in their grief. Finally, she maintained strong and regular contact with those persons identified as being especially helpful to her in times of crisis—her sister, good friend, and minister.

Lamont emphasized how well Mindy had pulled herself together. He commended her for having the strength to do so. He also *suggested how the coping methods she had discovered and was using might help her again in future times of need.* Lamont wished Mindy the best. This case of crisis intervention was terminated.

A Few Words About Helping People Cope with Grief and Loss

There are a number of suggestions for how you, as a professional, can help someone coping with death, a terminal disease, or virtually any type of extreme loss.

1. Encourage clients to talk about their loss, both with you and supportive others. Talking about grief eases loneliness and allows them to vent their feelings. Talking with close friends gives people a sense of security and brings them closer to others they love. Talking with people who have had similar losses helps put clients' problems in perspective. They will see that they are not the only ones with problems. Other people with similar crises may be able to give them positive suggestions about coping. Finally, clients may enhance their own self-esteem and sense of well-being when helping others.
2. Understand that many negative feelings may surface when a person is struggling to cope with a crisis. They might include anger, depression, or grief. Encourage expression of even these negative feelings so that clients might begin coping with them and moving forward.
3. Convey verbally and nonverbally that you are willing to talk about any concerns of the client. What you want to convey to clients is that you are emotionally ready to help them cope with their grief and to provide them with support. Remember,

(continued)

however, that clients may always choose not to share their feelings with you. You can encourage, but you cannot force them.

4. Do not discourage crying. Rather, people should be encouraged to cry as they feel the need. Crying releases tension that is part of grieving.

5. Answer questions as honestly as you can. Sometimes, this task is especially difficult. For instance, if you are dealing with a crisis where a client or someone close is dying or very ill, questions may be unpleasant. Answers may be awkward and even painful. Nonetheless, being as honest and straightforward as you possibly can is important. If you do not know an answer, seek out someone (e.g., a physician) who will accurately provide the requested information. Evasion or ambiguity in response to a dying person's questions only increase his or her concerns. If there is a chance for recovery, this fact should be mentioned. Even a small margin of hope can be a comfort. The

chances for recovery, however, should not be exaggerated.

6. If the crisis involves a dying person, help that person become the *star* of his or her own death. In other words, provide the person with requested information and help the person participate in decisions concerning death. Many people, when dying, reach a point where they want to tie up their loose ends.

They want to consciously set their affairs in order, clarify their will, and discuss their wishes regarding their funeral. Avoiding such topics is easy for other people, because of their own fears of death. Instead, many people feel more comfortable avoiding the painful topics and trying to remain unrealistically cheery. You, as a helping professional, can help your clients continue to appreciate their personal significance even when death is near. You can also urge your clients' loved ones to remain involved with your clients until the very end.

Crisis Intervention at the Mezzo Level

Although Highlight 7.3 portrays an example of crisis intervention in micro practice, in many ways, this example converges with mezzo practice. Mindy's two sons were also indirectly and integrally involved in the helping process, even though they did not actually meet with the crisis-intervention practitioner.

Golan summarizes the relevance of crisis intervention to mezzo practice with families:

In general, whether a family is considered to be in a state of collective crisis because of the role disruption of one of its members or whether one member's state of crisis acts as the hazardous event that disrupts the rest of the family system, intervention efforts should include evaluation of the family's strengths and weaknesses, of their capacities and motivation for change, and of the resources at their disposal, no matter who the designated client may be. (1987, p. 368)

A crisis affecting one or more members of a family affects the entire family. Likewise, intervention efforts directed at some member or part of a family influence the entire family group.

Golan states that crisis intervention is also relevant within the context of small groups:

Crisis-oriented groups are frequently used as support systems to avoid hospitalization or institutionaliza-

tion, to deal with potentially hazardous crises, such as impending surgery and dislocation, to resolve parent–child or marital conflicts, and to migrate acute eruptions among members of chronically disordered families or groups. (1987, p. 368)

Crisis Intervention at the Macro Level

In our introduction to crisis intervention, we cited how the approach is frequently used in response to crises involving major population groups suffering from natural disasters. Floods, earthquakes, droughts, and famines all require crisis intervention efforts on a massive scale. A macro perspective on crisis intervention could potentially involve countries, states, nations, and even continents, depending on the scope of the natural disaster. These other systems could contribute food, clothing, shelter, medical supplies, or funds to purchase what people in the crisis area need. This type of crisis intervention is at the macro level.

Crisis intervention could also be applied in economic and political situations. For example, human services workers or agencies are often involved with groups coping with plant closings and other economic emergencies. At another macro level, the former Soviet Union was in need of economic assistance when it disbanded its political structure and was coping with massive economic repercussions.

HIGHLIGHT 7.4

Definitions of AODA Terms

Familiarizing yourself with a number of terms commonly used in substance abuse intervention is useful. The jargon tends to revolve around the terms *alcohol, drug,* and *substance* (often referred to as *psychoactive substance*). In everyday usage, the term *alcohol* refers to any type of fermented or distilled liquor containing alcohol, such as whiskey or beer. *Drug* refers to a wide range of materials that alter mood or consciousness when ingested, including amphetamines, cannabis, cocaine, and hallucinogens. *Substance* is commonly used to refer to mind-altering drugs, including alcohol (hence the term *alcohol and other substance abuse*). In the context of abuse, described below, the terms *substance* and *drugs* are often used interchangeably (Gray, 1995).

Several other terms used in conjunction with alcohol, drugs, and substances are *dependence, tolerance, withdrawal, abuse, intoxication, alcoholism, alcoholic,* and *addiction.*

The *Diagnostic and Statistical Manual of Mental Disorders (DSM-IV-TR)*[a] published by the American Psychiatric Association (APA) (2000) defines substance *dependence* as "a cluster of cognitive, behavioral, and physiological symptoms" resulting from continued use of the substance despite significant resulting problems (p. 192). It occurs when three or more of the following happen within a one-year period:

1. *Tolerance*—the user requires increasingly more of the substance to reach the same level of mood alteration, or the substance's effects diminish significantly with continued use.
2. *Withdrawal*—these are symptoms that develop as a result of discontinued use of the substance or the compulsion to absorb the substance to avert these symptoms. Despite discontinued use, the user still craves the substance. Withdrawal symptoms may include severe abdominal pain, convulsions, anxiety attacks, depression, and uncontrollable trembling.

3. The user takes greater amounts of the substance over a longer time period than he or she meant to.
4. The user expresses an ongoing desire or failed attempts to decrease or control substance use.
5. The user spends huge amounts of time participating in activities aimed at obtaining or using the substance and recuperating from its aftermath.
6. The user curtails or avoids significant social, work, or recreational involvement due to substance use.
7. The user continues to use the substance despite being aware that the substance is causing or intensifying continued physical or psychological difficulties.

The *DSM-IV-TR* defines *substance abuse* as "a maladaptive pattern of substance use manifested by recurrent and significant adverse consequences related to the repeated use of substances" (APA, 2000, pp. 198–199). This is reflected by one or more of the following criteria in any 12-month period:

1. repeated failure to accomplish major work, educational, or social responsibilities due to substance use;
2. repeated use of the substance at times when it could cause physical harm (such as when driving);
3. repeated use of the substance that results in legal problems (such as tickets for driving under the substance's influence or arrests for disorderly conduct);
4. continued use of the substance despite the fact that it causes frequent interpersonal problems.

The *DSM-IV-TR* adds one other criterion for abuse, namely, that it involves people who have never been diagnosed with substance dependence.

The *DSM-IV-TR* indicates that a primary difference between the technical definitions of substance *dependence* and *abuse* involves the consequences for each. *Abuse* does not include the symptoms of tolerance, withdrawal, or compulsive use. Rather, *abuse* focuses on the negative outcomes of repeated use, emphasizing the user's interaction with or impact on other people and systems (such as experiences involving legal or interpersonal problems). Often an individual suffers substance *abuse* as an early user before the symptoms of substance *dependence* clearly emerge; however, many individuals can experience substance *abuse* over a long period of time without encountering symptoms of *dependence* (APA, 2000). Substance *abuse* might be regarded as "less problematic" than substance *dependence* because many of the physical and psychological symptoms associated with *dependence* are not yet evident (Barker, 1999, p. 470).

(continued)

a. This manual is the official authority for defining and explaining mental disorders and their symptoms. It is used to enhance accurate communication among human service and other professionals regarding clients' conditions. It is also used to provide diagnoses for eligibility to receive third-party payments (e.g., Medicare or private health insurance).

Intoxication, linked to drug abuse and dependence, is the development of a series of symptoms, often involving psychological or behavioral changes, directly related to intake of the substance and its influence on the central nervous system. Specific symptoms may include inability to think clearly, distorted perception, temporary euphoria, and impaired motor functioning.

Alcoholism is "a chronic disorder characterized by repeated excessive use of alcoholic beverages and decreased ability to function socially and vocationally" (*Random House Webster's Collegiate Dictionary,* 1999, p. 31). *Alcoholics* are people who suffer from alcoholism. *Addiction* is a term referring to dependence on some substance, having the same consequences as those described above; the term *substance dependence* is now commonly replacing *addiction* (Barker, 1999).

Terminology can be confusing (Gray, 1995). The same words are used differently in various contexts and treatment settings. Note that several terms are used to refer to professionals counseling people who abuse or are dependent upon alcohol or other mind-altering drugs. These include *substance abuse counselors, AODA counselors,* and *chemical dependency counselors.* Practitioners counseling people who abuse or are dependent upon alcohol may be called *alcoholism* or *alcohol abuse counselors.*

With respect to substance use problems, in everyday usage the term *abuse* often is used to include symptoms evident in the technical definitions of both abuse and dependence. Hence, we refer to counseling people for substance abuse or dependence as *substance abuse counseling.* Similarly, alcoholism counselors work both with people who abuse alcohol and those who are dependent on alcohol, often referring to both conditions as *alcohol abuse.* Therefore, in our ensuing discussion we will include *dependence* under the umbrella of *abuse* for alcohol and other substances.

Often, people have a substance of choice. That is, they prefer the type of mood alterations produced by one drug over that produced by another. For instance, one person may prefer beer over cocaine. Another person may feel just the opposite.

Being aware of the resources available to psychoactive substance abusers of any type is important for human service professionals. A large-scale self-help organization is Alcoholics Anonymous (AA), which is open to anyone who feels that he or she has encountered difficulties due to alcohol. Begun in 1935, AA now has thousands of chapters throughout the country.

Related to AA is Al-Anon. Anyone can choose to join this self-help group who feels that he or she needs help because of problems related to alcohol caused by someone other than themselves. Most members are family members of alcoholics. As with other self-help groups, Al-Anon allows members to provide each other with support, encouragement, and suggestions for dealing with problems related to alcohol.

Crisis intervention in most of these situations requires a multidisciplinary approach. Many professionals and citizens are called upon to pool their efforts and address major crises. Human services practitioners may become one segment of the total intervention effort.

Alcohol and Other Substance Abuse

Generalist practitioners need a background in substance dependence and abuse, also referred to as alcohol and other drug abuse (AODA), for three basic reasons (Gray, 1995; Roffman, 1987). (Please see Highlight 7.4 for definitions of terms.) First, human services professionals may be employed by agencies specializing in treatment for substance abuse.

Second, practitioners with graduate degrees "also function as program or agency administrators, as analysts with local or state government bureaus responsible for drug abuse services, and as aides to legislative committees" (Roffman, 1987, p. 484). These positions require knowledge of substance use and abuse even when not providing direct service to clients.

The third reason for needing some background in substance use and abuse involves your role as referral agent. Even if you do not work in a specialized substance abuse setting, you will still probably have clients or family members of clients with alcohol and other drug problems. Thus, you must be capable of making appropriate referrals. (See Highlight 7.5, which identifies a range of resources, and Chapter 15, which discusses brokering services.)

Raskin and Daley (1991) explain how alcohol and other substance abuse is often masked by and interrelated to many other problems:

HIGHLIGHT 7.5

Your Role as a Referral Agent

When you assess that alcohol or other substance abuse is a problem for a client, you need to know what resources are available to help them. We have indicated that Chapter 15 addresses brokering or referral skills in depth. Most resource agencies have similar goals in treating substance abusers. Their intent is "to educate the . . . [client] and significant others, to raise self-awareness, and to assist in the change process" (Marion & Coleman, 1991, p. 115). Marion and Coleman (1991, pp. 115–125) cite at least nine resources commonly available in communities which you can use for referrals:

1. *Detoxification.* Detoxification is "the process of removing drugs or other harmful substances from the body for a sufficient length of time to permit the restoration of adequate physiological and psychological functioning" (1991, p. 115). The client is forced to refrain from the addictive substance, while being given "rest, proper diet, health care, medication, psychological support, and social services" (Barker, 1999, p. 125). Education about the drug and its use is also provided. Detoxification usually occurs in a hospital setting, where clients remain for three to seven days. Strong encouragement is also provided to enter a rehabilitation program at the end of the stay.

2. *Outpatient services.* Outpatient services are those received by visiting a treatment facility without staying overnight. People who are drug dependent can remain in their own homes and still have services made available to them. Four types of clients are usually suitable for outpatient treatment: drug-dependent people not yet ready to commit themselves to a more extensive level of treatment; people making a transition from inpatient treatment back into the community; people who seek treatment early enough in the progression of dependency that they can respond to this level of treatment; and family members of drug-dependent people (Marion & Coleman, 1991).

3. *Intensive outpatient rehabilitation.* Dependent clients may still remain in their own homes but receive 10 to 30 hours of rehabilitative services each week. Thus, treatment is more concentrated than ordinary outpatient services.

4. *Inpatient treatment.* Clients remain in inpatient treatment all day and night. It provides a comprehensive, structured environment that maximizes control of the treatment process. In essence, it is "a safe, behaviorally oriented environment in which the patient begins to look at what addiction has done to his or her life," with the entire staff actively participating in the treatment process (Marion & Coleman, 1991, p. 117).

5. *Specialty programs and tracts.* Specialty programs target the needs of specifically designated populations. For instance, they may involve "programs for adolescents, the elderly, pregnant women … relapsers," or specifically designated ethnic or racial groups (Marion & Coleman, 1991, p. 117).

6. *Halfway houses.* Halfway houses are "transitional residences for individuals who require some professional supervision, support, or protection but not full-time institutionalization" (Barker, 1999, p. 207). Recovering abusers reside with other recovering abusers in a supportive setting, where they begin to adjust to life outside such a structured setting in the real-life community. Emphasis is on gradually increasing each resident's ability to handle responsibility at his or her own pace.

7. *Personal care homes.* People with extensive physiological damage caused by alcohol or other substance abuse may be admitted to personal care homes. Such facilities focus more on meeting basic, daily physical needs than on the provision of treatment for recovery.

8. *Mutual self-help groups.* Self-help groups are "voluntary associations of nonprofessionals who share common needs or problems and meet together for extended periods of time for the purpose of mutual support and exchange of information about activities and resources that have been found useful in problem solving. These groups usually meet without the direction of a professional" (Barker, 1999, p. 432). Specific programs include AA, Narcotics Anonymous (NA), and Cocaine Anonymous (CA). These groups provide exceptionally relevant treatment approaches in view of their established success. Support from peers in the process of recovery is especially critical (Marion & Coleman, 1991).

(continued)

In view of its prevalence, we will focus on AA here. This nationwide group provides support, information, and guidance necessary for many recovering alcoholics to maintain their recovery process. The organization's success rests upon several principles. First, other people who "really understand" are available to give the recovering dependent person friendship and warmth. Each new member is given a "sponsor," who can be called for support at any time during the day or night. Whenever the dependent person feels depressed or tempted, there is always the sponsor to turn to.

Additionally, AA provides the recovering alcoholic with a new social group with whom to talk and enjoy activities. Old friends with well-established drinking patterns usually become difficult to associate with. The recovering alcoholic can no longer participate in drinking activity. Often, social pressure is applied to drink again. AA provides a respite from such pressure and the opportunity to meet new people, if such an opportunity is needed.

AA also helps the recovering person to understand that alcoholism is a disease that the alcoholic cannot cure alone. He or she need no longer feel guilty about being an alcoholic. All that needs to be done is to stop drinking.

AA also encourages self-introspection. Members are encouraged to look inside themselves and face whatever they see. They are urged to acknowledge that they have flaws and will never be perfect. This perspective often helps people to stop fleeing from the pain of reality and hiding in alcohol and drugs. It helps them to redefine the expectations for themselves and to gain control. Within the context of this honesty, people often can also acknowledge their strengths. They learn that they do have some control over their own behavior and that they can accomplish things for themselves and others.

Organizations are also available to provide support for other family members and to give them information and suggestions. For example, Al-Anon is an organization for the families of alcoholics, and Alateen is designed specifically for teenagers within these families.

9. *Pharmacological adjuncts.* Some alcohol or other substance-dependent people need the help of prescribed medications (e.g., Antabuse, used to combat alcoholism) to help them begin the recovery process. This medication, of course, must be carefully monitored by medical staff (Marion & Coleman, 1991).

The addicted [drug dependent] person may seek help in a medical setting, a crisis clinic, a mental health agency, a family service agency, or from a private practitioner or a public assistance agency. In the medical setting, the presenting problem may be pancreatitis, liver disease, traumatic injury, or broken bones. In the mental health setting, the person may present depression, suicidal feelings, self-destructive behavior, anxiety, psychotic symptoms, or problems associated with an organic brain syndrome. Each of these problems may be the result of alcoholism or drug addiction. (p. 25)

Thus, regardless of your practice setting, you will probably need to address substance abuse problems. Training you to be a substance abuse counselor is far beyond the scope of this text. However, we will discuss some of the basic terms, individual and family dynamics, and treatment trends involved.

There are many similarities between alcohol abuse and other substance abuse in terms of biological, psychological, and interpersonal implications (American Psychiatric Association, 2000). However, elaborating upon the effects of the numerous varieties of drugs available today is also beyond the scope of this book. Therefore, we will primarily focus on alcohol abuse.

The Alcoholic Person

Levin (1995) describes alcoholism as "drinking more than is good for one over an extended period of time. There are three essential elements in this definition: (1) the drinking does serious harm of various sorts to the drinker; (2) the drinking continues despite its harmful consequences (that is, it is compulsive), and (3) the harmful drinking continues over an extended period of time" (pp. 88–89).

Denzin (1987) describes four progressive phases of alcoholism: "prealcoholic, prodomal, crucial, and chronic" (p. 10). The *prealcoholic* phase involves drinking in order to reduce anxiety or stress. During this phase, the person will look for social experiences that involve drinking. The person enjoys drinking and may drink more than those with whom he or she associates.

Prodomal, the second phase, signals increasing loss of control. Blackouts occur, in which memory losses mark blocks of time. During this phase, the individual who starts drinking finds that he or she cannot stop.

The *crucial* phase reflects even greater loss of control over drinking. The individual drinks more and more frequently and is increasingly less able to restrain him- or herself.

Finally, the *chronic* phase "occurs when the drinker begins morning drinking and feels the need to drink every four or five hours. He or she has become physiologically dependent upon alcohol. If a drink is not taken, nausea and shaking of the hands may concur. Alcohol removes these withdrawal effects" (Denzin, 1987, p. 10).

With each of these phases comes increasing loss of control. Drinking begins as a means of escaping stress and becomes the alcoholic's only way of coping with reality. Denzin emphasizes that "alcoholism is but a symptom of the alcoholic's other problems of living" (1987, p. 10). He continues, then, that there must be a two-pronged approach to treatment. First, the alcoholic must quit drinking. Second, the problems from which the alcoholic tried to escape in the first place by turning to drinking must be addressed.

Kingery-McCabe and Frances (1991) stress that each individual responds differently to alcohol dependence in terms of severity of physical and psychological effects and the length of time it takes to become dependent. They note four major facets of life are typically affected: "physical and medical, psychological or emotional, social or family, and spiritual" (1991, p. 58).

Physical repercussions of alcoholism may involve a number of organ systems, including the digestive, cardiovascular, nervous, endocrine, reproductive, respiratory, and immune systems (Anderson, 1995; Levin, 1995).

Psychological consequences are massive (Anderson, 1995). Kingery-McCabe and Frances (1991) explain that:

Addiction affects virtually every area of psychological functioning, including cognitive, emotional, and behavioral areas. The alcoholic or drug addict typically utilizes defense mechanisms (e.g., denial) that allow the addiction to continue. Self-esteem is adversely affected, and developmental tasks may be impeded or delayed as a result of impairments associated with the addiction. And in many cases, addiction can exacerbate or mask psychiatric disorders. (p. 67)

Alcoholics and other substance abusers typically adopt a series of defense mechanisms to protect themselves from having to deal with the problems caused by alcoholism. They include "minimiza-

tion," "denial," and "rationalization" (Perkinson, 1997, pp. 56–57, 114–116). Each defense mechanism serves to avoid taking responsibility for one's own behavior.

Minimization means assigning little importance to drinking or its consequences. "Minimizing says, 'It's not so bad'" (Perkinson, 1997, p. 56). Here the alcoholic acknowledges that drinking is occurring but admits to very little and tries to make it unimportant. An alcoholic might fill a ten-ounce glass halfway with whiskey instead of pouring it into a much smaller shot glass. This becomes "just one drink." Or, an alcoholic might say, "I really don't drink that much," while drinking three six-packs of beer a night.

Rationalization involves making excuses for the problems caused by the dependence on alcohol. For example, an alcoholic might say to him- or herself, "I really didn't flunk that exam because I had a hangover; the professor made the questions much harder than she said she would." Or, "It's been a rotten day. I deserve a drink or two."

Denial, the most prevalent defense used by alcoholics, involves insisting to oneself that nothing's wrong; there's no problem. Denial means distorting reality so that you just don't see the truth. An alcoholic who drinks a fifth of vodka or a 12-pack of beer a day might say to him- or herself, "I don't really have to drink." Or, such an individual might totally ignore spousal complaints about spending money on booze or being verbally abusive when drunk. Out of sight, out of mind. If you don't think about it, it doesn't exist.

Numerous social and relationship problems result from alcohol and other substance abuse. They include marital and family difficulties, disruptions in friendships, trouble in work and school performance, accidents when operating vehicles, and being arrested for crimes committed while under the influence.

Alcohol or another substance of choice (i.e., the preferred substance) becomes the abuser's "best friend." It is something the abuser can always depend on. The effects are pleasantly predictable, and the abuser can escape from life's stresses whenever he or she wants. People can be disappointing or place pressure on you, but a drug always acts the same.

Alcohol and other substance abuse also affect a person's spiritual life, which involves the core of how people feel about themselves, God, and the world. Abusers are out of control, but they are desperately trying to avoid the responsibility of dealing with that fact. Abusers frequently report having feelings of "guilt and shame" (Kingery-McCabe &

Frances, 1991, p. 75). They know that they are doing something wrong but cannot allow themselves to face up to it.

Guilt entails feeling bad about something you have done that was not right. For example, an alcoholic gets into a fight while drunk, which he regrets seriously the following day. He really feels guilty having to pay the $250 fine he received when arrested for fighting. Guilt also might involve something you should have done but failed to do. For instance, while drunk you "forgot" to attend your little sister's birthday party.

Shame, on the other hand, involves feeling that you are a bad person. It is not feeling badly about *something* but, instead, feeling badly about *yourself* (Curtis, 1999). Additional spiritual effects can include losing religious faith, becoming inactive in your church, inability to display caring and concern for the ones you love, decreasing your expectations regarding how you and others around you should behave, and generally feeling that life has less and less value.

Alcoholism and Family Relationships

Wegscheider (1981) maintains that alcohol abuse is a family disease, involving and affecting each family member. Although she focuses on the families of alcoholics, much of what she says is also frequently applied to the families of other types of substance abusers. She identifies a number of rules or norms with which alcoholics' families struggle to comply. In reality, these norms serve to sustain the drinking problem.

First, the alcoholic's alcohol use becomes "the most important thing in the family's life" (Wegscheider, 1981, p. 81). The alcoholic's top priority is getting enough alcohol, and the family's top priorities are the alcoholic, the alcoholic's behavior, and keeping the alcoholic away from alcohol. The goals of the abuser and the rest of his family are at completely opposite poles.

A second norm in an alcoholic's family is that alcohol is not the cause of the problem. Denial is paramount. A third family norm maintains that the alcoholic is really not responsible for his or her behavior and that the alcohol causes the behavior. There is always someone or something else to blame. Another rule dictates that no one should rock the boat, no matter what. Family members strive to protect the family's status quo, even when the family is miserable. Other norms prohibit discussing family problems either within or outside of the family and consistent avoidance of stating one's true feelings.

Families of alcoholics traverse through seven phases that synchronize with the four phases of alcoholism; they include "denial, adjustment, disorganization, attempts to reorganize, attempts to escape the problem, reorganization of part of the family, and recovery and reorganization of the whole family" (Denzin, 1987, p. 12). Like the alcoholics themselves, family members first try to *deny* that there is a problem or minimize how bad it really is.

Often, a family member plays the role of *chief enabler* (Curtis, 1999; Wegscheider, 1981). This person assumes increasing responsibility for maintaining family functioning and making excuses for the alcoholic. In essence, this role enables the alcoholic to continue drinking, yet assume less and less responsibility for the consequences of that behavior.

The second phase, *adjustment,* involves family members trying to get rid of the problem. A spouse may nag the alcoholic to stop drinking or even threaten to leave for good. Family members might try hiding the alcohol. They might attempt to minimize the problem by making jokes about it. Such tactics are hardly ever successful.

Meanwhile, the problem continues to worsen. During the third phase, *disorganization,* family members find pretending that the problem does not exist difficult. Instead, they adopt roles to try and maintain their denial.

The fourth stage through which the alcoholic family progresses, namely, *attempted reorganization* of part of the family, involves attempts to restructure the family. During this phase, the chief enabler takes over. The alcoholic assumes little or no responsibility anymore. The alcoholism problem may not seem as severe as before, because family members' expectations for the alcoholic's behavior are extremely low.

The fifth stage entails attempts to *escape* from the problem. Many times, the spouse will leave. Sometimes, the family fixates at this stage for some time. The alcoholic has had most responsibilities usurped. Again, because of low expectations, the problem may appear less severe. Thus, family members may escape from the problem by avoiding it.

The sixth stage in the alcoholic family involves family members *reorganizing the family without the alcoholic member's involvement.* If the alcoholic seeks treatment and begins recovering, the family will begin the seventh and final stage, *recovery and reorganization* of the whole family, including the recovering alcoholic.

Your Role in Intervention with Alcoholics

We have already indicated that your career path may or may not lead you to become a specialized alcohol and other substance abuse counselor. However, it is still important that you maintain an awareness of the problems involved, include related information in the assessments you do regardless of your practice area, and make necessary referrals for treatment interventions.

The following section will address the professional attitudes necessary for effective work with alcoholics. It will also discuss assessment of dependence, some specific micro intervention techniques used by alcohol abuse counselors, the significance of mezzo interventions, and possible macro approaches to intervention.

Effective Professional Attitudes

Denzin (1987), McNeece, and DiNitto (2002), and Miller and Rollnick (1991) identify a series of principles for working with alcoholics. They help to shape the appropriate professional attitude for working with alcoholics and their families.

1. *An alcoholic is able to recuperate and improve.* Many alcoholics do not recover. On the other hand, many do. Maintaining an optimistic attitude is important. Working with alcoholics is made difficult because of denial, relapses, and the resulting frustrations. Yet, to see a person return to a useful, productive, caring life can be infinitely rewarding.

2. *View alcoholism for what it is, namely, a disease that is out of the alcoholic's control.* Demeaning alcoholics and blaming them for their own problems is easy. To help them get better, do not rebuke and doom them. Help them to regain control. Remember that they are not rotten people—they are desperate people struggling to get better.

   An important concept related to that of disease is recovery. A recovering alcoholic "is a once-active alcoholic who has stopped drinking" (Denzin, 1987, p. 11). The assumption is that if you have the disease, you can only recover by stopping all drinking. Recovering alcoholics remain in recovery the rest of their lives.

3. *Be alert to symptoms that indicate an alcoholic problem.* Be sensitive to the signs of alcoholism (we will discuss assessment issues later). Does the person seem to be out of control when drinking? Does the person drink in secret? Does the person get in trouble during or after drinking? Is the person involved in arguments about drinking with those close to him or her?

4. *Remember that alcoholics have lost control.* You may think that an alcoholic getting "plastered"
at obviously noticeable and inappropriate times is odd. For instance, take the dean who staggered up to the stage to address 180 parents of incoming college freshmen. His speech was slurred beyond recognition. Or consider the woman who passed out cold at a party honoring her promotion. Once alcoholics start drinking, they cannot stop. Drinking often starts as a means of relieving stress.

5. *Employ motivational interviewing.* While earlier intervention models relied on confrontation, this approach tends to be less effective than more supportive techniques. Motivational interviewing presents "objective information to the client, deemphasizing that it is necessary to accept the label of alcoholic or addict to change, emphasizing client choice and responsibility for change, focusing on the client's concerns, addressing client denial with reflection" while the therapist and client work out the goals of intervention together (McNeece & DiNitto, 2002, p. 602).

6. *The alcoholic must assume responsibility for his or her own behavior in order to get better.* This guideline is related to the previous point in that alcoholics must eventually take responsibility for it. Until they become responsible for behavior, they will not be able to change it.

7. *The entire family is part of the alcoholic problem* (Curtis, 1999). We have established how an alcoholic's family passes through stages. Maladaptive roles and rules are established. Children can suffer and take their pain with them into adulthood. Thus, other family members need to address the abuse problem as early as possible so that they do not develop related problems of their own. The entire family needs attention in intervention.

8. *Know what resources are available.* Multiple problems are involved in alcoholism, as it touches so many aspects of people's lives. Become aware of counseling facilities, inpatient programs, and such self-help groups as AA and Al-Anon. (See Highlight 7.5 for a description of potential resources.)

9. *Avoid placing any labels on the alcoholic.* The chances are likely that alcoholics have already been blasted with accusations and slurs about their drinking. Part of the denial process involves becoming increasingly resistant to being called an alcoholic, drunk, or addict. If you plaster a label on them, they are likely to turn you off. AA emphasizes the importance of their coming to the

conclusion that they are alcoholics. Only then can they begin the recovery process.

Assessment of Alcohol and Other Substance Dependence and Abuse

Raskin and Daley (1991) suggest that information on the pattern of use is vitally important in a thorough assessment. Highlight 7.4 identifies the diagnostic criteria for abuse and dependence. Such information can be obtained either directly from the client or from others involved with the client. The following questions illustrate the types of information that can be gathered:

- "What drugs have been used?"
- "How old were you when you first started using?"
- "What was the last day that you used the drug?"
- "When do you usually use the drug? At what time of the week or day? How often during the day? Do you use every week or every day?"
- "How do you consume the drug?" (Obviously, you drink alcohol. However, other drugs can be injected, inhaled, smoked, or swallowed.)
- "Are you certain that the needles you used were clean? Do you ever use needles after they've been used by other people?" (If applicable)
- "Have you noticed any change in your drug tolerance level (that is, you need to take more or less of the drug than before to achieve the same effect)?"
- "Do you suffer from any withdrawal symptoms (for example, physical symptoms like 'the shakes' or nausea, or psychological symptoms like radical mood swings) when you don't use the drug for a long period of time?"
- "Do you ever experience more serious consequences of your drug use? For example, have you ever overdosed? Do you ever experience blackouts?"
- "Have you ever received any citations for driving under the influence (DUI)? If so, what were the circumstances?"
- "Has drinking ever affected your performance at work or school? If so, in what ways?"

Micro Practice Techniques for Implementation with Alcoholic Clients

Denzin (1987) describes an interpretative therapy approach to intervention. Such therapy focuses on four major points. First, alcoholics are excessively "self-centered" (1987, p. 25). They have given their "best friend," alcohol, top priority for a long time. Treatment, then, should focus on examining the alcoholics' sense of self. They need to realign their priorities and give more and better attention to the people they love.

When alcoholics drink, they feel much more important than they do when sober. They also avoid the stresses they dread in everyday life. The second focus of treatment involves the negative emotions the alcoholic is trying to flee. How does the alcoholic feel about him- or herself? How can you help the alcoholic more objectively evaluate personal strengths and weaknesses? How can alcoholics learn to accept and appreciate themselves for what and who they are?

Third, alcoholism distorts one's perception of time. Alcoholic time goes much faster or slower than normal time. Additionally, the alcoholic avoids living in the present by reverting to the past or dreaming about the future. In reality, alcoholics avoid the bad things haunting them in the past and the presumed things threatening them in the future through the drug.

A fourth focus of treatment is the distressed interpersonal relationships alcoholics suffer. They have probably disappointed, frustrated, humiliated, deserted, and disgusted many of the people closest to them. Thus, significant relationship repair work is probably in order.

Jacobs (1981) explains a variety of techniques for addressing problems encountered in micro intervention with alcohol abusers. Discussed here are denial, relapses, client mistrust, and arriving at an interview drunk.

The Problem of Denial

The major symptom of alcohol abuse is denial (Levin, 1995; Massella, 1991). Jacobs suggests that:

> During the early phases of treatment, it can be difficult to differentiate between clients who genuinely do not believe they have a problem and those who privately fear they can no longer control their drinking. One surefire way of losing clients before the distinction can be made is to demand total abstinence. Even if clients are willing to return, they are likely to be hostile and resistant, because the counselor has unwittingly compelled them to entrench their denial more deeply. (1981, p. 10)

Jacobs also states that goals of the first sessions should be basic. For example, the client might simply agree to return for the next session. We have already established the need to help the dependent person accept responsibility for his or her own behavior and its effects. When working with persons who deny they are alcoholics, confrontation should be as "unthreatening" as possible (1981, p. 10). The practitioner might ask, "If you were to stop drinking, do you think your life would be any different? If so, in what ways?" or "Do you ever get the feeling that you're having trouble controlling your drinking?"

More direct use of confrontation should be used only after a stronger relationship between worker and client has been established. Timing the confrontation is crucial. A problem at work related to alcohol or crisis in the marriage might provide good possibilities for confronting the client about the effects of drinking. The practitioner might then say, "It looks as if you're having a serious problem. Let's look at how it's related to drinking."

Many times, working with a genuine denier is tedious. Jacobs warns that the client will sometimes choose to discontinue treatment if the worker places greater demands on self-assessment. However, "the counselor can take solace in knowing that he or she has done all that can be reasonably expected" (1981, p. 12). The bottom line is that admitting that there is a problem is the client's choice and responsibility.

In conclusion, Jacobs notes that insight-oriented therapy, especially that which addresses reasons for drinking, is generally unsuccessful with denial. On the other hand, becoming involved in a group therapy situation may encourage deniers to assess themselves and their problem, as they compare themselves to others.

What If Your Client Has a Relapse?

Jacobs (1981) provides a series of suggestions for dealing with an alcoholic client who has a relapse. First, a worker should treat the experience calmly, compassionately, and briefly. The alcoholic very likely feels guilty and ashamed even of talking about it. The worst thing to do is to scold your client. When a supervisor or instructor scolds you, how do you usually feel about it? Angry? Downtrodden? Resentful? Rebellious? Clients generally feel the same way.

A second suggestion for addressing a relapse is to treat the ordeal in as beneficial a light as possible. Emphasize what the client has learned from it. Identify the negative consequences that have been suffered and relate how awareness of these consequences might help him or her abstain in the future.

This approach leads us to the third suggestion. Stress to your client that situations such as the one that led to the relapse should be shunned. Your client can learn that the conditions leading to the relapse (e.g., returning to the old tavern with "the

boys" after work as he used to do before recovery) only leads to another downfall and loss of control.

A fourth suggestion for addressing relapses entails helping your clients manage the stress that in the past has led to drinking. First, your clients need to become aware of the physical and psychological reactions indicating high stress levels. Next, they need to learn how to control that stress. For example, teaching them such stress management techniques as specific approaches to relaxation can be helpful.

A fifth suggestion concerns helping your clients avoid relapses in the first place. Using role plays of various alcohol-seductive situations before the situations occur can help clients learn to react to unexpected situations. If they have the chance to think through a tempting situation beforehand, they may be more likely to respond to it in a thoughtful, responsible way.

How Do You Get Your Client to Trust You?

Many alcoholics are used to failure. Perhaps they have tried to quit before with only temporary and limited success. Maybe they have been in treatment with alcohol abuse counselors who were unable to help them. At any rate, prior bad experiences together with the alcoholic's tendency toward secrecy and denial pave the ground for mistrust. Because of the severity of their own problems, some clients will not trust you no matter what you do.

Jacobs (1981) makes several suggestions for approaching client mistrust. First, be straightforward and honest about your own abilities. Do not pretend you can wave a magic wand and cure your clients. On the other hand, do not be self-conscious and apologetic. Rather, emphasize that helping a person recover takes a lot of hard work on the parts of both worker and client. You might indicate to your clients "that you will do everything in your power to help them" (Perkinson, 1997, p. 1). If you have had successes in the past, say so. On the other hand, you can say frankly that you are unable to make any promises. State what treatment will involve. Do not be secretive. One of your objectives will be to give direct feedback to your clients about their behavior. Your intent is to help your client face, rather than hide from, reality.

What If Your Client Arrives Drunk?

Counseling cannot proceed effectively if a client comes to an interview drunk (Jacobs, 1981; Sheafor et al., 2000). Jacobs (1981) cites four variables to consider when handling any incident: Is the client relatively docile and submissive; is the client "verbally aggressive" (1981, p. 75); is the client physically defiant and threatening; and what should you do about your future work with the client?

Docile clients should generally be calmly told to go home. Trying to work with a client who is drunk is *always* useless. You may decide to confront the drunken behavior at some later time when the client is sober. However, do not chastise the client while he or she is drunk. This disapproval may only make a manageable client volatile.

A client may appear both drunk and verbally assaultive when coming for an interview. In these cases, your main goal should be to minimize the disruption and send the client safely home (i.e., in a taxi or with a friend; your client, of course, should not drive his or her own car). If possible, you might take the client aside to a place where he or she will pose the least disturbance. Isolating yourselves from others, just in case the client becomes violent, is not a good idea. You should never place yourself in physical jeopardy. Allow the client to vent feelings. You might empathize via reflection if appropriate. For example, you might say, "I understand how angry you are right now." Do not disagree with the client. That tactic is useless. Rather, let the client settle down until he or she can be sent home. Once again, you can decide to address this behavior and its ramifications in the subsequent meeting when the client is sober.

You should not take any unnecessary physical risks if a client appears drunk and physically assaultive or aggressive. Stay in an area where others are. You might state your reactions honestly. For instance, you might say, "This is scary for me. I will need to call for help if you won't settle down." Do not try to do any counseling. Simply try to minimize the risk that something violent will happen. Someone other than you should call the police. Likewise, someone other than you (as the focus of animosity) should request that the client depart.

The fourth variable to consider is whether to continue treatment with the client. This consideration is regardless of the type of behavior the client manifested. Jacobs reflects:

Should a counselor continue to work with clients who have arrived in an intoxicated state? With the exception of those who presented a direct physical threat, in most instances, the answer is yes. If the anger directed toward the counselor was without any reference to physical threat, whether or how the counselor proceeds depends greatly upon how upsetting the experience was. (1981, pp. 76–77)

In a situation in which the practitioner no longer feels safe with the client, that practitioner should discontinue working with the client. When terminating the relationship, the worker should tell the client the truth. For example, the practitioner might say that he no longer feels able to work with the client because he no longer feels safe; additionally, he feels that he and the client would no longer be able to make much progress together. A referral to another resource, such as those described in Highlight 7.5, might be in order.

Implementation at the Mezzo Level

You will most likely fulfill one of two roles in mezzo level practice when working with alcoholics. You will make assessments and subsequent referrals to self-help groups such as AA, and you will work with the alcoholic and his or her family.

Several concepts are critical to direct implementation with families (Wegscheider, 1981). First, family members must realize the extent of the problem. They need to identify the alcohol abuse as their major problem. Second, they need to learn about and evaluate their family dynamics. They need to evaluate their own behavior and break out of the roles maintaining the alcoholic's abuse. The chief enabler, especially, must stop making excuses and assuming the alcoholic's responsibility. If the alcoholic is sick from a hangover and cannot make it to school or work the next day, it must be the alcoholic's responsibility, not a parent's or spouse's, to call in sick.

Third, family members should learn to deal honestly with alcoholics and give them accurate information about their behavior. For instance, family members should be encouraged to tell an alcoholic exactly how he or she behaved during a blackout. If the abuser hit another family member while drunk, this needs to be brought out. The confrontation should occur not in an emotional manner, but in a factual one.

Fourth, the family needs to learn about the progression of the disease. We have already discussed some characteristics of alcohol abuse. At first, only occasional relief drinking occurs. Drinking becomes more constant. The alcoholic then begins to drink in secret and feels guilty about drinking. Memory blackouts begin to occur and gradually increase in frequency. The alcoholic feels worse and worse about the drinking behavior but seems to have less and less control over it. Finally, the drinking begins to seriously affect work, family, and social relationships. A job may be lost or all school classes flunked.

Perhaps family members leave or throw the alcoholic out. The alcoholic's thinking becomes more and more impaired.

Finally, the alcoholic "hits rock bottom." Nothing seems left but despair and failure, and the alcoholic admits complete defeat. It is at this point that alcoholics may make one of two choices. Either they will continue on the downward spiral to a probable death related to alcohol, or they may desperately struggle to help themselves. Typically, during this period, alcoholics will make some progress only to slip back again. Vicious circles of drinking and stopping are often apparent. Finally, alcoholics may express an honest desire for help.

Implementation at the Macro Level

Implementation approaches at the macro level are those that go beyond the extent to which alcohol or other substance abusers and their families receive or do not receive treatment. Macro approaches concentrate on how abusers in general are treated and on what solutions to substance abuse problems society proposes.

HIGHLIGHT 7.6

Integration of Policy and Practice: Managed Care Dilemmas

A chapter on implementing generalist human services intervention may seem an odd place for a highlight on managed care. However, that practice can only occur within the overshadowing macro context of policy, regulations, and resource allocations must be stressed. Managed care is now a critical component of human services "practice in many settings including health, mental health, family, child welfare and a wide range of other public social service settings (Corcoran, 1997, p. 191).

Although "there is no standard definition of managed care," a number of concepts tend to characterize it (Edinburg & Cottler, 1995, p. 1639). Broadly stated, managed care is "a generic label for a broad and constantly changing mix of health insurance, assistance, and payment programs that seek to retain quality and access while controlling the cost of physical and mental health services" (Lohmann, 1997, p. 200). An identified group or range of health and mental health care providers contract with agencies to provide health care at a negotiated rate. This group serves to save agency administrations from the cost and inconvenience of providing employees with traditional health insurance. Managed care programs often provide services beyond those typically prescribed by health insurance (e.g., prevention and family services). Two primary principles promoted by managed care include *retention of quality*

and access while *controlling cost.* That is, health and mental health services should be of high quality and readily accessible to clients, on the one hand. On the other, they should be cost effective.

Managed care "fundamentally transformed" traditional relationships between clients and workers (Lohmann, 1997, p. 201). Historically, human services professionals in agency settings established treatment plans in conjunction with clients, while stressing informed consent and confidentiality to comply with ethical standards. Managed care takes these decisions out of workers' and clients' hands and puts them into the hands of removed third-party decision makers. A managed care representative, often a utilization reviewer or case manager, then reviews documentation and regulates "the services that clients receive, especially what specific services will be provided and at what cost" (Corcoran, 1997, p. 194). To Lohmann, managed care "represents the complete (and seemingly sudden) triumph of financial management concerns over virtually all other professional considerations" (1997, p. 202).

As generalist practitioners, we must work within our employing agency setting. However, we are also responsible for maintaining ethical practices and for making certain clients' needs are met. Several ethical issues may be raised concerning managed care.

The first involves the potential conflict between "the gatekeeping role of some managed care organizations and client self-determination" (Corcoran, 1997, p. 196). When subject to managed care, clients will no longer have the right to choose their service provider. Rather, the managed care utilization reviewer can make this determination.

(continued)

Similarly, managed care may conflict with the ethical principle of informed consent:

Informed consent requires that the client know in advance the clinical procedures, the risk of those procedures, and the available alternative procedures. Managed care may destroy informed consent by restricting the available procedures to a limited number. For example, a managed care company may determine the preferred practice and the preferred providers, with little consideration or disclosure of alternative procedures. (Corcoran, 1997, p. 196)

Managed care also has the potential to violate client confidentiality (Corcoran, 1997). Human services professionals are bound by the ethical standards that emphasize respect for clients' privacy. However, if a managed care organization demands information before providing services, what should the worker do? What if the worker does not agree with the organization's expressed need for information and feels the regulations violate clients' right to privacy? Workers may be required to report confidential information, whether they feel it is ethical or not (Chapter 2 discussed ethical issues in depth).

The point is not to get depressed about the managed care environment. Rather, practitioners must respond to the potential ethical dilemmas posed. Edinburg and Cottler (1995, p. 1641) argue that advocacy is the preeminent role for *human services professionals to help "patients and families in dealing with managed care delivery systems. Patients and families will need to know what their entitlement benefits are and how to obtain proper services."* They also note that advocacy is essential to enhance *"the health care system by serving on advisory committees and lobbying their legislators."*

At least five specific provisions could improve legislation to protect clients and their rights ("Managed Care," 1998); they could:

. . . guarantee patients the right to choose a doctor outside their health plan's networks if they agree to share the cost of services; ensure patients access to detailed information about coverage, treatment options . . . ; require companies to cover emergency care without prior authorization . . . ; make health plans comply with state and federal laws that protect the confidentiality of . . . health information; and require companies to set up procedures under which providers could appeal denials of coverage. (p. 1)

Macro issues focus on at least three major areas. The first deals with the adequacy and effectiveness of treatment programs. Are adequate services available to all abusers and their families? Are our clients being served with the resources they need? An answer of no to either of these questions leads to the possibility of macro implementation. Do new programs need to be developed or old programs improved? Does the client's managed care program adequately cover substance abuse treatment? Highlight 7.6 discusses managed care dilemmas.

A second macro issue involves the accessibility of alcohol and other substances to abusers. In the case of illegal substances, is our legal system adequately regulating their distribution? Obviously, there are problems, or there would not be abusers. What should be done to address these problems? Should abusers, dealers, or major drug kingpins be the target for legal action and control? What policies and programs should be developed to curb substance abuse problems?

In the case of alcohol, an accessibility issue involves the degree to which social policies should be permissive concerning its use. Should 18-year-olds be able to purchase alcoholic beverages? How about if they are only allowed to buy beer? Should 19-year-olds be able to purchase beer, or 20-year-olds, for that matter? Another serious issue related to alcohol involves driving under its influence. What is a permissible blood alcohol level?

A third macro issue concerns prevention of alcohol and other substance abuse. Should more and better drug education programs be developed? Should prevention focus on "early identification and treatment of alcohol-dependent individuals" or rather, on "education . . . aimed at the entire citizenry" (Anderson, 1987, p. 141)? What might the best methods be to stop alcohol and other substance problems before abuse occurs?

InfoTrac College Edition

This chapter discussed several implementation applications focusing on areas of practice that included child protective services, empowerment techniques with the elderly, crisis intervention, and alcohol and other drug abuse. For further information on these areas, enter the following search terms:

child abuse
crisis intervention
alcohol abuse
drug abuse
family preservation

 On the Internet

Because of the very dynamic nature of the Web, URLs are subject to change. Therefore, be sure to check out the companion Website for this book at http://www.humanservices.wadsworth.com, where links will be updated periodically.

157.142.136.54/cm/cmhome.htm
www.cs.umd.edu/users/connie
www.ncoa.org
www.arf.org
www.alcoholics-anonymous.org

CHAPTER 8
Evaluation and Termination in Generalist Practice

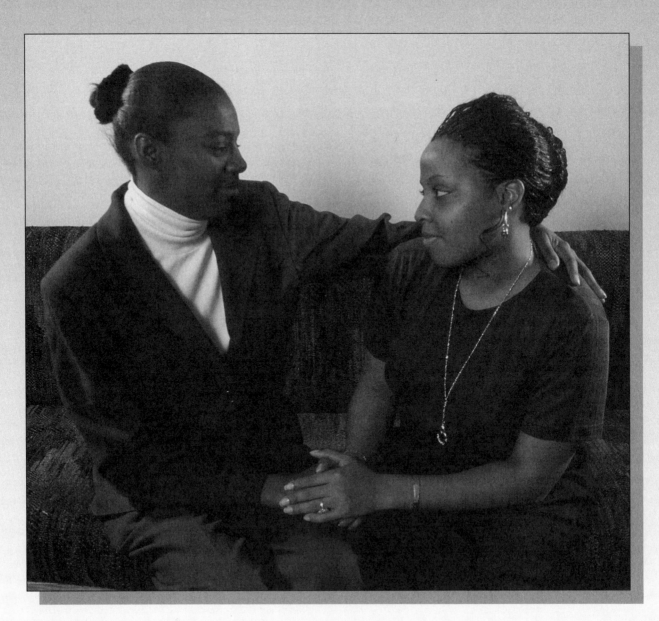

As a human services professional you may be confronted with any of the following tasks:

- Evaluating whether your efforts to help a juvenile delinquent stay out of the criminal justice system are working. (In other words, has he remained out of jail and in the community?)
- Proving to the county board of supervisors the effectiveness of a new parent nurturing program designed to reduce child abuse among low-income parents.
- Determining whether your assertiveness-training program is increasing group members' assertiveness. (To what extent have group members increased their assertiveness without aggressively violating the rights of others?)
- Measuring the effectiveness of a foster parent recruitment program you have implemented. (How many more foster parents have you been able to recruit since the program began compared to the period before the program was instituted?)
- Helping a previously aggressive client in a group home for behaviorally disordered adolescents prepare to return to her home, school, old friends, and community.
- Assisting a family (coping with a recent suicide attempt by its 14-year-old member) in the ending phase of a six-week family therapy program.
- Easing the transition of a frightened yet strengthened mother leaving the safety of a battered-women's shelter.

Introduction

To be effective as a human services professional, you must know whether or not the interventions you employ are working. This knowledge may seem simple enough in the abstract, but developing effective strategies to evaluate our practice is not always easy. Even when we have a clear plan for evaluating the outcomes of our practice or our programs, many things can challenge our conclusions about our effectiveness.

The evaluation process typically is ongoing in that we must always be alert to whether or not the goals we hoped to reach are being achieved (see Figure 8.1). Evaluation may also be thought of as an endpoint activity, often leading to the mutual client–worker decision to terminate the professional relationship. The last part of this chapter focuses on the knowledge and skills needed for effectively concluding professional human services professional–client relationships. In summary, this chapter will help you to:

- define evaluation;
- identify and use appropriate methods of evaluating your practice;
- identify commonly used methods for program evaluation;
- differentiate between various concepts important to evaluation of practice, including validity,

Figure 8.1   *Evaluation in the Generalist Intervention Model (GIM)*

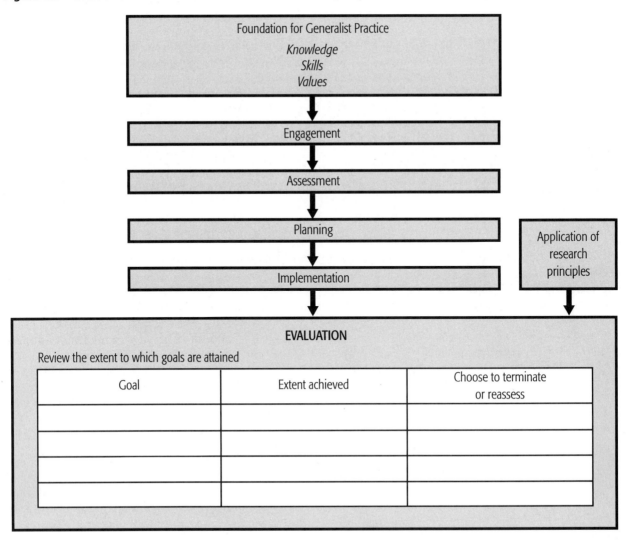

reliability, generalizability, baseline, formative, and summative evaluation;

- recognize common problems associated with attempts to evaluate human services practice;
- prepare the client for the termination phase;
- help the client recognize and manage termination-related feelings such as anger, anxiety, disappointment, and so on;
- recognize and manage your *own* termination-related feelings;
- recognize typical behavior and feelings common to the ending of counselor–client relationships;
- plan for and carry out appropriate termination activities with individuals, families, groups, organizations, and communities;
- plan for and carry out maintenance of change efforts.

 ## Evaluating Human Services Practice

Evaluation of human services practice has only recently been emphasized. It has been spurred by several factors, including demands for accountability, interest in improving human services practice, and the accreditation requirements of several professional human services organizations.

Increased emphasis in human services and in related fields on using "best practices" is also stressing the importance of evidence as a guiding factor in selecting interventions and designing programs (Gambrill, 1999). Evidenced-based practice (best practices) ensures that we use only knowledge that has been adequately tested using some degree of scientific rigor. It stands in opposition to authority-based practice, which relies on opinion and testimonials to support specific interventions. As Gambrill so correctly points out, none of us would want our physician to treat us based only on what she heard from a colleague nor would we want her to rely solely on the results of a single interesting study. Rather, we would want treatment based on carefully monitored trails with attention paid to scientific methods. This is one of the reasons why evaluation of our practice and programs is a critical, professional obligation of the generalist human services professional.

Definition and Purposes of Evaluation

Evaluation "is a process of determining whether a given change effort was worthwhile" (Kirst-Ashman & Hull, 2001, p. 322). You would not make repeated visits to a lawyer who rarely was successful in defending her clients. Neither would you consult a physician who forgets what his diagnosis was 30 seconds after making it. We all engage in a certain degree of evaluation each time we use the services of a professional, organization, or business. We notice whether our expectations were met, whether the service we received was appropriate, and how well we were treated. When this evaluation leaves us with a conclusion that the experience was negative, we do not patronize that person or service again.

At the micro practice level, evaluation is designed to help us determine to what extent our work with a specific client was successful. We are concerned with whether the intervention goals were achieved and how satisfied clients were with the services we provided. Evaluation aids in judging our competence as well as the methods, theories, and perspectives we use in generalist practice. Similarly, evaluation is concerned with explaining why a particular outcome occurred. Therefore, evaluation also focuses on process or determining how we got where we did.

At the mezzo level, we want to know if the treatment or educational group achieved its purposes. We are interested in whether group members reached the goals they set for themselves. In a task group we need to decide whether or not the tasks were accomplished in a timely fashion. Because of the differential nature of the two group types, we are less concerned about whether task group members had their individual goals met.

Macro practice evaluations are focused on whether entire programs accomplished their purpose. Also of concern is the relative cost of providing a program. Two programs providing similar services with nearly identical outcomes but at vastly different costs will not exist very long. Few of us would knowingly choose a service that was more costly but produced exactly the same result as a less expensive service.

As you can see, evaluation has a clear purpose at each level of generalist practice. Of course, there are many other reasons for undertaking evaluations. Evaluation is a normal step in the planned change process described in the Generalist Intervention Model (GIM) (see Chapter 1). It can no more be ignored than can assessment. As practitioners, we are interested in knowing whether what we are doing is working. This curiosity is natural. Our own interest is buttressed by human service ethical standards that make evaluation an ethical obligation of each human services professional. Providing services that we know are ineffective is unethical. We also do evaluations because we must continually try to improve our professional skills and knowledge. To increase your own effectiveness as a worker requires feedback from others. We want to know how client systems experienced their work with us, which gives them a chance to be heard and gives us important information. Finally, evaluation helps build the knowledge base of the profession. Both practice wisdom and published knowledge increase as we document the success of our efforts. Highlight 8.1 discusses other purposes for evaluating community programs.

External Factors in Evaluation

As sources of funding for human services programs have become increasingly scarce during the last 25 years, the demands for evaluation of those programs have increased. Governmental and private funding sources wanted proof that their money was being put to good use. They demanded greater assurance that the money they allocated for programs was accomplishing the intended purposes. While many agencies had been providing some kinds of evaluation, their emphasis was largely on output or measuring what the agency did. For example, the worth of an agency might be justified by noting that the agency staff provided ten thousand hours of one-on-one work with first offenders. Therefore, the implication is that the agency is productive. Still another agency might report that its caseload this year increased by 25 percent with no corresponding increase in staff. Thus, the agency implies its current staff is working all the harder. These types of measures supplied us with some information about what agencies do. However, they did nothing to satisfy the basic questions. Did the agency accomplish its purpose, and was it actually successful in helping its clients?

Besides the economic importance of evaluation, political pressures played a role in demanding accountability from social programs. Elected state and federal officials called for increased emphasis on evaluation to justify the continued expenditure of funds, which was especially true for those skeptical of, or opposed to, social programs.

Simultaneously, a growing consumer movement was affecting human services programs across the country. It maintained that users of products or services had a right to know about their effectiveness. Consumers wanted some assurance that they were getting what they were paying for, whether the product was cornflakes, cars, or counseling.

The result of this confluence of political pressure, economic necessity, and consumer interest is a heightened awareness of the importance of accountability (Hudson & Grinnell, 1989). Accountability involves "the state of being answerable to the community, to consumers of a product or service, or to supervisory groups such as a board of directors"; it also involves the profession's "obligation . . . to reveal clearly what its functions and methods are and to provide assurances to clients that its practitioners meet specific standards of competence" (Barker, 1999, p. 3). How can you, as a generalist practitioner, prove you are accomplishing what you say you are? In the following sections, we will look more closely at what evaluation means and the kinds of things that it achieves.

Obstacles to Evaluation

For workers to want to know the outcome of their efforts or to know that the program in which they work is effective may seem logical. Still, strangely

---

HIGHLIGHT 8.1

Evaluating Programs

Evaluation of either agency or community programs achieves several important purposes. These include:

1. Providing data that will assist current program improvement;
2. Helping agency administrators keep track of new programs still in the development stage;
3. Assisting agencies to determine which programs are most effective and should be continued;
4. Identifying programs with limited effectiveness to be considered for elimination;
5. Demonstrating to funding bodies that their money is being spent in accordance with their expectations;
6. Proving to donors, legislators, and other organizational supporters that their support is justified.

enough, evaluation has not been an ongoing concern for many workers. One reason is that the very act of evaluating a practitioner's own work leaves the practitioner vulnerable. Workers might ask themselves, "What if I'm not successful with every client? What if some clients actually get worse? What if my caseload is so large that I don't have time to follow up on my clients' progress? What if my agency charges a lot of money for services I'm not sure really work?"

These are all legitimate concerns that have served as obstacles to workers evaluating their own practice. After all, evaluations make judgments about what was accomplished in the change process. These judgments might not always be favorable to the worker, especially if clients were worse off after receiving help.

A second reason for the lack of a routine system of evaluation is that workers are often too busy for any kind of formal evaluation. High caseloads and busy schedules often make finding time to evaluate results in more than a cursory, haphazard fashion difficult.

A third reason for the lack of evaluation effort is that many agencies have not emphasized its importance. Simply counting cases seen or hours of service given was considered an adequate measure of an agency's effort. In addition, agencies did not have the money or time for extensive evaluation studies. Recording information and evaluating it is time consuming and expensive.

Another likely explanation was that most human services professionals lacked training in the use of evaluation approaches. Until accrediting bodies enacted standards requiring that human service–related education programs teach students specifically to evaluate their practice, most schools and universities neglected this content. While students routinely took research classes as part of their work, these courses were generally not focused on evaluation of one's own practice. Rather, the primary goal was to produce a graduate who could read the professional journals and be an intelligent consumer of human services research. Today, most students learn a variety of methods for evaluating their practice and for evaluating agency programs.

Typically, evaluations have one of two major thrusts. First, they can monitor the ongoing operation (effort) of an agency. Second, evaluations can assess the outcomes (effects) of a program or intervention. Monitoring and evaluation functions are complementary; monitoring looks at the process of giving service, and evaluation looks at the effectiveness of the service provided. The ultimate goal is to generate information that increases the effectiveness (and efficiency) of

interventions. Effectiveness involves succeeding at what you set out to accomplish. Efficiency concerns doing it at a reasonable cost. In other words, evaluations can focus on effort or activity, outcome, adequacy of performance, or efficiency.

Evaluations can also focus on the process of giving help. Let us use an example to illustrate how this process might work. Assume you are a worker who has attempted to help a woman become more assertive.

Cloe described herself as always being "shy." She was terrified of meeting other people and had virtually no friends. Additionally, she found asserting herself at work difficult. As a result, she felt that her colleagues, health care aides at a small nursing home, took advantage of her.

Of course, you cared whether or not Cloe became more assertive, which was the outcome the client desired and the goal toward which you both worked for the past six months. Also, you probably wanted to know which of your interventions proved most helpful and which did not. You want to determine which techniques to continue using in the future and which to omit. Thus, you may be focusing on your *efforts* or *activities* on behalf of your client.

Your agency, on the other hand, may be interested in different areas. For instance, the agency might want to evaluate the *adequacy of your performance*. For instance, the approach you were using with the client might not be as effective as others that are available. Similarly, the board of directors might be wondering whether this service is provided at the *lowest possible cost*. Their interest is in *efficiency* (the relationship between the resources used to effect change and the actual outcome). If another agency provides similar results at lower cost, the board may decide that it cannot afford you or your program.

As you can see, there are many facets to evaluation. In the next section, we will look at the evaluation process itself, focusing on goals and some key concepts in doing evaluations.

The Evaluation Process

You will recall the emphasis we placed in earlier chapters on clearly identifying the objective of your work with client systems. The GIM approaches client systems with a clear plan for helping resolve problems, improve quality of life, and address broad client and human service needs. To accomplish this objective, in the planning stage we used data from the assessment stage to help clients frame goals and objectives that were specific, measurable, and clear. Without clear goals and objectives, knowing if we (client and worker) accomplished what we set out to do is difficult. As with other steps in GIM, the success of succeeding stages depends upon the quality of effort that went into previous stages. Just as poor assessments lead to poor planning, hazy or sloppy objectives set in the planning stage affect our ability to do later evaluations.

Evaluation of practice follows the same planned change approach as in human services practice itself. For example, first we must define the problem to be evaluated. Once defined, the worker must consider the types of research approaches that might be appropriate (assessment). The best approach is then chosen (planning), and the research is carried out (implementation). Finally, the worker must examine and evaluate the results of the research effort.

As is evident, this approach mirrors almost exactly the way in which a worker deals with a problem involving an individual, family, group, organization, or community. As you might expect, there are some key terms and ideas that are essential to understanding and conducting research on human services practice. These concepts include formative evaluation, summative evaluations, baselines, validity, reliability, data-gathering methods, independent variables, dependent variables, and generalizability.

Formative Evaluation

We have indicated earlier that evaluations may be conducted for monitoring ongoing progress. Such *formative* evaluations assess the adequacy or amount of effort directed at solving a client system's problem and gathering data during the actual intervention.

Formative evaluations focus on the process of providing help instead of the end product of help giving. For example, Toseland and Rivas (1998) suggest that one can have group members complete a questionnaire following each individual group session. The questionnaire might ask the group members their opinions on what occurred in the group, perhaps focusing on what they learned. The results of the clients' evaluations would be used to help plan subsequent meetings. Formative evaluations help us assess whether or not the anticipated progress is achieved. For example, in educationally focused groups, the members may be given a pretest at the beginning of a session and a posttest after the session. These tests would help determine achievement of goals for that specific session. In other words, exactly how much did group members learn during that particular session? Similarly, the worker and client who periodically review progress made by the client over the past six meetings are engaging in

a type of formative evaluation. The PERT chart described in Chapter 13 is also a kind of formative evaluation. For example, a PERT chart provides a visual representation or diagram that "looks at program objectives and indicates all the activities that need to be performed, the time required for each, the sequence in which they should take place, and the resources required" (Barker, 1999, p. 381). At any point in the process, one can look at the chart and know what is to be done, by whom, and by what date. This chart allows us to know whether the process is proceeding as planned. It also enables us to make changes as necessary to reach our goals.

Most students are familiar with one form of formative evaluation, namely, course or instructor evaluations. These evaluations provide the instructor and the instructor's department with information to assess how well that teacher is conveying information to students. Although course evaluations occur at the end of a student's experience with an instructor, they are actually formative evaluations. These types of evaluations are used because they are intended to affect how the instructor teaches the course in the future.

Summative Evaluations

Frequently, we want to know whether or not the outcome we anticipated at the beginning of our planned change process has been achieved. This process requires that we conduct an evaluation after completion of the planned change process. We call such evaluations *summative,* because they occur at the end of the process. In one sense, end-of-semester examinations in a college course are summative evaluations. They help determine whether or not you have learned the material outlined in course objectives.

You may be a bit unclear about the distinction between summative and formative evaluations. The important thing to remember is that formative evaluations occur while a planned change process is continuing. Summative evaluations, on the other hand, occur at the conclusion of the planned change process, looking backward. Their goal is to summarize what has already occurred. Formative evaluations, on the other hand, are oriented towards the future. Their goal is to affect or influence what is yet to come.

Baseline

Another key concept is that of baseline. Baseline is a measure of the frequency, intensity, or duration of a behavior. *Baseline* is a term taken from behavioral research and is important in assessing the progress of some helping relationships. Take, for example, the case of Veronica Cecret. Veronica went to a human services professional for help because she and her daughter, Marty, fight furiously over Marty's boyfriend. Veronica says the fights occur "a lot, every day." Marty describes the frequency of fights by saying they occur "constantly." If the worker is to judge whether her efforts and those of the family are working, it will be important to learn whether the fights are decreasing or not. Without definitive information on the frequency of the fighting, it will be nearly impossible to know whether things are improving.

Before we can tell whether or not the behavior is changing, we must know how often it occurs. Thus, the worker might ask both Veronica and Marty to record individually the number of fights they have in a week. This information would provide some basis for knowing whether the frequency of the fights is diminishing, increasing, or remaining the same.

In some situations, having several baselines might be useful. Perhaps the fights between Marty and Veronica are affecting Marty's schoolwork. Marty's grades in certain subjects must be an additional measure to help determine whether the worker and clients are making progress.

Ideally, a baseline should be based on several observations made over a period of time prior to intervention. As you can see, baselines are important in the helping process and are required to conduct certain kinds of evaluations. We will discuss these types of evaluations later.

Validity

According to Marlow (1993, p. 91) "validity refers to the extent to which we are measuring what we think we are measuring." When we evaluate a practice situation, using appropriate measurements is important. Assume, for example, that you are a human services professional in a deferred prosecution program. This program involves working with a group of first-time adult offenders (e.g., shoplifters or drunk drivers) referred to your program by the court system. If they successfully complete your program, they will have their records wiped clean. The assumption behind the existence of your program is that early intervention with first offenders will reduce the tendency toward recidivism (further contact with the criminal justice system).

A new coworker suggests that perhaps one measure of the success of your program is whether or not the participants feel positively about the experience.

He suggests that you ask each member to rate the group experience on a scale of one to ten.

What is the problem with such an approach? The primary problem is that the purpose of the group is to reduce recidivism among this group of first offenders. The measure suggested—that is, a client questionnaire focusing on feelings—has nothing to do with the real purpose of your program, namely reducing actual recidivism. Such a measure is simply not a *valid* means of assessing the outcome of this group.

Validity is a significant concern in evaluation. It is entirely possible, for example, for the group members to have enjoyed the group experience and still continue a life of crime. A client questionnaire asking group members to report any contacts with the criminal justice system would have greater validity than one that asked them to rate the group experience. An even more valid method of knowing whether or not the goals of the group were met would be to follow up on each group member at periodic points in time (six months, one year, and so on) to see if there were any further arrests. Concluding that the intervention worked if only a small percentage of group members had subsequent arrests would be easier.

The matter of validity is a bit complicated, because there are really several types of validity. We can speak, for instance, of face validity. *Face validity* is simply a professional judgment about whether the measure actually measures what it is supposed to. Most of us would react strongly to a human services test containing questions unrelated to our course. If a statistics test asked us to reproduce Einstein's theorem, we would be confused and angry. The test was supposed to measure our mastery of statistics, not the math involved in Einstein's theorem. In this case, the test questions lack face validity. We would expect the final examination in a history of social welfare course to ask about the Elizabethan poor laws, Social Security amendments, Hull House, and the War on Poverty. As one might expect, achieving face validity is comparatively easy.

Another type of validity is concurrent validity. Concurrent validity exists when scores on one instrument correlate well with scores on another instrument that is already considered valid. Let us say we have a new test for depression that has not yet been determined valid. To test for concurrent validity, we might give the test to a group of patients who had previously been assessed as depressed using a valid depression scale. If the new test yields similar results, we can say it has concurrent validity. That is to say, the instrument has a clear relationship to the thing we hope to measure, namely, depression.

Predictive validity is another important form of validity. A measure has predictive validity if it can be used to predict future events. In theory at least, your internship performance should be predictive of how you will do in actual human services positions. To the extent that an instrument accurately predicts later performance, behavior, or outcomes, it is said to have predictive validity.

Not all the types of validity have been included in this chapter. Your research course will likely provide much greater depth on this matter and further hone your practice evaluation skills.

Reliability

Most of us would probably object to the following situation: A three-credit course on interviewing is required for graduation. The total course grade is based on a one-time observation by one faculty member. That faculty member would be drawn at random from a pool of faculty, including those in psychology, sociology, and human services. The rater would thus be assigned to you by chance. Our objection would probably be based on the realization that each of the potential raters might have different criteria they would use to judge us. One person who rates us on our interview might think we did a good job. Another rater, however, might come to a different conclusion. Even if the whole pool of faculty came from the human services program, there would probably be some differences in their judgments.

While all might be competent to judge interviewing skills, there still might be little consistency in their grading. The very same interview might be given an A2 by one and a C1 by another. Clearly, we want observers and instruments capable of making consistent judgments. This situation brings us to another concept of importance—reliability.

Reliability is "the extent to which an instrument measures the same phenomenon the same way each time it is used" (Toseland & Rivas, 1995, p. 385). The key phrase here is *each time*. In the previous example, we might be more comfortable if each observer were using the same rating form with clearly defined criteria. If there is a high level of consistency among the raters, we have what is known as interrater reliability, a desirable characteristic.

Let us take a slightly different look at reliability. Assume we have an instrument that purports to measure assertiveness. A reliable instrument will produce similar results each time it is used. If a person scores low on the instrument one week and high the next, we would question if the measure is reliable. Reliable instruments produce consistent results over time. In theory at least, the only thing that should result in changing one's score on the assertiveness test is assertiveness training or some similar intervention.

There is also a clear relationship between reliability and validity. If an instrument (or rater) does not produce consistent results on subsequent trials, we cannot depend on its accuracy. However, for a measure to be reliable but not valid is possible. Let us take an obvious example. Your score on a written test of French vocabulary might be reliable in that it will always produce the same result, namely, a low score. If, however, the purpose of the test is to judge your ability to *speak* French, not *read* it, the written test is a much less valid measure of spoken vocabulary, because it does not really test this area at all.

Just as you would want to be evaluated in a manner that is both valid and reliable, so too should you want to evaluate your practice in a manner that is both valid and reliable. Sometimes, this goal is relatively easy to accomplish. If you wanted to know whether or not a depressed client was becoming less depressed, you might administer to that client one of the available depression scales. You could develop your own instrument, but it would likely prove costly, time consuming, and of less validity and reliability than existing methods. Using instruments where validity and reliability have been demonstrated is certainly easier.

Whenever possible, we attempt to use multiple measures or indicators to help ensure that we are getting valid and reliable information. For example, a student doing field placement in a hospital outpatient setting used both weight loss and cholesterol levels as measures of whether clients were achieving the goals of a health-improvement program.

If possible, getting independent verification of subjective items is also preferable. While a client may accurately report a change in his or her behavior, having a report from other observers to substantiate the client's claims is often better. Clients may report improvement not observable to significant others. This raises questions about the accuracy of the client's information.

Data-Gathering Methods

The choice of which or how many data-gathering methods to use is determined largely by the goals of the intervention. Human services professionals use many methods depending upon need. Commonly used methods include surveys, interviews with significant others (parents, teachers, and so on), collected data (such as school attendance records and grades), and observations of the researcher and others involved in the change effort (Gibbs, 1991).

Surveys or interviews may be structured (using a specific set of questions in a structured format) or unstructured (using open-ended questions in an informal discussion). Observations may be direct (person-to-person) or recorded in some way (e.g., videotaping). *Self-reports* (information provided by the client) are used when what must be measured is subjective. Feelings and beliefs of a client are examples of situations where self-reports are appropriate. Because you cannot "see" what the client believes, you must resort to asking the client to report on this area. Many instruments have been developed based on this premise. Methods frequently used to gather subjective data include depression scales, assertiveness schedules, and other devices. Highlight 8.2 refers to a number of such instruments.

Products, achievement of a specific task or change in behavior, are often used in the data-gathering process. A withdrawn child who talks to no one on the playground is exhibiting a specific behavior, that of silence. The worker can certainly assess change in that behavior by noting if the child begins to talk to other children. Likewise, a client who is trying to lose weight can easily measure progress by stepping on the scale.

Observational measures are those that rely on others to observe a change in the client's behavior. They are used when observing specific behavior in a situational context is relatively easy and appropriate. Consider, for example, evaluations of a student's interviewing technique. One of the most anxiety-producing parts of becoming a human services professional is learning how to interview clients. Unlike other courses in college, this skill requires students to demonstrate that they can conduct an interview meeting the prescribed standards. They can achieve this accomplishment by using audiotape, videotape, or actual live interviews. Faculty then observe and rate the interview. Such a procedure provides a more valid indicator of interviewing skill than a pencil-and-paper test. The instructor is able to look for certain kinds of skills and judge whether or not the

---

HIGHLIGHT 8.2

Finding Valid and Reliable Instruments

Locating a valid and reliable instrument to assist with your practice and evaluation efforts is sometimes quite easy. There are instruments to measure all of the following:

- assertiveness
- peer relationships
- depression
- parenting skills and knowledge
- anger
- fear
- marital happiness
- alcoholism
- social skills
- anxiety
- argumentativeness
- self-esteem
- sexual interaction

This list is only a small sample of the types of measures available. Existing measures such as these usually have information on validity and reliability as well as normative data so that comparisons with "normal" populations can be done.

There are a variety of sources for these instruments:

- Beck, A. (1991). *The Beck Depression Inventory Manual.* San Antonio, TX: Psychological Corporation.
- Corcoran, K., & Fischer, J. (1994). *Measures for clinical practice* (2nd ed.). New York: The Free Press.
- Hudson, W. W. (1982). *The clinical assessment package: A field manual.* Homewood, IL: Dorsey Press.
- Hudson, W. W. (1984). *The Clinical Assessment System.* Tallahassee, FL: Walmyr.
- Magura, S., & Moses, B. S. (1986). *Outcome measures for child welfare services: Theory and applications.* Washington, DC: Child Welfare League of America.
- McCormick, I. A. (1984). "A Simple Version of the Rathus Assertiveness Schedule," in *Behavior Assessment,* 7, 95–99.
- Pietrzak, J., Rauler, M., Renner, T., Ford, L., & Gilbert, N. (1990). *Practical program evaluation.* Newbury Park, CA: Sage.

student has exhibited those skills in the interview. Ideally, the skills must be carefully defined and clearly known to both student and teacher. In addition, the observer must be competent to judge the presence or absence of the skill. In other words, the rating must be valid.

Independent and Dependent Variables

Two other concepts important in practice evaluation are independent variable and dependent variable. The *independent variable* is the factor we think is responsible for causing certain behaviors, reactions, or events. For example, taking a toy from a child may precipitate crying or a temper tantrum. Taking the toy away is the independent variable that leads to the child's behavior, which is the dependent variable. In a human services professional context, the helping process itself is considered the independent variable. We believe our efforts to assist the client (the independent variable) will cause or contribute to changes in some aspects of the client's life (the dependent variable). Results (dependent variable) depend on our intervention effort (independent variable).

The *dependent variable* is the outcome or end product of the helping process. The assumption is that the outcome is dependent upon the helping efforts, hence, the name "dependent variable." If a client is part of a self-esteem group, the level of self-esteem would be the dependent variable. In a new program designed to teach anger management to men who abuse their spouses, the ability to control their anger is the dependent variable.

In practice, we know that the independent variable (our helping) is not totally responsible for the outcome. Too many other intervening variables exist to make such a claim. For example, a client attempting to lose weight may join a weight-loss program that meets weekly. While the weekly sessions are helpful in many ways, other factors affect the client's life. The reactions of other persons (spouse, children, friends) may have an enormous influence on the client. If significant others praise the client's willpower and acknowledge how much better he looks, the results of the group sessions will be enhanced. If, on the other hand, no one shows any recognition of the client's efforts or, worse yet, belittles the effort, the outcome may be negatively affected. Remembering that many variables affect people's behavior is important. The worker's effort to help is simply one of these factors. We will discuss the importance of these alternate explanations for change later in this chapter.

Generalizability

Generalizability is the ability of a set of results in one situation to fit another circumstance or instance. Assume for a minute that we have been extremely successful in our efforts to help clients or that the program we are part of has had unusual success. Our feelings of success have been supported by the evaluation techniques we have used. Moreover, to begin thinking that these methods may prove useful to other similar groups is logical. We are now beginning to *generalize* the results of our research to other groups or populations.

Generalizability is a desirable characteristic of any successful program. However, the very limited size of our sample (a handful of individuals or groups) is too small to make generalizing appropriate. A substantial number of cases are necessary to establish that positive change has not come about simply by chance or other intervening factors.

In addition, for the results of a project to be generalized, we must have confidence that the group members are representative of, or similar to, others who might benefit from this program. Without this assurance, attempts to generalize from these clients to others are pure speculation. We shall refer to this matter again when we look at issues and problems in evaluation.

The concepts we have discussed so far include formative and summative evaluation, baselines, validity (face validity, concurrent validity, predictive validity), and data-gathering methods. We also discussed reliability, independent, dependent, and intervening variables, and generalizability. Each concept is important to the practitioner, whether one is looking at one's own practice or attempting to evaluate an entire program. In the next section, we will be looking at several techniques that can be used to evaluate practice.

Evaluation Designs for Direct Practice

Most of you will be involved in direct practice with client systems. Those client systems may be individuals, families, groups, organizations, or communities. The nature and level of your practice will be dependent upon your knowledge and skill, level of education, requirements of your agency, and the clientele served by your agency. Therefore, being familiar with a variety of techniques to evaluate direct practice is important. Among the most common are single-subject designs, goal-attainment scaling, task-achievement scaling, and client satisfaction questionnaires.

Single-Subject Designs

Single-subject designs are research methods aimed at determining whether or not an intervention was successful. The name is based on the fact that they are often used with a single case or client. Yegidis and Weinbach (1996) indicate that single-subject designs have had many names, including single N or $N = 1$ research, single-subject research, single-subject design, single case-study design, single-system design, and time-series research or design. Of course, the "single subject" may really be a family, a group, or some other size system. The structure of single-subject research is fairly simple. In its most basic form, we have a client with a problem, the problem is attacked through the intervention of the worker, and we have an outcome of that intervention. The outcome of the intervention is then compared to the state of affairs prior to intervention. Sometimes, this process is called the *AB design,* with A representing the preintervention state and B the intervention. Figure 8.2 shows an example of this design using a simple illustration.

The client here is in a halfway house for chemically dependent adults. The primary goal is helping the client find a job. The first objective is to encourage the client to engage in job-seeking efforts. Before intervention, the client applied for one job per week, information shown on the Phase A baseline. Phase B includes the period of time after the worker begins coaching the client in job-seeking skills. The

solid vertical line represents the start of intervention. The dots show that the number of job applications increased following intervention and then stabilized at four per week.

Clearly, the client has made progress. He now makes significantly more job applications per week. This increase indicates that the intervention—namely, coaching the client in job-seeking skills—has been effective to some extent.

The steps in implementing the single-subject evaluation are straightforward. First, an easily measured goal is identified (e.g., one goal might be to get a nursing home resident out of her room from after breakfast until the noon meal). Then a baseline is done showing the frequency of the behavior prior to intervention, which is called Phase A. Finally, a record of the frequency of the behavior is kept during and following intervention. A graphical representation of the change can be prepared quite readily. Sometimes a baseline can be constructed using information from a case record. However, frequently this source of information is not possible. For example, consistent or easily measurable types of information might not have been recorded.

In the event that there is no opportunity to establish a baseline, the worker can still maintain a record of the behavior following intervention. This is called a *B design.* Only the behavior occurring during and at the end of the intervention phase can be measured. The example shown in Figure 8.3 reflects an intervention with an adolescent who repeatedly violated his parents' curfew restrictions.

One should note that we consider results that occur in Phase B to be caused by the intervention.

Figure 8.2   *Single-Subject (AB) Design*

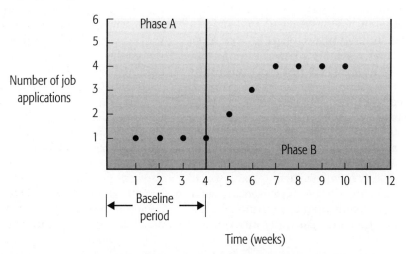

Figure 8.3 *Design without a Baseline*

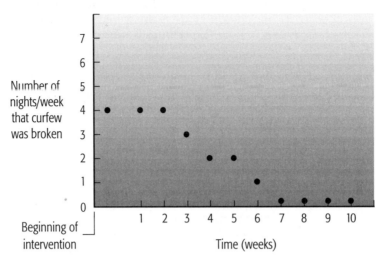

We know from our previous discussion that this notion is relatively simplistic. Many other variables may be contributing to cause the changes seen following intervention.

There are other types of designs that fall into the single-subject design category. For example, we might have a situation where an *ABC design* is possible. A baseline is constructed (as might occur when we keep track of how long the client stayed out of her room in the nursing home between the hours of 8 A.M. and noon). The period prior to intervention is the A Phase. When the human service professional begins to provide an intervention, we have the B Phase. Four weeks into the intervention, an additional treatment (C Phase) was prescribed (perhaps the client began to take medication). We now have an ABC design, where C represents the medication phase. Figure 8.4 is an example of this design.

Clearly, single-subject designs work well when there is an obvious behavior that can somehow be measured. A student used this method to chart arguments between two residents sharing a room in a nursing home. Both the residents and the nursing staff found the situation intolerable. The nursing staff maintained a record of when and how many arguments occurred, thus providing a baseline.

Efforts to increase or decrease the frequency of a given behavior are particularly appropriate for single-subject design. As was noted, this design can be used with client self-reports or where there is some sort of pre–post data-gathering device employed. That is, some specific instrument is used to measure a behavior prior to intervention and again after intervention.

The Rathus Assertiveness Scale (McCormick, 1984) is an example. Scores on this instrument can be used to measure levels of assertiveness prior to and following intervention.

Additional Perspectives on Single-Subject Designs

Looking over these various models, you may recognize other possibilities. Consider, for example, a family seeking help with their 13-year-old daughter, who is out of control. There is not sufficient time to do a baseline on either the daughter's or the parents' behavior. You begin the B phase by providing counseling to the daughter separately. Parental complaints about broken curfews, school absences, and angry outbursts represent possible baselines. Although the parents reject the need for their involvement in family counseling, they agree to the worker's request that they keep a chart of how often these three behaviors occur. Thus, we have three items we could measure in some way: broken curfews, angry outbursts, and school absences. These multiple baselines are fairly common when dealing with complex problems.

After four sessions leading to some improvement in the target behaviors, the family leaves for Christmas vacation. Shortly after returning from vacation the parents agree to additional help in the form of family counseling. Family counseling is really the introduction of a second intervention. Figure 8.5 shows this BAB design with multiple baselines.

One should note that single-subject designs can be adapted to other situations. For example, a group of adolescents learning about the risks and dangers

Figure 8.4   *ABC Design*

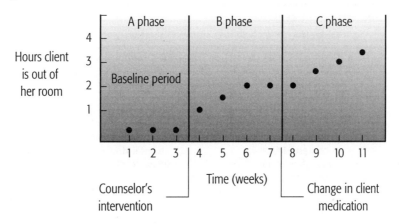

Figure 8.5   *BAB Design with Multiple Baselines*

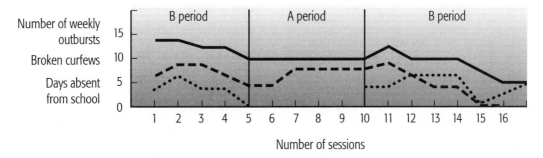

of drug abuse might be tested at the first group session and again at the end. This testing would provide a measure of knowledge at the start and conclusion of the intervention period. Pre–post tests of this sort are especially appropriate when the objective of intervention is increased knowledge.

Goal-Attainment Scaling

Goal-attainment scaling is a method used when achievement of the goal is sufficiently important to be used as the primary outcome criterion. It is positive in its connotation because it focuses on a desired state (e.g., employment) rather than on a problem (e.g., being unemployed). It is also used when a goal does not lend itself to the kind of charting and evaluation needed for single-subject designs. Perhaps it is a situation where the client has multiple goals, many of which are related to one another. Perhaps the goals are not as easily measured by counting behaviors, as was the case in the nursing-home situation mentioned earlier.

With goal-attainment scaling, various steps toward achieving a goal can be measured. Table 8.1 provides an example of these steps. The client is a mother of two children; all of them are living in a shelter for battered women. The client has three goals she wants to work on: (1) getting a temporary restraining order (TRO) from the court, which would prevent her husband from contacting her; (2) finding a job, so she will be less dependent upon her husband for financial support; and (3) reestablishing her social support network (composed of family and friends). Although the client may not achieve the ultimate goal of leaving her husband, finding a good job, and developing many new friends, she may still make progress toward increasing her self-esteem and becoming more independent. This progress can be charted using goal-attainment scaling.

McMahon (1996) employs another type of goal-attainment scale using a point system. A slightly modified version of her goal-attainment scale is shown in Table 8.2. As you can see, the system is essentially similar to the one in Table 8.1. The difference is that the

Table 8.1   *Goal-Attainment Scaling*

Levels of Predicted Outcomes	Objective 1[a]	Objective 2	Objective 3
Least favorable outcome	Client returns home to abuser, gives up goals	Client returns home to abuser, gives up goals	Client returns home to abuser, gives up goals
Less-than-expected outcome	Client contacts Court about TRO	Client applies for one job	Client calls one old friend
Expected level of success	Client obtains TRO from court	Client applies for a few jobs	Client spends time with friend
More-than-expected level of success	Client's spouse does not contest TRO	Client offered a job, but turns it down	Client spends time with a few friends
Most favorable outcome	Spouse leaves home so client can live there	Client accepts good job	Client develops new friends

Source: H. Hagedorn et al. (1976). *A Working Manual of Simple Program Evaluation Techniques for Community Mental Health Centers.* Washington, DC: U.S. Government Printing Office.
[a] One might substitute the objective listing at the top with a brief description of the problem being addressed.

Table 8.2   *Modified Goal-Attainment Scaling*

−3	−2	−1	0	+1	+2	+3
Goal given up	Much worse than at start	Little worse than at start	Starting point	Little better than at start	Much better than at start	Goal attained

Source: M. McMahon (1995). *The General Method of Social Work Practice.* Englewood Cliffs, NJ: Prentice-Hall, p. 252.

possibilities are arranged from the worst outcome (goal given up) to the best outcome (goal attained). This system can be easily modified and used with a wide variety of goals or client problems.

Task-Achievement Scaling

Task-achievement scaling is a method of evaluating the degree to which an identified set of tasks has been accomplished. Many human service intervention activities are discrete, or task-oriented. For example, brokering, advocacy, and service coordination-type tasks cannot be easily measured using single-subject designs or goal-attainment scaling. A good example is a hospital human service professional doing discharge planning. Primary goals for a given client may consist of arranging home health care for a client being discharged or checking on financial arrangements needed for admission to a nursing home.

Task-achievement scaling allows us to measure the extent to which the worker and client have completed agreed-upon tasks, such as arranging transportation or filing an insurance claim. This model is especially useful for situations in which there is limited contact between worker and client, as often happens in hospital discharge-planning units. It begins with the expectation that both client and worker agree on the tasks to be performed and who is to perform them. The focus is on results, not on effort. Typically, a five-point scale is used. Reid and Epstein (1977) use the following description of the points on the scale, ranging from 4 (completely achieved) to 0 (no opportunity to work on task).

A rating of 4 (completely achieved) applies to tasks that are fully accomplished (e.g., a job has been found, a homemaker secured, financial assistance obtained). It may also be used for tasks that are fully accomplished "for all practical purposes" (1977, p. 289). In the case of a couple whose goal was to reduce quarreling, a rating of 4 could be given if they reached a point where hostile interchanges occurred infrequently and no longer presented a problem, and they saw no need for further work on the task.

A rating of 3 (substantially achieved) indicates that the task is largely accomplished, though further action may be needed before full accomplishment is realized. Thus, if the task is to improve work performance, significant improvement would merit a rating of 3 even though further improvement would be possible and desirable.

When a rating of 2 (partially achieved) is chosen, demonstrable progress has been made on the task, but considerable work remains to be done. For example, if the task is to obtain a job, a rating of 2 could be given if the client has actively sought work and found a job he could take but was reluctant to. Or this rating would be appropriate for a couple who had made some headway on a shared task of finding things of mutual interest to do together even though they and the counselor were dissatisfied with their progress.

A rating of 1 (minimally achieved [or not achieved]) is used for tasks on which no progress has been made or on which progress has been insignificant or uncertain. If a client's task were to enroll in a suitable vocational training program, a rating of 1 would be given if the client was unable to locate a program, even though much effort had gone into searching for one.

A 0 rating indicates no opportunity to work on the task. An example would be a client who cannot carry out a task in the classroom because school is closed due to a teachers' strike.

Table 8.3 shows one example of a task-achievement scale. Here, we are dealing with an elderly client who will be confined to her home following a serious injury. She is physically able to care for herself but will need many services in order to remain at home and avoid moving to a nursing home. Five tasks were identified as important in keeping the woman in her own home. Two of the tasks, arranging for meals on wheels and locating a hospital bed, have been completely achieved. The client will receive homemaker services in about a week, although the original goal was to have these provided immediately. Snow shoveling

services have not yet been acquired, but the client has a list of people who might provide this service. Finally, the son and daughter-in-law are out of town, making contacting them difficult.

As can be seen from the example in Table 8.3, one case may have many tasks that must be accomplished. In some situations, all tasks may be achieved while in others only partial completion is possible. The task achievement scale allows for a rough assessment of the percent of tasks accomplished.

Here is how progress illustrated in Table 8.3 might be calculated. There are a total of 5 goals, each with a maximum point rating of 4 (completely achieved). Multiplying the number of tasks (5 tasks) times the maximum points possible (4 points), we have a total of 20. Now if we add the number of actual points under the rating (3, 4, 4, 2, 1), we find we have a total of 14 points. If we divide that total (14 points) by the maximum points possible (20) we end up with a 70 percent achievement rating for all goals (14/20 = .70). This is, of course, a very rough form of calculation. However, it does help us get some sense of how we are doing in achieving important tasks associated with a given case. It is a particularly useful method for task-oriented interventions (i.e., where specific tasks are identified to achieve specific goals).

Client Satisfaction Questionnaires

In certain situations, knowing the client's reactions to our interventions is important. Businesses routinely use *client satisfaction questionnaires,* which are a series of questions designed to learn the customer's reactions to various aspects of a product or service. For example, automobile purchasers are commonly surveyed about their satisfaction with recent acquisitions. They may be asked to identify any problems with the vehicle or to provide feedback about the person who sold them the car or the

Table 8.3   *Task-Achievement Scaling*

Task	Degree of Achievement	Rating
1. Homemaker services arranged	Client on short waiting list for services. Services will begin in about one week.	3
2. Meals on wheels services secured	Meals will begin the day client is discharged.	4
3. Hospital bed acquired	Hospital bed rented, will be delivered day client is discharged.	4
4. Snow shoveling assistance	Have list of possible people who might provide service.	2
5. Contact son and daughter-in-law	No progress—family is out of town for two weeks.	1

Source: W. Reid and L. Epstein (1972). *Task-Centered Casework.* New York: Columbia University Press.

service department's performance. Similar activities are undertaken by restaurants and other service-oriented businesses.

Client satisfaction questionnaires may be used with a single case, a group of clients all served by the same worker, or all clients served by an agency. In this way, they can be used for both evaluation of direct practice and evaluation of entire programs. One goal might be to help the agency identify service problems or areas where the service is insufficient. Sometimes, such questionnaires help identify unmet needs.

Client satisfaction questionnaires are designed to be used following an intervention. However, they may also prove useful for monitoring progress while service is being given. Toseland and Rivas (1998) suggest that there may be value in using client questionnaires during ongoing group meetings to gather information about the process. The method has been used routinely by some educational groups to help assess the effectiveness of each individual session. One advantage of this approach is that it can be used during intervention, immediately following termination of services, or at some later point in time.

Figure 8.6 shows one page from a client satisfaction questionnaire provided to clients seen by the admission staff of a nursing home. Other questions on this questionnaire asked whether the human service professional explained admission material clearly enough and whether the social service department helped to make the admission process as smooth as possible. There was also additional space for extended comments at the bottom of the questionnaire. This particular questionnaire was attempting to gather information about the social service department itself as well as about the performance of a particular human service professional.

Figure 8.6   *A Client Satisfaction Questionnaire*

Please circle the number that corresponds to your chosen response.

1. How would you rate the overall quality of your admission process at the Center of Care?

4	3	2	1
Excellent	Good	Fair	Poor

Comments: _____

2. Did you get the kind of service you wanted?

1	2	3	4
No, definitely not	No, not really	Yes, generally	Yes, definitely

Comments: _____

3. To what extent has our worker met your needs?

4	3	2	1
Almost all of my needs have been met	Most of my needs have been met	Only a few of my needs have been met	None of my needs have been met

Comments: _____

4. If a friend needed a similar nursing home, would you recommend this social service department to him or her?

1	2	3	4
No, definitely not	No, I don't think so	Yes, I think so	Yes, definitely

Comments: _____

This figure shows the potential versatility of client satisfaction questionnaires.

One disadvantage of such questionnaires is their potential for misuse. Asking a cocaine-addicted client and drug dealer if she benefited from an intervention aimed at keeping her out of the criminal justice system amounts to using the wrong tool for the job. Just as you would not use a screwdriver for driving a nail, you must carefully choose the tools you use in your evaluation efforts. Client satisfaction questionnaires cannot be used in lieu of other methods that produce more valid conclusions about the intervention's effectiveness.

Target-Problem Scaling

Target-problem scaling is another method of evaluating changes over time. It is a process where a problem is identified, a plan is implemented, and changes in target problems are measured to determine if the problem has changed in severity or seriousness.

The original problems are rated by degree of severity. Subsequent ratings are completed using the scale shown in Table 8.4. This form was completed by the teacher based on the rating scale at the bottom of the table. The child was one of several children in a group led by a school counselor. Each child had been referred for problems related to classroom behavior. This chart reflects changes in one of the group members. The degree of change in each identified problem is also assessed following intervention and a month later. In the case noted in Table 8.4, improvement has occurred in both problems, hence the change in degree of severity ratings. The degree of change also is rated positively by the teacher. Finally, a global or average rating reflects an overall picture of the problems being addressed.

Other practice evaluation systems do exist. One is peer review, which involves "a formal evaluation by a relevant peer group of an individual's general competence or specific actions" (Barker, 1999, p. 355). Unlike some of the methods previously described, peer review focuses almost exclusively on the process rather than the outcome of intervention. For example, an agency might adopt a system of evaluating monthly whether or not a worker's case files contain agreed-upon items such as a fact sheet, initial contact and assessment information, and written intervention plan. Each month a different worker's files would be reviewed to determine if the worker was meeting the professional standards adopted by the agency. (For a more detailed description of this method, see Sheafor et al., 1997.)

 ## Evaluation Designs for Programs

Up to this point, we have been talking primarily about evaluating direct practice. The data-gathering mechanisms described above were mostly useful for human service workers evaluating what they do as individual professionals. Some of the approaches discussed also have potential value for evaluating entire programs. Program evaluation can help us determine whether or not one program is more effective or efficient than another. Program evaluation includes periodic as well as ongoing evaluation of the process and the outcomes. In the following section, we will look very briefly at five program evaluation tools: needs assessments, evaluability assessments, process analysis, program outcome analysis, and program monitoring (Evaluation Research Society, 1982; Yegidis & Weinbach, 1996).

Table 8.4   *Target-Problem Change Scale*

Name of Rater:
Teacher:

Target Problem	Target-Problem Rating (Severity Scale)[a]			Target-Problem Rating (Degree of Change)[b]		Global Improvement Rating
	Start	Time 1	Time 2	Termination	Follow-Up	
Talks without raising hand	VS	S	NP	4	4	
Follows directions on assignments	ES	VS	NVS	3	5	4

[a] Degree of Severity Scale: NP (no problem), NVS (not very severe), S (severe), VS (very severe), ES (extremely severe)
[b] Improvement Scale: 1 (worse), 2 (no change), 3 (a little better), 4 (somewhat better), 5 (a lot better)

Needs Assessments

We will discuss needs assessment more in Chapter 13. *Needs assessments* are considered forms of front-end analysis. They are systematic efforts to help an agency determine whether, and to what extent, a program is needed. They also can be used after a program has been in operation for a period of time to determine if unmet needs still exist. They may be useful for identifying gaps in service and helping an agency decide whether a need for a service still exists (Marlow, 1993).

Evaluability Assessments

Evaluability assessments are methods designed primarily to answer the questions, "Can this program be evaluated? Is the agency evaluation ready?" (Pietrzak et al., 1990, p. 22). While one might think any program can be evaluated, this is not always true. For example, if either the intervention or the goals are not defined with sufficient clarity, arriving at an assessment will be most difficult. Sometimes outcomes cannot be readily measured because the program objectives or products are vague or undefined.

Other factors that might interfere with the ability to evaluate a program are lack of accurate identifying information about clients (which might preclude using client satisfaction questionnaires), high cost of conducting a particular type of evaluation, and poor program record keeping. For example, an agency may be unable to determine whether they are serving gay or lesbian youth because this information is not among the data they have collected in the past.

You can begin to see the importance of doing an evaluability assessment prior to launching into any evaluation of the program. Once an agency learns that it cannot adequately evaluate itself, it has two options. First, it can make changes that will allow future assessments (Love, 1991). Second, it can continue on without change. The latter choice carries high risk, because ultimately some sort of evaluation will be demanded of almost every agency.

Process Analysis

We briefly mentioned process evaluations (analysis) or formative evaluations earlier in this chapter. You will remember that they are designs used to evaluate the way interventions in the agency are carried out. Client satisfaction questionnaires can be used for this goal as can peer reviews. Both of these have been previously described and will not be covered again. At its most basic level, *process analysis* might focus on numbers of clients served or the kinds of services provided. It might also be focused on productivity ratios, such as the actual per-child cost of a program screening infants for malnutrition. Process analysis can also help an agency improve service by looking at the ways in which service is provided. If clients are being transferred from one unit in an agency to another unit, are such transitions conducted smoothly? What could be done to make them better? Process analysis depends largely on gathering information from both the producers and consumers of the process, namely human service professionals and clients.

There are a variety of instruments available to assist in process assessment. Clearly, the instrument to be used will be affected by the information desired. Pietrzak and colleagues (1990) provide a fine review of process evaluation and examples of available instruments.

Program Outcome Analysis

A *program outcome analysis* is an evaluation designed to tell us whether or not a program is working. It may also help us find out if a program is cost effective; that is, if the results merit the expense. There are multiple means of assessing program outcomes. If the program objectives have a consumer-satisfaction component, then we might want to use the client satisfaction scales we discussed earlier.

Perhaps a program hopes to increase the client's knowledge, skills, or attitudes. Consider, for example, a group training program for prospective adoptive parents of hard-to-place children (e.g., children who have disabilities or are older). The goal was to help these applicants learn about the difficulties experienced by many of these hard-to-place children. The program began because many prospective adoptive parents did not have accurate information about the problems experienced by these children. In this example, the parents were given a pretest to determine their knowledge prior to intervention and a posttest at the conclusion of the group training. This information, along with a consumer satisfaction questionnaire, was used to assess the outcome of this program.

There are other questions for which we might like answers. Perhaps we want to know if the new family resource unit is accomplishing its purpose. Do clients in the nurturing program learn any new skills that they use at home? Are the short-term changes noted at termination continued over a six-month period? How often do group members served by our substance abuse team reach the goals they set at the onset of intervention? Are there problems or problem areas for which our interventions are not successful?

As you think about these questions, you might realize that an agency whose workers routinely evaluated their practice would be in a better position to respond. Let us say, for example, that goal-attainment scaling is completed on many or most of the agency clients, which would allow the agency to gather a sizable chunk of information useful for program outcome analysis. Similarly, single-subject designs routinely used with clients could produce a volume of information as part of an outcome assessment. One should understand by now that assessing some program outcomes is easier if there is an ongoing attempt to assess the work of individual components (workers or units) in the agency. Pietrzak and colleagues (1990) provide excellent examples of outcome evaluation with a specific focus on child abuse programs.

Continuous Quality Assurance Evaluations

Continuous quality evaluations are focused on measuring attainment of previously identified program goals. The program goals are usually specific indicators that the agency has accepted as evidence of best practices. For example, one mental health agency used three indicators to assess quality service to clients. One indicator was the extent to which written assessments were completed within a 72-hour time frame following initial client contact. The agency goal was to have 99 percent completion rate in that period.

A second indicator was accuracy in the classification of clients by the human service professional. The goal was 100 percent accuracy, because correct classification directly affected whether the agency received reimbursement and payment for services provided to clients. Classification errors cost money.

The third indicator was client satisfaction with a goal of 100 percent. This indicator was measured by using specific questions from a client satisfaction survey mailed to all clients following culmination of their work with the agency.

Continuous quality evaluation emphasizes determination of whether the agency is achieving its goals. It can be concerned not only with the outcomes of human services professionals' intervention with clients but also with more mundane issues such as timely completion of paperwork. Although it is usually used to evaluate programs, it can clearly be used to assess aspects of the individual worker's performance. For example, a pattern of worker performance characterized by inaccurate classifications or a failure to complete assessments within target deadlines could result in a worker receiving additional training or supervision or more serious consequences such as suspension. Thus, this approach has implications for both program and practice evaluation. Table 8.5

Table 8.5   *Continuous Quality Assurance Evaluation, Northwest Center for Strong Families (July 1, 1999–June 30, 2002)*

Item	7/1/99 to 6/30/00	7/1/00 to 6/30/01	7/1/01 to 6/30/02
Required forms are completed and in file	73%	85%	94%
Initial intervention plan is appropriate	97%	95%	98%
Vocational rehabilitation needs are accurately assessed	89%	97%	100%
Discharge plans are documented	91%	98%	99%
Adequate follow-up is documented	80%	87%	95%
Total	**86%**	**92%**	**97%**

shows the results of a family service agency's continuous quality evaluation. The average total of all items for a single year allows a rough assessment of the extent to which the agency is achieving a desired quality of service.

Program Monitoring

Program monitoring is an ongoing activity designed to provide information to the agency on all aspects of its operation. Data may be collected on presenting problems, client demographics, services provided, and outcomes achieved. Agencies develop information management systems so that they can routinely assess how various aspects of their programs are progressing. An agency might decide, for example, that they no longer have sufficient numbers of children placed for adoption to justify continued offering of adoption services. Another agency providing specialized services in the area of sexuality might notice that the type of client has changed over the years. Instead of working with mostly intact couples needing accurate information, they are now helping clients with very serious sexual dysfunctions.

From these examples you can see how important maintaining accurate and complete records is. An ongoing effort at program monitoring is essential to improve services within the agency or organization and to manage agency resources wisely.

Issues and Problems in Evaluation

Any evaluation program employed by the worker or the agency has the potential to be misused or interpreted incorrectly. Part of this potential is due to the nature of the research tools available to us. Still other parts are inherent in any evaluation effort. For example, normally we are not able to randomly assign clients to treatment and control groups so that we will meet the high standards of the experimental model. Clients often need immediate help. Additionally, there are ethical concerns inherent in refusing clients an intervention because we wish to compare them with a group that is receiving service. We often must use quasi-experimental methods (i.e., experiments in natural social settings where some aspects of experimental design can be applied, albeit less rigorously than in a laboratory situation) rather than experimental methods. This is a limitation with which we must live. The next section will consider some of these issues.

Problems in Generalizability

As was mentioned earlier in this chapter, there is always a temptation to take evaluation results demonstrating a successful program and apply those results to other groups. We have also suggested that a program that is effective with a given group of clients may not work well with others. We often have no way of knowing if the clients we work with are representative of other clients. When we decide to evaluate our success with only a subset (sample) of the clients we have served, the potential for threats to generalizability to other client groups is obvious.

One of the reasons we attempt to obtain random samples when we survey people is that the mathematical characteristics of random samples allow us to infer from the sample to a larger population. A *random sample* is one in which all elements in a population have an equal probability of being included in the sample. An agency might wish to obtain a random sample of its clients. Staff can assign each client a different number and then use a table of random numbers to select those to be included in a sample. The idea is for the small subset of people being asked for information to resemble other people in the entire population as closely as possible.

Sometimes, there are problems with this process. Let us say you wanted to know the views of all students majoring in human services. You decide to select a random sample of the majors and to use a questionnaire to gather their views. Although a random sample should result in a subset or group similar to all human services majors, you could end up with no males in the sample simply because males compose only about 12 percent of all undergraduate human services majors. If you think that there may be a difference between males and females in the way they will answer the questionnaire, you might want to ensure that males will be proportionately represented in your sample. *Stratified random sampling* is a method of sampling that ensures some important subset or strata of a population (such as males) is not accidentally left out of a typical random sample. To create a stratified random sample, you must assign numbers to both male and female majors, and then, using a table of random numbers (located in most statistics texts), randomly select a proportionate number of males. If there are 100 human services majors and 88 percent are female, then 88 percent of your sample should also be female. There are a variety of other sampling methods that one may employ in the interests of ensuring that the sample is representative. A more detailed listing of these is included in Marlow (1993). Achieving a representative sample is essential if we hope to generalize the results of our evaluation.

Wrong Choices of Evaluation Tools

We have already noted that an evaluation instrument can be used inappropriately. Using a client satisfaction questionnaire to assess whether or not a program achieved its goal of reducing delinquent behavior is equivalent to hammering a screw into wood. The wrong tool is being used in both cases. The questionnaire is the wrong tool because the goal was to reduce delinquent behavior, not to entertain adolescents. In this case, the most appropriate measure of success should include some means of assessing whether the level of delinquent behavior went up, down, or stayed the same. Asking the client if he liked the group home experience (client satisfaction questionnaire) is of little value. There is a possibility that he liked the group home very much because he learned some new techniques for burglarizing homes. Perhaps he has even become a more accomplished criminal as a result of this experience. As you might imagine, the use of inappropriate measurement systems is a potential problem when agencies first begin evaluating outcomes.

Failure to Involve Clients in the Evaluation Process

Ideally, clients should be involved in the evaluation process to the greatest extent possible. Doing research on clients and not informing them that it is being done is ethically wrong. Clients should be promised confidentiality. Only aggregate data omitting individual identification should be released. Clients' rights should be carefully protected. Moreover, client knowledge of the evaluation process may increase the effectiveness of the intervention and their level of satisfaction (Campbell, 1988).

Staff Distrust of Evaluation

We indicated earlier that many agencies do not routinely engage in evaluation of practice or programs. When a research effort is suggested, fear or distrust by those who will be evaluated is not uncommon. The motives of the agency in asking for the evaluation may be questioned. Staff may feel they are being criticized or condemned. Unless the agency can gain the trust of those being evaluated, the chances are likely that the process will be fraught with problems.

Evaluation Process Interference with Service Giving

Ideally, program evaluation should be accomplished so that it does not interfere with giving service to clients. An effective management information system can make this process go more smoothly, because much of the data needed can be computerized and retrieved with relative ease. If, on the other hand, clients must complete lengthy questionnaires after each session or maintain detailed logs between sessions, this evaluation may affect the intervention. Clients may find the process time consuming or intrusive. They may cease coming or provide insufficient data to allow the evaluation to be carried out. Similarly, data collection should be a manageable undertaking rather than overburdening the workers (Bloom, Fischer, & Orme, 1995). If this situation happens, the evaluation process has begun to interfere with the service giving process.

Alternative Explanations for Program Outcomes

When a client or program achieves the desired objectives, attributing the results to the intervention employed is tempting. The tendency to confuse two events, one following the other, with cause and effect is natural. This thinking implies that because one event precedes the other, it naturally caused the other—which is often not the case. There are often multiple explanations for the occurrence of any event. The outcomes of our interventions are no exception. Highlight 8.3 includes a partial list of those factors, many of which are also called threats to the interval validity of the study design. That is, they represent influences that can cloud or obscure the real reason change occurred.

There are many other possible explanations for change that could confound the results of one's evaluation. Gibbs (1991) and Yegidis and Weinbach (1996) have developed extensive lists and clear explanations of alternative or confounding causes. The important thing to remember is that multiple explanations may exist for changes that we observe following an intervention. These possible explanations should act as a caution to the worker evaluating the results of any intervention.

Unanticipated Consequences

Not infrequently, we discover that a program has had consequences or outcomes we did not envision.

HIGHLIGHT 8.3

Alternate Explanations for Outcomes

- *History* is any event that occurs prior to the end of an intervention. Not infrequently, changes happening in the environment can affect the outcome of an intervention. For example, a 25 percent increase in the number of jobs in an area because of several companies expanding their workforce might explain why a job placement program was so successful. In the absence of these new jobs, the rate might have been quite different. There is also a possibility that the same number of unemployed people would have gotten jobs without the job placement program.
- *Maturation* is the process of aging. Sometimes, the results of an intervention can be attributed to changes being experienced by the subject. For example, most delinquent children reduce their delinquency as they age. A program that works with children from age 13 to 17 might be claiming success with its clients when the results may be more attributable to maturation.
- *Mortality* is the loss that occurs when some of the people in the sample begin to drop out. The result is that a select group is now being measured. One cannot extrapolate from this group to the original population. Client self-selection is operating here in that clients themselves may have made the decision about whether or not to continue in a program. Ideally, a program ought to include as failures those who dropped out along the way rather than just those who stayed to the end without reaching their goals.
- *Creaming* is the tendency of some programs to take only the very best candidates for a program. One danger is that evaluating only the best may reflect significantly greater effectiveness than if all similar candidates in the population were included. Another danger is that perhaps these "best" candidates would have changed anyway. For example, many first-offender programs take those they consider good candidates for the program. Thus, they tend to bias the outcome.

   The selection of clients by the worker often creates a form of bias that can be quite powerful.

Sometimes, workers are not aware they are selecting clients with specific characteristics.
- *Regression toward the mean* is the tendency for extreme scores to move toward the mean over time. This tendency occurs when those in the program were chosen because they varied greatly from the average. Take, for example, choosing all children with low scores on a self-esteem scale and exposing them to the treatment. This exposure will almost always result in their having higher scores the next time they are evaluated using the same scale. This is the result of a mathematical or statistical tendency for high scores (or, in this case, low ones) to move toward the mean (or average) on subsequent testing. Scores far from a mean may be the result of statistical error, and a second testing would produce a score more in line with the expected mean.
- *Reactance* is the reaction or change of behavior that occurs simply because of a new situation or environment. Reactance occurs when people are merely reacting to something new. As soon as people get used to the situation, their reactions change, or they revert to former ways of behaving. Think about how you and your family interact when a stranger is present. Often one behaves differently because of the presence of an observer. Typically, the presence of a new treatment (or worker) may produce something of a honeymoon effect, where people begin to act naturally only after they are comfortable with the new situation. Evaluation results may be skewed (distorted) because people are acting unnaturally and will return to their old behavior after they get used to the presence of the worker or the treatment.

   In program evaluation, one might be able to control some of these variables by comparing the results of the program with other situations where the program is not being used. This process is an attempt to create a control group of sorts and to use the experimental method of research. For example, the results of a first-offender diversion program in a city of 50,000 might be compared with the recidivism rate of first offenders in a city of comparable size that lacks such a program.

These may be categorized as either side effects or regressive effects (Sieber, 1981). Further, some side effects may be classified as harmful to clients, and others may be neutral in their impact or beneficial. A person learning to be more assertive, for example, may adopt this new approach with an employer. The employer, unused to the employee's newfound assertiveness, reacts by firing the employee. This outcome might be viewed as a negative side effect of the client's assertiveness training. Another example involves a couple learning to communicate their needs more clearly to each other through a marriage-enrichment program. They may discover that they really have incompatible goals in life. This leads them to a decision to divorce. This marriage-enrichment program may then be seen as having an unintended impact on the couple's marriage.

Another example of unanticipated consequences involves a policy decision made at the macro level. During the Clinton administration there was considerable interest in reducing the discrimination faced by gay and lesbians in the military services. A "don't ask–don't tell" policy was implemented that was intended to discourage the military from removing gay and lesbian soldiers. Unfortunately, the so-called "don't ask–don't tell" policy has resulted in even larger numbers of gay and lesbian military personnel being discharged from the armed services. Clearly, unintended consequences can occur at any level.

Regressive effects, as the name implies, mean that a situation gets worse as a result of the intervention. An example or two should illustrate how regressive effects can happen. Mr. Jones was referred to a counselor by another counselor who was moving away. An assessment of Mr. Jones's situation had been made by the previous counselor and by the consulting psychiatrist. The primary symptom, as described in the record, was anxiety. During the first interview, the counselor noted that the client was having trouble sleeping, had lost his appetite, and suffered from disinterest in his work. His relationship with his wife was also deteriorating. He was particularly anxious because his inability to concentrate at work was threatening his job. Mr. Jones had been receiving counseling about his anxiety and was taking tranquilizers prescribed by the psychiatrist. No one, it seemed, had recognized that Mr. Jones was suffering from depression. The medication prescribed for him was depressing him further. To make things even worse, he had been treated for the wrong problem.

Another example is drawn from the research on program effectiveness. The "scared straight" programs, in which juvenile delinquents are exposed to hard-ened criminals at maximum security prisons, have been extremely popular in the United States. The goal of these programs is to scare the delinquent youth into a law-abiding life. Adolescents are brought to a prison, and experienced criminals verbally threaten them and graphically suggest what their fate will be should they continue their delinquent behavior. Surely, one would think, such a program would be effective, because it would bring delinquents face-to-face with the future consequences of their actions. Unfortunately, research on the scared straight program indicates that "controls" (i.e., delinquents who did not go through this program) committed fewer delinquencies than those who participated in the program (Finckenauer, 1982). In addition, the offenses the controls committed were less serious than offenses committed by delinquents who had been "treated" in this program (Finckenauer, 1982; Lipsey, 1992).

The important thing to remember is that some of our helping efforts may have the opposite effect. Unintended consequences sometimes occur despite our best intentions. Finally, interventions that work for one client may not work as well with others. Gibbs (1991) has provided an excellent set of guidelines for practitioners tempted to use untested interventions or approaches that have limited research support.

Attempting to identify the factors that cause harmful side effects and modify the program accordingly is important. Offering clients help in overcoming negative experiences arising from prior agency contact is also important.

The completion of the evaluation phase leads to one of two conclusions. Either the client system has achieved the goals previously identified, or goals have not been reached. If the goals have not been attained, the worker needs to explore with the client whether or not continued intervention will be helpful. If both parties decide that continued work is needed, this decision may lead to a new process of planned change. If goals have been reached or there are other reasons for concluding the intervention, we then enter the termination phase of the helping process.

Culturally Competent Evaluation

As should be evident from other chapters, each step in the planned change process must be grounded in cultural competence. This is required because, just as in assessment, planning, and intervention, cultural variables play a significant role in research and evaluation. Highlight 8.4 identifies a number of ways that our efforts to evaluate practice can be enhanced by cultural awareness and sensitivity.

Termination

Termination is the end of the professional worker–client relationship. All relationships between human services professionals and clients must eventually come to an end. The ending may be scheduled or unexpected, successful or unsuccessful. Despite the circumstances of the ending, the worker must be prepared to manage this phase of the planned change process.

The tasks of termination are similar whether we are working with an individual, a family or group, a community, or an organization. This portion of the chapter focuses on the knowledge and skills needed for effectively concluding the professional human services professional–client relationship.

HIGHLIGHT 8.4

Cultural Competence and Evaluation

Research and evaluation might seem like topics for which issues such as ethnic diversity and cultural competence have little relevance. However, Cherry (2000) reminds us that "one of the primary purposes for doing research in the helping professions is to give practitioners another view of reality." He notes a true picture of reality is possible only if we are sensitive to racial, cultural, ethnic, and gender differences. In the past, without this sensitivity, we have ended up with biased research. Biased research has led to assumptions about the life experiences of women based solely on the experiences of males. It has led to conclusions applied to members of all ethnic groups when the only people studied were Caucasians. And it has fed stereotypes about many oppressed groups. Listed below are some ways in which cultural competence can be applied to our evaluation efforts (Cherry, 2000; Williams, Unrau, & Grinnell, 1998).

1. Ensure that samples chosen for research accurately reflect the diversity and characteristics of the entire population. Men and women may have different experiences with our helping efforts and programs. Similarly, asking questions about respondents' sexual orientation may help us understand what impact programs have on gay and lesbian people.
2. Be sensitive to data-gathering approaches that may be less effective with some groups. Probing questions in interviews may be very threatening to individuals from cultures prizing privacy and saving face.
3. Recognize that language differences and lack of facility with English may place respondents from other cultures at a disadvantage in terms of understanding either written or oral interview questions.
4. Whenever possible, involve members of minority groups, people of color, women, and gay and lesbian people in the planning stages of research that affects them.
5. Recognize that questionnaires and other data sources that have worked well with men or white people may not work as well with women or people of color.
6. Use culturally sensitive language when developing instruments.
7. Where needed, use interpreters to ensure that respondents understand the question and the researcher understands the response. Minority interviewers may also be needed.
8. Avoid unnecessary emphasis on problems with oppressed populations. Focus on strengths to the extent possible.
9. Avoid generalizing findings to any other group than that represented in the study.
10. Look for differences among participants that may help understand differential outcomes. For example, do gender or ethnic differences affect the level of satisfaction with a particular program?
11. Ensure that all questions are gender neutral and not biased toward the life experiences of any particular group. For example, don't ask about employment unless you also leave an option for homemakers who are not employed outside the home.
12. When giving choices on questionnaires, make certain that you have not overlooked critical options such as ethnic group or require forced choices that do not apply. For example, it may be better to allow respondents to check all cultural/racial groups with which they identify to avoid forced choices that are not truly relevant.

Ethical Practice and Critical Thinking About Termination

The ethical standards of many human services professions provide some guidance about when we may terminate services to clients. These standards usually require termination when services are no longer needed or serving a client's interests. Termination should not occur precipitously, and the worker should always arrange continued service through referral when this is indicated. Of course, termination, when it occurs, should be done for reasons relating to client needs and not based upon worker needs. Some standards allow termination of a client who fails to pay for services when payment is a clear condition of service and the consequences of ending the relationship have been thoroughly explored with the client.

Termination must be based upon clear evidence that the goals and objectives have been achieved. Gut-level feelings or impressions on the part of the worker do not represent a solid basis for such judgment. The worker is also obligated to use critical thinking skills at this stage of the planned change process. Assisting the client in considering if termination is appropriate given actual progress is helpful. For example, a client may feel immediately better in the early stages of work with a practitioner and come to believe that her problems are now manageable. The worker can help her analyze her reactions and challenge unwarranted assumptions. Or consider a client victimized by her partner's battery. She might assume that her spouse's sudden change of heart and contrition are evidence that she no longer needs to be involved in a support group for domestic violence survivors. The worker can help her assess whether this assumption is grounded in fact or hope.

Terminating Professional Relationships

As stated above, all professional relationships must terminate at some point. When a client no longer needs service, the relationship will expectedly come to an end. However, not all terminations occur as one might hope. Sometimes, terminations occur unexpectedly and for reasons that the worker could not have predicted. Being aware of these possibilities and prepared to act professionally in any case is important for a human service professional.

In this section we will look at several issues: the tasks of termination; timing and preparing for termination; reasons for termination; reactions to the termination phase; and making appropriate referrals.

Tasks of Termination

Termination of the closing phase of the planned change process involves a number of concrete steps (see Figure 8.7). Hepworth and colleagues (1997), Brill (1998), and Toseland and Rivas (1998) identify a similar set of tasks that the generalist worker and client system must undertake during the termination process. These tasks include:

1. *Deciding when to terminate the professional worker–client relationship.* Sometimes, we know from the onset exactly when the relationship between worker and client system will end. A six-session educational group lasts for precisely that many sessions. The hospital counselor helping a client being discharged tomorrow morning also knows exactly when their professional relationship will end. In other situations, the ending point will be determined depending on when the intervention's objectives have been achieved. Sometimes, the ending can be anticipated; other times it may not.

2. *Evaluating achievement of objectives.* One key intervention task is evaluating whether or not the agreed-upon objectives have been achieved. Termination may occur when the desired outcomes have occurred or when further progress is no longer possible. An appropriate activity for the worker is summarizing achievements and helping the client system recognize growth.

3. *Maintaining and continuing progress.* The accomplishments that the worker and client system achieved in the helping process must be maintained following termination. The shy, introverted youth who became more outgoing in the group must maintain this assertiveness outside of the protected group environment. The group can no longer shelter him from the environment. Similarly, the neighborhood association that successfully lobbied the police department for more foot patrols must continue their involvement and community-building activities. If they do not, things may begin to slip as other police priorities occur. Sometimes this is called generalizing or stabilizing the change effort.

4. *Resolving emotional reactions of the worker and client.* Reactions to termination can range from sorrow to relief or from a sense of loss to an anticipation of increased freedom. Both worker and client may have emotional reactions that need to be recognized, discussed, and resolved.

Figure 8.7   *Planned Change Steps in the Generalist Intervention Model (GIM)*

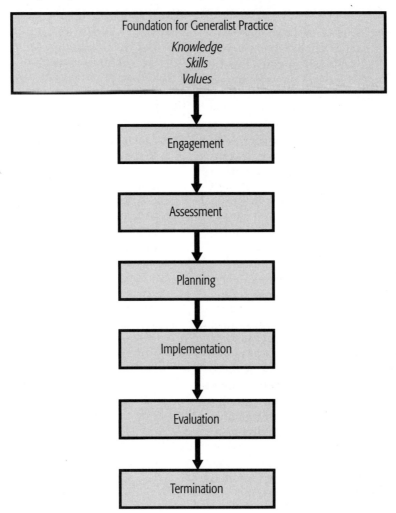

5. *Making appropriate referrals.* When the termination process indicates that clients need additional help, the worker must make appropriate referrals. These referrals can be made to a specific individual such as a psychiatrist or to an agency providing the type of help clients need.

Ultimately, the goal at termination is to empower the client system. This empowerment means that clients will learn to use their own resources (instead of those of the counselor) to manage future difficulties they may encounter. Empowerment is the real importance of stabilizing the change effort. Later in this chapter we will discuss each component of termination. Evaluation has already been discussed.

As you can see, there is considerable agreement about the activities that must be undertaken as a relationship ends. One of the first steps is deciding when to terminate. We will look at this topic next.

Planned Terminations

As has been suggested, one can easily predict that a worker–client relationship will eventually conclude. Thus, the worker will consider the timing of the termination as an important part of the helping process. Determining when to terminate is one of the most important tasks the worker must accomplish.

Frequently, an ending point is identified at the start of the professional relationship. For example, in task-centered practice situations the sessions are expected to continue for some set time period and then conclude. Let us look at a family that contracts to see a counselor for six weekly sessions. The family (and the worker) expect that the professional relationship will end after the sixth week. Similarly, consider the situation of a school counselor who is helping to develop an individualized educational plan for a child with learning difficulties. She knows that the relationship will terminate following the end of the school year. The timing of the termination in each of these examples can reasonably be predicted in advance, and, by definition, these are planned terminations.

Unplanned Terminations

Unfortunately, not all terminations can be planned for, and many are unexpected. Terminations may also occur for reasons not under the control of either client or worker. Some terminations occur because no progress has been made or because problems are getting worse, not better. Brill (1998) has suggested that lack of progress may be due to a misunderstanding between client and worker, incorrect or misinterpreted data, or incorrect definition of the problem. Perhaps the wrong problem was selected for intervention, the goals selected were not attainable, or the alternative selected was inappropriate. Maybe the wrong intervention was made. In other situations, the expectations placed on the client by the worker–client contract are too demanding, too complicated, or too simple. Sometimes, unexpected negative consequences of a change effort require premature termination. Likewise, termination may

be appropriate when there are relationship difficulties between client and worker.

Still other situations may bring about termination before either party would prefer. For instance, a school counselor may not continue seeing a client during the summer. Another example is a field practicum student who ends her placement while the client continues with the agency. Sometimes the worker must terminate with a client who is being referred to another worker or specialist. Additionally, a client may simply quit coming without notifying the worker. McMahon (1996) states that termination may occur when the area being probed is too sensitive and the client cannot tolerate opening the matter up. Some clients end their sessions because the feelings associated with ending are too painful to discuss (we will discuss some typical feelings about endings in a later section). Others simply drop out because terminating their sessions appears to them to be a way of controlling the ending. In other words, by taking the first step of quitting, they avoid the pain and discomfort of dealing with the end of a relationship. This situation is a bit like a person who quits her job because she anticipates getting fired anyway. Finally, some clients drop out because they are dissatisfied or lack the resources to continue. Highlight 8.5 illustrates some reasons for unplanned terminations in groups.

Other Points About Termination

Clearly, professional relationships can end for many reasons. Some of those reasons are under the control of the worker, and others are not. Some can be anticipated and others cannot. What is most important is

HIGHLIGHT 8.5

Unplanned Terminations in Groups

Group members may leave a group prematurely for any number of reasons. These may include any of the following factors:

1. Lack of motivation;
2. Changes in life that reduce interest in the group (such as moving, family death, and the like);
3. Problems with group meeting schedules;
4. Feeling out of place in the group;
5. Inability to form appropriate relationships with other group members;
6. Discomfort with strong feelings expressed in the group;
7. Insufficient orientation to therapy;
8. Feeling scapegoated in the group;
9. Problems arising from concurrent individual and group therapy;
10. Lack of financial resources to continue in the group;
11. Satisfaction with current changes that have occurred.

that the worker recognizes that unplanned terminations are fairly common. Whenever possible, the worker should plan for terminations and involve the client in that process.

If a client drops out prematurely (in the worker's opinion), it is appropriate to attempt to discover reasons for the client's decision. Perhaps, this effort will result in the client returning, perhaps not. Still, it is part of one's professional responsibility to follow up on a client who has terminated early. Ultimately, the client's right to self-determination must guide the worker. That is, the bottom line is that clients have the right to quit if they want to. Given the goal of helping the client become self-sufficient and less dependent upon the worker, it may even be a positive sign when clients decide they no longer need the worker's help.

Reactions and Feelings in Terminations

Feelings and reactions about termination are a somewhat controversial topic. Most authors spend a great deal of time declaring that clients experience a significant sense of loss when the relationship with the worker comes to an end. Other researchers have come to opposite conclusions. We shall try to include both perspectives here. Each is based on significant clinical and empirical research.

Extent and Range of Emotional Reactions

Several factors determine the extent to which clients experience given feelings about the termination process. For example, open-ended relationships in which the client and worker have had an extensive, ongoing professional association are more likely to result in stronger emotional reactions (Hepworth et al., 1997). Educationally focused groups experience significantly weaker emotional reactions than is true for treatment groups (Toseland & Rivas, 1998). Task groups (such as committees) frequently experience endings as positive. Members may even feel relieved that their job is done.

Client reactions to terminations are affected by a variety of things. These include the nature of the problem, the duration and intensity of contact, whether the ending was natural or forced, client strengths and support systems, whether goals were achieved or not, and whether or not the termination ends service or results from the client being transferred to another worker (Hellenbrand, 1987). Generally, a client system's sense of loss is directly related to the extent to which the relationship focused on personal problems (such as depression, anxiety) as opposed to environmental issues (such as housing).

Amount of Contact

In some situations, the amount of contact between client and worker is so limited that even the concept of termination seems inappropriate. The hospital human service professional who simply arranges for a client to get a hospital bed in her home while she recovers from a broken hip may terminate after only one or two short contacts with the client. There has often been such a limited degree of relationship building that perhaps the only reaction of the client would be gratitude.

Size and Type of System

Similarly, the size and type of system one is working with will have some bearing on the reactions to termination. For example, consider a worker who helps a community identify a number of major problems and come to consensus on those of greatest priority. He leaves the community with several functioning task groups, each aimed at coping with an identified problem. The degree of dependency and level of self-disclosure in this relationship are likely to be quite low. The relationship spans a relatively short period of time, and the issues dealt with were related to conditions in the community, not the personal lives of the clients. Reactions of community residents are positive but the amount of emotional content was limited.

Contrast the termination described in the section above to that found in the ending of a one-to-one relationship between a worker and a client recovering from depression. In the latter situation, the client and worker have been together for over nine months. The client has talked with the worker about a variety of personal issues. Subsequently, he has gradually developed increased self-confidence and feelings of well-being. Because of the relationship's intense nature, ending it is likely to be emotionally charged. Table 8.6 summarizes factors affecting reactions to termination.

Mixed Feelings

Mixed feelings often characterize the conclusion of professional relationships. The ending of any relationship in which strong emotional sharing has occurred is typically bittersweet. A sense of loss is

Table 8.6   *Factors Affecting Reactions to Termination*

Factors Likely to Produce More Intense Reactions	Factors Likely to Produce Less Intense Reactions
Open-ended relationships	Time-limited relationships
Frequent worker–client contact	Infrequent worker–client contact
Personal problem–focused	Environmental problem–focused
Absence of other client support systems	Presence of other client support systems
Individual or family client system	Organizational or community client system
High level of emotional content	Low level of emotional content
Treatment groups	Task groups

common. Some clients also experience anger and feelings of rejection in these situations. Others feel pride, satisfaction, optimism, and a sense of achievement or mastery because of what they have accomplished. Some clients report that old problems, long since overcome, reappear. New problems sometimes develop. At other times, clients object to the relationship ending, claiming they are not ready yet. Still others will deny that the end is approaching or that they have any feelings about the upcoming event, distancing themselves from the inevitable. Some clients report feeling a "sense of abandonment and loss and feelings of rejection and betrayal or hurt or anger. Clients may be anxious about managing alone and sustaining gains . . ." (Hellenbrand, 1987, p. 767).

Epstein (1980) has argued that clients do not routinely experience negative feelings at termination. She is an advocate of task-centered approaches, which are designed to reduce client reliance on the human services professional. According to Epstein:

It is a rare client indeed who truly becomes unhappy or adrift when termination occurs. Practitioners tend to overestimate the value they have as persons for the client's well-being. The rewards of termination for a client are great: fewer expenses, more time, more independence. A practitioner may provoke unhappiness in a client about termination if the practitioner has overvalued the relationship and if excess valuation has been communicated to the client by word or deed. (1980, p. 257)

In summary, while there is potential for strong termination feelings to exist, the worker should not assume that all clients will experience the same reactions.

Worker Reactions to Termination

Interestingly, clients are not the only ones who may experience strong feelings at termination. Human service professionals themselves sometimes experience reactions to the end of a professional relationship. The extent and intensity of those feelings is likely to be controlled by the same set of factors previously described. In other words, workers are subject to the same potential feelings as clients, depending upon a variety of factors. Human services professionals may feel a sense of disappointment, loss, or guilt. In these situations, a bit of self-disclosure, in which workers share their own feelings with clients, may have positive results. Such sharing may free clients to address their reactions to the termination. On the other hand, workers who are having trouble dealing with their own reactions ought to discuss this with a trusted supervisor or colleague. Seeking consultation in such instances is an appropriate use of supervision.

Helping Clients at Termination

One positive characteristic of termination is that it can always be anticipated. The exact timing of termination may vary but, like death and taxes, it will not go away. Usually, the worker can help clients at the termination point, and this section will look at a number of techniques for doing so.

Planning for Termination

Perhaps the most important way in which the worker can help a client at termination is to ensure that the topic of termination is addressed early in the relationship, preferably at the beginning. Planning for the termination and discussing it with the client will help reduce emotional attachment of the client to the worker and any resulting dependency. It also helps to temper the sense of loss we have already described. In time-limited interventions, termination is expected to occur at some specified point. A group that has planned to meet for seven sessions knows at the start when termination will occur. Residents of a halfway house may be told initially that they must move back into the community at the end of nine months.

The worker can help this process along by reminding the client about the approaching date of termination. Ideally, this should occur several sessions before the last meeting. The worker should leave time in later sessions to talk about termination, especially when termination is occurring earlier than expected. This situation might happen when the worker moves out of the geographical area or the agency discontinues a particular program.

Addressing Feelings About Termination

As discussed earlier, terminations often produce feelings for both the client and the worker. One worker task is to help the client express feelings associated with termination. The worker might say: "You've seemed sadder the last two times we've met. I wonder what you're feeling." Another way to raise the issue is through what's known as the "generalized other." The worker might state: "Some of the other boys who have left here have said they felt good about leaving. Others said they thought it had been a waste of time. How about you?" Here, the worker lets the client know that other persons in the same situation have felt a certain way and invites the client to share his own reactions, which may or may not be similar.

Sometimes, sharing the worker's own feelings about the approaching termination can be helpful. For example, consider a practitioner who has been working with a 15-year-old adolescent. For a year, the boy has been living in a residential treatment center for adolescents with problems related to delinquency or behavior disorders. He was admitted to this center after a history of criminal behavior in his home community. Nearing the boy's release and the coinciding termination of the worker–client relationship, the worker might say, "You're going to be finishing the program at the center in another couple of weeks. I want you to know that I feel very good about how hard you've worked here. I also want you to know that I'm going to miss you." In this way, the worker reminds the client of the upcoming termination and shares his own feelings about it. Frequently, this type of modeling by the worker is especially important for clients who have been socialized not to share feelings. It is through this kind of patient, sensitive work that the worker helps the client to address feelings about the ending process. Highlight 8.6 addresses termination feelings in groups and families.

Summarizing Progress

One of the important tasks of the termination phase is to recognize client accomplishments or achievements. Let us take the example of the boy mentioned in the previous paragraph. The worker might broach the topic of client growth by asking the client to summarize his progress over the time they have worked together. He might ask, "Can you

 HIGHLIGHT 8.6

Termination Feelings of Family and Group Members

Reactions to termination may vary in groups and families as well as among individual clients. For example, continuing members of a group may react to the departure of another member with guilt or anger. They may also raise questions about the value of the group, thereby challenging the leader.

Loss of several group members may ultimately result in the group ending because of an insufficient number of members. This situation is the ultimate threat to a group. Family members will still have each other to rely on after a family therapy session concludes. However, a group composed of unrelated adults from a large community is unlikely to offer members this degree of continuity. The latter may have lost a significant social support system. A family, on the other hand, continues to perform this supportive function. Members of contrived groups will have different reactions than members of family groups. However, recognizing that individual family members may each have their own reactions to the loss of an important worker–client relationship is important (Hellenbrand, 1987).

remember back when you first came here? You wouldn't even talk to me. Now you've progressed from Step 1 all the way to Step 10, the highest level in the cottage. What's made the difference between the old Pat and the new?" This question helps the client begin to identify the areas of growth that have occurred. It focuses attention on positive experiences and helps to increase the client's sense of accomplishment.

The techniques of planning for termination, uncovering termination-related feelings, and summarizing progress are three primary activities of the termination phase. Equally important, however, is ensuring that changes occurring during an intervention will be sustained after the relationship ends. The stabilization of change process will be discussed next.

Stabilization of Change

There is sufficient evidence that changes that occur in the context of therapeutic relationships do not necessarily carry over into the other areas of a client's existence. Changes that have occurred in individual behavior, for example, may not generalize to other situations in a client's life. The young woman who stops using drugs while in a treatment program is going to find it much harder to maintain this drug-free state when she returns to her old friends. Ultimately, the goal is that change in one area carries over into others.

Toseland and Rivas (1998) suggest seven things that workers can do to help clients maintain and generalize changes:

1. *Helping clients select relevant and appropriate situations to work on.* This selection can be accomplished by helping the client select important problems or concerns to work on. For example, focusing on a client's job-seeking skills when the primary problem is unemployment would make sense. While other issues (e.g., marital relationships, parenting skills, and so on) might be important, they are not as relevant to the basic problem of being out of work.

2. *Helping clients build confidence in their own abilities.* One of the ways the worker can assist is through helping clients review their work together. This review focuses on achievement of goals and sets the stage to talk about the future. Clients leaving a professional relationship often need reassurance. Discussing the client's progress can help to boost self-confidence.

3. *Using multiple situations and settings when helping members learn new behaviors.* Clients learning new skills and behaviors should be given multiple opportunities to use these. For example, people learning to be more assertive should be given the assignment to practice this with family, friends, coworkers, and strangers. The more situations in which the client can successfully employ a newfound skill, the greater the likelihood the skill will be used following termination.

4. *Using naturally occurring consequences rather than creating artificial ones.* Ultimately, clients will be confronted with the real world without the support of the human services professional. To ensure that they are eventually prepared, clients need to be given every opportunity to practice their new behaviors in natural settings. For example, a client who is trying to improve communication skills should eventually practice these skills in the real world. Away from the supportive environment of the worker or group, the client experiences the barriers encountered when people try to change their own behaviors. A client who can be assertive only in the assertiveness-training group has benefited little from the group experience.

5. *Extending treatment through use of follow-up sessions.* Follow-up contacts between client and worker often serve as "boosters" to help clients maintain their changes over time. Whether the focus is on weight loss, learning new parenting skills, or becoming more assertive, follow-up sessions remind clients that others remain concerned about their progress. Seeing the worker or other group members may rekindle clients' dedication to their goals or reinforce efforts to maintain their growth.

6. *Reducing setbacks in other environments such as school, the workplace, or the home.* Sometimes the clients' progress is undermined by other aspects of their environment. An example could be the student who is too easily influenced by his peers and gets into delinquent behavior when around them. To help the client keep his distance from these "friends," the worker might enlist the help of parents or school officials. If multiple figures in the boy's life are working in concert to encourage and maintain positive behavior, the chances that the changes will last are more likely.

7. *Helping members confront future problems by teaching them a problem-solving process.* Finally, most clients must learn to live without the worker's constant support and encouragement. One way of reducing dependency is to teach clients the same planned change approach the worker uses. Once clients learn to confront problems from this framework, many seemingly insurmountable problems disappear. At the very least, the clients learn a system that can be used effectively in most areas of their lives. In essence, as the worker you are trying to put yourself out of business by teaching clients what you know. The goal is often to teach them practical planned change skills. They will no longer need you and will be able to accomplish goals by themselves.

Stabilizing Change in Small Groups

Most of the approaches described earlier will work as well with small groups as with individuals. However, there are techniques that are especially effective with groups of various sizes. For example, many community-based programs take clients through a series of ever-increasing steps to independence. These steps finally culminate in the client's return to the community with a minimum of formal supervision. A shelter for battered women, for example, operates a halfway house in addition to the shelter itself. Many clients, after staying in the shelter for a period of time, are ready to move into a more independent living arrangement. At this point, the client may elect to move to the halfway house and remain there until she is able to make it on her own. The halfway house serves as a transition between the shelter and full return to the community. It also gradually reduces the role of the shelter staff so that clients do not become overly dependent on them for help.

There are other effective strategies when working with client groups. One such technique involves varying the use of group activities. For example, in the early stages of a group having members engage in activities that are group-building in nature (e.g., enhancing warmth and trust) is common. Thus, clients may be asked to do ice-breaking activities such as having members interview each other and introduce the interviewee to the group. The ice breaker is designed to increase the "we" feeling of the group.

Conversely, group activities can be used to decrease this "we" feeling. For example, the leader

may choose group activities that foster independence and reduce group cohesion. Take the members of an adolescent girls' group that have spent several weeks learning and practicing how to express their feelings to one another. In the last couple of sessions, the worker has asked the members to begin describing the ways their new communication skills are affecting relationships with parents and peers. By asking the members to focus their attention away from the group, the worker is helping to reconnect them with the larger environment in which they live.

Sometimes, groups plan ceremonies to help intensify the sense of ending and to acknowledge the clients' progress in a program. Group homes for chemically dependent clients frequently have "graduation" ceremonies as clients prepare to leave the shelter of the group home environment.

Stabilizing Change in Large Systems

The guidelines previously described work well with individuals, families, and groups. However, additional approaches are needed to stabilize change in communities and organizations. Kettner, Daley, and Nichols (1985) suggest the importance of change stabilization for work with large systems and provide important suggestions.

Routinize Procedures and Processes. One of the goals when attempting to change large systems is to ensure that whatever is accomplished continues indefinitely. One way this goal is accomplished is for procedures and processes to become routine. This can occur when changes are written into policies or rules or laws that ensure they will exist for the foreseeable future.

Clarification of Policies and Procedures. One way to help stabilize change in larger systems is to ensure that newly created policies and procedures are clear. Sometimes, individuals have "understandings" about what was decided or agreed upon. Later, no one can seem to recall exactly what was decided, or there is a major disagreement regarding what really transpired. To avoid this situation, you can follow the old bureaucratic adage and "put it in writing." Policies and procedures that are written down are less likely to be affected by faulty memories.

One approach is to use "memorandums of understanding." These are nothing more than memos or letters that restate in written form what has been agreed to verbally. Let us say the officer of an organization has verbally told you the organization will contribute $500 toward a new recreation program in your community. You could confirm this agreement by writing the person a letter reiterating what he has told you and thanking him for the organization's generosity. For example, you might simply state, "Thank you so much for your $500 pledge toward our new recreation program. Your generosity is very much appreciated." This "memorandum of understanding" is just a technique formalizing informal policies, agreements, or procedures. It helps prevent problems later on when people's memories become ragged.

On the same note, if a new policy is agreed to, the sooner it is entered into the organization's policy manual, the better. Most social agencies have manuals containing their policies and operating procedures. These manuals are important documents because they control what workers can and cannot do. The same is true for most large organizations. Policies that are articulated in policy manuals are more likely to be followed than those that are unwritten.

Reducing the Influence of the Change Agent.   There is another way to help maintain change and to increase the client system's opportunities to operate independently, namely to reduce the worker's and agency's influence. This method is often accomplished by reducing the frequency and intensity of contact between the worker and client systems. For example, a community worker might reduce the frequency of attendance at many committee meetings. Eventually, local members of the community will need to take leadership of the committees, and the worker's role becomes one of consultation. Finally, even this role is dropped as the indigenous leaders develop confidence and skill in leading their committees. The worker deliberately reduced the level of involvement to facilitate the development of natural community leaders. In this way, positive changes would be maintained on an ongoing basis.

Addressing Ongoing Needs of Clients

The worker in the termination phase of the helping process must attend to the ongoing needs of the client system. We have already discussed the importance of discussing with the client resources for future needs. Letting the client know that the worker and agency remain available should future help be required can also be helpful. The worker should probably not offer to extend service without

clearly knowing that a specific goal can be reached. This method prevents the client from becoming overly dependent upon the worker or agency. Still, keeping the door open for the client is important. If the termination is occurring prematurely, letting the client know of the worker's and agency's availability is especially important. The worker might say, "Denise, I know that you believe we have accomplished what you initially wanted to. I, too, feel we have come a long way. I think we were beginning to get into some other areas that don't seem so critical to you right now. I respect your right to bring this phase of our work together to a close. Still, I want you to know that I am available if you decide you would like additional help." The goal is to ensure a continued good relationship between the agency and client. Thus, the client can return should she need to.

If necessary, referrals to other service organizations or persons may be made. Referrals should always be made to specific persons, if possible. In some situations, you may decide contacting the new agency while you and the client are together is best. This way there is no confusion about what was said. Be sure to check if the client can get to the new service provider and to give written directions if necessary. Because of the possibility of clients falling between the cracks, reminding clients to let you know if there are any problems receiving needed services from the new agency is usually helpful. Chapter 15 discusses the referral process in more detail.

 InfoTrac College Edition

This chapter examined the processes of evaluation and termination in generalist practice. Both practice and program evaluation methods were discussed, as well as critical concepts in the evaluation process. Successfully managing the termination phase of the planned change process was also a focus. For additional information on related topics, please use the following search terms:

best practices
evidence-based practice
outcome evaluations
program evaluation
practice evaluation
single-subject designs
goal-attainment scaling

On the Internet

Because of the very dynamic nature of the Web, URLs are subject to change. Therefore, be sure to check out the companion Website for this book at http://www.humanservices.wadsworth.com, where links will be updated periodically.

www.pitt.edu/~cedar
www.aarf.org
www.ssrc.msstate.edu/publications
www.ericae.net

PART THREE

Intervention with Multiple Systems

CHAPTER 9
Working with Individuals

How can you get people to open up and tell you about their problems?

- Do you have to have an answer to every question?
- What if you do not know how to solve someone's problem?
- How do you work with a client who does not want to be there?
- What if the client will not say anything?
- How do you handle a hostile or angry client?
- What should you do if a client starts to cry?
- How much should you tell a client about your personal life?
- What if a client wants to be friends with you?
- What should you do if you think a client is not listening to what you are saying?

These and many other questions arise in the interpersonal relationship between a human services professional and a client and are especially important for beginning practitioners. Being able to work with individuals is a critical step in learning generalist practice. You must understand interpersonal dynamics and have interviewing skills before being able to work with groups of people and larger systems.

Introduction

The Generalist Intervention Model (GIM) follows a six-step planned change process, including engagement, assessment, planning, implementation, evaluation, and termination. Chapters 5 through 8 elaborated on what occurs during each of these phases. The worker needs to direct and control each worker–client interview during all of these stages. Interviewing provides a major means for gathering data during the assessment phase of a problem situation. There are a number of specific interviewing techniques that help workers to gather data, and this chapter will focus largely on those basic skills.

Sometimes, interviewing is broken up into beginning, middle, and ending phases. Most of the techniques described here are useful at almost any point of the interviewing process. However, some—such as how to introduce yourself to a client—are more oriented toward a particular interviewing phase.

This chapter focuses on the techniques necessary for communicating with individuals. Later chapters discuss how these techniques are useful throughout the intervention process. Also, keep in mind that these techniques form the foundation for learning and applying mezzo skills (working with groups) and macro skills (working with agencies, organizations, communities, and social systems). Learning how to communicate well and to work with individuals is a necessity for any type of human services practice.

This chapter addresses numerous questions like the ones listed at the beginning and discusses techniques to answer them. Specifically, this chapter will:

- relate how micro practice techniques are involved in the generalist planned change process;
- explore how to establish rapport and build a relationship with a client;
- examine issues in verbal and nonverbal communication;
- suggest effective ways to initiate the interviewing process, conduct interviews, and terminate them;
- describe and illustrate a variety of interviewing techniques;
- explore enhancing cultural competency through ethnographic interviewing;
- propose techniques to address interviewing issues such as dealing with diversity, confrontation, hostility, uncomfortable periods of silence, and involuntary clients;
- propose ways for terminating interviews.

Micro Skills and the Generalist Intervention Model (GIM)

Micro skills involve relationship building, the effectual use of verbal and nonverbal behavior, and proficiency in interviewing. They focus on your ability to relate to other individuals and communicate effectively. The planned change process entails ongoing interaction and communication with many individuals in your work environment including clients, colleagues, administrators, and other decision makers.

We have established that micro skills form the basis for working with groups (mezzo systems) and organizations and communities (macro systems). You must effectively interact with individuals in groups, organizations, and communities in order to get anything done. Micro skills are used through each phase of the planned change process—engagement, assessment, planning, implementation, and evaluation—whether you are pursuing micro, mezzo, or macro change.

Engagement requires establishing an initial relationship with an individual or each of a group of individuals regardless of what type of change you seek. During this phase, you use verbal and nonverbal skills to establish rapport and introduce your purpose and role. For example, a practitioner working at Planned Parenthood must establish an initial rapport with a client who may be feeling embarrassed or frightened. The client may be seeking some form of contraception or be distressed by an unwanted pregnancy. The worker must use micro skills to make the client feel comfortable enough to communicate her concerns and to begin looking at alternatives. The initial use of effective micro skills is critical if the worker eventually decides to focus on the client's individual plans (micro intervention), suggest an educational group (mezzo intervention), or pursue a statewide policy change concerning contraception or abortion on the behalf of this client and others like her (macro intervention). The worker who eventually pursues mezzo or macro intervention must use micro skills to establish rapport with individuals in those settings in order to achieve mezzo or macro change.

Assessment, likewise, involves interaction and communication with other individuals with micro, mezzo, or macro change. Through it, you strive to solicit enough information about the issue or problem involved to initiate positive change. You must talk and relate to other individuals effectively in order to accomplish this task. For example, consider a human service professional at an AIDS Support Network (an agency aimed at providing a range of services to people who are HIV positive). The worker must gain information about each client's health, social, financial, and emotional conditions before they can plan together what to do. Assessment proceeds after the initial engagement has been successfully completed. The client must feel comfortable and safe with the worker. Micro skills are necessary whether or not the worker and client pursue individual counseling (micro intervention), working with the client's family or involving the client in a support network (mezzo intervention), or advocating for greater resources on behalf of this client and others in similar situations (macro intervention). Any level change concerns interacting and communicating effectively with the individuals involved.

Similarly, the remaining steps in GIM—planning, implementation, evaluation, and termination—all require interaction and communication with other individuals. Planning involves working integrally with the client to establish a plan of action. Implementation entails working with targeted others in the environment to achieve the plan's goals. For example, a plan might entail seeking financial support for an elderly person with failing health. This plan necessitates working directly with other individuals who control the distribution of such support.

Evaluation concerns establishing that the implementation of a plan has been effective, which often entails using micro skills to communicate with the client and others involved in the change process to procure information and validate accomplishments. Finally, workers use micro skills to terminate relationships with clients in a considerate, planned, positive manner.

Interviewing: A Key Micro Skill

Communication with clients is obviously necessary to work with and help them. Interviewing provides a primary means for such communication and is a core skill in micro practice. Kadushin and Kadushin (1997) describe an interview: "The simplest definition of an interview is that it is a conversation with a deliberate purpose that the participants accept. An interview resembles a conversation in many ways. Both involve verbal and nonverbal communication between people during which they exchange ideas, attitudes, and feelings" (p. 4).

In generalist human services practice, interviews are more than pleasant conversations because they have a specified purpose. This purpose is to "exchange information in order to illuminate and solve problems, promote growth, and plan strategies or actions aimed at improving people's quality of life" (Hepworth & Larsen, 1987, p. 996). For example, you usually meet with a client to find a solution to some problem or to pursue some necessary change.

In addition to a designated purpose, an interview has two other characteristics, a "formal structure with role, time, and location constraints" and a "process and development orientation" (Kadushin, 1995, p. 1527). Formal structure and role involve how you assume the role of worker and professional helper. The client assumes the role of one needing assistance and assuming the unilateral focus of "attention, concern, and help" (1995, p. 1527). The interview's formal structure involves time constraints, appointment times, and location (often the worker's office). The interview's process in terms of what transpires resembles GIM's steps of engagement, assessment, planning, implementation, and termination. Later, we will address some techniques commonly used in the beginning, middle, and closing portions of the interview.

A place to start when learning how to interview and work with individual clients is to examine the skills of how to establish a good worker–client relationship. These skills form the foundation for engagement, GIM's first step. Because they are important throughout the intervention process and are among the bases for micro practice, we will elaborate upon them here.

Beginning the Worker–Client Relationship

When learning how to work with clients, examining how to establish a good worker–client relationship is useful. Some people are naturally popular, others are not. There are some basic behaviors and characteristics that make a person more appealing to others. Similarly, in worker–client situations, certain behavior and personal qualities tend to nurture interpersonal relationships. When manifested by the worker, these traits and deeds tend to put clients at ease and make them feel important and cared about. This chapter begins by discussing how verbal and nonverbal behavior can enhance worker–client relationships.

Verbal and Nonverbal Behavior

At the most basic level, human interaction and communication involve both verbal and nonverbal behavior. Verbal behavior is what is being said. Nonverbal behavior is communication in ways other than spoken words. People communicate by facial expressions, hand movements, eye contact, the manner in which they sit, and how close they stand to you. Any aspect of a person's presence that conveys ideas or information without being spoken is nonverbal communication.

An example is a student who is ten minutes late for a statistics exam (she was up until 4:30 that morning "cramming" in a panic and, for whatever reason, her alarm did not go off). She runs into her academic advisor, a talkative individual who starts to chat about next semester's registration. The student does not want to offend the advisor by dashing off. However, she needs to get to her exam right away. She fidgets, looks repeatedly at her watch, frequently glances in the direction she needs to go, and starts edging away step by step. Without actually using words, she is trying to nonverbally tell the advisor, "I don't want to be rude, and I appreciate the time you're taking to talk to me, but please stop talking and let me sprint to my stats exam." The advisor finally gets the nonverbal hint and asks, "Oh, are you in a hurry?" It probably would have been much more efficient, thoughtful, and straightforward for the student to have verbally stated those words to the advisor in the first place. Assertiveness was addressed in Chapter 4.

There are many aspects of nonverbal behavior. Here we will focus on four of them: eye contact, attentive listening, facial expressions, and body positioning.

Eye Contact

Looking a client directly in the eye is usually important. Direct eye contact means that you hold your head straight and face the client. This positioning of the head establishes a rapport and conveys that you are listening to the client.

You may know people who have difficulty looking you in the eye. This inability to make eye contact often conveys that they are afraid or insecure. It might also imply disinterest or dishonesty. On the other hand, maintaining continuous eye contact can make a person uncomfortable. Additionally, it can also be tedious, as if you were in a who-can-hold-out-and-not-blink-the-longest contest. Eye

contact is a complex nonverbal behavior. Moderate eye contact, somewhere between no eye contact and constant eye contact, seems to put people at ease most (Cormier & Hackney, 1999, p. 37). Thus, direct eye contact with an occasional glance away at your hands, a bookcase, or simply into nowhere is probably most appropriate.

One more point about eye contact must be mentioned. In some cultures, direct eye contact is considered disrespectful, uncomfortable, insincere, or rude (Cournoyer, 2000; Sheafor et al., 2000). This fact reinforces the need to become knowledgeable about and sensitive to cultural differences between you and your clients. Chapter 3 addressed skills for working with people of different cultural backgrounds.

Attentive Listening

Of course, you are supposed to listen to what a client is saying, right? In reality, listening is not so simple. First, the distinction must be made between *hearing* and *listening*. Listening implies more than just audio reception of words that are said. It focuses on comprehending the meaning of what is said.

There are a number of barriers to attentive listening involving three aspects of communication. First, the person sends a message with some *intent* of what needs to be conveyed (what the sender wants the receiver to hear). Second, the message receiver tries to decipher the meaning of what was said. Thus, the message has some *impact* on the receiver (which refers to what the receiver thinks the sender said). What the receiver actually hears may or may not be what the sender hoped the receiver would hear. Third, there may be environmental barriers impeding communication of the message (see Figure 9.1).

The first cluster of communication barriers mentioned involves the sender, in this case the client. The client might not be using words, phrases, or concepts that are clear to you. The client may say something vague. The sender's *intent* may not be the same as the *impact* on the receiver.

Or the client may view things from a different cultural perspective where the same words have different meanings. For instance, a Chicano father says, "The problem is that my daughter disobeys me and goes out with boys." A white middle-class human service professional may interpret this statement to mean that the daughter is seeing a number of men. Sexual activity and related issues such as pregnancy and sexually transmitted diseases may enter the worker's thinking. Finally, the possibility that the father is overly domineering may be a concern. However, what the Chicano father really

Figure 9.1   *Barriers to Attentive Listening*

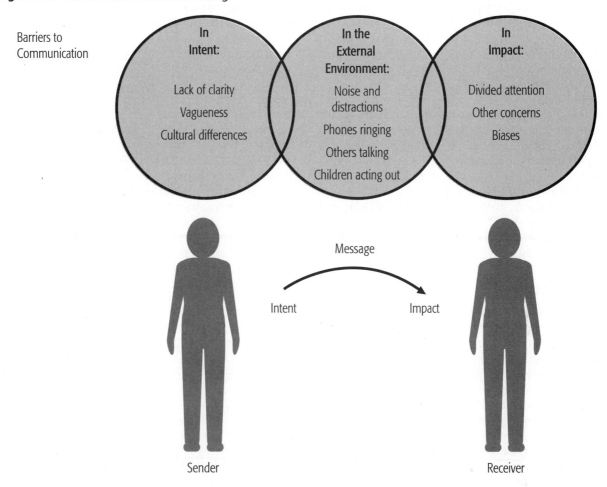

Source: The concepts of *intent* and *impact* were taken from the film *Behavioral Interviewing with Couples,* available from Research Press, Dept. 98, P.O. Box 9177, Champaign, IL 61826.

means is that his daughter thinks she is in love with a boy and is sneaking out to see him. In their Chicano culture, such behavior is inappropriate if a couple is not engaged to be married and, in any case, a chaperone is still needed to supervise them.

The second type of communication barrier involves the receiver, in this case, the human service professional. The worker's attention may be divided between what the client is saying and what the worker is going to say next. Likewise, the worker may be focusing on what direction the interview should go in the future. Paying full attention to the client and listening to all that is said is not easy.

The third cluster of communication barriers to attentive listening involves the external environment and potential noise and distractions. For example, a human service professional visits a client's home. The television is blaring, and four young children are running through the house with toy rifles playing "GI Joe." Such environmental distractions make organizing one's own thoughts difficult, let alone listening to what the client is saying.

In summary, listening is not easy. It demands concentration, perceptiveness, and the use of a range of interviewing skills. A number of these skills will be described in this chapter.

Facial Expressions

Facial movements and expressions provide an excellent means of communicating. A furrowed brow may convey intense concentration, uncertainty, or concern. A casual smile may indicate pleasure and even warmth. Raising the eyebrows can indicate surprise or sudden interest. In contrast, a blank expression conveys little or no information about what you mean or think.

Facial expressions can be used to reinforce what is said verbally and corroborate the fact that you mean what you say. However, two aspects about using facial expressions should be noted. First, being aware of your facial responses so that you know how you are communicating is important. Second, make certain that your facial expressions correspond with both your other types of nonverbal behavior and with what you are saying verbally. Giving a client a mixed message by *saying* one thing, while *looking like you mean* another, is not helpful. Such action can convey doubt that you are being truthful. For instance, if you say, "Oh, I'm so glad to see you," with a scowl on your face, you communicate inconsistent messages.

Body Positioning

Body movement and positioning also provide information to others. The tense/relaxed and formal/informal continuums are especially important.

Body tension involves how rigid or tense our muscles appear as we position ourselves and most frequently coincides with emotional tension. If we look uptight, we probably feel uptight inside. Such tension can be demonstrated by sitting perfectly straight and allowing minimal movement of extremities. Tension is also apparent when a person makes quick, nervous gestures, such as continuously tapping a foot or finger or jingling loose change in his or her pocket.

The opposite of a tense stance is a relaxed one. Relaxation can be portrayed by slow, loose movements and a decidedly casual, informal presentation of self. The most extreme form of a relaxed stance would probably be to lie down. The term *laid back* is often used to refer to such a relaxed approach.

When working with a client, being aware of how you nonverbally present yourself is important. Extreme tension may convey lack of confidence or excessive nervousness. It may put distance between you and your clients and make feeling comfortable and trusting you difficult for them.

On the other hand, an extremely relaxed stance may convey to a client that you do not care much about what happens. It may also damage your professional credibility.

Ideally, presenting yourself somewhere in between the two extremes is best. To some extent, body positioning is a matter of personal style. You need to appear genuine, that is, that you are reflecting aspects of your true individual personality to the client. Being aware of your body positioning and how it affects your interaction with clients is crucial.

The second continuum, formal/informal, relates to some extent with the tense/relaxed continuum. Being more rigid and tense reflects formality, while being relaxed is associated with informality. Formality implies greater structure and less warmth. To the extent that you are more formal with a client, you are less personal. You allow less of your true personality to show through the professional facade. On the other hand, complete informality or lack of structure impedes getting anything done. A worker–client relationship is not a friendship; it exists for the purpose of solving a problem or attaining a goal. This fact implies some degree of formality and structure.

As with the tense/relaxed continuum, the extent of formality often relates to personal style. The best approach lies somewhere between being extremely formal and extremely informal. The important thing is to be aware of how you are presenting yourself, how you feel most comfortable, and how the client reacts and relates to you.

A student once asked an instructor a question before undertaking her very first interview (which happened to be a relatively simple, very structured social history). She wondered if, while doing the interview, she should act like a "human service professional" or act like herself. The instructor thought to herself, "Hmmmm, what does a human service professional act like?" The answer is to use the techniques and planned change focus inherent in generalist human services practice (which the rest of this book is all about), yet to do so as yourself. Ask questions in the manner and tone of voice with which you feel comfortable. Smile when you feel like smiling. Use the gestures and personal presentation that reflect your true personality.

The use of personal space—the actual space or distance between you and the client—is another part of body positioning. Hall (1969) identifies four distances or zones that we set in our daily interactions: the intimate zone, the personal zone, the social zone, and the public zone. Each zone respectively demonstrates more formal and less intimate relationships. The *intimate* zone is just that. It ranges from skin contact to about 18 inches and is reserved for close personal relationships. The *personal* zone ranges from about 18 inches to 4 feet, the *social* zone from 4 to 12 feet, and the *public* zone outward from 12 feet. Contact with clients most likely should occur in the closer half of the social zone. This zone allows for comfortable discussion, yet provides an adequate degree of personal space so that a client does not feel threatened. Keep in mind that these distances tend to be culturally determined. Hence, they may not be the same for all people, depending upon their cultural background.

Another aspect of body positioning and defining personal space involves where workers sit in their offices in relationship to where clients sit. Typically, an office has a desk, and you as a worker may have some flexibility regarding placement of that desk. Sitting behind the desk and talking to a client seated in front of the desk implies greater formality and difference in status and may be appropriate in some settings where the worker feels such formality is needed. For instance, a probation officer might find it useful to sit behind a desk in a more formal situation where the goal is to monitor a client's adherence to prescribed probationary conditions. However, in many other situations, having the desk's front side abutting the wall, sitting behind the desk, and being able to turn your chair in order to talk to a client can convey greater informality and warmth.

Warmth, Empathy, and Genuineness

In generalist human services practice, a variety of relationship-enhancing characteristics can be defined and learned. Demonstrating these characteristics involves employing the appropriate corresponding verbal and nonverbal behavior. Three specific relationship-enhancing traits are warmth, empathy, and genuineness. These attributes characterize the human services literature as among the most basic and important in developing relationships with clients (Fischer & Gochros, 1975; Halley et al., 1998; Hepworth et al., 1997; Kadushin, 1995; Sheafor et al., 2000).

Warmth

Displaying warmth involves conveying a feeling of interest, concern, well-being, and affection to another individual. Warmth is a vehicle for acceptance. "Respectful and valuing statements about the client are accompanied by a smile, appropriate touching, pleasant surprise, and enthusiasm for the client's rendition of personal experience" (Keefe & Maypole, 1983, p. 62). Showing acceptance of clients, warts and all, also communicates warmth. Conveying warmth also involves enhancing the positive feelings of one person toward another. It

promotes a sense of comfort and well-being in that other person.

Warmth can be communicated to a client both verbally and nonverbally. Such behaviors can be defined, practiced, and learned. The following are examples of verbally communicating warmth:

- "Hello. It's good to meet you."
- "I'm glad we have the chance to talk about this."
- "It's pleasant talking with you."
- "It's good to see you again."
- "Please sit down. Can I get you a cup of coffee."

These are just a few of the many statements you can make to show that you respect the client and are glad he or she is there. These statements help to convey a sense of concern for the client and for the client's well-being. Similarly, there are many ways to communicate warmth to a client nonverbally. We have discussed how eye contact, attentive listening, body positioning, and tonal quality all can be used to a worker's advantage.

Empathy

Empathy is a second basic characteristic that has been found to enhance a worker–client relationship. Hepworth and Larsen (1987) refer to it as "the work-horse of interviewing" (p. 998). Empathy involves not only *being in tune* with how a client feels, but also *conveying to that client* that you understand how he or she feels. It does not necessarily mean you think the client's feelings are positive or negative, nor does it mean that you are having the same feelings yourself. Empathy is purely acknowledgment that you understand the client's situation. For instance, consider the case of Ms. Wilson, who has been referred to a protective services worker for abusing her 2-year-old son, Tyrone. A neighbor reported Ms. Wilson after seeing odd, straplike, black bruises on her child's arms two weeks in a row. During the interview, Ms. Wilson says, "Tyrone never does what he's told. He runs away from me when I call him. He gets into all of my things and breaks them. Sometimes I get so angry, I could kill him. I tie him up to the bed with old ties just so I can get some peace."

The worker empathetically responds, "Two-year-olds can be very difficult and trying. I understand how sometimes you feel like you're at your wits' end." This response conveys that the worker *understands* the situation and Ms. Wilson's feelings. However, it does not *condone* Ms. Wilson's behavior.

Empathy can be used to demonstrate to clients that you are on their side. Clients who feel that you have listened to how they feel and that you are not against them are much more likely to be willing to work with you toward finding solutions to problems. Empathy communicates to a client that you are there to help solve the problem (see Highlight 9.1).

In this example, what do you think Ms. Wilson's reaction would have been if the worker had responded with her statement by saying, "How can you hurt your own child like that? What kind of mother are you? Don't you have any feelings?" The latter statement criticizes Ms. Wilson and communicates to her that the worker does not understand her feelings and her situation. It totally lacks empathy. Ms. Wilson could easily view the worker as "the enemy," someone to fight with or avoid.

Establishing initial rapport is only the first among a number of reasons for employing empathy; Hepworth and colleagues (1997) cite several other uses. Empathy enables the worker to keep up with the client and the client's problems and concerns throughout the worker–client relationship.

Empathizing with positive emotions can also be helpful. For example, if a client appears exceptionally happy one day, an empathetic response may get at the reason. Maybe some problem has already been solved. Perhaps, a new client strength can be identified that can be used in the change process. Acknowledging positives may help in the maintenance of the worker–client relationship.

Additionally, empathic responding may elicit feelings and discussion about previously unmentioned issues. Empathy provides the worker with a

---

HIGHLIGHT 9.1

Practicing Empathic Responses

There are a number of leading phrases that you can use to begin an empathic statement. Here are some examples:

- "My impression is that ... "
- "It appears to me that . . ."
- "Is what you're saying that . . . ?"
- "Do I understand you correctly that . . . ?"
- "I'm hearing you say that . . ."
- "Do you mean that . . . ?"
- "Do you feel that . . . ?"
- "I feel that you . . ."
- "I'm getting the message that . . ."
- "You seem to be . . ."
- "When you say that, I think you . . ."
- "You look like you . . ."
- "You sound so _____. Can we talk more about it?"
- "You look _____. What's been happening?"

The following are several vignettes about client situations. Formulate and practice your own empathic responses for each one. The first vignette provides an example.

Example

You are a human services professional in foster care. You are visiting one of the foster homes on your caseload.

The purpose is to talk with both foster parents and determine how things are going with their 9-year-old foster child, Katie. The couple has three children of their own, all of whom are in college. In the past, the foster couple has expressed interest in adopting Katie. When you arrive at the home, only the mother is present. After polite greetings, the foster mother says, "Katie certainly doesn't like to read very much like the rest of us. I think she gets bored when she's not doing something active. Many times I just don't know what to do with her."

Possible empathic responses include:

- "You sound as if you're having some problems with Katie that you didn't expect. Can we talk more about it?"
- "It seems that you're somewhat frustrated with Katie these days."
- "I feel that you're telling me that Katie's more difficult to take care of than perhaps you thought."

Vignette 1

You are a human services professional in a health care facility for the elderly. Helen is a resident who has been living there for approximately two years. All rooms have two residents, which has consistently been a problem for Helen. Her current roommate is Emma, a quiet woman who rarely interacts with any of the other residents. Helen is very possessive of her things and wants no one else to touch them. Additionally, Helen does not like to share the means of getting at feelings that are not expressed verbally. For example, a worker can say, "When you frown like that, it looks as though you're very worried about something." The client now has an opening to talk about what is on his or her mind, even though it has not been expressed verbally.

Yet another use of empathy involves "making confrontations more palatable" (Hepworth et al., 1997, p. 116). Empathy can be used to disperse hostility. For example, a client enters a worker's office and demands his financial assistance check right now instead of five days later when he is supposed to receive it. He is breathing fast, his face is red, and his vocal tone is loud, gruff, and hostile. The worker chooses not to respond initially to what the client said. The worker does *not* say something like, "You're here five days early, and you can't have the check until it's ready."

Instead, the worker can make an empathic response by saying, "Mr. Carlton, you sound so angry. It seems that you desperately need the money right now." This latter response is much more likely to help Mr. Carlton calm down and talk about his problem. The worker may or may not be able to get Mr. Carlton his check. However, an empathic response will more likely convey to Mr. Carlton that the worker is on his side. He should be much more likely to settle down, talk about what is wrong, and pursue possible alternative courses of action.

Nonverbal communication can also be used to enhance empathy. A worker's gestures can mirror how a client feels. For instance, furrowing the brow can convey a serious focusing of attention and reflect a client's grave concern over some issue. Nonverbal communication can also emphasize or

---

bathroom, which is also used by the two residents in the next room. Helen, a strong, outspoken woman even at age 97, approaches you and says, "Emma keeps using my bathroom and moves my things around. I want her out of there right now! You do something right now!"

You empathetically respond . . . (Remember that you *do not* have to solve the problem right now. You only need to let your client know that you understand how she feels.)

Vignette 2

You are a school counselor. Romy, age 16, was in the men's bathroom when several other students were caught using drugs. Romy insists the others are guilty but that he is innocent, he just happened to be in the restroom at the same time. The teacher who found the boys could not distinguish who was guilty and who was not, so he put them all on "penalty," which means detention after school and exclusion from any sports for two weeks. Romy is furious. He comes up to you and says, "It's not fair! It's just not fair! I'm innocent, and I'm getting punished anyway. I should've used the drugs if I'm going to get the punishment."

You empathetically respond . . .

Vignette 3

You are a human services professional at a diagnostic and treatment center for children with multiple disabilities. Your primary function is to work with parents, helping them to cope with the pressures and connecting them with resources they need. A mother of a 5-year-old boy with severe cerebral palsy talks with you on a weekly basis. Her son is severely disabled and has very little muscular control. He cannot walk by himself or talk, although the other therapists feel he has normal intelligence. The boy's father belongs to a religion that denies the existence of disease and physical impairment. Thus, he denies that his son is disabled. The burden of caretaking rests solely upon the mother. She loves her son dearly and is generally enthusiastic in doing what she can for him. She enters your office one day, says hello, and sits down. She immediately puts her hand to her eyes and breaks down in tears.

You empathetically respond . . .

Vignette 4

You are an intake worker at a social services agency in a rural area. Your job is to take telephone calls, assess problems, and refer clients to the most appropriate services. You receive a call from an adult male. After identifying who you are and asking what you can do for the caller, he responds, "I just lost my job. Nothing's going right. I feel like I want to kill myself."

You empathetically respond . . .

enhance verbal empathic responses. For example, consider a client who appears happy. Smiling while making an empathic verbal response indicates more convincingly to the client that you really understand how the client feels.

Genuineness

The third quality found to enhance client–worker relationships is genuineness, which involves "sharing of self by relating in a natural, sincere, spontaneous, open, and genuine manner" (Hepworth & Larsen, 1987, p. 998). Genuineness simply means that you continue to be yourself despite the fact that you are working to accomplish goals in your professional role.

Personality refers to the unique configuration of qualities and attributes that make you an individual. Some people have effervescent, outgoing personalities. Others have more subdued, quiet temperaments. Some people relate to others using a sense of humor, while others prefer to relate in a more serious manner. The point is that there is no one type of personality that is best for a professional role. Rather, it is more important that you be yourself and not pretend to be something or someone that you are not. Genuineness conveys a sense of honesty to clients and makes them feel that you are someone they can trust.

Two sisters, Karen, a human services professional, and Susie, an occupational therapist, illustrate this point. Both women have worked with similar clients, primarily children and teenagers with behavioral problems. Karen is extremely outgoing, fast-moving, excitable, and tries to make jokes at every opportunity. Others have often labeled her "hyperactive" and frequently complain that she talks too fast. Susie, on the other hand, is calm, evenly paced, and sedate. Her manner has often been labeled "dignified." If Karen accidentally put her hand on a hot burner, she would utter a piercing scream, dash around frantically, and spew forth a stream of colorful obscenities. If Susie placed her hand on the same hot burner she would calmly lift her hand, look at it, and quietly reflect, "Oh, I burned my hand." (One might note that Susie's husband has commented that if you put Karen and Susie into a giant blender together, mixed them up, and poured them into two equal portions, they would turn into two "normal" human beings.) The point is that despite extreme differences in personality and style, both sisters worked effectively with similar clients. Each was herself, while still performing her professional functions (although Karen did have to carefully monitor her tendency to utter obscenities).

Client Self-Determination and Empowerment

In addition to demonstrating warmth, empathy, and genuineness, maintaining a commitment to client self-determination enhances a positive relationship between worker and client (Kadushin, 1995). Our ethical standards promote the right of clients to self-determination. Self-determination is each individual's right to make his or her own decisions.

An assumption about self-determination is that human services professionals have the responsibility to help clients make the best informed choices and decisions possible (Barker, 1999). This responsibility means practitioners must use their skills to provide clients with necessary information. Workers must also assist clients through the decision-making process by helping them identify the positive and negative consequences of their various alternatives.

For example, Myrtle is a single mother of three small children who applies for public assistance. In order to receive assistance, she must enter a six-week work training program after which she must actively seek and gain employment in order to continue receiving assistance. Available programs involve instruction in basic work habits in addition to more specialized training in food preparation, building maintenance, reception, construction, day care, or initial secretarial work. Esther, Myrtle's assigned human service professional, is responsible for providing Myrtle with enough information about each training program and helping her weigh the pros and cons of each so that she can decide which she should pursue.

The situation increases in complexity because Myrtle needs day care for her children. She has no available friends or relatives to help with child care. There are a few publicly subsidized day care programs available, but their reputations are fairly poor. Myrtle surely could not afford private day care. Esther must help Myrtle review her training and day care options to establish a plan that Myrtle feels is best for her. With Esther's help in exploring and evaluating options, Myrtle decides to enter the day care training track. Myrtle feels that she might then work in the same day care center that cares for her children and, thereby, observe and monitor their treatment.

Maximizing client self-determination to whatever extent possible is a practitioner's responsibility. Sometimes, this responsibility is more difficult, such as when a client is mentally incompetent or intends to hurt himself or others. Chapter 2 discussed such instances and the dilemmas involved more thoroughly.

Self-determination is related to empowerment, a major concept in the definition of generalist practice. We have defined empowerment as "the process of helping individuals, families, groups, and communities to increase their personal, interpersonal, socioeconomic, and political strength and to develop influence toward improving their circumstances" (Barker, 1999, p. 153). In micro practice and during the interviewing process, clients' involvement, input, and participation are paramount to intervention's effectiveness.

 ## Starting the Interview

The major goal of any interview is effective communication with the client. Interviews make use of communication with clients to solve problems, encourage positive change, and maximize clients' "quality of life" (Hepworth & Larsen, 1987, p. 996). We have talked about the importance of both verbal and nonverbal behavior in communication. We have also established that warmth, empathy, and genuineness are qualities that help foster professional relationships with clients. Now we will propose some specific suggestions for *starting* and, subsequently, *conducting* the interview. The emphasis is on planning and action. As a practitioner, you are there to help your client clearly identify what the problems are and what can be done to solve them. In this section, we will discuss typical interview settings, how to dress and prepare for interviews, initial introductions, alleviating clients' anxiety, conveying confidence and competence, and stating the interview's purpose. Skills for addressing these issues are absolutely necessary for the engagement step in the GIM's planned change process. Because most are basic micro skills that continue to be essential for later meetings and ongoing involvement, they will be discussed here.

The Interview Setting

Interviews may occur in a variety of settings, depending on the field of practice and type of agency. Some interviews take place in hospitals or schools. Many occur in the worker's own office, which gives him or her more control over the environment. We have already discussed positioning the desk and chairs to enhance the client's comfort level. Offering the client a cup of coffee, whether it is accepted or not, is another way of displaying warmth.

Human services professionals need to be sensitive to the overall impression their office environment itself presents. There are no absolute guidelines for dictating office decor. Putting pictures you like on the walls and trinkets you enjoy on the shelves is appropriate. However, you need to be aware of their potential effect on clients. If you paint your office bright orange and put giant posters of your favorite rock stars or rap artists on the walls, you need to be aware that this environment may be unnerving to some clients. On the other hand, if your clients are primarily adolescents who like some of the same pop icons you do, such posters may provide a means of making a connection with your clients. (The orange walls, however, should probably go.)

Some interviews will take place in the client's own home, which provides the advantage of seeing where and how he or she lives. However, home visits may have the disadvantage of distractions such as children, pets, and television, which can make controlling the interview more difficult. Home visits often provide an excellent means of making assessments and were discussed more extensively in Chapter 5.

How to Dress for the Interview and for the Job

The main thing to remember when deciding how to dress for interviews with clients and for human services positions in general is that your appearance will make an impression, and it is to your advantage to make a good one. A basic rule is to start out dressing "nicely" and "relatively conservatively." What this rule means is up to individual interpretation. Noting how other workers in your agency dress is important, because each agency has its own personality. Some agencies are formal, while others are informal.

Paying attention to clients' reactions to how you and the other workers in your agency dress is also important. If you are a woman who works in a corrections institution for delinquent youth, wearing three-inch-high heels and tight short skirts may be inappropriate. You may be expected to participate in recreational activities with clients, or, in the event that they lose control, help to physically restrain them. More informal clothing then would be to your great advantage.

Or, if you are a practitioner working in a protective services unit who must go out and interview families in poverty-stricken areas of the city, you may not want to flaunt wealth. In other words, wearing expensive three-piece gray flannel suits may not enhance clients' impression of you or your relationship with them.

On the other hand, it might. Some clients may perceive such efforts of formality as a demonstration of your professionalism and respect for them. Jeans and a T-shirt might have the opposite effect. Thus, carefully watching clients' reactions to you and dressing in a way that enhances your professional performance are important.

Thinking Ahead About an Interview with a Client

Before the interview begins, the worker needs to think ahead about at least three variables. First, is there any specific information that will be needed, such as addresses and phone numbers of specific resources? Can you anticipate any questions the client might ask for which you should be prepared?

Second, the interview's time frame should be clearly specified. The time frame means when the interview is scheduled to begin and when it needs to end. The meeting should start punctually. Making the client wait beyond the scheduled starting time may imply that the client's time is not important and that you have better things to do. A timely start conveys common courtesy and respect for the client. In the event that you are late for whatever reason, an appropriate apology should be made.

The interview should have a timely ending, and the next client should not be kept waiting. One means of alerting the client that the interview is coming to a close is to make a statement such as, "Well, we only have another ten minutes left, so perhaps we should talk a bit about our next meeting."

The third variable that needs consideration prior to the interview is the interview's purpose. According to Kadushin and Kadushin, "preparation involves specifying the interview's purpose and translating goals into specific items that need to be covered. . . . [I]nterviews need to ask how, in general, the purpose can be achieved, what questions they need to ask, what content they need to cover, and the best sequence in which to introduce such content" (1997, pp. 77–78). In other words, the worker should have some general idea about what he or she wants to accomplish by the end of the interview.

Initial Introductions

Initial introductions resemble those in other formal and informal interactions. Names are exchanged with typical pleasantries such as "It's nice to meet you." Using surnames is usually in your best interest, as they imply greater respect. Handshakes are also often appropriate. However, you need to be aware of the client's levels of comfort and anxiety. If a client cringes as you extend your hand, nonchalantly take it back and continue with a verbal interchange.

Sometimes, ethnic or cultural differences require you to behave differently than you normally would. For instance, the Hmong, who migrated to the United States during the past few decades from Southeast Asia, initially abhor the type of physical contact involved in shaking hands. Immigrants who have been here for a while, on the other hand, have quickly adopted this traditional greeting.

When beginning the interview, initiating brief, innocuous exchanges about some bland topic like the weather may also be appropriate. For example, "I'm glad you made it here despite the heat (or the blizzard)." A short interchange can be used to soften the formal edge of the interview and make the situation warmer and more human.

Alleviating the Client's Anxiety

"Starting where the client is" is a phrase human services professionals often use to describe how they begin an interview. The first important aspect of this concept is to think about how the client must feel coming into the initial interview with you. Put yourself into the client's shoes. You too would probably be anxious about approaching an unknown situation and would not feel in control. The client may wonder, "Will this 'professional' interrogate me under bright lights as if I were a foreign spy? Will this human service professional criticize all the things I'm doing wrong? Will I be attacked for something I did or didn't do?"

Many clients will approach the interview with anxiety; others, however, may arrive with resentment or hostility. For instance, if clients are forced to see you for some reason, having negative feelings is logical for them. The important thing is for you to pay close attention to their verbal and nonverbal behavior. Empathy is essential to communicate and begin the problem-solving process. Specific suggestions for how to deal with difficult situations such as hostility are discussed later in this chapter.

Other conditions that may be affecting a client's perspective and attitude should also be considered. Is your office hard to find? Did the client have to wait a long time before the appointment? Was there a bad experience with your agency in the past? Did the client have a flat tire on the way in to see you? Being aware that these and many other variables may be affecting a client's feelings is important (see Highlight 9.2).

HIGHLIGHT 9.2

Using Direct and Indirect Questions

Questions can also be categorized as being either *direct* or *indirect*. Direct questions are those that clearly ask for information and usually end in a question mark. Examples are:

- "Did your mother ask you to see me?"
- "What do you see as the major problem areas?"
- "How did you arrange for your transportation here?"
- "When do you intend on completing that plan?"

Indirect questions ask questions without seeming to. They provide an excellent vehicle for gathering information. Examples include:

- "Many mothers would find having three children under the age of five difficult."
- "You seem like you're under a great deal of stress today."
- "Taking care of your brother after school each day must make it hard to find time to play with your friends."
- "I wonder how you manage to care for little Johnny and your aging mother at the same time."

In each of these indirect questions, the interviewer is asking the client to respond but is not stating a direct question. Notice there are no question marks ending the sentences. This technique can be helpful in gathering information from clients without asking a tediously long list of direct questions.

Portraying Confidence and Competence

A common situation many new workers, especially those who are in their early and middle twenties, encounter is a client questioning their level of competence. A client might think, say, or both, "How can somebody your age possibly help me? I'm old enough to be your parent." In some cases, the last part of the statement is true.

A similar situation arises when a worker without children must work with clients who have problems with their children. Such clients may ask how a childless individual can possibly understand and help them.

There are at least five things a worker can do about these types of situations. First, when a client says something that is true (even if you do not want to make an issue of it), acknowledge that it is the truth. You can do this at least silently to yourself or make a statement to that effect. For example, you might say, "Yes, I am younger than you are," or, "No, I don't have any children." This statement gets the cards out on the table, so to speak, and prevents you from seeming defensive.

A second approach to addressing client concerns is to respond to the client with a question. You might say, "Is it important to you that I have children?" or, "Does my being younger pose a problem for you?" Again, this tactic gets the issue out on the table without making the worker appear defensive.

The third thing a worker can do is to follow up the true statement with another statement of truth. You might share examples of your competence. For instance, you could say, "I have an undergraduate degree in human services and have been trained to help solve problems just like yours. Why don't you give me a chance to show you what I can do for you?"

The fourth thing a worker can do in a situation where his or her competence is questioned is simply to rely on the relationship-building skills that we have already discussed. Keep warmth, empathy, and genuineness in mind. Be assertive verbally and nonverbally. Speak calmly and look the client in the eye. As the client gains trust in you as a professional, the question of competence will cease to become an issue. The best way to convince a client of your competence is by your own behavior. When you actually help a client, that client will probably perceive you as competent.

The fifth thing you can do to demonstrate competence is to be knowledgeable. Planning the interview conveys to the client a sense of organization and purpose. Knowing your role and where to find information the client needs also reflects your competence.

Beginning Statement of Purpose and Role

Not only must the purpose of the interview be clearly identified in the worker's own mind, it must also be clearly understood by the client. There are four major tasks that should be undertaken at the beginning of the interviewing process. The first, as we have already indicated, is to clearly explain the interview's purpose to the client. An example of this purpose involves a worker in an alcohol and other drug abuse (AODA) assessment unit in a large urban social services agency. The worker meets with her 27-year-old male client for the first time. After the initial introductions, the worker says, "I'm happy to talk with you today. I understand that you voluntarily came in for some help with controlling your drinking. What we need to do today is to find out more about you and your drinking, so I'd like to ask you a few questions."

In this example, the worker expressed warmth and concern. Without blaming the client, she indicated the need to work together. Finally, she explained in straightforward terms that her goal was to assess his drinking problem.

The second major task in an interview's beginning phase is to explain the worker's role to the client (Kadushin & Kadushin, 1997; Shulman, 1999). We have discussed how clients often have significant apprehension about interviews for a variety of reasons. Explaining your role does not mean reciting a job description. However, it does mean describing in general terms to the client what you intend to do and talk about.

For example, let us return to our original example of the AODA assessment worker with the 27-year-old client. After clarifying the interview's purpose, the worker might say, "I will be asking a number of questions that are typically asked when people want to work on controlling their drinking. Some of the questions may seem odd to you. They ask about a lot of things from work to friends to family to personal interests to the drinking itself. These questions help me get to know you better and give me a better idea about where we can start in helping to change."

The third important task in the initial interviewing process concerns "encouraging the client's feedback on purpose" (Sheafor et al., 2000, p. 144; Shulman, 1999). This encouragement means that the worker should ask how the client feels about the identified purpose. Actively involving the client from the beginning of the change process is necessary. Back to our AODA example, the worker might say, "I feel like I've done most of the talking so far. How do you feel about what I've said? Do the plans so far sound good to you? Is there something you'd like to change or add?"

The final task in the initial interview involves making a statement about the usefulness of the intervention process. In other words, the worker can convey to the client that there is hope to begin to solve his or her problems. For example, the worker might say, "When you talk about your drinking, I hear you say how worried you are. I think it is a serious problem. However, I give you lots of credit for having the courage to come in and talk to me about it. There are a number of excellent techniques we can use and alternatives we can look at. It's hard, but I think we have a good chance at helping you over the next few weeks and months."

These statements reflect only one combination of words and ideas for accomplishing the four tasks. In other words, there are many ways to define the purpose of the interviewer or to ask for feedback. The interview may indeed have any number of purposes. The intent may be to help a 15-year-old decide whether to have an abortion or to assist an 85-year-old in deciding where it would be best for her to live. The words used to define the purpose vary as dramatically as the actual intent of the interview. The important thing is for the client to understand why he or she is there and what you intend to do.

The discussion of the four tasks previously mentioned is oriented primarily toward one of the initial interviews with clients. Subsequent interviews with clients will not require such extensive, detailed explanations of purpose and other facets of the interviewing process. Clients already will have learned about your general intent. However, these tasks are good to keep in mind even with clients whom you have seen a number of times. In review, the four tasks include defining the interview's specific purpose, explaining what you will be doing, asking clients for feedback, and expressing hope that things can improve. All four help provide direction to interviews and enhance your positive interaction with clients.

 ### Conducting the Interview

Regardless of the specific purpose of the interview, its major function is communication with the client. Communication, of course, involves exchange of information. There is a variety of specific skills and techniques that can facilitate the exchange of information. Using these techniques helps to maximize the chances that your *intent* matches your *impact* on the client and vice versa.

There is also a vast array of communication techniques for workers to use, such as ways of initiating communication with a client or responding to something a client says. We will define and explain a number of specific methods of responding to clients that place the focus of attention on the client. Next, we will examine a number of issues and difficulties frequently encountered in interviews.

Remember that the pursuit of cultural competency is an ongoing process for practitioners. Becoming familiar with client's cultural values, expectations, and issues should always be on a worker's mind. Highlight 9.3 introduces the concept of enhancing cultural competency through ethnographic interviewing.

Verbal Responses to the Client

Some techniques that enhance worker–client communication are used to solicit information, while others encourage the client to enhance the worker–client relationship. The approaches include simple encouragement, rephrasing, reflective responding, clarification, interpretation, providing information, emphasizing clients' strengths, self-disclosure, summarization, and eliciting information.

Simple Encouragement

Encouragement is the act of prompting someone to continue, often by raising that person's level of self-confidence. Many times, a simple one-word response or nonverbal head nod, while maintaining eye contact, is enough to encourage a client to continue (Cormier & Hackney, 1999; Ivey & Ivey,

---

HIGHLIGHT 9.3

Enhancing Cultural Competence: Ethnographic Interviewing

An ongoing quest of human services practitioners is to continue learning about and appreciating the infinite facets of human diversity. Lum (1999a) maintains that a critical part of "cultural awareness . . . centers on ethnographic interviewing" (p. 75). *Ethnographic interviewing* focuses on learning about a client's cultural world, including values, behavioral expectations, and language. This is done by using conversation to gather "information in a nonthreatening manner" and working with the client to develop intervention plans that comply with both the client's right to self-determination and cultural perspective (Leigh, 1998, p. 12). Leigh (1998) explains:

> The ethnographic model . . . [emphasizes] that the expert on construction of meanings of any culture is a member of the culture . . . Ethnographic interviewing is a method of cultural discovery that requires the [professional] to move beyond professionally bound methods of conversation with those who request assistance in solving personal or social-generated problems. The person being interviewed becomes the [professional's] cultural guide, and this notion has an impact on the professional relationship. In some aspects the person is

> a teacher guiding the [practitioner] as a student through the intricacies of the contrasting culture. The [practitioner] has to become a skilled listener. (p. 12)

Green (1999) emphasizes the special orientation of ethnographic interviewing:

> "Empathy" and "openness" as primary techniques are inadequate because they presume an ability to enter into the sensibilities of another without first learning the context from which those sensibilities arise. The real skill in cross-cultural human services, as in any kind of cross-cultural learning, is to comprehend what the client knows and how that information is used in the mundane traffic of daily activities. Stylized "caring responses" are not an effective way of doing that. Rather, it is what our clients tell us about themselves, and how they do the telling, that is crucial to genuine understanding and insight. (p. 129)

Three concepts relate to preparing for the ethnographic interview and initiating the engagement and assessment processes. Used sequentially in practice, they are global questions, cover terms, and descriptors (Green, 1999; Leigh, 1998).

Global Questions

Global questions are initial, general inquiries posed to solicit information about culturally relevant aspects of the client's life. Their purpose is to enhance a practitioner's

(continued)

ability to successfully initiate and undertake the intervention process. Such questions focus on areas with which you are unfamiliar and yet would enhance your understanding of the client's environment and situation. It's a good idea to "list topics of general interest, write questions, and arrange them in an order that seems to make sense" prior to the interview (Green, 1999, p. 134).

For instance, Green (1999) tells of a mental health worker newly assigned to an area of New York City with a large Puerto Rican population. The worker (whom we will arbitrarily call Mariah) is unfamiliar with the community and speaks no Spanish. She drives through the area noting her impressions and questions. A more seasoned colleague traveling with her talks about how housing is deteriorating, overcrowding is escalating, schools are underfunded, most jobs pay only minimum wage, and there is a swelling demand for public health services. Mariah watches residents of various age groups actively converse with each other as they participate in life and work on the streets. She observes that numerous Spanish posters announce festivals, community projects, and events. Despite the obvious poverty and related social problems, Mariah perceives that there is a strong sense of community, active resident interaction and participation in neighborhood activities, and a strong adherence to a Hispanic heritage. Mariah observes that there are several publicly funded health centers and outpatient clinics in addition to private physicians' offices and pharmacies in the area. However, she also sees that "[t]here are *botanicas* or herb shops, and many *centros,* small storefront or basement 'churches' " where adherents of traditional spiritual beliefs both gather for worship and to receive "indigenous forms of mental health treatment, *consultas,* provided by specially trained folk healers" (Green, 1999, p. 135). Mariah carefully considers what she sees and thinks about how cultural beliefs and traditions might affect her ability to practice with this population. As a result, in the hope of enhancing her own ability to serve potential clients concerning their mental health needs, she identifies the following global questions to investigate with them:

1. What are the various activities of the *centros?*
2. How is a healing session conducted?
3. What other persons assist the healer, and what do they do that is important?
4. How are healers trained, and what specific skills do they say they have?
5. What distinguishes problems that are physical, supernatural, or both in their origins?

6. What are some examples of diagnoses the healer makes?
7. What are the causes of the problems healers see in their practice?" (p. 136).

Note that such global questions are only starting points. Answers to each might only initiate numerous questions to clarify ideas and refine Mariah's understanding of the culture.

Cover Terms

Cover term is a word that covers a realm of concepts, ideas, and relationships within a cultural context and has significant and special meaning to members of the cultural group. Cover terms often surface repeatedly as clients respond to global questions. Often, a worker unfamiliar with the cover term's depth of meaning initially will fail to understand the word's significance and relevance within the cultural context.

For example, the term *Issei* has immense implications for Japanese Americans (Green, 1999). Murase (1995) comments on the significance of this concept in terms of family values, cultural acceptance, and assimilation into the dominating culture:

> The traditional Japanese values and practices were most evident in the immigrant generation (the *Issei). As succeeding generations of Japanese Americans have become acculturated, there has been a change in the family structure and behavior. The original patriarch, male-dominated family network has given way among the second generation (the* Nisei) *to an increasingly important role for women in family affairs. The devastating World War II experience of incarceration in concentration camps also took its toll. Many* Nisei *parents tried to dissociate themselves and their children from traditional Japanese culture and become model Americans in the Anglo-Saxon tradition, often at great psychological cost. (Nagata, 1991, p. 243)*

Workers must pay close attention to what clients say in order to detect the presence and significance of important cover terms. Cover terms can initiate topics and open doors to greater understanding. However, they only scratch the surface. More detail is still needed in order to better comprehend a client's cultural world.

Descriptors

Descriptors are words solicited to explain cover words. In ethnographic interviewing a practitioner starts by thoughtfully preparing global questions, then identifies cover terms, and finally seeks out descriptors to fill in more of the cultural picture. For example, consider the words *extended family* within a cultural context (Green, 1999). A client might mention the words several times during an interview. The concept can serve as a cover term. But what does it really mean within a particular client's cultural context? The meaning probably is quite different "among immigrant Vietnamese from what it is among the Amish, Louisiana Cajuns, or *barrio* [neighborhood community] residents of East Los Angeles" (Green, 1999, p. 141). Depending on the cultural context, extended family might involve aunts, uncles, great-aunts and uncles, cousins, second cousins, nieces, nephews, parents, grandparents and great-grandparents, other relatives who are much more distant, or even members of other families who are emotionally or economically close to the client's family.

Finding descriptors through ethnographic interviewing helps practitioners fill in gaps of information and more fully enhance understanding of clients' cultural view of their world. Other examples of cover words are infinite. For instance, consider a male adolescent who angrily states, "I got my ass kicked yesterday" (Leigh, 1998). What does "ass kicked" really mean for that young man in his own cultural environment? Does it mean that members of a neighborhood gang tied him up and beat him until he bled? Does it mean his father caught him doing something wrong and beat him with his fists, all the while lecturing him about how he should never do the bad thing again? Or, does it mean he lost $40 in a basketball bet?

Summary

In summary, global questions, cover words, and descriptors are just a few of the concepts inherent in ethnographic interviewing, one important means of developing cultural competency. Becoming culturally competent is an ongoing learning process.

1999). Vocal clues such as "mm-mm," "uh-huh," "I see," or "please go on" demonstrate to clients that you are listening to what they are saying. Such responses may also be used to keep a client on the right track in conjunction with the purpose of the interview.

Rephrasing

Rephrasing is stating what the client is saying but using different words. Rephrasing has a variety of purposes. It can communicate to clients that you are really trying to listen to what they are saying. On the other hand, if you had not heard the client's real intent, it can give the client the opportunity to clarify his or her meaning. It can also help the client take time out and reflect on what was just said.

One example of rephrasing is a client who says, "I feel really miserable today." The worker may respond, "You really don't feel well at all today." Rephrasing does not involve offering an interpretation of what the client has said. It simply repeats a statement by using other words.

Reflective Responding

Reflective responding is translating what you think the client is feeling into words. It is a means of displaying empathy. Such responding conveys that you understand what clients are going through and how they feel about it. A typical scenario involves a client who is *talking about* problems but does not really articulate how he or she *feels about* them. Part of your job as the worker is to bring these feelings out into the open so the client knows they are there and can begin to work on them. Both verbal and nonverbal behavior can be used as cues for reflective responding. For example, a client comes to you with her shoulders slumped and her eyes downcast. She slumps into a chair and says, "Yep, he dumped me. He finally told me to get lost. He's been talking about it for months, but the old coot finally did it."

As a worker, you might respond, "You sound like you feel crushed and angry that your boyfriend left you. You also sound like you're a bit surprised even though he's been threatening for a long time."

Clarification

Clarification is making certain what the sender says is understood. Clarification is typically used in one of two ways (Benjamin, 1981; Kadushin & Kadushin, 1997). First, you can help clients articulate more clearly what they really mean by providing the words for it. The process is clarification for the clients' benefit. Second, you can use a clarifying statement to make what the client is saying clearer to yourself. This latter type of clarification is for your benefit. Many times clarification will benefit both worker and client. An example of this involves a client who comes to a worker and says, "I just lost my job. Everything's gone. What will I do? Where will I go?"

The worker may respond, "You mean you lost your income along with your job, and you're wondering about how to pay the rent and other bills this month?" This example depicts the worker's attempt to clarify what the real issues are that must be addressed and to help the client proceed from the more global to the specific. Trying to solve the problem of losing "everything" is difficult. However, determining the exact amount needed to pay the rent and other bills, or even finding an alternate residence, are more concrete, doable goals. Helping clients to specify what they really mean makes a problem much more workable.

Clarification is used when there is a question about what clients mean. Restatement, on the other hand, involves understanding clients and simply paraphrasing what they have said. Finally, reflective responding adds the dimension of emotion and feeling to clients' statements.

Interpretation

Interpretation is seeking meaning beyond that of clarification by bringing to a conclusion, enlightening, or pursuing a greater depth of meaning than what has been stated. Interpretation helps lead clients to look deeper into themselves and their problems. It enhances clients' perceptions of their own situations.

For example, a client says, "I hate it when my mother tells me what to do. And, yet, if I don't do what she says, she makes me feel guilty. She makes me feel like I don't care about her anymore." The worker might respond, "It seems that you have very ambivalent feelings toward your mother. You want to be independent, yet you don't want to hurt your mother's feelings. Perhaps, on some level, she realizes that, doesn't want to lose you, and is able to manipulate you."

To interpret means to take a statement a step beyond its basic meaning. In the preceding example, the worker went beyond the client's feelings of anger, guilt, and resentment. Instead, the worker focused in on both the client's and the mother's motivations for their behavior. The worker attempted to provide some insight into both of their feelings.

Providing Information

Sometimes, *providing information* to clients is appropriate. Providing information is educating clients by giving them data they need. They may ask you frank questions. They may not know where to find resources or how a social services system works. Or they may not understand why they must provide certain information or follow some rule. Sometimes, they will be misinformed, and accurate information will need to be provided.

For example, a female teenager asks a worker, "My friends tell me you can't get pregnant the first time you do it. Is that true?"

To this the worker might respond, "No, that's not true. You're just as likely to get pregnant the first time as any other time. There are some other things to consider, though, any time you choose to have sex. Would you like to talk about them?"

Empowerment: Emphasizing Clients' Strengths

Human services professionals deal with the most difficult human problems. Their clients are often those people who are most oppressed and have the most obstacles to living healthy, happy lives. Many clients are so overwhelmed by their problems that focusing on anything but problems is difficult for them. They assume a tunnel vision, that is, they have difficulty focusing on anything but this long, dark entrapping tunnel of stressful life issues.

Sometimes, identifying clients' strengths will be quite difficult because their problems will seem so insurmountable. However, as we discussed in earlier chapters that focus on the planned change process, emphasizing clients' strengths is critical throughout implementation and helps in several ways (Hepworth et al., 1997; Saleebey, 1997; Sheafor et al., 2000). First, it reinforces a client's sense of self-respect and self-value. Second, it provides rays of hope even in "tunnels of darkness." Third, it helps identify ways to solve problems by relying on the specified strengths.

Client strengths may be found in three major areas. The first involves behaviors and accomplishments. The second concerns personal qualities and characteristics. Finally, the third revolves around the client's material and social resources. Highlight 9.4 illustrates how to focus on client strengths.

Self-Disclosure

Self-disclosure is a worker's divulgence to a client of personal thoughts, information, feelings, values, or experiences. Many generalist practitioners, especially those new to the field, wonder to what extent they should disclose information about themselves.

What and how much about yourself should be disclosed during a professional interview has been,

HIGHLIGHT 9.4

Stressing Client Strengths

The following examples are statements workers might use to emphasize a client's strengths in three basic areas.

Client Behaviors

- "You've done a nice job of following those suggestions. Look what you've accomplished."
- "Sometimes you emphasize all the things that have gone wrong, but look at all the things you've done well. You've kept your family together even when your husband left you and you lost a primary source of income. You've managed a tight budget and kept your children fed, housed, and in school. You're going back to school part-time. I think that's wonderful."

Personal Qualities

- "You're very bright and easy to talk to."
- "I think you're very motivated to work on this goal."
- "It's nice to work with you. You're so cooperative."
- "You have a very pleasant personality. I think you will do very well in the group."
- "You brighten up when you're happy. It makes people feel good to see your cheery smile."
- "You look very nice today."

Client's Resources

- "I know it's been hard, but you've found yourself a part-time job and have worked out a schedule for paying your bills. That's a great start."
- "It's really good that you have close friends (or a minister or a relative) to talk to. It helps."
- "Your family is very supportive. That's really good."
- "There are several resources available to you here at the agency that can get you off to a good start."

historically, a controversial issue (Okun, 1997). On the one hand, some amount of self-disclosure can enhance relationships (Kadushin & Kadushin, 1997; Okun, 1997; Sheafor et al., 2000)—people are more apt to like others who reveal things about themselves. Similarly, the more you reveal to someone, the more likely that person will be to self-disclose to you. On the other hand, we all know people who seem to never stop talking about themselves. They are so interested in their own issues and activities that they never think of asking how you are. We also all know our reactions to people who behave this way: "Let me out of here!"

We have already established that warmth, empathy, and genuineness are important characteristics to demonstrate in professional worker–client relationships. To some extent, self-disclosure is necessary to give feedback to the client. Feedback involves providing input about how the client is functioning and how others perceive the client. This feedback is an important aspect of working through the planned change process.

Cormier and Hackney (1999) cite four major types of self-disclosure. The first three involve communicating something about the worker–client relationship and the ongoing interviewing process. These types of self-disclosures also frequently overlap with some of the other interviewing techniques mentioned earlier. They focus directly on the worker–client role and the purpose of the interview.

First, you can give information *about your professional role.* Second, you can share your feelings and impressions *about the client and the client's behavior* by giving feedback. Third, you can provide feedback *about your perceptions concerning your ongoing interaction and relationship with the client.* These latter two types of self-disclosure are especially useful when you cannot think of anything else to say during an interview. You can share your feelings about what is happening with the client inside or outside of the interview, or self-disclose what you feel is happening in your relationship with the client at that point in the interview.

The fourth type of self-disclosure, however, differs significantly from the other three. It involves *relating aspects about your own life or problems* in some way to the client's feelings or situation. This approach can convey empathy to the client and indicate that you really understand. It can also provide a "positive role model" under some circumstances by showing the client that others have learned to live through similar problems (Okun, 1997, p. 274).

The amount you choose to self-disclose about your own life is, ultimately, an individual decision. Some people are naturally more outgoing and self-disclosing than others. Regardless, when you as a worker choose to self-disclose, there are some basic guidelines.

The first guideline is to make certain that the self-disclosure is really for the client's benefit and not for your own. Friendships provide arenas for mutual self-disclosure and support, but professional worker–client relationships exist to benefit the client only (see Figure 9.2).

A second guideline is to make the self-disclosure relevant to the client, which involves demonstrating both "genuineness" and "timeliness" (Ivey & Ivey, 1999, pp. 289–290). In other words, self-disclose for some definite purpose. For example, the client may need some reassurance that talking about a particular issue is all right. Or at some specific point you

can make an empathic self-disclosure about an issue related to that of the client and he or she will feel more comfortable.

The third guideline for making self-disclosures is that they should be short and simple. You want to share a small slice of your life, feelings, or experience for a specific purpose. Details are unimportant. Most likely you just want to convey to your client that to some extent you really do understand how he or she feels.

Sometimes, clients will initiate asking you uncomfortable personal questions such as, "Are you married?" "Are you going with anybody?" "Did you sleep with your spouse before you were married?" or "Did you ever drink when you were underage or try any drugs?"

Figure 9.2 *Personal versus Professional Relationships*

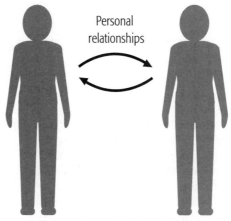

Personal relationships

Both people need their needs met.

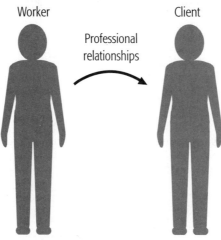

Worker   Client

Professional relationships

The purpose is to meet the client's, not the worker's, needs.

Under such circumstances, you have two choices. First, you can answer honestly, briefly, and simply. Then you can say something like, "I think we'd better get back on track. The important thing we're here to work on is your problem and what to do about it."

Your second choice is to avoid answering the question by instantly focusing on something else, such as the client or the interviewing process. In other words, you can ignore the question and talk about how the client is participating in the interviewing process. For example, you might say any of the following:

- "You seem really anxious to get off the topic today. What's on your mind?"
- "It seems as though you don't feel like talking about the problem right now. Is something bothering you?"
- "That really doesn't have much to do with what we're talking about here. We don't have that much time. Let's get back to the subject."
- "I feel as though you're trying to avoid my questions. What do you think are the reasons for that?"

This second approach of avoiding the answer may or may not work. If it does not, you may have to simply and honestly say something like, "I really don't feel comfortable answering that. Let's get back to the matter at hand."

Self-disclosure requires judgment about when, what, and how much to share with a client. When you carefully and thoughtfully select the information you provide to the client, you are also engaging in what is called "professional use of self." You are using your knowledge, experience, and perceptions in the professional worker–client relationship in a planful manner. In so doing, you may be modeling appropriate behavior for the client or demonstrating the willingness to deal nondefensively with difficult topics. In each case, you are monitoring what information you disclose and how it is used based upon what is needed at this point in time. Your sharing is not done because it feels good to you to get something off your chest. Rather, it is done to facilitate the relationship building and planned changed efforts.

Self-disclosure may also be especially helpful when working with cultural groups suspicious of, or uncomfortable with, the worker. Sharing items of personal information may help the client feel a greater closeness or comfort with the worker (Hull, 1982). However, the focus should be shifted back to the client as soon as feasible. You do not want clients to think that you need more help than they do.

Summarization

Summarization is restating the main points of an interview or a portion of an interview in a brief and concise manner. Periodic summarization helps the client focus on the main points covered during a portion of the interaction and also helps keep the interview on track. It can be used "as a transition to new topics, or to review complex issues" (Whittaker & Tracy, 1989, p. 137). Summarization is difficult in that the worker must carefully select and emphasize only the most important facts, issues, and themes.

Summarizing what has been accomplished during the interview is helpful when bringing it to a close because it allows the client to leave on a positive note. Also, summarizing recommendations about who is to do what before the next meeting crystalizes the plans that have been made in both the client's and the worker's minds. Summarization as a major aspect of terminating the intervention process is also covered in Chapter 8 (see Highlight 9.5).

Eliciting Information

As a part of the communication process, a worker must *encourage a client to reach for and share information.* One way of doing this is simply to ask questions. There are two basic types of questions, open-ended and closed-ended. Closed-ended questions include those that seek simple "yes" or "no" answers, such as:

- "Are you coming tomorrow?"
- "Did you have a nice time?"
- "Is Harry here?"
- "Did Francesca take the dog out yet?"
- "Are you getting along better with your wife?"

Closed-ended questions may also involve those where there are a number of clearly defined answers to choose from. They do not encourage or even allow for an explanation of why the answer was chosen or for an elaboration of thoughts or feelings about the answer. For example, consider these questions:

- "Are you male or female?"
- "Do you want chocolate, vanilla, or super-duper tutti-frutti ice cream?"
- "Are you working at Burger King, Mac's, or Heavenly Hash Heaven next summer?"
- "How many brothers do you have?"
- "What is your birthdate?"

In each of these instances, a simple response is required. The choices for the response are established

HIGHLIGHT 9.5

Telling a Client What to Do

Can you make suggestions to clients without interfering with their right to individual choice? Should you give a client advice? Should you urge clients to pursue an alternative when you are absolutely certain it is the best thing for them to do?

These are often difficult questions that may be encountered. There is some controversy regarding the extent to which a worker can direct a client into taking some particular action. A major problem is that if you tell a client what to do, in a way you are taking responsibility for the result. In other words, if it turns out that the result of the action is bad for whatever reason, the client has you to blame.

Another problem involves the difficulty of putting yourself in another person's shoes. Can you really understand being that person and understand his or her values and ideas? Is it ethical for you to tell other people what route is best for them to take when you do not have to suffer any possible consequences yourself?

Helping a client identify the alternatives available to him or her is one thing. Directing the client as to which one is the best is another. An underlying theme in the planned change process is to help clients explore the pros and cons of the various alternatives available to them. As a worker, you can help them think through what each possible action really would mean to them.

Consider a teenager with an unwanted pregnancy. More than likely, each of us has a strong opinion about what the teenager *should* do, or, rather, about what *we think we would do* in her situation. However, she has her own life situation with worries about her future, parents, friends, school, guilt, and religious ideas. The choice needs to be hers.

This is not to say that there are never times when encouraging a client to pursue the alternative he or she has chosen to be the best is appropriate. Sometimes, for a client to get going and move onward is difficult and

scary. In those circumstances, a worker needs to use professional judgment regarding how forcefully to encourage the client to proceed. A helpful thought is to emphasize to the client that taking no action is indeed a decision to take one alternative. Making no decision has definite consequences. For example, if the pregnant teen decides not to make a decision and ignore her pregnancy, at five or six months' gestation, she has already narrowed the alternatives available to her. She has begun to make a decision by not making a decision.

There will be times when clients will pressure you to tell them what to do. For instance, I once worked with a woman who had a variety of crises in her life and in her marriage. She spoke about a married man with whom she once had an affair. She said that she still thought about him often, even though the affair had ended over five years ago. She had not seen him since then because he lived in another city. She asked me point-blank if I would call him if I were her. Bewildered, I replied, "I can't answer that because I'm not you." The woman never spoke to me again.

After much thought, there would have been a number of more effective replies. For instance, I could have said, "That's a difficult thing for me to answer. Help me think through how you feel about this man, your husband, and your marriage, so that I can better understand your situation." In this way, I could have gotten back on the track of helping her think through her own decision.

There are some instances where encouragement to take some action may need to be more forceful. One example of this approach is crisis intervention, which was discussed more thoroughly in Chapter 7. In a crisis situation, clients may need to be pushed out of their frozen, emotional, and perhaps illogical state. Once again, however, this is a matter of professional judgment.

There's one other thing to consider when thinking about telling a client what to do. Namely, how do *you* feel when someone tells you what you *should* do? Do you run right out and do it readily? Or, do you resent the intrusion and ignore the advice, or even take off in the opposite direction?

ahead of time and have a closed number of options. Your job is simply to choose one. Even the last two questions have a limited number of responses. The number of brothers must be from none to probably under 20. A birthdate is limited to specific days in the 12 months of the year.

"Machine-gunning" or bombarding the client with one closed-ended question after the other is easy, especially for beginning interviewers. Frequently, this situation occurs when a worker is anxious and trying to keep the interview going. Often, the worker wonders why the client is not saying much or initiating any discussion on his or her own.

The answer to this dilemma is to use open-ended questions. Instead of requiring simple, established answers from a predetermined selection, open-ended questions seek out the client's thoughts, ideas, and explanations for answers. They encourage elaboration and specifics about answers unique to particular clients and situations. Consider the following examples:

- "What are your reasons for wanting to leave home?"
- "How are you feeling about the situation?"
- "What do you plan on doing in the future?"
- "What are the people in your family like?"
- "How are you planning to accomplish this?"

Each of these questions allows for a more detailed answer, unique to every individual and situation. For example, how you would describe your family members at any particular point in time would be different from the way anyone else would.

The Use of Why?

One thing to consider when formulating questions for clients is if and when to use the word *why*. This word can be threatening to clients because it is "intrusive" (Cormier & Hackney, 1999, p. 82) and often implies that the person to whom it is directed is at fault (Westra, 1996). For example, a student enters a classroom three minutes late. The instructor asks in front of the whole class, "Why are you late?" This question places a demand on the student to explain her reasons for doing something wrong by not being on time. The following are other examples:

- "Why do you beat your children?"
- "Why do you drink so much?"
- "Why don't you get a job?"
- "Why don't you get straight A's?"
- "Why do you always nag me so much?"

The word *why* also can put the burden of seeking out a solution on the individual to whom it is directed. The solution often involves reaching inside one's mind for facts, organizing one's thoughts and ideas, and presenting them in an understandable form right then and there. The following questions illustrate this:

- "Why does it take at least four years to graduate from college?"

- "Why does the sun shine?"
- "Why don't I have enough money?"
- "Why do they have that rule?"
- "Why can't I do what I want to?"

In summary, being cautious when using the word *why* is best.

Overlap of Techniques

Sometimes labeling a technique specifically as being a "clarification" or a "self-disclosure" is difficult. Some responses fulfill only one purpose and fit obviously into one category, while others combine two or more techniques if they fulfill two or more functions. The important thing is to master a variety of techniques and thereby become more flexible and effective.

Roles Human Services Professionals Play

Human services professionals use these various interviewing and micro practice techniques while playing a wide range of roles. Figure 9.3 depicts a number of them.

 ## Challenges in Interviewing

A fascinating aspect about working with and helping people is that you never really know what to expect. Every person, problem, and situation is different. However, you must frequently deal with a number of issues in order to continue with the planned change approach, often posing dilemmas for workers about how to proceed. Among these issues are dealing with diversity, silence in the interview, confronting clients, involuntary clients, and suspicion of untruth.

Dealing with Diversity: Cross-Cultural Awareness in Interviewing

We have established that appreciation of diversity is one of the founding concepts of generalist practice. Understanding the client's "ethnic reality" is critical. This reality involves "a group's cultural values as embodied in its history, rituals, and religion . . . , a group's migration experience or other processes through which the encounter with mainstream culture took place . . . , [and] the way a group organizes its family systems" (Devore & Schlesinger, 1999, p. 55). These experiences affect the way designated groups function, thrive, or face oppression within

Figure 9.3 *Human Services Roles with Micro Systems*

Human services professionals play many roles. The following diagrams illustrate some of the roles commonly assumed in micro practice. Circles are used to represent worker, client, and macro systems. Lines and arrows depict how systems relate to each other. Macro systems are usually organizations or communities. Client systems illustrated in these particular diagrams are individuals.

However, you should note how working on behalf of individuals often involves helping your clients deal with the many other systems with which they interact. The distinctions between micro, mezzo, and macro practice blur. Your goal as a professional is to help your clients solve problems, obtain resources, and address issues by using the most effective means possible. These illustrations are what being a generalist practioner is all about.

Enabler

The *enabler* role involves providing support, encouragement, and suggestions to a client system so that the client may proceed more easily and successfully in completing tasks or solving problems. The diagram above illustrates how workers can provide such support. An arrow pointing from the worker circle to the client system circle depicts the worker's support. The desired result is that the client system will be better able to cope with problems and to pursue some course of action.

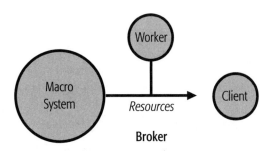

Broker

The *broker* role involves linking clients with needed resources. The line from the worker circle to the arrow in the above diagram portrays the worker's role. It illustrates the worker's active involvement in obtaining resources for the client. The arrow points from the macro system circle, which provides resources, to the client system circle, which receives them.

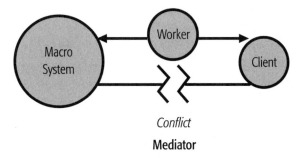

Mediator

Mediators work to help conflicting parties settle disputes and agree on compromises. A mediator maintains a neutral stance between the involved parties, taking no one's side. In the above diagram, the broken line beneath the worker circle depicts the two parties' broken lines of communication and their inability to settle differences.

Here the worker is mediating between a client system and a macro system. However, mediation can occur between virtually any size systems including between two macro systems or two micro systems. Consider, for instance, divorce mediation, where disputes are settled and agreements made between divorcing spouses.

the macro environment. Understanding the dynamics involved to empathize with clients and help them evaluate alternatives is essential for workers. Working with clients that have diverse backgrounds in terms of culture, ethnicity, and race requires several dimensions of cross-cultural awareness.

The first dimension involves the fact that learning about people from other cultures is an ongoing, continuous process. Cultural variations are almost endless. Not only are there multitudes of cultural and ethnic groups, but cultures and values diverge significantly within groups. A wealthy person from

Educator

As an *educator*, a worker conveys information to a client, as the diagram above illustrates.

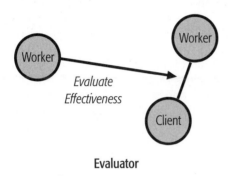

Evaluator

All practitioners need to assume the role of *evaluator* in terms of the effectiveness of their own practice. The arrow in the above diagram portrays the worker evaluating his or her own intervention with a client.

Case Manager/Coordinator

Many clients have multiple problems and are involved with many other systems. One role social workers often assume is that of *case manager* or *coordinator*. This role involves seeking out resources, planning how they might be delivered.

The box enclosing the macro and client systems represents the coordinated interactions between these two systems. The arrow pointing from the worker to the box depicts the worker's active involvement in coordinating all the systems involved. Although the diagram illustrates the coordination of one macro and one micro client system, such coordination can occur among any number of macro, mezzo, and micro systems.

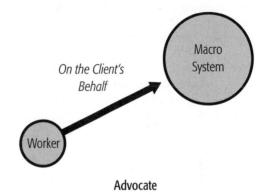

Advocate

Advocates champion the rights of others. They usually advocate with the goal of empowering their clients. The arrow in the diagram above, which leads from the worker to the macro system, is exceptionally thick. This line represents the significant amount of energy needed to have an impact on larger, more powerful systems. Advocacy is an extremely significant role in generalist practice.

northern India has different preferences, lifestyles, and even choices of cuisine than an impoverished person from southern India. People from Germany differ in language, cultural values, and lifestyle from people in Norway, despite the fact that most of them have a similar white European background. The

important thing is to keep your mind open and seek out information about your clients' cultural groups, whatever they may be.

Green emphasizes that the first step in learning about another culture involves going through "the trouble to learn some of what members of a culture know, including their beliefs about their history, their values, and what they see as their relationship to the rest of the world" (1999, p. 86). You can accomplish this "by combining reading, listening, watching, and consulting with knowledgeable insiders" (1999, p. 86). For example, when working with Hispanic clients, "prime features often regarded as ethnically significant" include "national origin, language, family names, religion, racial ascription, and immigration or citizenship status" (Castex, 1994, p. 290). Likewise, when working with Alaskan natives, important values include "respect for elders, love for children, respect for others, respect for nature, domestic skills, humility, sharing, cooperation, hard work, hunting skills, family roles, humor, spirituality, knowledge of language, knowledge of family tree, avoidance of conflict, and responsibility to clan or tribe" (Lally & Haynes, 1995, p. 198).

But learning is only the beginning. Cultural knowledge involves understanding people's values, actions, preferences, and expressions. This understanding includes observing "such overt activities as singing, dancing, arguing, playing, and working," in addition to "offhand comments, facial expressions, joking relationships, exchange of favors, and styles of demeanor" (Green, 1999, p. 86).

When working with people from other cultures and racial groups, remembering the concept of individualization is important. *Individualization* is the human services value maintaining that every person is unique with unique characteristics, distinguished from those generally characterizing a cultural, ethnic, or racial group. Individualization is a crucial concept in human services practice (Hepworth et al., 1997; Johnson, 1998; Sheafor et al., 2000). Workers must remain vigilant to individual values, preferences, and choices that may not reflect those generally embraced by the client's particular ethnic or cultural heritage. Proctor and Davis (1996) emphasize that "respect and professional courtesy are particularly important with minority clients, to whom society frequently gives less" (p. 102). Listening carefully to individual differences and appreciating personal values is one significant means of showing respect.

A second dimension of cross-cultural awareness involves understanding the extent to which clients are assimilated into the mainstream culture. This measure requires great sensitivity and perceptiveness to communicate with clients as effectively as possible. For example, newly migrated Afghanistani immigrants probably are much more embedded in their native culture and its values than those who have lived in the United States for a decade or more. Residents gradually assimilate some values and customs.

Likewise, differences develop between Hmong who migrated here as adults and those who were born and grew up here. The values of Hmong adolescents who join gangs diverge significantly from those of their parents. The family is traditionally "the most important influence in the lives of Hmong people," members' major goals being to enhance "its dignity and well-being" (McInnis, 1990, p. 29). Discord swells when teenagers' loyalties to gang and family conflict. Devore and Schlesinger (1999) reflect that "[t]he sense of family cohesion often diminishes in the second and third generation of immigrants or migrants. The family as transmitter of old values, customs, and language is often seen as restrictive by members of the younger generation" (p. 145).

A third dimension of cross-cultural awareness concerns attention to the stereotypes, prejudices, discrimination, and oppression negatively affecting people from various ethnic and racial groups. A *stereotype* is a fixed mental picture of members of some specified group based on some attribute or attributes that portray an overly simplified opinion about that group without considering and appreciating individual differences. *Prejudice* is a "preconceived judgment or opinion" about some individual, group, or concept that is not founded on fact and that usually involves a negative opinion or hostility directed at that individual, group, or concept (*Merriam Webster's Collegiate Dictionary*, 1994). *Discrimination* is "the prejudgment and negative treatment of people based on identifiable characteristics such as race, gender, religion, or ethnicity" (Barker, 1999, p. 132). *Oppression* involves putting extreme limitations and constraints on the members of some identified group.

Prejudice based on stereotypes often results in discrimination and oppression. Alternatives are limited for the oppressed group, and behavior is restricted. Nurturing their awareness of these conditions is absolutely essential for practitioners in order to understand clients' positions and establish viable alternatives for action. For example, a school counselor must seriously consider the wisdom of referring a shy, withdrawn Native American boy to a local recreation center whose members are renowned for their racist attitudes. Similarly, a practitioner would avoid referring a Jewish woman to a support group composed of neo-Nazis wrought with anti-Semitism.

A fourth dimension of cross-cultural awareness involves the importance of self-awareness, one's own ethnic and cultural background, and how that background may affect a worker's ability to practice (Devore & Schlesinger, 1999; Schlesinger & Devore, 1995). Questions you might ask yourself include:

- How do I view members of this cultural, ethnic, or racial group? What adjectives immediately come to mind?
- Do I have stereotypes and prejudged expectations about how these group members will behave? Do I have negative expectations not based on fact or that fail to take individualization into account?
- How does my own cultural, ethnic, and racial background affect my view of various groups and of the world in general?
- How can I open my mind to cultural differences and view them with objectivity and appreciation?
- How can I nurture my ongoing learning about cultural differences? What can I do to learn more?

Silence in the Interview

What if, try as you might, the client will not say much? Kadushin and Kadushin (1997) make some important comments about how silence can operate within human interaction such as an interview. First, "when people come together with the intent of talking to each other, silence generates social anxiety and is embarrassing. But the [practitioner] feels a professional anxiety at the thought that continued silence signals a failing interview" (1997, p. 213). In other words, a worker may feel threatened, inadequate, boring, or out of control if long periods of silence occur during the interview. Silent times almost seem to demonstrate the uselessness or lack of substance of the interview. However, in reality, "something is happening all the time, even when the participants appear to be totally passive. Silence is a period filled with lack of speech, in which both interviewer and interviewee participate" (1997, p. 214). In other words, silence is meaningful and may occur for a number of reasons.

Client-Initiated Silence

Silence in the interview is either client-initiated or worker-initiated (Cormier & Hackney, 1999). Client-initiated silence means that the client is taking responsibility for having the silent period happen. This silence occurs for different reasons (Cormier & Hackney, 1999; Fine & Glasser, 1996; Kadushin & Kadushin, 1997). First, the client may be addressing an issue, then come to a point of uncertainty as to where to go and need time to organize thoughts. Second, the client may be trying to pressure the worker to give some answer, response, or solution to a problem. A third use of silence is to offer resistance or to reject the worker's authority.

Negative Worker-Initiated Silence

The other type of silence in an interview is worker-initiated—that is, the worker has been talking and feels responsible for the silence (Cormier & Hackney, 1999). The first negative scenario involves a worker who demonstrates a quiet, noninvolved, nonassertive personality style. For this worker, working that hard at directing the interview is not natural. Such behavior is inappropriate and a "cop-out" for a professional. Professional skills must transcend individual personality styles.

The second negative type of worker-initiated silence occurs when the worker's mind becomes a blank and he or she cannot think of anything to say. This form of silence occurs more frequently with new workers who are anxious about their own performance.

Focusing on the Client Instead of Yourself

When a human services professional comes upon a new situation or new type of problem, becoming anxious is easy if you are not sure about what to do next. The answer to this dilemma is to tune in to your anxiety and do one of two things. First, you can allow yourself a brief period of silence in order to get your thoughts together. (This type of silence will be discussed further in the next section under therapeutic worker-initiated silence.) Second, you can think about what is happening in the interview and label it. For example, you might say, "It's pretty quiet in here. Where are your thoughts?" or "It seems like you're taking some time to think about the issue. That's all right. We can start again when you're ready."

Therapeutic Worker-Initiated Silence

Cormier and Hackney (1999) cite four ways that worker-initiated silence can be beneficial or therapeutic: "pacing the interview," "silent focusing," "responding to defenses," and "silent caring" (p. 53). Each type assumes that the worker initiates or is in control of the silent period.

Sometimes, conversations and information move rapidly during the interview, and there is not enough time for the client to keep up or to absorb all that is transpiring. *Pacing the interview* involves using small periods of silence to allow time to think about and assimilate what is occurring.

A second type of therapeutic silence involves *silent focusing*. This period of silence is a bit longer than those used to pace interviews and is only allowed to occur after some significant revelation has surfaced. Silent focusing enables the client to focus in on and think more intensively about an issue without having to rush right into something else.

The third type of therapeutic silence concerns the worker *responding to defenses* in the client. The silence occurs when a client has an emotional outburst directed toward the worker. Usually, the client is angry at something else (e.g., spouse, children, an agency that is denying benefits, landlord, in-laws, and so on). However, clients may vent their intense emotions at you the worker just because you are there. Becoming defensive yourself or immediately trying to provide insight into the client's behavior may be tempting. But a period of silence with congruent nonverbal behavior (e.g., maintenance of direct eye contact with the client and a somber facial expression) may give clients time to think about how and why they are acting the way they are.

Silent caring is the fourth type of therapeutic silence. Sometimes, there will be a period of intense emotion during an interview, often involving profound sadness, grief, or regret. Many times, a client will cry during these moments. Culturally, we are often taught that crying implies weakness and is essentially bad. This view is a misconception, however, because crying allows for an honest expression of emotion and an opportunity to let pain out and experience it. Unless such poignant emotions are identified and allowed expression, people cannot work through them and get on with life. A period of silent empathy during an interview may best convey your caring and understanding. Incidentally, subtly offering the client a tissue, or at least having a box readily available should a client need them, may also be appropriate.

Finally, one should note that there are distinctive cultural differences regarding the treatment of silence in conversations and interviews. Being sensitive to these nuances and respectful of the client's values about silent communication is important.

Confronting Clients

Confrontation in almost any situation is difficult for many people. To confront means to disagree with another person and make a point of stating that disagreement. Confrontation also involves risking a negative or hostile reaction from the person you are confronting.

Nonetheless, confrontation is an important tool in the problem-solving process of generalist practice. *Confrontation* is "the direct expression of one's view

of the conflict and one's feelings about it and at the same time an invitation to the opposition to do the same" (Johnson, 1997, p. 407). Confrontations involve identifying and examining participants' issues, needs, and emotions. A confrontation in human services practice often involves pointing out to clients their incongruencies or inconsistencies between what they say and what they do (Cormier & Hackney, 1999; Kadushin & Kadushin, 1997). Any confrontation first involves clearly identifying the existing discrepancy and then working toward some resolution (Ivey & Ivey, 1999). In other words, confrontations are necessary to help clients face factors that block progress toward attaining goals and, thus, heighten their motivation to make positive changes (Hepworth et al., 1997).

There are at least four types of discrepancies that practitioners frequently target for confrontation, including those "between two statements," "between what one says and what one does," "between statements and nonverbal behavior," and "between two or more people" (Ivey, 1994, p. 192; Ivey & Ivey, 1999). The following are examples of such discrepancies:

- A client states "I want to stay here and work on the problem. I really want to go home now."
- After having gone out to "hang one on in a big way" the prior evening, a client says, "I don't drink anymore."
- While chewing her fingernails, tapping her foot, and grimacing, a client says, "I feel so at ease here talking to you."
- A worker is interviewing two parents. The focus is on child behavior techniques. One parent states, "I really am responsible for all the discipline of the children." The other parent replies, "You're all talk and no action. I'm the one who does all the disciplining around here."

There are a number of reasons for these discrepancies (Hepworth et al., 1997; Ivey, 1994; Ivey & Ivey, 1999; Whittaker & Tracy, 1989). Sometimes, confrontations are necessary when clients are trying to resist intervention for a certain reason. At other times, clients may not be certain whether or not they want to be helped and are hesitant to cooperate. Still other times, for reasons of their own, clients will not want to follow through on recommendations. Sometimes, clients will find making actual changes in their behavior too difficult. Clients may also make excuses for behavior that you feel are unacceptable. Finally, clients may be behaving in ways that are contrary to their own best interests.

Hepworth and colleagues (1997) postulate that confrontations involve four components. First, the worker should communicate caring about the client and interest in the client's well-being. Second, the worker should clearly express the client's stated goal within the problem-solving process. Third, the worker should illustrate exactly what the discrepancy is. Finally, the worker should indicate the realistic results of the discrepancy.

For example, a worker in a sheltered workshop for adults with cognitive disabilities might say to a client:

- "I like you and I care about how you perform here" (communication of caring).
- "You've told me that you'd like to continue working here for a long time" (client's stated goal).
- "However, you say you like working here, but every half-hour of work you take a half-hour break" (identification of the discrepancy).
- "You know that everybody here is expected to work two hours straight, and then they get a half-hour break. You know that you and everyone else must follow these rules or you can't continue working here" (realistic results of the discrepancy).

There are several additional suggestions for maximizing the use of confrontation. First, as a worker, consider whether or not your relationship with the client is strong enough to withstand the potential stress caused by confrontation. For instance, confronting a client within ten minutes after the initial interview with the client has begun would probably be unwise.

Second, be aware of the client's emotional state. If a client is extremely upset, agitated, or anxious, a confrontation probably would have little value (Hepworth et al., 1997). Clients who are preoccupied with other issues probably will have little energy left to respond positively and helpfully to confrontations.

Third, use confrontations infrequently and only when you have to (Compton & Galaway, 1999; Hepworth et al., 1997). Confrontations are often difficult and imply some risk to the relationship. If they are used as an integral part of a confrontational style, the client may feel downtrodden and terminate the worker–client relationship.

Fourth, continue to demonstrate respect for the client throughout the confrontation (Nunnally & Moy, 1989). This respect involves listening to what the client is saying whether or not you agree with it and also acknowledging the fact that the client ulti-

mately has the right to choose his or her own course of action. Respect concerns keeping in mind that, as the worker, you are there to help the client, not to get the client to do what you want done.

Fifth, remain empathic with the client throughout the confrontation (Hepworth et al., 1997; Johnson, 1997) and do not get overly involved in trying to get your own way. Continue to work on understanding how the client feels and views the problems from his or her own perspective.

Sixth, use "I" statements during the confrontation (Sheafor et al., 2000). Simply rephrasing your thoughts to include the word "I" enhances the quality of personal caring and empathy. This technique emphasizes the fact that you are giving feedback instead of criticizing or blaming. For example, a worker might say, "*I* would like to share with you some inconsistencies I've noticed between what you've been saying and what you've actually been doing." This statement is far more personal and far less blaming than, "*You've* been saying one thing and doing another."

Seventh, have patience and allow the client some time to change (Hepworth et al., 1997; Johnson, 1997). Applying intense pressure for a client to change may be a turnoff because people are likely to resent being told what to do. Johnson (1997) emphasizes that a worker should not demand change unless he or she is God. Additionally, expecting instantaneous change is inappropriate. Clients need time to integrate new information, think things through, and make gradual changes in their lives and behavior.

Involuntary Clients

Voluntary clients are those who willingly seek counseling and help attaining their goals. For example, "spouses may voluntarily seek marital counseling from family service agencies; parents may ask for assistance in dealing with tensions to avoid abusing their children; and substance abusers may voluntarily participate in counseling to reduce the frequency of their undesirable behaviors" (Ivanoff, Blythe, & Tripodi, 1994, p. 5).

However, many human services professionals find themselves in the position of trying to help involuntary clients who do not want and were compelled to be there. Involuntary clients may be either *mandated* or *nonmandated* (Ivanoff et al., 1994, pp. 5–6). Some involuntary clients are legally required or mandated to receive services. These include prisoners, people in institutions or residential treatment centers, and others under court order. "Other examples of involuntary services include counseling for alcoholics involved in automobile accidents, group therapy for wife batterers, and parenting skill training for neglectful parents" (1994, p. 5).

Nonmandated involuntary clients are those "who are pressured by important persons in their environment to seek assistance" (Ivanoff et al., 1994, p. 5). These clients include an employer urging an alcoholic employee to get help from the company's Employee Assistance Program,[1] one spouse forcing the other into marriage counseling under threat of divorce, or staff and family pressuring an elderly person in a nursing home to cooperate with treatment plans.

There is no question that working with people who do not want to work with you is difficult. However, there are a number of suggestions that can help the intervention process along even when clients are involuntary.

First, acknowledge to yourself that the client is indeed involuntary. Do not ignore the fact that the client does not want to be there. Rather, accept it. Instead of trying to force the client to like being there with you, start where the client is.

Second, try to put yourself in your client's shoes (Kadushin, 1995). We have already discussed some of the negative feelings with which clients may come to interviews. They may be wary and suspicious. They may have had bad experiences with your agency or others before. They might be trying desperately to maintain their own homeostasis and thus strongly resist any attempt to change. Just looking at the reality of the situation instead of trying to fight it is a good start (see Highlight 9.6).

The third suggestion for working with involuntary clients involves labeling and helping them express their negative feelings (Kadushin, 1995; Whittaker & Tracy, 1989). If the client is resistant, bring that out into the open. For example, you might say, "I get the strong impression that you don't really want to be here. I'd like to know how you're feeling right now."

Identifying the reasons you suspect for the client's resistance is also helpful. For example, if appropriate, you might say, "I know it's been difficult for you to come in and see me. I realize that you're required to do this by the court." Once again, labeling the reality of the situation often both

disperses anxiety and introduces opportunities for clients to get their real feelings out on the table.

A fourth suggestion involves knowing the limits of your authority and, in effect, power over the client (Epstein, 1985). Giving the client the idea that you are the master and he or she must do what you say is usually a turnoff. However, you do want to clarify, at least in your own mind, the ultimate consequences of the client's involvement or lack of involvement with you. Depending on the circumstances, you may even want to state these consequences in the interview. For instance, the client's alternative to working with you might be incarceration. As a worker you might say, "I hope you choose to work with me on this problem. As we both know, your alternatives are limited to this or going to jail. That's a pretty coercive situation."

The fifth suggestion for involuntary client situations involves figuring out what you can do for the client that he or she wants. This requires careful *listening* to what the client says. What is really important to the client? What can you do that will make the intervention worthwhile? Your usefulness is often best demonstrated to the client in "an immediate and concrete way (e.g., by arranging for a needed service such as transportation, medical or dental care, and so on)" (Sheafor et al., 1988, p. 213).

The sixth suggestion concerns "cultivating hope and conveying encouragement" (Kadushin & Kadushin, 1997; Whittaker & Tracy, 1989, p. 143). You might try suggesting some potentially positive outcomes of the intervention that the client may never have considered. You might indicate that, although the beginning of the process is difficult, you have seen many other people work their problems out and make great gains.

The seventh suggestion involves allowing the client time to gain trust in you and in the intervention process (Hepworth et al., 1997). Expecting instant motivation is illogical. Allowing the client to get to know you as a competent professional while you establish a positive worker–client relationship is important.

The final suggestion for working with unwilling clients involves accepting the fact that, ultimately, the client has the right to choose whether or not to cooperate with you (Kadushin, 1995). After you have done your best, clients still may decide not to work with you. This choice is their right, and clients must live with the consequences of their decisions. You can help clients explore the negative and positive consequences of their decisions; however, they get to make the decision.

---

1. "Employee assistance programs (EAPs) focus on helping to prevent and remediate personal, work, or family problems that interfere with employees' optimal productivity" (Van Den Bergh, 1995, p. 842).

HIGHLIGHT 9.6

Handling Hostility

Sometimes clients will be angry when they arrive for your interview. They may raise their voices and even scream, shake their fists, scowl, snarl, be sarcastic, or behave aggressively in other ways. Displaying hostility is one way a client has of dramatizing a conflict. Conflicts may involve disagreements, disappointments, or general displeasure. What is certain is that something is making the client mad.

Johnson (1997) points out that, although conflicts are generally viewed as being unpleasant incidents to be avoided, there are some positive aspects to conflict. For example, conflicts bring to the surface issues that are of serious concern to clients. Instead of hiding their negative feelings, clients may voice some hostility. A worker then knows what he or she is up against and can begin to address the issues involved. Additionally, conflict can provide motivating arenas for change. A client who is uncomfortable enough with a situation to voice hostility may be more motivated to work to resolve the problem causing the discomfort. Only then can the client revert to a calmer, more comfortable state.

In addition to the suggestions provided for working with involuntary clients, the following propose ways for dealing with client hostility:

1. Do not get angry or defensive. Recognize your own reactions. Remember that this is a professional and not a personal issue.
2. Focus on the client's hostile *behavior* instead of labeling the client a hostile *person.* Label the hostile behavior and other dynamics as they occur.
3. Allow the client briefly to voice his or her anger. Be empathic. See the situation from the client's perspective.
4. Emphasize the client's personal strengths. Do not attack the client. You want to close, not widen, the rift in communication.
5. Know the facts regarding the client's situation. To help the client deal with reality, you must know what reality is.
6. Focus on the present and future. Avoid allowing the client to dwell on the past. Emphasize what can be done positively—not what has already happened negatively and can't be changed.
7. Look at the various alternatives open to the client and their consequences. Help the client evaluate the pros and cons of each alternative.
8. Do not moralize. (Remembering the times someone has moralized to you about what you *should* do and how annoying it was.)
9. *Summarize* what has occurred during the interview and what *recommendations* have been made. Sometimes, this summarization helps the client to keep on track. You want to help the client deal objectively with his or her reality, not go off on tangents of emotional outbursts.
10. Establish short-term, initial goals with a hostile client. These might include calming the client down and making a basic agreement to discuss a particular issue or to come to another appointment. These goals are quite different from addressing major problems as part of the intervention process.

Suspicion of Untruth

There may be times when a worker has a *gut reaction* that a client is not telling the truth. Gut reactions involve feelings that you get in reaction to situations where you feel in the back of your mind that something is occurring or something is wrong. Are details consistent? Are there gaps or inconsistencies in what the client is saying? Do some things not make sense to you? Becoming adept at identifying your gut reactions is useful because they often provide excellent clues about what is happening in any given situation.

Although we would probably prefer it otherwise, clients are not perfect. They may choose to lie for various reasons. Unfortunately, practitioners most often dislike addressing the issue of whether or not a client is telling the truth. Such confrontation often violates a worker's idea of "starting where the client is" and respecting the client. Confronting a possible lie is uncomfortable. For one thing, you may be wrong. The client may really be telling the truth.

Regardless, lying sometimes occurs. There are four suggestions regarding what to do if you think a client may be lying to you. First evaluate the situation logically. Do you have a feeling that something is not right? Are there discrepancies in facts? Or does the client's story not have a realistic sense to it?

Consider a 3-year-old child with odd-looking, round burn marks on the tops of his hands. The parent explains that the burns are the result of accidentally spilling some hot water on his hands. Your gut reaction, however, is to question how such a hot water burn resulted in small circular burn marks instead of a large reddened area. Logically, you might think such burns are more likely to result from a lighted cigarette. Such a gut reaction may give you a clue that child abuse may be occurring. At least it is a possibility to investigate.

The second suggestion for dealing with possible lying is to examine the client's pattern of prior behavior. The examination, of course, can only be done if you have a history of interaction with the client or if you have access to records about how the client has behaved in the past. Has the client omitted facts or lied before? Have you suspected lying before? Or is this the first time such behavior is suspected?

The third suggestion is that you may choose not to confront the client if this is the first time the possibility of lying has come up. You might give the client the benefit of the doubt.

The fourth suggestion about a client's lying is to evaluate the costs of believing or not believing your client. Is losing the client's trust more costly than you expressing disbelief? Or is ignoring what you think is not true and risking possible severe consequences more costly? For example, if you strongly suspect that a pregnant mother is lying about abusing cocaine, can you afford to ignore the lie at the expense of the fetus's health?

 ## Terminating the Interview

Sometimes, bringing an interview to a close is difficult or uncomfortable. You may think the client is finally feeling comfortable with you. During the last five minutes of an interview, the client may raise strikingly significant issues. The client may express the strong need to continue talking. Terminating the intervention process in general is addressed in Chapter 8. However, there are several points about how to end interviews and worker–client relationships that are relevant here. First, before the actual interview termination (e.g., five, ten, or even fifteen minutes before), mention exactly how much time is left (Kadushin & Kadushin, 1997). You might say

something like, "We're starting to get into some things you feel very strongly about. We've got another ten minutes to talk about them today, and then we can continue them in our discussion next week." This referral to the time communicates that the ending is approaching. It acts as a guidepost for how much more the client will be able to pursue, and it also sets a time limit so that the client is not abruptly surprised when the interview draws to a close.

The second suggestion involves "sharing ending feelings" (Cournoyer, 2000, p. 378). You can tell the client about how you feel as the interview is coming to a close. Statements may include positive feelings you have toward the client and about what the client has accomplished. Of course, these statements must reflect genuine feelings. For example, you might say, "I've really enjoyed working with you. I think you've made great strides toward achieving your goals."

A third recommendation for terminating interviews concerns asking clients to summarize what they think they have learned and accomplished (Fortune, 1995; Shulman, 1999). As the intervention progresses, the client should become increasingly articulate about what goals have become established and attained. How to identify and monitor goals was discussed more thoroughly in Chapters 6 through 8. Summarization helps a client focus in on the core meaningfulness of the intervention. Additionally, clarifying exactly what has been learned so it can be used to address new problems and situations again in the future helps a client.

The final suggestion for terminating interviews involves encouraging clients to share their own feelings about the intervention process (Fortune, 1995). Not only can you as a worker share your feelings about the interview and intervention process, but you can also draw out your client's reactions. As we have discussed earlier, expressing feelings openly allows clients to deal with them and move on with their lives. For example, a worker might say, "You seem awfully anxious right now. We've been working together for quite a while. Sometimes, it's scary to move on alone. How are you feeling?"

 ## InfoTrac College Edition

This chapter introduced a number of concepts and topics related to micro practice skills with individuals. To learn more about some of these topics, please enter the following search terms:

nonverbal communication
cultural competency
involuntary clients
facial expressions
empathy
empowerment

http://fbhc.org/Professionals/CulturalComp/home/
html
http://www.air-dc.org/cecp/cultural/default.htm
http://zzyx.ucsc.edu/~archer
http://www.advancingwomen.com/workplace/
empathy.html

 ## On the Internet

Because of the very dynamic nature of the Web,
URLs are subject to change. Therefore, be sure to
check out the companion Website for this book at
http://www.humanservices.wadsworth.com, where
links will be updated periodically

CHAPTER 10
Understanding Families

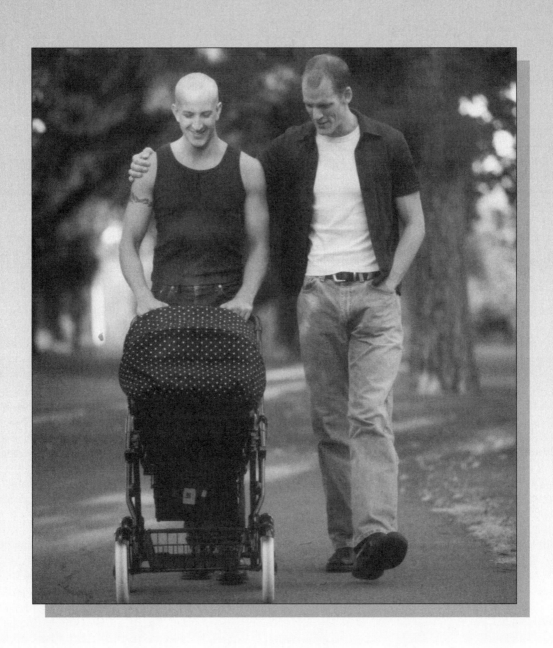

Television images of families have often reflected a version of real life that was somewhat idealized. Families, as displayed on "Leave it to Beaver" or "The Brady Bunch," were characterized by two heterosexual parents present in the home living a middle-class lifestyle. The family faced such typical life challenges as kids spending too much time on the phone and helping children learn to deal with successes and failures. Dad usually worked outside the home while Mom stayed home to care for the kids. If Mom had to work, there always seemed to be a surrogate parent to help raise the kids, clean the house, and prepare meals. Life was sometimes stressful but always manageable.

Consider real-life families today. June and Ward

> . . . *meet at the office (she's in marketing; he's in sales) and move in together after dating a couple of months. A year later, June gets pregnant. What to do? Neither feels quite ready to make it legal, and there is no pressure from parents, all of whom are divorced and remarried themselves. So little Wally is welcomed into the world with June's last name on the birth certificate. A few years later, June gets pregnant with the Beav. Ward is ambivalent about second-time fatherhood and moves out, but June decides to go ahead on her own. In her neighborhood, after all, single motherhood is no big deal; the lesbians down the street adopted kids from South America, and the soccer mom next door is divorced with a live-in boyfriend. (Kantrowitz & Wingert, 2001, pp 46–48)*

Six months after the Beaver is born, June's company moves its operations to Mexico to reduce costs, and she is unemployed.

Ward married the daughter of the company's vice president, moved to Texas, and no longer has any contact with his kids. Over the next few years, June uses up her unemployment insurance, goes on TANF, gets a job at significantly less pay, and moves in with Hank, a man she recently met. As his drug abuse problem becomes more serious, Hank begins to abuse Wally and June. Wally's schoolteacher reports suspected abuse to the local protective services office, and the family receives services for the next year. Finally, June moves to a domestic violence shelter after realizing that Hank's abuse is not going to stop. She gets a restraining order against him so that he is not allowed to have any contact with her or her kids. June and her boys are no longer in danger of abuse, but June discovers she is pregnant again. After considering her options and receiving counseling, June seeks an abortion. She tells no one about the abortion because it is against her religion. For years she has mixed feelings about her decision but has little time to worry about it because she has responsibility for raising two boys by herself. To make life harder, the Beav is diagnosed as hyperactive and having attention deficit disorder, while Wally is coping with the reading disorder, dyslexia. Though she has medical insurance through her employment, her HMO will not authorize a new medication that treats the Beav's disorder without the potential side effects of Ritalin. Sometimes, June thinks, "This is not the way I envisioned my life when I was 15."

The whole point of this chapter opener is that the nature of the family and of "typical" family problems has changed drastically in the past few decades. There have been awesome technological advances, massive upheavals in world economics, and major shifts in family structure. The problems families now face are very different than those confronted by the two-parent-with-children, male-dominated, unified family in which our culture has traditionally been rooted.

Of course, the Cleaver example only illustrates some of the changes in family life. For example, there are the changes in gender role expectations with respect to earning a living. Then, there are the moral dilemmas now being faced concerning sexuality and intimacy. Also, there are the effects of advancing technology.

There are some changes in the basic nature of families that the Cleavers do not illustrate as well. The Cleavers are very white and very middle-class. They do not reflect the increasing proportion of the population previously labeled as "minorities," in other words, people of nonwhite heritage. Nor do they clearly demonstrate the increasing proportion of women and children who compose the poor and homeless.

Working with families, regardless of their specific individual circumstances, is a major facet of generalist practice. Practitioners need to understand the basic dynamics of today's family relationships and the problems these families face. The family needs to be viewed from several perspectives. These include the family system as an entity in itself, the individual people making up the family system, and the impacts of the social, political, and economic environment upon how the family functions. These issues are what this chapter is all about.

 ## Introduction

Families continue to remain the foundation of most people's lives. They can provide the security, support, and intimacy people need. Human services professionals often encounter individual clients who initially appear to have individual problems. However, another way of looking at problems is from a family perspective. That is, you might view a problem not as belonging to the individual, but rather to the individual's entire family.

For example, take a 24-year-old man who abuses alcohol. His alcoholism not only affects him, but his wife, whom he slaps around when he returns home drunk. It also affects his three children. His primary interactions with them involve hitting, screaming, and ignoring. Finally, it affects the man's parents and other family members when he typically bursts into fits of alcoholic rage at family gatherings.

An 87-year-old woman whose health is rapidly failing provides another example. Of course, her health is *her* problem. However, it is also the problem of her middle-aged son and daughter, both of whom live at least 75 miles from her home. Should one of them take her in and care for her? If so, which one? Both of their spouses hate the idea. The spouses see the older woman's presence as a terrible disruption of their own families' lives. So should her children put the elderly woman in a health care facility? Should they force her to go even if she hates that idea? If she does enter a facility, which one? And how often do they need to visit? How can either of the elderly woman's children cope with their burden of guilt over not taking her in themselves?

Still another example involves an active 13-year-old boy who slips on the mud as he runs down to the river to swim. Although he has run down that same riverbank hundreds of times before, this time he slips and breaks his neck. What impact does his individual problem, namely that of being a quadriplegic, have on his parents, his siblings, his grandparents, and other members of his extended family?

Thus, generalist human services practitioners will often be called upon to work with an entire family to solve a problem. This task does not mean that generalist practitioners are family therapists. In describing what family therapists do, Brock and Barnard (1999) state, "The task of the family therapist is to change the structure and interaction processes of the client family (p. 2).

Family therapists are specialized. Their focus of attention is the family unit. Their goals involve changing family members' patterns of communication and interaction. Family therapists help clients make changes in how they think, both about themselves and about other family members. Therapy typically takes place in the therapist's office and can be somewhat long term.

Generalist human services professionals, on the other hand, must address a broader variety of problems. As we have discussed, many of these problems involve outside systems. For example, a client may have lost her job. Part of a human services professional's role then might be to help this client find other employment. Linking a client with employment agencies and other potential sources of jobs is one means of handling this case. Or the worker might help the client get temporary financial help until she can once again support herself. Still another possibility is helping the client become involved in job training.

A second example of the broad range of problems addressed by generalist practitioners is homelessness. A generalist practitioner can help a homeless client find temporary shelter and resources. Subsequently, that worker might help that client find employment or become linked with other services and financial aid. Likewise, the client may require help in getting needed health care.

Still another example of a problem addressed by generalist practitioners involves helping the 13-year-old with quadriplegia mentioned earlier. He is likely to need help in a variety of ways. He may have difficulty coping with the reality of his disability. Likewise, the impacts of the accident on other family members may need attention. Generalist practitioners may help the boy with quadriplegia and his family deal with these issues or refer them to someone else to do so. The options available to family members (such as pursuing resources) will probably need to be addressed. For instance, a generalist practitioner can work to help the 13-year-old get physical and occupational therapy and transportation services. A worker can find out what resources are available and help link him and his family with these resources. If services are not available, a generalist practitioner may advocate on the client's behalf so that the community and agencies within the community begin to respond to the client's needs.

Thus, generalist practitioners must adopt a broader view in helping individuals and families solve problems. They need a wide range of skills. They need to be able to tackle a variety of problems and try to solve them in whatever ethical manner they can figure out.

The family remains a significant force in people's lives. Family relationships are intimate and complex. In some ways, working with families in human services practice is different from working with individuals, other groups, or larger systems. Working with families is often considered to lie somewhere on a continuum between micro and mezzo practice. Therefore, human services professionals need a solid base of skills directly related to the planned change process with families.

Specifically, this chapter will:

- examine information useful in the assessment phase of the Generalist Intervention Model as it applies to families;
- review a spectrum of communication skills including verbal and nonverbal communication, in addition to specific avenues of communication within families;
- explore family structure with emphasis on the family as a system;
- identify family life cycle adjustments;
- describe common family conflicts and problems;
- relate policy issues in macro practice to families' basic needs;
- discuss variations in family structure, including single-parent families and stepfamilies;
- recognize several concepts concerning cultural competency and family assessment.

 ## *Families and the Generalist Intervention Model*

Work with families follows the Generalist Intervention Model (GIM) just like any other type of human services intervention. A worker must engage a family, conduct an assessment, develop a plan, implement the plan while amending it as necessary, evaluate progress, and terminate involvement with the family. A majority of this chapter and Chapter 11 will focus on these steps. Understanding family dynamics in order to conduct an assessment and proceed with intervention is critical for family treatment. Therefore, this chapter will address assessment issues, emphasizing step two in the planned change process. Chapter 11 will focus on practice techniques, beginning with engagement, step one, and proceeding with planning through termination.

 ## *Family Assessment*

As we know, assessment in generalist practice involves getting information about the client system and the client system's problems in order to decide how best to intervene. Here we will investigate some aspects of assessment that relate specifically to families. The entire family itself will be viewed as the client system.

There are various ways to define *families*. One definition is "a primary group whose members assume certain obligations for each other and generally share common residences" (Barker, 1999, p. 166). Another definition of *family* is "a grouping that consists of two or more individuals who define themselves as a family and who over time assume those obligations to one another that are generally considered an essential component of family systems" (e.g., caring for children or providing economic support) (Barker, 1995; NASW, 1982, p. 10). Proctor, Davis, and Vosler (1995) reflect that the latter "definition acknowledges the diversity of family types, including families headed by women; extended family households and a concept of 'kin' that is not restricted to relationships through blood, adoption, or marriage; and lesbian and gay couples and their children" (p. 942). Once the family has been identified as your client system, there are a variety of dimensions in which the family's problems and interactions can be assessed. These include communication, family structure, life-cycle adjustments, and impacts of the impinging social environment (Hepworth et al., 1997; Holman, 1983; Janzen & Harris, 1997; Thorman, 1982).

It's important to appreciate the richness of diversity in families and the strengths each unique family has. Highlight 10.1 focuses on some of the strengths tending to characterize gay and lesbian families.

Assessing Family Communication

How family members communicate with each other relates directly to how effectively the family flourishes as a system. Therefore, assessment of communication is essential in preparation for intervention. Several aspects of family communication will be discussed here. They include verbal and nonverbal communication in addition to the various avenues of communication.

Verbal and Nonverbal Communication

As we discussed in Chapter 9, regarding skills for working with individuals, communication involves transmitting information from one person to another. Both verbal and nonverbal communication are important in conveying meaning. That the *impact* on the receiver (what the receiver understands the sender to be say-

HIGHLIGHT 10.1

Strengths in Lesbian and Gay Families

Despite the fact that lesbian and gay people must deal with additional stressors such as homophobia (the irrational fear and hatred of gay and lesbian people) and lack of legal support for couples (e.g., being unable to marry in any state except Vermont and frequent ineligibility for partner's health insurance), many strengths tend to characterize lesbian and gay families. It's important for human services workers to seek out, emphasize, and support these strengths.

Tully (2000) cites the following realities:

Lesbian and gay male couples live in relationships that last from one date to a lifetime (just like nongay couples) . . .
Gay and lesbian relationships traditionally are more egalitarian [providing similar or equal levels of power for each partner] than nongay ones . . .
Gay and lesbian persons have friends of both sexes . . .
Gay men and women are indistinguishable from nongay persons . . .
More and more lesbians and gays are opting to have and raise children . . .
Children raised by lesbian or gay persons mostly grow up to be heterosexually well-adjusted adults with a high tolerance for diversity and show no ill effects from the experience of being raised in a nontraditional two-parent family. (p. 168)

It's also important to be aware of the numerous and varied community and agency resources available to

gay and lesbian families. These include recreational, social, and supportive groups and services. Examples of Websites providing information include:

- Gay and Lesbian Medical Association: http://www.glma.org/home.html
- Lesbian, Gay, Bisexual & Transgender Community Center: www.gaycenter.org
- Children of Lesbians and Gays Everywhere (COLAGE): www.colage.org

Still another source of strength for gay and lesbian families involves the wealth of cultural activities, events, and accomplishments (including literature, film, poetry, and music) generated by gay and lesbian people. Van Wormer, Well, and Boes (2000) reflect on how:

. . . there are many avenues of pride for gay or lesbian youth [and adults] seeking affirmation of who they are. . . . [People working with] this population (and who does not?) would do well to further engender this pride first by familiarizing themselves with some of the vast resources at hand and with the local organizations, events, and newsletters. . . . Gearing isolated gays and lesbians toward the richness of gay/lesbian heritage and of contemporary cultural and festive events can empower them in ways that all the therapy in the world cannot. In the European–North American part of the world where gay/lesbian identity is a force for identity and solidarity, there is a life of fulfillment to be had, a strength in likeness, a fortification against the daily cruelties and insults. And above all, there is fun and merriment to be enjoyed. (pp. 62–63)

ing) closely resembles the *intent* of the sender (what the sender means to say) is very important. As we know, inaccuracies or problems at any point in this process can stop the information from getting across to the receiver. At any point, distortion may interfere with the communication process.

Verbal communication patterns inside the family include who talks a lot and who talks only rarely. These patterns involve who talks to whom and who defers to whom. They also reflect the subtle and not so subtle aspects involved in family members' relationships. These qualities might involve hostility, pride, rejection, or overinvolvement.

Nonverbal communication patterns are also important in families. Frequently, a receiver will attribute more value to the nonverbal aspects of the message than the verbal. Nonverbal communication can involve facial expressions, eye contact, and posture. It can also involve seemingly trifling behaviors. See Highlight 10.2 for an example.

The situation illustrated in Highlight 10.2 may seem a bit unrealistic, but it really did happen. It illustrates several points about family interaction and communication.

First, what one family member might say in words to another one may not be what that sender

HIGHLIGHT 10.2

An Example of Conflict Between Verbal and Nonverbal Communication

Patti and Larry, a married couple, both work outside the home in professional careers. Because of their involvement in their respective jobs and the long hours they work, they see little of each other during the week. When Friday night rolls around, they typically relax together and enjoy talking about their work and future plans.

Patti made it a point to get home early one Friday and made Larry a relatively elegant beef stroganoff dinner—as elegant as it could get when it was started late Friday afternoon. The two, by the way, usually shared the cooking tasks.

Patti timed the dinner to be ready at 6:30 P.M., about the time Larry usually got home. Patti turned on the television and waited . . . and waited . . . and waited. Seven o'clock came and went. Seven-thirty rolled on by. Eight o'clock passed into oblivion. Time moved on from nine and finally to ten o'clock.

First, Patti took the dinner off of the stove and let it cool. An hour later she put it in the refrigerator so it would not spoil. Initially, Patti had been worried. What if Larry had been in a car wreck? But, no, the police would have called to let her know. Where was Larry? Why could he not call her to tell her he would not be home?

By 10 P.M., Patti had transcended far beyond her initial worry and even her anger. Her fury at Larry's inconsiderateness had escalated to immense proportions. As the evening had progressed she had gone beyond turning the roll of toilet paper in the bathroom upside down, a behavior that really annoyed him. She usually only resorted to such nonverbal behavior to get her point across when it really mattered and verbal communication

simply did not work. She not only vigorously squeezed the toothpaste down to the middle of the tube (another behavior which really aggravated Larry), but squeezed it all the way down to the bottom. He consistently and carefully liked to squeeze his toothpaste toward the top. Eventually, she had taken both the toilet paper roll and the toothpaste tube and thrown them in the garbage.

Patti then heard someone at the door. She, in addition, had also locked the door, another nonverbal means of displaying to Larry her serious disapproval. Someone out there was fidgeting with a key. There was scratching at the lock. Then, suddenly, the door burst open. There was Larry beaming a wide grin. He said with a somewhat drunken slur, "Well, hi ya, how're you doin'?"

Patti responded with a face of stone, her eyes black with rage, "I'm fine." She promptly left the room and went to bed.

Larry knew he was in the proverbial doghouse. Even after some unknown number of beers, he knew he should have called to tell Patti about Harvey's going-away party after work. He knew Patti was not "fine." He really knew how not "fine" she was when he discovered the missing toilet paper later that night and the phantom toothpaste the next morning.

Patti and Larry eventually talked the situation out. She told him how she thought he knew how she always looked forward to their Friday nights together. She told him how she had wanted to please him with dinner and how worried she had later become when he did not appear. She told him how she had felt he just did not care about her feelings. All he would have had to do was call her and tell her he would be late.

Larry apologized and said he would never do it again. Patti's nonverbal emphasis concerning the issue drove the point home. Later, verbal elaboration helped Larry understand the issue more clearly. However, to this day, Larry emphasizes how Patti "hates it when he has fun."

---

really means. Patti was not "fine," although she verbally stated she was. However, because of her anger and her feelings that Larry did not care about how she felt, she was not ready to express herself accurately with words.

Second, nonverbal behavior can provide important clues regarding what a sender really wants to convey. Patti did silly, although aggravating, things to convey to Larry that she was angry.

Third, critical nonverbal communication may involve any number of seemingly petty behaviors. Each of us has our "things" that, trivial as they may be, annoy us to no end. An annoyance may be how someone else puts the glasses into the dishwasher the wrong way or forgets to turn out the hall light at night. It might be how someone close to us forgets to put a plastic garbage bag in the waste container before dumping chicken bones into it. Or, it might be parking the car the wrong way in the driveway. Family members can use any of these things to communicate with each other.

A fourth point is that nonverbal behaviors often transcend trivial behaviors. They reflect feelings that the individual is unable or does not want to put into words. Emotions are strong among family members. Petty nonverbal behavior can wield formidable blows to those close to us.

There is a fifth point with respect to the story. Patti and Larry were able to unravel the problem themselves, despite the fact that Larry still feels Patti "hates it when he has fun." However, many times a generalist practitioner will be called upon to disentangle confused verbal and nonverbal communications. Helping communicators within the family to have their *intents* more closely match their *impacts* will be up to the worker.

The basic skills for micro practice clearly relate to working with families. In addition to understanding verbal and nonverbal communication, these skills include: being warm, empathic, and genuine; using interviewing techniques; and overcoming hurdles that often occur during the interviewing and problem solving processes. Family interaction and communication are more complicated because more individuals are involved.

Avenues of Communication

Perez (1979) cites "five avenues of communication," any or all of which family members may use in a given day; they include "consonance, condemnation, submission, intellectualization, and indifference" (p. 47). Evaluating how a family communicates using these avenues provides clear clues regarding where change is needed.

Consonance.   Consonance refers to the extent to which the communication receiver accurately hears and understands the sender of the communication. In other words, to what extent does the sender's *intent* closely resemble the receiver's *impact?* Healthy families are likely to have high levels of consonance in their communications. In other words, family members understand each other well. Unhealthy families, on the other hand, often have low levels of consonance. Members of these families do not communicate clearly with each other.

Condemnation.   Condemnation involves family members severely criticizing, blaming, negatively judging, or nagging other family members. More

than occurring only once or twice, condemnation involves a regular pattern of family interaction. This pattern may involve any number of the family members. In other words, one person may typically condemn another. Or that one person may typically condemn all the others. Likewise, all other family members may condemn one in particular. Or two or three members may condemn any one or more. Any configuration is possible.

People who form patterns of condemnation frequently do it to enhance their own self-esteem (Goldenberg & Goldenberg, 2000; Perez, 1979; Satir, 1972). Blaming or criticizing another person makes your own qualities and behaviors appear better or superior. For instance, take the 77-year-old woman who constantly condemned her husband of 55 years. He was 84. She regularly harped on how he was an alcoholic who could not keep a job. The strange thing, however, was that he had not touched a drop of liquor in over 40 years. Additionally, he had worked regularly as a carpenter for most of those years. However, when the woman dwelled on how bad her husband was, albeit for behavior that had occurred over 40 years ago, she made herself feel better. If he was so bad, then she looked good by comparison.

Submission.   Submission involves feeling so downtrodden, guilt ridden, or incapable that you succumb completely to another's will. You do not feel valuable or worthwhile enough to be assertive about your own rights and needs. Instead, you knuckle under the other person's will, submit, and obey. Perez (1979) sums up situations involving submission by saying:

> The submissive person, like the condemner, is difficult to live with. His [or her] feelings of ineptness and inadequacy put family members under constant pressure to support, to guide, to direct, to lead him. And again, when the dependency pressure becomes too demanding the family members may well respond via condemnation. (p. 49)

Intellectualization.   Intellectualization is the process of staging all communication within a strictly logical, rational realm. The existence of any emotion is denied or suppressed. A person who intellectualizes likes to evaluate a problem rationally and establish a solution as soon as possible. This person does not want illogical emotions to interfere with the process of dealing with and controlling reality. The problem usually faced by the intellectualizer, however, is that everyone has emotions, even the intellectualizer. Emotions that are constantly suppressed may build up and explode uncontrollably at inopportune times. Explosions may even result in violence.

Another problem with intellectualization occurs when the intellectualizer is unable to meet the needs of other family members. A person who intellectualizes can seem very cold and unloving. Traditional gender-role stereotypes that direct men to be strong, unemotional decision makers encourage intellectualization. This gender role often becomes a problem in relationships for women who traditionally have been raised to express emotions. A typical scenario involves a woman who seeks expressions of love and emotion from an intimate partner who instead intellectualizes.

Consider, for instance, one couple where the man states point-blank that he has no emotions; he says he is always happy. The woman responds with the question, "Well, then, what are you when you're yelling at me?"

The man replies hesitantly, "Then . . . I'm mad." At this the woman smiles silently to herself. She has made some progress by doubling her mate's emotional repertoire.

Indifference. Indifference involves remaining apparently unconcerned, not caring one way or the other, and appearing detachedly aloof. Two common ways indifference is manifested in families is through "silence" and "ignoring behaviors" (Perez, 1979, p. 51). One or more family members may not talk or respond to one or more other family members.

Indifference can be a very powerful and manipulative means of communicating. A mother who ignores her teenage daughter may convey a number of messages to her. Perhaps it makes the daughter feel her mother does not care enough about her to expend the energy. Or maybe the mother is angry at her for some reason.

In addition to being disturbing, being ignored can be very painful. For instance, consider the newlywed wife who was very emotionally insecure. During the first few weeks of marriage, she would ask her husband a dozen times a day if he really loved her. At first, he would answer, "Yes, dear, I do." However, he soon tired of her constant need for reassurance. He began simply to turn her off and ignore her. She was devastated. She needed to learn that her constant questioning was not eliciting the response she desired. Instead of making herself feel more secure, she was driving her husband away from her. This served only to escalate her insecurity.

Assessing Family Structure

Family structure refers to the organization of relationships and patterns of interaction occurring within the family. Here we will examine five dimensions of family structure. They include the family as a system, family norms, family roles, the balance of power within the system, and intergenerational aspects. Communication might be included as an aspect of family structure. However, because of its significance, not only in assessment but throughout planned change, we have already discussed it as a separate issue.

The Family as a System

Families are systems. The concepts involved in systems theory, which we discussed in Chapter 1, also apply to family systems. Family structure, then, can be assessed by thinking of the family in systems theory terms. As Holman articulates:

> In general systems terms, the family can be perceived as a dynamic system, consisting of a complex of elements or components (family members) directly or indirectly related in a network in such a way that each component (family member) is related to some other in a more or less stable way within any particular period of time. (1983, p. 23)

Viewing families from a systems perspective emphasizes "family interrelationships over individual needs and drives" and focuses on overall family functioning instead of individual pathology (Goldenberg & Goldenberg, 1998, p. 34).

Thinking of the family as a system is helpful when working with the family to help solve its problems. For instance, as in any system, all parts (family members) have relationships to all other parts (other family members). When assessing a family you need to assess all of the relationships among individuals, even those that superficially appear subdued and less significant.

Case Example—What Affects One Affects All.
Additionally, systems theory prescribes that an event affecting one family member will actually have an effect on *all* family members. For example, take Kay, age 16. She met a boy at a Friday night high school dance, went out with him for pizza afterward, and later got in a serious car accident. Ironically, the accident happened at about midnight on Friday the 13th. Another car pulled out in front

of the car in which Kay was a passenger. The driver in the other car tried to cut across the lane of his oncoming traffic to get to the other side of the boulevard. His car hit Kay's car head on. She was sitting in the middle front seat next to her new beau and was not wearing a seatbelt. Upon impact, her face was thrown down onto the radio in the dashboard. The result was a smashed right cheekbone, broken jaw, crushed nose, lost teeth, and several deep facial cuts.

In the four years following the accident, Kay went through a dozen plastic surgeries. Although the experience was painful, she later reflected that she had learned much from it. For instance, she quickly learned the old cliché that "beauty isn't everything." Her accident helped her to put things of real value such as her religious beliefs and personal relationships into perspective. The insurance money and a two-month trip to Europe were not so bad either. She eventually became a human services professional.

Her immediate family members, however, were traumatized by the car accident. Kay's 12-year-old sister promptly fainted during her initial visit to Kay in the hospital with her ruined face. Her parents were distraught. Not only did the regular trips to the hospital regulate how they would structure their lives over the next few years, but their worry over whether or not she would ever be able to live a normal life again because of her ugliness was devastating. Kay, now 39, reflects that her mother, Gloria, still maintains that Kay's accident was the worst thing that ever happened to her (meaning Gloria). Gloria stresses how it ruined her own life. Kay, of course, thinks this line of thinking is absurd because it was Kay's, not Gloria's, accident.

Boundaries and Subsystems. Two other systems theory concepts are exceptionally helpful when applied to family systems. They are boundaries and subsystems. Boundaries are "invisible lines of demarcation that separate the family from the outside nonfamily environment; they circumscribe and protect the integrity of the system and thus determine who is regarded as inside and who remains outside" (Goldenberg & Goldenberg, 1998, p. 32). In a family system, boundaries determine who are members of that particular family system and who are not. Parents and children are within the boundaries of the family system. Close friends of the family are not.

Inside the family, boundaries are invisible lines of demarcation that "differentiate subsystems; they help achieve and define the separate subunits of the total system" (Goldenberg & Goldenberg, 1998, p. 32). A subsystem is a secondary or subordinate system—a system within a system. The most obvious examples are the parental and sibling subsystems. Other more subtle subsystems may also exist depending on the boundaries established within the family system. A mother might form a subsystem with a daughter to whom she feels exceptionally close. Two siblings among four might form another subsystem because of their exceptionally close and unique relationship.

Boundaries separate the spouse subsystem within a family from the sibling subsystem. Each subsystem has its own specified membership. Either a family member is within the boundaries of the subsystem or he or she is not.

Boundaries between appropriate subsystems in families need to be maintained. For example, parents need to nurture and maintain their own subsystem as a marital couple. In an incestuous family, the marital subsystem boundaries may become blurred. The husband/father may form an intimate subsystem with one or more of his daughters. A family treatment perspective in this case might involve clarifying and strengthening the boundaries of the marital subsystem. Boundaries also need to be clearly delineated between the parental system and the children's subsystem.

Family Norms

Family norms are the rules that specify what is considered proper behavior within the family group. Janzen and Harris (1997) define family rules as "relationship agreements which influence family behavior" (p. 26). Many times, the most powerful rules are those that are not clearly and verbally stated. Rather, these are implicit rules or repeated family transactions that all family members understand but never discuss (e.g., see Highlight 10.2). Establishing norms that allow both the entire family and each individual member to function effectively and productively is important for families (see Highlight 10.3).

In families with problems, however, the family rules usually do not allow the family or the individual members to function effectively and productively. Ineffective norms need to be identified and changed. Positive, beneficial norms need to be developed and fostered.

The following is an example of a family in which there was an implicit, invalid, and ineffective norm functioning. The norm was that no one in the family would smoke cigarettes. A husband, wife, four children, and two sets of grandparents composed

HIGHLIGHT 10.3

Family Norms Vary Drastically from One Family to Another

Every family differs in its individual set of norms or rules. For example, Family A has a relatively conservative set of norms governing communication and interpersonal behavior. Although the norms allow frequent pleasant talk among family members, it is generally on a superficial level. The steaming hot summer weather or the status of the new variety of worms invading the cherry tree is fair game for conversation. However, nothing more personal is ever mentioned. Taboo subjects include anything to do with feelings, interpersonal relationships, or opinions about career or jobs, let alone politics or moral issues. On one occasion, for example, a daughter-in-law asked the family matriarch what her son and other daughter-in-law would name their soon-to-be-born first baby. With a shocked expression on her face, the matriarch replied, "Oh, my heavens, I haven't asked. I don't want to interfere."

Family B, on the other hand, has a vastly different set of norms governing communication and behavior. Virtually everything is discussed and debated, not only among the nuclear family members but among several generations. Personal methods of birth control, stances on abortion, opinions on capital punishment, and politics number among the emotionally heated issues discussed. Family members frequently talk about their personal relationships, including who is the favorite grandchild and who tends to fight all the time with rich old Aunt Harriet. The family is so open that price tags are left on Christmas gifts so each member knows what the other has spent.

The rules of behavior that govern Family B are very different from those of Family A. Yet, in each family, all the members consider their family's behavior to be normal and are comfortable with these rules. Members of each family may find it inconceivable that families could be any other way.

---

this family. Although never discussed, the understanding was that no one had ever or would ever smoke. One day the husband found several cigarette butts in the ashtray of the car typically used by his wife. Because no one in the family smoked, he deduced that these butts must belong to someone else. He assumed that his wife was having an affair with another man, which devastated him. However, he said nothing about it and suffered in silence. His relationship with his wife began to deteriorate. He became sullen, and spats and conflicts became more frequent. Finally, in a heated conflict, he spit out his thoughts and feelings about the cigarette butts and her alleged affair. His wife expressed shocked disbelief. The reality was that it was she who smoked the cigarettes, but only when no one else was around. Her major time to be alone was when she was driving to and from work. She took advantage of this time to smoke but occasionally forgot to empty the ashtray. She told him the entire story, and he was tremendously relieved. Their relationship improved and prospered.

This example illustrates how an inappropriate norm almost ruined a family relationship. Of course, there were other dynamics going on between the spouses involved. Relationships are complicated

entities. However, such a simple thing as the wife being a "closet smoker" had the potential to tip the balance and destroy the marriage. In this instance, a simple correction in communication solved the problem. The interesting thing is that eventually the entire family learned of this incident. The wife still smokes but still insists on doing it privately. The family now functions effectively with an amended family rule that accepts but never mentions her smoking.

Human services professionals need to identify and understand family norms so that inappropriate, ineffective norms can be changed. At any point, a human services professional can point out such an ineffective norm to family members, help them clarify alternative solutions and changes, and assist them in determining which solution is best to pursue.

Family Roles

Family roles are "individually prescribed patterns of behavior reinforced by the expectations and norms of the family" (Worden, 1994, p. 12). In families, these roles usually involve behaviors that work for the benefit of the family. For instance, the parental role prescribes behaviors helpful in supporting, directing, and raising children. Likewise, a parent might assume a "worker" role to earn financial sustenance for the family by being employed outside of the home. Children, on the other hand, might assume the roles of "student" in school and "helper" in household tasks (Holman, 1983, p. 29).

In addition to these more formal socially acceptable roles, family members may hold a variety of more informal roles, often related to individual personalities and interactional patterns among family members. For instance, such roles may include troublemaker, the oppressed one, the illustrious star, the one to blame for everything (scapegoat), Mr./Ms. Perfection, the old battle-ax, or the family's black sheep.

There is a broad range of roles that can be assumed in families. One family comes to mind that has a "white sheep" within its flock. The nuclear family consists of two parents and three children, two females and one male, the latter of whom is also the youngest, although all the family members are adults. The family is not "bad," really—all members except for the youngest male like to drink, party, and do their share of swearing. None are involved in any organized religion. The youngest male, on the other hand, is a fundamentalist pastor. Hence, he has become the "white sheep" of the family.

Because each person and each family are unique, there is no ideal formula for what roles are best. Each family must be evaluated on how its unique configuration of roles functions to the family's advantage or disadvantage on the whole.

Holman (1983) stresses that "the worker must examine how roles are performed and whether or not they meet the needs of the family" (p. 30); he proposes a series of questions to explore:

- What specific roles does each family member occupy?
- Do the various roles played work well together for the family's benefit?
- Are any of the roles ambiguous, redundant, or left empty?
- Is there flexibility among family roles so that the family is better able to adjust to crisis situations?
- Do the family's roles conform with basic social norms (e.g., society does not condone a criminal role)?
- Do the family's roles function to enhance the family's feelings of self worth and well-being or detract from these feelings? (p. 30)

Chapter 7 explained the chief enabler role and various norms commonly portrayed in families with alcoholics. These families are dysfunctional in that massive amounts of energy are wasted in trying to survive with a drug-abusing person in the family's midst.

Balance of Power within the Family System

Power is "the capacity of one [family] member to induce change in the behavior of another family member" (Hepworth et al., 1997, p. 295). Power is a vague concept that is difficult to specify clearly. It is usually related to holding a higher rank, having more prestige, being more respected, and having greater access to and control over resources than others in the system, in this case, the family system.

Power is relative. That is, one individual has more or less power than other individuals. It is irrelevant to one individual shipwrecked alone on a desert island.

Power is also complex and difficult to quantify (Hepworth et al., 1997). That is, different family members have more or less power over different matters. For instance, one parent who manages the checkbook and pays all the bills may have more influence over finances than the other parent. On the other hand, the other parent may have more control over family activities, such as what the family does from weekend to weekend. Influence varies depending on the issue.

Children, too, have power to various degrees. They can exert control over the behavior of parents and siblings. Take a 5-year-old boy who throws himself on the floor screaming whenever his single-parent mother takes him along to a supermarket. The child has power to the extent that he can force his mother to either leave the place or at least cut her shopping short.

Take another example: Christianne and Mortimer are a married couple. Christianne is very outgoing, assertive, and independent, while Mortimer is generally quiet, introspective, and not very socially oriented. Christianne will make virtually all of their social plans with little or no input from Mortimer. Although Mortimer goes along with most of Christianne's ideas, he has definite veto power. If he does not want to participate in a social activity, he simply says so. The activity is then either not planned at all or postponed. Hence, there is a balance of power in their relationship, at least concerning this particular issue.

Christianne and Mortimer also illustrate how power relationships are often hidden or concealed. External appearances do not always accurately represent the reality of the balance of power. Although Christianne outwardly appears to lead social activities in the relationship, she does so only with Mortimer's consent.

In assessing a family, the important question is whether or not the balance of power as perceived by each individual is adequate and fair. Situations where family members resent the balance of power may be ripe for planned change intervention. Take, for instance, an adolescent who feels hopelessly repressed and unable to express openly any opinions of her own. Or, consider one spouse who feels totally impotent and oppressed by the other spouse. Finally, consider a parent, either married or single, who feels he has no control over the children's behavior. Each of these families needs help.

Assessing Intergenerational Aspects of Family Systems

Another important aspect of family structure is historical. What is the family's history? Under what conditions were the parents or the single parent in a family brought up? How did the parents' and the grandparents' early environments affect each generation's behavior and way of life? Has there been a history of alcoholism in the family? Or has corporal punishment to the point of child abuse been considered a family norm?

Assessing Life-Cycle Adjustments

In addition to family communication and structure, assessing life-cycle adjustments can give clear insights into a family's problems. As families mature and progress through time, they must successfully complete tasks appropriate to that stage of their development. Problems surface when these tasks cannot be completed.

Several decades ago, the family life cycle and the types of experiences family members had during specified phases of the cycle were much more predictable than today. This predictability is no longer the case. There is no "typical" cycle. Carter and McGoldrick (1999b), emphasizing the difficulties in describing a normal family life cycle, explain:

Within the past few decades, the changes in family life cycle patterns have escalated dramatically, owing especially to the lower birth rate; the longer life expectancy; the changing role of women; very high divorce and remarriage rates; the rise of unmarried motherhood, unmarried couples, and single-parent adoptions; the increased visibility of gay and lesbian couples and families; and the increase in two-paycheck marriages to the point where they are the American norm. (p. 8)

The traditional family life cycle was conceptualized as having six major phases (Carter & McGoldrick, 1980). Each phase focused on some emotional transition in terms of intimate relationships with other people and on changes of personal status.

Traditionally, the first stage involved an unattached young adult separating from his or her family of origin. During this phase, the young adult established a personal identity and developed new interpersonal relationships. Stage two concerned marrying and realigning life's joys and responsibilities within a couple's framework. Stage three entailed having children and meeting the children's needs. Stage four concerned dealing with adolescent children, whose needs and strivings for independence called for very different types of interaction than that appropriate for younger children. Stage four also often marked refocusing the couple's relationship and addressing the needs of their own aging parents. Stage five involved sending children forth into their own new relationships, addressing midlife career issues, and coping with the growing disabilities of their own parents. Finally, stage six entailed adjustments to aging themselves and addressing the inevitability of one's own death.

Today, Carter and McGoldrick (1999a) propose that "no single list of stages [for a typical family life cycle] is sufficient or inclusive" (p. xv). The complications, unpredictability, and vast range of different cultural and interpersonal contexts cause family life cycles to vary immensely. Many people no longer choose to marry or have children. Many others choose to delay doing so until much later in life. Divorce and remarriage are widespread, causing massive restructuring in family life. Additionally, "vast differences in family life cycle patterns are caused by oppressive social forces: racism, sexism, homophobia, classism, ageism, and cultural prejudices of all kinds" (1999a, p. xv).

Poverty can pose immense consequences upon the life cycle of families. Kliman and Madsen (1999) explain how socioeconomic class can determine what opportunities and resources are available to family members and how these, in turn, affect a family's ability to weather crises:

Economic privilege buffers families physically and psychologically against the stressful effects of death, divorce, illness, disability, and trauma. Divorce deprives a realtor and her children of vacations and private college; it leaves their daycare provider's family without heat, pushing the oldest child out of school and into a dead-end job. . . . An elderly widow with a paid-off house and investments can afford home health care; her children and grandchildren need not organize themselves around her care. In contrast, a family sharing a grandmother's subsidized housing becomes homeless on her death, and the mother, who had already lost many work days because of the grandmother's illness, may be fired while apartment hunting. Homelessness makes regular school attendance impossible for the children, derailing their hopes for finishing school. (p. 93)

In other words, social class standing in the context of a family's surrounding community has huge implications regarding development of self-esteem and the ability to function effectively. It affects dreams of future accomplishments, basic opportunities, and what family members can realistically accomplish in the future.

Culture also affects the life cycle of families at every stage (Hines et al., 1999). They explain how families radically differ regarding the emphasis placed on various life transitions, depending on their cultural background:

[T]he Irish have always placed great emphasis on the wake, viewing death as the most important life cycle transition, which frees human beings from the suffering of this world and takes them . . . to a happier afterlife. African Americans, perhaps, as a result of similar life experiences with suffering, have also emphasized funerals. Both groups go to considerable expense and have traditionally delayed services until all family members can get there. Italian and Polish families have placed the greatest emphasis on weddings, often going to enormous expense . . . [celebrating and] feasting for lengthy periods of time, reflecting the importance these groups place on continuation of the family into the next generation. Jewish families [stress the importance of] the bar mitzvah and bat mitzvah, a transition to adulthood for boys and girls, respectively, reflecting the value placed on intellectual development, a transition that most other Western groups do not mark at all. (p. 70)

Carter and McGoldrick (1999a,b) stress the need to focus both on the individualized life transitions of clients and their dynamic interactions with the social systems enveloping them. Generalist practitioners are often called upon to help families when they are under their greatest stress. Being alert to the broad range of life's transitions and sensitive to families' needs as they progress through these phases can provide workers with significant clues for effective interventions.

Impacts of the Impinging Social Environment

The social environment involves the conditions, circumstances, and human interactions that encompass human beings. A family-in-environment focus provides an important perspective for understanding how families interact with the many other systems surrounding them in the social environment. These systems may include other individuals, friends, families, work groups, social service organizations, political units, religious organizations, and educational systems. All affect how family systems and individual subsystems within the family can effectively go about their daily operations and lives. The other point to remember is that what happens to any individual family member ultimately affects the entire family system (Thorman, 1982). Thus, macro systems have an impact on entire families by affecting individual members.

The following is an example of how macro systems influence family systems. The family consists of two parents and three children aged 9, 13, and 16. Both parents work in a small sausage-processing plant in a rural community of about 12,000 people. Due to deteriorating external economic conditions, the plant is forced to close. Both parents are laid off. Although the parents desperately seek alternative employment, none is available. Unemployment in the community skyrockets. Competition for jobs is intense.

The family's involvement with the many other systems in the environment continues. The family's lack of resources stresses their ability to pay the bills. They get pressure from their landlord and the utility companies. Under such heavy stress, the parents begin to fight. Their children subsequently react to the stress, their parents' fighting, and their newly imposed poverty by starting to rebel. Their work in school suffers, and truancy becomes an increasing problem. The school then contacts the parents about these escalating problems, which, in turn, add to the parents' stress. The parents' coping abilities are gradually eaten away.

This is just one of the multitude of examples that portray how family systems are integrally involved with the other systems in their environment. Families are not isolated units. Each member of a family system must constantly respond to surrounding environmental conditions.

Assessing a Family's Access to Resources

The previous example reflects the serious impact macro systems can have on families. Often, the systems involve the family's access to adequate resources. Limited resources can have a wide range of serious effects on a family's ability to function. Therefore, generalist practitioners must be acutely aware of any family's resource status.

There are numerous ways of examining how readily a particular family can obtain necessary, available resources. Vosler (1990) has developed the Family Access to Basic Resources (FABR) format, illustrated in Figure 10.1, which provides an excellent means of accomplishing this. Vosler explains:

The . . . FABR assessment tool can enable professionals, families, and individual family members to determine the extent of stress and stress pileup caused by

Figure 10.1 *Family Access to Basic Resources (FABR)*

Part 1–Monthly Expenses for a Family of This Size and Composition

Work Expenses		Health Care	
Transportation	$_____	Medical	$_____
Child Care	$_____	Dental	$_____
Taxes	$_____	Mental Health	$_____
Purchases for Basic Needs		Special Education (e.g., substance abuse)	$_____
Decent Housing	$_____	Family and Developmental (counseling) Services	$_____
Utilities	$_____		
Food	$_____	Procurement of Resources/Services (e.g., transportation)	$_____
Clothing	$_____		
Personal Care	$_____	Monthly Total:	$_____

Part 2: Potential Monthly Family Resources

			Yes	No
Money Income				
Wages (If parents' occupations are known, what are average monthly wages for these types of jobs?)	$_____	Clothing: Access to Used Clothing Store	_____	_____
		Personal Care and Recreation Access to Free Recreational Activities	_____	_____
Child Support (if applicable)	$_____	Health Care		
Income Transfers (for those unemployed or not expected to work)		Medicare?	_____	_____
		Medicaid?	_____	_____
Unemployment Insurance	$_____	Health Clinic?	_____	_____
Workmen's Compensation	$_____	Dental Clinic?	_____	_____
Social Security	$_____	Mental Health Services?	_____	_____
Supplemental Security Income	$_____	Special Services (e.g., drug abuse treatment)?	_____	_____
Aid to Families with Dependent Children[a]	$_____	Education		
Other (e.g., general relief, emergency assistance)	$_____	Public Education?	_____	_____
		Special Education?	_____	_____
Credits, Goods, and Services (free or sliding scale)				
Housing				
Section 8	$_____	Tutoring	_____	_____
Other housing Assistance (e.g., public housing, shelter, hotel/motel)	$_____	General Equivalency Diploma (GED)?	_____	_____
		Job Training?	_____	_____
Utilities Assistance	$_____	Family Development (counseling) Services		
Food		Family Services?	_____	_____
Food Stamps	$_____	Support Groups?	_____	_____
Women's, Infants', and Children's Supplementary Food Program (WIC)	$_____	Family Life Education?	_____	_____
		Procurement		
Food Bank, Food Pantry, and Other Food Assistance	$_____	Transportation?	_____	_____
		Monthly Total		$_____

Part 3–Current Resources
A. Access to Resources Last Month
Money Income

Wages (use net pay; then
subtract other work expenses
from Part 1 above, including
child care, transportation, etc.) $_____

Child Support $_____

Income Transfers $_____

Credits, Good, and Services
Housing $_____
Food $_____
Clothing $_____
Personal Care and Recreation $_____
Health Care $_____
Education $_____
Family and Developmental
Services $_____
Procurement $_____
Monthly Total $_____

B. Resource Stability
How stable was each resource over the past year (very stable, somewhat stable, somewhat unstable, very unstable)? Discuss for each type of resource.

Wages: Overall access to wages through employment? Types of jobs available? Part-time or full-time? Wage levels? Benefits? How would/do you deal with child care or supervision of youth? Quality of child care? Do you have choices? How would/do you deal with an ill child? How would/do you get to and from work? What education and training are needed for good jobs? What education and training opportunities are available? Have you been laid off or terminated or experienced a plant closing? Number of times unemployed? Length of time unemployed?

Child Support: How is this received? How was the amount decided? Are checks regular? Are payments up to date? Other problems?

Income Transfers: What experiences have you had in receiving benefits? What kinds of attitudes have you encountered? How adequate are benefits relative to your family's expenses? Has a check been cut? Has a check been delayed? Have you been dropped from benefits for reasons you didn't understand?

Housing: Rent or own? Choice? Maintenance a problem? Are utilities adequate? Have you been put on a waiting list or been dropped from Section 8 or other housing assistance? Have you had to move or been evicted because the landlord converted to higher rents, condominiums, etc.? Have you experienced homelessness?

Food: Quality? Variety? Have your Food Stamps or WIC been cut or delayed? If so, do you understand why? Has other food assistance been cut or changed?

Clothing: Variety for different roles?

Personal Care and Recreation: What kinds of recreation? Individual? Family?

Health Care: High quality? Choice? Available in crisis? Have you been dropped from health care coverage with an employer or from Medicaid? If so, why? Have you or another family member been put on a waiting list, for example, for medical or dental care, for counseling for a mental health problem, or for treatment for alcohol or drug abuse? If so, how long did the person have to wait for services?

Education: High quality? Available for all ages? For special needs? Choice? Have you participated in education or training paid for with loans? If so, how are you managing loan repayments?*

---

a. AFDC was "a public assistance program . . . funded by the federal and state governments to provide financial aid for needy children who are deprived of parental support because of death, incapacitation, or absence" (Barker, 1995, p. 14). The Personal Responsibility Act (PRA) passed by Congress in August 1996 abolished AFDC "which had provided support for poor children and their mothers since its inception as Title IV of the 1935 Social Security Act"; AFDC was replaced by "block grants for Temporary Assistance to Needy Families (TANF)" which "put a cap on federal funds provided to the states" and allowed states greater discretion in benefit distribution (Abramovitz, 1997, pp. 311–312). The purpose of the FABR questionnaire is to determine resources regardless of their source. Therefore, you might replace the AFDC category with other new programs providing benefits to children and families.

Family and Developmental Services: High quality? Choice? Available in crisis? Have you or another family member been put on a waiting list, for example, for family counseling? If so, how long did the person have to wait for services?

Procurement: Bus? Car? What's within walking distance? How reliable is transportation (e.g., bus and/or car)? How close are bus lines to home, work, child care, shopping, etc.?

Source: Nancy R. Vosler (1990). "Assessing Family Access to Basic Resources: An Essential Component of Social Work Practice," *Social Work, 35*(5), 436–437. Copyright © 1990, National Association of Social Workers, Inc. Reprinted with permission from the NASW Press, Silver Springs, MD.

inadequate or unstable basic family resources. . . . The FABR outlines assessment areas for exploration with the family so that both the [practitioner] and the family can begin to understand potential sources of chronic stress from the larger environment. (1990, p. 435)

When using FABR, completing parts 1 and 2 of the instrument before meeting with the family is best for the human services worker. FABR can provide the worker with some insights concerning a family's economic status before beginning work with the family.

Part 1 allows for a general estimation of what an average family (of the client family's size and composition) needs every month to function effectively. Such information can be obtained from a variety of sources. Public agencies may have these figures available as a result of their regular data-collection procedures. Sometimes, census data is helpful. If information is not readily available, "agencies or a local advocacy group could be called upon to develop estimates based on adequate resources needed for a *long-term decent standard of living* for various household sizes and family configurations" (Vosler, 1990, p. 438).

One should be aware that the poverty line established by the U.S. government is an estimate of what a person needs to subsist and is probably significantly lower than what a family actually needs to thrive.

Part 2 of FABR focuses on what resources macro systems in the client family's social environment can potentially provide. What resources are actually available to this family to help them reach the input level they need? What types of local, state, and national assistance can the family potentially use?

Part 3 of FABR can be completed by the family itself during one of the worker's early meetings with the family. This portion identifies what resources the family actually has. Part 3 is divided into the family's "access to resources last month" and its "resource stability." The section on resource stability helps establish whether the resources obtained last month were abnormally high or low and whether or not the last month's input reflects that which is typical for the family.

A family's actual access to resources, then, can be calculated by taking the family's total "access to resources last month" (Part 3A) and subtracting that from the total "monthly expenses for a [typical] family of this size and composition" (Part 1). The remaining amount refers to what the family needs to function but is not getting. Subsequently, Parts 2 and 3B help the worker identify specific problems in the family's access to resources.

Part 2 supplies clues for what resources the family is not getting but potentially could be. What services has the family not been aware of or taken advantage of in the past? How could the worker act as broker to link family members with the services they need?

Part 3B alerts the worker to problems in ongoing acquisition of resources. For instance, one question asks, "Have your Food Stamps[1] or WIC[2] been cut or delayed?" (Vosler, 1990, p. 437). Such questions can help the worker begin identifying problems in service delivery and exploring potential intervention approaches for positive change. What obstacles exist in impinging macro systems that prevent the family

1. "The Food Stamp program, which was created to supplement the food-buying power of low-income people, is the nation's response to its hunger problem. Monthly benefits in the form of coupons used to purchase food are entirely federally financed. . . . Eligibility for the program is restricted to households that meet income, resource, and work requirements prescribed by law" (Wells, 1987, p. 628). Note that the Personal Responsibility and Work Opportunity Reconciliation Act of 1996, which established TANF, also placed significant restrictions on Food Stamp accessibility.
2. WIC is the Special Supplementary Feeding Program for Women, Infants, and Children administered under the Department of Agriculture. The intent is to provide low-income women and their children at risk of insufficient nutrition with food subsidies.

from getting needed resources? What macro systems are potential targets of change?

On one level, FABR indicates what the family needs in order to function adequately. It provides cues for how the worker should proceed. The worker can target where resources are lacking or not being used and establish plans to enhance the family's access to them.

On another level, FABR indicates what resources impinging macro systems are failing to provide. By emphasizing the importance of the family's access to resources, it highlights the significance of the family's interactions with multiple macro systems. FABR thus establishes links among micro, mezzo, and macro levels of practice. FABR can provide documentation regarding where resources are lacking and where changes are needed in macro systems. When families have poor or no access to basic resources, interventions may need to involve "social planning, advocacy, and lobbying within larger social systems, including work at neighborhood, local, state, and national levels" (Vosler, 1990, p. 438).

Difficulties in Soliciting Personal Information

One should note that soliciting such personal information from clients as much of what the FABR addresses may be difficult. People may be proud and feel uncomfortable talking about the public assistance they receive. There are several suggestions for helping them share information.

First, acknowledge the fact that solicitation may be difficult. Be conscious of how you phrase questions and how clients react to these questions. Second, "be a warm, giving, and dependable person" who uses "a liberal dose of self-disclosure to help the client see you as a real and genuine person" (Sheafor et al., 2000, p. 270). The more you can effectively engage clients and form a positive relationship with them, the more comfortable they will feel in answering questions. Third, you might start out with asking less-sensitive questions. Some informal chatting may soften the interviewing process. For example, soliciting information about children's names and their recreational interests might portray your interest and concern about the family's well-being. A fourth suggestion for soliciting difficult information involves being tactful (2000). Avoid criticizing clients or insensitively hurting their feelings.

A fifth suggestion concerns the situation when clients refuse to provide information. Sheafor and colleagues (2000) suggest that you:

. . . follow up with an effort to engage the client in a discussion of general reasons why some topics might be hard for people to discuss and why people often want to withhold and protect certain information. These reasons might include feelings of shame and embarrassment, not knowing what words to use, not knowing how the [worker] will react, not knowing if the worker would understand, fear that the worker might be judgmental, fear of a lack of confidentiality, fear that the information will be used to exploit the client, and so on. (p. 271)

Addressing these issues straightforwardly may enhance clients' trust in you and increase their comfort level in sharing personal information.

Family Conflicts, Problems, and Their Resolutions

Conflict can be defined as "a struggle over . . . resources, power and status, beliefs, and other preferences and desires" (Bisno, 1988, p. 13). Hostility, strife, disharmony, arguments, or disunity all can be involved. Conflicts are destined to occur in any group. As a matter of fact, many times conflicts are positive and desirable. Groups, including family groups, are made up of unique individuals, each with individual opinions and ideas. Conflict can represent the open sharing of these individual ideas. It can serve as a mechanism for improving communication, enhancing the closeness of relationships, and working out dissatisfactions.

Although each family is unique, conflicts and problems can occur in a number of categories (Goldenberg & Goldenberg, 1998; Janzen & Harris, 1997; Thorman, 1982). First, there are relationship problems between primary partners who are, for example, spouses or significant others. Second, there are difficulties existing between parents and children. Third are the personal problems of individual family members. Finally, there are stresses imposed on the family by the external environment.

Family problems do not necessarily fall neatly into one of these categories or another. Frequently, families experience more than one category of problems. Nor are these problem categories mutually exclusive. Many times one problem will be closely related to another. Take, for instance, a woman who is a wife, mother, a legal librarian, and the primary breadwinner for her family. The law firm at which she has worked for the past 11 years suddenly decides to hire a lawyer to replace her. Despite massive efforts, she has not been able to find another job with similar responsibilities and salary. This situation can be considered a family problem caused by stresses in the environment. However, it is also a personal problem for the woman. Her sense of self-worth is seriously diminished as a result of her job loss and inability to find another position. As a result, she becomes cranky, short-tempered, and difficult to live with. The environmental stress she is experiencing causes her to have difficulties relating to both children and spouse. The entire family system becomes disturbed.

We will now examine each of the four problem categories. They include partner difficulties, parent–child relationships, personal problems of individuals, and external environmental stresses. Some intervention directions will be proposed.

Partner Difficulties

Couples may bring many issues to counseling including disagreements about raising children, domestic violence, sexual problems, conflicts over money and recreational time, and unfaithfulness. Communication issues often surface as a primary concern (Hartman, 1995; Worden, 1994).

One frequent purpose in interventions involving couples and larger families is to enhance the congruence between intents and impacts as individuals communicate. A practitioner can help each partner communicate more effectively by giving suggestions about how to rephrase statements using words that reflect more clearly what the speakers really mean. Another suggestion is to encourage feedback, that is, to examine what happens when the receiver shares reactions about a message with the sender. For instance, refer to Highlight 10.4. Instead of responding to Lavidia's demands defensively, Buell might be encouraged to tell her, "I love you very much, Lavidia. I need to keep in shape, and I need some time to myself. How can we work this out?"

Eventually, Buell and Lavidia used a planned change approach to iron out their difficulties. The accuracy of their communication gradually improved through counseling. Each learned how to better communicate personal needs. Instead of their old standoff, they began to identify and evaluate alternatives. Their final solution involved several facets. First, Buell would continue to go to the club to work out three nights each week. However, Fridays would be spent with Lavidia. It turned out that she was exceptionally annoyed at not being

able to go out with Buell on Friday nights. Lavidia, who also was an avid believer in physical fitness, would occasionally go with Buell to the health club to work out. This gave her the sense of freedom to join him when she chose to. The important thing was that she no longer felt restricted. In reality, she rarely went with him to the club. Lavidia also chose to take some postgraduate courses in her field on those evenings when Buell visited the club. She enjoyed such activities, and they enhanced her sense of professional competence. The personal issues of Buell's need to feel free and Lavidia's lack of self-esteem demanded continued efforts on both spouses' parts. Enhanced communication skills helped them communicate their ongoing needs.

Parent–Child Relationship Difficulties

The second major type of family problems is difficulties in the relationships between parents and children. Sometimes this entails the parents having trouble controlling children. Frequently, especially as children reach adolescence, this involves communication problems.

There are many perspectives on how best to manage children's behavior and improve parent–child communication. Two major approaches include applications of learning theory and Parent Effectiveness Training (PET) developed by Thomas Gordon (1970).

Practitioners can help parents improve their control of children by assessing the individual family situations and teaching parents some basic behavior modification techniques. Behavior modification involves the application of learning theory principles to real-life situations. For instance, getting into a punishment rut with a misbehaving child is easy for parents. Take Freddie, age 4, who spills the contents of drawers and cabinets in the kitchen area whenever he is unobserved. His parents have seen enough flour, honey, silverware, and plastic bags in heaps on the floor to last them several lifetimes. In their frustration, they typically respond by swatting Freddie on the rump. He then cries a little bit until the next time he has the opportunity to be in the kitchen alone and start all over again.

In family counseling, Freddie's parents were taught several new behavior-management techniques (i.e., behavior modification techniques applied to specific child-management situations). First, they were taught the value of positive reinforcement. These reinforcements are positive experiences or consequences that follow a behavior and increase the likelihood that it

HIGHLIGHT 10.4

An Example of Communication Problems within a Marriage

Buell and Lavidia, both in their mid-30s, have a communication problem. They have been married one year. The marriage occurred after a lengthy dating period that was filled with strife. A primary source of stress was Lavidia's desire for the permanent commitment of marriage and Buell's unwillingness to make such a commitment. In view of Lavidia's threats to leave him, Buell finally decided to get married.

Prior to the marriage, a major source of difficulty concerned the time that Buell and Lavidia spent together. They each owned their own condominiums, so they did not live together. Buell was very involved in a physical-fitness program. He went to work out at a health club four nights each week, including Fridays. Buell also had numerous close friends at the club with whom he enjoyed spending his time. Lavidia was infuriated that Buell restricted the time he spent with her to only some of the days when he didn't work out at the club. Her major concern, however, remained Buell's inability to make a commitment. Lavidia felt that things would change once they got married.

After marriage, things did not change much. Although Lavidia and Buell now lived together, he still worked out at the club with his friends four nights a week. This schedule continued to infuriate Lavidia.

In a discussion, the spouses expressed their feelings. Lavidia said, "I hate all the time Buell spends at the club. I resent having him designate the time he thinks he can spend with me. I feel like he's putting my time into little boxes."

Buell responded, "My physical health is very important to me. I love to work out at the club. What should I do—stay home every night watching television and become a couch potato?"

One way of assessing this couple's communication is evaluating the *intent* (what the speaker wants to have communicated to the receiver) and the actual *impact* of the communication, that is, what the listener actually hears (Gottman et al., 1976). Many times, the intent and impact of communication are different. A therapeutic goal is to improve the accuracy of communication, that is, the extent to which the intent of the speaker and the impact upon the listener resemble each other.

There were other difficulties within Buell and Lavidia's relationship that are too lengthy to describe. Here we will limit our discussion to some of the issues involved in the simple communication addressed earlier. In a recent discussion, the following scenario developed. Lavidia verbally stated that she hated seeing Buell go to the health club so often. The impact on Buell was that he felt Lavidia was trying to control him and tell him what to do. He loved Lavidia but was also very wary of losing his independence and what he viewed as his identity. When Lavidia placed demands on him, he became even more protective of his time.

Lavidia's intent in her communication was different than her impact; she felt that he thought the club and his friends were more important than she was. These feelings were related to her basic lack of self-esteem and self-confidence.

Buell's response to Lavidia's statement also had serious discrepancies between its intent and impact. Buell was verbally stating that he loved to work out. The impact on Lavidia, that is, what she heard Buell say, was that he liked the club and his friends more than he liked her. Buell's actual intent was to tell Lavidia his physical health and appearance were very important to him. He also wanted to communicate to her that his sense of independence was important to him. He loved her and wanted to be committed to her, yet his long-term fear of commitment was related to his actual fear that he would lose his identity in someone else's. He was afraid of losing his right to make choices and decisions and being told what to do.

---

will recur. Instead of relying solely on punishment (i.e., rump swatting), the parents were taught to react more positively to Freddie during those times when he was behaving well (i.e., playing appropriately and not emptying drawers). By closely examining Freddie's behaviors and the circumstances surround-ing him, his parents gradually learned to view Freddie in a different way. They learned that he felt he was not getting enough attention in general. In order to get the attention he needed, he resorted to the destructive drawer-emptying behavior. Providing Freddie with structured positive playing times when they gave Freddie their sole attention was much more effective. This technique, in addition to making positive comments about his good behavior, helped to diminish Freddie's need for getting attention in inappropriate ways. Freddie's parents also learned that their punishment was having the opposite effect of what they had intended. That is, instead of stopping his bad behavior, they were unwittingly encouraging it. Punishing Freddie was actually a form of positive reinforcement because it gave him the attention he wanted. Thus, he continued his drawer-emptying behavior.

As an alternative to punishment, Freddie's parents were taught the time-out technique. Time-out involves a procedure where reinforcement is withdrawn resulting in a decrease in the occurrence of the behavior. Instead of swatting Freddie when he emptied drawers, his parents were directed to place him in a corner with his eyes to the wall for five minutes. A few minutes should be the maximum duration of a time-out, as it loses its effectiveness after a very short length of time (Kazdin, 2001; White, Nielsen, & Johnson, 1972). It was also important to administer the time-out to Freddie immediately after his inappropriate behavior occurred. This quick response was necessary for him to relate the time-out directly to his misbehavior. Time-outs provided Freddie's parents with a method to deprive Freddie of attention without hurting him. Because attention was what Freddie really wanted, this became a very effective behavioral control technique. It should be emphasized, however, that Freddie needed continued attention and positive reinforcement for appropriate behavior. He would not have misbehaved in the first place had he not been trying to let his parents know about an important need, namely, his desire for attention.

Parent Effectiveness Training (PET) is a second method frequently used when parent–child relationship problems occur. Two principles involved in this approach include active listening and the sending of "I-messages" (Gordon, 1975; Sheafor et al., 2000; Westra, 1996). Active listening resembles the intent–impact communication approach described earlier when discussing couples' communication. It involves two basic steps. First, the receiver of the message tries earnestly to understand the sender's feelings and messages. Another way of explaining this process is that the receiver tries to understand the actual intent of the sender. In the second step, the receiver puts this "understanding into [his/her] own words . . . and feeds it back for the sender's verification" (Gordon, 1975, p. 53).

For instance, 13-year-old Tyrone says to his mother, "Dances are boring. I'm not going to that boring old dance on Friday."

His mother works hard at active listening and tries to see the situation from Tyrone's perspective. She replies, "You mean you'd really like to go but you don't think you can dance very well."

Tyron responds, "Yep." His mother had accurately heard his real concerns.

A second technique involved in PET is the use of "I-messages." Such messages do not blame or threaten but rather tell the receiver how his or her behavior is affecting the sender. The speaker leaves responsibility for changing the behavior squarely on the receiver. I-messages should be used to convey both positive and negative feelings and allow the receiver to get to know the sender.

For instance, a mother is trying to teach her 16-year-old daughter how to drive. The daughter gets on the freeway for the first time and pushes the gas pedal to the floor. The speedometer zooms to 85 miles per hour. The mother could choose to say, "You're driving way too fast! Do you want to kill us both?" This is a blaming, threatening statement. Instead, she chooses to say, "I'm really scared driving so fast." In other words, the mother takes responsibility for her own feelings without placing blame on the receiver of her statement.

Personal Problems of Individual Family Members

Sometimes, a family will come to a practitioner for help and identify one family member as being the problem. A basic principle of family therapy is that the entire family owns the problem (Goldenberg & Goldenberg, 1998; Street, 1994; Worden, 1994). In other words, sometimes one family member becomes the scapegoat for malfunctioning within the entire family system. The practitioner is then responsible for helping the family define the problem as a family group rather than an individual problem. Treatment goals are then most likely to involve the restructuring of various family relationships.

For instance, a family of five came in for treatment. The family consisted of a 48-year-old husband and father, a 45-year-old wife and mother, and three children: Rob, 19; Ralph, 16; and Julie, 13. The family came from a rural Wisconsin town of 8000 people. The father was a successful businessman who was involved in town politics. The mother was a homemaker who did not work outside of the home. Rob was a freshman at the University of Wisconsin at Madison. The identified problem was Ralph. For the past year, Ralph had been stealing neighbors' cars whenever he had the chance and running down people's mailboxes. To say the least, this activity became annoying to the local townspeople. The family came to counseling as their last resort to try controlling the problem.

After several sessions of family members pointing blaming fingers at Ralph, Julie quietly commented to her parents "Well, you never say anything about *his* problem," and proceeded to point at Rob. Suddenly, as if a floodgate had been opened, the entire family situation came pouring out. Julie had been referring to her parents' difficulties in accepting Rob's recent announcement that he was gay. Rob was going through a difficult period as he was "coming out," in terms of making lifestyle decisions and relating to old friends and family members. Father was terrified that the local townspeople, who had extremely negative and irrational fears of gay people (homophobia), would find out. Father feared that he would lose precious social status and that it would damage his political career. Mother turned out to be a serious alcoholic, a secret that the entire family had worked hard to keep. Mother and Father had not had a sexual relationship for 10 years; they slept in separate bedrooms. Father was a harsh, stern man who felt it necessary to maintain what he considered absolute control over family members, including Mother. He was very critical of them all and never risked sharing his own feelings. Finally, Julie was having serious problems both with her grades and attendance in school. She was also sexually active with a variety of young men. Both she and her parents lived in constant fear of her potential pregnancy.

As it turned out, Ralph was one of the better-adjusted individuals in the family. He attended school regularly, got straight B's, and was active in high school sports (before being suspended for his car-stealing, mailbox-crushing behavior). This family provides a good illustration of a family-owned problem. The entire family system was showing disturbances. Ralph was the scapegoat, the identified problem. All Ralph was doing was calling attention to the family's many more global problems.

External Environmental Stresses: The Impact of Social and Economic Forces

The fourth category of problems frequently found in families includes those caused by factors outside of the family in the external environment. These problems can include inadequate income, unemployment, poor housing conditions, poor access to means of transportation and places for recreation, and inadequate job opportunities (Johnson & Wahl, 1995). Included in the multitude of other potential problems are poor health conditions, inadequate schools, and dangerous neighborhoods.

To begin addressing these problems, practitioners need sharp brokering skills. That is, they need to know what services are available and how to make a connection with families in need of these services.

Many times appropriate services will be unavailable or nonexistent. Practitioners will need to advocate for clients. That is, they will need to plead actively the cause of their clients, often far beyond what is minimally required (Helton & Jackson, 1997). Sometimes, services will need to be developed. Other times, unresponsive agency administrations will need to be confronted. Legal assistance may be necessary. There are no easy solutions to solving nationwide problems for families such as poverty or poor health care. This is a constant, ongoing process. Political involvement will be necessary. Many external environmental stresses are difficult to change and diminish. However, such environmental stresses pose serious problems for families that practitioners will not be able to ignore.

 ## Variations in Family Structures

Changing values, issues, economic support, and technology have had an awesome impact on family life over the past few decades. Generalist practitioners cannot assume that the families on their caseloads will consist primarily of intact, two-parent families with two to four relatively well-adjusted, blood-related siblings. Practitioners today will address a wide variety of family structures and issues. Thus, being aware of the broad range of dynamics that can operate within these various structures is important. Here, we will consider two of these variations, namely single-parent families and stepfamilies.

Single-Parent Families

The traditional family configuration (two parents, one a mother who remains in the home to provide full-time care) is becoming less and less common, demonstrated by the following facts:

- Twenty-nine percent of U.S. families with dependent children are supported by single parents (Renzetti & Curran, 1999).

- A great majority (86 percent) of single parents are women (Renzetti & Curran, 1999).
- Almost 60 percent of all women over age 16 work outside of the home (Renzetti & Curran, 1999). One-half of mothers with infants under one year old are employed outside of the home (Sapiro, 1999).
- Although 74 percent of white families with children under age 18 have both parents living within the home, only about 36 percent of African American families and 64 percent of Hispanic families have both parents living there (U.S. Department of Commerce, 1998).
- While the overall poverty rate for all families is almost 11 percent, the rate for married-couple families is almost 6 percent and that for female-headed families is over 33 percent (Stout & McPhail, 1998).
- Women earn less than 75 percent of what men earn (Rotella, 1998).
- Poverty rates are significantly worse for families headed by women of color (Stout & McPhail, 1998).
- Female-headed families of color are worse off than they were 20 years ago, in that their adjusted median incomes fell while those of married couples increased (Strand, 1995).
- The economic status of U.S. single mothers is lower than that in most other Western industrialized countries (Strand, 1995).

These statistics have at least two clear-cut implications for generalist human services professionals. First, human services professionals must be flexible regarding what is considered a "typical" or "normal" family. Second, poverty and lack of resources are characterizing a growing number of American women and children.

As in two-parent families, such issues as effective communication among family members and satisfactory child management are vitally important. Likewise, a focus on the family's relationships with other systems in the environment is important. However, two aspects should be highlighted for single-parent families. First, there are often greater pressures brought to bear on a single parent to assume virtually all of the parental responsibilities by him- or (more frequently) herself. Chapter 4, which addressed gender-sensitive human services practice, discussed some of the special issues women face.

The second aspect to emphasize in single-parent families is their even greater likelihood of impoverishment. At one level, linking families with needed resources is critically important. Chapter 15, on brokering, addresses this in greater depth. On another level, advocacy on the behalf of children and their families is often called for. Chapter 14 describes this likeliness of impoverishment further.

Single Teenage Parents

A group of single parents deserving special attention is that of single teens. The pregnancy rate for teens in the United States is significantly higher than those in other industrialized nations; additionally, "teen births are especially heavily concentrated among the poor and among African-American and Hispanic-American mothers" (Renzetti & Curran, 1999, p. 37). Teen parenthood can place momentous responsibility on people who are children or almost children themselves. The increase in teen parenthood is attributed to a variety of factors including increased sexual activity among young people, failure to use contraception, and failed contraception.

Lott (1994) comments on young women's motivation for pregnancy:

> . . . teenagers may see having a baby as a route to adulthood. Related to this is the hopelessness widespread in poor ghetto communities in which young people have little expectation of getting a good job and feel isolated from the larger culture. . . . A baby can make an adolescent girl feel like an adult and a caregiver, someone of significance and importance in the life of another, and a person from whom competence is expected. . . . Teenage pregnancy is linked to limited opportunities and a bleak future. (p. 87)

Chilman, Nunnally, and Cox (1988) caution that we should not blame teen parenthood as "the main cause of early school leaving, youth unemployment, poverty, and welfare dependency" (p. 38). Rather, they continue to say that the real causes of these problems lie in our social structure fraught with "institutional racism" and its serious unemployment problem "especially among minority youth" (1988, p. 38).

Weatherley and Cartoof (1988) propose a series of suggestions for working with single adolescent parents; they focus on "a continuum of services thought to be appropriate at various stages of adolescent pregnancy and parenthood" (p. 39). These include the following.

Preventing Pregnancy.   Primary pregnancy prevention refers to preventing the problem altogether, assuming that the pregnancy is a problem. To attempt prevention, adolescents need both information and ready access to contraception so that they can make responsible decisions. Research indicates that sound sex education programs can delay first intercourse, reduce the frequency of intercourse, decrease the number of partners, and increase condom use (Hyde & DeLamater, 2000). In effect, such programs "make students less permissive about premarital sex than students who do not take these courses" (Caroll & Wolpe, 1996, p. 641). Effective sex education programs "focus on reducing risk-taking behavior," "are based on theories of social learning," "teach through experiential activities that personalize the messages," "address media and other social influences that encourage sexual risk-taking behaviors," "reinforce clear and appropriate values," and "enhance communication skills" (Hyde & DeLamater, 2000, p. 626).

Access to methods of birth control also seems to be important. Components that appear to increase adolescents' use of clinics include "free services, an absence of parental notification, convenient hours for students, walk-in service, a diversity of locations, and warm and caring staff" (Weatherley & Cartoof, 1988, p. 39).

Promotion of chastity has been proposed as a means of pregnancy prevention. However, research has not established that this approach works (Hyde & DeLamater, 2000; Weatherley & Cartoof, 1988). "Just say no" is easy to say but hard to do. Several pictures come to mind. One possible scenario involves just saying no to a hot fudge sundae if you absolutely adore hot fudge but are desperately trying to stay on your liquid-protein diet. Another is just saying no to a friend offering you a cigarette when you are out at a bar where everyone in the world seems to be smoking and you just quit this morning. One final scene involves one of those hot, passionate, decision-making moments when you are madly in love and you are simply certain it will last forever (again). Just saying no is not always so easy.

Help during Pregnancy. Providing support during pregnancy can be important. Becoming depressed and isolated during that time is easy. Physical changes may have impacts, especially in view of the great emphasis placed on physical appearance, attractiveness, and popularity during adolescence. One junior high teacher once said that talking about the responsibility of pregnancy and teen parenthood had absolutely no effect on her students. However, the young women sat up with serious faces and widened eyes when told that once you

have a baby, you often have stretch marks on your abdomen for the rest of your life. To these young women, stretch marks were serious consequences.

Pregnant adolescents may need help relating to friends and family members, which involves maintaining good communication with and emotional support from others around them. Many times a human service professional may need to do active outreach to the pregnant teen. Home visits may be especially useful. Counseling can be provided either individually or in a group.

Pregnant teens most often need counseling about good nutrition and the impacts of lifestyle upon the fetus. For instance, they need to be well-informed about the results of alcohol and drug use during pregnancy. Teens also may need help in determining what to do about the pregnancy and other future plans involving living conditions, day care, education, and employment.

Helping Adolescent Fathers.   Not forgetting that babies born to adolescent mothers also have fathers is important. Despite myths to the contrary, most teen fathers are significantly affected by their child's birth and are involved to various degrees in the child's early life (Carroll & Wolpe, 1996; Strong, DeVault, & Sayad, 1999; Weatherley & Cartoof, 1988).

An adolescent father may need help in expressing his feelings, defining his role, and contributing where he can in taking over responsibilities for his child. Many adolescent fathers have psychological repercussions as a result of the pregnancy (Carroll & Wolpe, 1996; Elster & Panzarine, 1983; Strong et al., 1999). Because of their tendency to do less well educationally and economically (Bolton & MacEachron, 1988; Carroll & Wolpe, 1996), they may need help and encouragement in pursuing educational and vocational goals.

Helping Mothers after the Pregnancy.   Keeping the continuum of service in mind is important. This mother's needs do not suddenly stop after the baby is born. The case is not automatically closed. Weatherley and Cartoof (1988) cite three major areas where adolescent mothers may need ongoing help:

1. They may need help in learning about positive parenting and child-management skills. Several aspects have been found to enhance this training. For one thing, training should be "flexible, informal, and individualized" (Weatherley & Cartoof, 1988, p. 49). For another thing, training is more helpful when provided after the

baby is born rather than during the pregnancy (McGee, 1982). Finally, all involved family members and caregivers, including the child's father, should participate in the training (Furstenburg & Crawford, 1978).

2. Adolescent mothers often need help in avoiding more pregnancies. Pregnancy is no guarantee that they have an adequate knowledge of decreasing chances of conception or of birth-control methodology. Both information and ready access to contraception are necessary.

3. Young mothers often need assistance in their future life planning. Issues include continuing their education, gaining employment, finding day care for their child, and determining where and how they will live.

Assessment and Personal Values

A few comments about personal values are warranted here. Clarifying their own personal values and prohibiting these values from interfering with assessment and other aspects of practice is critically important for workers (Loewenberg et al., 2000). Reamer (1995a) reflects that workers' "personal values influence their views of clients, intervention frameworks and strategies, and definitions of successful and unsuccessful outcomes," in addition to workers' responses to clients (pp. 894–895).

Working with pregnant adolescents provides a useful example of how personal values may be in direct conflict with clients' values. Strong opinions are involved. You may personally feel that a 13-year-old female is unable to care adequately for an infant. You may think that for this 13-year-old's mother to assume primary responsibility for the infant's care is unfair. You may strongly favor or reject the concept of abortion. Regardless of your personal values regarding an individual case, helping a client assess all available alternatives is still important for you. Only she can evaluate which course is best for her. Chapter 2 discussed values and ethics in much greater depth.

Remarriage and Stepfamilies

A stepfamily is "a primary kinship group whose members are joined as a result of second or subsequent marriages" (Barker, 1999, p. 465). Visher and Visher (1988) stress that stepfamilies differ from intact nuclear families in that they are more likely to experience certain problems. Because of the increased prevalence of such blended or reconstituted families, being aware of their special issues and needs is important for generalist practitioners. For one thing, loyalty conflicts may arise (Sager et al., 1983). Which parent of the divorced or separated couple should the children be loyal to? How does a newly married stepparent fit into the family's scheme of things? Should a remarried parent devote more attention to his or her new spouse or to children from the prior marriage?

Defense of territoriality is often another major issue in blended families. How is power and authority reestablished and changed when new parts of family systems are melded together? Many questions arise in newly blended families. Will the stepchildren resent the new stepmother assuming the same parental authority as their biological father and, for that matter, their biological mother? How will the new spouse get along with the stepchildren's other biological parent? Because of old interactional patterns, how difficult will it be for a new stepparent to adjust to all the firmly established interactional patterns of the old family system? How will stepchildren adjust to new stepparental rule?

Visher and Visher (1988) propose that "the basic struggle for a stepfamily is the search for its identity as a family unit" (p. 224); they go on to identify at least seven aspects characterizing stepfamilies. Each merits the worker's attention when working with such families.

The first area needing attention is that of "change" on the one hand, and "loss" on the other (Visher & Visher, 1988, p. 225). Members of stepfamilies are subject to massive changes. Place of residence may change. Schools may change. Daily family procedures may be altered. When and what the family eats may be modified by the new stepparent's wishes. Children may have to modify their bedroom sleeping arrangements to incorporate new stepbrothers and sisters. Where the family traditionally spends Thanksgiving, Christmas Eve, Hanukkah, or Easter may change. Members of stepfamilies are forced to make a broad variety of adjustments. These range from major alterations in basic living conditions to minor adjustments in everyday habits.

Additionally, a stepfamily suffers losses (Goldenberg & Goldenberg, 1998). Sometimes it loses regular contact with the absent parent. Other times, it loses friends or possessions. Perhaps the children never see their grandparents on one side of the family anymore.

The point is that attending to the vast array of changes, including losses, that confront stepfamily members is especially important for practitioners. These changes may provide clear clues regarding what direction interventions need to take.

A second aspect of stepfamily life important for workers to address is the idea of "unrealistic belief systems" (Visher & Visher, 1988, p. 227). Modeling our idea of the perfect family on the intact nuclear family is easy. There may be pressure for parents in newly blended stepfamilies to try to make these new families conform to old rules that may no longer be appropriate. For example, there is the idea that step-brothers and stepsisters should become emotionally close and get along almost immediately like an instant family. This idea is unrealistic. Relationships take time to develop. Positive feelings take time to be nurtured and grow. The practitioner may need to help the family set more realistic expectations for its interaction. However, some individual family members may never come to like each other.

A third important issue to address with stepfamilies is that of "insiders versus outsiders" (Visher & Visher, 1988, p. 228). Outsiders may include "a step-parent without children who joins a parent with children, a fourteen-year-old girl who comes to live with her father and stepmother after they have been married for five years, or a mother and her two children who move into her new husband's former home" (1988, p. 228). Practitioners need to watch out for family members placed in outsider roles. Feeling like an outsider in what is supposed to be one's own home inevitably causes problems. The human services professional may need to help the family define ways in which it can make all members become insiders and feel "at home."

The fourth important aspect operating within stepfamilies is that of "power" (Visher & Visher, 1988, p. 229). Power is a complicated concept that is difficult to define concisely. It involves who controls or influences whom within the stepfamily. It concerns the hierarchy of command. In other words, who will be paid attention to before someone else? Power also involves the amount of respect various stepfamily members have for each other. Usually, the ranking system places the biological parent living with the children first, the biological parent not living with the children second, the stepparent living with the children third, and the stepparent not living with the children last. More complex custody arrangements such as joint custody may complicate the power hierarchy even more.

Problems arise when people feel powerless in stepfamilies. A problem can easily develop when step-parents feel stepchildren do not listen to them.

A situation can be difficult for a child who feels divided between two stepfamilies and unable to control his or her own life. Likewise, a non-custodial parent refusing to follow the terms of the custodial agreement and collecting or returning children unpredictably can be problematic (see Highlight 10.5)

At any rate, when power is an issue, the worker needs to help the family clarify to the best extent possible *who has what power* and *what that power involves*. That all family members feel they're valuable family participants and not simply helpless pawns is important.

Power conflicts may also result from differences in parenting styles among households. Children in stepfamilies frequently trek from one household to another, depending on parental involvement, custodial agreements, and visitation arrangements. Frequently, each household will have different rules, expectations, and parenting styles (Goldenberg & Goldenberg, 1998). Goldenberg and Goldenberg (1998) stress the importance of learning coparenting. This process involves maintaining open communication and consistency between households where children reside at different times.

The following is an example of a power conflict where coparenting could be improved. Becca, who is 8 years old, lives with her biological father; biological brother Daniel, 10; stepmother; and stepsister. Becca and Daniel spend every other weekend and designated holidays with their biological mother. On visitation weekends, Becca's mother dresses Becca in tight, seductive clothing and encourages her to paint her nails. When Becca returns to her biological father's home, he forbids her to wear such clothing at home or school. He also forbids her from using nailpolish, as she has spilled it on the carpet several times. This situation is only one of numerous conflicts in childrearing practices. Becca's biological parents detest each other, never having recovered from a bitter divorce process. Unfortunately, their differences in child treatment give Becca numerous double messages. Who is right? Whom should she believe?

"Loyalty conflicts" involve the fifth problem commonly found in stepfamilies (Visher & Visher, 1988, p. 231). Children may feel pulled between two divorced parents. A parent may feel torn between loyalty to a new spouse and loyalty to children from a prior marriage. Because of the new mixing of people and the more complicated structures involved in stepfamilies, such loyalty conflicts are understandably common occurrences.

A human services professional faced with these issues needs to help make the family understand

HIGHLIGHT 10.5

An Example of Life within a Stepfamily

One stepmother, Cathy, after one and a half years of marriage, made some wise comments about stepfamily life. Cathy married for the first time in her mid-30s to someone a few years older than herself. He was divorced and had two teenage daughters.

Both of these daughters lived with Cathy and her new husband. Cathy spoke of how she naively entered the marriage and stepfamily life, never anticipating the struggles that were about to occur.

Cathy, a counselor by profession, described her stepdaughters as beautiful but spoiled. Discrepancies in values between stepmother and stepdaughters were huge. Problematic issues in stepfamily life were ominous. Cathy's stepdaughters would associate only with "upper-class" people (meaning people who had a lot of money) and people of their same race. Neither daughter liked poor people very much. Additionally, one daughter kept things fastidiously clean and the other maintained a disorganized mess. Cathy's own approach to housework was somewhere in between. The daughter who emphasized cleanliness was also anorexic. This made family meals and eating in general a continual struggle. For instance, Cathy confided that sometimes she would bake muffins for her anorexic stepdaughter, which the latter loved. On the outside these looked like ordinary muffins high in fiber content and low in calories. On the inside, however, they were packed with a special, highly caloric substance made for people who needed additional nutrition. Hence, the muffin appeared to be 80 calories by looking at the outside, but in reality it exceeded 800. Her anorexic stepdaughter would eagerly eat two or three muffins at a sitting. In this way Cathy could trick the anorexic into getting her needed nutrition. Cathy said the anorexic daughter probably "would've fainted dead away" had she had any inkling regarding how many calories there really were in what she considered a "diet" muffin.

Cathy also commented on how difficult feeling automatic love towards her stepdaughters was. She did not have the loving, nurturing childhood years (at least, these years should be such theoretically) to develop a strong relationship with them. The common daily struggles and annoyances of teenagers versus parents in addition to the major differences in values made it very difficult for positive feelings to bloom.

A positive aspect about the family was that Cathy and her husband maintained a good relationship between them. Her husband worked hard at not taking sides against her on behalf of his daughters.

Due to the conflicts and the anorexia, the entire family entered family counseling. Cathy expressed profuse relief at being able to step out of her human services role and say how she really felt as "the wicked stepmother." She felt the sessions were very helpful to the family as communication began to improve. Although the family did not become blissfully happy, at least it could function and accomplish its daily activities. Cathy continued to work at her marriage. Cathy also recognized that the daily living problems with her stepdaughters would gradually decrease as the girls matured and moved into their own living arrangements for good. She was willing to bide her time.

that people do not have limited quantities of love that must be divided between some finite number of people. Rather, love can be shared and expressed in many ways. It might be the task of the practitioner to help family members establish ways of displaying love and affection differently and more effectively than they have in the past.

"Boundary problems" make up the sixth area important to monitor in stepfamilies (Goldenberg & Goldenberg, 1998; Visher & Visher, 1988, p. 232). As we have discussed, appropriate boundaries are important to maintain in any family. For instance, the spouse system needs to maintain its special, unique status. However, in stepfamilies boundaries may easily become vague or confused because of the complex nature of relationships.

The seventh potential problem area in stepfamilies involves "discrepant life cycles" (Visher & Visher, 1988, p. 232). When two 25-year-olds marry and start out together, their life cycles are synchronized. They are progressing through their life stages at the same pace and are experiencing major life events more or less coincidentally. However, when remarriage is involved, other variables often come into play. There may be a substantial age difference between spouses. One's children may be preschoolers while the other's are in high school. One may not have children at all.

An issue that commonly surfaces is that of whether or not to have children together in this new family. There is no ideal decision to make about this issue. Each individual couple needs to examine the pros and cons of each choice, including how strongly each feels about the issue. As with other issues addressed in families, generalist practitioners can facilitate family members in making such decisions.

Intervention with stepfamilies is similar to that of intact families. Of course, some attention needs to be directed to the special issues we have described in addition to problems common in intact families. However, many of the same techniques can be used in stepfamilies to achieve similar ends.

Enhancing Cultural Competency: Family Assessment and Keys to Empowerment

Cultural and ethnic diversity are essential aspects of family life. Although Chapter 3 discussed ethnicity in greater depth, it is so basic to family assessment and understanding that several concepts will be introduced here. These concepts include acculturation, immigration history, school adjustment, employment (Lum, 2000, p. 230), "typical male/female interactive patterns, [and] the role of the extended family" (Goldenberg & Goldenberg, 2000, p. 52). Understanding cultural values can help practitioners emphasize a family system's "strengths and resiliency" rather than "the families' presumed deficiencies or weaknesses" (Proctor et al., 1995, p. 944). Each of these interrelated concepts is addressed in this section.

Acculturation

On the one hand, human services professionals must develop sensitivity to a family's cultural roots. On the other, practitioners must attend to each family's individuality. An important concept is *acculturation,* which is "the adaptation of language, identity, behavior patterns, and preferences to those of the host/majority society" (Lum, 2000, p. 231). Acculturation, then, involves the extent to which family members have been assimilated into the majority culture and to some extent relinquished traditional ethnic values

and behaviors. The point is not to assume that a family automatically fits an ethnic profile. Rather, be sensitive to cultural variation and assess each family as a unique entity, because "[e]very client should be understood from his or her unique frame of reference" (Ridley, 1995, p. 82).

Immigration History

Establishing details about immigrants' experiences is important. Major differences exist for families experiencing different circumstances ranging from: those who have recently arrived and may be struggling with language difficulties; those composed of foreign-born parents and American-born children; those who are second-generation immigrants; and those whose immigrant heritage dates back several generations (Goldenberg & Goldenberg, 2000). The following four factors can seriously affect a practitioner's ability to establish a relationship and solicit assessment information: "(1) how long ago newcomers arrived; (2) the circumstances of their arrival; (3) the support system they found upon arrival; and (4) the degree of acceptance they found here" (Goldenberg & Goldenberg, 2000, p. 53).

Ahearn (1995) comments on illegal aliens (i.e., citizens of other countries who illegally take up permanent residence in the United States):

> There is no accurate count of the number of illegal aliens in the United States; estimates range from one million to twelve million individuals. Among these individuals are Mexicans and Central Americans who have crossed the Rio Grande or the Arizona and California borders, Chinese brought by boat in exchange for a promise of several years of servitude, and thousands of Irish, Nigerians, and Pakistanis who have entered legally as tourists and have never returned home. (p. 773)

A Hispanic family illegally immigrating to the United States from Mexico would logically be wary of contact with human services professionals or other representatives of "the system." In order to understand family functioning, human services professionals must be sensitive to such people's vulnerability, potential emotional turmoil, and possible traumatic experiences (Ahearn, 1995).

Another aspect of assessing immigration history relates to acculturation. A third-generation Vietnamese family may be more assimilated into the mainstream culture than one immigrating six months ago. Language poses an additional factor.

Recent immigrants may have had less chance to learn English and thus face a greater communication barrier.

School Adjustment

When children are involved, the school environment is critically important to a family's well-being (Lum, 2000). One question to pursue concerns whether or not the school is safe. Does the school environment pose physical danger to children by other children? Are children of various ethnic heritages exposed to racist treatment and discrimination? Another question concerns the extent to which the school is conducive to learning. Are cultural differences valued and celebrated? Are students treated equally? Are their individual strengths emphasized?

Employment

A "reliable, steady job" is the most critical element in establishing family stability (Lum, 2000, p. 232). As the FABR establishes, assessing economic resources is a vital part of understanding a family and its issues. Ethnic groups often face the additional barrier of discrimination when trying to enter the majority culture's labor force. Human services professionals must address this issue and, if necessary, advocate for change.

Lum (2000) provides examples of how ethnic groups have adapted to the work force. Southeast Asian immigrants "have pooled their resources to open restaurants, croissant and donut shops," and other creative businesses (p. 232). Many "African Americans have taken out small business loans to start small enterprises in the inner city and have employed African American service and construction workers" (2000, p. 216).

Male and Female Interactive Patterns

Male and female interactive patterns are processes dictating how men and women interact with each other based on their gender and respective roles. For example, Balgopal (1995) describes gender-related aspects of Asian culture:

Asian families are generally patriarchal, and in traditional Asian families, age, sex, and generational status determine the roles that members play. The father is the head of the family, and his authority is unquestioned;

he is the main disciplinarian and is usually less approachable and more distant than the mother, who is the nurturer and caretaker. (p. 234)

Practitioners should be sensitive to the values and expectations of different cultural groups. Helping family members explore alternatives that coincide with cultural values is the human services professional's job.

Role of Extended Family

An extended family includes those relatives, including grandparents, aunts, uncles, cousins, second cousins, and the like, who have family relationships extending beyond the nuclear family (i.e., parents and children) (Barker, 1999). Extended families can provide great strength and support to individual members.

Longres (1995) describes Hispanic families:

Although nuclear-family households prevail, family life ideals espouse the goal of male-headed, tightly knit, extended heterosexual units. Latinos wish to create ties that solidify marriage, bind siblings, reach across generations, and incorporate relatives and godparents. (p. 1215)

In African American families, relatives other than parents often assist in raising children (Goldenberg & Goldenberg, 2000; Logan, Freeman, & McRoy, 1990). Likewise, a Native American child "may have available innumerable family members who assume responsibility for care" (Devore & Schlesinger, 1999, p. 83).

InfoTrac College Edition

This chapter covered content important for assessing families. This included communication skills useful with families; family structural issues; family life cycle, conflicts, and problems; and policy issues affecting families. For further information on these areas, enter the following search terms:

family assessment
family life cycle
family communication
family structure

On the Internet

Because of the very dynamic nature of the Web, URLs are subject to change. Therefore, be sure to check out the companion Website for this book at http://www.humanservices.wadsworth.com, where links will be updated periodically.

www.nida.nih.gov/Diagnosis-Treatment/Diagnosis5.html

www.gov.nb.ca/hcs-ssc/english/services/fcss/access.htm

www.statcan.ca/english/census96/oct14/fam1.htm

www.undp.org/popin

CHAPTER 11
Working with Families

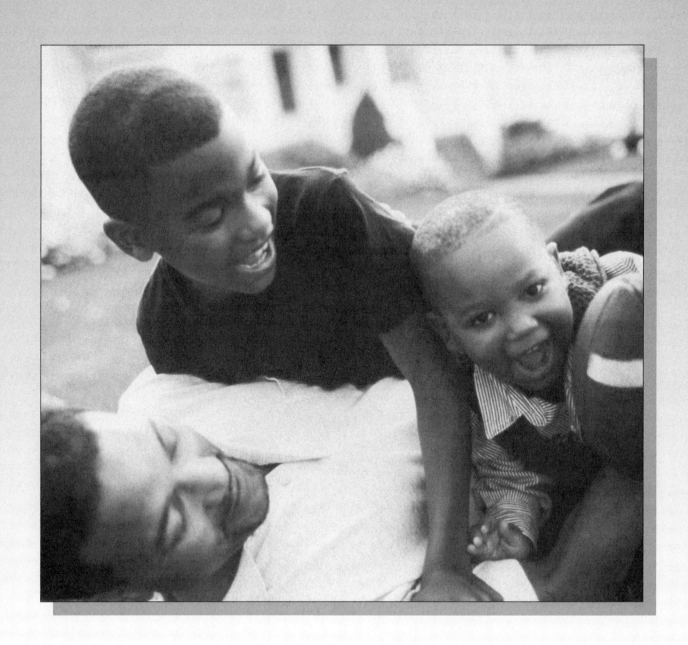

LaDonna did not know what to do. She was 36 years old and divorced. She had a 5-year-old son from her prior marriage. An attractive woman with fiery red hair and penetrating bright blue eyes, she was tremendously proud of being a junior in college. She had worked hard raising her son with no child support payments from his father, who was pretty much out of the picture. LaDonna's grades were excellent, and she looked forward to a bright professional future.

All these things had little or nothing to do with the problem upon which she was so intent. After dating a number of men steadily and some not so steadily, she had finally found a man with whom she would like to spend the remainder of her life. Jorge, age 40, was also divorced. LaDonna and he were deeply in love and were planning to marry within a few months.

Jorge also had a child from his prior marriage. His daughter Maria had just turned 18. Here was the problem: Maria had become pregnant when she was 17 and single. Her daughter, Denise, was born just two weeks after Maria turned 18. Maria, therefore, was considered an adult who was supposed to be a responsible guardian for Denise. The alleged father denied his paternity and wanted nothing to do with either of them.

However, Maria had a number of problems that interfered with her ability to be the responsible adult she was supposed to be. For one thing, she was addicted to crack and experienced radical swings in her feelings toward Denise. One minute Maria would hold Denise lovingly, and the next, she'd throw her down on the couch, run out the door, and leave the baby alone screaming wildly in their tiny, sparsely furnished apartment.

Once, Maria got so frustrated that she screamed she could not "stand it" anymore ("it" being the burdensome responsibility of parenthood,

Denise's crying, and the infant's constant demands for attention). She then picked Denise up, ran down the hall of her apartment building, stopped at the first door from which she heard music emanating, and knocked. She did not know the apartment's residents. Nonetheless, she almost threw Denise at the woman who answered and brashly told the woman to take care of her baby. Maria said she had something she must do and would return shortly. Maria did not return and pick up Denise for two full days.

LaDonna was terribly worried about Denise. Soon, LaDonna would become Denise's stepgrandmother. LaDonna would be an integral part of the family and would thus be one of the owners of the problem. LaDonna did not think Maria really wanted to keep Denise, yet Maria was terrified of giving Denise up.

LaDonna felt Maria was abusing and neglecting Denise and considered what she should do? Should she call Protective Services and tell them what has been happening? What would Maria think of her then? Denise is now two months old. How much longer can she stay in such an environment with Maria and not be seriously hurt? Should Denise be placed in foster care? But even then, how could LaDonna be certain that the foster care placement would be a good one?

LaDonna did have an idea. She had an aunt who lived 2000 miles away. Her aunt was 38 years old, married, and infertile. LaDonna felt her aunt would give virtually anything to have a baby of her own. Her aunt had difficulties applying for an adoptive child for a number of reasons, including being in her late thirties. On the other hand, LaDonna's aunt was doing well in the business she and her husband owned. They were financially well off.

LaDonna wondered if she should call her aunt and tell her about Denise. Would her aunt be interested? What if her aunt would pay Maria, perhaps, $20,000 to cover "adoption costs"? Maria was broke and would really like the cash, but what were the legal ramifications? Was such an adoption possible? Would Maria go for it? If LaDonna called her aunt, would she just be raising her aunt's hopes for nothing? What if Maria bluntly refused any such idea? Then, there is still Denise, poor, precious Denise, crying all the time. LaDonna did not know what to do.

Introduction

The story described above is true. It illustrates some of the infinite issues and problems that can confront families. Working with families can be phenomenally complex, monumentally frustrating, and yet fantastically fascinating. When the story left off, LaDonna was in the process of contacting a counselor to help her with some of her issues and questions. The problem obviously is difficult. Yet those with the worst problems can use the most help.

This chapter will examine how to work with families in generalist human services practice. Based on the content in Chapter 10, this chapter will explore specific approaches and techniques for helping families address their problems and issues.

Specifically, this chapter will:

- relate generalist practice skills to working with families;
- discuss the planned change process with families step-by-step;
- examine various approaches to implementing family intervention including reframing, teaching families problem-solving techniques, teaching child-management methods, offering families support, role playing, videotaping, and using homework assignments;
- address work with multiproblem families;
- explain family preservation;
- enhance cultural competency by exploring issues involved in working with gay/lesbian and African American families;
- appraise the current status of family services;
- examine macro practice with families.

Many of the skills that apply to other types of human services interventions also apply to families. Working with families is built upon the relationship building and interviewing skills discussed in Chapter 9. These skills are the basic ones necessary for generalist micro practice. Families are made up of individuals who communicate with each other. Planned change is based on communication. Therefore, many of the same skills are used when working with families. These include: monitoring your own and clients' verbal and nonverbal behavior; maximizing warmth, empathy, and genuineness; using verbal responses and initiators such as classification, interpretation, and summarization as part of the planned change process; and overcoming issues and hurdles such as clients who insist on not saying anything or on voicing extreme hostility.

Working with families also requires the skills to be discussed in Chapter 12, which we refer to as mezzo skills. These, of course, involve working with groups. Because a family is a special kind of group, these skills also apply. Group dynamics, decision-making strategies, and roles are concepts that also apply to families. Making assessments, formulating plans, and leading people through the intervention process occur in families much as they take place in other types of groups.

Finally, working with families often requires those skills that we will cover in Chapter 13, which emphasizes working in and with agencies and systems. Policies regarding how families are treated may be unfair. Families may not have access to the resources they desperately need.

Additionally, there are a number of more specific techniques that apply primarily or only to families. The main focus of this chapter will be the special approaches for working with families in view of the issues confronting them. As with any other generalist intervention, we will apply a planned change approach.

Family Treatment and the Planned Change Process

Working with or treating families follows the Generalist Intervention Model, just as any other type of human services intervention would. First, the worker must engage the family, that is, establish a professional relationship between him- or herself and the family system. Second, the practitioner must assess the family's needs from micro, mezzo, and macro perspectives (Chapters 5 and 10 explored various family assessment approaches and issues). Next, just as in any other type of intervention, a plan needs to be formulated. Some of the family's micro, mezzo, and macro aspects will be targeted for change. The next stage involves the implementation or actual carrying out of the plan. Following this process, the intervention needs to be evaluated to determine its effectiveness. Finally, termination needs to occur.

Strategizing for Family Intervention: Do You Always Have to See the Entire Family?

As we know, a family is a system. Every single part of a system is important because what affects any *part* of the system affects the *whole* system. Therefore, because each family member is an important part of the family system, each member should be involved in the intervention process. The term *conjoint* family treatment refers to meetings involving at least two family members (Goldenberg & Goldenberg, 2000, p. 436).

There are at least three advantages to seeing the entire family together. First, being able to observe the entire family in interaction can give great insight to understanding its dynamics (Janzen & Harris, 1997; Worden, 1999). When family members are missing, part of the family's interactional patterns are also lacking. For example, a single-parent mother and her 12-year-old daughter might consistently complain together about the 16-year-old son/brother in the family. They say he's "no good." He fights with them all the time, lies, steals, and is generally impossible to live with. Without being able to observe the mother's and daughter's interaction with this boy, the worker does not really know what is going on in the family. The worker can see neither the boy's behavior nor the family's problems from the boy's perspective. Perhaps the mother clearly favors her daughter and regularly criticizes her son. Maybe his acting out is his way of expressing his anger at the situation and demanding some attention.

This line of reasoning leads us to the second advantage of seeing the whole family together. It enhances the worker's ability to be fair and objective. In other words, the worker is better able to assess and understand the problem from the perspective of all family members. The worker is thus less likely to take sides on the part of one person or the other. Bandler, Grinder, and Satir (1976) emphasize that a person working with the family "must be careful not to assume any one member of the family is a spokesperson for the rest of the family" (p. 15).

A third advantage to seeing the entire family involves the opportunity to see communication patterns. As Sherman (1977) indicates, "Communication patterns within the family become the first and major focus of observation and response by the worker" (1977, p. 438). Assessing what you can observe right in front of you is much easier than hearing about it secondhand. The difference between how family members think they communicate and how they really do communicate is often a major part of the family's problem.

However, stipulating that the entire family must be present during problem-solving sessions often presents problems. Sometimes, there are family members who refuse to participate. At other times, questions may be raised regarding the need for everyone to be there. For example, if the parents are having sexual difficulties, is it appropriate for their four children, ranging in age from 8 to 18, to be present during the meetings? At yet other times, scheduling everyone together may be impossible or nearly impossible. For instance, parents may work opposite shifts and are only available on weekends when you do not want to work. Sometimes, family members live out of town. Finally, is it really necessary to solving the designated problems that all family members expend the time and energy to be present all the time?

Family treatment involves any practice interventions that serve to change a family (Janzen & Harris, 1997). The important thing is to help solve the family's problems. Although family treatment means that the end result should benefit the entire family unit, this result is accomplished in many different ways. On the one hand, seeing one or two individuals may be more advantageous. On the other, working with the entire family in order to effect needed changes may be necessary. The critical thing is that the family benefits from the change effort.

Seeing each family member at least once may be useful to solicit all members' perspectives. This can be done on an individual basis. The purpose is to assure that the worker does not assume what one or two family members say accurately represents how all family members feel.

Perhaps the best guideline is to see the entire family together at least once if the task is at all possible. From there, arbitrarily determine which subsystems are needed to work on which problems. If getting everyone together is not possible, then do the best you can. Get as many together as is possible and reasonable. As we have emphasized many times, human services professionals must be flexible. They need to do the best they can with what they have. Situations are rarely ideal. The important thing is to help effect change and solve problems.

For example, a "family therapist" is beginning treatment with a family consisting of a mother, a father, a 16-year-old daughter, and a 19-year-old son. The identified problem is the son, who is extremely depressed. The identified problem, by the way, is the reason the family stated it came in for treatment. The real problem may be something quite different.

This therapist believes that the entire family must be present in order for the therapeutic process to do any good. He believes treatment is useless unless all family members are involved.

As the interview progresses, a discovery surfaces that the son is gay. He is having a terrible time coping with the ramifications of the fact, which include the homophobic responses of other people and the realities of living outside of the heterosexual mainstream. He also has difficulties accepting himself for what he is, namely, a worthwhile human being.

The young man's father states adamantly that homosexuality is "bad and wrong." The father refuses to discuss his feelings during this interview or at any time in the future. He states that he will not attend any more therapy sessions until the son stops being gay. This, of course, devastates his son who, teary-eyed, is pleading for his father's acceptance.

After going around and around on the issue, the therapist responds that if the whole family does not attend therapy sessions, he will not continue therapy. That is that. This declaration is despite the fact that both mother and daughter express serious concern for their son/brother and commitment to the therapeutic process.

Perhaps the therapist is trying to force the father into participating in the treatment sessions. Or maybe the therapist sincerely believes working with the incomplete family system is useless, and that nothing can be achieved under such conditions. At any rate, the young man hangs himself the following week.

As a generalist practitioner, what would you have done with this family? What other alternatives might have been available? The therapist involved considered no other options. As a generalist practitioner in this situation, you might have considered seeing only those family members who were available and doing what you could within those limitations. Another possibility was to refer the young man to someone who could work with him individually. Still another option included referral to a gay support network or group.

That the young man killed himself was not the therapist's fault. We are all ultimately responsible for our own lives. However, the problem can be attributed to the lack of options presented to the clients. The family was cut off because of one member's unwillingness to comply with the therapist's rules. The young man may have killed himself anyway. No one will ever know. However, perhaps a more compassionate approach would have helped. Maybe providing him with some other options would have made the young man feel as though someone cared.

Engagement, Assessment, and Planning with Families

Janzen and Harris (1997) cite three primary goals when beginning to work with families. First, the worker needs to get a clear picture of the family's interaction, the problem itself, and how the family's interaction helps to maintain the problem. Second, the worker must gain the family's consent to begin treatment and their commitment to participate. This task may not be easily achieved. Some or all family members may deny that the problem even exists. They may insist that a certain family member or members are really to blame for the problem and, therefore, really should be the target of intervention. They may not even feel that anyone but the person with the identified problem should participate in treatment. The third goal when beginning an intervention with families is "to set procedures for change in motion. Family members should be able to leave with beginning confidence that they have been understood, that something new is being offered, and that something positive can happen as a result of agency contact" (1997, pp. 109–110).

Janzen and Harris (1997) also state that there are five phases to beginning treatment. These phases are examined in the following sections.

Phase 1: Alleviate or at Least Minimize Early Apprehension

The purpose of this phase is "to acknowledge the family members and make them somewhat comfortable in the office before moving on to the task at hand" (Worden, 1999, p. 25). A warm, cordial greeting and introduction is a pleasant way of initiating the worker–family system relationship (1999). The practitioner might comment about how pleasant meeting the family is. Some agreeable small talk can soften the meeting and enhance comfort levels (Street, 1994; Worden, 1999). For example, the practitioner might say, "Did you have any trouble finding the place?" or "I hope you haven't been waiting long." Other pleasantries might include comments about the weather, traffic, or family members' general health and well-being.

The human services professional might then complete family introductions by saying something like, "Let me make sure I have your names right. You must be Matilda. I'm glad you could come. You're 17, correct? What school do you attend? Don't you live in the Smartbrain District?" (Worden, 1999). Of course, the worker does not want to blast family members with one question after another but rather demonstrate interest in individual family members.

The worker can also clarify relationships during this phase. For instance, the worker might say, "Bob, you're Amelia's son by birth, and, Harvey, you're Bob's stepdad? Am I right?" (Street, 1994). Including children in all these processes as well as adults is important (1994).

The practitioner may relate a brief history of contacts with the family and what information about the family is at his or her disposal (1994). The worker also establishes the "ground rules for working together" (Helton & Jackson, 1997, p. 50). These rules may include emphasizing that: all family members' input is valuable; members are expected to demonstrate respect for each other verbally and nonverbally; members should refrain from interrupting each other; and the practitioner's job is to share perceptions and recommendations about family interaction and communication and answer any questions the family might have (Worden, 1999).

The intent of providing information is to help fill in the scary unknown with concrete information. The more family members understand the human services professional and the helping process, the more comfortable they are likely to feel. Thinking of how clients might be reacting as they enter this likely unfamiliar situation is important. Will this human services professional ask personal questions in front of everybody else? Will he or she cut me down to nothing? Will everyone have to lie down on couches? Do they still perform lobotomies? Therefore, alleviating unsubstantiated fears and beginning discussion about the realities of family intervention is crucial.

Still another technique for calming anxiety is asking each person to describe his or her thoughts and feelings about being there. Specific questions you might ask include:

- "What kinds of things did you expect when you first walked in? Is this anything like you thought it would be?"
- "Did you have a chance to discuss our meeting beforehand? If so, what kinds of things did you talk about?"
- "I know this is a new experience for you. How do you feel about being here?"

Many of the introductory techniques resemble those described in Chapter 9 on micro practice. However, there are two major differences between initial individual and initial family interviews. First, as the worker, you have more than one person to interact with and observe. Second, you need to make certain that each individual has the opportunity to voice opinions. Each individual needs to feel that he or she is important right from the beginning.

Phase 2: Ask Family Members to Explain What Is Wrong

The second phase in initial family intervention involves asking each family member to share their perception of the problem. There will likely be a wide variety of different perceptions. Asking for individual viewpoints allows the worker to observe each member's reactions to the rest of the family's definitions. One should note that this phase is not the time to start problem solving—it is a time for observation. The problem must be clearly understood before the change process begins.

Frequently, family members will point their fingers at one person and blame that individual for the problem. Confronting this blaming behavior and starting discussion about how the problem belongs to the entire family may be tempting for the worker. However, allowing the family to act as naturally as possible at this point is important. The worker wants to set the groundwork for change. The important thing here is to observe interactions, understand the problems, and target the most appropriate things for change.

Other issues may emerge. For instance, some family members may find restraining themselves from talking and waiting their turn difficult. They may burst in and interrupt. Parents may find it a challenge to be patient and allow their teenage daughter, the identified problem in their eyes, a chance to tell her side of the story. Old interactional patterns may kick in. The parents may immediately think how they have heard their daughter's side before and turn themselves off to it. In this case, the worker needs to establish one of the session's rules, namely, family members must not interrupt each other. All family members must feel their opinions are important. However, in this example, noting the interaction between parents and child is relevant for the worker. It probably dramatizes what typically occurs in their daily living situations.

At other times, there may be family members who will not say anything. The worker may then attempt to draw them out. For instance, the worker might say, "You're being awfully quiet right now. What are your feelings about the problem?" The important thing is to let the quiet person know that his or her feelings are also valued. For example, the worker might say, "Your ideas are important. I'd really like to hear them whenever you're ready." Clients should know that their input will be welcomed when they feel comfortable enough to give it.

Phase 3: Establish Agreement About What Is Wrong

After problem definitions have been elicited from all family members, the trick is to come to some agreement about what problem or problems should be worked on. Problems are usually complex. Reid (1985) addresses the difficulty of determining the "real" problem. In any family, having a clear, concisely agreed upon definition of the problem would be nice. He emphasizes "that all problems are 'real' to someone. It is usually impossible and fruitless to search for the one problem that has some quintessential reality, [i.e., the essence of the problem in its clearest, purest form] that others lack (1985, p. 31)." In other words, there is no crystal clear, absolute problem.

Perhaps, a more useful perspective is to think of most stated problems in terms of their "representativeness" (Reid, 1985, p. 31). Many families will verbalize superficial issues that are related to underlying problems. For example, a teenage son will state that his mother nags him about "everything all the time." His mother, on the other hand, says the problem is that her son will neither clean up his room like he is supposed to nor obey her curfew limitations concerning when he gets in at night. These perceptions are significant and important in the pair's day-to-day lives. However, a more pertinent issue involves the struggle for control between mother and son. The stated issues are really symptoms of the difficulties in the overall interaction.

Bandler and colleagues (1976) emphasize the usefulness of focusing "not on the problems and content, but on the processes of coping and communicating. This allows him to select useful information from the perspective of process, instead of being overwhelmed by detail. Transforming the system will entail change at the coping level, not at the content level" (p. 138). In other words, work with families often involves changing how family members interact and communicate. The end result is teaching them different means of problem solving than those they have used unsuccessfully in the past. Changing family processes enables the family to solve a wide range of problems, instead of the relatively limited ones they initially verbalize.

Let us return briefly to the example of mother and son cited earlier. The son probably will not agree that he is to blame for the real problem, because he neither cleans up his room nor gets in on time. Nor will the mother probably agree that the real problem is her fault, namely, that she criticizes and badgers her son excessively. However, a worker might get them to agree that the conflict occurring regularly between the two is a problem for both of them.

Reid (1985) suggests several techniques for engineering a problem consensus. The initial two summarize much of what we have already discussed. First, attempt to focus on a problem or some aspect of a problem over which the family will concur. Second, "recast problems expressed in individual terms as problems of interactions between family members or as problems of the family as a whole" (p. 35). This technique is one illustration of "reframing," which we will discuss more thoroughly later on in the chapter. Reframing "gives family members a different definition of the situation, one that may help them see the problem in a new light" (p. 36).

Third, help the family to articulate problems you observe in their interaction during the interview, problems that they are not able to express verbally themselves. For instance, consider a family where each member actively criticizes each other family member during the interview. However, they do not define the problem as involving excessive criticism. Rather, each family member states that the real problem is the behavior of other family members. For example, verbalized problems might include drinking excessively, running away, not being able to hold a job, or poor housekeeping. Each problem is expressed as being someone's else's fault. The worker might assume a totally different perspective. Intervention may focus on defining the family's hostile confrontational communication instead.

There is a fourth technique for establishing agreement about a problem. If several problems have surfaced, present them to the family in the order you consider them important. Ask each family member to rank the problems in the order he or she feels they are important. Then compare and contrast the results. Generally, problems that are considered more important by the most family members would be given higher priority. If there seems to be a tie between problems for top places, you can choose the problem you feel is the easiest to solve. Achieving some success in its treatment as soon as possible is important for the family.

The fifth technique for gaining problem consensus in a family must be used carefully. It involves preventing family members from pointing their fingers at some individual and making that person the family scapegoat,[1] at least during the process of coming to a consensus.[2] One way of doing this is to label the scapegoating as it occurs. Such feedback can help family members begin to identify their behavior and patterns of interaction. Another approach is to ask family members to stop the scapegoating in order to continue their progress toward a problem consensus.

Practitioners may also ask scapegoats to share their perspectives of the family problems. Likewise, scapegoats can be asked how they feel about being targets of blame. Soliciting scapegoats' feelings can serve to enhance empathy among family members. Additionally, such encouragement serves to tell scapegoats that their feelings are also important. No one should be made to feel the target of blame. Finally, encouraging such participation shows the family that each member's input is important. All family members should be asked at some point their personal perspectives concerning family issues. The family's problem concerns all family members. The practitioner can emphasize this to the family. Each person is involved and, thus, contributes to the problem. Helping the family develop this perspective is the worker's task.

Reid (1985) gives two additional suggestions for targeting the family's problems. The first is to limit the initial list of problems to three. The list can be changed at a later time. The second suggestion is that even a vague problem about which the family has a consensus is better than a list of minor, specific complaints. For instance, "improving family communication," although vague and global, would be more desirable than a list like "talks on the phone too long," "wears same socks for five days in a row," and "is sarcastic whenever asked a question," where there is no consensus.

Phase 4: Concentrate on How Family Members Relate to One Another

Focusing on how family members relate to and communicate with one another is the fourth phase in

beginning family treatment. This phase follows establishment of a problem consensus with the family. Typically, during this step the worker orchestrates discussion of the problem by family members. There are three structured ways of doing this.

The first way involves communication between the worker and individual family members. The worker directs questions to members that further explore the problem. Reid (1985) notes four major aspects of the target problem that can be explored. These include: how long the problem has existed and major events related to the problem since it began; the problem's intensity and incidence for the week or two prior to the interview; what family members have done to try to solve the problem in the past; and what barriers have been operating both inside and outside the family, which have prevented the problem's solution until now. Highlight 11.1 provides an example of how a target problem can be explored.

Hearing how each family member talks about the problem provides the worker with much information. She can find out how the problem evolved and how it has been intertwined in the family's interpersonal dynamics.

A second way the worker can structure how family members talk about a problem is through a discussion in which all family members participate.

The worker instructs the family members to talk to each other about the problem. At the same time, the family is instructed not to direct any communication to the worker. In this way, the worker can observe how family members participate in problem solving together and what some of the obstructions in communication are.

Janzen and Harris (1997) note some of the communication difficulties that can be observed in families. They state:

Communications may be unclear; topics may be changed before issues are resolved, statements interrupted, blame affixed, [and] support offered. Statements may be addressed to nobody in particular, and some individuals may attempt to speak for others. (pp. 118–119)

Additionally, family members may vie for power, initiate conflicts, form liaisons, or give support to each other. These are the interactions that the worker can observe and later use to help the family target ineffective interactions for change.

The third way a worker can structure a family's discussion of problems is to instruct only two family members to talk about how to solve the problem

---

1. A *scapegoat* is a family or group member who is "made to bear the blame for others or to suffer in their place" (*Random House Webster's College Dictionary*, 1999).

2. At other times during the planned change process, scapegoating might be allowed. For example, at some time during assessment, the practitioner will probably want to observe the family's genuine interaction in order to plan for effective changes. Practitioners must first observe problem behaviors before targeting them for change.

HIGHLIGHT 11.1

Four Ways of Exploring a Target Problem

The Situation

Rosie, age 58, works part-time as a salesperson at a small shoe store. She is married to Bob, age 61, a retired luggage department manager for Sears. Their three children, Sean, Shane, and Sher, are married and live in other states. The problem is Bob's mother, Yetta, age 87, whose health has seriously declined. She has difficulty walking, her sight is failing, and she is becoming increasingly forgetful. Yetta has been living in the same urban flat since her husband died 40 years ago. Rosie and Bob live in another area of the same city. Yetta has one other son who lives in another state and who rarely comes to visit her.

Yetta receives Meals on Wheels every day. This supportive service delivers daily noon meals to elderly persons in their own homes for relatively reasonable fees. One day, the delivery person finds Yetta disoriented and babbling. Yetta mumbles that she fell and hit her head.

The Meals on Wheels delivery person calls an ambulance, and Yetta is taken to the hospital where she remains for several days in order to evaluate her condition. Medical staff raise questions regarding whether Yetta is capable of living alone in her own home any more. The case is referred to the hospital worker.

Exploration of the Problem

The hospital worker arranges a meeting with Bob, Rosie, and Yetta to discuss Yetta's situation. Yetta is no longer disoriented, so is able to share her feelings. The worker proceeds to explore the problem by pursuing four major dimensions involving the following questions; she receives the information that is recorded after each:

1. *How long has the problem existed, and what were the major events related to the problem since it began?* Yetta's health has been gradually failing over the past three years. However, she has fallen only once prior to about a month ago. Until now she has never really hurt herself.
2. *How intense has the problem become in the past two weeks?* Yetta admits that she has fallen several times during the past two weeks. However, she emphasizes that she has never really gotten hurt until now. Bob and Rosie were unaware of any of the other falls.
3. *What have family members done to solve the problem in the past?* Bob has tried to talk to Rosie about the possibility of Yetta moving in with them several times since Yetta's health began to fail. Rosie, however, has consistently refused to talk about it. She would typically "cut Bob off" and state that they should just "leave well enough alone." Yetta has never raised the issue of moving to either of them.
4. *What barriers have been operating both inside and outside the family that have prevented the problem's solution until now?* Yetta has adamantly maintained that she does not want to move from her home. She is determined not to enter a nursing home.

Rosie has never gotten along very well with Yetta, who she feels is stubborn and overly talkative. She feels she has been good to Yetta and cares about her well-being. However, Rosie has consistently avoided discussing letting Yetta live with her and Bob. Rosie has been enjoying her time and relative freedom since her children have left. She dreads having to give these up to care for Yetta. Rosie does not feel that becoming a "full-time nurse" at her age is fair.

Bob worries intensely about his mother. Whenever he has tried to talk to Rosie about his concerns, she has abruptly refused. He feels Yetta should leave her flat and come to live with him and Rosie. He feels he has a responsibility to take care of his mother, and he wishes Rosie felt the same way. However, he also worries about how Rosie and Yetta would get along. He does not want to live on a battlefield. The family has no information about the nursing homes in the city. Nor do they know how to go about getting it.

Several external supports have been working to maintain Yetta in her own home. Thus, the problem of Yetta's failing health has not been addressed. First, Meals on Wheels has provided one hot meal a day, so Yetta has been getting adequate nutrition. Second, a concerned friend from Yetta's church named Alice Dicks looks in on Yetta almost every other day. Additionally, Alice, who is 20 years Yetta's junior, takes her to church activities when Yetta feels up to it. Yetta's minister also visits her regularly. Finally, Bob and Rosie call Yetta at least twice a week, frequently take her on outings, invite her for dinner, and help her with laundry and shopping.

Summary

The intent of this brief vignette involving Yetta and her family is to provide an example of how a human services professional might begin to explore at least four dimensions of a target problem. This problem situation has many other facets that are beyond the scope of this abbreviated description. In real life, many other questions could be asked and other issues examined.

So What Happens?

We will not take the time here to explain how all the specific steps in the Generalist Intervention Model are applied. However, we will tell you what happens.

Because Yetta remains insistent upon staying in her own home, she does so, at least temporarily. The human services professional obtains additional supportive equipment for her. This includes a walker which Yetta can lean on for balance as she walks and a "beeper" worn around her neck that will notify the hospital immediately if pressed when she has trouble and needs help.

For four months Yetta continues to receive support from family, friends, minister, and Meals on Wheels. However, she eventually falls again and breaks her arm. She, together with Bob and Rosie, then decide that she will move in with them. Rosie does her best to take care of Yetta. One year later, Yetta becomes extremely disoriented. Several times she wanders out of the house for no apparent reason and gets lost. Finally, she can no longer control her bladder.

Bob and Rosie go to the County Department of Social Services and ask how to go about finding a "good" nursing home placement for Yetta. There they are referred to the appropriate human services professional. They explore a variety of nursing homes, evaluate the respective pros and cons of each, and eventually place Yetta in the one they consider best for her.

Problems do not always have one best solution. Often, there are a number of possible solutions. Sometimes, as in Yetta's case, the solutions are progressive.

---

with each other. At any point the worker can establish parameters about how communication will occur (Janzen & Harris, 1997). For example, the worker can specify that one person may not interrupt another, discussion should not stray far from the targeted topic, and that speakers will take responsibility for their own feelings and avoid speaking for other people.

Any of these three approaches provides the worker with a small sample of the family's real-life interaction. In effect, a small laboratory is created. Working with families is difficult because there are so many dimensions and nuances involved. Sometimes, a worker can find out a lot about a family early on. At other times, learning about the family takes much longer. At the very least, however, structuring such communication at the beginning of family treatment shows the family the types of things that can go on in family intervention and prepares them somewhat for future work.

Phase 5: Establish Commitment to a Plan of Action

Establishing an agreement regarding what is to be done and who is to do it is an important aspect of planning (Helton & Jackson, 1997). In other words, we establish a contract with clients. This agreement is a major step in the planned change process of the

Generalist Intervention Model. The information in Chapter 5 on planning relates to contracting with families just as it relates to contracting with individuals, groups, organizations, and communities. The contract becomes both a map or guide for the implementation process and a seal of commitment of both family and worker. It reflects the primary problems to be worked on and the work assignments involved.

Implementation of Family Intervention

Human services professionals address a wide range of family problems and issues. Thus, the techniques and approaches used vary dramatically. A major "challenge for the worker is to select the interventive method best suited to the family and the presenting problems" (Proctor et al., 1995, p. 946). During the implementation phase, a practitioner tries to "help the family with issues and/or problems that are preventing optimal functioning" by carrying out goals established during the planning phase (Helton & Jackson, 1997, pp. 55–56). Implementation can involve a range of treatment approaches, which include reframing, teaching families problem-solving techniques, teaching parents child management methods, and offering support (Proctor et al., 1995). Additional practice techniques include role playing, videotaping, and homework assignments.

Reframing

Reframing means helping family members view a problem or an issue with a different outlook or understand it in a new way. It is also referred to as "relabeling or redefining" (Sheafor et al., 2000, p. 461). Within the family treatment context, this technique usually means helping one family member change negative thinking about another family member to a new, more positive perspective. Reframing often helps one person better empathize with another person or understand content more clearly from that person's perspective.

The following are some examples of a client's statement followed by a worker's reframing of the client's thought:

- *Client's statement:* "Johnny hates me. All he does is scream at me. I don't even want to go near him anymore."
- *Worker's reframing:* "You sound upset and hurt at how Johnny yells at you so much. Maybe he's upset and hurt, too. Maybe he feels you're avoiding him. If he didn't care about you, he probably wouldn't expend so much energy yelling at you and trying to get your attention."
- *Client's statement:* "My dad says I'm much too close to my grandmother. He says it's a sick relationship, that all she does is manipulate me."
- *Worker's reframing:* "It's interesting that he's so concerned about that relationship. Maybe he's jealous that you two are so close. Maybe he'd like to feel closer to you, too. After all, you visit your grandmother whenever you have the chance. Yet, you never visit him. Also, you've told me how he resents his own mother and how she tried to manipulate him when he was small. Maybe that has something to do with it."
- *Client's statement:* "All my parents do is try to control me. They're like two little dictators. They ask me who I'm going out with every second I'm gone. They tell me I'm supposed to have a 10 P.M. curfew. If I'm two seconds late, they're waiting for me at the door to ask me where I've been. They're driving me crazy."
- *Worker's reframing:* "You sound as though you're feeling suffocated by your parents. It sounds to me like they're very concerned about you. If they didn't really care what happened to you, they

wouldn't be interested in what you did. Maybe they don't see their behavior as controlling. Maybe they see it as being good parents and trying to keep you out of trouble."

Teaching Families Problem-Solving Techniques

Problem solving is a family's "ability to resolve problems at a level that maintains effective family functioning. A family problem is seen as an issue that threatens the integrity and functional capacity of the family" (Carlson, Sperry, & Lewis, 1997, p. 81). We have discussed how the terms planned change and problem solving can be used interchangeably. You can teach a family many of the same steps and substeps involved in the Generalist Intervention Model's six-step process. Just as you can use many of them in practice, so can a family learn to use many in its daily life. For example, consider goal setting, a major aspect of planning. A family can adopt the same who-will-do-what-by-when action step format for goals that you use in practice. The technique simply provides a means for getting things done. For example, a family might follow the plan that Mom and Dad will make an appointment to talk with the Humdrum School counselor about special testing by next Tuesday.

Please remember, however, that families with problems usually require help in improving communication among members before they can master other problem solving skills (Hartman, 1995). Only when members can work together by using effective communication can a family plan and implement positive changes.

Teaching Child-Management Methods

Teaching parents how to improve their children's behavior is a common goal in family treatment. Substantial research supports parents' ability to increase children's positive behavior and decrease maladaptive behavior through child-management skills (Kazdin, 2001; Orton, 1997). Chapter 10 introduced two techniques used for this purpose, I-language and active listening.

Behavioral approaches to child management have been found especially effective (Kazdin, 2001; Orton, 1997). Such approaches have successfully addressed many childhood problems, including anxiety, depression, eating disorders, underachievement, enuresis (unintentional emission of urine), deficiencies in social skills, and attention deficit hyperactivity disorder (a condition characterized by a persistent pattern of inattention, excessive physical movement, and impulsivity that appear in at least two settings, including home, school, work, or social contexts) (Orton, 1997). "Behavioral therapy's treatment goal is to increase infrequent appropriate behaviors or eliminate excessive inappropriate ones" (p. 339). It is far beyond the scope of this book to teach behavioral techniques, but basic principles include the following:

- *Positive reinforcement* is a procedure or consequence that increases the frequency of the behavior immediately preceding it. For example, a mother gives her daughter a warm hug every time the daughter gets an A on a test. Such hugging is positive reinforcement if it increases the child's studying behavior that results in getting A's on tests.
- *Negative reinforcement* is the removal of a negative or aversive event or consequence that serves to increase the frequency of a particular behavior. Consider a teenager grounded until his grades improved. Lifting the grounding when school grades improve is negative reinforcement, because the lifting ends an aversive event and increases the boy's attention to his school work.
- *Punishment* is the presentation of an aversive event or the removal of a positive event that results in the decreased frequency of a particular behavior. For example, a father sharply criticizes his daughter when she slurps her soup. This criticism is punishment—the presentation of an aversive event—if it decreases her soup slurping behavior. Likewise, the father might inform his daughter that she will not get dessert if she chews with her mouth open. Removal of a positive event (dessert) is punishment—if it inhibits her from chewing with her mouth open.
- *Modeling* is learning behavior by observing another individual engage in that behavior. For instance, parents often teach their children how to tie shoes by showing them how. By watching, children learn how to do it themselves. The parents have thus used modeling to teach behavior.

Offering Families Support

Providing support does not necessarily coincide with traditional, specialized family therapy where a family attends regular appointments in a therapist's comfortable office. However, "especially when working with young, economically disadvantaged, or socially isolated parents, it is helpful to offer support or to mobilize available support in the family's envi-

ronment" (Proctor et al., 1995, p. 946). Support can take the form of public assistance, school and educational services, job skills training, employment-seeking services, housing, help from religious institutions, health care, food, participation in formal support groups, or involvement with informal support systems "such as other families with similar problems, naturally formed support groups, extended family networks, close friends, and understanding co-workers" (Helton & Jackson, 1997, p. 56). A prime directive for human services professionals is to assess client systems' access to resources and advocate for resources when those available are inadequate, inaccessible, or nonexistent. Later in this chapter, on page 356, Highlight 11.4 discusses a number of policy areas human services professionals might address for macro-level change.

Role Playing

Role playing refers to having a person assume a different role or part than the one he or she would normally assume. It usually involves one of two scenarios. First, within the family treatment context, the worker directs one family member to assume the role or character of another. The major requirement is that the role player attempts to act and feel the way he or she thinks the other person does in real life (Okun, 1996). Role playing allows family members to understand more clearly how other family members feel from their own unique perspectives. Frequently, a technique called "role reversal" is used where two family members are asked to exchange and act out each other's roles. The intent is usually to help people see how they each perceive each other.

An example concerns a father and "uncontrollable" 14-year-old daughter who are asked to reverse roles. The father portrays his daughter by walking around in a huff, swearing at his role-play "father," and threatening to break things. On the other hand, the daughter acts out her father by screaming at her role-play "daughter," telling her she's grounded, and savagely raises her fist as if ready to strike.

The practitioner would then help the clients to begin talking about how each perceived the situation and how each felt. An intent of the discussion is to enhance empathy toward each other.

The 14-year-old then describes to her father how she feels about her situation and how her feelings were demonstrated by her role-play actions. She does not have a very positive self-concept. She feels making friends is difficult for her, so she hangs out with those who will accept her. She does not care if they shave half their heads and dye their hair in purple and orange streaks. She is caught in a no-win situation when her father tells her she cannot associate with them anymore. She feels she has no choice since without these friends, she will have no one.

Her father also explains his feelings and why he acted the way he did. In reality, he stresses, he feels worried and frustrated. He feels his daughter will not listen to him as children "should" respond to their parents. To him she looks like "a mental case" by the way she dresses. He is feeling like a failure as a parent because nothing he tries helps him get control over the situation. He is desperately worried that belonging to such a "wrong crowd" will only result in drug use, sex, and who knows what else.

Having these two people reverse roles and interact with each other may provide some interesting insights into their own behavior. When father walks around in a huff, swears at daughter, and threatens to break things, daughter sees how she looks to other people. On the other hand, when daughter screams at father telling him he is grounded and raises her hand to strike him, father may get some insight into his own actions. He may never have had any idea regarding how his behavior looked to anyone else.

Of course, family members will probably not get instantaneous revelations and have their problems miraculously cured by doing role reversal. However, there is potential for them to increase their empathy for others, broaden their view of problem situations, and become aware of alternatives never thought of before.

The second kind of role playing involves having people remain themselves but act differently than they normally would in some defined situation. This technique allows them to try out and practice new ways of behaving in fabricated situations, without taking the risks those new behaviors might pose in real life.

For instance, take a woman who is afraid to share her true feelings with her husband. She feels he is a domineering man and would not listen to her anyway. Via role playing, she can practice what to say and how to say it before ever really confronting him, which allows her to gain confidence in how to act. It also lets her think through ahead of time how she might respond to a variety of his possible reactions.

The bad thing about role playing is that the situation is obviously not a real one. Sometimes it seems "fake" to participants. However, the very good thing is that it allows people to plan what to do and practice before the actual situation takes place. Risk is minimal.

Video Recording

"I hate watching myself on video" is a frequent comment of students who are forced to make video recordings of themselves for their human services practice courses. They do not like the grating tone or the soft mumbling of their voices. They hate to see how they jiggle their feet or slump in their chairs. They think they look too fat or too lanky.

What video recording does is make people observe themselves as others see them. It makes them confront the effectiveness and appropriateness of their various verbal and nonverbal behaviors. So it also is with families.

When viewing recordings of their interaction, family members can be made to see themselves as others see them. When a mother tells her delinquent son, "I love you," she can see the scowl on her face and hear the angry, harsh tone of her voice. Video recording can be useful for pointing out double messages such as this. The mother was saying one thing verbally but communicating quite another thing nonverbally.

Video recording can be used to demonstrate family alliances. For example, a mother may observe herself sitting next to her young daughter and patting her daughter's arm lovingly and frequently during an earlier interview. Video recording can also dramatize conflicts. For instance, two partners who live together can watch themselves both talking at the same time, trying to cut each other off, and struggling to be heard.

There is one note of caution, however. Workers should use discretion regarding how much of a family session to play back. Time, of course, is valuable. Segments of family interviews should be selected to illustrate specific points related to target problems.

One other point to keep in mind is the fact that some families may initially feel uncomfortable or self-conscious when recorded. This, however, usually passes with time. Most become accustomed to the equipment being there and essentially forget about it. Video recording should never be used, of course, without each family member's clearly expressed permission.

Homework Assignments

Homework assignments are tasks given to clients to be completed at home outside of the interview. They can be given to individuals or entire families, depending on the assignment. The important thing is that they are clearly specified. They should incorporate at least one of the following elements:

1. Directions regarding specifically what is to be done (e.g., talk about a specified issue, study a handout, or rehearse a specified activity);

2. Specification regarding frequency or amount of times the homework should be done (e.g., do the homework two times each day or during three evenings next week);
3. Specification of how the homework is to be counted or kept track of (e.g., each time the specified homework is done, mark it down on a progress sheet);
4. Directions regarding what is to be brought to the next interview or meeting (e.g., bring your behavioral chart or a list of your partner's strengths);
5. Indications of what will happen under specified circumstance (e.g., you will earn 30 minutes of free time, gain one additional point, or place one dollar in the treatment account each time you participate in the specified behavior) (Sheafor et al., 2000; Shelton & Ackerman, 1974).

In other words, homework assignments should follow our general guidelines for specificity. Family members should understand the assignment's purpose. They should know who will do what and how by when. Finally, they should clearly understand the results of these actions.

Human services professionals are not required to give homework assignments to families. Sometimes, there are none that are appropriate. Other times, families are not willing to cooperate. However, such assignments do provide a viable option for enhancing family treatment time. That is, time to work on problem solving is expanded because some of it occurs outside of the session. Assignments also provide opportunities for families to apply what they have learned in treatment sessions to what they do in their real lives outside of treatment. In other words, they can practice new behavior and skills outside of the interview situation.

Evaluation and Termination with Families

Evaluating progress and goal achievement is as important with families as with any other client system. One facet of evaluation is determining when longer term goals have been met in preparation for termination. Goals should be as clear as possible so that a worker can easily measure their accomplishment. Another facet of evaluation is the ongoing measurement of progress (Street, 1994). For instance, a worker might ask at the beginning of a family session how things went since the last meeting. Were family members able to follow through on

recommendations and plans? Did any events occur to interfere with progress? Did family members accomplish homework assignments? What were the results?

As in termination with any client system, preparing the family for the end of contact with the worker and the agency is important for the worker. Street (1994) suggests asking family members to address a number of questions:

1. What is the current status of the problem?
2. How can the family explain the current status? What has happened since the beginning of intervention?
3. What roles have various family members played in the intervention process?
4. If a comparable problem arose again, how would the family handle it?
5. What issues and events brought the problem to a head in the first place? How has family members' thinking about the problem changed?
6. How do family members feel about ending the intervention process?
7. What factors would indicate the need for counseling again in the future? (pp. 148–150)

Helton and Jackson (1997) emphasize the relationship between follow-up and other aspects of the intervention process. They suggest that "one cannot evaluate a family adequately without referencing the future, that is, what is to follow" (p. 59). One aspect of follow-up is the identification of resources to continue maintenance of the family's homeostasis. Such resources include both what the family has learned throughout the intervention process and external supports they enjoy as a result of the process (such as support from schools, public agencies, or health care organizations).

Family Issues and Services

Several other issues and services concerning families are important to address. These include multiproblem families, family preservation, diversity in families, current family services, and macro practice with families.

Multiproblem Families

Many families that come to you for help will be overwhelmed with a horde of problems. For instance, one family of five may have the following problems affecting one or more of its members:

poverty, physical disability, delinquency, alcoholism, developmental disability, marital or partner discord, inadequate housing, and unemployment. Families will often come to you because they have nowhere else to turn. They will probably be desperate. A state of crisis is likely (crisis intervention was discussed in Chapter 7).

What will you do? Where will you start? How will you begin to sort out the problems and plan strategies to solve them?

Thorman (1982) relates how

. . . one of the most successful approaches to helping the multiproblem family is a problem solving model that enables the family to untangle the web of problems it confronts to establish specific goals to be achieved, and develop the skills needed to solve their problems. (p. 112)

When you work with problems having such multiple levels, there are five primary points to remember:

1. *Do not get overwhelmed yourself.* Stay calm. Try to remain objective. Avoid getting emotionally involved with a series of small crises. You can be of no help to the family unless you retain your professional objectivity and judgment.

2. *Follow the planned change process as you would with any other problem situation in micro, mezzo, or macro practice.* Keep on track. Engage, assess, plan, implement, evaluate, and terminate. Clarify for yourself where you are in the planned change process at all times.

3. *Partialize and prioritize the problems involved.* Partialize or divide the problems up. Define what each problem involves and specify the family member(s) it most affects. Next, prioritize the problems as you would prioritize them for any other case situation. Which are felt to be most important by all family members? Which are most critical? For which do you have a good potential for achieving solutions?

4. *Determine which, if any, problems you can work on yourself.* Part of planning for implementation involves translating client problems into needs. The next logical step is to review what services are available to satisfy these needs. What intervention possibilities fall within your own skill level and job description? Which are services that your agency readily provides? Which are possible to accomplish within your caseload responsibilities and time constraints? Meeting all

the needs evident in a multiproblem family is usually humanly impossible for one practitioner.

5. *Identify and use relevant community resources.* Which client needs demand resources and services that can best be supplied by your agency's staff other than yourself or by other agencies entirely? Making this decision necessitates your need to know about the resources available in your community. Chapter 15 stresses and explains the importance of brokering and case management for a wide range of interventions including those targeting multiproblem families.

Family Preservation

Family preservation services are "intensive services generally delivered in the client's home over a brief, time-limited period. These services were developed to help prevent unnecessary out-of-home placements, keep families together, and preserve family bonds" (Tracy, 1995, p. 973). The concept of family preservation has become a major thrust in agencies throughout the country. It involves doing everything possible to keep the child in the home and provide treatment for the family. Family preservation services are also referred to as family-based services, "home-based services, or in-home treatment" (Berg, 1994, p. 4).

Six goals of family preservation services are: "(1) to protect children, (2) to maintain and strengthen family bonds, (3) to stabilize the crisis situation, (4) to increase the family's skills and competencies, (5) to facilitate the family's use of a variety of formal and informal helping resources, and (6) to prevent unnecessary out-of-home placement of children" (Tracy, 1995; Tracy et al., 1991, p. 1).

In past decades, working with families usually involved focusing on protecting the child. This protection, in turn, often meant removing the child from the home. Services were then provided in a segmented manner by a variety of workers. For example, consider an alleged case of child abuse. One protective services intake worker would gather the intake data when the child was initially referred. Another outreach protective services worker might provide services to the family. Still another would work with the foster family if the child had been placed there.

Family preservation, on the other hand, emphasizes service provision to the family unit in a more coordinated fashion. For instance, one worker might do the majority of the engagement, assessment, planning, intervention, evaluation, termination, and follow-up process. The child would be likely to remain in the home during the entire process. All services would be provided or coordinated by a designated worker with the intent of helping the intact family solve its problems. Under this coordinator's direction, services could be "provided by a treatment team" proceeding with a coordinated and unified effort (often made up of case manager, worker/therapist, and such support staff as the parent educator, homemaker, and so on) (Berg, 1994, p. 5).

Major Themes in Family Preservation

Maluccio (1990) identifies eleven concepts characterizing family preservation programs. They include:

1. *Crisis orientation.* Family preservation is based on intervention when a crisis is taking place within the home. Workers can then take advantage of the family's motivation to alleviate the stress it is experiencing.

2. *Focus on family.* The family is all important. The family is considered the optimum place for children to remain. All intervention emphasis is directed toward keeping the family together and strengthening its members.

3. *Home-based services.* Services are provided in the home whenever possible. The ongoing thrust is improving the home environment.

4. *Time limits.* Because family preservation workers intervene during times of crisis, they work quickly. The intervention process in most models ranges from four to twelve weeks, although some extend longer than that. Setting time limits helps workers and their clients evaluate progress regularly.

5. *Limited, focused objectives.* All intervention objectives are clearly specified. The primary goal is to alleviate the crisis situation and strengthen the family unit so that a crisis is less likely to erupt again.

6. *Intensive, comprehensive services.* Workers' time and attention is concentrated on the families and their progress. The Child Welfare League of America's (CWLA) *Standards for Service to Strengthen and Preserve Families with Children* (1989) suggests that family preservation workers have small caseloads of two to six families. Workers may spend as much as 20 to 25 hours each week arranging for resources and providing services themselves (such as

problem-solving counseling and parenting skills education).

7. *Emphasis on education and skill building.* The family preservation approach is a positive one. The assumption is that people can improve if they are provided with the appropriate information and support.

8. *Coordination.* Because intervention is intensive and numerous resources often are involved, coordination is important. Frequently, a practitioner will assume a case-management role.

9. *Flexibility.* Each family is different, having varying problems and needs. Flexibility enables practitioners to match a wide range of services and resources with the family's needs.

10. *Accessibility.* Workers in family preservation must be readily accessible to families in crisis. Their work is intensive and time limited. Workers' caseloads typically are small so that they can concentrate their efforts.

11. *Accountability.* Accountability, the obligation to accept responsibility for your actions and practice, is considered important. The emphasis on focused objectives and time-limited interventions enhances workers' ability to evaluate their effectiveness.

Family Preservation and Planned Change

A family might be identified as a candidate for family preservation services upon initial intake. There are four criteria for inclusion in such a program (Quinn, 1993). First, "one or more of the children in the family is at imminent risk of out-of-home placement" (p. 30). Second, the family, or at least one adult member of the family, agrees to the service" (p. 30). Third, a "less obtrusive community resource" such as "a parent aide or family counseling" is unavailable or not considered potentially effective (p. 30). Finally it is determined that children's safety will not be compromised by having them remain in the home during service provision.

During engagement, the practitioner works to establish a positive, trusting relationship with family members. The worker should use active listening and a nonjudgmental tone of voice when attempting "to connect with the family and understand their perspective and their wants and desires" (Tracy, 1995, p. 976). The worker can talk with the family about agency roles, responsibilities, and goals (Quinn, 1993). Often, the worker seeks a concrete way to help the family such as making a referral or providing a service to meet an immediate need (Tracy, 1995).

Assessment seeks information about the total family's functioning. Special emphasis is placed on safety issues for children and others in the family in addition to the family's access to necessary resources (including food, shelter, transportation, medical care, and child care) (Tracy, 1995). The worker also assesses "skills in parenting, coping, behavior management or child discipline, and communication" (p. 977). Practitioners can assess family members' concern about issues by observing clients' emotional reactions, verbal and nonverbal cues, expressed desire to work on issues, and level of hopefulness about improvement (Berg, 1994). Throughout assessment, emphasizing clients' strengths is critical (Berg, 1994; Saleeby, 1997). Berg (1994) gives the example of a 22-year-old single mother of a 5-year-old child. A worker should focus on the fact that this mother was able to work through the difficulties and responsibilities of motherhood, while she herself was still a child. This woman "had to solve hundreds of the large and small problems of daily living at a young age. This reframes her as being a competent woman, rather than an irresponsible, unwed teenage mother" (1994, p. 40).

Planning for family preservation intervention involves goal-setting and contracting just like intervention in other generalist practice scenarios. Common goals for individual families might be "to improve parenting, communication, and anger management skills" (Tracy, 1995, p. 977). Berg (1994) makes several suggestions for goal formulation. First, the client must feel that goals are significant. Goals cannot be one-sided on the worker's part. Clients must be committed to working on them. Second, goals should emphasize social interaction both among family members and between them and others in the social environment. The focus of the change process is on the whole family within its own social and economic context, not a particular individual. Third, goals should be "small, simple, and realistically achievable" (1994, p. 70). Like any goals established during planned change, they should be clear and behaviorally specific (Tracy, 1995).

Fourth, goals should be viewed in terms of what can be done positively instead of focusing on problems. For example, consider a situation where a worker focuses on a problem and asks a mother, "When Billy pokes his finger in his little brother Herman's ear, what do you do?" The mother responds, "Well, I scream at the top of my lungs for him to stop or he'll break Herman's eardrum." The worker could rephrase the question to focus on positive rather than negative behavior by asking the mother, "How do you think you can get Billy to keep his fingers to himself and play more appropriately with Herman?" The mother might then respond, "Maybe I could give him some activity projects and praise him for staying on task."

A fifth suggestion for goal formulation is to emphasize that goals are difficult to achieve. In reality, even small goals may be difficult for clients when they involve changing well-established behaviors. If the client fails to achieve a goal as well as could be, you can blame the problem's difficulty, not the client, for failure. Similarly, the client who achieves a difficult goal can take pride in the achievement.

Implementation of a plan can involve a broad range of service provision. Some implementations emphasize "education and skill-building" (Tracy, 1995, p. 977), which include "direct intervention aimed at improving self-esteem, improving communication between family members, teaching anger control, teaching stress management, increasing frustration tolerance, and increasing the caregiver's repertoire of parenting skills" (Quinn, 1993, p. 32). Other services are "concrete" or "hard" (Tracy, 1995, p. 977). These services include "advocacy, information and referral, case management, respite care, and homemaker services" (Quinn, 1993, p. 32). Housing or financial benefits are more examples of concrete services.

Evaluation in family preservation on one level involves determination of whether or not individual family goals were met during the four-to-twelve-week intervention process. On a programmatic level, evaluation concerns whether or not family preservation services are effective. Rzepnicki, Schuerman, and Littell (1991) comment on the usefulness of program evaluation for family preservation services:

> First, they can provide descriptions of program characteristics and clients. The major purpose of this type of evaluation is to monitor service utilization; to provide data for purposes of program funding, program development, or replication; or to monitor compliance with legislation that requires services to be provided to particular categories of clients. Second, evaluations may focus on outcomes to examine the effectiveness of home-based and intensive family preservation services in keeping families together and reducing service costs. (p. 71)

In view of family preservation's time-limited approach, termination is actually introduced during the first family visit when the date is set (Tracy,

1995). The whole service provision process is focused on accomplishing goals and completing itself. There are two dimensions to termination (1995). First, termination establishes the extent to which service goals were achieved for the family. Second, termination should involve linking families to ongoing resources. Family preservation does not intend to cure families of all their ills. Rather, it provides families with necessary skills and connects them to continuing resources in order to keep the family unit intact.

Enhancing Cultural Competency: Diversity and Families

No two families are alike. We have been discussing some of the general techniques that can be applied in a broad range of work with families. Now we will discuss two subgroups of the total pie of families, namely, lesbian and gay families and African American families.

Lesbian and Gay Families

Many of the issues faced in families where parents are gay or lesbian closely resemble those addressed in families with heterosexual parents. However, generalist practitioners need to be aware of some special issues affecting lesbian and gay families. The five issues that we will address here are the impacts of homophobia, lesbians and gay men as parents, coming out to children, special custody issues, and special environmental issues in gay relationships.

Homophobia. Homophobia is "obsessive hostility and fear toward homosexuals" (Masters et al., 1995, p. 385). Whithan and Mathy (1986) potently describe the extent of homophobia:

> Not only are homosexuals criminalized, victimized, and labeled pathological, they are also regarded by some religious groups as sinners deserving to be put to death, a view reminiscent of the Inquisition. There are very few, if any, groups in American society which evoke more hostility than homosexuals. (p. 180)

Lesbian and gay people are women and men "who have a preferential sexual attraction to people of their same sex over a significant period of time" (Masters et al., 1995, p. 372). They cannot legally join the FBI, the CIA, or the military. The Roman Catholic Church has decried homosexual behavior as sinful. In many Protestant churches (although not all denominations), lesbian and gay people are not allowed to join the clergy. Lesbian and gay people have been denied or lost jobs and housing purely on the basis of their sexual orientation. Violence against lesbian and gay people has risen dramatically in the past few years.

Generalist practitioners need to examine homophobia from two perspectives. First, they need to explore and cope with their own homophobia. Second, they must be aware of the oppressive impacts homophobia wreaks on the families of lesbian and gay clients.

Confronting your own homophobia may be very difficult (see Highlight 11.2). It may involve serious soul-searching to identify and evaluate your own

---

HIGHLIGHT 11.2

Confronting Homophobia

Lesbian and gay people live in a heterosexual world. To help understand what being gay or lesbian is like, viewing the world from their perspective is useful. Assuming that you are heterosexual, what would living in a world where the mainstream of society was gay be like? Consider the following questions:

1. What do you think caused your heterosexuality?
2. Have you ever been attracted to someone of your same gender?
3. Do your parents know that you are heterosexual?
4. Are you not worried that your children may also turn out to be heterosexual?
5. Do you ever suffer any discrimination because of your heterosexuality?
6. Why do you not try homosexuality? You might like it.
7. Would you not rather fit in with everybody else in our homosexual society?
8. In view of the fact that there is such a high failure rate in relationships among persons of the same gender, would not sharing a life with someone of the opposite gender be even more difficult?

personal values. A possible consequence may be making some hard distinctions between your own personal opinions and professional values. Some people have expressed serious religious convictions that condemn homosexuality. On the other hand, the human services profession emphasizes individual clients' rights to make choices about their own lives. As a professional, assisting people in solving their problems is your job. Professionally and ethically, you cannot tell clients what to do or how to act.

The second perspective on homophobia involves the oppression lesbian and gay people and their families suffer. We have already noted some aspects of discrimination. Gay people may be denied access to certain jobs and residences. They may be ostracized socially. They may live in constant fear that they will be fired from their jobs if found out. You may need to address the additional problems generated by homophobia just as any other problems your clients may have.

Lesbians and Gay Men as Parents. Many lesbian and gay people have children (Henry, 1993; Laird, 1995; Morales, 1995; Perez, DeBord, & Bieschke, 2000). However, giving an exact number is impossible because no accurate studies exist of how many people are gay (Henry, 1993). Estimates of lesbian and gay adults with children vary from 1.5 to 5 million; and the estimates of the number of children raised in lesbian or gay homes are between 8 and 10 million (Laird, 1995). Realizing that myths prevail about gay and lesbian parents with respect to their children is important. For example, one involves the idea that gay people will goad their children into being gay. This belief is not the case. Children raised by gay or lesbian parents are no more likely to "become gay" than children raised by heterosexual parents (Bailey et al., 1995; Goldenberg & Goldenberg, 1998; Hyde & DeLamater, 2000; Moses & Hawkins, 1982). Looking at this belief in another way, perhaps children with gay parents are raised to be more aware and acceptant of individual human differences in general (Woodman, 1995). Sexual orientation is only one of many ways in which human beings differ from one another.

Coming Out to Children. "Coming out" is the process of "acknowledging to oneself, and then to others, that one is gay or lesbian" (Hyde & DeLamater, 2000, p. 389). Coming out to their children is an issue that many gay and lesbian parents must address. Gay and lesbian people are recommended to come out to their children at the earliest opportune time (Berzon, 1978; Moses & Hawkins, 1982). Morales (1995)

suggests that "being honest, truthful, sincere, and sensitive and using words children can understand are crucial" (p. 1090). Moses and Hawkins (1982) cite at least four reasons for coming out to children early. First, hiding one's homosexuality creates an atmosphere of secrecy. It can give children the impression that sexuality is something to be ashamed of. Second, evading the issue hinders positive, straightforward communication between parents and children. Children may get the idea that they cannot talk to their parents openly about other issues in the same way they cannot talk about their parents' relationships and sexuality. Third, avoidance of the issue runs the risk that children may be informed about their parents' homosexuality from others. Such information may be conveyed in a negative and critical manner. This "information" may only validate for children the homophobic idea that being gay or lesbian is bad. Fourth, the effort of maintaining such secrecy may put pressure on family relationships. Problems such as resentment, anger, rebelliousness, or communication lapses may result.

Human service professionals may be placed in the position of helping gay and lesbian parents come out to their children. Moses and Hawkins (1982) suggest a number of ways in which human services professionals can help parents do this. First, gay and lesbian parents need to be comfortable with the fact that they are gay or lesbian. The more secure gay parents are in their identity as gay people, the more likely the experience of telling their children will be positive (Morales, 1995, p. 1090). The parent may initially express resistance and voice concern about coming out to children. In this case, the human services professional can also help the parent explore reasons for these feelings. Are these reasons valid? Or is the parent painting an exceptionally dark picture? The parent needs to understand that the children eventually will find out anyway. A human services professional can help parents evaluate the possible results and repercussions if they tell the children themselves versus if the children find out from some other source. A human services professional can help gay and lesbian parents explore the contrast between explaining their sexual orientation as a positive aspect of life as opposed to finding out about it as a surprise in a possibly negative way.

Second, gay and lesbian parents need to plan exactly what to tell their children about sexual orientation (Morales, 1995). A human services professional can help them think through what they want to say and how they want to say it, assisting them in role playing the scenario before it actually occurs. Parents can also be prepared for the potential negative responses of their children. As a human services professional, you can suggest ways that parents can react to and cope with such less than desirable reactions. Thinking through the entire situation ahead of time can decrease parents' anxiety and help them to feel they are in greater control.

The third suggestion for helping gay and lesbian parents come out to their children involves timing. If possible, coming out to children who are young is probably least difficult. Becoming familiar and comfortable with an environment in which differences in sexual orientation are considered "normal" helps children incorporate the concept as just another part of life. Sexual orientation then becomes nothing out of the ordinary with which they need to become concerned.

One should note that very young children may not be able to hide the fact of sexual orientation from others very well. They may not be able to discriminate between when sharing this information is appropriate and inappropriate. Children are not sophisticated enough to analyze the effects of telling someone they have parents who are gay or lesbian. Therefore, gay and lesbian parents who come out to very young children need to be prepared to come out to everyone, even if they would choose not to.

An example comes to mind. Take Tabitha, the 6-year-old daughter of a lesbian mother living with her lifetime lover and partner. Tabitha's teacher was talking to Tabitha's first-grade class about the upcoming parent–teacher conferences. Her teacher was saying that she hoped both mothers and fathers would be able to attend. Tabitha raised her hand and, when called upon, blurted out, "I don't have a dad, but both my moms are coming. They sleep together." One's response might be, "So much for subtlety."

Telling older children about being lesbian or gay involves some different issues. Adolescents, adjusting to their own developing sexuality under colossal peer pressure, "are often particularly vulnerable to peer cruelty" (Laird, 1995, p. 1611). Moses and Hawkins (1982) reflect how older children "may be embarrassed by their gay parent(s) in public, and may worry that their friends will find out" (pp. 206–207). They continue, however, that "these worries usually subside after an initial period of time, but they are worth anticipating. An atmosphere of openness and trust will make it easier for children to communicate their reactions directly" (p. 207).

Harry (1988) found that children with gay fathers frequently used "impression management" to control intimidation and criticism by others (p. 110). For example, these children closely scrutinized how they phrased things about their family. Likewise, they would avoid being seen by their friends when with both their father and his lover.

Another idea is to teach children contextual alertness. In other words, teach children to evaluate each situation and the potential reactions of specific individuals involved. They can learn to formulate questions in their heads. For example, does this person seem like one who might be open to homosexuality? What might the negative results be if this person were told? On the other hand, what might the positive results be? Might simply remaining silent be best?

Lesbian and Gay Parents and Child Custody Issues.

Child custody issues often become a major concern for gay and lesbian parents. Therefore, this may be an issue over which gay and lesbian parents may come to you as a human services professional for help. Lesbian and gay parents have experienced major difficulties in custody debates over their children because of their sexual orientation (Berger & Kelly, 1995; Perez et al., 2000). Numerous courts have denied parents custody simply because of being lesbian or gay (Berger & Kelly, 1995). For example, Laird (1995) comments on the courts' treatment of the lesbian family: "Because the lesbian family is not recognized in most social and legal definitions of family, it is also excluded from the social sanctions and benefits that accompany such recognition. Courts have often acted to destroy lesbian family bonds, removing children or making custody of children contingent on the biological mother's living alone and forsaking contact with other lesbians" (p. 1606).

One example is a San Francisco mother who was forced to endure court-mandated personal restrictions concerning custody and visitation of her three children (Lewis, 1980). The court ordered that as a condition for custody the mother see her female lover only at specified times. These times included when her children were at school or when they visited their father. It is legitimate to ask whether such conditions would have been imposed had her lover been a male.

Judges presiding over custody disputes can make arbitrary judgments concerning what is in a child's best interest (Laird, 1995; Moses & Hawkins, 1982). Some judges may have homophobic ideas, which have the potential of influencing their decisions. For instance, one lesbian mother felt forced to move from one state to another. She moved from a state where judges were known to make oppressive decisions concerning gay and lesbian people to another having more liberal legislation and judicial precedents on the part of gay and lesbian parents. The move was triggered by her fear that her ex-husband would attempt to regain custody of their three children if he found out she was lesbian, despite the fact that he had not seen his children for over five years. Additionally, when her family lived with him in the past, he had been physically abusive both to her and to the children. She moved because her chances of winning a potential custody battle were poor in the former state and much improved in the latter.

Human services professionals can help gay/lesbian parents fight and win these custody battles in several ways (Moses & Hawkins, 1982). First, the parent must realize that although progress has been made, the odds for gaining custody are still not good. The parent needs to realize that such cases usually take considerable time and energy. Court cases also frequently cause burdensome stress for both parent and children, in addition to being expensive. Teaching the client such skills as assertiveness, stress management, and problem solving are frequently useful. Another suggestion is to make certain to get a highly competent attorney. Referring the gay parent to support groups is also helpful. Finally, educating the gay parent by providing reading material is often beneficial.

Social and Economic Oppression of Lesbian and Gay People. There are a number of special environmental circumstances characterizing gay relationships. Human services professionals need to be aware of these special conditions in order to help gay and lesbian families cope with them. The first issue involves the right to marry. No state in the nation will allow same-sex couples to marry (Berger & Kelly, 1995; Tully, 1995). California and Hawaii have "domestic partnership systems" where same-sex couples gain some privileges (AASECT, April 2000). Some communities have established a local "domestic partner registry, which extends no city benefits, but provides same-sex couples the opportunity to formalize their relationships" (Wall, 2000, p. 1). Vermont has gone much further by passing a "civil union measure" that stops "just short of allowing same-sex couples to marry" (AASECT, April 2000, p. 6). In effect, same-sex couples may "apply for a license from a town clerk and receive a certificate of civil union." The law lists 24 legal arenas where "the law would treat gay and lesbian couples the same as straight couples, including child cus-

tody, probate court, workers' compensation, and family leave benefits" (AASECT, April 2000, p. 6). However, legal experts indicate that other states will probably not accept such unions as legal.

Heterosexual unions tend to be characterized by much celebration and legal support. Families and friends hold wedding showers, give gifts, and make the wedding itself a major social event. Gay people, however, do not have this legal alternative. "Partners" often cannot be included in health insurance policies. Nor can partners file joint tax returns.

The partner of a gay or lesbian person who becomes critically ill and needs hospitalization may be denied visiting privileges (Laird, 1995). Gay lovers and partners have no legal rights because they do not fall under the legal definition of family. Gay and lesbian couples are encouraged, therefore, to draw up a legal document involving the medical power of attorney; these may address "visitation rights, the right to be consulted and to give or withhold consent about medical decisions, and in case of death, the right to personal effects and the right to dispose of the body" (Schwaber, 1985, p. 92).

Wills and the exercising of their instructions are another source of difficulty for many gay and lesbian couples (Berger & Kelly, 1995; Tully, 1995). Absent a will, gay partners have no inheritance rights. All inheritance will be given to legal family members. Therefore, gay people are strongly encouraged to make a will clearly specifying what possessions will go to which people.

However, relatives may still challenge a will under the concept of "undue influence" (Peters, 1982, p. 24). This principle implies that unfair manipulation has occurred on the part of the gay partner to influence the dictates of a will. Gay people are therefore encouraged to update the contents of the will from time to time. Each time they should ascertain that the will accurately reflects their current assets and that all is well documented.

Being sensitive to the unfairness and oppression suffered by gay and lesbian people is important for human services professionals. Plans and interventions can target not only improving an individual gay or lesbian person's situation, but also at changing larger systems. At the macro level, practitioners can advocate for new laws that forbid discrimination on the basis of sexual orientation. Likewise, workers can exert pressure for the dissolution of old laws and policies that oppress gay and lesbian people.

Working with African American Families

Understanding the cultural expectations, economic conditions, and social realities of the various ethnically and culturally diverse groups whom generalist human services practitioners work with is a necessity. Lloyd and Bryce (1984) stress that workers "must understand the family's culture and values if they are to be effective helpers. Worker insensitivity to cultural values can result in unintended and unrealized attacks on any area of the family's life—language, appearance, relationship patterns, aspirations" (p. 25).

This section examines aspects of practice with African American families. Chapter 3 addressed culturally competent practice more thoroughly with a variety of ethnic groups.

The Many Strengths of African American Families.

Highlight 11.3 emphasizes the importance of understanding African American history in recognizing the oppression African Americans have suffered. "There is little question that individual and group history provide clues about how problems originate and suggest possible avenues for resolution" (Devore & Schlesinger, 1999, p. 140). Developing an appreciation of the many strengths African American families have evolved in response to this oppression is just as important. First, African American families tend to have "strong kinship bonds among a variety of households" (Hatchett & Jackson, 1999; Ho, 1987, p. 180). There is a strong support network developed beyond the simple nuclear family. Viewing this family structure as inferior and inadequate is easy for workers coming from a white mainstream orientation.

For instance, one practitioner worked for a day treatment center that offered both special education and therapy for adolescents with behavioral and emotional problems. A 12-year-old African American client at the center was the source of unending frustration to the human service professional and the other staff. The boy seemed to change his place of residence on a weekly or biweekly basis, which required repeated updating of the bus route responsible for picking him up every day. Additionally, it made working with the boy's family difficult for the boy's human services professional. For one thing, knowing who the primary caretakers were was challenging, because there were so many people involved. For another thing, that kind of extended family structure simply did not fit into the family counseling model to which the worker was accustomed. The worker, by the way, was white and middle-class. She had been trained to work within the context of a nuclear family where the child's two parents were supposed to take total responsibility for the child's welfare.

In this case, the worker could have assumed a more appropriate and effective perspective. She could have looked at the substantial extended family network as a strength rather than a deficit. There were many caring, involved resources and role models available to this boy instead of the one or two provided by parents.

A second strength often available to African American families is the flexibility of family roles (Ho, 1987). Contrary to traditional gender stereotypes, both men and women can assume either emotionally expressive or economically supportive roles. This versatility in roles allows greater flexibility in terms of improving family functioning. It follows that, in a family where both parents are present, a worker should not assume a matriarchal structure just because the mother/spouse makes her points strongly. Marital relationships in African American families tend to be egalitarian by nature.

A third strength inherent in many African American families is their dedication to spirituality and serious involvement in their churches (Ho, 1987; McAdoo, 1987; Schiele, 1999). African American churches provide a massive resource for hope and spiritual growth, social support, and a range of services to meet members' needs. Such services may include "senior citizen activities, child care, educational groups, parenting groups, and housing development" (Ho, 1987, p. 182).

Human Services Practice with African American Families.

McAdoo (1987) identifies three major roles for human services professionals to assume when helping African American families. First, the worker needs to develop empathy for the oppressive cultural context in which African American families must live. Second, the worker must maximize the use of practice skills and available resources to improve the social and economic conditions of African American families. Third, the practitioner must advocate on behalf of African American families to change the policies, regulations, and expectations that act to discriminate against African Americans.

Additionally, Ho (1987) cites at least four major approaches that are useful when working with African American families: (1) engaging the client or family; (2) assessing the family in past and present; (3) setting mutual goals; and (4) identifying the target system for change.

HIGHLIGHT 11.3

The Impacts of History and Oppression on African American Families

This text is a practice text that describes practice skills. However, examining the historical and current social context in which African American families live in order to best apply these skills is important.

McAdoo (1987) relates some of the major historical conditions having an impact on African American families. Initially, of course, African Americans as slaves were often "forced to lie polygamously," "were bred as animals," and saw "a domestic pattern of mother–child units" evolving as the result of plantation life (1987, p. 196). Families had little control over their destiny. Couples were torn apart at the whim of their owners.

Later, during Reconstruction, McAdoo continues, individuals striving to gain and maintain power and white supremacy (e.g., the Ku Klux Klan) worked to make life as restricted as possible for African American people. Many African Americans were forced to move west, leaving extended family behind. Later, in the 1930s, African American families also migrated to the hubs of industrialization in the north. There they could find jobs, despite, once again, leaving much of their extended family network behind.

McAdoo (1987) stresses that "since the mid–1970s, [African Americans] have faced another form of disrup-tion—increased levels of impoverishment and deterio-rating social conditions which have led to further eco-nomic and structural changes in their families" (p. 196). Contributing to this are things such as "lower marital fertility, increases in the rates of divorce and separation, the earlier sexual activity of [African American] youths, the reluctance to give children up for adoption outside the familial networks, delays in marriage, the imbalance in the ratio of men to women, and the high unemploy-ment rate of young [African American] men" (p. 198). African American people are much more likely to be poor than white Americans. African American families are over three times more likely to be poor than white families; 29 percent of African American families in the United States live in poverty, compared to 8 percent of white families (Leashore, 1995). Although "the gap in the educational status of African Americans and whites has been substantially reduced over time . . . differences remain, especially in rates of high school completion and college enrollment (p. 108). Because of deficient conditions, "African Americans have more health prob-lems than do whites" (Leashore, 1995; McAdoo, 1987, p. 202), in addition to a higher death rate (Leashore, 1995; McAdoo, 1987).

Thus, prevalent values in African American families have resulted both from the history of slavery and from ongoing oppression suffered since those times. Human services practice with African American families needs to proceed within the context of the resulting social and economic conditions.

Engage the client/family. Regardless of race, empathizing with a family and its situation is important. The referral process may have been tedious or confusing. Family members may have had bad experiences with agencies in the past, which can eat away at trust.

Understanding the initial silence and apparent lack of communication often posed by African American family members is also important. This silence may convey their lack of faith and confidence either in your ability to help them while in the role of worker or in the agency's commitment in and abil-ity to do so. Family members may be experiencing their own anger at how they have been treated by white society. Their resentment may indirectly be projected onto you.

Reasons for communication blocks need to be addressed just like any other issues raised in the problem solving process. If you are not African American and especially if you are white, you may want to discuss straightforwardly any racial tensions you may perceive. Do not be defensive if family members express anger. It is logical for them, if they have negative feelings, to vent them at you just because you are there. These feelings must be addressed and placed within perspective before the problem solving process can proceed.

On the one hand, be understanding. However, on the other, also be strong and assertive. Most African American families will expect the worker to compe-tently and straightforwardly lead the intervention process.

Finally, realize that most African American families will react most positively to an intervention process with clearly identified goals and with constraints on how long it will take to get results. In other words, telling an African American family that the change process will take an indeterminable amount of time will probably not be well received.

Assess the family in past and present. Understanding dynamics in African American families is as critical as it is in other families. Most African American families are more interested in what is going on in the present than in the past. Therefore, the reasons for soliciting information about more historical issues (e.g., how parents themselves were raised by grandparents or what family incidents occurred several years ago that had serious impact on the family) need clear explanation regarding why they are important.

Set mutual goals. Goal setting is just as important when working with African American families as any other families. The chances are likely that the African American family will be plagued by a number of concurrent problems. Therefore, the worker must both be problem-oriented and maintain a focus on how circumstances outside of the family fuel the problem. An African American family would probably consider solving an economically related problem (like unemployment) much more important than resolving interpersonal conflicts (e.g., a disagreement between partners). The family's top priorities need to be addressed first. Additionally, the faster a problem can be solved, the more cooperative family members will probably become.

Identify the target system for change. As with any other family, the worker needs to identify the systems in need of change. This identification should be done in a prioritized order. Sometimes, the problem can best be solved by targeting an external entity like the schools or the health care system. At other times, interpersonal change is needed within the African American family system.

The Current Status of Family Services

Family services are those provided by human services agencies that focus on the needs of families and couples. In other words, a broad array of agencies can provide services to families as long as these agencies clearly state that families are to be the primary recipients of service. One survey of North American Family Service agencies (Family Service America, 1984) found that "the major concerns of families are unemployment, single-parenthood, increased family violence, incest, blurred sex roles, depression and loneliness, and alcohol and drug abuse" (Erickson, 1987, p. 593). Erickson also states that programs include various types of counseling, "educational programs, financial assistance programs, employee assistance programs, and programs geared toward effecting social or institutional change" (1987, p. 593).

The types of family services available in any particular community depend on what the community needs, on the one hand, and what it can afford to pay for, on the other. Thus, the services available to families vary drastically from one area to another. Most family service agencies provide services directly to individuals, groups of individuals facing similar problems, and the families themselves. For example, they might provide individual counseling for depressed family members, support groups for battered women, or family counseling for entire families.

However, there is also a definite macro practice aspect to the family service agency. It typically addresses problems held by a number of people in the community. When services are not available, the generalist practitioner may need to assess the community's needs. For instance, the worker may determine that substance abuse treatment services are inadequate to meet the needs of families within the community. That worker may then proceed to gather data to document that the need truly exists and subsequently to advocate for the expansion of current programs.

In another situation, the worker may discover that substance abuse services are available but are not getting to the people who really need them. In this case, the worker may investigate what is causing this blockage and try to remedy the problem. For instance, are available treatment programs not being publicized adequately? Is the red tape so thick that cutting through it and getting service is difficult for people? Or, for some reason, are agency policies making the neediest people ineligible?

Whatever the reason, family service agencies can provide effective and flexible resources to help satisfy community families' real needs. Generalist human services professionals may be called upon not only to serve individuals, families, and groups but also to advocate for changes in agency policies, governmental legislation regarding how resources are distributed, and expansion of services that are already there.

Erickson (1987) emphasizes the importance of empowering people via family service agencies; in other words, he stresses "helping people to help themselves" (p. 592). One aspect of the generalist human services professional's macro role is to help people join and work together in order to bring about their own changes.

Macro Practice with Families: Promoting Social and Economic Justice

Thorman (1982) cites insufficient income, inadequate housing, lack of job opportunities, and deficient services both for transportation and recreation as being primary problems among the families who turn to family-based service agencies for help. He continues that "our nation's professed belief that the family is the cornerstone of our society is not matched by public policy. We have not really addressed the question of how to guarantee all families the conditions necessary for family support" (1982, p. 91). Unfortunately, this situation has not improved in the past two decades. Unavailability of health insurance, lack of supportive day care services for the children of parents who work, and a dearth of strategies to train workers for skilled vocations where jobs are available are among the myriad of problems confronting America's families.

Generalist practitioners in agency positions often feel frustrated and overwhelmed at the concept of changing the system because it is not working right. They often feel they have enough to do with their daily micro and mezzo practice concerns. However, the roots of clients' problems should always be kept in mind. Sometimes there might be an opportunity to amend an agency policy, even a relatively minor one, so that clients are better served. A worker may be able to assist in a political campaign to elect people who are more sensitive to families and their needs. Or, a worker might be able to advocate for clients to prove the need for some service and to succeed in making that service available to people who really need it. Highlight 11.4 proposes six policy areas meriting practitioners' attention.

The Generalist Intervention Model emphasizes constant awareness of the impacts of macro systems. The potential to make improvements in agencies, organizations, and systems should never be forgotten as one means of effecting positive change for clients.

Poverty is a major stumbling block obstructing the progress of multitudes of American children, and, in effect, their families (Coulton & Chow, 1995). A different configuration of services could be made available to American families if policies geared towards family were improved (Kamerman, 1995). Generalist practitioners should best keep these concepts in mind when considering intervention alternatives. Sometimes, macro level changes may be possible. Improved family service policies would follow a number of principles.

First, all families should have access to the services they need regardless of their income bracket. Second, services should be distributed along neither racial nor economic lines. In other words, the same quality of services should be available to everyone. Agencies providing family services would have a mixture of races and economic levels characterizing its clientele. Third, services should be convenient for everyone. All families should have access to coordinating referral and appointment centers that they could contact. Fourth, families should have as many options as possible so that they could select the service of their preference. Fifth, parents should be given significant input into the agencies and their policies serving families. Sixth, more volunteers and paraprofessionals should be used to aid in service delivery. Using such people to perform less specialized tasks would minimize the cost of expensive specialists. Finally, seventh, more resources should be devoted to preventing problems before they occur rather than applying Band-Aids after the problems already exist. A more superficial view sees prevention as an extravagance that is not absolutely necessary. Therefore, the programs and services that could prevent and minimize problems often rest at the bottom of priority lists. When money runs out, programs aimed at prevention are frequently among those first cut.

InfoTrac College Edition

This chapter applied generalist practice skills to working with families and using the planned change process with families. Skills include reframing and teaching problem-solving skills and child-management methods. Other skills covered included family support, role playing, video recording, and using homework assignments. Related topics include working with multiproblem families and issues involved in working with gay/lesbian and African American families. For further information on these areas, enter the following search terms:

teaching families
family support
child management

HIGHLIGHT 11.4

Families, Macro Practice, and the Integration of Policy and Practice

Because of the major focus on resources and their availability to families, the importance of macro practice is easily stressed. Needed resources are only available if agencies and organizations provide them. These agencies offer them only if their policies and procedures allow them to do so. Sometimes, agency and social policies restrict resources. Other times, policies simply deny that such potential resources exist. Hence, as a generalist human services practitioner, you may have to advocate and work for changes in organizational and social policies so that resources are made available to the people who need them.

There are a number of policy areas that critically affect the well-being of families (Kamerman, 1984, 1995; Kamerman & Kahn, 1981). The policies existing in these areas merit careful attention and scrutiny. Each policy issue has dramatic and direct effects upon your clients, including both families and individuals. They include the following six.

1. Employment

How family members can work to gain income is dictated by policy. World and national policies determine where jobs will be located and what kind they will be. For example, if the cost of running a farm continues to escalate and small U.S. farmers cannot compete with others in the world, small U.S. farmers may go bankrupt. However, the government can subsidize these farmers. For example, the government can (and does) formulate policies to help farmers pay their farming costs. Other policies can add charges to imported farm produce so that U.S. farmers can compete with foreign prices. Such policies tend to decrease the farmer's potential for bankruptcy.

Another example involves providing money for job training. Programs can be developed to pay for training certain segments of the population for jobs that need to be filled. Training takes money. If poor people in an urban ghetto or a rural enclave cannot afford training, they will not get it. Thus, they will not get the jobs. However, if training is provided and paid for in another way, these same people will get jobs.

What if the unemployment rate in your clients' community is more than 50 percent, as is the case for many young people in urban ghettos? Even then, those who are employed receive minimum wages and no benefits (such as health insurance, sick leave, or vacation). What can you do to help your clients gain adequate employment under such circumstances if no programs and policies exist to help you?

This book is neither an economics nor a policy text. You probably guessed that. However, the book does intend to depict clearly how policy at various system levels has direct impact on clients and what they are able to do. It also, of course, affects what *you* can *do* for clients.

2. Direct provision of income or substitutes for income

How income is provided or not provided to designated groups of people is a policy matter. How much money is provided to a family without resources varies drastically from one state to another. This money directly affects the family's quality of life. Thus, the greater level of public assistance payments provided in one state allows the same family greater potential for a better quality of life there than lower payments in another state.

Substitutes for income, otherwise referred to as "in-kind income transfers," can also provide resources to families. Food stamps, which can be exchanged only for groceries, are a good example. Criteria for who is eligible to get food stamps and how many they can get vary drastically from state to state.

What do you do when your clients are not eligible for enough cash and in-kind income transfers to survive? What do you do if policies neglect clients who are slowly starving to death?

3. Health care

Policies determine who is or is not eligible for publicly financed health care such as Medicaid or Medicare. Even those who are eligible find that such programs either do not pay enough or do not cover certain health needs at all. Additionally, many health care facilities will not accept such payments because they do not pay full costs, are administratively burdensome, or take too long to actually arrive.

Even for those with private insurance (many millions of people have none), policies also determine what is paid for and how much. For instance, a deductible of

$1000 that must be paid before the insurance company will begin paying anything might as well be a billion dollars for clients who do not have ready access to money at all.

Designated maximum amounts for specific health services create other problems. For instance, take an insurance policy that allows $500 for alcohol and drug rehabilitation services. If the entire program costs $7000 or more, what good will the measly $500 do?

4. Homeless people

More and more families, especially those including only women and children, are homeless. Rents are escalating. Affordable housing is becoming increasingly difficult to find throughout the nation. What do you as a human services professional do if there are no programs with policies to provide your clients temporary shelter, food, and longer-term housing? What do you do if families are living literally on the streets?

5. Day care

Most women work. More specifically, most women with children work. Adequate day care for their children is difficult, if not impossible, to find. It is also expensive, and the quality is highly variable. Should the federal, state, and/or local governments establish policies to provide resources for day care so that parents can work? Are you and others willing to pay taxes to finance these services?

What if your client is a single parent who receives public assistance payments barely allowing her to subsist below the poverty level? What if she wants to go out, get a job, and support herself, but is unable to because she cannot afford the available day care? What policy changes might help her?

6. Child support maintenance

Policies dictate how much support divorced fathers provide their children. (Of course, mothers may also be required to provide support to children living with their fathers.) Policies also mandate how the receipt of that support is monitored. In other words, if the family does not receive the financial support it is supposed to, then what happens? Do existing policies indicate that a portion of the father's salary can be garnished, that is, legally removed from his pay and sent to his family before he receives his paycheck? Will policies mandate that this happens automatically, or must the mother seek legal counsel to advocate for her? What happens if the father moves to another state? Will that state's policies allow the garnishment of wages?

What if your client, a single parent and mother of two, works for a minimum wage, cannot afford adequate housing on that income, and desperately needs support payments to subsist? Even minimum wages are determined by policies. How will policies help or prevent you from helping her get her due resources?

The problems evident in all six policy issues are difficult to solve. The questions raised are hard to answer. However, these are questions and issues that generalist practitioners must face every day. What provides the direction is the human service professional's ethical perspective of seeking the best route for the common good. Many times, advocacy on behalf of clients is paramount. Searching and working for policy change may be critical.

gay families
African American families

 On the Internet

Because of the very dynamic nature of the Web, URLs are subject to change. Therefore, be sure to check out the companion Website for this book at http://www.humanservices.wadsworth.com, where links will be updated periodically.
www.cwla.org/
www.thegayconnection.com/
www.cglbrd.com/
www.lesbian.org/lesbian-moms/
www.nbcdi.org

CHAPTER 12

Human Services Generalist Practice with Groups

Six young adults sat around the room fidgeting nervously and avoiding each other's eyes. Each wondered what the others were thinking. All would describe themselves as shy, inadequate, and depressed. This was despite the fact that their individual personalities varied drastically. All had tried to kill themselves at least once, which is why they were gathered together in that room. The six were about to begin their involvement in a treatment group. The group's initial purpose was to help the participants explore the reasons for their sadness and begin to build more fortified self-concepts and lives. The counselor entered the room. Group treatment was about to begin.

Juanita Curacoa, chairperson of the group, felt increasingly anxious. She had already interrupted Mr. Fischer twice. There he was rambling on again about irrelevant details. He simply would not stop talking, and she had only 23 more minutes to bring the group to a consensus. This group was a task group trying to initiate a plan for publicizing a new child abuse prevention program. Finally, at her wit's end, she stated loudly and assertively, "Excuse me, Mr. Fischer. I appreciate your ideas and input. Our time is very limited. We need to hear what the other group members have to say." The rest of the people in the room seemed to breathe a simultaneous sigh of relief. The meeting proceeded.

Lamar is a 9-year-old with cognitive disabilities who has lived with foster parents almost since birth. Lamar has a number of serious delays in development including intellectual, language, social, and physical (both fine and gross motor). Even though he resides in foster care, he remains involved with his biological parents and his seven siblings still living with them. The biological family struggles with a multitude of problems including poverty, truancy, illness, and the mother's own cognitive disability. The foster parents and the biological parents do not like each other much and quarrel regularly. Lamar visits his biological family on a weekly basis.

A number of professionals sit around a large rectangular table discussing Lamar and his situation. Each had evaluated his case and now will make professional recommendations. They all are participating in an interdisciplinary team staffing (i.e., a planning meeting involving a number of different professional disciplines). A human services professional is the case coordinator. It is her job to run the meeting and help bring the team to conclusions regarding the best plan to help Lamar. The speech, physical, and occupational therapists, along with the nurse, physician, psychologist, and psychiatrist would all share their findings. Together they would formulate plans to help Lamar, his foster family, and his biological family. As case coordinator, the human services professional is responsible for pulling together a broad range of information so that it makes sense. Her task is to lead the group in formulating effective intervention plans.

 ## *Introduction*

The previous examples illustrate the types of groups that human services professionals might lead. Much of human services occurs within, by, or for groups. A human services professional, therefore, needs both group knowledge and skills. Increasingly, human services professionals use groups for a variety of purposes. A group is defined as "a collection of people, brought together by mutual interests, who are capable of consistent and uniform action" (Barker, 1999, p. 201). Groups help chemically dependent people and those trying to lose weight. Groups help children cope with the divorce of their parents, teach new foster parents about the effect of separation and placement on foster children, and help family members deal with many problem areas. They assist persons with psychiatric disabilities to live in their own communities through such mechanisms as peer-led recovery groups, advocacy groups, and family support groups (Mackelprang & Salsgiver, 1999). Human services professionals also play a role in some self-help groups such as Parents Anonymous.

In addition, human services professionals use groups to gather information about clients and to help plan interventions. In many settings, human services professionals participate in staffings where colleagues from other disciplines share their knowledge about a particular client. Case conferences are common in medical settings and other types of agencies.

Finally, most human services professionals will participate in agency staff meetings where the focus may be on new policies, in-service training, or agency problems. In each case, the human services professional will need specific knowledge and skills to participate as an effective group member, leader, or facilitator.

This chapter will:

- examine two major types of groups, treatment and task;
- describe the various roles generalist practitioners frequently assume in groups;
- formulate a framework for understanding groups;
- outline the skills needed to work effectively with groups;
- discuss basic elements that have an impact on group dynamics, such as group culture and norms, size, and composition;
- explore various decision-making approaches used in groups;
- review micro skills essential for working with groups.

 ## *Types of Groups*

There are different ways to categorize the types of groups with which human services professionals are frequently involved. Perhaps the most common approach is to divide groups into either *task groups* or *treatment groups*. Each of these two basic types can be further divided into more specific categories.

Task Groups

As their name suggests, task groups exist to achieve a specific set of objectives or tasks. Concerted attention is paid to these tasks, and attainment of the desired ends assumes great importance. The objectives help determine how the group operates as well as the roles played by members. The following list is not exhaustive but provides examples of the types of task groups with which the human services professional may come in contact. They include boards of directors, task forces, committees and commissions, legislative bodies, staff meetings, multidisciplinary teams, case conferences (staffings), and social action groups. The possible roles the human services professional might play are described under each type.

Boards of Directors

A board of directors is an administrative group charged with responsibility for setting the policy governing agency programs. The board is a legal entity established by the bylaws, organizational charter, or articles of incorporation. Normally, the board hires and supervises the agency director and determines policy within which the agency must operate. Such policy has direct impact on what agency practitioners can and cannot do for clients. Boards often establish subgroups or committees responsible for such things as personnel policies, finance, and building.

Members of the board are not usually experts in the operation of the agency but are elected or selected based upon other contributions they may make. For instance, they are often prominent community citizens and may financially support the agency.

Human services professionals working with a board of directors for the first time may find it challenging. Board members know a great deal less about the organization than many agency staff members and must be kept well informed. As laypersons, they may not understand why a program exists and may not share all the values of agency staff. Because their position is one of authority (remember, they hire and fire the director who can hire or fire you and your supervisors), working with board members takes tact and finesse. Because they provide the agency with a strong connection to the community and are often instrumental in fund-raising, board members are an irreplaceable asset for the agency.

Task Forces

Task forces are groups established for a special purpose and usually disbanded after completion of their task. They may be created by any of the other task groups mentioned in this section. For example, a board of directors might appoint a task force to explore new funding approaches for the twenty-first century. A United Way task force may be established to consider better ways of distributing funds to new agencies. Members of the task force usually are appointed because of their special expertise or interest in the topic under consideration. They are expected to study the idea or problem, consider alternatives, and prepare a report. After completion of the report, the task force usually goes out of existence.

Committees and Commissions

Committees are groups responsible for dealing with specific tasks or matters. They may be formed by people in virtually any agency or organization. Members of a committee may be appointed or elected, depending upon the type of committee. A board of directors may create a personnel committee to develop personnel policies for the agency and evaluate the agency director's performance. An agency may appoint a committee to plan the annual holiday party. Committees typically work in a particular area and may be either standing or ad hoc. A standing committee is one that exists on a continuous basis. It may be provided for in an organization's bylaws (e.g., an executive committee or finance committee) or it may be established by agency administrators (e.g., a speakers' committee).

An ad hoc committee, like a task force, is set up for one purpose and expected to cease operation after completing its task. A committee to revise an organization's bylaws is a good example of an ad hoc committee. Much like task force members, committee members may be selected because they have a particular interest in the committee's task or because of their expertise.

Commissions are similar to committees in that they also are responsible for a particular task. They are usually ongoing in nature. A community may have a city planning commission, a nondiscrimination and affirmative action commission, and a police and fire commission. These groups exist to help city officials with particular tasks. The planning commission may review all requests for new buildings or consider only those falling into a certain category. The nondiscrimination committee may investigate charges of discrimination in application of city laws and regulations. The police and fire commission may help set policy for the police and fire departments. Commission members may be elected but usually are appointed by an administrator with approval of the governing board. Members of such groups are called commissioners.

Legislative Bodies

Legislative bodies include city councils, county boards of supervisors, state legislatures, and the U.S. Congress. Composed of elected representatives, these bodies have legal responsibility for establishing laws and appropriating funds for programs established by law. A human services professional's interaction with these bodies can occur in many ways. Human services professionals currently serve as elected members of each of these bodies. They may also be called upon or choose to testify before legislative bodies considering laws affecting clients, which might include funding for social programs, family leave legislation, or Social Security policy. Sometimes, a human services professional may serve on the staff of a legislative body, handling details such as scheduling, locating meeting sites, and ensuring that identified tasks are carried out. Because legislative bodies establish policies (laws) that affect which social programs are created and funded, being familiar with how these bodies operate is important for human services professionals. They also must be prepared to testify about the need for programs and to work with members of legislative bodies to achieve human services purposes. Such purposes might include licensing of human services professionals at all levels and funding for social programs. Finally, they must be willing to serve as members of legislative bodies.

Staff Meetings

Staff meetings are meetings composed of agency staff members who assemble periodically for some identified purpose. Some agencies have meetings of all staff members on a regular basis. Others assemble only small groups regularly (such as all supervisors or all members of the foster care staff). Staff meetings occur for the purposes of explaining new policy, keeping all participants informed about changes in the agency, or introducing new staff. Sometimes, the meetings have the social or emotional function of bringing all staff members together to enhance the sense of commonality or "we" feeling. Often, the agency director or other supervisory personnel preside over the staff meeting. Depending upon the type of agency (and preferences of the director), the meeting may consist of an administrator announcing new policies and

everyone else listening, or it may be a discussion session where all members are equally free to contribute ideas and reactions.

Multidisciplinary Teams

Multidisciplinary or M teams are groups of professionals from various disciplines that meet to discuss specific clients with whom team members are working. In a state institution for patients with severe cognitive disabilities, a team may consist of a human services professional, nurse, medical doctor, psychologist, and aide. In a hospital healthworks program, the M team may include a registered nurse, human services professional, dietician, and psychologist. One member of the team often serves as the leader, but all members are responsible for their specific area of expertise. Typically, the team meets regularly.

Case Conferences and Staffings

A case conference is "a procedure often used in social agencies and other organizations to bring together members of a professional staff and others to discuss a client's problems, objectives, intervention plans, and prognoses" (Barker, 1999, p. 62). Case conferences, also called staffings, are similar to multidisciplinary teams. One difference is that, unlike the M team, the members who compose the case conference may not be perceived as, or see themselves as, a team. They may meet on an as-needed basis instead of regularly. Depending upon the type of agency, members participating in the case conference or staffing may be from the same or different disciplines.

Sometimes an entire department will staff a client. Here, all members can contribute to the decision making. For example, one juvenile probation department staffs all cases where the probation officer's presentence investigation includes a recommendation for incarceration. Other probation officers look at the same evidence gathered by the investigating officer and consider whether or not the recommendation was appropriate. The purpose of a staffing is to bring the wisdom of others to bear on a particular situation to arrive at the best solution or recommendation.

Social Action Groups

Social action is

a coordinated effort to achieve institutional change to meet a need, solve a social problem, correct an injustice, or enhance the quality of human life. This effort may occur at the initiative and direction of professionals in social welfare, economics, politics, religion, or the military, or it may occur through the efforts of the people who are directly affected by the problem or change. (Barker, 1999, pp. 446–447)

The purpose of social action groups is to change the physical or social environment (Toseland & Rivas, 1998). Beneficiaries of this change may be either members of the social action group or other nonmembers. Goals might include getting the city to enforce health and building codes, changing the eligibility requirements for a specific social program, or modifying rules or laws that discriminate against a particular class of persons. Highlight 12.1 provides an example of a social action group.

Another example of a social action group might be composed of human services professionals testifying before a legislative body requesting funds for drug and alcohol treatment programs. Yet another example would be citizens asking the city council to rezone their neighborhood to stop the conversion of existing homes into multifamily housing. The human services professional may be a group member or serve as the group's leader. Another possible role is a staff or resource person to the group. In this role, the worker might help arrange meetings, provide the names of contact persons within existing agencies and organizations, or assist the group in whatever ways are needed. Having the skill to help the group reach its goal, while ensuring sufficient stability of the group until completion of the task, is important for the worker (Toseland & Rivas, 1998). For example, the worker might help the group over rough spots such as early setbacks or failures by encouraging and supporting their efforts and then might follow up on all decisions to make certain that the group's wishes are carried out.

Treatment Groups

Treatment groups are any groups where the primary focus is on members' emotional and social needs. Five types of treatment groups will be discussed: growth, therapy, educational, socialization, and support (Toseland & Rivas, 1998). In each group, there is a presumption that the individual member of the group is going to benefit directly from the existence of the group. Usually, individual change occurs within group members, and that change is often the reason for the group's creation.

Growth Groups

As the name suggests, growth groups are designed to encourage and support the growth of the individual group member. The presumption is that this growth can be done by helping the member achieve insight or self-understanding. The group experience may consist of various activities designed to help participants reach their goals. One example would be a group focused on helping couples learn to communicate better. A series of exercises might be done emphasizing listening skills, value clarification, and

---

HIGHLIGHT 12.1

Social Action Within a University

The staff members in the university counseling and health office were becoming increasingly concerned about policies and procedures being initiated by the program director. The policies and procedures did not seem directed toward helping students and appeared increasingly erratic. The director often threatened to fire staff who disagreed with him and implied that all his actions had the backing of his immediate supervisor. Although he possessed a nursing degree, the director was also making decisions beyond his level of training and competence. After several failed attempts to talk directly to the director, staff members met and decided that additional steps would be necessary to change the situation and restore harmony within the program. Each staff member wrote to the vice-president for Health and Counseling Services (the program director's supervisor) and identified individual concerns. A copy of each letter was sent to the director so that he was made aware of the staff's continuing concern. The letter also clearly stated that the staff had decided to follow the appropriate chain of command to create change. In other words, the staff was committed to take the issue up to the director's supervisor and even higher levels, if necessary. Following discussions between the vice-president, the director, and members of the staff, the director chose to resign his position, and a search was conducted for a replacement.

sending clear messages. Another example is a group composed of women who have sought refuge in a domestic violence shelter. The group meets twice a week with a focus on helping the members explore what they want from their lives. Activities include a time for each person to talk about her immediate and long-term goals and didactic presentations on the pattern of violent relationships. The group also makes the women aware of alternatives open to them, such as court-imposed restraining orders and financial resources in the community, and supports them in their efforts to be free of abuse. Growth groups focus on helping individuals achieve their potential and building on their strengths. There is no presumption that members necessarily have a "problem."

In growth groups, the worker is a facilitator, helping the group members attain their goals. As with all groups, the worker's role involves a higher level of activity in early stages and less activity as the group develops.

Therapy Groups

Therapy groups help clients who have an identified goal of changing some aspect of their behavior. The term includes groups where the objective is recovering from problematic life experiences. Such groups include a hospital-sponsored group for clients 20 percent or more overweight, an inpatient group for chemically dependent patients, and a group for people who abuse their children. The focus is on correcting a perceived intrapersonal or interpersonal problem or learning better problem solving and coping styles.

The worker role is one of higher visibility in this type of group. The worker may begin as a director, expert, or leader, depending upon the needs of the group, but probably will become more of a facilitator as the group progresses. Working with therapy groups generally requires an advanced degree in human services.

Educational Groups

Educational groups include a variety of groups designed to provide members with information about themselves or others. The purpose, as suggested by the name, is to educate or teach the group members about some issue or topic. This education may be done through didactic presentations, role playing, activities, and discussions. Examples include a group for prospective adoptive parents, natural childbirth groups, and practical parenting groups. Educational groups are similar to growth groups in that there is no presumption that members have a

"problem." Educational groups tend to have less interaction among leaders and members than growth or therapy groups.

As in the therapy group, the worker in an educational group is often a group leader who may be doing much of the presentation of new information and serve as the group expert. In a group focused on teaching parents new child nurturing skills, a undergraduate human services practicum student developed the curriculum after reviewing similar programs, put together the charts and exercises to be used by participants, and led the group through each session.

Socialization Groups

Socialization groups assist participants in acquiring skills necessary to become "socialized" into the community. The presumption is that the group members have a deficit of some sort in social skills. For example, a group might be developed for adolescents who have been involved in delinquent behavior. By their actions, they have demonstrated an inability to abide by society's norms. Socialization groups frequently make great use of structured experiences or activities as a medium for change and rely less on member-to-member discussion. In some cases, the activities become the primary or only intervention that occurs. Adventure-based or experiential counseling programs are one example. These adolescent programs include heavy emphasis on physical skill, testing one's courage, and building both teamwork and self-reliance. The programs increase the self-confidence of group members, improve their social skills, and redirect their energies into socially approved activities. In these programs, group members are challenged by a series of physical hurdles, including climbing over barriers, rappelling down a cliff, and crossing a stream on a rope.

A current events group at a nursing home is another example. In this case, group emphasis is on getting the residents to interact with one another by discussing current events. The group also has a goal of helping to keep the residents' minds active and oriented to the present.

The human services professional's role in socialization groups is often one of highest visibility. This visibility may include serving as director or expert, designing the program, and leading members through the process and exercises. As with other types of groups, that role may change as the group enters later stages of development.

The role of the human services professional in each of these treatment groups has some similarities and some differences. To summarize, the leader will have the highest visibility in educational, therapy, and socialization groups. In each case, the worker may be a director, expert, or leader. In the growth group and some therapy groups, the leader may be more of a facilitator, simply helping the group members attain their goals. Commonly, the worker is more active in the early stages of all groups. Once a group becomes established, the worker's role often changes to that of a consultant, expert, and role model. Group needs usually determine the role to be played by the human services professional. Therefore, human services professionals must be flexible and modify their type and level of involvement as needed. They also need to use a variety of skills, depending upon the group's stage of development, the skills of the members, and the type of group.

Support Groups

Support groups are groups of people sharing certain characteristics who get together to provide one another with "encouragement, information, and sustenance" (Barker, 1999, p. 474). They typically have a professional leader and may be formally or informally organized. Because they exist to accomplish a variety of goals, they may share some characteristics with the groups we have already discussed. For example, one support group is the La Leche League. This group is devoted to encouraging breast-feeding of infants and to helping parents better understand the advantages of this method over the use of baby formula. In some ways, this organization is similar to the educational group in that members are not presumed to have a "problem." Rather, they share the characteristic of being parents (or prospective parents) of infants. As might be expected, much of the activity in group meetings is educational in purpose.

Another example is a support group offered by a domestic violence shelter. This program, aimed at older women, deals with topics such as medical insurance, money management, and age discrimination in the workplace. Meeting twice a month for one and a half hours, the group provides emotional support, fosters learning opportunities, and helps more mature women experiencing domestic violence recognize their unique strengths, problems, and options.

The term *support group* is sometimes used interchangeably with *self-help group,* because both share a goal of having members provide support to one another. Self-help groups, however, are less likely to have professional leadership. To further complicate matters, you will recognize that many different types of groups provide members with advice, emotional support, information, and other help. Examples include support groups for people with chemical dependency problems, educational groups for new foster parents, and treatment groups for men who batter. Thus, support might be considered a component of many different types of groups. As a result of this confusion, the term *support group* is less clearly delineated than the other types of groups previously discussed. What is most important to remember is that the term is frequently used in human services to refer to groups with a strong mutual support emphasis.

All of the group types identified earlier are merely examples of the range of groups used in human services. In practice, seeing two or more group approaches used within the same group is common. For example, Plasse (1995) reports on a treatment group for recovering addicts that combined therapy for substance abuse, education on child development and family management, and growth content on improving communication skills. Activities used in the group included role playing, values-clarification exercises, and creative writing. While the group was primarily therapeutic, it contained elements found in several other group types. Plasse termed this approach a "psycho educational model," reflecting the merging of educational and socioemotional approaches.

Brennan (1995) describes using a psychoeducational group for work with patients experiencing bipolar psychiatric disability.[1] Using a strengths-based model, he combined education with group support to help patients and their families learn problem-solving skills and acquire knowledge about this illness, its treatment, and community resources.

 ## Worker Roles in Groups

That human services professionals play multiple leadership roles in groups will be clear from the many examples in this chapter. This section briefly discusses some common human services professional roles and describes how they are used in work with groups. The roles are broker, mediator, educator, and facilitator.

---

1. Bipolar disorder, formerly called manic-depressive illness, involves an impairment of mood characterized by some combination of hyperactivity and depression or sadness.

Broker

Brokers help group members obtain needed resources by connecting them with community agencies. This process requires that the worker be familiar with community resources, have general knowledge about eligibility requirements, and be sensitive to client needs. A broker may help the client obtain emergency food or housing, legal aid, or other needed resources. A worker may act as a broker either in one-to-one situations or in a group.

Community resource books or interest-based directories can prove helpful to new and experienced workers. These books typically describe most services in a community, including eligibility requirements, contact persons, addresses, and telephone numbers. Brokers can use such listings to augment those with which they are familiar. To be most helpful, the worker should attempt to aid the client through referral to specific staff members. Clients going to a new agency without having a contact person or much information about how to use the resource can have a bad experience and become discouraged from using the agency. A more detailed review of the broker role appears in Chapter 15.

Mediator

Mediators help group members resolve conflicts or other dissension (Toseland & Rivas, 1998). To be most successful in this role, the worker must believe that different sides to a disagreement are legitimate and help each side recognize that its views are valid. Avoiding win-lose situations (described later in this chapter) is an important task of the human services professional as mediator. Therefore, the worker must help the parties identify the points of disagreement and of mutual interest. The worker then must focus on finding a solution that meets the needs of all. Finally, on another level, the worker may help group members negotiate with the environment or other systems. This negotiation is especially important when the client finds resource systems intimidating and impersonal. The worker can help bridge this gulf and build on the broker role described earlier.

Educator

As a teacher, the human services professional provides group participants with new information, structures the presentation of that information, and uses modeling to help members learn new skills. This role will be discussed later.

Facilitator

The facilitator, as the name suggests, guides, eases, or expedites the way for others. This fact is true when the problem is between individuals and their environment or when it is between members in the same group. In a task group, the facilitative role may involve helping the group stick to the agenda, creating a safe environment for open discussion, encouraging all to participate and supporting their contributions. It also includes helping members test new skills and summarizing what has been accomplished (Corey & Corey, 1992).

Clearly, the human services professional must play various roles depending upon the needs of the group and the problems confronted. Conceiving human services as being made up of a series of roles is important. This line of thought coincides with the idea that generalist human services professionals have numerous responsibilities. It also helps the worker think more clearly about what a group needs at any given time in its developmental life.

 ## Basic Group Dynamics

Human services professionals who have dealt with various types of groups frequently comment about how the group seems to develop a life of its own. Each group has its own unique configuration of varied individual personalities, as well as its own set of dynamics that affect what is said or done, the roles that members play, and how the group relates to the leader. There have been repeated efforts to provide a framework for understanding group dynamics and to help those working with groups. Many frameworks attempt to explain group development through a single model. Each of these approaches has strengths and weaknesses. This section focuses on five broad areas: group development; group culture, norms, and power; group size and composition; duration; decision-making patterns; and group roles.

Group Development

Most groups proceed through an identifiable set of four steps or stages. This pattern of development has allowed group observers to describe the stages and to predict what may occur in each stage. In the first stage of development, most groups display *a strong reliance on the leader*. Members expect the leader to provide direction, and they tend to be more hesitant or reluctant to participate actively. The leader assists members in this stage by encouraging participation, supporting positive group norms (informal rules of behavior), and helping members rely more on one another.

In the second stage, the group members begin to assert themselves more. During this time, *some level of conflict is common*. Power and control issues arise more frequently as members become more comfortable with each other and take greater responsibility for what happens in the group. There may be disagreement over goals agreed upon in the previous stage and challenges to the leader that can be unsettling. That the leader encourage open discussion of the conflict so that the group will ultimately be responsible for its decision is important. Recognizing that conflict is expected, acceptable, and often even healthy is also important.

Once past the conflict stage, the group is ready to go ahead with the primary work facing it. Group productivity increases, and there is greater attention to achieving its goals. This level is stage three, the *"working" phase* of the group. Members frequently feel positive about the group, may have developed affection or liking for it and its members, and are more willing to share their ideas and reactions. Trust has developed among members as roles become more clear and a group culture has developed. The role of the leader is likely to change during this phase. There is more need for a leader who can serve as consultant, advisor, or resource to the group instead of a director.

Finally, there is usually a fourth phase, *separation,* where the group has reached its goals and members begin to separate emotionally from the group. In this phase, there are often feelings of loss when the group ends, but there also may be angry feelings. Again, the worker should expect and realize that members may need help to accept and discuss their feelings.

The group stage model (see Highlight 12.2) appears to apply well to growth or treatment groups (groups that focus on changing the individual group member) and to many task groups (committees, teams, social action groups). However, the ongoing nature of task groups (agency staff meetings, boards of directors, and so on) may complicate or mix up some stages. Because some staff groups do not have a separation phase where members prepare to leave, there is less likely to be the same kinds of reactions found in other groups with a defined ending period. Open-ended groups, such as Parents Anonymous, where members enter and leave the group at different times, may change how the group develops. The previous model fits most closely those groups where members join and leave the group together (closed groups), such as the teen group described in Highlight 12.2.

There may also be a difference in group development between formed groups and those that exist naturally. Formed groups are those where the members have been brought together by an outside agency, organization, or individual. Therapy groups created by the human services professional are an example. Natural groups are those where the members have come together through bonds of friendship or kinship. One type of natural group, a family, already has an established pattern of interacting with one another, which may also be true of a gang. Formed groups composed of clients with similar problems or characteristics (e.g., substance addicted or delinquent girls) are perhaps more likely to fit the model described. Thus, when group members achieve their treatment or personal goals, the group will enter phase four, where separation occurs.

Realizing that any development model for groups is only an abstraction is important. Individual groups may not proceed exactly as outlined earlier. Some groups will seem to skip a stage or move backward instead of forward from time to time. Remember, failure to proceed in the precise manner described earlier is neither an unhealthy sign nor necessarily problematic. The human services professional must be flexible and adaptable when working with groups because they vary so drastically in purpose, composition, and dynamics.

Group Culture, Norms, and Power

All groups have an identifiable culture that is the traditions, customs, and values/beliefs shared by group members. Culture affects how members react and interact with one another and the leader, typical coping styles used, how work is done, and how status and power are distributed. Sometimes, this culture exists prior to the worker's involvement, as with families or groups of friends. At other times, it occurs after group formation. Norms are unwritten expectations about how individuals will act in certain situations. Norms are part of the culture of all groups and can help or hinder the accomplishment of group goals. The worker has a role in helping to create norms that support attainment of these goals. For example, a norm of openness and a willingness to admit mistakes can be encouraged by a worker who models these characteristics for group members. Evidence of a positive group culture includes free expression of ideas, open

HIGHLIGHT 12.2

Stages in Teen Group Therapy

Stage 1 in a Teen Group: Reliance on the Leader

As she looked around the group of teenagers, Shantia was reminded once again about the effect a group can have on its members. Shantia had been assigned to work with this group because she had previously had some group experiences during her practicum placement. Having read the files on all of the members, Shantia knew something about each of the girls present in the teen center meeting room. Jacque was quiet, which for her was unusual. She was always the most talkative person in any group. Belinda was whispering to Angel, and both were smiling knowingly. Cindy was looking down and flipping absentmindedly through her notebook. Alice stared out the window. When Shantia got up to close the door, the room became as quiet as a tomb. Each girl looked up at Shantia expecting her to say something.

Stage 2 in a Teen Group: Addressing Conflict

Shantia had asked the group to agree on the major activities they would pursue during the next six weeks. Although there had been ample time to decide, the group seemed hopelessly deadlocked. Jacque was arguing that the group should hold a party, and Cindy testily reminded her that they were in this group because they partied too much. Belinda asked if they could have a session focused on getting along better with parents. When Shantia responded favorably to Belinda, Angel said she did not want to talk about her parents. After ten more minutes, the group was no closer to a decision than when the meeting started.

Stage 3 in a Teen Group: Working

When Alice said she felt her parents did not care what happened to her and began to cry softly, Jacque reached over and put an arm around her. "Maybe they just don't know how to show they care," Cindy said. "I mean, we can't know what's in someone else's head." "That's right," said Belinda, "don't assume anything about parents." As the group meeting came to an end, Shantia smiled and said quietly, "I'm very proud of how the group reached out to Alice and used the ideas we've been talking about the last few weeks. You've really supported one another."

Stage 4 in a Teen Group: Separation

For the last meeting, Shantia had asked the girls what they wanted to do that would appropriately conclude their work together. They decided to write each other brief notes stating what good qualities they learned about one another during the past few weeks. This method of saying goodbye was encouraged by Shantia, who had also arranged for milk and brownies for the meeting. The group had spent the last week talking about their feelings as the group ended and reviewing the various plans group members had for the summer. Shantia told them she would miss their weekly meetings and encouraged them to stay in touch with her and with each other.

---

disagreement, and a safe atmosphere in which the contributions of members are respected and considered. The worker can help ensure development of such a culture by describing for members what is desired or expected in the group, modeling appropriate behavior, and supporting group members as they interact within the group.

Value differences among group members may contribute to difficulties within the group. For example, within a group of teens discussing sexual behavior, it is likely that some members will view sexual activity as a part of adolescence and others (because of religious or other values) may not want to talk about the topic. The worker should encourage members to discuss the values they brought to the group and to listen carefully to the values of other members. When a climate of trust and safety exists, members are more likely to accept individual differences and allow fellow members to express their individuality. If members do not sense such a climate, they are less likely to be honest in expressing opinions and more guarded in what they say and do. This type of climate is less likely to lead to positive outcomes. The leader should help to establish a culture where members are free to talk and are supportive of each other. This openness permits the business of the group to be accomplished in an open and frank manner.

Power issues always exist within groups. In many groups there is a period in which the group or individual members of the group vie with the leader for power. In most groups, individual members have different levels of status and power. Those accorded the highest status by other group members are more likely to be listened to. Subgroups may develop as two or more members find themselves holding similar views and feeling at odds with other group members. Struggles over decisions may occur, exacerbated by these divisions.

Group Size and Composition

Sometimes both the size and composition of a group are established ahead of time, and the worker lacks control over these elements. For example, consider families and other preexisting groups. The size of the family is not within the control of the worker, nor is the composition. In other situations, the worker is responsible for making decisions about who will be included as members and how large the group will be. For instance, a worker leading a parent nurturing group may set the limit on members at seven or nine and not allow a larger group.

Group size has a definite impact on what occurs within a group. It affects both the level and type of interaction in addition to members' feelings about the group. Large groups tend to be less popular with members because of lessened opportunity for discussion and interaction. Members of larger groups are more likely to feel inhibited and will often participate less than members in smaller groups. "Education groups usually have from four to fifteen members; discussion groups usually have from five to eight. Ideally, personal growth groups, support groups, and therapy groups have from five to eight members, although there can be as few as three and as many as twelve" (Jacobs, Harvill, & Masson, 1994, p. 37). Many human services groups have as many as ten members, and some groups are much larger. Larger groups may be more effective at handling difficult and involved problems because the number of possible contributors is greater. Thus, the task or objectives of the group may be a factor affecting group size. Although composition of a group may be beyond the control of the worker, many situations do allow the leader to select the members. Formed groups lend themselves nicely to this kind of selection, because the worker often chooses individual members.

The worker must decide the degree of heterogeneity and homogeneity appropriate for a given group. A heterogeneous group has members with different problems and personality characteristics. A homogeneous group has members with similar problems and personalities. Practically speaking, few groups are completely homogeneous, because as human beings we all differ from one another in many ways. Workers must take these differences into consideration when selecting members for a group.

We must also remember that there may be real advantages in selecting people for a group who are alike in some ways and different in others. For example, selecting people who share similar problems (e.g., child abusers) but who have differing personalities might make sense. For another example, selecting seven nonverbal group members would not be wise. A healthy mix of talkers and listeners is likely to be more useful.

Age also may be a factor in composition. Different levels of development probably preclude starting a group composed of children ranging in age from 8 to 15. The difference in interests and attention spans could be especially problematic. Ultimately, the purpose of the group should be considered when deciding group size and composition.

Gender also may be an important consideration. Gender similarity may be important in groups of children, but gender diversity is desirable among adolescents when the objective is helping group members develop socialization skills. Bertcher and Maple (1974) suggest selecting members with similar descriptive characteristics such as age, sex, and level of education but with dissimilar behavioral attributes. Behavioral attributes include aggressiveness, verbal ability, and leadership skills, among others. Having some group members who will serve as models for other members might be preferable. Human services professionals need to give this matter careful consideration when composing a group. As Fatout and Rose (1995) note, groups require sufficient homogeneity for stability but enough heterogeneity for vitality. Finding this exact balance is not often easy, however, because predicting how well a particular group's members will function together is often impossible.

Duration

Determining the duration of a group requires that the worker decide how many sessions will be held and how long each will last. Having groups meet for one and a half to two hours per session is common, which provides enough time to conduct the business of the meeting without becoming drawn out. Specifying in advance the length and number of sessions helps members focus on the topic and discourages non-functional behavior such as wasting time on irrelevant topics. A group planning to meet for six sessions is more likely to stay on task than one meeting for twenty sessions. A general observation is that the closer to the ending point a group gets, the more likely group members will attend to the task. This phenomenon is familiar to many students who find their interest in, and efforts to write, a class paper increase as the deadline approaches.

Flexibility is helpful in the matter of duration. If a preselected length of time proves counterproductive, the worker should feel free to suggest a change. The judgment of the worker and clients about what works best is as important as any set of guidelines.

Decision Making in Groups

How groups, especially task groups, make decisions is important to understanding why some groups are more successful than others. Task groups, like com-

mittees, administrative groups such as boards of directors, teams, treatment conferences, and social action groups (Toseland & Rivas, 1998), must often make decisions. These task groups share some similarities, yet each is different from the others in some important ways, including how they interact and come to decisions. In this section, several common approaches to group decision making will be discussed: consensus decision making, compromise, decision making by majority, rule by an individual, persuasion by a recognized expert, averaging of opinions of individual group members, and persuasion by a minority of the group (see Highlights 12.3 and 12.4) (Johnson, 1994). In addition, we will review three special techniques to help groups make decisions and solve problems: nominal group technique, brainstorming, and parliamentary procedure.

Decision Making by Consensus

An attractive, albeit time-consuming, approach to making decisions is through consensus. Consensus

---

 ### HIGHLIGHT 12.3

Approaches to Decision Making

Decision Making by Consensus

The Blackwell City Council was at an impasse. After a year of study, debate, and argument, the new library was no closer to fruition than when the council started discussing the idea. The primary issue that had stymied the group was the proposed location. The library board had proposed that the new building be located on an undeveloped site near Lake Prosper, a recommendation supported by two or three council members. Other members wanted the new library adjacent to the old library, a location that many felt was too small to meet future needs. After a lengthy debate, Geraldo Velasquez, a human services professional on the city council, suggested holding an advisory referendum on the location, allowing the residents of the city the opportunity to voice their opinion. Council members were all in agreement with this proposal, a consensus decision that was unusual for this body. At least temporarily, it got the issue off their agenda and offered hope of a clear mandate from the voters.

Decision Making by Compromise

"Finally, a package we can live with." Charmaine was exhausted. As president of the human services union, she had been deeply involved in the negotiations for the contract for the next year. After an initial (and unacceptable) offer from the finance committee, the union representatives had been going through the usual process of making proposals and rejecting them. Finally, a package was agreed to. It contained salary increases agreeable to the union and gave management more flexibility to move workers within the agency. It was a compromise for both parties, because it did not give either side exactly what they would have liked. It was a classic labor agreement, something for everyone but less than each side had desired.

Decision Making by Majority Rule

The five agency supervisors were in the second hour of what was supposed to be a one-hour meeting. The issue that had stymied efforts to conclude the meeting was a proposed reorganization of services and service units. Don was unhappy with the proposal because it would increase the workload of his unit slightly at a time when he felt his workers were already overloaded.

Still, the proposal would give the agency an opportunity to offer a very specialized service, which a previous needs assessment had determined was long overdue. Finally, the agency deputy director asked for a show of hands for those who supported the proposed change. All supervisors but Don voted in favor of the proposal. The deputy director said, "Don, I know you are not crazy about this idea, but it has the support of the others, and we're going to go with the majority this time. I will see, however, what I can do about getting another position assigned to your unit to help with the overload."

Rule by an Individual

The Millard School Rec Club was having difficulty choosing an activity to mark the end of the high school year. In past years, the group had held pizza parties, donated gifts to the school, and contributed their time to a neighborhood cleanup project. Marcus, the captain of the baseball team and a respected student, argued forcefully that the club should donate money to the school to purchase a pitching machine. Other members of the group were reluctant to express their opinions for fear of appearing to oppose Marcus's suggestion. When no one spoke up, Marcus then said, "Well, then it's settled. I'll tell the principal and the coach." The group had just allowed one member to rule (make a decision) for the entire club.

Persuasion by an Expert

When it came time to discuss how the new human services program would be evaluated, everyone on the administrative staff looked to Kobe for guidance. He was considered the resident expert on program evaluation and was familiar with a variety of approaches that could be used in different situations. Though Jack had some reservations about a couple of Kobe's ideas, his opinions did not sway the staff group very much. Jack knew in advance that Kobe's recommendations would be accepted by the group based on his reputation and past experience. Sure enough, when the meeting was over, Kobe's ideas were approved and his plan for evaluation accepted.

Averaging of Individual Opinions

Angelina had asked her foster care unit to evaluate her performance as a supervisor. Angelina had only recently become a supervisor after several years as a line human services professional. Most of the people in the foster care unit had been her friends before her promotion six months ago. Now she wanted to get their feedback on her work as their supervisor.

After much discussion, unit members decided to rate Angelina on five different characteristics they considered important in a supervisor. When they were done, they decided to present Angelina with a composite picture of how the unit felt about her leadership. Rather than give her their individual ratings, the unit members decided to average their individual ratings on each of the five characteristics and give her one set of ratings. This method eliminated extremes at both ends (e.g., very high or very low ratings) and gave a more "middle-of-the-road" view of her performance.

Persuasion by a Minority

The night was getting quite late as the Franklin Avenue Neighborhood Association neared the end of its agenda. The last item to discuss was what to do about the vacant house at the end of the block. The property had been abandoned by its owner and was attracting children and local teenagers who sought access through its broken windows and door. Because the house was really on the edge of the neighborhood, many members did not see it as a matter of great concern. There was even a question of whether the property was part of Franklin Avenue, because it faced a side street.

Quietly, but firmly, Mr. Alison and Mrs. Gonzales spoke of the dangers to the neighborhood children and the way the property detracted from the quality of the neighborhood. Ms. Washington, usually rather quiet, then spoke passionately about how this house was a danger to her small children. She angrily asked how the other members would feel if the house was next door to their homes. She demanded that the group take a position and ask the city to have the house torn down or renovated. The group decided to follow her recommendation, less out of commitment and more because of her ardent and outspoken position on a matter of relatively less concern to them.

The Family Treatment Program: Recognizing Conflict

The new specialized family treatment program was barely six months old when problems began to appear. It was designed to provide intensive in-home treatment by a team of family workers with low caseloads. The program had initially been greeted as a very positive approach to working with multiproblem families. Within a few months, the team was beginning to prove the merits of the idea. At the same time, workers who were not part of the specialized unit began to complain.

Soon, the source of the complaints became clear. With several workers attached to the special program, those remaining were being asked to handle larger caseloads. Many saw the benefits of the new program but felt their extra work was unfair. Those with larger caseloads felt they were assuming too much of the burden and resented it.

When designed, the new program had no alternative plans to handle an increased caseload. Nor was any thought given to how removing workers from the regular family unit would affect the workload of those who remained. Clearly, the agency administration had a problem.

---

refers to "the process in which individuals and groups achieve general agreement about goals of mutual interest and the means to achieve them" (Barker, 1999, p. 99). Consensus decision making is attractive because, when concluded, all members accept and support the decision even if they were not initially so inclined. To make decisions by consensus requires an atmosphere of openness in which all members have an opportunity to be heard and influence the final outcome. This approach presumes that members can present alternate ideas, that opposing views are solicited, and that creative solutions are encouraged. The emphasis is on finding the best solution instead of getting one's way. The real advantage of consensus decision making is that it increases the commitment of group members to the decision. In situations where this commitment is particularly important, there is no adequate substitute.

Decision Making by Compromise

Most of us have been involved in decision making by compromise. In these situations, the group attempts to reach a solution that most, if not all, members, can support. In some cases the compromise pleases no one entirely but is viewed as the best that can be done under the circumstances. Each side gives up something to reach an agreement with the other side. Groups that begin with an idea, amend it repeatedly to satisfy divergent points of view, and then approve the final product usually are making decisions by compromise.

Decision Making by Majority

Most deliberative bodies (e.g., legislatures, boards of directors) make decisions by majority rule. In this model, a decision occurs when over one-half of the decision makers support (or vote) for an idea. Decisions made in this fashion typically are accepted by the winning side and disliked by the losing side. Losers do not necessarily feel as compelled to support the outcome of the group decision making as is true with consensus. Because majority rule is a less time-consuming method, large groups often use it. When a matter is of little consequence, majority rule may be a satisfactory method for making a decision. When the matter is complex or requires a high level of commitment from the group to the decision, this method is problematic. Losers may not support the decision and may passively undercut the proposal. In some cases, losers may be resentful and actively work to make the idea fail. Alternate methods of arriving at majority rule involve increasing the percent of votes required for passage (revisions of bylaws or constitutions of organizations frequently require a two-thirds majority) or developing a weighted system of voting. While these methods help increase the percent of members who support a decision, they do not truly overcome the disadvantages of this style of decision making.

Rule by an Individual

Many groups make decisions by default and allow one individual to make choices that affect the entire group. This situation may occur because of the forcefulness of the speaker, members' fear of offending the decision maker, disinterest in the decision itself, or lack of assertiveness. Essentially, one member makes a decision, and the rest of the group acquiesces. Sometimes, there is discussion among the members about the options; at other times there is none.

Persuasion by a Recognized Expert

Many groups have members with expertise in a certain area. For example, one member of an educational group may have had experience placing a loved one in a nursing home. Other group members typically listen to members who are perceived to be knowledgeable about a given subject. When a group comes to making a decision, it may accede to the recommendations of the "expert."

Averaging of Individual Opinions

In some groups, decisions are made by averaging the opinions of individual group members. This process is done most easily when the opinions are really able to be averaged. That is, the opinions may be in the form of numerical ratings that can be averaged using standard mathematical techniques. Unlike a compromise, there is really no giving in by individual members but rather an acceptance that one's opinion will be merged with those of the rest of the group. This technique has the advantage of not requiring people to give up their opinion or change it in response to group pressure.

Persuasion by a Minority

Persuasion by a minority often occurs when one or more members of a group feel strongly about a particular decision. It happens more frequently when a subgroup has intense attitudes and the rest of the group has less invested in the matter at stake. A vocal and persuasive individual (or group of individuals) thus may be successful in swaying the opinions of a larger group.

Nominal Group Technique

One of the more interesting techniques used to help groups make decisions is the nominal group. Its intent is to help "assess existing problems, needs, interests, or objectives" (Barker, 1999, p. 328). This approach can be used by groups of various sizes. To begin, members receive a problem statement and list their ideas about the problem. Each member does this without consulting other members; once this process is completed, the leader goes around the group one by one asking each member to provide

one of the ideas from his or her list. This process continues until all items on each person's list have been exhausted. Members may choose to pass when they no longer have any ideas to contribute. They are also free to contribute additional ideas they thought of while listening to other members. The worker writes each idea on a board or flip chart visible to all members. No evaluation of ideas occurs during this round-robin procedure.

Once all the ideas are collected and listed for the members, the leader begins to go through each idea briefly. This process helps ensure clarity and allows each member to explain the merits of an idea. No lengthy discussion of any idea occurs at this point.

In the third stage, members review the ideas on the board and list those they believe are the most important or have highest priority. They may be asked to select a specific number such as five or fifteen. The goal is to reduce the overall list by one-half to three-quarters. Once completed, the leader places a check mark by each idea supported by a member. This tabulation may be accomplished by the member listing the best ideas on a card and handing the card in or by going around in round-robin fashion again. When completed, the group has a list of those ideas that showed the most promise.

In the final stage, members rank the new list of ideas. Usually, the priority list will be small, with only five ideas permitted. These are listed on index cards, one idea per card. The cards are collected, and the leader tallies the results on the flip chart. The highest priority idea receives a point value of five and on down to the lowest priority item, which receives a one. A mean rank for each idea is computed by adding the numbers together and dividing by the number of members. Once completed, the idea or ideas that have the greatest support and should be undertaken by the group are usually clear.

The nominal group technique can produce a larger number of alternatives than most other approaches (Scheidel & Crowell, 1979). This approach is usually enjoyable for the participants. It is an effective technique for developing alternatives, because it encourages participation of all members. It also allows all points of view to be expressed and discourages making decisions without adequate discussion. Finally, it increases members' commitment to the outcome.

Brainstorming

Brainstorming is a group technique used to encourage members to produce a variety of ideas about a specific topic. It is an efficient way to develop alternate solutions to a problem. Useful in both large and small groups, brainstorming begins with a problem to be solved. Each member presents one idea, and then another member has a turn. This process continues until the leader lists all ideas on the board or flip chart. No attempt is made to rate or evaluate the ideas. Members should be free to present ideas they thought of after hearing other members' contributions and should raise their hands before participating. The leader should encourage all contributions and clarify any ideas that are not clear.

Unlike the nominal group approach, the evaluation phase does not closely follow the idea-generating phase. Ideas tend to be better if the problem is clearly and specifically defined. Brainstorming can produce large numbers of ideas and works best when the goal is generation of multiple alternatives. It does not work as well with complex situations or those in which there is only a single correct answer. There is, however, no clear evidence that brainstorming is more or less effective than the nominal group approach. Because both methods rely on an atmosphere of openness to new ideas, the worker should encourage this process and resist premature attempts to evaluate the ideas presented. In either case, ideas that receive immediate evaluation, especially a negative assessment, are less likely to be followed by other ideas. Members may feel threatened because someone ridiculed or challenged their idea and will be less likely to risk offering other ideas to the group.

Parliamentary Procedure

Parliamentary procedure is a highly structured technique used by groups of various sizes to make decisions and conduct business. The model of parliamentary procedure described in *Robert's Rules of Order* (Robert, 1989) was devised over 100 years ago and remains the most common set of guidelines in use today. Groups agree in advance to use the rules, so that there is no last-minute disagreement about how decisions will be made. Most deliberative bodies (legislatures) and large task groups and many smaller task groups use *Robert's Rules* to facilitate their work. While parliamentary procedural rules are clear and designed to help the group, they are not always followed closely. Sometimes, the procedures called for in the rules become barriers to accomplishment of group goals. For example, smaller committees may decide to operate by consensus and dispense with voting on items where the group is in agreement. In this case, parliamentary procedure

may be too time consuming and unwieldy. In legislative bodies a person can easily waste the body's time by endlessly speaking on a matter before the group. Called *filibustering,* this method may stymie a body and prevent it from conducting its normal business. In these situations, groups may decide to temporarily suspend some of the usual rules of parliamentary procedure, thus preventing filibustering.

In parliamentary procedure, the business of the group occurs in the form of *motions,* which are proposed actions that the group is asked to support. A member of the human services student organization may make a motion to buy paint to refurbish the child-care center. The motion might be stated as follows: "I move we purchase three gallons of paint for the child-care center." If others support this motion, one member would say, "I second the motion." The motion or proposal would then be open for debate or discussion by the members. Motions generally fall into two major categories, primary motions and secondary motions. *Primary motions* bring business to the group for consideration. The motion to purchase paint is an example of a primary motion. Primary motions include both main motions (example above) and incidental motions. *Incidental motions* are used for such purposes as adjourning the group and repealing an action already taken.

Secondary motions are those used to act upon the primary motion. They include motions to amend a main motion, to refer a matter to another body, or to defer action on a motion (postpone or table). They also are used to limit debate on a motion, to reconsider a motion, or to bring up for discussion an item that had been previously tabled. Lastly, secondary motions include motions to challenge improper actions and to request information (e.g., point of order or point of information). For example, a member who wished clarification on why the body is dealing with a matter that seems to belong to another group would raise a hand and address the presiding officer by stating: *"Point of information."* The chair would then ask the member to state the point of information and would attempt to respond to the question the member has raised. Similarly, if a group strays in their debate and is now discussing a matter that is not related to the motion on the floor, a member might state: *"Point of order."* The member would then remind the group that they have not yet voted on the motion before them and have begun to debate some other matter. The chair would then rule on the member's point of order, ask if there is any additional debate on the motion on the floor, and then call for the vote.

Other motions do exist, but they are used too infrequently to mention in this chapter. *Robert's Rules of Order* should be consulted by those who frequently use parliamentary procedure.

The primary principle established by parliamentary procedure is that each person has a right to be heard without interruption. The person who makes a motion speaks first on a topic. All members must have an opportunity to speak if they so wish. Debate must be related to the motion on the floor and cannot be on superfluous matters. Once each person who wishes has had a chance to speak, the leader (chair) asks if there is any further debate. If there is none, the group will then vote on the proposal. Sometimes a member of the group will wish to stop debate and bring a matter to a vote. This is achieved by saying "I call the question." This motion is not debatable—it immediately halts discussion on a matter if supported by two-thirds of those present.

When the group is ready to vote, the chair will say "All those in favor of the motion, say aye." Restating the motion to be voted on or having the secretary read the motion may be best. At that point, all favoring the motion will respond "aye." Then the chair will call for all no (or nay) votes, then all abstentions. The chair will decide which side prevailed based on this voice vote and announce the results. Sometimes, members vote by raising their hands or by using paper ballots, especially when the vote appears to be close. Normally, a simple majority must approve a motion. If a tie occurs in the voting, the motion does not pass. Sometimes, the chair may vote to break a tie or to create a tie.

As mentioned earlier, a motion may be amended. This *amendment* means it may be changed by a member proposing to add or delete something in the original motion. To amend the previously mentioned motion, a member might say "I move to amend the motion to place a limit of 50 dollars on the amount to be spent for paint." This amendment also needs a second and would be voted on. If approved, the amendment would then become a part of the original main motion. After all amendments are considered and voted on, the main motion (as amended) would be voted on.

There are other rules governing parliamentary procedure. These include specification of a *quorum* (the minimum number of group members that must be present to conduct business) and use of an *agenda* (an ordered list of the topics to be covered in the meeting). Most groups have a leader or chairperson responsible for helping the group conduct its business. A secretary is charged with the task of keeping the minutes (official record of a group's actions). Other officers, such as a treasurer or vice-chairperson, may be needed depending upon the type and size of the group.

In larger groups there may be subgroups or committees to which certain business is sent for review. For example, to have both standing (ongoing) committees (such as finance committee and personnel committee) and special ad hoc committees set up to handle specific bits or categories of business is common. Committee members and the chairperson of the committee are appointed by the chair of the larger group. The smaller the committee, the less likely it is to use more formalized parliamentary procedures.

A human services professional skilled in the use of parliamentary procedure can be of enormous assistance to task groups. Knowing how to make and amend motions and otherwise properly handle the group's business can make the group's task go smoothly. Parliamentary procedure provides a set of rules to guide groups in their deliberations; it was never meant to serve as an obstacle. In the final analysis, the wishes of the group must prevail even if a violation of *Robert's Rules* occurs.

Group Roles

Observers of most groups have concluded that there are two types of basic functions that each group must fulfill: task functions and maintenance functions. Task functions help to keep a group on task and working toward agreed-upon ends. Maintenance functions, on the other hand, ensure that the needs of group members receive attention. Both task and treatment (therapeutic) groups require members who attend to task and maintenance functions. In task groups, we are typically less concerned about the needs of the individual member and more focused on the group task. In contrast, within treatment or growth groups, the needs and interests of individual members receive more attention. Remembering that no group operates without attending to both functions is important. The emphasis placed on each function will vary depending upon the group.

In practice, the members of the group are the people who often carry out the various functions described earlier. This process occurs through one or more roles that members (and leaders) play in the group.

Task Roles

As mentioned previously, task roles are functional roles designed to help the group reach agreed-upon goals. Members of a group engage in particular behaviors that help facilitate this process. One such role is *information seeking* from the leader or other members. In addition to seeking information, a member may solicit the opinions of group members to help determine how people perceive some topic. *Opinion seekers* often want this information before stating their own position. *Elaborators* expand on ideas proposed to the group and help to ensure that a complete explanation is provided for all ideas.

Other members may engage in teaching or *instructing* roles. These members often clarify and remind the other members about previous decisions they have made. Still other members will *evaluate* or make judgments about the wisdom or appropriateness of any particular idea or course of action.

Some members engage in an *energizing* role by showing excitement and enthusiasm for projects; by force of their interest, they bring other members along. Energizers are the spark plugs in any group.

Once a group has made a decision, some members will serve as *recorders,* or unelected secretaries, by keeping a log or record of decisions reached or actions taken. Some may actually jot down these items, while others maintain only a mental notebook. Recorders are sometimes assisted by other members who remind the group to follow some agreed-upon rules or procedures as they continue their deliberations. The *recorder* is helpful because it helps the group stay on task, and the recorder serves as the unofficial historian in a group. The *procedural technician* helps the group follow their own agreed-upon ways of making decisions.

Persons playing task roles are interested in the group completing its agreed-upon task and try to help this process. They tend to be more committed to the task and may be less concerned about the importance of group maintenance.

Maintenance Roles

Group maintenance is an important function needing attention in any group. Group maintenance roles are more concerned with improving, enhancing, or increasing group functioning. Task groups often pay less attention to this facet than treatment groups do, but the function of group maintenance cannot be ignored. Group maintenance roles include harmonizer, compromiser, encourager, follower, tension reliever, and listener. The titles assigned to these different roles are less important than the behaviors that members perform to accomplish the group maintenance function. As suggested by the titles, group members focusing on group building and maintenance encourage other members to participate *(encourager),* and they listen carefully *(listener).* They also follow the directions of others *(follower),* emphasize harmony and compromise *(harmonizer* and *compromiser),* and relieve rough moments in the group, often through humor *(tension reliever).* The goal is to attend to the group's socioemotional climate and help the group maintain its "we" feeling.

Paying attention to the needs of individual members naturally occurs in most treatment groups. Members are selected for, or join, these groups with the expectation that their social and emotional needs will be given concerted attention. Task groups, on the other hand, often assume that members' personal needs are secondary to the group's purpose. A balance between meeting the two types of needs, task and socioemotional, must occur in all groups. There almost always will be more attention to the task of the group and less to individual needs of the members in a board of directors or a multidisciplinary care conference in a hospital. Likewise, a group for men who abuse their spouses or a group for women surviving breast cancer will have a greater emphasis on individual needs and feelings of the members. Ultimately, all groups need members who attend to both functions. Task groups that ignore the feelings and needs of members are not likely to endure, because members will drop out or otherwise avoid participating. Treatment groups without sufficient task focus will not reach their goals of changing individual behavior. Group members will become frustrated because they see no progress. Eventually, a therapeutic group that does not maintain a task focus will lose members, funding, or both.

Nonfunctional Roles

Not all the behavior of group members can be classified into the two categories described previously. Some roles played by members meet only their own needs. These behaviors include aggressiveness, blocking, seeking recognition for self, dominating the group, seeking help, and confessing past errors. These roles, however, do not further the progress of the group.

Aggressive members attack others and, by putting them down, attempt to raise themselves. Such members are likely to challenge the ideas and motives of others and soon become a problem for the group. *Blockers* are usually the ones to say "Yes, but . . ." to all the ideas or solutions proposed in the group. No matter what the proposal, they will always have a reason why it will not succeed. *Recognition seekers* will engage in a variety of behaviors, all of which are designed to focus the group's attention on themselves. Like the people who dominate *(dominators)* the group by talking incessantly or people who seek help from the group for their own problems, those *seeking recognition* have personal needs that are not being met. That behavior indicates a need to which the group cannot respond. The person who confesses *(confessor)* past mistakes often embarrasses the group by inappropriately disclosing personal behavior. For example, at the first meeting session, when members take turns introducing themselves, one member remarks that she had an abortion once. This disclosure makes some members of the class uncomfortable and shows the member's insensitivity to the usual boundaries experienced within such groups. These roles are important because they indicate the needs of the individual member, but they often do not help the group toward its goals. A member who behaves in this fashion often risks rebuke from the group and slows the group in its achievement of objectives.

Other nonfunctional roles include the scapegoat, deviant member, defensive member, quiet member, and internal leader (Shulman, 1992). *Scapegoats* draw upon themselves the wrath of other members and serve as someone to blame when things are not going well. *Defensive members,* on the other hand, do not accept blame for anything and deny responsibility for their actions. *Deviant members* engage in behavior they know the group will oppose or find annoying, such as continuing to speak out of turn,

interrupting others, or refusing to participate in group activities. *Quiet members* simply do not participate and make getting to know them impossible for anyone. Finally, the *internal leader* may vie for leadership of the group and attempt to wrestle control from the designated leader. Internal leaders are often members with significant natural leadership ability or influence over other members.

Groups need guidance and help from the leader to recognize and confront nonfunctional roles. At various times in the developmental history of a group (i.e., as a specific group develops and changes over time), different roles may be needed. The leader must be familiar with task and group building or maintenance roles and skilled enough to model them for group members. Leaders also must be keenly aware of what the group needs at any time. They then must either address that need themselves or draw upon other group members who will play the proper role. Continued nonfunctional role playing by a group member usually suggests that the group itself is not functioning well. Such behavior should not be ignored or allowed to continue unabated. Table 12.1 summarizes the wide variety of potentially positive and negative group roles as well as those considered nonfunctional.

 ## Micro Skills in Groups

Chapter 9 discussed a variety of skills important for micro or one-on-one practice, such as relationship-building skills with clients (warmth, empathy, and genuineness) and attending skills (including eye

Table 12.1   *A Variety of Group Roles*

Potentially Positive Roles	Potentially Negative Roles	Nonfunctional Roles
Instructor	Aggressor	Scapegoat
Information Seeker	Blocker	Deviant Member
Opinion Seeker	Recognition Seeker	Defensive Member
Evaluator	Dominator	Quiet Member
Elaborator	Help Seeker	Internal Leader
Energizer	Confessor	
Recorder		
Procedural Technician		
Harmonizer		
Compromiser		
Encourager		
Follower		
Tension Reliever		
Listener		

contact, active listening, facial expressions, and body position.) In addition, Chapter 9 described a number of interviewing skills, including encouragement, reflective responding, rephrasing, clarification, interpretation, providing information, summarizing, and self-disclosure. As might be expected, these skills are as applicable in groups as they are in one-on-one interviews. In therapeutic or growth-oriented groups, the worker is likely to use these skills and to encourage group members to do the same. Part of the worker's function, indeed, may be to teach these skills to members of the group. For example, members of a parenting skills group will benefit from learning how to listen actively to their children. Members of chemical dependency treatment groups will need to engage in self-disclosure; modeling this behavior is not uncommon for the leader.

Task groups typically have less emphasis on such matters as self-disclosure because it is not usually related to the purpose of the group. Likewise, interpretation of behavior and reflective responding is used less often in a staffing for a nursing home patient. Listening skills and the ability to summarize, clarify, and provide information are, however, just as important in task groups as they are in one-on-one interviews and in treatment-oriented groups. Viewing the development of skills as a continuing process is important. Some skills essential for one-on-one situations must be used in small groups and when working with larger system levels such as an agency or large governmental organization. At the same time, a worker with a group must use additional skills that include playing task and group maintenance roles, and using parliamentary procedure and nominal group and brainstorming techniques.

 ## Groups and the Generalist Intervention Model (GIM)

The ability to utilize the steps in the Generalist Intervention Model (GIM) is also important with groups. For example, the engagement step is important in treatment groups where the worker develops a professional relationship with group members and conveys warmth, empathy, and other indicators of interest in all of them. In task groups, engagement is often seen in the behavior of the worker who introduces him- or herself and seeks introductions from other members. It is also evident in the listening skills used by the worker whether playing the role of leader or member.

The assessment step occurs in both task and treatment groups as members seek to understand the purpose of the group, the needs and potential contributions of members, and their commitment to the group. Recognizing and acknowledging the strengths of each group member helps maintain the focus on growth and helps empower the group. Group members must identify issues or problems they will work on while considering the role that the larger environment plays in causing or maintaining the problem.

Planning occurs in both treatment and task groups. The planning step identifies the actions that need to be taken to address the task of the group. It includes prioritizing the issues to be dealt with, including translating problems into needs. Consideration of alternative solutions is done by group members in both task and treatment groups. Selecting goals and objectives, which then suggest concrete steps that members or the group itself will take, is required in all types of groups. For example, a group for women experiencing domestic abuse might discuss alternatives available to a member considering whether to return to the abuser or not. A board of directors will review various possible ways to increase income and reduce expenses for the agency. Treatment groups often use a general working agreement (or contract) whereby members might commit themselves to meet for six sessions to learn assertiveness skills.

The implementation phase of GIM is sometimes referred to as the working stage of the group. Individual members wrestle with the goals and objectives they have set for themselves. In task groups, the day-to-day discussion and decision making is what occurs. Groups follow (and sometimes revise) the plans made during the planning stage. Progress toward goals is monitored and acknowledged.

Evaluation is a critical activity in groups. Both task and treatment groups have goals and objectives that can be measured or otherwise assessed. Those struggling with substance abuse issues can tally the number of days away from drug use. Patients recovering from surgery can determine the extent to which they feel more in control of their lives and confident about the future. A multidisciplinary team can determine if they devised a thorough set of recommendations for helping a particular client.

All groups reach a point of termination, which may occur when the six sessions for learning anger management techniques have ended or when the ad hoc committee has completed its set of recommendations.

Both task and treatment groups are concerned about the need for follow-up. A task group that failed to come up with a proposal may be asked to continue or be replaced by another group. A treatment group where clients have ongoing individual needs may suggest an appropriate referral. GIM is an important tool for workers involved with groups.

Task and Treatment-Group Skills

Whether the human services professional is leading a task group or facilitating a treatment group, there exist several essential skills. These skills include conflict resolution, modeling and coaching, team building, confrontation, consultation, coordination, and using structure.

Conflict Resolution

Conflict is a fact of life. It occurs routinely within relationships and can have positive or negative consequences, depending upon how it is handled. Conflict may arise from power or status differences, personality disagreements, or from opposing values or belief systems.

Conflict tends to be viewed as negative because too often it is not resolved or managed successfully. Friesen (1987) has suggested applying a four-step problem-solving framework to conflict management. The four steps include recognition of actual or potential conflict, assessment of the conflictual situation, choosing a strategy, and intervening.

Recognizing Conflict

Recognizing conflict is easy when people do not talk to one another or are openly hostile, unnecessarily polite, or outright rude. Ideas suggested by one side may be routinely rejected by the other. The conflict may be between individuals or groups. It may be created by jealousy and other personal reactions, confusion, or misunderstanding. The example in Highlight 12.4 (on page 372) suggests how even the best plans can create conflict.

Assessing Conflict

Assessing conflict usually requires talking directly to the parties involved. Often, the source becomes clear during this process. In the situation in Highlight 12.4, the source was readily identified. Sometimes, other problems mask the source, or the problem is the result of miscommunication. In the latter case, the problem can be more easily resolved. Highlight 12.5 gives a simple example.

Creating a problem does not take much effort. Undoubtedly, unclear messages between sender and listener cause their share of conflictual situations.

Choosing a Strategy and Intervening

Identifying the source of a conflict is an important step in resolving it. Once identified, appropriate strategies can be considered or devised. For example, if the problem is simply between people a variety of approaches can be used. These include bargaining or negotiating (discussed in Chapter 13) and other methods designed to separate those in conflict. When a structural problem (one related to agency

HIGHLIGHT 12.5

That Is Not What I Said: Assessing Conflict

Rafer was in his second month as director of the Eastern Washington Service Center (EWSC). The agency had been wracked with scandal before Rafer became director. Under a recent director, the agency had lost its entire building fund because of poor stock investments. Rafer's task was to return the agency to a healthy financial footing and restore its reputation. In his first report to the board of directors, Rafer explained recent changes in EWSC and tried to highlight some of the accomplishments. To help improve staff morale and productivity, he announced he had recently bought some chairs. Almost immediately one board member at the other end of the room exclaimed angrily, "What?" Rafer was momentarily perplexed. Surely purchasing a couple of office chairs was not a matter of major concern to a member of the board of directors. Then the board member asked, "Did you say you bought shares or chairs?" Rafer quickly assured the board that he had indeed purchased desk chairs, not shares of stock, the cause of the earlier scandal.

design or organization) is causing the conflict, the solution must also be structural. For example, a disagreement over assignments may be resolved by modifying the assignment system or redistributing an unfair workload. Sometimes, an interpersonal problem can be resolved through structural means. Highlight 12.6 illustrates this point.

While positive outcomes are not always possible, and some conflicts cannot be managed, progress can usually be made. In some cases, the following strategies will prove effective.

Win–Lose and Win–Win Situations

One of the ways we can avoid becoming involved in conflict is to recognize when a win–lose conflict situation is developing. The nature of competition often produces a win–lose mentality. Much of our society is structured around the idea of winning or beating the competition. In group meetings, there are always clues to win–lose situations. When you feel yourself lining up on one side or the other, you are probably becoming involved in a win–lose incident. Sometimes our language gives us away. If we say or believe that our way is the only way or the best way, we are implicitly giving a message that the other person's point of view is wrong. Eventually, win–lose situations become lose–lose situations, because neither side benefits. The side that loses feels bad and may be

resentful. They often lose their sense of being part of the group and may even sabotage things if sufficiently upset. Losers stop listening to the other side and soon see additional areas where they disagree. Resolving win–lose situations requires that we first be aware of them. Once alerted, there are a number of skills and techniques that can be employed to defuse the situation. Zander (1983) has suggested some strategies that are often successful for resolving or avoiding win–lose situations in groups:

1. Asking each person to listen actively to the other. Active listening requires that you demonstrate your understanding of what the other person has said by paraphrasing it.
2. Role playing for the parties to show how their communication looks to an outsider.
3. Asking both sides to list their areas of similarity and agreement.
4. Attempting to identify goals that transcend the differences between the parties and working for solutions that fulfill these goals.
5. Finding objective criteria or values that can be used to evaluate other solutions.
6. Seeking agreement from each side to make concessions that will meet the needs of the other.

Once agreements appear to be reached, testing to make sure they have happened is important. Asking

---

HIGHLIGHT 12.6

Square Peg in a Round Hole: Choosing a Strategy

Both workers and clients complained about the treatment they received from Dee. With responsibility for the reception area, Dee was supposed to greet all clients and visitors, notify workers of their arrival, answer phone calls and direct them to other staff, and keep track of clients when the worker came to the front desk to meet them. Workers considered her rude to clients and felt she was impatient and irritable most of the time. She was likened to Charles Dickens' character Scrooge.

The agency administrative staff had discussed the situation before, and the supervisor had talked to Dee, all to no avail. Dee would try to improve, but things always seemed to end up the same. The administrative

staff was working on a reorganization plan that would require assigning new responsibilities to one supervisor and reassigning an additional experienced clerical staff member. After a brief discussion the group decided to reassign Dee to new duties and move her from the reception desk to the clerical pool. A new receptionist would be hired, and Dee would be working with day care providers and foster parents. She would handle financial details and report to a new supervisor. Within days of the administrative reorganization, Dee was hard at work on her new tasks. She stopped complaining, treated everyone with respect, and underwent a remarkable transformation. This change continued, and Dee was never again reported for abusive or rude behavior. The agency reorganization had not been designed to end the problem in the reception area but had the effect of doing so. Once away from the stress of being the receptionist, Dee developed into a highly valued member of the agency team.

both sides to describe explicitly their understanding of the agreed-upon solution is wise.

Miscommunication that originally caused a problem can just as easily disrupt the solution. The ability to resolve conflict successfully, or at least to manage it, is an important skill for any human services professional.

Modeling and Coaching

Albert Bandura's 1986 work on modeling suggests the enormous importance that watching others has on our behavior. Human services professionals may find modeling helpful in a number of situations, including teaching new skills, showing clients alternative methods for resolving problems, and helping clients develop a repertoire of responses to problematic situations. An example of this is presented in Highlight 12.7. Bandura has identified conditions that enhance the likelihood that a model's behavior will be copied. These conditions include: (1) the observer's attention level or awareness of the model; (2) the observer's retention of the modeled behavior; (3) the observer's ability to perform modeled behavior; and (4) the observer's motivation to perform the behavior. Awareness of the factors that influence effective modeling allows the human services professional to increase the likelihood that the modeled behavior will

be performed by the observer. In groups, this modeling can be achieved by several methods, including:

1. asking the observer to pay special attention to the model's behavior;
2. describing for the observer why the modeled behavior is important;
3. having observers role play the modeled behavior to ensure that they understood and can perform it;
4. using praise both for the observer and for others who perform the appropriate behavior; or
5. giving observers immediate corrective feedback when they attempt a new behavior.

Coaching is a skill that includes giving the client specific information as well as corrective feedback. For example, a human services professional may suggest a new way of approaching a difficult coworker, ask the client to role play it, and then will provide feedback about ways to improve. In coaching, the worker may choose to intervene immediately after a client has engaged in a behavior. If the behavior to be changed includes verbal communication, the worker may wish to ignore the content and focus on the process (Hepworth et al., 1997). Describing the group member's behavior, instead of evaluating it, is always appropriate. Evaluative comments typically

---

HIGHLIGHT 12.7

Teaching Disciplinary Techniques: Modeling and Coaching

The second meeting of the practical parenting group began with a review by the human services professional, Marjorie, of what had been learned in the first session. Marjorie then discussed the program for the day. The major goal was to learn two new, nonpunitive techniques for disciplining children. The first technique was a time-out procedure. Marjorie told the group they would see a brief video of a mother using the time-out technique with her child. Group members were asked to watch the mother carefully and take notes on what she did. Marjorie emphasized the importance of this technique for managing certain kinds of situations that commonly arise between parent and child. She quickly

summarized the research on this approach as well as her own experience with its use.

(Using the approach described, Marjorie was demonstrating two of the guidelines for modeling: asking the observer to pay special attention to the model and describing why the modeled behavior was important.)

After the video had been played twice, Marjorie asked one of the parents to volunteer to model the time-out technique with Marjorie playing the child's role. Then each parent took a turn playing the roles of parent and child. Marjorie praised good examples of the time-out technique and suggested improvements for group members who were having more difficulty.

In this last section, Marjorie used the remaining guidelines. She asked the group members to role play the desired behavior and used praise or corrective feedback, depending upon how well the person performed the desired behavior.

exacerbate problems instead of assisting communication skills. People often resent direct criticism.

One approach to coaching would be to ask a group member to speak directly to another member, rather than to the group as a whole or to the worker. This method is especially helpful if the group involves family members or others with whom the speaker frequently interacts. For example, in the couples group Jayson tells the human services professional that he would like his wife to be more affectionate. The human services professional asks Jayson to turn directly to his wife and tell her specifically what he would like her to do. In this way, Jayson must address his wife, who is ultimately the only person who can solve his problem. This approach forces Jayson to be more specific, because "being more affectionate" has many meanings.

Coaching also involves encouraging members to try new behavior. A common barrier to behaving differently is fear that one will look stupid or perform poorly. The worker can help overcome this fear by encouraging and supporting the member. This technique is especially effective if the behavior to be copied has already been modeled. Assertiveness training typically uses a combination of modeling and coaching to help group members develop and use new skills. When used by the worker in tandem, these skills can increase the likelihood that the members will adopt and continue the new behavior or communication patterns.

Team Building

Team building is the process of creating a group of individuals with the expertise, dedication, and characteristics needed to achieve a specific purpose. It requires both careful consideration of those who will compose the team and attention to the conditions that will enhance the team's ability to perform. The importance of working as a team member should be clear by now. The use of multidisciplinary teams, staffings, and similar work groups is sufficiently common in human services that every worker can expect to become a member of one such team or another. Whether or not the team works effectively is often a result of the team-building efforts that have occurred. Johnson (1998) and others have identified some of the problems that frequently interfere with the ability of a team to develop. Our emphasis here is on strategies to build a team, while overcoming common barriers.

Team building can best occur when there is strong organizational support for the team. This

support can be shown through several means. First, that the place of the team within the organization is clear is important. This process requires providing sufficient time for the team to meet independently of their case-handling responsibilities so that team meetings will not be an additional burden competing with their regular job responsibilities. If the only time the team meets is around individual cases, there will likely be limited ability to develop the "we" feeling so important to effective functioning. Adequate time for team building also allows the team to agree on goals and roles and responsibilities ahead of time. These responsibilities include not only decision-making processes but also who will assume leadership responsibilities.

Leadership for the team can be handled in a variety of ways. The leader can be selected by the team members or appointed by an outside supervisor. That the leader be well qualified is crucial. That is, he or she should have experience working on teams and making decisions as part of a team. Although members bring varying levels of expertise to the team, all should be seen more or less as equal participants. Clear status differentials among members may impair group functioning.

Some team building will occur as members become more familiar with their colleagues. This familiarity includes communication patterns, terminology, disciplinary jargon, and interpersonal styles. Quite simply, it involves getting used to each other and how the team interacts. A well-functioning team will be composed of members who understand and respect one another's expertise, carry out agreed upon tasks, and are cooperative. Individual members must be comfortable working in an interdisciplinary environment and not lose sight of their professional orientation.

The work of teams is achieved in the same planned change steps described earlier in this text. The team must define the problem, select appropriate goals, use their collective knowledge to consider alternatives, develop an intervention plan, and carry it out. Evaluation of the plan and process must follow the implementation phase. Team members should agree in advance how this process will occur. If this process is done and the other tasks mentioned earlier are performed, an effective team is likely to result.

Confrontation

Confrontation within a group tends to be more discomforting than confronting individuals on a one-on-one basis. Yet, to be effective as a team player, group leader, or member, the worker must be able to use confrontation. Chapter 9 described some of the situations where confrontation is appropriate. In this section, we will discuss briefly the importance of confrontation in groups.

Chapter 9 described confronting discrepancies, primarily in relation to working with individuals. Discrepancies that occur within groups also require some level and type of confrontation. A worker in a treatment group who determines that a member has engaged in behavior warranting confrontation has a responsibility to follow through and confront that individual. There are, however, at least two ways to do confrontation that can make it more palatable and effective. When workers choose to confront a client directly, for example, because of a discrepancy between verbal and other behavior, this situation provides a good opportunity to model appropriate confrontation for other members. The worker engages in a nonblaming type of confrontation by pointing out the discrepancy and how it affects the worker, for example, by using an "I" statement.

A second manner of confrontation involves having the worker in a group ask the entire group to take responsibility for problem solving. Thus, a worker might say, "Is anyone else bothered by Mike's assertion that he is going straight, after saying that he was arrested again last night?" This approach places responsibility for confronting Mike on the group instead of the worker, underscoring an important principle in treatment groups.

Confrontation in task groups is also essential. Members must be able to confront other members who do not carry out agreed-upon tasks or who engage in other behavior that threatens the group. For example, a team member represents himself to the public as having more authority and responsibility in the group than what he really had. In other words, he believes he does most of the work and, therefore, wants most of the credit. The group, charged with planning a conference, takes responsibility for telling the errant member that no single member is appointed as a conference coordinator and that the group reserves this role for itself. In their view, they all put in a lot of effort and deserve to share the credit accordingly.

While there will usually be a brief moment of discomfort when confrontation is used, the costs of not being confrontational are too high to avoid this responsibility. As always, confrontation should be used judiciously and tactfully. One should have both empathy and respect for the sensitivities of the person being confronted.

Consultation

As described throughout this chapter, the worker may serve as a consultant to the group, while acting in a leadership role. Consider a worker who provided consultation to a Parents Anonymous group. The group's goal was to provide a supportive experience for parents who abuse their children and to help these parents avoid such behavior in the future. The worker's role included providing consultation on available community services, strategies for successfully negotiating agency bureaucracies, and nonpunitive ideas for child management. The worker informed group members about local resources, shared his knowledge of agency eligibility requirements, and helped clients assess the appropriateness of the service for meeting their needs. The consultant role is basically that of an advisor who provides information, suggestions, ideas, and feedback. A consultant lacks administrative power over the consultee but has special knowledge or expertise that is of value to the recipient. The consultee is free to accept, modify, or reject the advice.

Consultation may be either case consultation or program consultation, or it may include elements of both (Shulman, 1992). In *case consultation,* the focus is on a specific client or situation, and the consultation may be provided to any professional or group. An example would be consultation provided to a nursing home staff on a particular client.

Program consultation may occur when the consultant works with supervisory or administrative staff about ways to improve service. In this case, the focus may be on agency policies and practices instead of a specific client.

In one instance, a human services professional was asked to serve as a consultant to a family planning agency. The agency director believed that the intercession of a consultant could help ameliorate problems occurring among volunteers serving the agency. The problems seemed to focus on disagreements between and among volunteer group members and the director. Volunteers appeared resistive to suggestions and direction provided by the agency director. The consultant met separately with the director and then jointly with the director and the volunteers. Several salient issues of concern to the volunteers were identified during this meeting. The primary issue involved a perception that the director was favoring one member of the volunteer group over the others. The consultant suggested that the director address this issue directly with the group. The director publicly announced his engagement to the "favored" volunteer and took pains from that point on to ensure that his interactions with the group did not show favoritism. The end result was improved service delivery to agency clients, increased openness on the part of the director, and a greater sense on the part of the volunteers that they were making a valued contribution to the agency.

Although no single model of human services consultation has emerged, consultation does involve a purpose, a problem, and a process. Ultimately, the success of the consultation depends upon the relationship between consultant and consultee. The expertise and capability of the consultant is only as effective as the relationship between the two allows. Once again, skills important for one-on-one interventions are important when working with groups.

Coordination

Coordination "is the working together of two or more service providers" (Johnson, 1998, p. 354). Johnson describes the coordinating function as encompassing both collaboration and teamwork. To be successful, coordination requires that all parties have a common goal. The goal may relate to a particular client or include provision of services to a target population. There is an expectation that all parties believe that improvements will occur if coordination of services is accomplished.

Case management often involves coordination of services provided by a variety of professionals. The focus is on assuring that all services provided to a client are accomplished in a way that achieves common goals and meets client needs. Often the human services professional is the person who has the case management responsibility and ensures that agreed upon services are provided (case management will be discussed further in Chapter 15). Coordination is especially important when the service providers have different professional orientations or when both formal and informal resources must be used to help the client. To be most effective, the human services professional providing coordination must value and believe in the competence of services provided by others. The worker must also ensure that all important information is communicated to all parties. That sufficient time be made available for building relationships among the participants, in addition to participants having support for their efforts, is important (Johnson, 1998).

Using Structure

Structure describes the use of "planned, systematic, time limited interventions . . ." (Toseland & Rivas, 1998, p. 240). One of the facets of structure is the use of time. Group meetings should begin and end at an agreed-upon time. Material brought up at the last minute is best held for the next meeting.

Agendas help structure time, ensuring that topics or activities to be covered are known to all. This structuring places responsibility on all members to stay on task. Sometimes, the amount of time to be spent on each topic is specified, further structuring the use of time. In treatment groups, structure may include spending different amounts of time on each client's issues. In many groups, all members take turns sharing their progress since the previous meeting, with major focus on one member. This process is then followed in successive meetings so all members have opportunities to focus on their problems.

The worker is largely responsible for enforcing time constraints and models this for the members. Frequently, the entire intervention is highly structured. Many educational groups are well-structured and include blocks of time allocated for specific topics, group activities designed to teach important concepts, and even role playing. The degree of structure needed may vary from one type of group to another. The worker will need to be flexible in planning and working with groups.

InfoTrac College Edition

In this chapter, we discussed the skills needed for working with groups. Group types and practitioner roles also were reviewed. In addition, important aspects of group dynamics and decision making processes used by groups were considered. For more information on these topics, please enter the following search terms:

treatment groups
task groups

growth groups
therapy groups
support groups
psychoeducational groups

✳ *On the Internet*

Because of the very dynamic nature of the Web, URLs are subject to change. Therefore, be sure to check out the companion Website for this book at http://www.humanservices.wadsworth.com, where links will be updated periodically.
www.priory.com
www.payson.tulane.edu
www.mendezfoundation.org
www.parli.com

CHAPTER 13

Working with Organizations and Communities

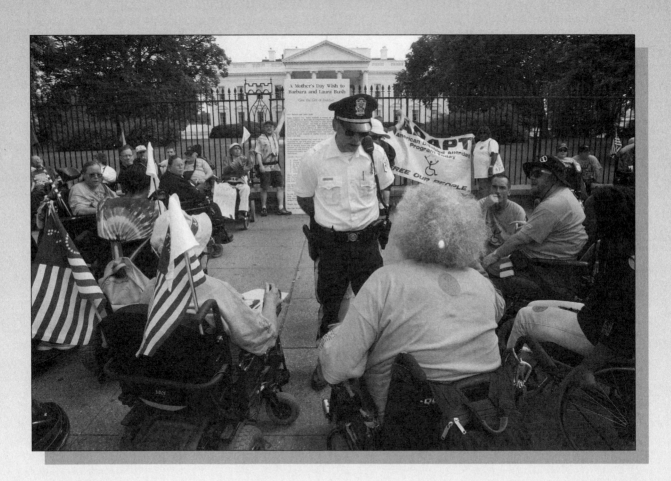

Georgette Harrison was dog-tired. Her primary job was to license foster homes, make foster home placements, and oversee her agency's receiving homes for children. The receiving homes provided temporary (up to three weeks) shelter while more permanent arrangements could be made (e.g., foster care or return to the child's own home). But this year had been an especially bad one for Georgi, as her friends called her, as well as for the county human services agency for which she worked.

First, she had become aware that fewer people were applying to be foster parents. She did not know the reasons why, but the lack of homes was becoming serious. Second, she recognized that her agency badly needed a group home for adolescent boys. Referrals for group-home care were increasing, and her traditional foster homes were not designed to handle half-a-dozen delinquent boys.

Georgi found that her colleagues were also confronting many problems. Too many sexually active young people had no access to family planning services. Many of them could not afford to see a physician.

Finally, her own agency seemed reluctant to provide clients with adequate resources unless administrators were legally pressured to do so. Past efforts to get the agency director to be more flexible were not particularly successful.

As a line human services professional (i.e., not a supervisor or administrator), Georgi did not think of herself as a community organizer or organizational change agent. However, in the next three years, Georgi would be involved in all of the following macro-level change activities:

1. developing a family planning clinic for low-income clients
   (she later served as vice chair of their board of directors);

2. creating community education programs designed to increase the number of licensed foster homes (she prepared radio and newspaper ads and appeared on local talk-radio shows);

3. writing of a grant to establish a group home for delinquent boys (she wrote the grant, defended it before a review panel, and supervised operation of the group home);

4. pressuring of her agency's director to recognize client rights and provide better service; and

5. creating a new program to provide part-time jobs as tutors for delinquent adolescents.

 ## *Introduction*

Macro practice in generalist human services involves working on behalf of whole groups or populations of clients. It transcends working with individual clients or small treatment groups. Macro practice involves questioning and sometimes confronting major social issues and global organizational policies. Sometimes, the services your clients need are not being provided; at other times the policies that govern your work are unfair or inhumane. At these times, you will need to consider whether or not to try to change the organization, policy, or system on behalf of your clients. You may need to assess the situation from a broad perspective, and you may have to evaluate what impact "the system" (whichever one may be involved) has on your clients.

Many, perhaps most, human services professionals, especially as they begin their practice, focus on working with individual clients or groups of clients. Thinking about changing "the system" is vague or overwhelming. The specific "system" that needs changing may be hard to define (e.g., "the system" may be the organization you work for, a county social services agency, your state government, or a federal bureaucracy). How to go about making changes in "the system" may be unclear. The work necessary to implement changes may not be included in your written job description. You might be awed by the amount of effort such change demands.

Core value themes in human services include the fundamental rights of people to have their basic needs met, to make their own choices (assuming such choices harm neither others nor themselves), and to maintain their human dignity. A central theme of the empowerment tradition in human services practice is the emphasis on expanding client resources especially for groups denied social and economic justice (Simon, 1994). There will be times when you will find these value themes violated. You will see inequities and unfairness that you will be ethically unable to tolerate. These instances are most likely to be the times when you will call upon your macro practice skills to implement changes outside the individual client or client group. Something in the environment, in some part of "the system," will need to be the target of your change effort. This chapter focuses on the skills needed to work *with* and *within* the various systems enveloping us. Most macro change efforts will be pursued within an agency context. Therefore, we will view macro practice primarily from an organizational perspective. Specifically, this chapter will:

- introduce an organizational context of practice;
- define and discuss major perspectives of macro practice, including social reform, social action, case advocacy, and cause advocacy;
- examine the concept of community and its relevance to human services;
- describe the application of micro and mezzo practice skills to macro practice;
- examine and illustrate the skills necessary for effective macro practice, including building and maintaining organizations, evaluating results, fund-raising, budgeting, negotiating, mediating, assessing needs, planning, using political skills, and working with coalitions;
- emphasize those skills necessary to exercise influence, including petitioning, working with

the media, educating, persuading, confronting, collaborating, and letter writing;

- examine those roles most useful in macro practice, including initiator, negotiator, advocate, spokesperson, organizer, mediator, and consultant.

Defining Macro Practice

Macro practice in the human services is designed to improve or modify some aspect of society. Improvements or changes can be sought in organizational or societal policies and procedures that regulate distribution of resources to clients. These improvements might occur when clients are either not getting needed resources or when the resource is not provided as effectively or efficiently as possible.

Similarly, macro practice is concerned with developing new resources when what clients need is unavailable. Sometimes, new policies and procedures must be developed and implemented. At other times, whole new groups, agencies, or organizations must be established.

Another task common to macro practice is helping clients get their due rights. Changes need to be made in "the system" so that clients can exercise their rights. Change is needed whether for the benefit of one client or ten thousand clients.

Macro practice targets "the system" to determine where and how changes need to be made. Numerous systems make up our "general society." They include political systems like town, county, state, and federal governments as well as legal systems involving the police, legislature, and courts. Additionally, they involve social service delivery systems like county social service agencies, residential mental health facilities, and federal Veterans' Administration services.

Macro practice often requires the use of advocacy on behalf of clients. Advocacy involves intervening in order to help clients get what they need. Sometimes, it means going further and working much harder than the specifications of your job description. This element of human services is one that makes human services special and distinct from other fields.

Finally, macro practice occurs frequently in an organizational context. In other words, most macro practice is carried out by those in agencies or organizations. Agencies have policies or constraints that often act to limit workers' behavior. This aspect differs from human services professionals who can act as independent agents, attack a problem, and do whatever they want. The following is a detailed exploration of this issue.

The Organizational Context of Human Services Practice

Most human services professionals spend all, or part, of their professional careers within formal organizations. Similarly, all persons live and practice within a community (rural, urban, suburban). The benefits of formal organizations include such tangible resources as office space, salary, clerical support, paper, telephone, and the like. They also provide less tangible benefits such as sanction for one's professional efforts.

Consider, for example, that the human services professional in a child welfare agency must complete investigations following allegations of child abuse. She was hired for that job, supported by the agency in her performance, and is generally respected by the agency and community for her efforts to protect vulnerable children. In pursuing the mandate for child protection, the worker has an office, telephone, mileage allowance, secretarial support, salary, and fringe benefits. These are provided because the agency and community believe in the potential good to be accomplished by the worker. Clearly, such formal organizations as social and other human services agencies provide much of value to the human services professional.

With the benefits of belonging to or working for an organization, however, come drawbacks. These include policies, rules and regulations that circumscribe behavior, and procedures that sometimes become a source of difficulty. The worker who has not found working within an organization sometimes troublesome or downright antithetical to professional obligations to the client is rare. Highlight 13.1 illustrates how an agency can sometimes become part of the problem. Moreover, a significant number of human services professionals move into macro level positions within a few years of graduation (York, Denton, & Moran, 1990). This transition also confronts human services professionals with the challenge of making their own agencies responsive to social and economic justice needs of clients.

Professional–Organizational Conflicts

Conflicts such as the one experienced by the worker in Highlight 13.1 are common in many human services agencies. Frequently, the problem is even more

When the Agency You Work for Is Part of the Problem

Gaylon had worked only a short time for the Macon County Department of Human Services. As foster care coordinator, he was responsible for recruiting, screening, training, and licensing of foster homes. It was a job of which he was very proud. He put in many extra hours meeting prospective foster parents in the evening, so neither foster parent would have to take off from work to meet with him. During one of their regular supervisory conferences, Gaylon's supervisor, Patty, said he was accumulating too much compensatory time and should stop the evening visits.

Gaylon liked Patty and generally felt that she was supportive of his work. Patty said that if people cared enough about becoming foster parents, most would come in during regular business hours. The new policy troubled Gaylon. In his view, foster parents were providing an important and irreplaceable service to the community and agency. Foster parents were always badly needed, and most of the couples interested in becoming foster parents had at least one parent working during the day. Most were in what some might call the lower-middle class, hardworking people with limited financial resources. Gaylon saw them in the evening because he was reluctant to ask parents to take time off from work and possibly lose income. Gaylon felt an obligation to the foster parents and a duty to follow the rules of his agency, and now these responsibilities seemed in conflict.

serious than the one in our example. Human services professionals who feel a sense of professional identity with the human services profession and subscribe to its ethical standards may find serious conflicts arising between their professional role as change agents and their responsibilities to the employing agency. These naturally occurring conflicts reflect the reality of professional practice within formal organizations. All human services professionals have an obligation to follow the policies of their agency, and most of the time this is not a problem. The conflict described in Highlight 13.1 was real, and the dilemma faced by the human services professional was challenging. Formal organizations require rules and regulations (policies) to function effectively. When these two obligations collide, the worker (and often the client) are frequently in the middle.

Limitations and Risk Assessment

When such a situation arises, the worker must decide how to handle it. The planned change process explained earlier in this text is applicable here. The worker must assess several items. Knowing, for example, whether Gaylon's view is correct, that foster parents should not have to take off from work to participate in the interviews, would be important. His position, however, rests largely on his values and nothing stronger. Knowing if scheduling meetings during the day discourages foster parents from participating might be important.

And learning why the supervisor felt the amount of compensatory time was excessive might also be helpful. Was there some agency rule that set the maximum amount that could be accrued? Was the supervisor just worried about how much evening work Gaylon was putting in? He needed to know where the problem lay in order to find a solution. Also, Gaylon was a new worker, albeit a valuable one. He felt challenging his supervisor would be difficult because of his newness.

Gaylon's reluctance illustrates the importance of assessing the risk inherent in trying to change any part of an organization. He was also aware of other rules that were equally problematic but seemed more intractable. Gaylon knew that there are limitations in how many, what type of, and how fast problems within an agency can be solved. A new worker who tries to change some part of an agency is in a vulnerable position. Before making efforts to change an organization, the worker must realistically assess the probability of success, the importance of securing this change, and the risks to him- or herself for pursuing such a change. This last risk cannot be accurately assessed without considering the strategies Gaylon might undertake to challenge the rule. Some strategies carry increased risk to the worker. Angering a supervisor is risky. Getting fired is unappealing. The worker is more vulnerable at certain times. Many agencies, for example, place a new worker on probation for six months. During that time, the worker may be fired for almost any reason without recourse to the usual protections afforded more experienced workers (union contract, personnel policies, and so on).

Theoretical Base for Organizational and Community Change

Netting, Kettner, and McMurtry (1993) have identified two broad theoretical perspectives that underlie practice with large systems—organizational theory and community theory. Organizations include any structures with staff, policies, and procedures whose purpose in operating is to attain certain goals. For example, schools, public social welfare departments, and an agency operating four group homes for developmentally disabled adults are all organizations.

Organizational theory is concerned with how organizations function, what improves or impairs the ability of an organization to accomplish its mission, and what motivates people to work toward organizational goals. Some approaches to organizational theory have focused on management or leadership style, while others have dealt with such structural issues as organizational hierarchy, planning, staffing patterns, budgeting, policies, and procedures.

Community theory has two primary components: the nature of communities and human services practice within communities. Warren and Warren (1984), major students of communities, argue that a community is a "combination of social units and systems that perform the major social functions" important to the locality (p. 28). The first major social function includes the production, distribution, and consumption of goods and services. According to their formulation, all community institutions (churches and businesses, professional and governmental organizations) provide a variety of goods and services.

The second function of a community is socialization, or the process in which knowledge, values, beliefs, and behaviors are taught to members of the community. Socialization is particularly important to children, because this process is the way they learn the community's expectations for them. Families are one of the primary socialization units in the community.

The third function is social control, which is the community's efforts to make sure members live within the norms of the community. Social control is exerted through laws, police powers, and the court systems.

Social participation, the fourth function, is the involvement of community members in various activities designed to enhance a sense of belonging. It is achieved through religious organizations such as churches, social clubs such as the Junior League, membership organizations such as NASW, and friendship groups. In addition, many businesses and governmental agencies encourage social participation through organized events such as sporting activities.

The final community function, mutual support, involves caring for the sick, helping the poor or homeless, and providing a variety of health and human services. Mutual support activities are carried out by individuals and families, social and religious organizations, and the government. It is easy to see how problems could occur in carrying out any of these functions. One can also envision how human services professionals might become involved in solving these problems.

Warren and Warren (1984) have also helped us conceptualize communities from multiple perspectives. For example, one may think of a community as having specific geographical boundaries, like a city, or as denoting a group with shared interests and beliefs, such as the human services community (see Highlight 13.2). The community may be seen as a target for change, as the problem, or as the context within which change occurs. The advantages of these perspectives become more apparent when assessing the problem, deciding among several possible interventions, and evaluating the outcome.

Human services practice in the community is the second component of community theory. Each of the following sections highlights a particular approach to human services practice in the community. As will be evident, however, some of the approaches, such as social action and advocacy (case and cause), can be employed to change organizations as well as communities. In both cases, the goal is change, but the nature and extent of change may vary dramatically.

Social Reform

Garvin and Cox (1995) have briefly discussed the history of social reform movements in the United States. The social reformer's basic concern is the development and improvement of social conditions. Early efforts at social reform included creation of kindergartens, recreational programs for children and adults, and educational programs for adults. The early social reformer fought large-scale problems

HIGHLIGHT 13.2

Community Organization: The Traditional Focus on the Community in Macro Practice

Historically, *community organization* has been the term used to refer to macro practice in human services. The methods and directions of human services practice have changed and evolved, just as the economic and social realities of the times have drastically changed. However, the concept of *community* continues to be very significant for human services professionals. You might ask how the word *community* can be clearly defined. Is it a neighborhood? Or is the community a group with common issues, problems, and concerns? For example, there is the human services community or the community of physically disabled persons. Does the word *community* connote a certain ethnic, cultural, or racial group? How large or small should a community be? Can the United States be considered a national community?

Barker (1999) defines the community as "a group of individuals or families that share certain values, services, institutions, interests, or geographical proximity" (p. 89). We have already described Warren and Warren's 1984 formulation of the city. Their perspective on the community is perhaps the best articulated and most well-respected.

Because of the wide range of possible meanings associated with the term *community,* we will focus here on some of the major concepts inherent in the Barker and Warren and Warren definitions. First, both Barker's and Warren and Warren's definitions concern a group of people related in terms of locality. Second, these people also have some interests or functions in common. Third, because of their common locality, functions, and/or interests, people in the community interact together on some level or at least have the potential to interact.

A fourth concept involved in community is important from a human services perspective. A community can be organized so that its citizens can participate together, solve their mutual problems, and improve their overall quality of life. Human services professionals can use their macro practice skills to mobilize citizens within communities to accomplish the goals they have set for themselves. Human services professionals have been involved in efforts to encourage the growth of new businesses and to counteract the human toll that occurs when a major employer goes out of business.

Historically, the three methods of community organization engaged in by human services professionals have included social action, social planning, and locality development (Rothman, Erlich, & Tropman, 1995). Using macro practice skills to advocate on behalf of communities of people is one logical application of

---

related to immigration and the impact of urbanization. Human services professionals helped develop vocational education, hot lunch programs, neighborhood playgrounds, and community housing codes. These changes came about through the reformers' involvement in the political process.

Like their forebears, human services professionals today actively pursue a legislative agenda designed to improve client services and meet large-scale problems with large-scale programs. The social reformer's focus is on modifying the conditions of society that seriously threaten the well-being of citizens or prevent them from developing their potential. The human services professional–reformer today works to maintain and strengthen such programs as Headstart; the Women, Infants, and Children (WIC) food program; and family planning. He or she fights homelessness and drug abuse and opposes changes in public assistance programs that will hurt or penalize the programs' recipients. In

summary, social reform is more concerned with problems on a larger scale and focuses efforts in such legislative arenas as Congress, state legislatures, county boards of supervisors, and city councils.

Social Action

Social action is a term given to at least three different but related types of activity: (1) advocacy around specific populations and issues such as homelessness and hunger; (2) working in local and national elections to elect sympathetic representatives and to support new programs designed to combat large-scale problems; and (3) networking with other groups pursuing a similar agenda. The latter may include organizations of women or gays and lesbians who combine efforts to combat such problems as sexist or homophobia-induced rules. Clearly, overlap exists between the roles of social reformer and social activist, although the latter model social action. Frequently, social action can be used to remedy imbalances of power. For instance, sometimes a city will draw its voting boundaries to guarantee that minorities will not be the majority in any single district. Some minority groups have forced communities (sometimes through legal action) to rewrite the boundaries for city voting districts so that they have an opportunity to elect a representative who would uphold their interests.

Social planning is "a technical process of problem solving with regard to substantive social problems, such as delinquency, housing and mental health" (Rothman et al., 1995, p. 30). The emphasis is to call in experts or consultants to work with designated community leaders to solve specific problems. People in the general community would have little, if any, participation or input into the planned change process. For example, a city might call in an urban renewal expert to recommend what should be done with a blighted area of the community.

Locality development is "community change . . . pursued through broad participation of a wide spectrum of people at the local community level" (Rothman et al., 1995, p. 28). The idea is to involve as many people as possible within the community in a democratic manner to define their own goals and help themselves. Locality development is consistent with human services values, because individual dignity and participation and the right of free choice are emphasized.

There is considerable debate regarding the paths human services macro practice should take. National and world politics have changed drastically since the three traditional methods of community organization were enthusiastically espoused. Resources continue to shrink, and hard decisions must be made regarding their focus. Many argue that macro practice in the real world is substantially different than it was a few decades ago.

The position of this text is that macro practice, which involves interventions with large systems and organizations on behalf of people, is still a major component of generalist human services. Systems and their policies need change and improvement. Oppressed populations need advocacy. The focus of change must not be limited to changing the behavior of individual clients or client groups. Rather, there is a cluster of macro practice skills that human services professionals can use to effect change. As we have already indicated, today, most macro practice takes place within an organizational context.

The basic concept of community is no less important now than it was 20 or 30 years ago. It remains just as important to focus on the benefits of large groups of people, their overall well-being, their dignity, and their right of choice. Community provides a wider, more global perspective within which human services professionals can view the world and set their goals.

emphasizes greater involvement in the change effort by the intended beneficiaries. Social reform frequently focuses on doing good *for* the client, while social action more often values doing good *with* the client.

Cause Advocacy

Barker (1999) defines *advocacy* as the act of directly representing or defending others (p. 11). *Cause advocacy* is a term used to describe advocacy efforts by human services professionals on behalf of an issue of overriding importance to a *group* of clients. It assumes that the expected beneficiaries are likely to share certain common characteristics. Examples of causes for which advocacy might be appropriate include education for children with disabilities, expanded medical insurance coverage for the elderly, or both. Sometimes, the terms *cause advocacy* and *class advocacy* are used interchangeably. The latter

term also suggests that one is advocating for all members of a particular class or grouping of persons (e.g., poor people, people with physical disabilities, or people of a particular ethnic group).

Case Advocacy

Case advocacy, as the name implies, refers to activity on behalf of a single case: an individual, family, or small group. Case advocacy typically involves different strategies from those used to advocate for a cause. For example, the focus may be on the way a particular rule is preventing a client from receiving services to which he or she is otherwise entitled. The expectation is that this client will benefit from waiving the rule or interpreting it differently, but there is no general sense that a large group of clients will benefit in a similar fashion. Because of its significance to generalist human services practice, Chapter 14 discusses advocacy in much greater depth.

Because of the similarities between organizations and communities, the planned change model discussed in Chapter 1 is clearly applicable. However, a problem need not exist for intervention to occur. A worker might, for instance, choose to intervene after identifying a potential problem, to prevent future difficulties, or simply to improve an already existing program or condition. The advantage of this approach is that it allows the human services professional to be *proactive* instead of *reacting* to problems or issues. Thus, a human services professional may recognize that a change in a particular program or policy might produce additional benefits or that greater efficiency could be achieved by modifying some aspect of the services provided.

A good example of this is Ramona, a human services professional practicing in a residential facility for adolescent clients with serious emotional disabilities. Ramona worked with adolescent males on the open unit that provided a less restrictive milieu for nonsuicidal/nonviolent residents. The open unit was a transition unit, housing residents who were preparing themselves to go home. Only residents who had made significant progress on the locked ward were placed on the open unit where they could be more autonomous. Open unit residents were expected to use their new skills in managing anger and depression and were able to go home on weekend passes. However, Ramona's agency had a policy that said all residents on either locked or open units must use their razors to shave only in the presence of staff. Ramona considered the policy problematic for several reasons. First, the residents were being treated as if they could not be trusted when the very purpose of the open unit was to demonstrate client strengths and progress and to encourage continued improvement. Second, the policy ignored the fact that residents went home on the weekends and used their razors without anyone monitoring them. Third, requiring staff to monitor each resident while shaving took them away from more important tasks.

Ramona discussed her concerns with other staff members and the unit manager. This led to a meeting between the staff and the chief psychiatrist, who vetoed any change in policy. The staff prepared a position paper reiterating their proposal and empowered clients to express their own views in the paper. After a couple of months of internal agency discussions, the policy on the open unit was changed. Shortly after, Ramona received a letter of commendation from the agency deputy director for her interest in the welfare of residents.

 ## Micro Skills for Organizational and Community Change

Earlier chapters have explained some key skills necessary for intervention at all system levels. The intent of this chapter is to briefly summarize the ways in which these skills apply when working for organizational and community change. Chapter 9 identified warmth, empathy, and genuineness as important attributes for working with individuals. Much of the work of organizational or community change occurs in face-to-face interactions. These interventions might be worker to client, worker to administrator or supervisor, or worker to elected or appointed official. The capacity for genuineness and empathy are equally important in these situations. The worker in Highlight 13.3, who was attempting to modify local procedures, was perceived as genuine and sensitive to the problems of decision makers. Most people respond better to warmth than to criticism, a fact applying to administrators or others in positions of power. There may be times where the worker does not wish to be considered sensitive to the target's position or where clear adversarial strategies are most appropriate. These situations, however, are much less common.

Usually, positively reinforcing others and the ability to form relationships with people from vastly different backgrounds and orientations are essential for work in the community. Finally, the capacity to observe and understand verbal and nonverbal behavior and to interpret and summarize the words of others and the ability to portray oneself as confident and competent are important skills for organizational or community change.

 ## Mezzo Skills for Organizational and Community Change

Much of the work of human services professionals occurs on a one-on-one basis or through working in small task groups. These groups have several advantages. Groups are often better equipped to handle complex activities or to undertake projects beyond the ability of a single person. In addition, participants in the group are usually more committed to the outcome when they are involved in the decision-making process. Chapter 12 discussed groups in greater detail, and no attempt will be made here to

HIGHLIGHT 13.3

Human Services Professionals Can Help Improve Delivery of Services

The meeting room of the Algoma City Council was full—an unusual event, because hardly anyone ever attended the council's bimonthly meetings. Residents of the small community simply allowed the council the freedom to conduct business and rarely asked to address the body.

Tonight, the situation was different. Residents in the Knollwood subdivision were out in force to protest a business park proposed for property next to their residential neighborhood. Each resident spoke and shared misgivings about the potential effect this development might have on their property values. They also expressed anger at not being formally notified about the proposal. Council members stated their sensitivity to the plight of the residents and agreed to gather additional information before making a decision. They also promised that residents would have an opportunity to review any proposed building in the business park.

When a speaker said that many members had attended this meeting because their neighbor had seen the topic on the council agenda, another potential problem surfaced. If residents did not know about a proposed development, they could not voice their concerns. The present system relied mainly on word of mouth to inform people about issues pending before the council. Suspicion existed in such circumstances and prevented an impartial review of the proposal.

Finally, a human services professional attending the meeting proposed a solution. A brief amendment to the zoning law would provide for residents within 300 feet of a proposed development to be notified about the changes under consideration. Most residents believed this would provide ample warning, allow citizens to voice concerns, and allay fears that some secret development would adversely affect their lives. The result would be better communication between city government and the citizen and prevention of the angry and disenfranchised feelings that emerged tonight. Over time, both sides would benefit from the change.

recap that material. Instead, an example of a successful project involving a task group within a community is provided in Highlight 13.3.

As our example in Highlight 13.4 suggests, mezzo skills useful for organizational and community change include the following:

- conflict resolution
- developing win–win outcomes
- team building
- public speaking
- consultation

The final mezzo skill needed is coordination. In Highlight 13.4, several steps had to be achieved simultaneously, while others followed a sequence. The worker sought examples of other landmark ordinances that could be used as a model. He arranged meeting times and places for the group. He also helped plan a lobbying campaign and assisted the group in each of its chores. Because some members of this task group were also members of other community groups, avoiding overlap in meeting times was essential. Ensuring that each member knew exactly who to talk to regarding the ordinance

was also important. Skill in coordinating the efforts of group members is essential to any organizational or community change effort.

Macro Skills for Organizational and Community Change

This chapter will address nine major skills important in macro practice: evaluating results, fund-raising, budgeting, negotiating, mediating, influencing decision makers, needs assessment, planning, and working with coalitions.

Evaluating Outcomes

Evaluating the outcome or results of one's practice has become increasingly important. Clients have a right to expect their human services professional to be competent for the task at hand. Wanting to improve one's practice is also incumbent upon the human services professional. Learning what does and does not work and in what situations is essential.

HIGHLIGHT 13.4

Saving a Community: A Task Group at Work

Clearwater had once won an award for its beauty. The growth of the university and the concomitant destruction of Victorian-era homes had left many in the town in a state of despair. Not only were the remaining homes being converted into student housing, but the lovely elm trees lining the streets had died, leaving a denuded landscape.

At the request of local officials, the community development specialist called a meeting at which citizen concerns would be explored. Using techniques such as nominal group (a combination of brainstorming and prioritizing issues by the group), the worker helped the group identify three major problem areas. Three groups were formed, each in response to a particular problem. One group focused on trying to save the remaining historic homes, a second worked on community beautification, and a third looked at downtown business development. The worker met separately with each group to help them get started. Periodically, all three groups met together to discuss accomplishments and future tasks. The historic preservation task group studied the problem and considered the work of other cities with similar problems.

Eventually, this group wrote an ordinance protecting historic buildings from destruction or unsympathetic remodeling. They lobbied the city planning commission and the city council, organized mailings to council members, and spoke at various public meetings. Despite vigorous opposition from the most powerful property owner in town, the council adopted the ordinance and established a permanent landmark commission to enforce it.

Achieving this was not easy. Overcoming opposition and resolving areas of conflict were formidable tasks. Conflict resolution, described in Chapter 3, is equally important at both the organizational and community levels. The ability to diffuse potentially problematic situations, to find a satisfactory middle ground, is critical. Win–win outcomes, where all parties benefit, are desirable and should be the worker's goal whenever possible.

Similarly, the ability to use the disparate strengths of many individuals and to build an effective task group requires skill in team building. In this case, the worker assessed the strengths and weaknesses of each group member and helped the group accomplish its goal by building on the former and overcoming the latter. Thus, members who were more comfortable speaking in public presented the group's ideas to the city planning commission, the city council, and the chamber of commerce. Others wrote letters, telephoned people, and addressed envelopes.

After the historic preservation group became an effective body, the worker adopted a consultant role, offering ideas and providing feedback to the group leaders. Skill in offering consultation is important because workers may not continue indefinitely as leader. Yet they will want to provide for a certain degree of continuity or stabilization of the change effort.

The human services professional should always operate under the dictum that governs medical doctors: "First, do no harm." Without a plan for evaluating interventions, we run the risk of inadvertently hurting the people and causes we are trying to help.

Chapter 8 took a more in-depth look at types of evaluations useful for human services professionals. For purposes of this section, however, we will identify two major approaches: practice evaluation and program evaluation. *Practice evaluation* is evaluating the effectiveness or results of what individual human services professionals do. It may take the form of single subject designs, task achievement scaling (Reid & Epstein, 1972), client satisfaction surveys, or goal attainment scaling (Alter & Evens, 1990), also called goal accomplishment (McMahon, 1996).

Program evaluation is evaluating the effectiveness and results of entire programs. Program evaluation techniques might include needs assessments, evaluability assessments, process analysis, outcome analysis, and cost-benefit analysis (Grinnell & Williams, 1990). These approaches were discussed further in Chapter 8.

Fund-Raising

For most people, asking for money is a difficult task. In the human services context, asking for money is called fund-raising. Social programs usually cannot exist without financial support. Money is needed to pay staff, buy equipment, and rent space. It is also required for such consumables as paper, pens, and so on. Fund-raising may be needed to purchase equipment for refurbishing a park in a low-income section of the city. Money may be required to support an AIDS awareness project being started by a local social service agency. The shelter for survivors of domestic violence may undertake fund-raising to pay staff or purchase groceries. Many social programs depend upon a combination of public funding and private donations to cover operating costs. In addition, political campaigns require money. Human services professionals may be called upon to raise funds and should be familiar with the basics of fund-raising.

The fund-raiser should keep multiple sources of funds in mind. Flanagan (1980) divides these into individual donors, corporate donors, foundations, membership dues, and benefits. In addition, church organizations and service clubs often provide funding if the area to be supported falls within their sphere of interest. Foundations and corporations tend to have the resources to make major contributions to a cause or program. On the other hand, they can be the most difficult and time consuming to solicit. Individual donations are more easily acquired, but the amounts received are likely to be limited. While individuals typically give once for a cause, corporations are often willing to provide continuing funds. Foundations are also more likely to give matching funds if their program promises to raise an equal amount from other sources. This type of fund-raising is often an effective way to start up a program but does not guarantee any long-term support. Service clubs and church groups often provide small donations for specific projects. They may offer to purchase a piece of equipment or provide time and money to build a wheelchair ramp.

Membership dues are generally free of the restrictions that other kinds of donations carry. Because they depend upon membership, the size of the member pool becomes important. Membership dues are ongoing, but often the dollar amount raised is low when compared to other sources. Equally limiting are benefits. Most of us are familiar with benefits of one type: the bake sale or car wash.

While benefits can take this form, the most successful benefits in terms of money raised are those involving some activity in which the public can participate. A musical program, comedy show, raffle, or dance that will attract the public holds more promise than such things as bake sales. Held annually, benefits can be very successful and become a continuing source of funding.

Fund-raising takes time, hard work, and dedication by the human services professional. There is only one real secret to fund-raising: You must ask for money. Asking others to donate is scary; it is a taboo subject with many people. Flanagan suggests starting by selling a product, such as a sweatshirt or cookbook, which is produced at minimal cost and sold at a good profit. Later, requesting money specifically for support of your cause may be possible. Some organizations sell memberships to the public, aware that the purchaser is not likely to attend any of their meetings. Joining the organization simply allows one to give indirectly to support the group's goals.

In many situations, making the program's request through a formal presentation will be necessary for the fund-raiser. The audience may be the entire membership, such as with a service organization or a select group such as a foundation's board of directors. In other scenarios, all fund-raising may be achieved through mail solicitations. This scenario is not uncommon when raising money for political campaigns. In these situations, the fund-raisers begin by listing those likely to support the cause. Next, they decide the best person to make the request. Direct person-to-person solicitation uses a similar process. If the contact is through a letter, making it clear why the potential donor should give to the cause is important. Making the request as relevant to the individual donor as possible is desirable. Some letters suggest an amount to be donated, while others leave this up to the donor. In fund-raising drives dedicated to purchasing equipment, listing the cost of the items may be helpful. Some who receive the solicitation may choose to donate money for a specific item or to donate the equipment itself.

In more extensive solicitations, especially to foundations or corporations, a packet of materials about the program may be developed. Formal presentations may include visual aids or videotaped information and printed materials. Whatever the source of funding, providing a "thank you" is critical. This appeal should include at least a note of appreciation, preferably handwritten, and perhaps an oral "thank you" as well.

Finally, remembering that people usually do not give to a cause without being asked is important. The person doing the fund-raising must believe in the cause and be willing to explain to potential donors why they should support the project. Once begun, the process of asking for money becomes easier, and even the novice fund-raiser becomes more self-confident. Remember, if you want something, you have to ask for it.

Budgeting

Budgeting involves money, which is critically important to all agencies and organizations where human services professionals function. Budgeting is an important concept to understand. Most beginning generalist practitioners will not be responsible for actually making up a budget. However, the budget and the budgeting process will *always* affect them.

A budget is "a statement of probable revenues," that is all types of income "and expenditures during a specified time period" (Barker, 1999, p. 43). We all have budgets, that is, specific allotments of money we can spend for rent or food or fun. The key thing about budgets is that they involve some predetermined and limited amount of money. If more money is spent on one thing, such as rent, there is less money to be spent on other things, such as food and fun.

The same principle applies to social agencies and organizations. Each has a budget regarding how much money it can spend and on what. When more money is spent on one item (e.g., provision of financial assistance to clients), then less money is available to spend on other items (e.g., human services professionals' salaries). The amount of money allotted to you (as salary and benefits) and to your clients (as services or resources) is critically important.

In effect, different parts and functions of an organization compete for the same money or portions of that money. When you work for an agency, there will be times when you strongly feel that clients have needs that are not being met at all or at least not satisfactorily. When advocating for these clients, you will need to understand budgets and this competition for funds.

For instance, a human services professional at a private day-treatment center for children and adolescents with behavior disorders was concerned about the "snacks" given to the children each morning upon their arrival. Day treatment provided troubled children with therapy and special education during the day. Yet, the children returned to their own homes each night. Many of the children came from severely impoverished homes with little, if any, food in the house. When they arrived at the center in the morning, they were hungry. The "snack" they received then was often the only nourishment they would get until the lunch the center provided at noon.

The day-treatment program was owned by a private individual who sold the agency's services to surrounding counties that did not provide these services themselves (this is referred to as "purchase of service," in that public agencies buy some kind of service from someone else who provides it). All staff at the day-treatment center, including human services professionals, received very high salaries. However, these salaries were at the expense of the other services. For instance, the offices and classrooms were poorly furnished, and the building was badly in need of repair.

Additionally, there was the problem of the "snacks." The owner of the agency apparently had gotten a "deal," by purchasing a whole truckload of crumb cakes at little expense. After three weeks of crumb cakes every morning, the center's clients were becoming tired of them. Despite their hunger, the children began to refer to the cakes by a quite vile term. The teachers and human services professionals, also quite sick of the cakes, found reprimanding the children for their vocabulary difficult, as the staff was beginning to feel the terms were almost appropriate.

The human services worker we initially talked about was worried over the lack of adequate nutrition because these cakes were all most of the children were getting. She was also concerned about the sugar-initiated "high" the children experienced immediately after eating the cakes and the subsequent drop in energy level. Many children already had problems with being overly active, controlling their behavior, and attending to classroom tasks. Should the worker approach the higher-level administration about this problem? Was the issue important enough to do so? She did not want to seem as though she was the type of person who complained about everything.

She finally did approach the center's director (who was one level below the owner). His response was that having the crumb cakes at such a reduced rate helped to keep the agency within its budget. Was she willing to take a cut in salary to improve the quality of morning snacks?

How would you have responded to the director's question had you been this human services professional? Would you have said, "Oh sure, I'll gladly take a cut in pay"? Would you have sheepishly backed away? Or would you have countered the director's question with a statement suggesting that money could be redistributed from some other part of the budget?

The point is that budgeting is extremely important. The greater the depth of your understanding of your agency's budget and of the budgeting process, the more potential you will have to impact budgeting decisions.

The task of preparing and managing a budget for any enterprise is similar. Usually, one establishes the budget for a given period (such as a year). Three types of budgeting may be encountered: line item, program or functional, and incremental (Sheafor et al., 1997).

Line-Item Budgets

A line-item budget is a statement of expenditures for a designated period of time, usually one year, where each cost item is noted on a separate line. Items are then added to portray the total budget expenditure. A line-item budget depicts how money will be spent without describing what the agency does (Skidmore, 1990). For example, one might have a category called personnel (further divided into salary, fringe benefits, and so on), another called equipment, and as many other categories as needed. An agency may operate multiple programs, such as protective services, foster care, and juvenile court services, but the costs of each program are not separated and identified. In effect, costs of these programs (and any new ones) may be invisible, because everything is lumped together into one big budget.

Setting initial budgets or continuing budgets may represent something of a guess. In the former situation, there is no existing budget to use as a model. With continuing budgets, there is an existing budget, but the estimates for future years must be prepared before the current year has been completed. Many social agencies use this method of budgeting.

Program Budgets

A program budget is a statement of expenditures where cost items are broken down according to programs the agency provides (Skidmore, 1990). It relates directly to how the agency spends its money in addition to the amount the agency spends. A program budget, also known as a functional budget, uses the same structure as line-item budgets. It also identifies functions such as the adoption program, delinquency project, or group home. This process allows the cost of each program to be identified and is useful in making decisions about spending priorities. Such a system is not perfect, because it relies on estimates of certain items. For example, in one agency the secretary spends a portion of her time typing for the adoption program and another portion doing bookkeeping for the group home. To assign her salary into the proper categories depends upon the accuracy of the estimates of the time she contributes to each program. This estimation is not always a simple chore. When accomplished, program budgets are helpful for accountability, in that they indicate where money is actually being spent. They also allow some measure of cost-effectiveness. In short, they can help establish that money is being put to the best use.

Table 13.1 compares two budgets for the same agency. One is a line-item budget, and the other is a program budget. The line-item budget reflects the entire cost of running the agency but does not give detailed information on either of the two programs operated by Happy Daze Family Services. The program budget shows the relative expenses and income from the two programs. As is evident, the family counseling program actually brings in more income than it costs to operate. On the other hand, the international adoption program costs over $100,000 more to operate than it brings in. The family counseling program subsidizes or helps pay for the adoption program, a fact which would not be evident without a program budget.

Line-item and program budgets are common ways of describing existing budgets. In other words, they describe how the current budget is organized. Once a budget exists, the common system for dealing with requests for budgets for subsequent years is an incremental budget.

Incremental Budgets

An incremental budget is a system in which an agency's budget from last year is used as a starting point for this year's budget. Typically, one would plan for the next year's budget by starting with the existing budget and then acting according to assumptions. If one assumes, for example, that income and expenditures will rise at the same rate as inflation (e.g., 3 percent), then the existing budget will be increased by 3 percent for next year. If the rate increases differently across categories (e.g., personnel or equipment), these differences should be reflected in the increment used. If salaries are going up at the rate of 5 percent and equipment at 2 percent, one would raise the amount budgeted for both categories accordingly.

Similarly, a decrease in revenues would result in reductions of anticipated income and expenditures of a given amount. This method is a common form of budgeting.

Negotiating

Negotiating is a process in which at least two individuals participate in a face-to-face interaction in order to reach a mutually acceptable decision. Negotiations

Table 13.1 *Comparison of Line-Item and Program Budgets*

2002 Line-Item Budget Happy Daze Family Services, Inc.		2002 Program Budget Happy Daze Family Services, Inc.	
		FAMILY COUNSELING PROGRAM	
Expenses		**Expenses**	
Personnel		Personnel	
Professional Staff	$250,000	Professional Staff	$100,000
Support/Clerical Staff	50,000	Support/Clerical Staff	20,000
Travel	5,000	Travel	2,000
Rent	35,000	Rent (40% of total)	14,000
Maintenance/Cleaning	4,500	Maintenance/Cleaning	1,800
Utilities	34,750	Utilities	13,900
Phone	19,750	Phone	7,900
Total Expenses	$399,000	Total Expenses	$159,600
Income		**Income**	
Fees for Service	$150,000	Fees for Service	$25,000
Donations	10,000	Donations	500
United Way Allocation	75,000	United Way Allocation	75,000
State Contract	164,000	State Contract	164,000
Total Income	$399,000	Total Income	$264,500
		INTERNATIONAL ADOPTION PROGRAM	
		Expenses	
		Personnel	
		Professional Staff	$150,000
		Support/Clerical Staff	30,000
		Travel	3,000
		Rent (60% of total)	21,000
		Maintenance/Cleaning	2,700
		Utilities	20,850
		Phone	11,850
		Total Expenses	$239,400
		Income	
		Fees for Service	$125,000
		Donations	9,500
		Total Income	$134,500
		Total Expenses for Both Programs	$399,000
		Total Income for Both Programs	$399,000

occur over any issue where people disagree or conflict with each other. Sometimes, disagreements are marginal. For example, you might think your client needs a clothing allowance of 50 dollars, and your supervisor thinks 25 dollars is sufficient. At other times, disagreements reflect opposite opinions. For instance, you think your client needs services; another worker thinks she does not.

Negotiating (sometimes called bargaining) can be problematic. When one side gains and the other loses, bad feelings often result. Such outcomes contribute to a long list of problems and interfere with future working relationships. Homan (1999) summarizes some possible guidelines for effective negotiation.

First, separating the problem from the people involved is important. In practice, this separation means we cannot personalize the differences that exist. To do otherwise is to create an adversarial situation when a problem solving approach would be more effective. Disliking the *ideas* or *demands* of others without disliking the *person* is possible.

The second step is to direct attention to the mutual interests of both parties and not to the positions they are taking. Both sides have goals they value highly and others that they feel are less important. Negotiating based on this approach allows for creative problem solving and increases the likelihood that both sides will be pleased with the outcome.

The third step requires devising new options or choices that benefit both sides. The value of this approach is that it steers away from the tendency to think there is only one answer. It also creates alternatives that help meet the needs of both sides in the negotiation. Flexibility is important.

Consider saving the most difficult issues for last, raising them only after you have resolved less troublesome items. This approach builds on the success of earlier negotiation. This method works, however, only when all issues have been placed on the table at the beginning of the bargaining session. Obviously, if all the issues are not on the table to begin with, it would be impossible to determine which are likely to be more difficult. Consequently, piecemeal negotiation in which each topic is brought up in random order should be avoided, if possible.

If needed, you can have a third party suggest a compromise or agree to use some objective criteria to decide an issue. For example, some state child welfare agencies, in an effort to garner more funds from legislators, have used the Child Welfare League of America[1] standards as an outside arbiter to illustrate appropriate staffing and funding levels. The use of such external means for settling disagreements does require agreement on the part of both sides that the third party is fair and impartial.

Negotiation allows both you and your opponent to win and makes the chances that each of you will be satisfied with the outcome more likely. Achieving this goal is not always easy, but it will result in more positive feelings on both sides.

Mediating

Mediating is also a process used to resolve disputes between opposing parties. However, unlike negotiations, in mediation both parties meet with a third party who serves as an impartial referee or peacemaker. Mediation is becoming a more common approach to solving differences of agreement in many areas. Mediating is common in divorce situations where the husband and wife disagree over such things as custody arrangements, child support, and maintenance.

Mediation has grown as an approach used by human services professionals spurred by state legislation that permits alternative ways of resolving disputes. The result has been increased satisfaction for participants and a resultant empowerment for clients who actively participate in the process. Like other processes discussed in Chapter 12, mediation can lead to win–win solutions of conflicts between individuals and groups (Severson & Bankston, 1995).

Mediation settles disputes between neighbors, vendors and customers, and landlords and tenants. The limited research on mediation suggests that it produces positive outcomes from the perspective of the individual parties. Shulman (1999) discusses the value of the worker recognizing the legitimate interests of both parties. As in negotiating, the goal of mediation is to work toward the common interests of each member, focusing on the specific areas of disagreement. The goal is to produce an outcome satisfactory to both sides (Toseland & Rivas, 1998). Human services professionals may be involved in mediating between clients and such institutions as schools, social agencies, and government agencies. The worker's task is to motivate and help each side reach out to the other.

For example, a school might object to the dress or hairstyle of a student and suspend her from school. As a mediator, you could work with the school, student, and parents to reach a compromise all could live with. Of course, another approach to this particular situation is to serve as a negotiator on behalf of the student and her family. As a human services worker, you may be involved in both roles at different times. In your role as negotiator, you will represent yourself or another party and attempt to reach a settlement that satisfies you or the party for whom you are negotiating. Hopefully, it will also produce an agreement the other side can live with. As a negotiator, you are clearly on one side of the issue or dispute. As a mediator, you are positioned right in the middle; you can not be seen as favoring one side or the other, or you will lose your credibility with the other side. Thus, in mediation you are the third party to whom both sides can look for fairness and helpfulness. Your task is to motivate and help each side reach out to the other. While both negotiation and mediation can result in each side feeling like they have achieved their goals, they are fundamentally different roles.

---

1. Child Welfare League of America is the best-known national organization promoting the interests of children in the United States. The organization establishes standards of practice and advocates for the needs of children.

Influencing Decision Makers

Chapter 12 identified several common ways that groups make decisions. Of course, not all decisions are made by groups. Some decisions are made by individuals acting alone or by only a couple of people acting together. In many instances, human services professionals want to influence those who make the final decision, especially when that decision has a major impact on our clients and the programs of which we are a part. In fact, influencing others is a common role for human services professionals. Sometimes, this influence is direct—as in the role of probation officer. At other times it is indirect—such as when one models behavior for a client. In many areas of human services practice and in one's life, there is a need to influence other people, particularly those with decision-making power such as supervisors, administrators, elected and appointed officials, and others in similar positions. The tactics one adopts often depend upon several factors: the target, the ability of the human services professional, the likelihood of success, and the risk to both client and worker.

If the target is an individual, the tactics may differ from those used when dealing with an organization. We also must consider our own ability to bring about change, including such aspects as our ability to influence others, our power, and our resources. In addition, some approaches may be more or less likely to bring success in certain situations. For example, a letter-writing campaign may not be effective against entrenched individuals who do not care what others say or think.

Finally, all large system interventions carry some risk to both the client and worker. In many situations, the risks are minimal, entailing no more than perhaps a few ruffled feathers for a short time. Yet other cases may involve the risk of losing a job or position. In all cases, we must recognize that the decision to select a strategy is a serious one with a variety of components.

In the next section, we will discuss seven strategies for influencing decision makers, although each is not equally effective in all situations.

Petitioning

Petitioning is the collecting of signatures on a document asking an organization or person to act in a particular manner. Petitions have a section where supporters may sign their names as a show of support for the ideas presented. Petition signatures are somewhat easy to obtain and, therefore, not as effective as other methods. For example, it is common to sign a petition when asked by a friend, even when holding views opposite to those expressed in the petition. In one instance, a group opposed to City Councilman Jones gathered enough signatures to force a recall election. When the election occurred, Jones' opponent received fewer votes than there were signatures on the recall petition. In some situations, however, petitions can be effective. The example in Highlight 13.5 illustrates this point.

Working with the Media

Any type of media, including television, radio, and newspapers, can be employed with good results. Working with the media is an effective way to bring attention to one's cause and to influence decision makers. For instance, you might use the media to help get transportation services to therapy sessions for children with physical disabilities whose parents can't afford transportation costs. A newspaper article or a segment on television illustrating the plight of these children can gain public support. The public might subsequently pressure the city or county government to finance transportation services.

 HIGHLIGHT 13.5

Petitioning Works

The Evergreen City Council was preparing to vote on whether or not to build a bypass highway around the city. Several members of the council had already stated their support for the bypass. They argued that it would reduce congestion on the city's main street and make crossing a dangerous street easier. Prior to the vote, Mrs. White, who owned a small antique business on Main Street, presented the council with a petition signed by most of the businesses located on Main Street. The petition opposed building the bypass highway because it might negatively affect some businesses along the street. During balloting, not a single member of the council voted to build the bypass. Even stubborn council members who supported the bypass were influenced by a petition signed by so many business leaders.

You can also use the media to inform the public and promote your own agency. For example, one large urban children's hospital sponsors a five-mile run each year. The purpose is not only to raise funds but also to publicize its services and increase public use and support.

The decision to use media often occurs when no other method has proven effective or will have the same degree of effectiveness. There are several general guides to using the media (Sheafor et al., 1997). First, reach out to the media. Contact them early before problems arise and provide ideas for stories regarding your agency.

Second, build contacts within the media. Just as we develop resources of other agencies to which a referral can be made, media contacts should also be nurtured.

Third, if you are speaking for an organization or agency, be certain you are authorized to do so.

Fourth, provide ease of access for media representatives to contact you. Give them both home and office phone numbers and addresses and suggest the name of someone else they may contact if you are unavailable.

Fifth, learn the timetables necessary for all media. Newspapers have deadlines as do radio and television. Reporters appreciate timely notice of newsworthy events.

Sixth, do not play favorites. Give all forms of media the same opportunity to present your story, unless you are granting an exclusive interview. In these cases, no one else will have access to the story until it appears in the media.

Seventh, if the media make a mistake, consider your reactions with care. If a correction is necessary, be tactful and explain the reasons for your request. Usually, minor errors should be left alone. Like everyone else, media representatives react to praise and support. If you thank them for the exposure and express satisfaction with the result, they are more likely to cooperate in the future.

Finally, if you gave your story, posed for pictures, and waited in vain for the article to appear, you are not alone. Many articles do not get printed because more important news supersedes the story. Reporters do not like this situation to happen, because it affects them as well, but they recognize it as an occupational hazard. Again, thank the reporter for the effort and state your willingness to work with them again.

In certain situations, you will have to prepare a media release. A media release is a public announcement that may acknowledge the opening of an agency, the creation of a new program, or a problem which needs attention from the community. A sample press release is shown in Figure 13.1. Writing a press release requires a degree of careful planning. Remember that the media like news and fresh information for their customers. Just because you think something is interesting does not mean the media will consider it newsworthy. Rose (1995) provides excellent suggestions for developing an effective news release. For example, think about what would make your information of interest to the public. Identify the primary theme for the release such as a compelling statistic on teen pregnancy or the unusually effective outcomes experienced by a particular program. Perhaps the release responds to an issue that has been in the headlines recently. Do not go overboard in the release. Provide factual information focusing on such possible items as an announcement of an event or activity, critical background information on an issue, human-interest topics, or follow-up on a community event.

The first paragraph of the news release should include the most crucial information. Subsequent paragraphs should include (in priority order) those ideas that you believe elaborate on the first paragraph. Remember also that the media still tend to use the five W's—who, what, when, where, and why. Do not neglect any of these items. If the editor chooses not to print a specific piece of information, that is the paper's right. You, however, do not want to leave out critical information that is key to whether or not the news release gets the editor's attention. Following up a news release with a phone call solely as a matter of courtesy is permissible. The call will serve as a reminder to the editor and could lead to a request for further information, a news feature, or other more extended coverage.

Educating

Educating is providing information and teaching skills to others. Often, decision makers are not as familiar with every aspect of a situation as others may be. Thus, the circumstance may only take educating a decision maker about a situation to produce the desired outcome. This is often the case with such public officials as legislators, who must represent many varied viewpoints. For example, a legislator with little understanding may not feel allocating resources to combat child abuse and neglect is important. As a human services professional you may need to inform or educate that legislator about the problem's seriousness before she is convinced spending the necessary money is worthwhile.

Sometimes, simply presenting the information in written form and in person will convince the deci-

Figure 13.1   *Using the Media: An Example of a News Release*

> Rural Mental Health Clinic
> 12 East North Street
> East North Overshoe, Vermont
> (802) 658-0371
>
>
> For Immediate Release:
>
> Drug and Alcohol Program a First in State
>
> EAST NORTH OVERSHOE, VT—June 28, 2002. The Rural Mental Health Clinic has
> added a drug and alcohol program to their new service center in East North Overshoe.
> According to the director, Jim Stevens, the new program is the first in the state to offer
> both inpatient and outpatient service to chemically addicted individuals. The clinic has
> added three staff members and will be hosting an open house on Friday, July 12th, from
> 1:00 p.m.–3:00 p.m. The office for the new program is located at 232 Spring Street.
>
> For further information, contact Jim Stevens at 658-0371 or 658-9981.
>
>
> ###

Note: The release should be typed double-spaced with margins of at least $1\frac{1}{2}$ inches on each side.

sion maker about your position. In other situations, it will require repeated efforts. It is important to remember that people don't like to appear ignorant or to be treated as if they were. Avoid talking down to the decision maker but present the information as matter-of-factly as possible. Sometimes, sending a written position statement as background is helpful before proceeding to the point of an in-person interview. It allows the target to become familiar with your ideas and to have some basis for beginning a dialogue with you. Often, the educating function is an adjunct to the next skill, persuading.

Persuading

Persuading is the process of presenting your point of view with the intent of getting another person to concur. Persuading people or organizations to change may be easy or difficult, depending upon several variables. Persuasion is easiest when the target or decision makers share your values and perspectives. Persuasion is more difficult when the target shares similar values but does not perceive the problem in the same light. Persuasion is most difficult when the target neither shares similar values nor accepts your identification of the problem. These variables must be carefully considered when attempting to persuade. Chapter 14 provides a more detailed discussion of persuasion.

We are not suggesting workers persuade clients to adopt a position similar to their own. Client self-determination is still a cardinal value. Instead, we are recommending that this knowledge can be put into practice on behalf of client systems, especially when the target for change is an agency or larger system. Persuasion is a positive alternative to the next skill to be discussed, confrontation.

Confrontation

Confrontation is the act of challenging another, usually in a face-to-face meeting. Few of us like confrontation. When asked why they decided to become human services professionals, many students reply, "Because I want to help people." Helping people and confronting people sometimes seem like opposing ideas. In actuality, much of human services practice involves confrontation. The clinician confronts a client about lying or confronts a patient who says one thing and does another.

Confrontation is common in work with the chemically dependent, correctional clients, and others who have in some way violated community stan-

dards. Confrontation requires certain assumptions concerning action and target systems (Patti & Resnick, 1972). An *action system* is "the people and resources in the community with which the [human services professional] deals to achieve desired changes. For example, the action system for a client being evicted might include the other residents of the apartment building, local housing officials, and the media, contacted by a worker in an effort to change a landlord's policies" (Barker, 1999, p. 5). A *target system,* on the other hand, is "the individual, group, or community to be changed or influenced to achieve" our goals (p. 480). Confrontations may be appropriate under the following circumstances:

1. *Action system goals* and *target system goals* are in sharp contrast to one another.
2. The action system poses a credible threat to the target system. (This threat usually means that there is an availability of coercive power the action system can use against the target system.)
3. The target system's position is somewhat immutable because of its investment in the status quo or fear of the outcome of the proposed change. It may also lack information about economic costs of the change or be concerned about loss of support from groups that favor the existing system.

Confrontation can take many forms, but the two most difficult are legal action and public embarrassment. In taking legal action, the human services professional is proceeding with the belief that the target has violated a law, code, or other regulation and that other methods have not borne fruit. Legal action may involve reporting a landlord for violating city building or health codes by failing to provide hot water or allowing vermin to exist within a building. It may include pressing charges against the target for violation of a criminal law, such as battery or violation of a court order. Another possibility is filing a civil suit against a person for violating one's rights. Examples include getting fired from a job because of one's race or gender. Pursuing the latter forms of legal action is potentially expensive, time consuming, and lengthy. The outcome is uncertain, and there is always some risk for the worker and client. Other strategies should be used whenever possible, because they provoke less emotion and are more likely to lead to win–win results.

Another form of confrontation is public embarrassment, which occurs when the worker makes the target system's shortcomings or errors public knowledge. An example of this situation is shown in Highlight 13.6.

Such tactics are dramatic and extreme and do not always succeed. Yet, in certain circumstances, they may be effective in forcing change in larger systems. Confrontation may not be an easy route to follow. However, the needs of clients and the worker's obligation to the client should take precedence over any initial discomfort about tactics.

Ultimately, client empowerment is heightened when the worker clearly communicates the risks involved with confrontation tactics. Client systems should know the possible outcomes and consequences of specific tactics and be directly involved in undertaking the change efforts. By this involvement, clients develop the political/social power and personal empowerment that is a goal of most social and economic justice interventions (Cowger, 1997).

Confrontation is the approach most likely to raise potential ethical concerns for human services professionals. Hardina (2000) identified a variety of tactics that human services professionals found raised ethical problems. These include "violence, deceit, and causing personal degradation or harm" (p. 13). Specific objectionable activities included destroying property, lying, and stealing, while other respondents felt that causing emotional harm by demonstrating at a target's home was unethical. Reisch and Lowe (2000) identify some additional ethical issues that affect human services practice in the community. These include conflicts between human services professionals' obligation to employers versus their responsibility to clients, concerns about how best to allocate scarce resources, and drawing a line between the public interest and the interests of individuals or groups we represent. Chapter 2 discussed ethical guidelines and dilemmas in some detail.

Collaborating

Collaboration is the procedure in which two or more persons or systems work together to serve a given client. If the target system is rational and will listen to new or challenging ideas and is acting with good faith, collaboration is the preferable route. The client may be an individual, family, group, or community. Collaborative strategies include all of the following:

1. Supplying facts about the actual problem because the target does not know much about the existence of a particular problem.
2. Offering options for resolving the problem to help the target consider other solutions that the action system believes are or will be effective.
3. Asking permission to try a solution on a trial basis because it does not commit the target to an open-ended agreement with unknown consequences.
4. Requesting permission to set up a committee to consider the problem and possible alternatives. This increases the target's involvement in the problem and expands the number of people aware of the situation. It is less threatening, because the only request is for a study committee.
5. Requesting increased opportunities for target and action (or client) systems to get together and share interests. This may be somewhat more threatening to the target, but it gets the two parties talking about their respective concerns.
6. Appealing to the values, ethics, or scruples of the target system assuming that the values or ethics of the target are consonant with those of the action system.
7. Convincing the target system through rational debate and discussion, especially when the

---

HIGHLIGHT 13.6

Embarrassing a Landlord

The Smith Apartments tenants were angry. No matter how much they complained to the city and their landlord, their living conditions remained the same. The building in which they lived was in violation of many city ordinances, and the landlord refused to make any changes. The city did not follow through on its enforce- ment responsibilities, and the situation remained deadlocked. Finally, the tenants decided to try a different approach. Late one afternoon, they gathered in front of the landlord's home in an exclusive suburban neighborhood and picketed, their signs expressing anger with his neglect. The group called the news media, and television crews appeared at the site to record the event for the evening news. Both city officials, who had been lax in their enforcement of the building codes, and the landlord himself experienced enough embarrassment to undertake the changes demanded by the tenants.

target and action system share certain values or when the data presented leads to a conclusion the target system can accept.

8. Identifying adverse outcomes that arise from continuation of the present situation. This can be effective if the negative outcomes are realistic or have a realistic probability of occurring (Patti & Resnick, 1980).

Collaborative strategies should generally be attempted before using adversarial approaches. Adversarial approaches run the risk of alienating both the target and those not directly involved in the situation, such as coworkers. Collaborative strategies are good-faith efforts to change the target system based on positive assumptions about the target. Only when they fail should other approaches be used.

There may be times when collaborative and adversarial strategies work together or when a given tactic may be used differently than previously described. For example, the petition case described in Highlight 13.5 was not an adversarial tactic, as defined by Patti and Resnick, but a collaborative effort to let the target system (city council) know of a potential problem that could be caused by their decision to relocate the highway. Ultimately, the actual mechanisms used to cause change depend on many factors. These mechanisms include the competence of the worker, the desires of the intended beneficiary, assumptions about the target system, and the risks of one strategy versus another.

Letter Writing

Letter writing is not always recognized as a strategy for influencing decision makers, yet it can be effective in certain situations. Elected officials frequently receive letters on topics and often keep a tally of how many letters arrive on a particular subject. Virtually any issue—from the need for alcohol and other drug abuse prevention programs to nuclear war—may be addressed. Sheafor and colleagues (2000) provide suggestions for writing better letters, which are incorporated in Highlight 13.7.

Needs Assessment

Needs assessments are systematic appraisals used to gather data on clients'

> . . . problems, existing resources, potential solutions, and obstacles to problem solving. In social agencies, needs assessments are made on behalf of the clients who receive clinical services and in communities, on behalf of all the residents. The purpose of needs assessments is to document needs and establish priorities for service. The data come from existing records such as U.S. Bureau of the Census and local government statistics as well as from interviews and research on the relevant population. (Barker, 1999, p. 323)

Needs assessments are used for a variety of purposes, but their primary role is to estimate the extent of demand for a particular service or program.

 HIGHLIGHT 13.7

Letter-Writing Strategies

To be effective, letters should:

1. Be carefully planned, revised, polished, and proofread.
2. Include letterhead (with address), date, salutation (Dear _____), body, complimentary close (Sincerely), and both typed and written signatures.
3. Be businesslike and pleasant.
4. Be brief (preferably one page) and discuss only one topic.
5. Open with a positive comment.
6. Be factual and simply written.
7. Request a response.

Less effective letters include those that appear identical, those copied out of newspaper advertisements, or clearly mass-produced letters (e.g., duplicated copies instead of originals). Letters attacking the reader are less likely to work and may backfire. Some people advocate handwritten letters, but the advantages of a clear, typed message outweigh those of handwritten communication.

If letters are to be mass produced, as might be desired when a group is trying to sway the reader, vary the letters so that they don't appear identical. Written letters are helpful in certain situations and help create a record of communication with the decision maker. They should be used as an adjunct to, not instead of, other more personal forms of contact. Person-to-person communication is still superior to written messages as a means of influencing people.

There exist a variety of ways to conduct a needs assessment. The five primary methods include the key informant approach, the community forum approach, the rates-under-treatment approach, the social indicators approach, and the field study. Each method is briefly described in the following list using the models explicated by Warheit, Bell, and Schwab (1977):

1. The *key informant* approach asks especially knowledgeable individuals about the needs of a given community, such as a county judge or other local officials. These individuals would be approached to seek their opinions about needs in a particular area.
2. The *community forum* approach assumes that the general public also has knowledge of a community's needs. A series of widely advertised meetings are held to bring in a cross section of the population.
3. The *rates-under-treatment* approach counts the people who seek and receive a given service (e.g., supportive home care) to estimate the actual need in a community.
4. The *social indicators* approach uses information in existing public records, such as the census, to estimate the actual need for a service.
5. A *field study* needs assessment relies on gathering actual data in the community through interviews and observation.

All but the last of these methods are inexpensive and relatively easy to use. When undertaking a needs assessment, thinking through the exact information that one wishes to gather is important. One must define goals and decide how the goals will be measured and what data should be collected. Sometimes those collecting the data will need special training or orientation. A needs assessment is an effective method for determining unmet need in a community and, sometimes, for determining the existence of an overlap of services. Each human services professional should be able to conduct a needs assessment using one or more of the above approaches.

Planning

Planning hardly seems like a topic that deserves much attention in a human services text. After all, everyone plans something, and most people have had experience in various activities for which planning was required, whether for a party, a picnic, or a trip. Planning with large systems, however, requires a higher level of skill than the aforementioned activities. Several techniques exist to assist the planner identify all steps, establish a time frame, and assign specific tasks to responsible parties. One of the more useful approaches is the Program Evaluation and Review Technique (PERT). PERT assists the planning process for both business and social services (e.g., one author used this technique to plan a group home program and to prepare for accreditation of two human services programs). In PERT, there are four steps that must be undertaken: (1) identifying major tasks to be accomplished; (2) placing them in sequential order; (3) determining the probable time needed for completion of each step; and (4) identifying those responsible for completing each specific task.

Once these steps are completed, it is possible to map out the total project graphically, showing what will occur, when it will occur, and who is responsible. The sample PERT chart in Figure 13.2 uses planning for a party as the project.

The chart shows the tasks to be accomplished and the date by which each step is to be completed. If a committee planned this party, each task might be

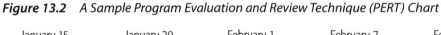

Figure 13.2   *A Sample Program Evaluation and Review Technique (PERT) Chart*

delegated to a particular subcommittee, and the chart would reflect this assignment. Assignments may be shown by coloring in the chart, a different color for each responsible party, or by placing initials in the lower corner of a square. Sometimes, two or more tasks occur simultaneously, and this would be reflected by a vertical line connecting the two boxes, one box placed under the other as in Figure 13.2. If the tasks are complex, a detailed work plan can be drawn up to show the activity, describe the steps within, identify those responsible, and specify the date for completion. The PERT system allows planning larger projects and allows for constant monitoring of tasks. It shows what will be accomplished while holding people responsible for their assignments. It is simple, easy to use, and applicable to many tasks or projects.

Working with Coalitions

Many tasks associated with changing large systems require the concerted efforts of multiple groups. A coalition is "an alliance of various factions or ideological groups in a society brought together to achieve a goal" (Barker, 1999, p. 83). The types of groups forming a coalition may be similar or diverse. For instance, well-to-do business owners and single parents receiving public assistance might form a coalition to help their community combat drug abuse. Environmentalists and area residents might work together to prevent locating a hazardous waste facility in or near a poor neighborhood.

Toseland & Rivas (1998) note that coalitions may be effective because they combine resources of multiple groups or organizations. Having several groups with like interests work together to achieve ends that each group desires is quite common. For example, the efforts to create licensing laws for human services professionals often involve coalitions between professional organizations representing various groups, such as marriage and family therapist associations and social workers. This bringing together of coalitions frequently occurs because few laws pass through the efforts of only one group. Coalitions are often essential when the task is large and will require a complex effort by several participants. Perhaps the primary advantage of working with coalitions is the increased strength that occurs when several groups combine forces.

Coalitions may be designed to be ongoing or developed to respond to a specific problem. Sometimes, a coalition created to respond to a particular problem may continue indefinitely as the groups or individuals involved recognize advantages

of the new structure. Of course, any coalition may cease to exist after achieving the initial goal. Permanent alliances are difficult to maintain but are potentially effective in uniting diverse interests in a common cause.

Deciding which groups to include in a coalition is relatively easy. One must be aware of the network of community groups already in existence. Knowing the primary goals of each group and assessing the compatibility of these goals with those of your organization is important. Knowing which groups are and are not influential and attempting to align with them if possible are also important. Begin by listing organizations already working in a specific area. An organization focused on youth might determine that it shares interests with many other groups. Examples include groups focused on the developmentally disabled, service clubs giving to youth causes, scouting organizations, teacher organizations, YMCAs or YWCAs, and so on. Arranging a meeting with the leadership of these groups to explore the possibility of working together to establish a drug education program is one example. If the leadership of several organizations can work together well, the process becomes easier to manage. Individual personalities or styles can be either a barrier or an asset to this collaboration.

After the coalition is created, the real work begins. While there is enormous strength in coalitions, they also suffer from serious shortcomings. Sometimes a coalition can be broken apart by playing up the differences among or between organizations that form it. Opponents use this tactic to try to sidetrack or otherwise weaken the group.

Similarly, keeping every coalition member informed of what is happening is important. This fact is especially true where there is a history of organizations not working together or where there is an unequal balance among the various subgroups.

If one group is clearly the strongest and has the most to gain from the effort to organize and use the coalition, having the leaders of the stronger group keep the others apprised of what is happening is essential. Weaker partners fearing being left out of significant decisions may drop out.

The importance of shared leadership is obvious. Making certain that all groups in the coalition are represented on some sort of coordinating board or steering committee helps them to feel they have a stake in the outcome.

The governing committee members must often take any plans developed by the governing body back to their respective groups for approval. This process is cumbersome, but it ensures that no group will be dragged into a project against the wishes of its members. For ongoing coalitions, the decision by one group not to participate in a specific project is unlikely to threaten the coalition. On the other hand, an ad hoc coalition formed to pursue a specific purpose is vulnerable to dissolution if one or more of the component groups withdraw.

Coalitions are most effective when the task is clear and the responsibilities are specified. Coalition members may continue to work on other projects, but individual goals must be sacrificed for the good of the coalition. This sacrifice means each organization in the coalition must agree that the primary goal is of sufficient importance and that achieving it supersedes the petty jealousies and difficulties that traditionally exist. A decision must also be made about the contributions to be provided by each group. In addition, assessing which group is more likely to be effective with which tasks is important. Just as in any other endeavor, assigning tasks to those most competent to carry them out makes sense. An effective coalition can multiply exponentially the capacity to achieve desired ends.

Creating a coalition from existing groups is easier than building an individual membership organization with the same goal. In the end, the former is more likely to accomplish its goals, to shorten the time needed to achieve desired ends, and to build a reputation for effectiveness.

Worker Roles in Organizational and Community Change

Thinking of a practitioner's work as a series of roles is possible and sometimes helpful. This section will briefly describe several key roles assumed when working for change in organizations and communities. They include initiator, negotiator, advocate, spokesperson, organizer, mediator, and consultant. Some of these roles are also used at the micro and mezzo levels of generalist practice.

Initiator

The initiator is the person or group that calls attention to an issue. The issue may be a community problem, a need, or simply a situation that can be improved. It is important to recognize that a problem need not exist before attention can be called to

it. Often, preventing future problems or enhancing existing services is a satisfactory reason for creating a change. Thus, a human services professional may recognize that a policy is creating problems for particular clients and bring this to the attention of the supervisor. For example, the agency's office hours may force clients to come at difficult times, resulting in lost pay and jeopardizing their jobs; or a client may identify ways that service could be improved. In each case, the person is playing the role of initiator. Usually, this role must be followed up by other kinds of work, because just pointing out that a problem exists is no guarantee that it will be fixed.

Negotiator

In some situations, the worker may find him- or herself in the role of negotiator, representing an organization or group trying to wrestle something from another group. For instance, a worker may negotiate better police protection for a neighborhood hit by a rash of drive-by shootings. As mentioned earlier, negotiators who can construct a win–win situation are more likely to be successful than those who adopt a win–lose approach. Successful negotiators also remain calm when others are more emotionally involved. Negotiators cannot personalize the attacks or comments of the other person or group with whom they are negotiating. The task is to find a middle ground that satisfies both sides. Negotiators need the skills of an advocate to push for achievement of organizational goals and those of a mediator to find a satisfactory compromise.

Advocate

Advocates speak out and act on behalf of clients. They decide what their clients are entitled to and what problems are keeping clients from receiving what they need. The worker must also assess the adversary to figure out its strengths and weaknesses. While some adversaries may quickly meet the advocate's requests (demands), the chances are that additional work will be required. This might include assessing the client's situation to determine if advocating for the client is likely to cause further problems. The client may be in a vulnerable situation, and the worker would not want to worsen things. Sometimes documenting a problem so that the adversary understands the reasons for the client's concerns is possible. In other situations, documentation alone will not suffice. As discussed earlier, an opponent who does not share your values or perception of the problem will not accede to your wishes. Consider an agency director who is more concerned about saving money than serving needy clients. Documenting that many clients receive only a portion of the services they need is unlikely to sway the director who believes additional services will increase agency costs. In addition, few people or groups give up power willingly. Thus, the advocate must expect to use skills such as negotiating or bargaining with the adversary or use pressure tactics to achieve desired ends (Connaway & Gentry, 1988). Advocacy is discussed in much greater depth in Chapter 14.

Spokesperson

A spokesperson is someone authorized to speak on behalf of others. This role is sometimes a troublesome one. Sometimes, the spokesperson begins to personalize the information provided until it reflects more the spokesperson's ideas than the organization's. Spokespersons should seek to present the organization's views and positions without coloring them with their own views, which is not always easy. In addition, a special problem exists when you disagree with the position taken by your organization or group. The dilemma can be resolved in two ways. First, you can cease to speak for the group, ending your role as spokesperson. Second, you can reflect accurately the organization's position and submerge your own hesitation or disagreement. Doing anything else, such as presenting the group's opinion in a way that satisfies your own beliefs, is violating the principle of representing the group.

Marshall Winston learned about this limitation the hard way. Marshall was the president of the West Bend Community Service League (CSL), a membership organization dedicated to improving the city of West Bend. The League's Board of Directors had recently decided not to undertake a community recreation project because a clear need had not been demonstrated. Marshall did not agree with the board's decision, which was final. When Sally Wombat asked Marshall—as CSL president—to speak at the next Rotary Club meeting about needs in the community, he presented the recreation project as critical for the community. In so doing, he went against the wishes of his own board of directors. At the next board meeting, several members raised concerns about Marshall's right to speak as the president of CSL when his comments clearly did not reflect the opinion of the organization.

Organizer

An organizer coordinates individuals or groups to pursue some designated function(s). The organizer may be organizing individuals or groups. As mentioned earlier, organizing existing groups is usually easier and more effective than creating groups from scratch. Organizers' tasks include developing the potential of others to serve as leaders, stimulating others to act, identifying likely targets for change, serving as a staff member or facilitator, and linking the organization with others sharing their interests (Rubin & Rubin, 1986). The tasks vary, depending on the nature of the problem and the strengths and limitations of the components to be organized. Where indigenous leadership already exists, the worker may serve as a consultant or advisor; where it is not present, the worker may become a mentor or teacher. In either case, organizing others is a formidable role. One example is Alicia Gunn, who organized a group of human services professionals all dealing with the juvenile court in Porter County. Membership in the group was composed of probation officers, protective services workers, foster care workers at the local family and children agencies, and adoption workers from the State Department of Human Services. Alicia's goal was improving services to children and adolescents who ended up in the juvenile court system. She believed that if all of the agencies and workers dealing with children coming in to the court system could sit down and talk about the situation, service improvements could result.

Mediator

As Chapter 1 explains, mediators are neutral persons who resolve disagreements among various systems in conflict. Mediators can achieve several desired ends. Mediators may help two sides work out a compromise. To do this requires understanding both parties' positions and finding a suitable compromise. This compromise requires listening to each side and drawing out feelings and beliefs about the disagreement (Hepworth et al., 1997). The worker as mediator can clarify positions, recognize miscommunication about differences, and help both parties present their ideas clearly. The mediator helps take emotion out of the situation, allowing better problem solving. Mediation skills are becoming increasingly important in such situations as divorce and child-custody disagreements.

Consultant

A consultant is someone who provides advice, suggestions, or ideas to another person, group, or organization. Consultants advise cities on zoning laws, suggest better ways of structuring human services programs, and help groups become more effective. There are two requirements for consultants. First, they must know more than the individual consultee. This knowledge may be specific on a particular topic, such as zoning laws or better ways of problem solving. Second, consultants must be able to see their advice ignored without becoming offended. A consultant does not have supervisory or administrative power over the consultee. If the consultee chooses to ignore the consultant's advice, no matter how good, the consultant must accept that the client has this right. The principle of self-determination is clearly operable in such situations. With accepting consultation comes the concomitant right to take or ignore the advice provided.

For example, the Central State Hospital for Developmental Disabilities invited in a team of human services practitioners, nurses, and physicians experienced in services to clients with developmental disabilities. The consultant team's role was to identify how the hospital could become more effective in serving its clients and recommend strategies to foster independence for residents. While the recommendations were all well-developed and documented, the hospital implemented only the suggestions that administrators felt would not increase costs.

The Generalist Intervention Model (GIM) in Macro Practice

As we have seen in each of the preceding chapters, the Generalist Intervention Model (GIM) involves a series of steps used to create change. These steps are guidelines for planned change efforts with individuals, families, groups, organizations, and communities. Consider Manuel Gossett, a human services professional with the La Casa social service agency. La Casa serves Hispanic clients in the community, providing bilingual counseling for individuals and families, outpatient treatment groups for chemical dependency, and a homeless shelter. Manuel's supervisor asked him to prepare a needs assessment to determine if the agency should consider establishing an inpatient program for clients with substance abuse. As part of his task, Manuel was to meet with directors of other agencies who were already serving clients with chemical dependency problems. Manuel followed each of the GIM steps in more or less the correct order. He decided to use a couple of needs assessment approaches rather than relying on any single model. Not only would he gather information from key informants, but he would also incorporate statistics from existing programs to document the need for additional programs.

Because Manuel did not know all of the agency directors beforehand, he realized that he would need to meet each of them and establish a relationship that would foster his goal of gathering information. Thus, he entered the first step—*engagement*. He used a number of micro skills, including conveying warmth and genuineness, attentive listening, and using rephrasing and clarification to ensure he understood the information being provided by each person he interviewed. He also planned ahead and developed a set of questions that he wanted to ask each director.

As he gathered his data from these interviews and other sources, he made a tentative *assessment* about the need for an inpatient chemical dependency program. He concluded there appeared to be considerable need for such a program. However, he also identified a number of potential concerns expressed by each of his key informants. He noted, for example, that several new group-home-like programs in the city had met with resistance from neighbors who opposed such programs in their backyards. He also noted that health insurance companies' funding was getting reduced or restricted through forms of managed care. Manuel decided that he needed to include these concerns in his report.

When he turned in his completed needs assessment, Manuel's supervisor was quite impressed, so impressed that he asked Manuel to proceed to the next step, which was to develop an agency plan for creating a new program. In the *planning* stage of GIM, Manuel prioritized the problems he had identified in his report. He also developed appropriate solutions for each problem after thoroughly considering the pros and cons of each alternative. He noted, for example, that the neighborhood-related problems experienced by other residential programs probably would be much reduced in the Hispanic community served by his agency. He knew of at least two occasions where new group homes had been sited without anyone raising the kind of fuss mentioned by the other agency directors. He also drew up a plan for including neighborhood residents on an advisory board for the new facility.

As another part of the *planning* stage, Manuel also specified the goals and objectives of this effort, which included a tentative timetable and a list of tasks to be completed by La Casa staff. Implementation of the plan was more complicated. Because Manuel was not a supervisor or administrator, he decided that *implementation* would require a concerted effort by his superiors in the agency. He volunteered to monitor progress toward achieving the objectives and to suggest changes in the plan where needed. However, Manuel felt that details such as locating and renting space, hiring and training human services professionals, and dealing with health insurance companies needed more expertise than he possessed. This understanding was an appropriate assessment of his own level of competence and the mark of a good human services professional. At the same time, he could certainly monitor whether a given step had been achieved or where plans were not being carried out.

Six months later Manuel prepared an *evaluation* report for his supervisor to take to La Casa's Board of Directors. The report noted that a final contract was being negotiated to rent a large two-story home about six blocks from the agency's main office. Advertising was being prepared to hire one more human services professional. The agency had tentative agreements with 14 other agencies interested in referring clients to the substance abuse program. A small purchase-of-service contract was being presented to the county human services agency that would pay La Casa a set amount for each client admitted to the facility. (The county agency found it easier to pay other agencies to provide inpatient services than to start its own facility.) A local college human services program was helping to design an evaluation plan that could be used to determine the new program's effectiveness. Manuel included all of this information in his report. His supervisor, duly impressed with the fine work that went into this effort, told Manuel that he would use his talents again when such special projects were

being considered. Manuel smiled and asked if this recognition would come with a salary increase. His supervisor was still laughing as Manuel headed down the hallway.

 ## InfoTrac College Edition

This chapter reviewed some important skills for working with organizations and communities. Among the topics covered were the organizational context of practice, major definitions related to macro practice, the application of micro and mezzo skills to macro practice, and specific macro practice skills. Additional information on these topics is available using the following search terms:

organizational theory
social control
social action
cause advocacy
case advocacy
fundraising
needs assessment
press releases

 ## On the Internet

Because of the very dynamic nature of the Web, URLs are subject to change. Therefore, be sure to check out the companion Website for this book at http://www.humanservices.wadsworth.com, where links will be updated periodically.
www.acf.dhhs.gov
www.tuw.org
www.advocacy.org
www.uhcan.org
www.acorn.org

CHAPTER 14
Human Services Advocacy

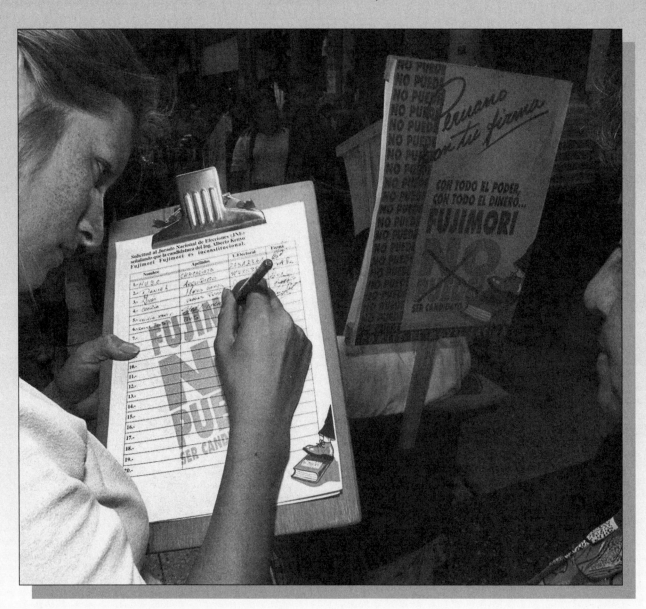

Shari Montero ran into a brick wall. Trying desperately to find housing for her homeless client, she had finally located a house that met the family's needs. The house was large enough to accommodate Mr. Vue and his four children, eliminating the need for the family to continue sleeping in their car. (Mr. Vue was a Hmong who had immigrated from Vietnam with his family.) The only problem was that the house had to be approved by the Indian Falls City Housing Authority if Mr. Vue were to receive a housing subsidy. The subsidy was a monthly payment from the housing authority that would help Mr. Vue pay the rent on this house.

When Shari called the housing authority requesting approval of the house, she learned that it would be several weeks before the home could be inspected and certified for inclusion in the housing subsidy program. Shari knew that Mr. Vue did not have several weeks. His children were not in school, he lacked food, and the family could not be expected to continue living out of his car. Frustrated, Shari decided it was time to try a different approach. Assuming the advocate role, Shari contacted Betty Sardinia, her representative on the Indian Falls City Council. She explained the situation to Councilwoman Sardinia and asked if there were anything she could do to speed up the process. Within the day, Shari received a call from the housing authority. Councilwoman Sardinia had called an official she knew at the housing authority and exercised her influence to speed up the process. The housing authority representative would inspect the house the following day.

Shari was elated. She arranged for the house to be cleaned before the visit by the housing authority and notified Mr. Vue of the good news. Following the visit, the house passed inspection, and the Vue family finally had a home. Shari then helped Mr. Vue enroll his children in school. She followed up with him for the next few months to ensure that his transition to his new home was proceeding satisfactorily.

Introduction

In this chapter, we will place the preceding example within the context of the human services role known as advocacy. Specifically, this chapter will:

- define advocacy and discuss its relationship to the profession of human services;
- discuss the assumptions associated with advocacy;
- explore various assumptions about power, organizations, clients, and different approaches to advocacy;
- review the knowledge and skills advocates require;
- review the assessment process used in advocacy situations;
- describe strategies and tactics used by the advocate;
- discuss different models of advocacy.

Defining Advocacy

One of the most important objectives of human services is to help people obtain needed resources. Often this objective occurs through the brokering role discussed briefly in Chapter 1 and in detail in Chapter 15. The broker role requires that the human service professional help clients by connecting them to appropriate agencies or services. The broker is providing clients with information about options and referring clients to agencies or organizations that can best respond to their needs. Sometimes the worker must act as a mediator between the client and a resource. This role might be required, for example, when a client has been refused service of benefits through a misunderstanding or confusion about whether or not the client was eligible for the service.

In other situations, the worker must assume another role, namely that of advocate. Barker (1999) defines *advocacy* as including representing, defending, and "championing the rights of individuals or communities through direct intervention or through empowerment" (p. 11).

Briar (1967) was one of the first to argue the importance of case advocacy. He argued that the advocate is the client's supporter, advisor, champion, and representative in "dealings with the court, the police, the social agency, and other organizations" (p. 28). Human services professionals use their position and professional skills to "exercise leverage for needed services on behalf" of individuals and groups (Brown, 1991, p. 212). As part of the human

services profession's obligation to serve the most vulnerable populations, we must expect that many clients will need our assistance. Isolated clients, those with disabilities, deinstitutionalized clients, and children are examples of situations where advocacy may be essential. Many organizations exist specifically to advocate for certain issues or categories of clients. Examples include Mothers Against Drunk Driving (MADD), the Alliance for the Mentally Ill, and the Gray Panthers.

Advocacy is "a concept borrowed from the legal profession," according to Mailick and Ashley (p. 625). They view the advocate as an "unequivocal partisan serving the interests of the client, even, in the extreme, in opposition to the policies of his or her own agency" (p. 625). Sheafor and colleagues (1997) state that the advocate "speaks, argues, manipulates, bargains, and negotiates on behalf of the client" (p. 502).

Advocacy and the Generalist Intervention Model

Advocacy is an implementation strategy in the Generalist Intervention Model (GIM). That is to say, it is the means the worker chooses as the most effective way of bringing about change. Because it is more complex and potentially more problematic than other approaches, advocacy must be carefully considered during the assessment and planning phases. We have included some general thoughts to consider as you contemplate a situation where advocacy may be required.

Case Advocacy

Case advocacy, as the name implies, refers to activity on behalf of a single case. It is usually employed in situations where the individual is in conflict with an organization, perhaps over benefits that have been denied. As we described in Chapter 13, the "case" may be an individual, a family, or a small group.

Effective case advocacy requires several types of knowledge:

- knowledge of the agency's policies, regulations, and administrative structure;
- knowledge of the agency's appeal procedures;
- knowledge of available legal remedies;
- knowledge of the agency's formal and informal power structure;
- knowledge of external forces to which the organization responds;

- knowledge of the consequences (for both client and others) of escalating issues (Kadushin & Kadushin, 1997; Sheafor et al., 1997).

The reader may be wondering at what point case advocacy becomes cause or class advocacy. The line between advocating for a single client and engaging in macro practice (working on behalf of whole groups or populations of clients) can become somewhat blurry. For example, a successful appeal of a decision in the case of a single client may result in a new interpretation of old rules benefitting all clients in similar situations. Yet, a discouraging reality of case advocacy is that while the advocate may successfully challenge the agency on behalf of a specific client, no long-term change in agency policy is guaranteed. Consequently, other clients face the same hurdles in their interactions with the agency.

While there are similarities between the two approaches, case advocacy generally involves strategies and tactics different from those employed for cause advocacy. These differences are especially true when we look at legislative advocacy, a form of cause advocacy that will be discussed later in the chapter.

Cause Advocacy

Cause advocacy involves human services professionals' efforts to address an issue of overriding importance to some client group. The emphasis on *cause* means that this type of advocacy affects multiple groups of clients or potential clients. It is also sometimes called class advocacy.

For example, early human services professionals were active in efforts to develop kindergartens, to create laws prohibiting child labor, and to require education for persons with physical disabilities. The beneficiaries of these efforts were not individual clients but entire categories of people. A more current example might involve a human services professional advocating to serve a category of clients more effectively within his or her own agency. Perhaps the location and office hours of an agency make using the agency's services difficult for low-income clients. A worker might attempt to get the agency to open an office in a different, more accessible location or to extend agency office hours further into the evening. Similarly, a worker might work to change laws that discriminate against gay or lesbian persons.

Let us re-examine the case involving a social worker named Gaylon, described in Chapter 13. You may recall that Gaylon's supervisor wanted prospective foster parents to come in during the day for their appointments, even if it meant taking time off from their work. In this case, Gaylon used cause advocacy. He advocated for all prospective foster parents as a large group and tried to convince his supervisor that the agency should be more flexible. He argued that the agency should expand its hours in the evening so more foster parent candidates could have access to its services.

The need for class advocacy may become more obvious after repeated cases arise having similar characteristics. You may notice patterns in case records or observe striking similarities in the types of problems clients are having.

At the agency level, individual human services professionals may conduct cause advocacy working alone. Beyond the agency level, advocates are much more likely to involve themselves in coalitions with other workers and agencies because some forms of advocacy require major effort. Consider a new state law that requires community agencies to serve formerly institutionalized clients but does not provide any funding for such services. Because the problem is at a level far above the individual agency, advocacy will require many groups working in concert if a change in this law is to be achieved.

Cause advocacy often involves resistance because it requires significant change in the status quo. You may have to use tactics involving conflict to overcome this resistance. We have established that people in power usually do not want to give it up.

Let us refer back to Gaylon's case. Pressuring his agency to expand its hours has implications and repercussions. More hours require spending more money to staff the agency longer. Agency administrators may resent being pressured to dig up more funding or to allow workers to accrue compensatory time. They might resist any change in the status quo. People in administration also tend to resist being told or pressured regarding what to do, which is especially the case when it involves employees theoretically under their control.

Some cause advocacy has resulted in lawsuits challenging official regulations and governmental inaction. Sheafor and colleagues (1997) observe that ". . . within the past twenty years, most of the reforms in the areas of mental health and mental retardation grew out of lawsuits" (p. 545). Lawsuits can be extremely threatening to an agency's or organization's administration. They usually involve potentially significant conflict. Lawsuits make problems public. They are also expensive. For all these reasons, many administrators will avoid them like the plague.

Cause advocacy, then, often involves risks, both to the agency and to the worker initiating it. These risks are why advocacy requires such sensitivity, tact, and skill. As an advocate, you want to facilitate change for the well-being of your clients. However, you probably do not want to get fired.

Useful Skills in Advocacy

The effective advocate will need to know how to use government documents and other data sources. Often documenting the existence of a problem will be necessary. You may need to know where to get facts, information, and official statistics.

Comfort with and ability to use the political process are also important. Most of the rules, regulations, and funding for human services programs are derived from state or federal laws. Changing laws require that you know how the political process works and can use this process to achieve client-sensitive goals.

Whether the target is an agency supervisor, a board of directors, or a legislative committee, the advocate must be comfortable speaking in public. For example, you may find yourself needing to present arguments or ideas to groups such as legislators or members of an agency board of directors. Public speaking skills will make advocating easier.

A level of tolerance for conflict is also important. Change is often difficult for others, and resistance is common. You must be comfortable in situations where people disagree with you or your ideas.

 ## The Goals of Advocacy

The advocate (either alone or in concert with others) is attempting to "influence another individual or group to make a decision that would not have been made otherwise and that concerns the welfare or interests of a third party" (Sosin & Caulum, 1989, p. 534). We have emphasized throughout this text the planned change framework that is used by human services professionals. Advocacy is simply a more radical approach to planned change. The purpose of client advocacy is "to secure benefits or services that the client is entitled to but . . . unable to obtain" (Sheafor et al., 1997, p. 502). The nature of this task is such that advocacy is more likely to involve confrontation than most other approaches to intervention (1997).

Making a distinction between two aspects of advocacy is important. On the one hand, advocacy involves making certain that clients have *access to existing rights and entitlements*. On the other hand, advocacy also concerns *social action to secure new rights and entitlements*. We have discussed social action in previous chapters and will revisit the topic again later in this chapter. Essentially, the advocate is working to help clients reach goals they have defined as desirable. Those goals usually require some action on the part of a decision maker. That decision maker may have to change a previous decision, reinterpret rules, or modify procedures to benefit the client. On the other hand, you may be asking an organization to abide by and enforce existing rules or regulations. In the case opening this chapter, the goal was to influence the decision maker (representative from the housing authority) to act immediately in a crisis rather than following the usual procedures of first-come, first-served.

 ## Targets of Advocacy

Targets of advocacy may include individuals, groups or organizations, elected or appointed officials, public and private human services agencies, legislative bodies, court systems, or governmental entities (such as the housing authority). Any of these persons or organizations may impede client access to service or treat clients inhumanely. By doing so, they become potential targets of advocacy because, as human services professionals, we adhere to several principles.

First, we work to increase accessibility of social services to clients. Not only should needed services exist, but clients should be able to use them without undue difficulty. For example, clients for whom English is not their primary language will have difficulty completing lengthy forms written in that language. If they cannot complete the forms, they will not receive the services.

Sometimes, the services themselves are satisfactory, but other problems prevent clients from using them. For example, services may be available only during the day when clients work. Or there may be long waiting periods before services can be received. Another problem entails services offered at locations that are inaccessible to clients, such as when a building is not accessible to people with disabilities or when services are offered at sites far from clients' homes.

A second principle is that advocates promote service delivery that does not detract from clients' dignity. In other words, clients should not be put in humiliating or embarrassing situations in order to receive services. For instance, consider a situation where clients must wait in a filthy, crowded waiting room for hours to receive needed public assistance. Advocating that such conditions be changed because they are an affront to the clients' dignity is appropriate.

Sometimes, services are provided in a fashion that is demeaning to clients. For example, one large county social services agency provided workers with desks located within a giant facility that resembled a remodeled warehouse. There were no walls or partitions between workers' desks. Thus, anyone within sight or hearing of the desks could easily find out what the client and the worker were talking about. Privacy was almost nonexistent.

A third principle to guide advocates involves working to assure equal access to all who are eligible. For example, service delivery that is more accessible to white clients than to African American or Hispanic clients is unacceptable.

Hepworth and colleagues (1997) provide additional examples in Highlight 14.1 of situations where advocacy may be appropriate. As you will see from the examples, the targets of advocacy may vary depending upon the individual situation.

 ## The Realities of Advocacy

The human services professional playing the advocate role is operating under a different set of realities than is true in roles such as broker or facilitator. The realities represent a starting point in understanding how change takes place, the influence of advocates and clients in the planned change process, and the role of power in advocacy situations. As such, they help guide the advocate in interactions with client systems, organizations, and other targets of advocacy. The realities do not detract from our belief that change in large systems is possible but they do temper our sense of the possible. These realities cover three areas:

- realities about power.
- realities about organizations.
- realities about clients.

Realities About Power

There are five facts about power that are helpful in understanding advocacy:

1. Those who hold power are generally reluctant to give up that power.

2. Those who hold power generally have greater access to resources than people with less power. For instance, those with more money have more access to legal services, education, and health care.

 HIGHLIGHT 14.1

Indications for Advocacy

Advocacy is likely to be the role of choice in any of the following situations:

- when organizational barriers to services are created by agency policies or procedures;
- when clients are refused legally entitled benefits or services;
- when existing services are inadequate to meet identified needs of individual clients or groups of clients;
- when services provided to clients are inhumane or dehumanizing;
- when agencies or staff discriminate against clients because of gender, race, religion, sexual orientation, or for other reasons;
- when services or benefits are not provided to clients in a manner consistent with the immediacy of their

need (e.g., refusing to provide timely services in crisis situations);
- when multiple clients clearly have the same need for which no services or benefits yet exist;
- when clients cannot adequately protect their own interests or act on their own behalf;
- when existing services or benefits make the situation worse;
- when clients are denied civil rights or other legal protections;
- when clients are denied a voice in the planning for or creation of services;
- when human services professionals can help clients mobilize in their own interest to obtain services or benefits routinely available to those with more resources;
- when human services professionals can help achieve social and economic justice for individual or groups of clients. (Hepworth et al., 1997, pp. 468–472)

3. Resources in general, including power, are not distributed equally. Some people simply have significantly more power than others.

4. Conflict between people and between people and institutions is inevitable, especially when those in power treat those with less power unfairly. People do not want or like to be under-dogs. For example, Devore and Schlesinger (1996) see an inherent conflict in minority–majority group relations. They argue "dominant institutions dominate minority people, and advocacy identifies with clients who are subjects of domination" (p. 147).

5. You must have power in order to change existing organizations and institutions. Otherwise, large systems are resistant to change. Change takes effort and work. Systems tend to cling to the stable state they are used to, whether or not that state is effective. Thus, having access to sufficient power to influence the outcome of the change effort is necessary for the advocate.

Later in this chapter we will discuss ways in which workers can garner power to enhance their advocacy.

Realities About Organizations

We have established that advocacy involves thinking about and manipulating power. Advocacy also entails working with organizations and their policies. Understanding organizations can help us to target them and their policies more effectively. Within the advocacy context, we have four major organizational realities to consider:

1. There are many reasons why organizations and institutions fail to meet client needs. Sometimes, the system does not recognize a problem or chooses not to address it. Other times, agencies and organizations serve their own needs rather than their clients' needs. Organizations may be experiencing a budget crisis. Top administrators may be more concerned about their own reputations than about serving clients' needs, or caseloads may be so great that clients cannot be served adequately.

2. Agencies and organizations, just like people, *do* have potential to change. Advocacy grows out of a philosophy that people have the same rights to tax-supported social services and benefits as they do to such things as public

education and city streets. It is a fact of life that benefits and services are not distributed equally in any society. Some individuals and groups receive a greater share because of a variety of circumstances, ranging from luck to political, social, or economic power. The advocate's role is to help right the imbalance by working on behalf of those with less luck or power. Human services professionals believe that agencies and organizations can change to meet client needs. Influencing the organization to change requires that the worker mobilize resources on behalf of less-powerful clients. Of course, accomplishing this is often not a simple task.

3. Many agency leaders would prefer that workers not advocate for changes in their organization. Agency board members and administrators usually find that maintaining the status quo is easier if you do not have people urging you to change or expand services and resources. Therefore, attempts at change may be met with resistance. For example, the workers in a county human services agency wanted to provide each public assistance recipient with a booklet describing their rights and the benefits, to which they were legally entitled. The booklets, developed by a client advocacy group, contained factually correct information that encouraged clients to get the benefits they needed. A request to include these booklets in the regular monthly mailing of benefit checks was denied by the agency administrator. The administrator feared that clients might assert rights that the agency was unwilling to recognize, which would inevitably cost the agency more money. This increase, in turn, would raise the wrath of the county board. The administrator wanted to avoid this scenario at all costs. He adamantly refused to have anyone think he supported giving benefits to clients, other than those the agency was forced to provide.

4. Not only can agencies refuse to be helpful, but they may also subvert the rules or try to be secretive. Advocacy is needed because some human services agencies and institutions are insensitive to client needs or deny clients needed services. Additionally, agencies and organizations can fail to follow rules or hide how their workers and supervisors are really performing. Similarly, they can keep clients ignorant of their rights. Sometimes the clients are too discouraged or powerless to stand up for themselves. Sometimes clients receive inappropriate treatment or

mistreatment by the very agencies charged with responsibility to help them. Ultimately, the human services professional must understand the dynamics of organizations and institutions. That understanding will be helpful at the point of assessing and planning for change.

Realities About Clients

One of the most important realities about clients is derived from the human services conceptualization of the client in the environment. In this model, clients are never seen as existing separately from their environment. That is, clients both influence and are influenced by their environment. Whatever problems exist do so because of the dynamic interaction between the two.

In the past, the emphasis was on how people deserved what they got. When applied to clients, this meant that the clients' problems were their own fault. We now refer to this approach as "blaming the victim" and see that it is often the environment and how that environment influences clients that are really to blame for problems.

The second reality is that clients should be helped to help themselves. This means that workers should not act as advocates for clients when they can advocate for themselves. People tend to become dependent when we do things for them that they can do without us. Often, we can help people be advocates for themselves by teaching them to be assertive and modeling this ourselves.

A third point about advocacy is that it should never be carried out without the full knowledge and consent of the client. We will discuss the reasons for this caveat in the section on assessment of advocacy situations.

Knowledge Required by Advocates

Workers acting as advocates need to know many things. They need to know the rights of clients and the avenues of redress available to clients. They must know the resources that can be mobilized on behalf of the client. Finally, they must master strategies and tactics that are most likely to be effective.

Knowing the Rights of Clients

The effective client advocate must know the rights and entitlements of clients. "Rights are those protections and guarantees to which people or society have a just claim and cannot, in American society, be denied without due process of law" (Brill, 1990, p. 230).

There are two types of rights: individual rights and societal rights. Individual rights are those that you as an individual are guaranteed. Examples include the right to an education and freedom of speech. Societal rights, on the other hand, are the collective rights of the people as a whole that are considered more important than individual rights. For instance, you as a member of society have the right not to be murdered by another individual.

Sometimes, individual and societal rights are in conflict. For example, owning land along a river and using that land as you see fit (individual rights) are possible for you. The river itself, however, cannot be modified by the landowner. You cannot forbid people to use the river, nor can you alter the riverbank without permission (societal rights).

Another example of rights in conflict involves freedom of speech (an individual right). Saying whatever you want, however, does not allow you to shout "fire" in a theater when there really is no fire. Such exercising of freedom would threaten the safety of others (a societal right).

As you can see, there are limits even to the most basic rights we have as citizens. Understanding both the rights and the limitations of those rights is important. In view of societal rights, we cannot make unreasonable or illegal demands on agencies no matter how much clients want us to pursue their individual rights (Halley et al., 1998).

Avenues of Appeal

Challenging the actions of agency administrators or employees requires a thorough knowledge of the avenues of redress or appeal open to the client. For example, consider a decision that has been made by a line worker in the agency. To whom can this decision be appealed? Is the worker's supervisor the next step in the chain of command? Does the agency have an ombudsman (an individual designated to investigate charges and complaints) to whom complaints can be directed? Does the law provide for a fair hearing process in which clients can appeal decisions with which they disagree?

Entitlements are "services, goods, or money due to an individual by virtue of a specific status" (Barker, 1999, p. 155). The nature of the entitlement may dictate the avenues of appeal available. Entitlements may arise from several sources. First are those that are established or defined by law or regulation. These include federal, state, and local laws and regulations. Because laws or regulations are not always clear, a second category of entitlements is those based upon an interpretation of law or regulation. A third category is those based upon an organizations' own policies. And, finally, because policies can be just as confusing and debatable as laws, a fourth category of entitlements is based upon interpretation of organizational policy.

Knowing the source of the entitlement may help us decide what form our advocacy will take. For example, most entitlements guaranteed by law have specific appeal procedures built into the law. Agencies may or may not have identified appeal procedures for those who disagree with agency policy.

Frequently, appeal procedures appear in agency handbooks or regulations. Whenever possible, the established appeal procedures should be followed before considering other options. If you and the client have not exhausted the appeal system, brushing off your complaint is easy for the agency. The agency can always say you have not followed proper procedures, which is why knowing specifically how to appeal different kinds of decisions is important.

Available Resources

Often, human services professionals will seek the help of other resources in carrying out the role of advocate. Resources include both people and agencies and organizations that may help you and the client. One of the most important resources is assistance with legal questions. While knowing everything about every client's rights may not be possible, having access to those who do know is possible and advisable. Attorneys are important sources of information about certain kinds of rights such as those written into existing laws or guaranteed by the Constitution.

In addition, some organizations work actively to protect the rights of the individual citizen. For example, the American Civil Liberties Union exists to help ensure that individual rights are not abridged or limited, particularly by those elements of our society that are the most powerful (government and business). This organization may prove helpful to workers unsure about legal rights of a client.

Legal Aid is another organization providing pro bono (free) legal services. Sometimes, the worker will know an attorney who will provide free service or help at nominal cost. Perhaps an organization like the Alliance for the Mentally Ill will be available to help. In the assessment section of this chapter, we will discuss other possible resources.

Tactics and Strategies of Intervention

The worker will need to be familiar with a variety of techniques and approaches useful in advocacy situations. Some of these strategies and tactics resemble those used in other human services roles. Others are unique to the role of advocate. Much of the remainder of this chapter will be devoted to discussing strategies and tactics.

The successful advocate requires two types of skills. Required first are the generalist practice skills useful in virtually any type of intervention. These include skills in "interviewing, listening, observing, being empathic, supportive, confrontive . . ." (Hutchison, 1989, p. 409). The advocate also needs to understand group process—resistance to change, decision making in groups, nonverbal communication, and both formal and informal structures and procedures. That the advocate will need to know how to gather and present data is also likely.

The second category of skills required by advocates includes those needed specifically for particular situations. For example, political or legislative advocacy requires skills somewhat different from those needed in advocating for an individual client. We will discuss these skills later in this chapter.

 ## Assessment in Advocacy Situations

As in any assessment, there are several considerations you as an advocate need to take into account. On the one hand, examining your own position and potential ability to advocate is important. On the other hand, you need to assess aspects of the potential advocacy situation outside yourself. These aspects include the clients' resources and strengths, characteristics of the adversary (i.e., the person, organization, agency, or policy that needs to change), and the resources, strategies, and tactics available to cause change.

Self-Assessment

One of the first questions to address is the source of the advocate's sanction. In other words, who or what gives you the right to advocate? Does your job description include serving as an advocate for clients? Does the sanction come from the clients' clearly stated legal rights that are not being observed? Perhaps, the primary source of sanction is the ethics of the human services profession.

There are many barriers to successful advocacy such as internal agency policies and external obstacles. For example, sometimes you will experience a lack of support from colleagues and superiors. Placing client interests above those of your own agency may cause conflict with peers and others (Mailick & Ashley, 1989, p. 626). The combination of barriers can make your job stressful. Workers must realistically assess their own vulnerability. What risks exist in serving as an advocate? Are the risks minor or great? What is the source of the risk? What means exist to counter the risk? Are the likely gains worth the risk? Do the tactics considered increase or decrease the risk?

Another factor is the worker's ability to devote the necessary time to the change effort. Advocacy often takes more time because problems are more intractable.

In addition, workers must deal with their own discomfort about being advocates. When dealing with people in power, the worker is in the uncomfortable position of asking for help instead of giving it. Often, the people targeted for change by the advocate have great experience in avoiding the issue. Because such people are frustrating to deal with, the worker may have to risk appearing aggressive or antagonistic to get anything done (Kadushin & Kadushin, 1997). The worker should be aware of and prepared for this possibility.

What Are Your Sources of Power?

What sources and kinds of power do advocates have available to cause change? There are several different types of power, according to French and Raven (1968). *Legitimate power* exists when person A believes person B has the right to influence him or her. The right often derives from a person's authority, based on his or her position in an organization. For example, supervisors usually are perceived as having a legitimate right to direct the behavior of subordinates. Similarly, you usually step on the brake and pull over when you notice the police car with flashing blue lights in your rearview mirror. This action rests on your perception that the police have a legitimate right to direct you to stop (although you may argue with the officer for doing so).

Reward power is the ability to provide positive reinforcement to another person. Examples of rewards are salary increases, praise, promotions, and other things perceived by the receiver to be beneficial. Reward power may be lodged in any number of persons (e.g., parents, spouses, employers, friends).

Coercive power is the ability of someone to punish or use negative reinforcement on another individual. Here there is the real or potential threat that something bad will happen or something good will be taken away if you do not cooperate. In addition to their legitimate power, police officers have a certain amount of coercive power they can employ. The threat of a speeding ticket is supposed to coerce you to obey the speed limit.

What is experienced as coercive depends a great deal on the person being coerced. Because individuals vary so greatly, something considered coercive or unpleasant by one person may not be seen as bad by another. For example, sitting in a smoke-filled bar with extremely loud music playing might be a delight to one person and a noxious nightmare to another.

Referent power exists when one person is influenced by another person because of admiration for that individual. If you look up to others, admire their values or ideas, or otherwise would like to emulate them, you have accorded them referent power. Conversely, someone you find repulsive or unpleasant is not likely to have any referent power over you.

The final type of power is *expert power*. Expert power is available to those we consider to be authorities or especially proficient in some area. We generally accord physicians expert authority because we believe they know more than we do about the field of medicine.

Not infrequently, multiple sources of power exist in the same person or organization. For example, job supervisors may have legitimate power, coercive power, and reward power. Ideally, the advocate should attempt to marshal as many types of power as possible. If the adversary is vulnerable because he or she has broken the law, using legitimate power to cause change is possible. You may recall the case of the landlord who refused to fix up his slum apartments in violation of city law. Remember also in this case that tenants contacted the news media, which held the landlord up to public condemnation and ridicule, a coercive power.

Other Assessment Considerations

Three dimensions are important in assessment when contemplating advocacy. First is the nature of the problem situation. The second concerns the strengths, rights, and resources of the client. The third entails the characteristics of the adversary.

The Nature of the Problem Situation

Before beginning to advocate, you certainly need to understand the nature of the problem situation itself.

For example, will the change effort take place at the level of the decision maker or does it require change in agency policy, administrative procedures or regulations, or social policy? Is the problem occurring because the client has a special need that is not being addressed? Or is it because there is a bad relationship between the target system and the client?

You will remember that the target system is "the individual, group, or community to be changed or influenced to achieve our goals" (Barker, 1999, p. 480). Is there a deficiency of some sort in the target system (either structural or in personnel)? Is the problem a bad or ineffective social or agency policy? Is the target system a worker, administrator, policy maker, or legislator who is not functioning the way you think she or he should? Is the target system external to, or part of, the worker's own agency? What types of relationships exist between the advocate and the target system? The answers to these questions suggest different strategies and tactics.

Keeping an open mind about the situation and the target system is also important, at least at first. For example, do not automatically presume that people or groups acting as barriers are malicious, deliberate, or mean-spirited. Often target system actions may be inadvertent or result from different perceptions of the situation. Initially assuming the worst may create a self-fulfilling prophesy. Highlight 14.2 shows an example of a problem in which several alternative hypotheses are possible.

Sometimes problems occur because of staff ignorance of client cultural values and beliefs because the staff has not taken enough time to develop rapport with clients. Perhaps the client has not understood the necessity for certain information or misunderstood what was asked. Even the application forms clients must complete for specific entitlement programs (e.g., Medicaid) may cause problems. Questions may be vague or call for answers the client does not have. One can wonder whether the use of confusing application forms exists to discourage clients from applying for help or simply reflects an agency's lack of sensitivity.

Before advocating, you need to address a number of questions. First, is the goal to acquire new

---

HIGHLIGHT 14.2

When the System Is Not Working

Nathan Washington and Ramon Vallejo owned a duplex together in the mid-size college town of Fort Druid. They had lived there for almost 17 years and were happy in their quiet, residential neighborhood.

One morning, they were suddenly awakened by the eager rap, rap, rap of pounding hammers coming from the house immediately next door. The noise annoyed them. However, this noise was nothing compared to their annoyance and displeasure when they found the structure was being converted to tiny units of inexpensive student housing. They were infuriated. All they could envision was loud, pulsing music in wee morning hours and cases of empty beer cans strewn around the yard. Neither Nathan nor Ramon had been notified about this pending change.

It so happened that the city ordinance in Fort Druid is quite clear regarding such structural changes. Any time there is a major change proposed in the use of a building or in its structure, residents within 300 feet are to be notified. The city is required to send a letter describing the proposed action. For example, a request by a property owner to convert a single-family home into an apartment must have the approval of the city planning commission.

The commission must hold an open hearing (a meeting where anyone who wishes to come and speak can do so) and allow neighbors to present their views. The ordinance calls for notification of neighbors because changes in their neighborhood can have economic and quality-of-life significance for them.

If you were advocating on behalf of Nathan and Ramon, three issues would confront you. First, the owners of the house may not have obeyed the law by seeking permission to modify their building. Second, if they had sought proper approval, the failure to notify residents as required by law may make the actions of the planning commission illegal. Therefore, their approval of the house conversion may be invalid.

Third, there is the question of why the problem occurred in the first place. Were the neighbors not notified because the required open meeting had never been held? Or had they failed to read the notice when it was mailed to their home? Was it a mistake by an individual staff person in city hall who simply forgot to mail the notice? Was it an attempt to keep the neighbors from exercising their legal rights to present their objections to the planning commission? Were the notices lost in the mail?

What actions an advocate might take are clearly dependent on the problem's cause. Assessment is critical to identify these numerous potential causes, explore their substance, and target the one that appears to be real.

resources or improve existing ones? How long has the problem existed? How serious is it? How many people are affected by it? Is there any history of advocacy efforts that would add information to the current assessment? If past efforts failed, what were the reasons for these failures? Has anything changed that would make the decision to advocate more likely to succeed?

The answers to all of these questions should lead you to believe you can influence the decision maker. Your assessment should make you certain that you can persuade or coerce the target system into acting as you wish. Otherwise, you are probably wasting your time and should consider other intervention options (Sosin & Caulum, 1989).

Assessing the Client

Clients must be closely involved in the decision to select advocacy strategies. You need to assess their motivation to participate and their ability to do so. There are at least five reasons for this involvement. First, the chance for success is greatest if clients participate in planning the intervention. Second, clients are more likely to use and value resources they had a hand in developing. Third, resources are more likely to be appropriate when clients have helped develop or create them. Fourth, clients gain an important sense of efficacy when they participate in actions designed to reach their goals. Fifth, working with others helps produce a sense of participation and involvement that may be important for clients lacking self-esteem and a support network. You might ask yourself a number of questions. For instance, how important is the issue to the client? Is it an emergency or less pressing? Does the client have any ability to compromise, or is the issue too basic? Will this effort cause problems for the client at some later point? What resources and strengths does the client have (e.g., verbal skills, determination, leadership ability, social skills, intelligence)? Does the client have any other sources of power?

The answers to such questions will help you plan more carefully and wisely. For example, you can decide how quickly you need to act. You will also know if compromises are possible, and what role may be played by the client.

Assessing the Adversary

Understanding the adversary or target system well is critical. "What are the power system's structure, channels, lines of authority, processes, rules of procedure? How are decisions made?" (McMahon, 1996, p. 347). What are the adversaries like? What do we know about their jobs, their titles, motivation, and capabilities?

Perhaps the first question to address is: How *open to change* is the adversary or target system? Additionally, to what degree do you and the target system share the same views about client needs? You must know whether or not the target system (adversary) will be receptive to change. The target may be resistant, sympathetic, or indifferent to our efforts. Receptivity may be a function of the type of objective pursued. For example, if the objective is to increase access to already existing resources, the target system might be more open to change. If, on the other hand, you are seeking changes in the basic policies or procedures of an agency, expect more resistance.

You also want to know the *degree of vulnerability* of the adversary. Is the person violating agency policy (which is somewhat minor) or violating a law (which is much more serious)? Is the action taken permitted within the discretion normally granted the decision maker, or has the person exceeded that authority?

Knowing how this adversary *handled complaints or challenges in the past* may be important. For example, does the person respond best to face-to-face meetings, or are all decisions made by reviewing written materials? Does the person usually make quick decisions or need time to think about requests? Does the person consult others before deciding?

Finally, knowing the *values* of the adversary would be helpful. What are the person's goals? Is this person likely to be more sympathetic to the client's viewpoint or to the worker's? Substantial differences in values and goals decrease the probability of quick solutions. The greater the divergence between values and goals of the client and adversary, the more power is required to change the situation. Determining the availability and potency of power is an important part of the assessment process.

Planning in Advocacy Situations

Planning in advocacy situations requires considering the knowledge gained from the assessment steps previously identified and selecting the most appropriate interventions. The first step in planning is to consider the resources, strategies, and tactics that you will employ to bring about change.

Resources may include money, power, prestige, authority, commitment, and any other means you can muster to help reach your goal. You as an advocate, your client, or some aspect of the environment may be tapped for resources. Outcomes depend partly on the resources of the change agent and the receptivity of the target system. The most effective advocates use this information and adopt a variety of resources and techniques.

Strategy concerns broad issues and your plan for approaching advocacy. For example, a strategy might entail the amount of conflict you plan to use in an advocacy effort. What strategies make the most sense given the available resources? As in the planning phase of the planned change model, you must select a strategy based on the problem, the objectives, your sanctions, and characteristics of the change agent and target systems.

Tactics represent the specifics of your plan such as how conflict is used and when. For example, confronting the adversary immediately with an overwhelming show of support for your ideas might be important. Remember the case mentioned in Chapter 4, where the city council was intent on supporting a bypass highway around the city. By quickly confronting the city council with a petition signed by almost every business owner on the highway, the proposed bypass was rejected immediately.

One of the most important factors in the decision to advocate is the resources available to use in the intervention effort. Are there others who will join in to work on the problem? From whom can you expect support and opposition? Do you have some influence with the decision maker? Is some amount of money or power available to you?

The Ultimate Decision

Ultimately, the human services professional must make a decision about when and when not to advocate. This decision is sometimes difficult. Fruitless efforts to change target systems are demoralizing to clients and workers. When the assessment phase points to the eventual failure of the intervention, stopping before committing further resources to the endeavor is better. In the words of the song "The Gambler," sung by Kenny Rogers:

> *You have to know when to hold 'em, know when to fold 'em,*
> *know when to walk away, know when to run.*

Intervention: Advocacy Strategies and Tactics

Following assessment and planning, the worker and client must decide the appropriate strategy and

tactics to use for a given advocacy situation. In this section, we will look closely at the techniques that advocates often employ (see Highlight 14.3). They include persuasion, fair hearings and legal appeals, political and community pressure, using the media, and petitioning. Some of these were discussed in Chapter 13 and will only be addressed briefly here.

Persuasion

Persuading others to take certain actions can be simple or extremely difficult. It depends on several factors, including the nature of the problem, the degree of resistance experienced, the client's wishes, and the capabilities of the worker.

Because advocacy work usually involves challenging the status quo, resistance will occur. We often select a strategy based on our perception of how difficult influencing the adversary will be. Adversaries who share your views will probably require little persuasion. You may then need only to define the issue clearly and present your evidence that a problem exists that the adversary can resolve. In other words, persuasion is more likely to work when the target system understands the client's needs and values, accepts the worker's perspective, and shares the values of the worker (Toseland & Rivas, 1998). In these cases, collaborative strategies are possible and recommended. Collaborative strategies are synergistic. That is, working together gets more accomplished with less effort than people working alone. Collaboration involves giving and clarifying information. In a sense, advocates can then educate their adversaries. Joint planned change is possible, and both parties can begin working together on a solution.

Effective persuasion of adversaries is a challenge. Human services professionals are recommended to approach this challenge by using the following steps:

1. Clearly state the issue of concern (i.e., a policy, procedure, decision, or process) you believe is a problem.
2. Allow adequate time for discussing the issue and answering questions. Do not attempt to hurry the process. People who feel pressured are more likely to say no just to get rid of the pressure.
3. Identify exactly what you want done. Do you want a policy or rule changed, a different decision, or an exception made?
4. As the discussion unfolds, summarize areas of agreement between you and the adversary.

HIGHLIGHT 14.3

Guidelines for Advocacy

The following guidelines for advocacy are useful in almost all situations where you may serve as a client's advocate and where persuasion, fair hearings, appeals, petitioning, and more confrontational strategies are used.

1. Serve as an advocate only with clear permission of your client. Clients have a right to decide if they wish you to undertake advocacy on their behalf.
2. Acknowledge to the client and yourself that acting as an advocate can affect your relationships with other people and organizations. This impact can be positive or negative.
3. Advocacy is appropriate only to help the client, not to pursue your personal agenda.
4. Get the facts first. Your credibility is influenced by having accurate information, such as dates, times, actions, statistics, and other hard data. Do not go into a situation unprepared.
5. Always enter an advocacy situation with a clear list of concerns and questions. Know exactly what you want and be prepared to assertively ask the target to meet your request.

6. Look at issues from both sides. Put yourself in the shoes of the adversary. Can you employ your empathy and other practice skills to see how things look to them? Being able to convey this understanding, while demonstrating respect for your opponent, leaves the door open for that person to give in. No one appreciates being put down, misunderstood, or treated badly.
7. Keep a record of things that are said in meetings that relate to your goal. If you are told something is true, check it out. If you are getting different messages from different people, determine which is true or whether the facts lie somewhere else.
8. Always find out who makes decisions at the next higher level. Learn the chain of command. If you are turned down at one level, knowing the next line of appeal is important. Inform your opponent that you intend to take the matter to his or her supervisor or governing board, depending on which is most appropriate.
9. Record all steps you take to resolve an issue. Note details such as time, place, date, decisions, and decision makers. Be prepared for taking the next step.

Sources: Sheafor et al. (1997); Kadushin & Kadushin (1997); Compton & Galaway (1999).

This summarization helps build a bridge of understanding and reduces the feeling of distance between your respective positions.

5. Attempt to find a common ground whenever possible. Seek areas where you have similar interests with the adversary.
6. Avoid vague statements and always make your positions, requests, and points clear to the opponent.
7. Be candid about what you will do if the problem is not remedied. This straightforwardness is not done in the form of a threat but only as a matter-of-fact statement of intent. If you intend to appeal a decision or assume a more conflictual stance, let the opponent know it. In some cases, using this method may get the opponent to reconsider his or her position.
8. Convey your sincerity and determination to resolve the matter.
9. Maintain eye contact and avoid any gestures (such as looking down) that might undercut your firmness.

10. Approach the adversary as if you both have a desire to resolve thing. Do not start by suggesting that the opponent is not willing to hear your position.
11. Do not filibuster or monopolize the conversation. Listen empathetically and allow the other person a chance to be heard.
12. Do not lose your cool. Getting angry is a mistake. Those who blow up emotionally lose power in these situations.

In other situations, you may choose different tactics. For example, you may try negotiating with the adversary, bargaining, or offering compromises to achieve as much of your goal as possible. This posture assumes, of course, that the matter of concern is one where compromise is possible and is sanctioned (supported) by the client.

When Persuasion Does Not Work

Sometimes, you may need to consider using confrontation and more conflictual approaches. These approaches are usually used when the advocate has little influence over the decision maker (Sosin & Caulum, 1989). This lack of influence suggests the need to take more drastic steps. Confrontational approaches involve three dimensions. First, you can threaten to disclose the adversary's failure to follow law or policy. Second, you can actually disclose the information and allow the natural consequences to occur. Finally, you can appeal through administrative hearings or the courts.

The latter option is not employed routinely because of the cost involved. It may be appropriate only when other alternatives fail. Administrative appeals occur much more frequently because they are often the only way to cause changes in rules and regulations or decisions based on those rules and regulations.

Fair Hearings and Legal Appeals

"Fair hearings and grievances are administrative procedures designed to ensure that clients or client groups who have been denied benefits or rights to which they are entitled get equitable treatment" (Kirst-Ashman & Hull, 2001, p. 366.) Normally, the clients notify the agency that they wish to have a fair hearing concerning the adversary's decision, which means that an outside person (usually a state employee) will be appointed to hear both sides of the argument. The fair hearing examiner may find the adversary has violated state or federal policies. Then the examiner may direct the adversary to comply with the rules and award the client his or her rightful benefits. Sometimes just the threat of using the formal appeal process will be enough to change an adversary's earlier decision. Other times, the agency may have no policy for a fair hearing or appeal, and other confrontational tactics can be employed. For example, seeking advice and assistance from an attorney is often possible. Not infrequently, an attorney's letter presenting the possibility of legal action is sufficient to cause adversaries to change their position.

Political and Community Pressure

Consider the case discussed earlier regarding finding housing for a Hmong client. The worker used an elected official (a city council member) to pressure a city agency to act in a responsive and timely fashion. Many political figures proudly tell their constituents of their efforts to combat bureaucracies at all levels on their constituents' behalf. For example, most members of the U.S. House of Representatives and Senate provide such help to constituents. The latter usually have expressed unhappiness about decisions or lack of action taken by the Social Security Administration and other federal agencies.

Don't ignore state representatives and senators either. One agency, faced with laying off almost a dozen staff members because of a proposed change in how the state contracted with providers of family services, wrote a persuasive letter to their state representative. The letter, outlining the concerns and problems, asked the legislator to meet with agency representatives to discuss the matter. Shortly thereafter the state agency backed down on their proposal (J. Campbell, personal communication, May 26, 1999).

In other situations, pressure may be brought through community groups such as the Alliance for the Mentally Ill. Advocacy organizations exist to work for their membership. They will often intervene to help their members cope with uncooperative systems. Organizational pressures of this type depend, of course, on the existence and availability of such supportive associations.

Using the Media

Advocates may be able to use the media as a confrontive tactic to cause change. For example, some television stations conduct public service programs that respond to viewer's written complaints about agencies or organizations. A reporter will investigate the situation and discuss it on the evening news. Often this type of pressure will result in a favorable change for the client.

One should note that the problem does not have to involve a government bureaucracy. Clients who have received unsatisfactory responses from businesses have used these television programs to publicize their complaints.

Advocates can also use the media to publicize wrongdoing. This tactic, you may recall, was used by the apartment residents to embarrass the landlord. The landlord was unresponsive to both his own tenants and to the city's feeble enforcement efforts until the television stations reported the situation on the evening news. This is really a combination of using the media and employing community pressure. A similar approach was used by All Together, an agency advocating for the rights of people with physical disabilities. The agency's clients complained that transportation services they needed were being denied or so restricted that they were hampered in their efforts to maintain employment and lead productive lives. Prior attempts at letter writing had been unsuccessful, and some clients felt they had been victims of retaliation for voicing their concerns. To demonstrate their unhappiness, the clients and staff of All Together picketed a fund-raising event for the transportation agency. Clients, many in wheelchairs, carried picket signs and chanted their concerns. The event, which was being attended by the news media, quickly focused attention on the transportation needs of clients with physical disabilities. It also caused community residents and transportation service board members to look more closely at the way the agency was meeting client needs. Within a short time afterward, the Board of Directors asked the transportation services director to step down and began a wholesale revamping of their services to clients with disabilities.

Petitioning

Another tactic you can employ as an advocate involves circulating petitions. We discussed this approach earlier, in Chapter 13. As you may recall, petitioning is the collecting of signatures on a piece of paper requesting some type of action. You might collect neighborhood signatures asking for stop lights at a dangerous intersection. Petitions can be effective. However, many people will sign petitions without real commitment to the cause. Because signatures on petitions are generally easy to get, many officials discount their importance. Therefore, you should carefully consider their potential effectiveness before using them.

Selecting a Strategy for Advocacy

Sosin and Caulum (1989) suggest that the advocate select the "strategy of least contest" (p. 537). This suggestion means that you should choose the approach requiring minimum effort and stress to achieve your desired goals. Their advice suggests that nonconfrontational approaches should be used before confrontational ones. For example, collaborative strategies should be applied before confrontational ones, if possible. Confrontation can be wearing on you. It can siphon your energy away from your other job tasks.

Consider three conditions before deciding to exert pressure and cause a confrontation:

1. You have already tried less confrontational ways of instituting change. For example, you have tried unsuccessfully to persuade your adversary.
2. You have enough proof that clients have been treated unfairly and are absolutely certain that your grievance is consequential.

3. You determine that you have a good chance at succeeding by exerting pressure and initiating a confrontation. You do not want to waste your energy if the cause is hopeless (Halley et al., 1998, p. 228).

Whistle-Blowing

Barker (1999) defines whistle-blowing as "informing those people in positions of influence or authority outside an organization about the existence of an organization's practices that are illegal, wasteful, dangerous, or otherwise contrary to its stated policies" (p. 517). Some organizations, such as those in the federal government, provide means for whistle-blowing to occur while maintaining the anonymity of the person reporting the problem. There are even laws designed to protect the whistle-blower from retaliation by supervisory and administrative personnel whose positions are threatened by the revelations. These laws notwithstanding, whistle-blowing carries a degree of risk that varies in direct proportion to the seriousness of the allegations. Whistle-blowers have been fired, have been reassigned to insignificant responsibilities at remote locations, and have been harassed into quitting.

The purpose of providing this caveat is not to discourage human services professionals from advocating for clients with their own agencies or with others who are not acting in an appropriate manner. Rather, it is to assure that the decision to advocate is an informed one that has taken into consideration the risks involved.

Legislative Advocacy

Earlier in this chapter we discussed case advocacy and cause advocacy. In this section, we will discuss a third type of advocacy called legislative advocacy. Legislative advocacy is similar to cause advocacy in that the human services professional is working for a broad category of clients or citizens. Legislative advocacy specifically entails efforts to change legislation to benefit some category of clients. In many cases, creation of new legislation is the most effective means of addressing the human services needs of large groups of clients. Kopels (1995) notes that the Americans with Disabilities Act (ADA) discussed in Chapter 3 represented an advocacy tool aimed at people with disabilities, a group she characterizes as "the poorest, least educated, and largest minority population in America" (p. 337).

Legislative advocacy also may embody efforts to defeat bills considered harmful in some way. For example, a proposed reduction in funding for the Head Start program would mean limiting or cutting off Head Start services previously available to clients. Head Start is a federal program established in 1965 to provide disadvantaged minority preschool children with education to compensate for previous social deprivation.

Another example of harmful legislation is a proposed bill to restrict access to reproductive health services such as Planned Parenthood. This agency provides information, contraception, counseling, and physical examinations, all directed at helping people (usually women) gain control over their own reproduction. Services are usually provided on a sliding fee scale. This means that fees are based on how much people can pay. Poorer people pay less than richer people.

Legislation limiting access might incorporate requirements such as forcing women under age 18 to provide written parental permission before they can receive any services. Another inhibiting proposal might involve denying state or federal funding if agency staff discuss abortion as a possible alternative to unwanted pregnancy. Both of these examples limit available services. The first places restrictions on the basis of age. The second limits the potential for informing clients of the options available to them.

Responsibility for legislative advocacy is part of being a human services professional. So many decisions affecting human services programs, human services professionals, and clients are made in the legislative arena that *not* to be concerned about and involved in legislative advocacy is impossible.

Some human services professionals may feel a bit awed at the prospect of trying to get laws passed and programs funded. Fortunately, legislative advocacy has one unique feature that makes this effort less difficult than it seems. The primary rule of legislative advocacy is that getting elected and reelected is the most important activity of most legislators (Haynes & Mickelson, 1997). Consequently, this "rule" means that most legislators like to know what their constituents want and are susceptible to their constituents' influence.

In addition, most legislators must make decisions about any particular proposed bill based on limited information. Many bills are complex, which increases the likelihood that the legislator will need to depend on others for information. As a consequence, legislators may very well be influenced by a small number of advocates or by a particularly persuasive argument about a given bill. In other words,

you are encouraged to tell your state and federal senators and representatives what you think should be done about bills and issues (see Highlight 14.4). You can also mobilize other workers or clients to write or call in what they think. This tactic is one means of gaining at least some power over which laws are passed or defeated in the political process. Comparing your views on various legislative issues with those of your elected representatives is possible by consulting the World Wide Web. For example, Project Vote Smart, a not-for-profit and nonpartisan research organization, has compiled ratings from almost 100 interest groups. You can look up your U.S. senator's or representative's voting records on any number of issues. The Web address is http://www.vote-smart.org.

Of course, there are realistic barriers that reduce the likelihood of getting new legislation passed. First, there is the fact that the majority of bills are not actually passed. Only about 20 percent of proposed bills eventually receive legislative approval and are signed by the governor or president to become law (Dear & Patti, 1981, p. 289). Moreover, most legislative sessions are somewhat short, lasting only a matter of months. The legislature might not even get to the bill you are interested in. Therefore, desired legislation may have to be reintroduced the following year, which often involves starting the whole process of influence again from scratch.

Additionally, legislative bodies are unpredictable. Turnover in membership from session to session after elections, changes in control from Republican to Democratic leadership, or economic news (e.g., lower than expected tax revenues resulting in less money available) make the entire legislative process more complicated. People in power also make unpredictable decisions that affect legislation. For example, in a recent race for governor, the incumbent ran for reelection based on his success in increasing the economic growth and well-being of the state. He emphasized how well the state was doing financially because of his wonderful work and effort. Three weeks after winning the election, he announced that the state was experiencing a multimillion dollar shortfall in revenue because of economic conditions. In other words, the state had millions of dollars less than it had been expected to have. This required a freeze on hiring and a reduction in budgets for all state agencies including social services. As a result, many social workers who had supported that governor felt betrayed. Thus, the unpredictability of the legislative process means that the advocate must remain flexible and ready to change strategies as needed (Haynes & Mickelson, 1997).

HIGHLIGHT 14.4
Writing Elected Officials

Human services professionals often have reason for writing to elected officials. It is important to use the correct form and address for such letters. Some common addresses and the accompanying salutation appear below.

Letters to the President
The President
The White House
1600 Pennsylvania Ave. NW
Washington, DC 20500
http://www.whitehouse.gov

Salutation
Dear Mr./Ms. President:

Letters to U.S. Senators
The Honorable (insert full name)
United States Senate
Washington, DC 20510
http://www.senate.gov/contacting/index.cfm

Salutation
Dear Senator (insert last name):

Letters to Members of the House of Representatives
The Honorable (insert full name)
U.S. House of Representatives
Washington, DC 20515
http://www.house.gov/house/MemberWWW.html

Salutation
Dear Representative (insert last name):

Letters to Cabinet Secretaries
The Honorable (insert full name)
Secretary of (insert name of Department)
Washington, DC (insert correct zip code)
www.whitehouse.gov/government/cabinet-secretaries.html

Salutation
Dear Secretary (insert last name):

Here are several additional guidelines for writing to elected officials:

- Write using your own words rather than sending a form letter. The latter carries less weight.
- Keep your letter brief and polite. Threats or impolite letters are likely to be ignored.
- Identify yourself as an informed constituent who is concerned about a specific, timely issue.
- Identify the specific action you would like, such as "vote for AB 297."
- Give clear reasons for your request, supported with facts and figures.
- Send a follow-up thank-you letter if your representative acts in accordance with your request.

Lists of your elected representatives can be acquired from the public library or by contacting your city hall. In addition, some states publish very detailed books listing all state officials. These lists may be found in your public library and often obtained free from your state legislator. You might also go on the Internet and check the Democrats' site (www.democrats.org/) and the Republicans' site (www.rnc.org/).

Legislative advocates soon realize that a bill may not be passed just because it is a good bill. Even documented evidence strongly supporting a bill will not guarantee passage if other factors intervene. These factors include economic conditions, political positions, lawmakers' personal values or life experiences, and legislative precedent. Each of these aspects may override logic and compelling arguments. Besides, even when legislators support a bill, it may be buried or defeated in a committee composed of a smaller group of legislators who evaluate the bill and prepare it for presentation to the entire legislature. Once on the floor of the legislature, a bill may be defeated or returned to committee. Finally, governors may veto bills for their own idiosyncratic reasons.

Factors Affecting Legislative Advocacy

Being successful as a legislative advocate requires that you understand some factors influencing whether or not a bill will be passed. For example, the fiscal consequences of a bill are extremely important to its chances for success. The cost of a proposed piece of legislation is perhaps the most important factor affecting its likelihood of becoming law. Logic might dictate that a bill's merit or usefulness is the most important aspect in making it pass, but this reasoning is not true in practice. Generally speaking, bills that ultimately require spending less money are more likely to pass.

The popularity of a bill also has some bearing on its potential success. The more popular a bill is, that is, the more support it has among constituents and legislators, the more likely it is to become law. Such bills are usually those that have little impact on social change and require little or nothing from the public. In other words, bills that are popular and do not affect most people directly are more likely to pass. A bill to increase the penalty for selling drugs is a good example. It is likely to be popular with the general public because its impact will only be on a relatively small group of people, and it supports commonly held values about selling drugs.

Steps in Legislative Advocacy

There are a series of steps legislatures follow to pass new legislation; likewise, there are coinciding steps a human services professional can take to advocate for the passage of a new bill (Dear & Patti, 1981). The steps for legislative advocacy include the following: developing a draft of the bill; figuring out who else will help you in support of the bill; getting specific legislators to sponsor the bill; asking your legislative sponsors to introduce the bill; educating the general public about the bill's worth and usefulness; trying to positively influence any legislative subcommittee members responsible for decision making about the bill; and trying to influence other legislators who will be voting on the bill's passage.

Step 1: Developing and Revising the Draft Bill

Formulating an original piece of legislation can be a formidable task. It requires both knowledge of the law and familiarity with existing regulations, policies, and programs related to the proposed bill. Consequently, most proposals are sent to an already established unit (sometimes called a legislative reference bureau), which is responsible for writing the first draft of a bill. This body is usually an arm of the legislature. Its staff members often prepare a summary of the bill to help legislators understand its intent. Once in draft form, the bill needs to be refined. Often, clarifications and changes need to be made so that the bill reflects its supporters' intentions.

Step 2: Identifying, Obtaining, and Maintaining the Bill's Supporters

Initially, identifying those who are natural supporters of a bill is important; that is, who is naturally interested in the bill's topic or will obviously benefit from the bill. Predicting who will be neutral or opposed to a bill is equally important. If you hope to see this bill become law, you will need to know who is likely to dislike the bill. Knowing those who are initially neutral may give you a basis for later persuading them to support the bill. These people may include legislators, their staffs, human services professional organizations, governmental agencies (e.g., the Department of Health and Human Services), and social service providers. Ironing out differences between factions supporting the bill is important. For example, people support a bill for many different reasons. Each supporter may have ideas about how to improve the bill. One group may dislike a particular word or section in the bill. These differing perspectives must be reconciled if you are to reach an agreement on the final bill. Keeping supporters on board is important, and modifying the bill may be one cost of achieving this consensus.

Arranging face-to-face meetings and providing copies of the draft bill to potential allies and adversaries may be necessary. Such tactics will allow these individuals a chance to explain their support (or opposition), and give you a chance to convince them to support the bill. This process also may result in changes in the bill as neutral or opposing groups come on board.

Attempt to get support from the governor and official state agencies affected by the bill. For example, a bill affecting who can be placed on probation would likely be of interest to the state bureau of corrections. State agencies are more likely to get bills they support through the legislature. Such agencies' opposition can be fatal to a bill because they are part of the arm of state government designed to administer bills passed by the legislature. Thus, they are considered to be experts on legislation affecting their respective areas of responsibility.

Step 3: Arranging for Sponsorship of the Bill

Finding legislators who are willing to introduce and work for a bill is a crucial step. Supporters who will do nothing to help a bill pass are not useful except to stay out of the way. If you are trying to get a bill passed, involve legislative staff members in discussions about the bill. Frequently, these staff (those who work for the legislator) have the greatest influence with the legislator. Making changes in the bill to gain their support can be especially important. For instance, they may be more likely to support a bill after you have made some compromises honoring their needs and wishes.

Past track records of legislators can be important as guides to how they will vote on any given bill. Have they supported similar bills in the past? Have they made public statements supporting the bill's intent? Or have they been critical of issues the bill addresses?

The "safety" of the legislator's seat also will be a factor. Those reelected by large margins or without opposition are often in stronger positions than legislators worrying that each vote may cost them the next election. Stronger positions may allow legislators to take greater risks. For instance, they may be more likely to support a bill that will require spending money if they believe in the merits of the bill.

Similarly, keeping away from legislative extremists who will never compromise is important. Compromise is the currency of politics. Unwillingness to compromise on a bill is likely to lead to its defeat.

If possible, obtain support of legislators in the majority party. Gaining support from members of both parties (bipartisan support) is even better. Obtain as many sponsors as possible for a bill because it will increase your support and the likelihood that the bill will pass.

Step 4: Introducing the Bill

Ask the legislative sponsors of your bill to introduce it before the legislative session or as early in the session as possible. Doing so leaves more time for lobbying and modifying the bill to satisfy additional supporters. Bills introduced late in a session often do not become law because of time constraints. Lobbying involves seeking "direct access to lawmakers to influence legislation and public policy. The term originated in the tendency of some of these people to frequent the lobbies of legislative houses to meet lawmakers" (Barker, 1999, p. 280).

Step 5: Working with Interest Groups to Broaden Support for the Bill

Every bill has many potential supporters, some of whom never participate in the legislative process. Often, potential supporters simply do not know that a bill has been introduced. Or they may not believe they can have much influence on the bill. Try to get as many potential supporters behind your bill as possible.

Step 6: Educating the Public

Educating the public is often difficult, because frequently bills do not appear to be of interest to many people. One example of public education occurred in a state in which human services licensing was being proposed. Articles appeared in newspapers around the state describing situations where unethical human services professionals continued to practice without licensing. Human services professionals and others sent letters to, and wrote articles for, newspapers stressing the importance of protecting the public from incompetent and unethical professionals. Such articles and letters served to educate the public about the issues and benefits of licensing human services professionals.

Step 7: Influencing Legislative Committee Consideration

All bills introduced in a legislature are referred or assigned to one or more committees prior to being considered by the entire body. Legislatures thrive on committees. Committees are formed of smaller groups of legislators charged with analyzing, refining, and making recommendations about proposed legislation. Committees typically have jurisdiction over matters on a particular topic. So, for example, there may be a committee on agriculture, health, and human services, another on judiciary and consumer affairs, and one on education, and so on. Legislators usually express an interest in serving on a particular committee. Committee appointments are normally made by the leadership of the respective legislative body. Thus, the Speaker of the House or the Senate president will have major influence over who gets on what committee.

In addition, subcommittees are formed within committees to investigate an even more narrowly defined area. For instance, the agriculture, health, and human services committee previously mentioned would probably have separate subcommittees on each of the three areas: agriculture, health, and human services.

Every bill must go through one (or more) committee or subcommittee. Committees can allow a bill to die by not acting on it and also can refuse to pass a bill that the sponsor will not agree to modify. Ultimately, if a bill is to go to the legislative body for a vote, it must have been approved by the respective committee to which it was assigned. Advocates must lobby committee members, ask for public hearings on a bill where a broad range of people can voice their views, and arrange for expert testimony at those hearings. Hearings increase the likelihood that a bill will pass and provide opportunities for further lobbying. They also offer chances to make compromises with opponents that will make the bill more satisfactory to a larger number of people.

Testimony at public hearings should be carefully planned to include who will speak, in what order, and what they will say. People who testify should provide a written copy of any testimony to the committee members before speaking. Not everyone who testifies needs to be an expert on a topic. The purpose of a hearing is to listen to all who wish to speak on the bill under consideration. Thus, both experts and interested parties are welcome to participate. There are a number of suggestions about how testimony should be structured and presented. These suggestions can apply to your own testimony or that of others you are helping to prepare for testimony.

First, the written statement should be able to stand on its own (i.e., it should not need any additional verbal clarification). Additionally, it should be worded so that it is clear, straightforward, and readily understandable by most adults. Jargon should be omitted. The statement should specifically explain why this law is important and what particular benefits it will have. Argue the case on its merits and never preach. Use factual material and cite its source (e.g., census data, specific government studies or publications). Potential on-line sources for information include:

- www.cdfactioncouncil.org
- www.urbaninstitute.org
- fjsrc.urban.org

Using case examples to illustrate the impact of a specific bill is also permissible. However, use humor carefully, because being perceived as a serious professional person is important.

Avoid hostility and focus testimony on the proposed legislation. Be brief, show respect for committee members, and be ready to answer questions, including hostile ones. Finally, when you are finished, thank the committee for the opportunity to speak.

Step 8: Influencing Action on the Floor

Bills may be amended or modified by legislators making motions from the floor. The advocate needs to anticipate this possibility and be ready to compromise in ways that will not destroy the bill. When a bill is on the legislative floor, only legislators can participate in what is done with it.

Outside of the actual legislative floor, you as a supporter can help by contacting uncommitted legislators and communicating your point of view. You can also help by seeking media coverage of the bill. Phone calls can be made to legislators within the 48 hours before voting commences. This time schedule helps ensure the legislator will remember the call when the bill is ready to be voted on.

Keep track of supporters and opponents. Advocates for legislation should contact both those who support a bill and those who oppose it. All who will vote on the bill need to know constituents are supporting it. Lobbying cannot be restricted to those already predisposed to the bill's passage.

Seek media coverage of the bill to reach and interest large numbers of constituents. You should plan to attend and be present for the debate on a bill. Doing so will help you understand any opposition to the bill, and you can then suggest to the legislator or his or her staff amendments or changes that might keep the bill on track. And, when contacting legislators or the media, you must be current regarding all the issues. Being present for the debate will help you in this regard.

You should not be discouraged by the amending process. Amended bills get through the legislature with much greater frequency than those without amendments.

Once a bill has received favorable action in one house of the legislature, the same eight steps are repeated in the other house. Generally, a bill may be introduced in either house first, although some state constitutions require that certain types of bills must originate in one house or the other. One hopes to see the legislative process end with the governor signing the bill into law.

One other aspect of legislative advocacy involves helping good legislators get elected. By "good," we mean people with values similar to our professional values. Helping a candidate win an election is an exhilarating experience. Because political campaigns require so many varied skills, finding a role in a campaign is always possible. Possibilities include campaigning door-to-door; distributing flyers door-to-door (called mail drops) or on campus; telephoning potential voters; soliciting or contributing money; transporting voters to the polls; putting up yard signs; placing a sign on your car; folding, stuffing, and sealing letters; and typing. The value of this work is clear. Elected officials remember who helped them and will be most sensitive to their helpers' views.

InfoTrac College Edition

This chapter was devoted to the topic of advocacy in human services practice. It defined the concept and identified the assumptions associated with its use. A variety of strategies and tactics related to advocacy were discussed, as were different models of advocacy. For additional material on these and related topics, please use the following search terms:

advocacy
advocate
case advocacy
cause advocacy
coercive power
persuasion
whistle-blowing
legislative advocacy

On the Internet

Because of the very dynamic nature of the Web, URLs are subject to change. Therefore, be sure to check out the companion Website for this book at http://www.humanservices.wadsworth.com, where links will be updated periodically.
www.advocacyguru.com
www.protectionandadvocacy.com
www.spanusa.org
www.fcae.nova.edu
www.whistleblower.org
www.healthlaw.org

CHAPTER 15

Brokering and Case Management

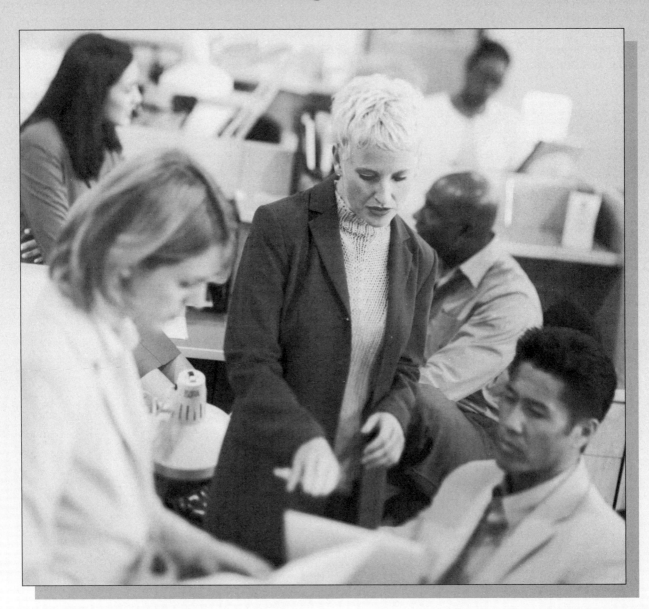

"Margie St. John, please call the E.R." As she heard the hospital loudspeaker page her, Margie tensed slightly. She knew that emergency room pages were always serious. Because she was already on the first floor, Margie walked briskly to the hospital's trauma center. The nurse on duty quickly explained the situation: Mr. C. Benjamin arrived at the trauma center after suffering a heart attack on the interstate highway. Attempts to revive him failed, and the emergency room physician was about to talk to his wife. The Benjamins, both in their late sixties, had apparently been traveling through the state on the way to visit relatives.

Margie accompanied the doctor to the trauma center waiting room where they met Mrs. Benjamin. A petite woman, Mrs. Benjamin looked very weary. The crumpled handkerchief in her hand was damp from tears. The doctor introduced herself and Margie. Margie then sat next to Mrs. Benjamin.

"Is he dead?" Mrs. Benjamin asked quietly. The doctor slowly nodded her head and responded, "Yes, he is."

Mrs. Benjamin put her head in her hands and cried softly for a minute. She raised her head and asked, "What am I going to do now?"

Margie said that she knew this must be a terrible time for Mrs. Benjamin. She offered to do everything she could to help Mrs. Benjamin and invited her to come to the human services office. As the doctor departed, Margie reached out her hand and helped Mrs. Benjamin to her feet. Together they took the elevator to Margie's office.

Margie again expressed her sensitivity to Mrs. Benjamin's situation and asked her if there was anything that she (Margie) could do. Slowly, Mrs. Benjamin described the events of the day that preceded the death of her husband. In a few minutes Margie discovered the following information.

The Benjamins, who were residents of Wisconsin, were traveling through Minnesota to visit relatives in Iowa. They had car trouble about 15 miles from the hospital. When Mr. Benjamin got out to check on the car, he fell to the ground. A passing trucker radioed a nearby highway patrol officer, and together they attempted cardiopulmonary resuscitation. An ambulance arrived shortly and transported Mr. Benjamin to the hospital. The highway patrol officer brought Mrs. Benjamin to the hospital with their pet, a small dog. Mrs. Benjamin said the car was still on the side of the highway and contained a large load of frozen meat in the trunk that was to be a gift to her daughter in Iowa. As they talked, Margie began to make mental notes of the tasks ahead. She also learned some information about Mrs. Benjamin that would prove helpful as they worked together to resolve the woman's concerns. Future tasks included:

1. Mrs. Benjamin needed to notify her daughter and son about the death of her husband.
2. Mrs. Benjamin needed a place to stay for the evening (a place that would allow dogs).
3. The disabled car would have to be towed into town.
4. The frozen meat in the trunk would need to be cared for before it spoiled.
5. Mrs. Benjamin would need to find transportation back to her home.
6. Mrs. Benjamin would need to arrange the funeral and transportation of her husband's body.

Margie also tactfully asked if this situation had created any critical financial problems for Mrs. Benjamin. Did Mrs. Benjamin have enough money to pay for lodging and meals? Could she depend on her daughter and son to be supportive in this time of grief? Did she know anyone in this area of the state?

Which of the problems or tasks could Mrs. Benjamin handle herself, and which would need Margie's intervention? As Margie and Mrs. Benjamin continued talking, the answers to each of these questions became clear. By the end of the day, each problem, in addition to several others, had been resolved.

Introduction

Place yourself in Margie's position. Would you know how to resolve each of these problems? In what order would you tackle them? Would you know what community resources might be appropriate to help Mrs. Benjamin as she copes with this crisis? This example is only a small sample of the many challenges facing a human services professional. The ability to provide service to a client often requires knowing what resources are available. Brokering is the subject of the first portion of this chapter. With reference to brokering, this chapter will:

- define brokering and explain the importance of the brokering role in generalist practice;
- review some of the characteristics of effective brokers and the types of resources with which they must be familiar;
- apply the planned change process to the brokering role.

Case management is the focus of the second portion of the chapter. Case management goes beyond brokering and involves coordinating the provision of a network of services. This chapter will also:

- discuss the concept of case management and relate its usefulness to generalist practice;
- apply the planned change process to case management with special emphasis on the intervention phase;
- review factors influencing the delivery of case management services;
- discuss the effectiveness of case management services.

A Definition of Brokering

Brokering is the linking of client systems to needed resources. Such resources can target a broad range of client needs. Brokering might include helping a client get needed financial, legal, or medical assistance. It might involve helping a client find quality day care for children. Similarly, it might focus on helping to place a family member in a nursing home or a group home for people with developmental disabilities.

By itself, the idea of brokering seems somewhat simple. A client has a particular problem, and the worker tells the client about a resource that matches the client's problem. Sometimes, this is referred to as providing information and referral. The professional provides the client with information about available resources and refers the client to the most appropriate resource. Of course, this explanation is a great oversimplification of what really occurs in generalist human services practice. It is oversimplified for a number of reasons. First, it assumes client needs can be met through existing services and resources. As discussed in earlier chapters, sometimes resources do not exist and must be created. These situations call for other human services roles, including advocacy, a topic discussed in Chapter 14. Second, services may not be accessible or affordable for clients. Third, clients may need more help than simply giving them a name and telephone number suggests.

The Importance of the Brokering Role in Generalist Practice

Sometimes, a human services professional's only role is that of broker. Other times, the broker role is combined with others, depending on client need. For example, in addition to being a broker, the generalist human services professional also might need to be an advocate for clients denied access to existing resources. For instance, a homeless person by definition has no address. An agency policy might require that an address is necessary in order for that person to receive financial aid. A worker might first have to advocate on behalf of the client to change the policy before helping the client to actually receive the resources.

Additionally, the worker may play any of the roles described in previous chapters (e.g., mediator or educator) either simultaneously or sequentially. Most simply, the generalist human services professional plays the broker role by helping clients assess their needs and locating appropriate resources to meet those needs. Once a resource is identified, the worker connects the client to that resource through a referral. Finally, the worker evaluates with the client the effectiveness of the resource in meeting the client's needs. First, we will discuss the importance of being familiar with various types of resources.

The Effective Broker

Becoming effective in the role of broker requires more than simply memorizing the names of available agencies. First, it requires knowledge of agency eligibility criteria (such as income or age limits).

Second, it necessitates familiarity with many different kinds of resource systems (e.g., emergency housing, food pantries, general assistance, Temporary Assistance to Needy Families [TANF]). Third, it requires that the worker develop a network of contact people to whom clients may be referred. In other words, you need to know specifically whom to call. You must also know who can and will give your client the most help.

Maintaining familiarity with eligibility criteria is perhaps the most difficult of the tasks facing the worker, because such criteria are constantly changing. New regulations, legislation, and evolving agency policies and procedures all affect eligibility criteria and complicate the job of the worker.

The Importance of Knowing Resources

A study of social workers in Maryland (Rauch & Tivoli, 1989) found that 52.8 percent did not know where to refer a person with a genetic concern. These types of concerns involve situations in which couples or individuals fear the possibility of some inherited or other genetic defect in future offspring. Over 30 percent of workers did not even know if such a service existed within a 30-mile radius of the agency, and 45 percent did not know if genetic consultation was available to their agencies.

One of the most challenging aspects of beginning your professional life as a human services professional is becoming familiar with the community or area in which you are practicing. Even human services professionals who grew up in a community may not know the myriad of agencies, services, and programs available in that area. The difficulty is compounded if you have just moved and have little knowledge of your new community. New workers often develop their own resource lists that include information on each new agency or service they encounter. However, this method is not very systematic, because the list contains only resources the new worker comes upon in a given period. Later in the chapter we'll discuss more thoroughly this matter of identifying resources.

Eligibility Criteria of Resource Agencies

It is unrealistic to believe that every human services professional is going to become intimately familiar with all criteria for each program, agency, or resource available in a community. A familiarity would require an extraordinary memory for detail. Even if you could remember it all, the information quickly becomes dated as criteria change. However, for you to become familiar with the broad categories of programs and to know generally the types of needs a program addresses is appropriate.

For example, you might refer a family with no food to a free pantry (operated by churches, hospitals, or other groups), the Salvation Army, or the local public assistance agency where the family could qualify for food stamps. Similarly, you might most appropriately refer a battered woman to a domestic violence shelter. In each case, you need to know what types of resources are available and be able to discriminate which clients likely qualify for which programs.

Conversely, you must be capable of determining which resources are inappropriate. For instance, you would not refer a sexual assault victim to a treatment group for sex offenders.

Because eligibility criteria do change, the worker will find remaining knowledgeable about specifics of each program difficult. This problem can be alleviated somewhat by creating a homemade database. The database could be computerized, on alphabetized note cards, or any other system fitting your organizational style. The database should contain information such as types of problems for which referral is appropriate, names of contact persons, addresses and telephone numbers, and notes about eligibility criteria. For example, knowing that a given agency provides assistance only to those having incomes falling below a certain level is helpful. While this level may change periodically, at least you would know there is such a level and have some idea about where the cutoff line has been. Finally, if you have an ongoing system of agency contacts, you can simply call the likely contact person to figure out whether a client fits agency criteria.

Characteristics of Resource Agencies

Besides the criteria used by an agency in determining eligibility, you should be aware of a variety of agency characteristics (Connaway & Gentry, 1988). Such characteristics affect how well services are delivered to your particular client. For example, is this agency extremely formal and rule bound, or does it have a flexible attitude toward solving client problems? What are the goals of the agency and the level of available resources? Does the agency provide assistance with fuel costs in the winter, and, if so, what form does that assistance take? Will the food pantry allow a person to come every week, or are there specified limits regarding the number of weeks food will be made available? How accessible is the building? Are ramps or elevators available to those with disabilities? Are there waiting periods before assistance can be given? Is there a long waiting list for certain kinds of service? What hours is the agency open? Is the service provided only seasonally (e.g., at Christmas time)?

Such information helps the client and worker decide about the appropriateness of a given referral. It also can prevent clients from being referred to an agency that cannot meet their needs. When inappropriate referrals occur, clients may become discouraged and withdraw entirely from the helping process. Besides knowing the broad criteria and characteristics of various agencies, the worker should develop a network of contact persons within each agency. The reasons for this network will be discussed in the next section.

Contact Persons in Resource Agencies

In larger communities, you cannot be expected to learn the names of each person in every agency. We are, however, capable of remembering the names of an extraordinary number of people. A person can easily remember the names of well over 100 people. If you doubt this fact, begin by writing down all the people in your family, nuclear and extended, and add to the list all your friends, people in your class, faculty members, and teachers. Add university staff, doctors, dentists, storekeepers, bartenders, and so on. As you can see, the list gets longer and longer. With the names of agency contact people, the task is easier because you will be listing these people on your database of resource agencies.

When arriving in a new community, spending some time visiting various agencies to become familiar with their programs and staff is helpful. Learning the names of staff who handle intake is especially important, because they may be the first person with whom your client will come in contact. Whenever you phone an agency, make a point of jotting down the names of the people you talked with and their areas of responsibility.

An advantage of having more than one contact person at an agency is that you can give a client alternatives. This information is helpful if the first person is not in when the client contacts the agency. Having alternative contacts increases the likelihood that the client will receive the desired service.

Finally, make a point to become involved in your community. Join a service club, participate in community meetings, sit in on city council meetings, or attend major community events (pancake day, fireman's chicken dinner, Fourth of July celebrations, and so on). These activities will increase your knowledge of community resources and enlarge the circle of people you can call upon in times of need. The smaller the community, the more important it is that you involve yourself in its life.

Types of Resources

The variety of resources in a community is almost limitless. One resource directory for three (mostly rural) Wisconsin counties turned up almost 400 different agencies (Hull & Zastrow, 1988). The challenge is to use the many available sources of information.

Community Resource Directories

Perhaps the most commonly used sources of information about community resources are published directories listing social or human services. These booklets are often put together by information and referral agencies, social service agencies, volunteer groups, or educational institutions. Ideally, the directory should contain both an alphabetical index of agencies and services and a problem-focused index. You should be able to look up not only the agency's name but also the type of problem you need to address. Highlight 15.1 shows a page from a single directory listing legal services, nursing homes, and nursing services. Under each topic is a list of specific agencies providing services that address these needs and the problems involved.

The listing for each agency in a directory should contain certain common items of information, such as:

- name of the organization;
- address and telephone number;
- office hours;
- executive director or contact person;
- services provided;
- eligibility guidelines;
- accessibility to the handicapped;
- geographical boundaries of services;
- source of funds.

Each directory should contain listings for various categories of services. These listings may include sources of emergency food, lodging, or clothing; financial help; and job and employment assistance. The directory should also list marital counseling or therapy; abortion and adoption agencies; services

HIGHLIGHT 15.1

Community Resource Directory Index

The following is an example of a directory used by a community services organization.

Legal Services

Attorney General's Office of Consumer Protection	71
Jefferson County Human Services	
(Domestic Abuse Victims)	136
Legal Action of Wisconsin, Inc.	146
Prairie State Legal Services, Inc.	177
Pro Se, Inc.	179
Rock County Juvenile Probation Dept.	188
Rock County Restitution Project	188
Rock County Victim/Witness Assistance Program	194
Rock Valley Victim Offender Reconciliation Program	197
Search Reports	199
State Public Defender, Office of	207
Stateline Area YWCA Family Shelter	208
Walworth County Child Support Unit	227
Walworth County Family	
Court Commissioner	228
WAVE-Domestic Violence Program	236

Nursing Homes

Beloit Convalescent Center	75
Beverly Terrace Nursing Home	86
Caravilla	93
The Carlyle	94
Cedar Crest, Inc.	95
Countryside Home	109
Credible Care, Inc.	110
Geneva Lake Manor	127
Lakeland Nursing Home of Walworth County	145
Marquardt Memorial Manor	153
Meadow Park Nursing Home	155
Memorial Community Hospital Long Term Facility	158
Sherwood Care Center	202
United Cerebral Palsy of South Central Wisconsin	215
Willowbrook Nursing Home	238
Willowfield of Delevan	238

Nursing Services

Alpha Christian Registry, Inc.	63
Beloit Home Nursing Service	77
Fort Atkinson Memorial Hospital	121
Holton Manor	127
Marquardt Memorial Manor	153
Memorial Community Hospital Home-	
Health Agency	159

Source: Adapted from G. H. Hull and C. Zastrow (1988). *Community Services Directory for Jefferson, Rock and Walworth Counties.* Whitewater: University of Wisconsin–Whitewater, Department of Social Welfare.

---

for categories of people such as the elderly, children, the physically disabled, and the chemically dependent; child care services; correctional services; hospitals; educational and recreational services; and volunteer organizations. Highlight 15.2 shows a sample listing for two such agencies.

Telephone Books

Of course, resource directories are not the only source of information about community services. Most telephone books have listings for a variety of human services. Typically, these listings appear in the Yellow Pages under a range of headings:

- Alcoholism Information and Treatment Centers;
- Associations;
- Attorney Referral Service;
- Career and Vocational Counseling;
- Crisis Intervention Service;
- Drug Abuse and Addiction Information and Treatment;
- Hot Line and Helping Lines;
- Human Service Organizations;
- Marriage, Family, Child, and Individual Counselors;
- Mental Health Services;
- Psychologists;
- Rehabilitation Services;
- Social Service Organizations;
- Human Services Professionals;
- Stress Management Services;
- Suicide Prevention Service.

These listings include not only formal social service agencies but also organizations and associations

HIGHLIGHT 15.2
Resource Directory Listing

Attorney General's Office of Consumer Protection

123 W. Washington Avenue
Room 170
P.O. Box 7856
Madison, WI 54707
(608) 266-1852
(800) 362-8189 (toll free)

MILWAUKEE
819 N. 6th St.
Room 520
(414) 227-4949

Office Hours
Madison: 7:45 A.M.–4:45 P.M.
Milwaukee: 8:00 A.M.–5:00 P.M.

Services
Processes consumer complaints; enforces state consumer fraud laws; may seek injunctions to stop businesses or individuals from engaging in fraud and deception; may order businesses to pay restitution; uses computer data bank to analyze consumer problems; may enjoin public nuisance; provides consumer information/education materials upon request.

Serves
Wisconsin consumers

Accessibility to Handicapped
Office located on mezzanine; reach by stairs and elevators from West Washington Ave. entrance—no stairs from side entrance, Hamilton St.

Area Served
State of Wisconsin

Source of Funds
State tax supported

Beginnings Group Home

502 E. Holmes
P.O. Box 802
Janesville, WI 53547
(608) 756-4900

Office Hours
Twenty-four hours a day, seven days a week

Director
Thomas Miles

Services
Individual and family counseling, crisis counseling, vocation exploration, instructive and corrective experiential living, educational planning, adventure-based recreation (Westbound Program), and behavior modification resident program.

Serves
Status and delinquent youth ages 13 to 17

Accessibility to Handicapped
Yes—ramp

Area Served
Rock County and surrounding counties

Sources of Funds
Rock County Department of Social Services and grants

that may provide assistance for particular kinds of activities or events. Examples include:

- American Red Cross;
- Boy Scouts;
- Camp Fire, Inc.;
- Epilepsy Center;
- Girl Scouts;
- New Concepts for the Handicapped Foundation, Inc.;
- Special Olympics;
- YMCA;
- YWCA.

Information and Referral Services

Consulting established information and referral agencies or services provides another useful source of information about community resources. Public libraries and human services agencies often provide such a resource. One of your first steps as a new worker should be to find out which agency provides information and referral services for your community. Often, a phone call is all you need to locate a particular service or resource.

Service Organizations and Clubs

Communities of every size have service clubs or organizations that offer a variety of resources. Examples of such organizations include:

- American Legion;
- Eagles Club;
- Elks;
- Exchange Club;
- JCs;
- Kiwanis;
- Knights of Columbus;
- League of Women Voters;
- Lions;
- Masonic Lodge;
- Moose;
- Rotary International;
- Shriners;
- United Way;
- Veterans of Foreign Wars (VFW).

The vast majority of these organizations provide specific services to their communities such as money to pay for special projects (e.g., neighborhood parks, equipment for people with disabilities, or medical treatment for specific handicaps). Others provide the labor needed to undertake and complete community projects. The Kiwanis, for example, donate money to help many community causes benefiting individuals, groups, and the community as a whole. Their members also donate hours of work for such projects as community beautification and building projects. The Lions have a particular interest in vision and eye-related problems. The Shriners operate a specialized hospital that treats burn victims.

Unless you know of such groups and understand what each sees as its mission in the community, you might miss an important resource. One human services worker successfully approached two service organizations to fund a year of college for her client. For another client with serious respiratory problems, the same worker successfully approached a local service club and convinced members to donate a much-needed air conditioner.

You can usually request listings of community organizations and service clubs from the local chamber of commerce or from the United Way. Once you receive a listing, you can make a point to learn more about these organizations. As your knowledge of these groups increases, they become yet another important resource for clients.

Internet Resources

The Internet can also provide useful information about resources. For example, locating substance-abuse counselors or treatment facilities by Zip code is now possible (http://www.samhsa.gov). It is also possible to fine-tune one's search to look for providers or services targeted to specific topics such as detoxification or using certain approaches, e.g., methadone. Information is also available on topics of interest to gay and lesbian clients. These include www.gay.com. Many sites have links to other resources including service providers, merchants, and products aimed at the gay and lesbian population.

Other organizations are using the Web to facilitate finding information on service providers and to provide general information. For example, the United Way provides a list of local offices at http://www.unitedway.org. Private foundations and government organizations are providing results of their research as well as sources of data on particular issues. The Annie E. Casey Foundation has important information on advocacy, while the Census Bureau provides data on such topics as education, poverty, and ethnicity.

FreeTranslation.com is a Web site that helps translate text written in a foreign language. Information about the homeless can be accessed at the National Law Center on Homelessness and Poverty (http://www.nlchp.org).

Similarly specialized resources can be located for people with specific disabilities. A list of some of these sites along with on-line addresses is shown in Table 15.1.

Other Informal Natural Resource Systems

As a generalist practitioner, you can use limitless creativity in identifying and brokering resources. Your supervisor and other workers may be additional resources for information. They may know of services or be able to suggest alternatives you have not considered. Even the Internet may be helpful in obtaining data or services. In addition, you may often identify and use informal or natural resource systems. Sometimes, they may ultimately have more importance in the lives of your clients than more formal structured resources. Informal natural resource systems include groups or individuals with which clients are naturally involved (e.g., relatives,

Table 15.1 *On-Line Resources for People with Disabilities*

AccessAbility, Inc.	Company providing products for those with visual disabilities	http://www.4access.com/main_no_frames.htm
Brain Actuated Technologies	Allows hands-free control of computers and other electrical items	http://www.brainfingers.com/cyberlink.htm
Disability Access Symbols	Graphics Art Guild Foundation	http://gag.org/resources-das/index.html
Family Village	Virtual community for persons with cognitive disabilities (formerly called mental retardation), their families, and providers of services and support.	http://www.familyvillage.wisc.edu
National Council on Disability	Independent agency makes recommendations to Congress and the president about issues affecting the disabled.	http://www.ncd.gov
NYC Consortium for Independent Living	Disability resources in New York City	http://www.nycilc.org
Zoom Text®	Screen magnification software	http://www.aisquared.com

friends, neighbors, or clergy). We sometimes refer to such systems as social networks. We will refer to more informal types of resources periodically throughout the rest of the chapter.

The Planned Change Process in Brokering

We have discussed the planned change process in greater depth in earlier chapters. This section will review briefly how that process applies to the role of broker, focusing primarily on the intervention phase.

Identifying and Assessing Client Needs

When clients come to us or are brought to our attention, gaining breadth and depth in understanding their needs is important. As part of the assessment process, we have the obligation to assess the urgency and priority of client needs. Cultural characteristics and group identification also play roles in how clients request and accept help for specific needs. The client's attitude and reaction toward accepting help may be a barrier to providing that help. For example, a Hmong client may be reluctant to accept help because doing so violates cultural expectations that one should rely on family in times of need. Accepting help may also imply that clients cannot manage their own affairs, which is also looked down on within the Hmong culture.

Human services values play a clear role in the identification of need process. For example, the decision about which resource to use is always ultimately the client's. Client self-determination plays an important role in the assessment of needs. The human services professional may believe that certain problems should have greater priority. Still, if the client will not acknowledge those problems or

thinks them less important, there is little the worker can do. As a worker, you can provide your client with alternatives. You can help your client identify the pros and cons of each. However, making the final choice about what to do or accept is your client's right and responsibility.

It is essential that the worker and client be absolutely clear about the client's needs. Without this clarity, evaluating the extent to which the resource system has helped will be impossible. Once the needs are clarified, the worker is in a much better position to identify potential resource systems. Chapter 5 addressed the process of assessing client needs in detail. Thus, this chapter will not elaborate further on the process except to note that assessment is essentially the same in most planned change situations.

Identifying and Assessing Potential Resource Systems

As the client's needs become clearer, the worker as broker begins to consider which of the available resources will be of most assistance in the particular situation. Perhaps there are informal resources the client has overlooked. These sources might include family, friends, coworkers, and others with whom the client has existing relationships. On the other hand, such relationships may be unavailable or inappropriate, and then the worker needs to help the client explore other options. At this point, a community resource directory can be of inestimable value.

As we have discussed, even if such a document is not available, the worker should have his or her own list of resource systems. As the worker, you should know the services provided by various agencies and have a rough knowledge of their eligibility requirements and other pertinent information. For example, you should know if the agency charges a fee for service and if financial help is available. You can share this information with the client, along with any other likely problems or obstacles the client may encounter. If clients are likely to be placed on a waiting list for service, you should alert them to this. Only when clients are knowledgeable about available options can they make informed choices. You are obliged to help clients make decisions based upon the best information available.

Helping the Client Select the Best Resource System

Many clients know little about existing agencies or services. Other clients will have rudimentary information but do not understand certain aspects of the service network. Still other clients will be experienced users of available services. By talking to the client, you can figure out the client's understanding of potential resources. If this understanding is inaccurate, you can help the client develop a more factual perspective. Helping the client make a choice is also your responsibility, which can be done by answering client questions. If appropriate, you can recommend a specific service based on your knowledge of its effectiveness.

While a wealth of options may seem positive, there is a possibility that the multitude of agencies, organizations, and services will only confuse the client. Also, what is clear to the worker may appear unduly complex to clients not accustomed to formal resource systems. Therefore, you need to make certain the client clearly understands what is involved.

Within the broker role there are essentially four alternatives for connecting clients and resource systems (Halley et al., 1998). First, a simple approach is to refer the client to an existing service. This option presumes that the client now has sufficient information about different agencies to make an informed decision.

A second option is to provide the resource yourself. This option is appropriate when the expertise needed is within your capacity as a helper and is sanctioned by your agency.

The third choice comes into play when existing services or resources do not meet the client's needs and the worker must be creative in finding or developing a resource. In this situation, the worker has a couple of options. One involves tapping the potentially most helpful resource, knowing full well that it will probably not solve the entire problem. This

alternative is perhaps the least desirable and should never be chosen without the client understanding that the outcome is likely to be somewhat unsatisfactory.

Another choice is to create a resource. The worker who sought and received assistance from a service club for a client's college tuition pursued this option. No existing service organization provided the kind of financial assistance needed. Nevertheless, the worker targeted an organization whose interests closely matched those of the client. She then convinced the organization's members to stretch their criteria to meet the client's needs. The worker's ingenuity and imaginativeness helped create a resource that had not previously existed.

Frequently, clients have multiple needs requiring the resources of more than one agency or organization. In these situations, the responsibility of the worker is coordination of existing resources. The goal is to oversee the timely and efficient distribution of resources to the client. Because this last option relates to the concept of case management, we will discuss it later in this chapter's section on case management.

Making the Referral

Making an appropriate referral requires more than simply giving a client the name and address of an agency. There are several actions you can take that will enhance the success of the referral. In the interest of client self-determination, offering clients as many resources as possible is better. Sometimes this method is not feasible, because only one agency provides the needed services. When a client makes a decision about a particular agency, you can facilitate the transition by writing out the necessary information about the agency and giving it to the client. These methods can include the agency's name and address, telephone number, names of contact persons, and even a brief description of what to expect. For frequently used agencies, you can prepare this information in advance.

Another valuable technique is to send the new agency a written description or referral outlining the client's needs. Sometimes this information is helpful because clients will not have to repeat all the information they already told you. Meeting with the worker or professional from the other agency to discuss the case and go over any written records may also be appropriate for you.

You can set the actual appointment time for the client before he or she leaves your office. For example, you or the client can call the new resource and establish the appointment time right then and there.

A final possibility is to accompany the client to the new agency. This technique occurs less frequently because it is time consuming. Still, this option makes sense when clients are hesitant to go and no one else is available to accompany them. This step may be particularly important when the client is under great stress or is undergoing a medical procedure, such as an abortion.

How much you do for the client should depend upon the client's ability. Clients suffering from serious mental impairment, for example, are more likely to rely on the worker. A general guideline is not to do things for clients that they can do for themselves. Creating unnecessary dependency in clients is undesirable.

In addition, you should avoid giving clients a falsely positive impression about what the new resource will or can do. Optimism is appropriate, but painting an unrealistic portrait of the helping agency is not (Hepworth et al., 1997). Clients will only become disappointed and disillusioned.

Helping the Client Use Resource Systems

Obviously, part of helping clients use resource systems involves giving them encouragement to do so. For a variety of reasons, clients may be reluctant to approach yet another agency. Many clients find the experience of having to discuss their problems quite traumatic. Verbalizing problems may conjure up images of accepting charity or having failed in a particular role (breadwinner, mother, and so on) or may simply be embarrassing. Other clients will be uncomfortable with anything that suggests accepting "welfare." An example involves an elderly client who feared placement in a nursing home. Her primary worry was that the cost of the nursing home placement would be paid for, in her words, by the "county." For her, this understanding meant she would be going "on welfare," which had a distinctly negative connotation for her. The worker reminded the client that she and her husband had spent their entire working life paying taxes to build roads, maintain schools, provide for needy families, and pay for social service staff. The client had been paying all these years for some services that she was just now getting a chance to use. When put in this context, the client became more comfortable about the impending nursing home placement. She believed she had already paid her fair share.

When clients have to explain their situation to more than one agency, you can help them in several ways. First, you can provide a written referral to the new agency. Or you can explain the basic details to a staff person in the new agency. You can also brief clients about the actual procedures used by the new agency and barriers that they might encounter. As mentioned earlier, clients should be given the names of more than one contact person in case the first person is absent when the client contacts the agency. You can also call clients right before their appointments to see if they have any last-minute concerns or problems. Such calls can act as boosters to encourage clients to keep appointments.

Follow-Up and Evaluation of Resource Systems

The most important measure of the success of a referral is whether or not it met the client's needs. To know the outcome, you must learn the result of the referral. This means either that you contact the client or that you ask the client to call you back after the referral. You can also schedule an appointment with the client following the referral visit. Such appointments can be set before clients visit the new agencies. In this way, you remind clients that you will be following up on the referral, thus providing another form of encouragement. Of course, if you accompany the client to the new agency, follow-up occurs on the spot.

If the client will be having several sessions at the new agency, you could choose to meet the client after each session. This method provides for direct follow-up and may be desirable to reinforce the client's participation. On the other hand, the client whose needs are met by the new agency may not want to continue meeting with you anymore because you are not providing service. Ultimately, respecting the client's rights is important. Following up on referral is part of your responsibility as a professional human services professional to evaluate your practice (Hepworth et al., 1997). You need to know if the client encountered barriers or if the referral itself was inappropriate. Perhaps the services were not available in a timely fashion. Or perhaps the agency did not operate according to your or your client's expectations.

Maybe the agency denied services that the client was entitled to. If so, you may need to assume the role of advocate to help cut through the red tape and bureaucratic subterfuge. Perhaps a higher degree of coordination is necessary if multiple resource systems have been involved. The worker needs this type of information if a realistic evaluation of the referral is to take place.

Workers may discover that a given agency is inadvertently creating problems for clients. Part of the worker's obligation to the client is to provide this knowledge to the agency as a way to help improve the functioning of that resource system.

A referral's success is evaluated according to whether the client's identified needs have been fulfilled. If the client was referred for job training, was the training provided? Was the job the client trained for appropriate? Did the client ultimately get a job in that field? Sometimes, a client satisfaction questionnaire will provide sufficient information to conclude that the referral was successful (Connaway & Gentry, 1988). Chapter 8 described several evaluation tools that can be used to assess goal achievement. Many of these can be employed to evaluate the success of the worker acting in the broker role. Choosing the correct one requires experience and good judgment.

Case Management

The concept of case management is not new to the profession of human services. Case management has existed since the nineteenth century but has received more attention in the past quarter century (NASW, 1992). One reason for this attention is that case management services are now required for specific categories of clients by both federal and state laws and regulations.

What Is Case Management?

Woodside and McClam (1998) and others identify case management as a method of service provision in which a worker assesses the needs of clients and (when appropriate) their families, and then arranges, coordinates, monitors, evaluates, and advocates for a package of multiple services to meet the specific client's needs. In practice, this method means that a practitioner, on behalf of a specific client, coordinates needed services provided by any number of agencies, organizations, or facilities. Moxley (1989) states that "services are said to be coordinated when the principal actors within the helping network are in agreement with one another regarding the client's care, and are moving in the same direction" (p. 12).

For example, take Larry Sensenbrenner, age 32, who suffers both from a chronic mental illness and from kidney disease. He was institutionalized at a state mental hospital at age 19 and is now being returned to his home community. Larry has no living family members and no place to live. He needs regular monitoring to ensure that he takes his prescribed medication. Larry needs a variety of services, including housing in the community, medical and mental health services, employment opportunities, and possibly financial aid. All these services must be coordinated so that they are working toward the same goal: keeping Larry out of an institution and functioning as independently as possible in the community.

Case management is the intervention of choice for clients like Larry who have multiple ongoing needs. The principles of case management have been articulated by Gerhart (1990):

- *Individualization of services.* Services are developed or designed specifically to meet the identified needs of the client.
- *Comprehensiveness of services.* Comprehensive services encompass all areas of the client's life, including housing, recreation, employment, social, financial, medical care, mental health care, and so on. This principle helps ensure that no need will go unfulfilled.
- *Parsimonious services.* The meaning of parsimonious services is that duplication of services will be discouraged and that costs for services will be controlled. Uncoordinated services may result in some needs being met by duplicate agencies, while other needs go unmet.
- *Fostering autonomy.* A major focus of case management is on helping clients become as self-sufficient as possible. It also means providing maximum client self-determination so clients make as many decisions regarding their own care as is possible.
- *Continuity of care.* Continuity of care means that as the client moves through life, requiring inpatient services and help in the community, case management services will ensure continued monitoring of needs. There is an expectation that most of the clients will require assistance throughout their lives, because the conditions that they suffer from are chronic and not subject to quick recovery. Such expectations are especially true in the cases of clients with chronic mental illnesses and those with significant developmental disabilities (p. 216).

Essentially, case management uses the same planned change process described throughout this text. The problems are typically multiple ones and need the interventions of many agencies and organizations. As in any worker–client relationship, the client's active involvement in the helping process is expected. Moreover, the chances are likely that the worker serving as case manager may have to advocate for clients in certain situations. If services or resources that the client is entitled to are not provided, the worker may take necessary steps to correct the problem. Existing resources are used to the maximum extent possible. If services or resources to meet client needs do not exist, the worker has an obligation to work toward the development of such resources.

As you can see, the case manager plays several roles, including broker, advocate, counselor, teacher, community organizer, or planner (Hepworth et al., 1997). Client needs determine the worker's role. Most importantly, however, case managers provide the link between clients and the human services system. Case managers know the comprehensive needs of clients, connect them to appropriate services, and ensure that those services are provided effectively.

This method requires the case manager to encourage clients to use services and to give them the emotional support they need to survive day to day. As might be expected, high-quality case management services involve frequent and intense client–case manager contact.

While case managers play a variety of roles, including that of broker, it is important to underscore that the concepts of broker and case manager are not synonymous. The role of case manager goes well beyond that of broker (see Highlight 15.3). The broker may refer clients to one or more specific services. The case manager has the broader task of ensuring that a wide spectrum of clients' needs are met in an efficient and effective manner. Both brokers and case managers require knowledge of community resources and where such information can be found. Both require good working relationships with service providers and organizations that may be used by clients. Ultimately, the case manager is responsible for coordinating, monitoring, and evaluating the service provided to clients, which are activities beyond the routine duties of a broker (Hepworth et al., 1997).

 HIGHLIGHT 15.3

An Overview of Case Management

1. Definition of Case Management: Human services case management is a method of providing services whereby a human services professional assesses the needs of the client and the client's family, when appropriate, and arranges, coordinates, monitors, evaluates, and advocates for a package of multiple services to meet the specific client's complex needs.

2. Purpose of case management
   a. Promoting the skills and capability of the client in using social services and social supports.
   b. Developing the abilities of social networks and relevant service providers to further the functioning of the client.
   c. Promoting effective and efficient service delivery.

3. Focus of case management: Formulating a client support network that integrates client skill development, involvement of social networks, and involvement of multiple providers.

4. Tasks of case managers
   a. Assessing of client needs, social network capabilities, and abilities of social service providers.
   b. Developing a comprehensive service plan that includes multidisciplinary professional involvement and maximum client involvement.
   c. Intervention directly with client to strengthen skills and capacities for self-care and/or indirectly with systems impinging on client.
   d. Monitoring of service plan implementation and tracking of client status, service delivery, and involvement of social network members.
   e. Evaluation of service plan effectiveness and its impact on client functioning, on social network's capacity to support client, and on the ability of the human services professional to work with client.

In reality, the case manager typically is directly involved in the care of some clients to an extensive degree. Hepworth and colleagues (1997) point out that the case manager has great responsibility for ensuring that the client receives services to meet a variety of needs.

One other important responsibility of the case manager involves integrating the formal support system (agencies and services) with that of the informal support system (e.g., family, friends, and others directly involved with the client). The case manager strives to help the client function independently by facilitating interpersonal relationships (Roberts-DeGennaro, 1987). This may involve negotiations between formal and informal support systems. For example, family members may be reluctant to work with an agency, or they may be unwilling to allow the client the independence needed to function in the community. Perhaps relationships between the client and family members are strained. In either case, the interpersonal problems prevent the client's needs from being met. Describing this dual role, Moore (1990) argues that the case manager is both an enabler and a facilitator whose primary responsibility is to help clients function independently. We will discuss Moore's perspectives in detail in a later section. Finally, Moxley (1989) provides an excellent overview of case management (see Figure 15.1), the steps of which parallel GIM.

The Importance of Case Management for Generalist Practice

Within this country, most states now either require or recommend case management services for certain categories of clients. Moreover, several federal laws have specifically identified case management as a

Figure 15.1 Worker Responsibilities in Case Management

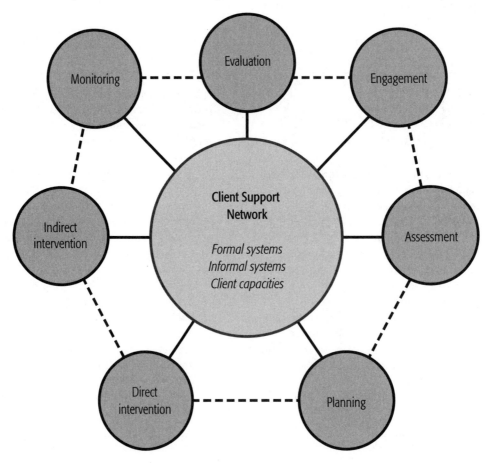

desired form of service to offer clients (Woodside & McClam, 1998). Within the field of human services, case management has been recognized as a major human services function.

Of a sample of 350 major companies, almost all were using case managers to help employees get appropriate rehabilitative care for job-related injuries and to reduce costs of that care (Institute for Rehabilitation and Disability Management and National Center for Social Policy and Practice, 1988). Interest in case management has spread so rapidly in recent years that private case-management firms are now in existence (Kaplan, 1990). They are helping clients receive homemaker services, alternative housing, day care, transportation services, chore services, and in-home meals.

Allen (1990) argues that "more families are likely to be affected by case managers than by treatment providers" (p. 1). The Developmental Disabilities Assistance and Bill of Rights Act (Public Law 95-602) specifically lists case management as a priority service. Case management is being used extensively in the developmental disability field, with those suffering from chronic mental impairment, and in the field of child welfare.

Of particular importance for the human services profession is the fact that case management is an approach consistent with human services' emphasis on the client's rights. Contrary to the implications of the term, the *clients* are not being managed, but the *services* are. Case managers need the skill to intervene with individuals, families, agencies, and the larger community. These same skills are needed by generalist human services professionals regardless of their practice settings (Hepworth et al., 1997). Case managers are currently being used by hospitals and health maintenance organizations.

Several factors are operating to increase the importance of case management for human services professionals, such as:

1. Increased emphasis on maintaining clients in the least restrictive environment;
2. The goal of keeping people out of institutions;
3. The objective of maintaining the elderly in their homes as long as possible;
4. Efforts to reduce or contain costs of providing health and other forms of care to clients;
5. Increased attention to rights of clients who often lack awareness of available resources;
6. Awareness that some clients cannot follow through on the ordinary referral because of their limited capacities (e.g., mental impairment);
7. Increased focus on how the environment contributes to client problems;
8. Decreased focus on the medical model of practice (the medical model tends to view clients' problems as "diseases"; hence, the client should be "cured"), and
9. Expansion of human services programs and increased complexity and fragmentation of services (i.e., greater specialization with no one taking overall responsibility for client service) (Stein, 1981).

Assessment

Assessment is the part of the planned change process where the case manager learns the current and future needs and problems of the client. Because so many clients have long-term needs, future needs have perhaps a higher priority than is true in other areas of human services. The assessment must cover medical, psychological, recreational, social, educational, and vocational areas.

Take, for example, a client who is physically disabled. Here several issues are involved. First, a problem may be caused directly by the disability itself. An example would be absence of mobility caused by paralysis of both legs. Second, a need may have no relationship at all to the disability. A client who lacks clothing or adequate shelter may have had the same problem even without the disability (e.g., if his company laid off many workers who then could not locate other employment).

A third source of problems could be caused by the client's informal support system. For example, a parent's attempts to protect a developmentally disabled young adult may prevent that person from learning skills that would help him to become independent.

Fourth, problems may occur in the formal resource systems designed to help clients. For instance, an agency may refuse to provide a service that the client is entitled to. The agency's policies may be inappropriately applied. Perhaps the person denying the client service dislikes the client or feels he is taking advantage of the agency. There is also a chance that the resource system simply lacks the ability to deliver a specific service. The budget may be inadequate, or maybe a specific resource cannot be located. An example of the latter is an agency that has been unable to hire a bilingual human services professional to serve as an interpreter for the agency's Hispanic clients.

There are obviously a variety of explanations that can exist for a given need discovered in the assessment process. These explanations mean that the assessment must concern itself with at least three areas, as discussed in the following sections.

Assessment of the Client's Ability to Meet Environmental Challenges

Environmental challenges include a client's self-care ability (e.g., to take care of hygiene, dressing, money management, and so on). In this process you need to find out what clients need from their informal and formal resource systems. A need can be anything that you and your client view as necessary for a positive quality of life. The first thing is to determine which needs can be met with little or no outside help. The focus is on the client's strengths and capabilities, not on deficits or shortcomings (Saleeby, 1997). You also need to determine which available services or resources the client can use. In assessment it is important not to make clients excessively dependent upon others nor to assume they can do more for themselves than is really the case. A simple example is a baby-sitter who carried a one-year-old baby all around the house because she just assumed that the child could not walk. She was astounded upon her arrival one evening to find the baby toddling after his parents. Thus, you will assess client skills that need to be maintained and those that will need to be enhanced.

Finding out why the client has sought assistance at this particular time may also be important. Does the request for help coincide with important changes in the client's personal resources (e.g., loss of job, eviction), changes in the client's primary support group (e.g., aging parents), or the recent availability of formal resources (e.g., a newly created program)? As in any assessment, you will want to find out something about the history of the problem as understood by the client or the client's family. For example, is it a problem for which other interventions have failed, or is it something the client is only now willing to admit? Will the client need ongoing service or only in times of stress? Does the client have effective relationships with informal resource systems? What is the client's involvement within formal resource systems?

Finally, as with any assessment, the case manager may have a role in determining if the client is eligible for service. This decision will largely be based on the information gathered above.

A good example of this assessment process is the situation involving Latisha, who is a 35-year-old divorced woman with a long history of schizophrenia (which is a serious form of psychosis characterized by disturbances in thoughts, mood, and behavior). She has been in and out of hospitals over the past ten years, mainly when she has gone off her medication and begun to wander the streets. Each time, she has become stabilized for a period of several months to years but then has quit taking her "crazy pills," as she calls them. She survives financially on a small trust fund left by her deceased parents. She has just been referred to a new community program designed to help people with chronic mental health problems. Noel, a human services professional with the new program, has just received the referral. Over the next several days he will assess Latisha's strengths, challenges, and resources and develop a service plan appropriate for her situation. One of the first things Noel does is to focus on Latisha's ability to meet environmental challenges.

Noel talks with a worker from the referring agency who has worked with Latisha. He also interviews Latisha and her sister and brother-in-law. From this information, Latisha seems to be able to care for herself (such as hygiene, dressing, and so on), and to manage her money when she is on her medication. She also can hold a job, although she has very few skills and no formal training past high school. That medication and support together are usually sufficient to keep Latisha from relapsing is also plain. The absence of either one apparently triggers her downfall. Noel concludes that Latisha has many strengths. She is employable, responds to medication and support for her condition, and can take care of herself in most situations. This step is the first in assessing her ability to meet environmental challenges.

Assessment of the Caretaking Ability of the Client's Informal Support Group

How capable are the client's family and friends to meet identified needs? These needs may include basic items such as food or shelter, or more abstract things such as social or emotional support. You will want to determine both immediate and extended family members and their relationships with the client. Are there others who serve as informal resources for the client? These resources might include friends, coworkers, neighbors, storekeepers, members from the same church or club, and schoolmates (Moxley, 1989). What kinds of assistance can the primary support group give? How do members of the primary support group interact with the client? How well does this resource system interact with formal resource systems?

From Noel's discussions with Latisha and her sister, the constant monitoring of Latisha appears to be hard on the family. While the sister and her husband are willing to have Latisha live with them, they sometimes get overburdened themselves. Latisha can be argumentative, boisterous, and difficult at times. The family feels as though they can never leave her alone for even a few days because they do not know if she will stay on her medication. The caretaker role is taxing both husband and wife. Latisha has no real friends. Her major love in life is bingo, which she plays every Thursday night down at the Hully Gully Church of the Doomed. She has a couple of acquaintances who play bingo the same night.

Noel concludes that the family is a potential resource for caretaking if additional support can be generated externally. The family cannot care for Latisha without outside help.

Assessment of the Resources of Formal Support Systems

The focus here is on the capability of formal resource systems to meet client needs. As we have seen, the formal system may not have the capacity to meet a client's needs (e.g., due to a lack of money). Perhaps, it denies the client services that he or she is otherwise entitled to. This may occur, for instance, because of confusion over eligibility or because of inappropriately applied policies.

As we assess each of these areas, we must focus on the availability, adequacy, appropriateness, acceptability, and accessibility of the resources (Moxley, 1989). The *availability* of a service is simply whether or not it exists. Absent services are not available. Sometimes resources are available to fill a need but remain unused because no one knows they exist (Hepworth et al., 1997). In other instances, a client's needs are not known because the client is isolated or protected by family members or because of the absence of a prior needs assessment.

There is also the possibility that a client has not shared a need with anyone. For persons with disabilities that are not visible to others (e.g., learning disabilities where they are unable to read), keeping their "secret" from all but a handful of friends is not unusual. Some may not share the information with anyone. Often, only an in-depth assessment will disclose the problem.

The *adequacy* and *appropriateness* of a resource system must also be considered. For example, a resource may be inadequate for a client in that it meets only a portion of the person's needs. Despite a resource's inadequacy, it may still be appropriate because at least a portion of the client's needs can be met. Ideally, a resource would be both adequate and appropriate.

In other situations, the *acceptability* of a resource may be low. Maybe the client refuses to accept help from a specific source. Perhaps the client is too proud to ask for help from a particular agency because of past bad experiences or the negative reputation of the agency. Perhaps the client believes there is a stigma in accepting help from the agency. Any of these factors may reduce the acceptability of the resource, even if it meets all the other criteria.

Accessibility of a resource becomes a problem when the client lacks transportation, mobility, or other means to access the resource. Much of the available housing in this country is not accessible to people with physical disabilities because of stairs, narrow doorways, or equipment that cannot be reached by clients in wheelchairs.

Of course, accessibility may be blocked by other factors. Perhaps the client does not have enough money to use the resource. Maybe the client does not qualify for a service because he or she has too much income. A program or service may be inaccessible because a health insurance program will not pay for a needed service. As you can see, many things can block access to a resource.

Assessment also may help us to understand the factors that cause or contribute to a particular problem. Allen (1990) points out that knowing a child is physically abused does not provide sufficient information to allow intervention. Here we know what the problem is but not necessarily what is causing it. Intervention needs to target the cause. Child abuse may be "the result of poor parenting skills, a historical pattern of family violence, stresses on the family because of unemployment, or many other potential factors. If the problem is unemployment, parenting classes will not be the most useful intervention" (p. 2).

The process of gathering information needed for assessment for case management is similar to other assessments. For example, the case manager reviews pertinent records (agency, school, and so on), interviews appropriate people (client, family, friends, and so on), and refers the client to specialists who can provide other kinds of data. This data may include psychological testing, vocational or educational assessment, medical examinations, and similar evaluations. Moxley (1989) summarizes the case management assessment process by noting it as:

1. *Need-based.* This means we focus specifically on client needs.

2. *Holistic/comprehensive.* This means we attempt to assess clients' needs in all areas, instead of just a few. We will concern ourselves with needs covering income, shelter, work, education, physical and mental health, social and other relationships, recreation and leisure time, transportation, legal, and so on.

3. *Interdisciplinary.* This suggests the importance of using the expertise of various disciplines to understand clients' needs. Examples include physicians, human services professionals, psychologists, speech pathologists, occupational therapists, physical therapists, and so on.

4. *Participatory.* The client is fully involved in assessing his or her own needs and maintains maximum self-determination.

5. *A process.* This concerns a simple recognition that assessment is an ongoing, changing, progressive type of interaction.

6. *Systematic.* This ensures that each area of potential need is explored in sufficient depth and breadth.

7. *A product.* When completed, the assessment should be in written form. It should be a product that guides planning and intervention (pp. 29–32, 33–37).

Noel must next assess the formal support system that may be available to help Latisha. His agency provides a clubhouse near the downtown area, where people with conditions similar to hers can interact with friends, relax, watch television, and talk with human services staff. Noel thinks that this program might be helpful to Latisha. It is located on the bus line, so transportation is available. It is also focused on developing friendships and mutual support groups for persons with chronic mental illness. Equally important, the clubhouse has four rooms that are available for temporary lodging for its members. These rooms are used for members when their caregivers need a respite. Noel is aware of the toll that caring for a person with chronic mental illness can exact on a family. Perhaps if the family can periodically take vacations or just get away from their

responsibilities for a while, they can carry their burden longer. Noel also knows that having Latisha visit the clubhouse daily will bring her into contact with others struggling with their own illnesses (and taking their medication each day). Seeing them maintain themselves may have something of a modeling effect on her. The primary challenge is to determine if Latisha is interested in receiving service from the clubhouse program.

Table 15.2 provides an overview of case management assessment that emphasizes two perspectives. The first is a focus on identification of client needs. The second involves the assessment of the capacities of the client (self-care), informal support systems (mutual care), and formal support systems (professional care). It also contains a brief description of the assessment process (Moxley, 1989).

In summary, the assessment process in case management and that described in Chapter 5 are essentially identical. Each must consider the capacities of client, clients' informal support systems, and formal support systems.

Planning

Planning in case management is a process of finding and securing needed services. These services may include those required for assessment of the client situation, planning, or implementation (intervention). The services used should match client needs to the greatest extent possible. The case manager is responsible for monitoring and evaluating the adequacy of services. The client must be involved to the maximum degree possible in the planning process and is always free to reject a given service.

Service Plans

In planning, the case manager creates a service plan that incorporates six dimensions:

1. Client needs are prioritized.
2. Goals and objectives of service are established.
3. Resource systems that will be involved are identified.
4. Time frames are identified within which services will be delivered and goals achieved.
5. Outcome measures are formulated that will be used to evaluate achievement of case plans.
6. Specific tasks are assigned to individuals and groups so that it's clear who is responsible for what.

Table 15.2   *The Structure of Case Management*

Characteristic of Assessment: Organizing Concepts	Identification of Client Needs: Unmet Needs	Assessment of Self-Care: Client Functioning	Assessment of Mutual Care: Social Network, Social Support	Assessment of Professional Care: Formal Human Services
Basic units of assessment	Income	Physical functioning	Social network structure	Resource inventory
	Housing/shelter	Cognitive functioning	Social network interaction	Availability
	Employment/ vocational training	Emotional functioning	Emotional support	Adequacy
	Health Mental health Social/Interpersonal Recreational/leisure Activities of daily living Transportation Legal Education	Behavioral functional	Instrumental support Material support	Appropriateness Acceptability Accessibility
Process of assessment	Review with client, others, and professionals the needs of client in key areas of daily living	Match needs with client functional areas to assess whether he can fulfill his own needs	Match needs with mutual care resources to assess whether social network can fulfill client needs.	Match needs with professional care resources to assess whether formal service can fulfill client needs.

Impact Goals

Planning in case management often involves setting impact goals. Impact goals include goals that result in changing some major aspects of the client's life and are the expected results of our intervention. One such goal might involve resolving the transportation needs of a young man who uses a wheelchair. Arranging for the acquisition of a vehicle that would accommodate the client's chair would be an impact goal with major consequences for several areas of the client's life. For example, it would provide transportation to work, give increased access to other community resources, and improve recreational opportunities. Another example would be providing for in-home medical care for a client, which would enable the client to remain at home rather than being placed in a nursing home.

Service Objectives

Service objectives should be differentiated from impact goals. They describe steps that must be undertaken to achieve an impact goal. For example, let us assume you have a client who lives in a home that is not accessible to someone in a wheelchair. The client is suffering from a condition that restricts her to a wheelchair indefinitely. Service objectives might include identifying the physical and structural changes needed in the client's house to make it accessible to her and locating a carpenter to make the changes (Moxley, 1989). Making the home accessible is the impact goal, and service objectives help achieve the impact goal.

Noel's service plan for Latisha is shown in Figure 15.2. Because of the importance of client involvement in the assessment and planning process, Latisha must sign off on the service plan. As you can see, his service plan has both impact goals and service objectives and indicates who will do what by when. It does not show the dates of accomplishment yet. These will be entered along with any notes as the case service plan progresses.

Another slightly different type of case plan is shown in Table 15.3. It describes the impact goal (expected results) and details what the intervention plan will be. It also shows who will do what and sets a date when the impact goal is to be achieved. The interventions described here are essentially a list of service objectives (e.g., apply for Medicaid, undergo eye exam). The plan is developed in cooperation with the client or the client's family, if the client is a child. As you can see, the case manager must have substantial familiarity with available formal resource systems and a working relationship with many different professionals. Following completion of the service plan, the implementation phase begins.

Figure 15.2   *Case Management Plan*

Client: Latisha Denver   Case manager: Noel Valtierra

Impact goal: Develop supportive services designed to maintain Ms. Denver's stability
Priority: #1

Service Objectives	Responsibility	Target Date	Actual Date of Accomplishment	Notes
Latisha visits downtown clubhouse	Noel/Latisha	3-13-04		
Latisha participates in weekly activities at clubhouse	Latisha	4-01-04		
Latisha uses clubhouse as temporary lodging while sister's family is on respite	Latisha	As needed		
Latisha's sister's family notifies Noel when respite is needed	Sister	As needed		
Explore having other clubhouse members attend bingo with Latisha	Noel	4-15-04		

Client's signature _____ Date: _____

Case manager's signature _____ Date: _____

Table 15.3   *A Completed Service Plan*

Problem	Expected Results	Intervention/Strategy	Timeline
1	Child has appropriate day care.	Client will go to Craven County Child Development Center. Parent will first visit center and make application. Center will provide structured program to enhance developmental skills of client.	9-27-04
2	Family receives food stamps until they are employed and can afford adequate food.	Speak with food stamp worker about emergency stamps. Establish an appointment.	5-20-04
2	The client's parents are employed.	Refer parents to job service. Give job suggestions to parents.	5-20-04
2	Client has medical coverage.	Check eligibility requirements for Medicaid. Refer family to make application with Medicaid. Client will be eligible since spend-down was met in March 1992.	5-30-04
3	Family knows if child has normal vision in both eyes.	Client will visit Dr. Jones for an eye exam.	5-30-04

Implementation

The implementation phase can be regarded as having two parts. One concerns the direct services provided by the case manager. The other involves indirect services provided by other resource systems. Some argue that the case manager should not provide direct services but simply arrange for others to do so. They reason that the time and effort needed to provide direct service may detract from more needed indirect service facilitation. Still, most writers agree that the case manager will provide some direct services to clients.

Direct Services

The case manager may be called upon to provide several direct services to clients. Although these services may not involve counseling or therapy, they will still be important to clients. Direct services may include crisis intervention (e.g., locating temporary housing for desperate, homeless people), supporting clients making difficult decisions, helping to modify clients' environments (e.g., arranging for transportation within the community), and helping clients overcome emotional reactions to their crisis situations (Moxley, 1989).

Other case managers may serve in the role of teacher. For instance, they might instruct clients in money management or personal hygiene. Sometimes, case managers share professional knowledge and judgment with a client or provide important information to clients trying to make decisions. Clients may need to be taught important job-seeking skills before gaining employment. Some teaching techniques available to human services professionals were described in Chapter 12.

Sometimes, case managers will need to motivate clients, especially when clients have experienced past failures in attempting to make positive changes in themselves or when they have experienced disappointments in getting the resources they needed. Simple discouragement can make clients doubt that anything could ever possibly be different. Frequently, you will need to continue motivating the client throughout the assessment and planning processes (Allen, 1990). Gerhart (1990) provides some excellent suggestions for motivating clients that appear in Highlight 15.4.

HIGHLIGHT 15.4

Motivating Techniques

The following eight techniques can be used to motivate disgusted, disheartened, or discouraged clients:

1. Begin by asking about the plans a client has for her- or himself. These might include completing school, learning a trade, living independently, getting along better with family members, or establishing an intimate relationship.
2. Contribute realistic suggestions aimed at enhancing the client's life and forestalling relapses. For example, tell the client exactly what to expect when approaching a new agency for help. Suggest ways the client might respond to a negative decision by the agency.
3. Discuss points of disagreement between worker and client and work out realistic compromises. For instance, identify options that satisfy both you and the client.
4. Develop a contract with the client specifying mutual goals.
5. Identify the steps that must be taken and the service providers that can help the client to reach agreed goals.
6. Provide the client with data about service providers. Such information might include eligibility requirements, location, transportation, the nature of services, or the length of service.
7. Discuss any of the obstacles the client can foresee in using the proposed services. For example, suggest the client bring certain forms of identification along when applying for a specific service, which might eliminate typical delays in qualifying for assistance.
8. Review what the responsibilities of each party will be in completing the linkage with a particular service provider. For instance, ask the client if he or she understands what you, as the case manager, will do and what the client is responsible for doing (Gerhart, 1990, p. 213).

Workers also will have to support clients through periods of change and help them survive and prosper in their environment. One way of providing this support is to give clients useful information. Another is to praise client changes and growth. As a case manager, you will be working both to help the client change and to assist informal networks in aiding the client. Clients will encounter multiple service and aid programs that are confusing and complex. Eligibility criteria may be unintelligible. Regulations may appear arbitrary. The worker will be providing direct service by helping clients negotiate formal resource systems.

Indirect Services

Indirect services provided by the case manager are largely limited to two roles. The first involves linking clients with needed resource systems. These systems may be formal in that they are existing social agencies. However, they also may include mutual care systems, such as associates from various sectors of the client's life (school, church, work). Self-help groups such as Alcoholics Anonymous, Parents Anonymous, Parents Without Partners, and the National Alliance for the Mentally Ill can also be used to provide mutual care services.

Perhaps, contacting other service-providing agencies either in person or in writing will be necessary for the case manager. In such instances, the advantage of knowing staff members in other agencies is critical. Johnson (1992) emphasizes how important respecting and valuing the contributions of the other caregivers is for case managers. Whether the needed care is given by you or some other resource system, remember that the ultimate goal is to help clients help themselves.

A second indirect service role involves advocating with various systems on behalf of clients. Much of a case manager's indirect service addresses this latter task. Changing the system to help the client is more difficult than asking the client to change. The case manager may have to develop new resources (often in collaboration with others) or improve access to existing resources. Sometimes such actions mean advocating and intervening with clients' informal resource systems (family and friends). Other times the worker must coordinate services so that clients get only those they need. Technical assistance and consultation to resource systems may be required as they attempt to deliver needed services to the client (Moxley, 1989). As needed, the case manager meets with the client and agency representatives to facilitate referrals and

service provision. Meetings also may be held to negotiate problems that exist between the informal system (e.g., family, friends) and formal resource systems.

As in other areas of generalist human services practice, the case manager's responsibilities and activities are determined largely by clients' needs. Those needs change over time and require the case manager to provide an ever-changing pattern of direct and indirect service. As the client becomes more involved with existing resource systems (formal and informal), the worker's role shifts to the next phase of the process, monitoring.

Monitoring

Monitoring is one of the primary tasks during the implementation phase. During the monitoring process, the case manager continues to communicate with service providers. This process involves two tasks. The first concerns determining if the service plan is being completed. The second focuses on whether or not the original goals are being accomplished.

During the monitoring stage, rewriting the case plan may be necessary. The case manager maintains necessary records and documentation. Managers look for gaps in service and fill them. If clients fail to appear for scheduled appointments, the case manager follows up to see what happened. If the client is receiving medication, the case manager will help assess whether the client is under- or overmedicated. If expected outcomes are not being achieved, the case manager will use assessment skills to figure out the cause (Allen, 1990). Are new needs emerging? Is the original process being followed, or have changes occurred? What can be done to improve service delivery and effectiveness?

Case managers continue to advocate for the client when the need arises. A case manager also serves as the contact person for the case. Thus, the manager represents the client to resource systems (both formal and informal) and represents those agencies and people in contact with the client. Monitoring also helps ensure that clients do not use the system inappropriately. For instance, a client might receive duplicate services or similar benefits from two or more resource systems. Appropriate coordination of services usually can prevent such problems from happening. The monitoring function occurs through the use of formal communications, formal and informal meetings, phone contacts, case recording, and formal evaluation devices (e.g., instruments, test results). The primary focus is on how services are provided. Though there is heed paid to the outcomes attained, primary attention to this matter occurs in the evaluation phase.

Additional Roles

The nature of case management is such that the worker provides a vast variety of services or roles. The absence of natural support systems (families, friends) may put the worker in a position of having to help the client develop such a resource. Other clients may infrequently use available services. Thus, the case manager may engage in outreach, namely, reaching out to potential clients who need and qualify for the service. This task might include public education about the availability of a service and what the referral process involves. It may also involve advocating with an agency to provide services in a different location or during different time frames to fit potential clients not previously served.

Evaluation in Case Management

The importance of evaluating the outcomes of case management services is critical. While some studies show that case management is cost-effective (i.e., receiving adequate or better services for the amount they cost), others do not (Kaplan, 1990). There is clearly more research needed to assess the effectiveness of case management.

As we have discussed, some evaluation occurs during the implementation phase. There we were concerned with whether or not the original case management plan and goals remained appropriate.

During the evaluation phase, we want to determine if impact goals have been achieved. Perhaps the first task is to decide how data will be collected. Do we use existing case records? Or are external assessments of the client's progress necessary, such as your own observations or calls to other agencies?

Another thing we need to do is look carefully at outcomes. Did the client get and keep a job? Has the major health problem that brought the client to our attention been alleviated? Does the client have a reliable form of transportation, thus allowing participation in the sheltered workshop program? Is the client taking the medication as prescribed? Has the client quit talking to walls and doors? Is the home now fully accessible to a person in a wheelchair?

Achievement of many of these goals can be easily assessed because the case manager, significant others, and the client can simply observe results. Other goals are not as observable and require more subjective judgments.

Sometimes we want to know if the case management services themselves were helpful. If they were helpful, in what ways? What was the impact of service delivery upon the client? Was the client satisfied with the service? Depending upon the ability of the client, client satisfaction questionnaires and surveys might be used. Similar instruments might be created to gather impressions from others involved with the case (e.g., family, friends, or formal resource systems).

Other targets of evaluation include the resource systems that served the client. Can these networks provide continued service to the client? Will they need to be augmented (increased or improved) in some way? Were there problems that have been overcome? What barriers remain?

These evaluations require more subjective judgments and are less easily measured. Yet they remain important questions. The answers may determine the continued effectiveness of the helping agencies to many other clients.

Termination in Case Management

Discussing terminating case management services is more difficult than other short-term interventions. Many clients receiving case management services have chronic, debilitating conditions. Some case management services continue throughout the client's life. In these situations, the only terminations will occur when the worker leaves or the client dies or moves away. When any of these situations happen, the termination issues described in Chapter 8 remain relevant. When case management services end, closure with both the individual or family and with those resource systems that have provided service are involved. As with any termination, the worker, client, and any others involved will experience a variety of potential feelings that must be dealt with. In addition, the client may need further referral to new and different services. The case example in Highlight 15.5 illustrates many of the steps and activities common to case management practice.

Factors Influencing Case Management Service Delivery

The amount of research on the effectiveness of case management is relatively limited. However, there is some evidence that smaller caseloads influence service delivery. When caseloads become too large, the managers have time to respond only to crises. Similarly, there is a corresponding deterioration in

HIGHLIGHT 15.5

Case Management for a Client Who Has Mental Disabilities

The police brought Oliver to the county crisis unit after he had caused a disturbance in a bank. The Crisis Unit staff had often seen Oliver before. Fifty-six years old, with organic brain syndrome caused by paresis, syphilis, and chronic alcoholism, he had been deteriorating mentally for the last several years. Because he was incoherent and threatening, he was placed in the inpatient unit at Marin General Hospital.

Henja got involved in the case after hospital staff decided that Oliver's crisis had passed. They determined, however, that he needed long-term treatment in a skilled psychiatric nursing facility. But no local facility would accept him for a variety of reasons, including the fact that they had no vacancies, they lacked the proper security, and the patient was dangerous or unmanageable. Henja was asked to find a psychiatric nursing facility in a neighboring county.

She did so, but the process was not simple. The work included:

- consulting with Marin General Hospital's inpatient staff, the patient's family, and the Transitional Services staff;
- reviewing Oliver's medical, psychiatric, and social history;
- clarifying his legal status;
- interviewing him to assess his current mental status and potential for violence;
- arranging funding through supplemental security income and MediCal, the state's medical benefit plan (similar to other states' Medicaid);
- presenting the information, including the potential for violence, to the facility's intake worker and convincing the facility to accept Oliver;
- asking MediCal to authorize treatment; and
- arranging transportation to the facility.

The case was not over, though. Oliver got worse. He started assaulting other patients and injured a staff member. Henja got a telephone call: Take Oliver away from here. When he returned to the Crisis Unit, a treatment conference determined that he needed to go to Napa State Hospital. But the hospital would not accept him. The director of admissions argued that the hospital was short of beds and that Oliver's prognosis was so poor that he would never be discharged.

Henja got on the phone and, at the request of a county mental health supervisor, she spoke to the director at Napa. Because Henja is a state employee who had worked at the hospital and knows the staff, she was in a position to influence the situation. "I worked out an agreement with the director," she recalls. "If he would assure me that the hospital would evaluate Oliver's condition and develop a treatment plan for him, I would promise to place him in a county facility as soon as he was ready."

Henja kept in weekly contact with Oliver and the hospital treatment team. Fortunately, Oliver responded to the lithium and therapy that were prescribed and became generally friendly and cooperative. But he retained symptoms of his organic brain syndrome and refused to acknowledge either his illness or his alcoholism. His plans for the future, he said, were to go back to work, continue drinking, and keep "fooling around with the ladies." Over four months, Henja and the hospital team developed a plan that would allow Oliver to be transferred to a locked skilled nursing facility, where he could continue treatment but also get passes out. With Henja's considerable trepidation, the transfer took place. Because Oliver has continued on lithium and has stopped drinking, the placement has worked well, and Oliver may soon be transferred to a less restrictive facility. In getting Oliver out of the state hospital, Henja kept her promise to the admissions director (Gibelman, 1982).

the case manager's relationship with clients (Moxley, 1990). Caseloads over about 30 begin to reduce the effectiveness and quality of services provided by case managers (Rubin, 1992).

Another factor influencing service delivery is the extent to which the case manager's responsibilities are clearly delineated. Typically, case managers with vaguely defined responsibilities end up largely providing direct service to the client instead of focusing on the diversity of services needed (Rubin, 1992).

The quality of supervision that supervisors provide to case managers has a bearing on the manager's performance. Rubin (1992) notes that supervisors could be an important source of support for case managers.

However, many supervisors do not know exactly what the case managers are doing. This lack of knowledge reduces the effectiveness of the supervisor as a source of support.

Stress and burnout of case managers are also factors influencing service to clients. The relatively high demands on individual case managers have prompted suggestions that the burnout might be prevented by assigning a team of workers to serve as case managers for specific clients. Presumably, the team would share responsibility for the client's well-being, reducing the burden on any single case manager.

Finally, Wolk, Sullivan, and Hartmann (1994) note that more effective case managers need to be aware of the

> . . . scope and nature of their work and at the same time need to be sensitive to their own interpersonal skills. Case managers interact with a diverse group of people who will be providing or expecting information, creating or solving problems, and obstructing or facilitating decision making. The case managers who attend to their conscious use of self in the performance of requisite managerial roles will be the managers who are the most effective in goal attainment with their clients. (p. 158)

InfoTrac College Edition

This chapter was devoted to the topics of brokering and case management. Both concepts were defined and described, and the characteristics of effective brokering and case management were discussed. To locate more information on these and similar topics, please use the following search terms:

resource systems
referrals
case management
case manager
support groups

On the Internet

Because of the very dynamic nature of the Web, URLs are subject to change. Therefore, be sure to check out the companion Website for this book at http://www.humanservices.wadsworth.com, where links will be updated periodically.
www.gaycenter.org
www.volunteermatch.org
www.cirs.org
www.singlemomz.com
www.confidentkids.com
www.al-anon.alateen.org

Bibliography

Abramovitz, M. (1997). Temporary assistance to needy families. In *Encyclopedia of social work supplement* (pp. 311–330). Washington, DC: NASW Press.

Abramson, J. (1982). The autonomy–paternalism dilemma in social work. *Social work, 27*(5), 422–427.

Abramson, J. (1988). Participation of elderly patients in discharge planning: Is self-determination a reality? *Social work, 33*(5), 443–448.

Abramson, M. (1990). Keeping secrets: Social workers and AIDS. *Social work, 35* (2), 169–173.

Aguilar, D. C., & Messick, J. M. (1974). *Crisis intervention: Theory and methodology* (2nd ed.). St. Louis, MO: C. V. Mosby.

Ahearn, F. L., Jr. (1995). Displaced people. In *Encyclopedia of social work* (19th ed., vol. 1, pp. 771–780). Washington, DC: NASW Press.

Alberti, R. E., & Emmons, M. L. (1975). *Stand up, speak out, talk back!* New York: Pocket Books.

Alberti, R. E., & Emmons, M. L. (1995). *Stand up, speak out, talk back!* New York: Pocket Books.

A. A. World Services, Inc. (1988). *A message to teenagers . . . How to tell when drinking is becoming a problem.* New York: Author.

Allen, J. A. (1995). African Americans: Caribbean. *Encyclopedia of social work* (19th ed., vol. 1, pp. 121–129). Washington, DC: NASW Press.

Allen, M. (1990). *Why are we talking about case management again? The prevention report.* Oakdale, IA: National Resource Center on Family Based Services.

Allgeier, E., & Allgeier, A. R. (2000). *Sexual interactions* (5th ed.). Boston: Houghton Mifflin.

Alter, C., & Evens, W. (1990). *Evaluating your practice.* New York: Springer.

Ambrosino, R., Heffernan, J., Shuttlesworth, G., & Ambrosino, R. (2001). *Social work and social welfare.* Pacific Grove, CA: Brooks/Cole.

American Association of Sex Educators, Counselors, and Therapists. (1994, November). Studies in short. *Contemporary sexuality, 28,* 10–11.

AASECT (2000, April). Quick hits: Sex in the news. *Contemporary sexuality, 34*(4), 6–9.

American Psychiatric Association (1994). *Diagnostic and statistical manual of mental disorders* (4th ed.). Washington, DC: Author.

American Psychiatric Association (2000). *Diagnostic and statistical manual of mental disorders* (4th ed., text revision). Washington, DC: Author.

A.A.A. Wisconsin Division Safety Department (n.d.). *Who has a problem?* Madison, WI: Author.

Amott, T., & Matthaei, J. (2001). The transformation of women's wage work. In G. Kirk & M. Okazawa-Rey (Eds.), *Women's lives: Multicultural perspectives* (2nd ed.). Mountain View, CA: Mayfield.

Anderson, S. C. (1987). Alcohol use and abuse. In A. Minihan (Ed.), *Encyclopedia of social work* (18th ed., vol. 1, pp. 132–192). Silver Spring, MD: National Association of Social Workers.

Anderson, S. C. (1995). Alcohol abuse. In *Encyclopedia of social work* (19th ed., vol. 1, pp. 203–215). Washington, DC: NASW Press.

Apgar, K., & Callahan, B. N. (1980). *Four one-day workshops.* Boston: Resource Communications, Inc.

Arredondo, P., Topper, R., Brown, S., Jones, J., Locke, D. C., Sanchez, J., & Stadler, H. (1996). *Operationalization of the multicultural counseling competencies.* Washington, DC: Association for Multicultural Counseling and Development.

Asch, A., & Mudrick, N. R. (1995). Disability. In *Encyclopedia of social work* (19th ed., vol. 1, pp. 752–761). Washington, DC: NASW Press.

Austin, C. D. (1995). Adult protective services. *In Encyclopedia of social work* (19th ed., vol. 1, pp. 89–95). Washington, DC: NASW Press.

Baer, B. L. (1979). Developing a new curriculum for social work education. In F. Clark and M. Arkava (Eds.), *The pursuit of competence in social work.* (pp. 96–109). San Francisco: Jossey-Bass.

Bailey, J. M., Bobrow, D., Wolfe, M., & Mikach, S. (1995). Sexual orientation of adult sons of gay fathers. *Developmental Psychology, 31,* 124–129.

Balgopal, P. R. (1995). Asian Americans: Overview. In *Encyclopedia of social work* (19th ed., vol. 1, pp. 231–238). Washington, DC: NASW Press.

Bandler, R., Grinder, J., & Satir, V. (1976). *Changing with families.* Palo Alto, CA: Science and Behavior Books.

Bandura, A. (1986). *Social foundations of thought and action: A social cognitive theory.* Englewood Cliffs, NJ: Prentice-Hall.

Barker, R. L. (1995). *The social work dictionary* (3rd ed.). Washington, DC: NASW Press.

Barker, R. L. (1999). *The social work dictionary* (4th ed.) Washington, DC: NASW Press.

Baruth, L., & Manning, M. (1991). *Multicultural counseling and psychotherapy.* New York: Merrill.

Bauman, R., Kasper, C., & Alford, J. (1984). The child sex abusers. *Corrective and social psychiatry, 30,* 76–81.

Beck, A. (1991). *The Beck depression inventory manual.* San Antonio, TX: Psychological Corp.

Beeler, N. G., Rycus, J. S., & Hughes, R. C. (1990). *The effects of abuse and neglect on child development: A training curriculum.* Washington, DC: Child Welfare League of America, Inc.

Behavioral interviewing with couples [videorecording]/ produced by Behavioral Images with Research Press; directed and written by Phil Stockton and John Gottman. Champaign, IL: Research Press, c. 1976.

Bellak, D. (1984). *Comparable worth: Issue for the '80s,* a consultation for the U.S. Commission on Civil Rights, June 6–7.

Bellos, N. S., & Ruffolo, M. C. (1995). Aging: Services. In *Encyclopedia of social work* (19th ed., vol. 1, pp. 165–173). Washington, DC: NASW Press.

Benjamin, A. (1981). *The helping interview.* Boston, MA: Houghton Mifflin.

Bennett, L. W. (1995). Substance abuse and the domestic assault of women. *Social work, 40*(6), 760–771.

Berg, I. K. (1994). *Family based services: A solution-focused approach.* New York: Norton.

Berger, R. M., & Kelly, J. J. (1995). Gay men overview. In *Encyclopedia of social work* (19th ed., vol. 2, pp. 1064–1075). Washington, DC: NASW Press.

Berliner, L. (1995). Child sexual abuse: Direct practice. In *Encyclopedia of social work* (19th ed., vol. 1, pp. 408–417). Washington, DC: NASW Press.

Berliner, L., & Elliott, D. M. (1996). Sexual abuse of children. In J. Briere, L. Berliner, J. Bulkley, C. Jenny, & T. Reid (Eds.). *The APSAC handbook on child maltreatment* (pp. 51–71). Thousand Oaks, CA: Sage.

Bernal, G., Martinez, A. C., Santtisteban, D., Bernal, M. E., & Olmedo, E. E. (1983). Hispanic mental health curriculum for psychology. In J. C. Chunn, P. J. Dunston, & R. Ross-Sheriff (Eds.), *Mental health and people of color* (pp. 65–96). Washington, DC: Howard University Press.

Bertcher, H. J., & Maple, F. (1974). Elements and issues in group composition. In P. Glasser, R. Sarri, & R. Vinter (Eds.), *Individual change through small groups* (pp. 186–208). New York: Free Press.

Berzon, B. (1978). Sharing your lesbian identity with your children. In G. Vida (Ed.), *Our right to love: A lesbian resource book.* Englewood Cliffs, NJ: Prentice-Hall.

Biegel, D. E., Shore, B. K., & Gordon, E. (1984). *Guiding support networks for the elderly: Theory and applications.* Beverly Hills, CA: Sage.

Bisno, H. (1988). *Managing conflict.* Newbury Park, CA: Sage.

Bloom, L. Z., Coburn, K., & Perlman, J. (1976). *The new assertive woman.* New York: Dell.

Bloom, M., Fischer, J., & Orme, J. G. (1995). *Evaluating practice: Guidelines for the accountable professional.* Boston: Allyn & Bacon.

Bolton, F. G., & MacEachron, A. E. (1988). Adolescent male sexuality: A developmental perspective. *Journal of Adolescent Research, 3,* 259–273.

Brandwein, R. A. (1987). Women in macro practice. In *Encyclopedia of social work* (18th ed., vol. 2, pp. 881–892). Silver Spring, MD: National Association of Social Workers.

Brassard, M., Germain, R., & Hart, S. (1987). *Psychological maltreatment of children and youth.* Elmsford, NY: Pergamon.

Brennan, J. W. (1995). A short-term psychoeducational multiple-family group for bipolar patients and their families. *Social work, 40*(6), 737–743.

Briar, S. (1967). *The current crisis in social casework in social work practice.* New York: Columbia University Press, pp. 19–33.

Brill, N. I. (1990). *Working with People.* New York: Longman.

Brill, N. I. (1998). *Working with people: The helping process* (6th ed.). White Plains, NY: Longman.

Brissett-Chapman, S. (1995). Child abuse and neglect: Direct practice. In *Encyclopedia of social work* (19th ed., vol. 1, pp. 353–366). Washington, DC: NASW Press.

Brock, G. W. & Barnard, C. P. (1999). *Procedures in marriage and family therapy* (3rd ed.) Boston: Allyn and Bacon.

Brown, L. N. (1991). *Groups for growth and change.* New York: Longman.

Bryson, R. B., Bryson, J. B., Licht, M. H., & Licht, B. G. (1976). The professional pair: Husband and wife psychologists. *American psychologist, 31,* 10–16.

Bureau of Indian Affairs (2000). Indian entities recognized and eligible to receive services from the United States Bureau of Indian Affairs. *Federal register, 65*(49), 13298–13303.

Burgess, A. W., & Holmstrom, L. L. (1974). *Rape: Victims of crisis.* Bowie, MD: Robert J. Brady.

Burstow, B. (1992). *Radical feminist therapy: Working in the context of violence.* Newbury Park, CA: Sage.

Burt, M. R. (1992). *Over the edge: The growth of homelessness in the 1980s.* Washington, DC: Urban Institute.

Byington, D. B. (1995). Sexual assault. In *Encyclopedia of social work* (19th ed., vol. 3, pp. 2136–2141). Washington, DC: NASW Press.

Campbell, J. A. (1988). Client acceptance of single-system evaluation procedures. *Social work research and abstracts, 24,* 21–22.

Carlson, J., Sperry, L., & Lewis, J. A. (1997). *Family therapy: Ensuring treatment efficacy.* Pacific Grove, CA: Brooks/Cole.

Carroll, J. L., & Wolpe, P. R. (1996). *Sexuality and gender in society.* New York: HarperCollins.

Carter, B., & McGoldrick, M. (1999a). *The expanded family life cycle: Individual, family, and social perspectives* (3rd ed.). Boston: Allyn & Bacon.

Carter, B., & McGoldrick, M. (1999b). Overview: The expanded family life cycle: Individual, family, and social perspectives. In B. Carter & M. McGoldrick (Eds.), *The expanded family life cycle: Individual, family, and social perspectives* (3rd ed., pp. 1–26). Boston: Allyn & Bacon.

Carter, E. A., & McGoldrick, M. (1980). *The family life cycle: A framework for family therapy.* New York: Gardner Press.

Castex, G. M. (1994). Providing services to Hispanic/Latino populations: Profiles in diversity. *Social work, 39* (3), 288–296.

Chaplin, J. (1988). Never married, single, adolescent parents. In C. Chilman, E. Nunnally, & F. Cox (Eds.), *Variant family forms* (pp. 17–38). Newbury Park, CA: Sage.

Chau, K. L. (1990). A model for teaching cross-cultural practice in social work. *Journal of social work education, 26*(2), 124–133.

Cherry, A. L. (2000). *A research primer for the helping professions.* Belmont, CA: Wadsworth.

Child Welfare League of America. (1989). *Standards for service to strengthen and preserve families with children.* Washington, DC: Author.

Chilman, C. S., Nunnally, E. W., & Cox, F. M. (1988). *Variant family forms.* Newbury Park, CA: Sage.

Coalition (1994). *Talking about disabilities: A guide to using appropriate language.* Nashville: COALITION for Tennesseans with Disabilities.

Collier, H. V. (1982). *Counseling women: A guide for therapists.* New York: Free Press.

Comas-Diaz, L. (1996). Cultural considerations in diagnosis. In F. W. Kaslow, (Ed.) *Handbook of relational diagnosis and dysfunctional family patterns,* pp. 152–168. New York: John Wiley & Sons.

Compton, B. R., & Galaway, B. (1999). *Social work processes.* Pacific Grove, CA: Brooks/Cole.

Congress, E. P. (1996). Dual relationships in academia: Dilemmas for social work educators. *Journal of Social Work Education, 32*(3), 329–338.

Congress, E. P. (1999). *Social work values and ethics: Identifying and resolving professional dilemmas.* Chicago: Nelson-Hall.

Connaway, R. S., & Gentry, M. E. (1988). *Social work practice.* Englewood Cliffs, NJ: Prentice Hall.

Conte, J. R. (1995). Child sexual abuse overview. In *Encyclopedia of social work* (19th ed., vol. 1, pp. 402–408). Washington, DC: NASW Press.

Corcoran, K. (1997). Managed care: Implications for social work practice. In *Encyclopedia of social work 1997 supplement* (pp. 191–200). Washington, DC: NASW Press.

Corcoran, K., & Fischer, J. (1994). *Measures for clinical practice* (2nd ed.). New York: The Free Press.

Corey, G., Corey, M.S., & Callanan, P. (1998). *Issues and ethics in the helping professions* (5th ed.). Pacific Grove, CA: Brooks/Cole.

Corey, M. S., & Corey, G. (1992). *Groups: Process and practice* (4th ed.) Pacific Grove, CA: Brooks/Cole.

Cormier, S., & Hackney, H. (1999). *Counseling strategies and interventions* (5th ed.). Boston: Allyn & Bacon.

Costin, L. B., Bell, C. J., & Downs, S. W. (1991). *Child welfare: Policies and practice* (4th ed.). New York: Longman.

Coulton, C. J., & Chow, J. (1995). Poverty. In *Encyclopedia of social work* (19th ed., vol. 3, pp. 1867–1878). Washington, DC: NASW Press.

Council for the Accreditation of Counseling and Related Educational Programs. (2000). *The 2001 Standards.* Alexandria, VA: Author.

Cournoyer, B. (2000). *The social work skills workbook* (3rd ed.). Belmont, CA: Wadsworth.

Cowger, C. (1997). Assessing client strengths: Assessment for client empowerment. In D. Saleeby (Ed.) *The strengths perspective in social work practice* (2nd ed., pp. 59–73). White Plains, NY: Longman.

Cowger, C. D. (1994). Assessing client strengths: Clinical assessment for client empowerment. *Social work, 39*(3), 262–268.

Cox, E. O., & Parsons, R. J. (1994). *Empowerment-oriented social work practice with the elderly.* Pacific Grove, CA: Brooks/Cole.

Cox, F. M., Erlich, J. L., Rothman, J., & Tropman, J. E. (1987). *Strategies of community organization.* Itasca, IL: Peacock.

Crooks, R., & Baur, K. (1999). *Our sexuality* (7th ed.). Pacific Grove, CA: Brooks/Cole.

Crosson-Tower, C. (1999). *Understanding child abuse and neglect* (4th ed.). Boston: Allyn & Bacon.

Cultural Information Service. (1984). *The burning bed: Viewer's guide.* New York: CIStems.

Curtis, O. (1999). *Chemical dependency: A family affair.* Pacific Grove, CA: Brooks/Cole.

Davis, J. (1982). *Help me, I'm hurt.* Dubuque, IA: Kendall-Hunt.

Davis, L. V. (1995). Domestic violence. In *Encyclopedia of social work* (19th ed., vol. 1. pp. 780–789). Washington, DC: NASW Press.

Dear, R. B., & Patti, R. J. (1981). Legislative advocacy: Seven effective tactics. *Social work, 6*(4), 289–296.

Denzin, N. K. (1987). *Treating alcoholism.* Newbury Park, CA: Sage.

DeRisi, W. J., & Butz, G. (1975). *Writing behavioral contracts: A case simulation practice manual.* Champaign, IL: Research Press.

Desselle, D. D., & Proctor, T. K. (2000). Advocating for the elderly hard-of-hearing population: The deaf people we ignore. *Social work 45*(3), 277–281.

Devore, W., & Schlesinger, E. G. (1996). *Ethnic-sensitive social work practice.* Columbus, OH: Merrill.

Devore, W., & Schlesinger, E. G. (1999). *Ethnic-sensitive social work practice* (5th ed.). Boston: Allyn & Bacon.

Dillard, J. M. (1983). *Multicultural counseling.* Chicago: Nelson-Hall.

Diller, J. V. (1999). *Cultural diversity.* Pacific Grove, CA: Brooks/Cole.

Dixon, S. L. (1987). *Working with people in crisis.* Columbus, OH: Merrill.

Downs, S. W., Costin, L. B., & McFadden, E. J. (1996). *Child welfare and family services: Policy and practice* (5th ed.). White Plains, NY: Longman.

Dunkle, R. E., & Norgard, T. (1995). Aging overview. In *Encyclopedia of social work* (19th ed., vol. 1, pp. 142–153). Washington, DC: NASW Press.

Duprey, M., McDonnell, C., Paymar, M., Regan, K., & Soderberg, J. (Eds). (1996) *Coordinated community response to domestic assault cases: A guide for policy development.* Duluth, MN: Domestic Abuse Intervention Project.

Dziegielewski, S. F., Resnick, C., & Krause, N. B. (1996). Shelter-based crisis intervention with battered women. In A. R. Roberts (Ed.), *Helping battered women: New perspectives and remedies* (pp. 159–171). New York: Oxford University Press.

Edinburg, G. M., & Cottler, J. M. (1995). Managed care. In *Encyclopedia of social work* (19th ed., vol. 2, pp. 1635–1642). Washington, DC: NASW Press.

Ell, K. (1995). Crisis intervention: Research needs. In *Encyclopedia of social work* (19th ed., vol. 1, pp. 660–667). Washington, DC: NASW Press.

Elster, A. B., & Panzarine, S. (1983). Teenage fathers: Stresses during gestation and early parenthood. *Clinical pediatrics, 22*(10), 700–703.

Englander-Golden, P., & Barton, G. (1983). Sex differences in absence from work: A reinterpretation. *Psychology of women quarterly, 8*(2), 185–188.

Epstein, L. (1980). *Helping people: The task-centered approach.* St. Louis, MO: Mosby.

Epstein, L. (1985). *Talking and listening: A guide to the helping interview.* St. Louis, MO: Times Mirror/Mosby.

Equal Employment Opportunity Commission (EEOC) and the U.S. Department of Justice (1991). *Americans with*

Disabilities Act handbook. Washington, DC: U.S. Government Printing Office.

Erickson, A. G. (1987). Family services. In *Encyclopedia of social work* (19th ed., vol. 1, pp. 589–593). Silver Spring, MD: National Association of Social Workers.

Erickson, M. F., & Egeland, B. (1996). Child neglect. In J. Briere, L. Berliner, J. A. Bulkley, C. Jenny, & T. Reid (Eds.), *The APSAC handbook on child maltreatment.* (pp. 4–20) Thousand Oaks, CA: Sage.

Evaluation Research Society (1982). Evaluation research society standards for program evaluation. In P.H. Rossi (Ed.), *New directions for program evaluation: Standards for evaluation practice.* San Francisco: Jossey-Bass.

Ewalt, P. L., & Mokuau, N. (1996). Self-determination from a Pacific perspective. In P. L. Ewalt, E. M. Freeman, S. A. Kirk, & D. L. Poole, *Multicultural issues in social work.* Washington, DC: NASW Press.

Fagan, J., Friedman, E., & Wexler, S. (1984). *National evaluation of the LEAA family violence demonstration program: Summary of major findings.* San Francisco: URSA Institute.

Family Service America. (1984). *Family service profiles: Agency staffing and coverage.* New York: Author.

Fatout, M., & Rose, S. R. (1995). *Task groups in the social services.* Thousand Oaks, CA: Sage.

Federal Bureau of Investigation. (1998). *Uniform crime reports for the United States, 1997.* Washington, DC: U.S. Government Printing Office.

Finckenauer, J. O. (1982). *Scared straight! and the panacea phenomenon.* Englewood Cliffs, NJ: Prentice Hall.

Fine, S. F., & Glasser, P. H. (1996). *The first helping interview: Engaging the client and building trust.* Thousand Oaks, CA: Sage.

Fischer, J., & Gochros, H. L. (1975). *Planned behavior change: Behavior modification in social work.* New York: Free Press.

Flanagan, J. (1980). *How to sell and how to ask for money.* Chicago: National Committee for the Prevention of Child Abuse.

Fong, R. (1993, February). *Family preservation: Making it work for Asians.* Paper presented at the Council on Social Work Education Annual Program Meeting, New York.

Fong, R., & Mokuau, N. (1996). Not simply "Asian Americans": Periodical literature review on Asians and Pacific Islanders. In P. L. Ewalt, E. M. Freeman, S. A. Kirk, & D. L. Poole (Eds.), *Multicultural issues in social work* (pp. 269–281). Washington, DC: NASW Press.

Fong, R., & Peralta, F. (1994, March). *Family preservation values and services: Cultural sensitivity toward Asian and Hispanic families.* Paper presented at the Council on Social Work Education Annual Program Meeting, Atlanta.

Forte, J. A., Franks, D. D., Forte, J. A., & Rigsby, D. (1996). Asymmetrical role-taking: Comparing battered and nonbattered women. *Social Work, 41* (1), 59–73.

Fortune, A. E. (1995). Termination in direct practice. In *Encyclopedia of social work* (19th ed., vol. 3, pp. 2398–2404). Washington, DC: NASW Press.

Fraser, S. (Ed.) (1995). *The bell curve wars: Race, intelligence, and the future of America.* New York: Basic Books.

Freeman, J. (1995). *Women: A feminist perspective.* Mountain View, CA: Mayfield.

French, J. R., & Raven, B. (1968). The bases of social power. In D. Cartwright & A. Zander. *Group dynamics: Research and theory* (pp. 259–269). New York: Harper & Row.

Friedrich, W. N., Grambsch, P., Damon, L., Hewitt, S. K., Koverola, C., Lang, R. A., Wolfe, V., & Broughton, D. (1992). Child sexual behavior inventory: Normative and clinical comparisons. *Psychological assessment, 4,* 303–311.

Friesen, B. (1987) Administration: Interpersonal aspects. In *Encyclopedia of social work* (19th ed., vol. 1, pp. 17–27). Silver Spring, MD: National Association of Social Workers.

Furstenburg, F., & Crawford, A. (1978). Family support: Helping teenage mothers to cope. *Family planning perspectives, 10,* 322–333.

Gambrill, E. (1997). *Social work practice: A critical thinker's guide.* New York: Oxford University Press.

Gambrill, E. (1999). Evidenced-based practice: An alternative to authority-based practice. *Families in society, 80*(4), 341–350.

Garvin, C. D., & Cox, F. M. (1995). A history of community organizing since the Civil War with special reference to oppressed communities. In J. Rothman, J. L. Erlich, & J. E. Tropman. *Strategies of community intervention* (pp. 64–99). Itasca, IL: Peacock.

Gelles, R. J., & Cornell, C. P. (1990). *Intimate violence in families* (2nd ed.). Newbury Park, CA: Sage.

Gelman, S. (1987). Board of directors. In *Encyclopedia of social work* (19th ed., vol. 1, pp. 206–211). Silver Spring, MD: National Association of Social Workers.

Gerhart, U. C. (1990). *Caring for the chronic mentally ill.* Itasca, IL: Peacock.

Gibbons, M., & Vincent, C. (1994). Childhood sexual abuse. *American family physician, 49,* 125–137.

Gibbs, L. (1991). *Scientific reasoning for social workers.* New York: Macmillan.

Gibbs, L., Gambrill, E., Blakemore, J., Begun, A., Keniston, A., Peden, B., & Lefcowitz, J. (1994). *A measure of critical thinking about practice.* Unpublished paper presented at the fall Conference of the Wisconsin Council on Social Work Education, Stevens Point, WI.

Gibbs, N. (1998). 'Til death do us part. In S. Ruth (Ed.), *Issues in feminism: An introduction to women's studies* (4th ed., pp. 326–333). Mountain View, CA: Mayfield.

Gibelman, M. (1982). Finding the least restrictive environment. *Practice digest, 4*(4), 15–17.

Gibelman, M. (1995). *What social workers do.* Washington, DC: NASW Press.

Gilbert, L. A. (1985). *Men in dual-career families: Current realities and future prospects.* Hillsdale, NJ: Erlbaum.

Gilson, S. F., Bricout, J. C., & Baskind, F. R. (1998). Listening to the voices of people with disabilities. *Families in society: The journal of contemporary human services, 79*(2), 188–202.

Golan, N. (1987). Crisis intervention. In *Encyclopedia of social work* (18th ed., vol. 1, pp. 360–372). Silver Spring, MD: National Association of Social Workers.

Goldenberg, H., & Goldenberg, I. (1998). *Counseling today's families.* (3rd ed.). Pacific Grove, CA: Brooks/Cole.

Goldenberg, I., & Goldenberg, H. (2000). *Family therapy: An overview* (5th ed.). Pacific Grove, CA: Brooks/Cole.

Good Tracks, J. G. (1973). Native American noninterference. *Social work, 18,* 30–35.

Gordon, T. (1970). *Parent effectiveness training.* New York: Peter Weyden.

Gordon, T. (1975). *P.E.T. parent effectiveness training.* New York: New American Library.

Gothard, S. (1995). Legal issues: Confidentiality and privileged communication. In *Encyclopedia of social work* (19th ed., vol. 2, pp. 1579–1584). Washington, DC: NASW Press.

Gottlieb, N. (1987). Sex discrimination and inequality. In *Encyclopedia of social work* (18th ed., vol. 1, pp. 561–569). Silver Spring, MD: National Association of Social Workers.

Gottlieb, N. (1995). Women overview. In *Encyclopedia of social work* (19th ed., vol. 3, pp. 2518–2529). Washington, DC: NASW Press.

Gottman, J., Notarius, C., Gonso, J., & Markman, H. (1976). *A couple's guide to communication.* Champaign, IL: Research Press.

Gray, M. (1995). African Americans. In J. Philleo & F. L. Brisbane (Eds.), *Cultural competence for social workers: A guide for alcohol and other drug abuse prevention professionals working with ethnic/racial communities.* Washington, DC: U. S. Department of Health and Human Services, 69–101.

Green, J. W. (1999). *Cultural awareness in the human services: A multi-ethnic approach* (3rd ed.). Boston: Allyn & Bacon.

Greenberg, J. S., Bruess, C. E., & Haffner, D. W. (2000). *Exploring the dimensions of human sexuality.* Boston: Jones and Bartlett.

Greene, G. J., Lee, M., Trask, R., & Rheinscheld, J. (2000). How to work with clients' strengths in crisis intervention. In A. R. Roberts (Ed.) *Crisis intervention handbook* (2nd ed., pp. 31–55). New York: Oxford University Press.

Grinnell, R. M., & Williams, M. (1990) *Research in social work: A primer.* Itasca, IL: Peacock.

Guidry, H. (1995). Childhood sexual abuse: Role of the family physician. *American family physician, 51,* 407–414.

Hagedorn, H., Beck, S., & Werlin, S. (1976). *A working manual of simple program evaluation techniques for community mental health centers.* Washington, DC: Government Printing Office.

Hall, E. (1969). *The hidden dimension.* Garden City, NY: Doubleday.

Halley, A. A., Kopp, J., & Austin, M. J. (1998). *Delivering human services: A learning approach to practice* (4th ed.). New York: Longman.

Hammond, J. L., & Mahoney, C. W. (1983). Reward-cost balancing among coal miners. *Sex roles, 9,* 17–29.

Hardina, D. (2000). Models and tactics taught in community organization courses: Findings from a survey of practice instructors. *Journal of community practice, 7*(1), 5–18.

Harkess, S. (1988). Directions for the future. In A. H. Strombery & S. Harkess (Eds.), *Women working: Theories and facts in perspective* (pp. 358–360). Mountain View, CA: Mayfield.

Harry, J. (1988). Some problems of gay/lesbian families. In C. S. Chilman, E. W. Nunnally, & F. M. Cox (Eds.), *Variant family forms.* Newbury Park, CA: Sage.

Hartman, A. (1970). To think about the unthinkable. *Social casework, 51*(8), 467–474.

Hartman, A. (1978). Diagrammatic assessment of family relationships. *Social casework, 59,* 465–476.

Hartman, A. (1995). Family therapy. In *Encyclopedia of social work* (19th ed., vol. 1, pp. 983–996) Washington, DC: NASW Press.

Harway, M. (1993). Battered women: Characteristics and causes. In M. Hansen & M. Harway (Eds.). *Battering and family therapy: A feminist perspective* (pp. 29–41). Newbury Park, CA: Sage.

Hasenfeld, Y. (1987). Program development. In F. M. Cox, J. L. Erlich, J. Rothman, J. E. Tropman (Eds.), *Strategies of community organization* (4th ed., pp. 450–473). Itasca, IL: Peacock.

Hatchett, S. J., & Jackson, J. S. (1999). In H. P. McAdoo (Ed.), *Family ethnicity: Strength in diversity* (2nd ed.). Thousand Oaks, CA: Sage, 171–190.

Hawkins. R. P., & Dobes, R. W. (1975). Behavioral definitions in applied behavior analysis: Explicit or implicit. In B. C. Etzel, J. M. LeBlanc, & D. M. Baer (Eds.), *New developments in behavioral research: Theory, methods and applications.* Hillsdale, NJ: Erlbaum.

Haynes, K. S., & Mickelson, J. S. (1997). *Affecting change* (3rd ed.). New York: Longman.

Hellenbrand, S. (1987). Termination in direct practice. *Encyclopedia of social work.* (18th ed., vol. 2, pp. 765–770). Silver Spring, MD: National Association of Social Workers.

Helton, L. R., & Jackson, M. (1997). *Social work practice with families: A diversity model.* Boston: Allyn and Bacon.

Henry, W. A., III. (Sept. 10, 1993). Gay parents: Under fire and on the rise. *Time.* 66–69.

Hepworth, D. H., & Larsen, J. (1987). Interviewing. In *Encyclopedia of social work* (18th ed., vol. 1, pp. 996–1008). Silver Spring, MD: National Association of Social Workers.

Hepworth, D. H., Rooney, R. H., & Larsen, J. A. (1997). *Direct social work practice.* Pacific Grove, CA: Brooks/Cole.

Herman, D. (1984). The rape culture. In J. Freeman (Ed.), *Women: A feminist perspective* (pp. 20–38). Palo Alto, CA: Mayfield.

Hines, P. M., Preto, N. G., McGoldrick, M., Almeida, R., & Weltman, S. (1999). Culture and the family life cycle. In B. Carter & M. McGoldrick (Eds.), *The expanded family life cycle: Individual, family, and social perspectives* (3rd ed., pp. 69–87). Boston: Allyn & Bacon.

Ho, M. K. (1987). *Family therapy with ethnic minorities.* Newbury Park, CA: Sage.

Hodge, J. L., Struckmann, D. K., & Trost, L. D. (1975). *Cultural bases of racism and group oppression.* Berkeley, CA: Two Riders Press.

Hoffman, K., & Sallee, A. (1993). *Social work practice: Bridges to change.* Boston: Allyn & Bacon.

Holder, W., & Corey, M. K. (1991). *Child protective services risk management: A decision making handbook.* Charlotte, NC: Action for Child Protection.

Holman, A. M. (1983). *Family assessment: Tools for understanding and intervention.* Beverly Hills, CA: Sage.

Homan, M. S. (1999). *Promoting community change* (2nd ed.). Pacific Grove, CA: Brooks/Cole.

Homma-True, R., Greene, B., Lopez, S., & Trimble, J. E. (1993). Ethnocultural diversity in clinical psychology. *Clinical psychologist, 46,* 50–63.

Hudson, J., & Grinnell, R. M. (1989). Program evaluation. In B. R. Compton & B. Galaway (Eds). *Social work processes* (pp. 691–711). Belmont, CA: Wadsworth.

Hudson, W. W. (1982). *The clinical assessment package: A field manual.* Homewood, IL: Dorsey Press.

Hull, D. B., & Hull, J. H. (1978). Rathus assertiveness schedule: Normative and factor-analytic data. *Behavior therapy, 9,* 673.

Hull, G. H., Jr. (1982). Child welfare services to Native Americans. *Social casework, 63,* 340–347.

Hull, G. H., & Zastrow, C. (1988). *Community services directory for Jefferson, Rock and Walworth counties.* Whitewater: University of Wisconsin–Whitewater Department of Social Welfare.

Hutchins, T., & Baxter, V. (1980). Battered women. In *Alternative social services for women* (pp. 179–234). New York: Columbia University Press.

Hutchison, N. (1989). Application of process in a community change endeavor. In B. R. Compton & B. Galaway *Social work processes.* (pp. 407–410). Belmont, CA: Wadsworth.

Hyde, J. S., & DeLamater, J. (2000). *Understanding human sexuality* (7th ed.). Boston: McGraw-Hill.

Iatridis, D. S. (1995). Policy practice. In *Encyclopedia of social work* (19th ed., vol. 3, pp. 1855–1866). Washington, DC: NASW Press.

Institute for Rehabilitation and Disability Management and National Center for Social Policy and Practice (1988). *Case management: The present and future tool for improving employment opportunities for people with disabilities.* Unpublished proposal.

Ivanoff, A., Blythe, B. J., & Tripodi, T. (1994). *Involuntary clients in social work practice: A research-based approach.* New York: Aldine de Gruyter.

Ivey, A. E. (1994). *Intentional interviewing and counseling: Facilitating client development in a multicultural society.* Pacific Grove, CA: Brooks/Cole.

Ivey, A. E., & Ivey, M. B. (1999). *Intentional interviewing & counseling: Facilitating client development in a multicultural society* (4th ed.) Pacific Grove, CA: Brooks/Cole.

Iwamasa, G. Y., Larrabee, A. L., & Merritt, R. D. (1995, August) *Are personality disorders ethnically and gender biased?* Poster presented at the annual meeting of the American Psychological Association, New York.

Jacobs, E. E., Harvill, R. L., & Masson, R. L. (1994). *Group counseling* (2nd ed.). Pacific Grove, CA: Brooks/Cole.

Jacobs, M. R. (1981). *Problems presented by alcoholic clients.* Toronto: Addiction Research Foundation.

Janzen, C., & Harris, O. (1997). *Family treatment in social work practice* (3rd ed.). Itasca, IL: F. E. Peacock.

Jayaratne, S., Croxton, T., & Mattison, D. (1997, March). Social work professional standards: An exploratory study. *Social work, 42*(2), 187–199.

Johnson, A. K., & Richards, R. N. (1995). Homeless women and feminist social work practice. In N. Van Den Bergh (Ed.), *Feminist practice in the 21st century.* Washington, DC: NASW Press.

Johnson, D. W. (1994). *Reaching out: Interpersonal effectiveness and self-actualization* (5th ed.). Boston: Allyn & Bacon.

Johnson, D. W. (1997). *Reaching out: Interpersonal effectiveness and self-actualization* (6th ed.). Boston: Allyn & Bacon.

Johnson, G. B., & Wahl, M. (1995). Families: Demographic shifts. In *Encyclopedia of social work* (19th ed., vol. 2, pp. 936–941). Washington, DC: NASW Press.

Johnson, L. (1992). *Social work practice: A generalist approach* (4th ed.). Boston: Allyn & Bacon.

Johnson, L. (1998). *Social work practice: A generalist approach.* Boston: Allyn & Bacon.

Johnston, S. (1987). The mind of the molester. *Psychology today,* February, 60–63.

Jones, L. (1987). Women. In *Encyclopedia of social work* (18th ed., vol. 2, pp. 872–881). Silver Spring, MD: National Association of Social Workers.

Jones, M., & Biesecker, J. (1980). *Goal planning in children and youth services.* Millersville, PA: Training Resources in Permanent Planning Projects.

Kadushin, A. (1995). Interviewing. In *Encyclopedia of social work* (19th ed., vol. 2, pp. 1527–1537). Washington, DC: NASW Press.

Kadushin, A., & Kadushin, G. (1997). *The social work interview: A guide for human service professionals.* New York: Columbia University Press.

Kadushin, A., & Martin, J. A. (1988). *Child welfare services* (4th ed.) New York: Macmillan.

Kagle, J. (1991) *Social work records.* Belmont, CA: Wadsworth.

Kagle, J. D., & Giebelhausen, P. N. (1994, March). Dual relationships and professional boundaries. *Social work, 39*(2), 213–220.

Kamerman, S. B. (1984) Women, children and poverty in industrialized countries. *Signs, 10*(2), 249–271.

Kamerman, S. B. (1995). Families overview. In *Encyclopedia of social work* (19th ed., vol. 2, pp. 927–935). Washington, DC: NASW Press.

Kamerman, S. B., & Kahn, A. J. (1981). *Child care, family benefits, and working parents.* New York: Columbia University Press.

Kanel, K. (1999). *A guide to crisis intervention.* Pacific Grove, CA: Brooks/Cole.

Kantrowitz, B., & Wingert, P. (2001, May 28) Unmarried with children. *Newsweek,* pp. 46–48.

Kaplan, K. O. (1990). Recent trends in case management. In *Encyclopedia of social work 1990 supplement.* Silver Spring, MD: NASW Press.

Kazdin, A. E. (1989). *Behavior modification in applied settings* (4th ed.). Pacific Grove, CA: Brooks/Cole.

Kazdin, A. E. (2001). *Behavior modification in applied settings* (6th ed.). Belmont, CA: Wadsworth.

Keefe, T., & Maypole, D. E. (1983). *Relationships in social service practice.* Pacific Grove, CA: Brooks/Cole.

Kemp, A. (1998). *Abuse in the family: An introduction.* Pacific Grove, CA: Brooks/Cole.

Kettner, P., Daley, J., & Nichols, A. (1985). *Initiating change in organizations and communities.* Pacific Grove, CA: Brooks/Cole.

King, J. C. (1981). *The biology of race.* Berkeley: University of California Press.

Kingery-McCabe, L. B., & Frances, A. C. (1991). Effects of addiction on the addict. In D. C. Daley & M. S. Raskin (Eds.), *Treating the chemically dependent and their families* (pp. 57–78). Newbury Park, CA: Sage.

Kirk, G., & Okazawa-Rey, M. (2001). *Women's lives: Multicultural perspectives* (2nd ed.). Mountain View, CA: Mayfield.

Kirst-Ashman, K. (1989, March). *Enhancing the relevance of human behavior and the social environment content.* Paper presented at the Council on Social Work Education Annual Program Meeting, Chicago, IL.

Kirst-Ashman, K. (1991, March). *Feminist values and social work: A model for educating nonfeminists.* Paper presented at the Council on Social Work Annual Program Meeting, New Orleans.

Kirst-Ashman, K. (2000). *Human behavior, communities, organizations, and groups in the macro social environment: An empowerment approach.* Pacific Grove, CA: Brooks/Cole.

Kirst-Ashman, K., & Hull, G. H., Jr. (2001). *Generalist practice with organizations and communities,* 2nd ed. Pacific Grove, CA: Brooks/Cole.

Kitano, H. H. (1991). *Race relations.* Englewood Cliffs, NJ: Prentice-Hall.

Kliman, J., & Madsen, W. (1999). Social class and the family life cycle. In B. Carter & M. McGoldrick (Eds.), *The expanded family life cycle: Individual, family, and social perspectives* (3rd ed., pp. 88–105). Boston: Allyn & Bacon.

Kolko, D. J. (1996). Child physical abuse. In J. Briere, L. Berliner, J. A. Bulkley, C. Jenny, & T. Reid, *The APSAC handbook on child maltreatment,* pp. 21–50. Thousand Oaks, CA: Sage.

Kopels, S. (1995). The Americans with Disabilities Act: A tool to combat poverty. *Journal of social work education, 31*(3), 337–346.

Koss, M. (1988). Hidden rape: Sexual aggression and victimization in a national sample of students in higher education. In A. Burgess (Ed.), *Rape and sexual assault II.* New York: Garland.

Kuramoto, F. H., Munoz, F. U., Morales, R. F., & Murase, K. (1983). Education for social work practice in Asian and Pacific American Communities. In J. C. Chunn, P. J. Dunston, & F. Ross-Sheriff (Eds.), *Mental health and people of color* (pp. 127–156). Washington, DC: Howard University Press.

Kurz, D. (1993). Physical assaults by husbands: A major social problem. In R. J. Gelles & D. R. Loseke (Eds.), *Current controversies on family violence,* 88–103. Newbury Park, CA: Sage.

LaFromboise, T. D., Berman, J. S., & Sohi, B. K. (1994). American Indian women. In L. Comas-Diaz & B. Greene (Eds.), *Women of color: Integrating ethnic and gender identities in psychotherapy* (pp. 30–71). New York: Guilford.

Laird, J. (1995). Lesbians: Parenting. In *Encyclopedia of social work* (19th ed., vol. 2., pp. 1604–1616). Washington, DC: NASW Press.

Lally, E. M., & Haynes, H. A. (1995). Alaska natives. In *Encyclopedia of social work* (19th ed., vol. 1, pp. 194–203). Washington, DC: NASW Press.

Land, H. (1995). Feminist clinical social work in the 21st century. In N. Van Den Bergh, *Feminist practice in the 21st century.* Washington, DC: NASW Press.

Landon, P. S. (1995). Generalist and advanced generalist practice. In *Encyclopedia of social work* (19th ed., vol. 2, pp. 1101–1108). Washington, DC: NASW Press.

League of Women Voters (1972). *Know your community.* Washington, DC: Author.

Leashore, B. R. (1995). African Americans: Overview. In *Encyclopedia of social work* (19th ed., vol. 1, pp. 101–115). Washington, DC: NASW Press.

Lee, C. C. (1999). Counseling African American men. In L. Davis (Ed.), *Working with African American males* (pp. 39–53). Thousand Oaks, CA: Sage.

Leigh, J. W. (1998). *Communicating for cultural competence.* Boston: Allyn & Bacon.

Levin, J. D. (1995). *Introduction to alcoholism counseling: A bio-psycho-social approach* (2nd ed.). New York: Taylor & Francis.

LeVine, E. S., & Sallee, A. L. (1999). *Child welfare: Clinical theory and practice.* Dubuque, IA: Eddir Bowers.

Levy, C. S. (1982). *Guide to ethical decisions and actions for social service administrators: A handbook for managerial personnel.* New York: Haworth.

Lewis, K. G. (1980). Children of lesbians: Their point of view. *Social Work, 25*(3), 203.

Lewis, R., & Ho, M. (1975). Social work with Native Americans. *Social work, 20*(5), 378–382.

Lindsay, M. (1995). *Understanding and enhancing adult learning.* Unpublished paper prepared for presentation at the Spring Conference of the Wisconsin Council on Social Work Education, Wisconsin Dells, WI.

Lindsey, D. (1994). *The welfare of children.* New York: Oxford University Press.

Lipsey, M. (1992). Juvenile delinquency treatment: A meta-analytic inquiry into the viability of effects. In T. Cook, D. Cordray, H. Hartman, L. Hedges, R. Light, T. Louis, & F. Mosteller (Eds.), *Meta-analysis for explanation: A casebook* (pp. 83–127). New York: Russell Sage Foundation.

Lloyd, G. A. (1995). HIV/AIDS overview. In *Encyclopedia of social work* (19th ed., vol. 2, pp. 1257–1290). Washington, DC: NASW Press.

Lloyd, J. C., & Bryce, M. E. (1984). *Placement prevention and family reunification: A handbook for the family-centered service practitioner.* Iowa City: University of Iowa.

Locke, P. (1973, August). Indian gifts of culture and diversity. In *Cultural Diverse Exceptional Children Conference Presentations* [Cassette recording]. Reston, VA: The Council for Exceptional Children.

Loewenberg, F. M., & Dolgoff, R. (1996). *Ethical decisions for social work practice.* Itasca, IL: F. E. Peacock.

Loewenberg, F. M., Dolgoff, R., & Harrington, D. (2000). *Ethical decisions for social work practice* (6th ed.). Itasca, IL: Peacock.

Logan, S. M. L., Freeman, E. M., & McRoy, R. G. (1990). *Social work practice with black families: A culturally specific perspective.* New York: Longman.

Lohmann, R. A. (1997). Managed care: A review of recent research. In *Encyclopedia of social work 1997 supplement* (pp. 200–213). Washington, DC: NASW Press.

Longres, J. F. (1991). Toward a status model of ethnic sensitive practice. *Journal of multicultural social work, 1,* 41–57.

Longres, J. G. (1995). Hispanics overview. In R. L. Edwards (Editor-in-chief), *Encyclopedia of social work* (19th ed., vol. 2, pp. 1214–1222). Washington, DC: NASW Press.

Lott, B. (1987). *Women's lives: Themes and variations in gender learning.* Pacific Grove, CA: Brooks/Cole.

Lott, B. (1994). *Women's lives: Themes and variations in gender learning* (2nd ed.). Pacific Grove, CA: Brooks/Cole.

Love, A. J. (1991). *Internal evaluation.* Newbury Park, CA: Sage.

Lum, D. (1999). *Culturally competent practice: A framework for growth and action.* Pacific Grove, CA: Brooks/Cole.

Lum, D. (2000). *Social work practice and people of color: A process-stage approach* (4th ed.). Pacific Grove, CA: Brooks/Cole.

Mackelprang, R., & Salsgiver, R. (1999). *Disability.* Pacific Grove, CA: Brooks/Cole.

Mackelprang, R. W., & Salsgiver, R. O. (1996). People with disabilities and social work: Historical and contemporary issues. *Social work, 41*(1), 7–14.

Magura, S., & Moses, B. S. (1986). *Outcome measures for child welfare services: Theory and applications.* Washington, DC: Child Welfare League of America.

Mailick, M. D., & Ashley, A. A. (1989). Politics of interprofessional collaboration: Challenge to advocacy. In B. R. Compton & B. Galaway (Eds.), *Social work processes* (pp. 622–628). Belmont, CA: Wadsworth.

Major, E. (2000, Winter). Self-determination and the disabled adult. *The new social worker, 7*(1), 9–16.

Maluccio, A. N. (1990). Family preservation: An overview. *Family preservation: Papers from the institute for social work educators 1990,* 17–28. Riverdale, IL: National Association for Family-Based Services.

Managed care curbs backed: Would establish reviews of payment denials. (1998, January). *NASW News,* pp. 1, 10.

Marion, T. D., & Coleman, K. (1991). Recovery issues and treatment resources. In D. C. Daley & M. S. Raskin (Eds.), *Treating the chemically dependent and their families* (pp. 100–127). Newbury Park, CA: Sage.

Marks, J. (1995). *Human biodiversity: Genes, race, and history.* New York: Aldine de Gruyter.

Marlow, C. (1993). *Research methods for generalist social work.* Pacific Grove, CA: Brooks/Cole.

Martin, H. P., & Beezley, P. (1976). Personality of abused children. In H. P. Martin (Ed.), *The abused child* (pp. 105–111). Cambridge, MA: Ballinger.

Martin, S. E. (1984). Sexual harassment: The link between gender stratification, sexuality and women's economic status. In J. Freeman (Ed.), *Women: A feminist perspective* (pp. 54–69). Palo Alto, CA: Mayfield.

Martin, S. E. (1995). Sexual harassment: The link joining stratification, sexuality, and women's economic status. In J. Freeman (Ed.), *Women: A feminist perspective* (5th ed.) Mountain View, CA: Mayfield.

Masella, J. D. (1991). Intervention: Breaking the addiction cycle. In D. C. Daley & M. S. Raskin (Eds.), *Treating the chemically dependent and their families* (pp. 79–99). Newbury Park, CA: Sage.

Masters, W. H., Johnson, V. E., & Kolodney, R. C. (1995). *Human sexuality* (6th ed.). New York: HarperCollins.

Mather, J. H., & Lager, P. G. (2000). *Child welfare: A unifying model of practice.* Pacific Grove, CA: Brooks/Cole.

Matsuoka, J. K. (1990). Differential acculturation among Vietnamese refugees. *Social work, 35*(4), 341–345.

McAdoo, H. (1987). Blacks. In *Encyclopedia of social work* (18th ed., vol. 1, pp. 194–206). Silver Spring, MD: National Association of Social Workers.

McCormick, I. A. (1984). Simple version of the Rathus Assertiveness Schedule. *Behavior assessment, 7,* 95–99.

McGee, E. (1982). *Too little, too late: Services for teenage parents.* New York: Ford Foundation.

McHugh, M. C. (1993). Studying battered women and batterers: Feminist perspectives on methodology. In M. Hansen & M. Harway (Eds.), *Battering and family therapy: A feminist perspective.* Newbury Park, CA: Sage.

McInnis, K. M. (1990). The Hmong family. In K. M. McInnis, H. E. Petracchi, and M. Morgenbesser (Eds.), *The Hmong in America: Providing ethnic-sensitive health, education, and human services.* Dubuque, IA: Kendall-Hunt.

McKibben, A., Proulx, J., & Lusignan, R. (1994). Relationships between conflict, affect, and deviant sexual behaviors in rapists and pedophiles. *Behavior research and therapy, 32,* 571–575.

McMahon, M. (1996). *The general method of social work practice.* Englewood Cliffs, N.J.: Prentice-Hall.

McMillen, L. (1997, January 17). Linguists find the debate over "Ebonics" uninformed. *The Chronicle of Higher Education,* A16–17.

McNeece, C. A., & DiNitto, D. M. (2002). Chemical dependency treatment. In A. R. Roberts & G. J. Greene. *Social Workers' Desk Reference,* pp. 598-604. New York: Oxford University Press.

Merriam-Webster's collegiate dictionary, 10th ed. (1994). Springfield, MA: Merriam-Webster.

Meyer, C. H. (1995). Assessment. In *Encyclopedia of social work* (19th ed., vol. 1, pp. 260–270). Washington, DC: NASW Press.

Miller, N. B. (1982). Social work services to urban Indians. In J. W. Green, *Cultural awareness in the human services.* Englewood Cliffs, NJ: Prentice-Hall.

Miller, W. R., & Rollnick, S. (1991). *Motivational interviewing.* New York: Guilford Press.

Minor, M., & Dwyer, S. (1997). The psychosocial development of sex offenders: Differences between exhibitionists, child molesters, and incest offenders. *International journal of offenders therapy and comparative criminology, 41,* 36–44.

Mokuau, N. (1990). A family-centered approach in native Hawaiian culture. *Families in society, 71*(10), 607–613.

Moore, S. T. (1990). A social work practice model of case management: The case management grid. *Social work, 35*(5), 444–448.

Morales, J. (1995). Gay men: Parenting. In *Encyclopedia of social work* (Vol. 2, pp. 1085–1095). Washington, DC: NASW Press.

Moses, A. E., & Hawkins, R. O. (1982). *Counseling lesbian women and gay men: A life-issues approach.* St. Louis: Mosby-Year Book.

Mosher-Ashley, P. M., Bogen, H., Ates, E. F., & Franklin, G. (1996). Placing elderly persons with psychiatric impairments in residential care homes. *Adult residential care journal, 10*(1), 38–53.

Moxley, D. P. (1989). *The practice of case management.* Newbury Park, CA: Sage.

Murase, K. (1995). Asian Americans: Japanese. In R. L. Edwards (Editor-in-Chief), *Encyclopedia of social work* (Vol. I, pp. 241–249). Washington, DC: NASW Press.

Nagata, D. K. (1991). Transgenerational impact of the Japanese American internment: Clinical issues in working with children of former internees. *Psychotherapy, 28*(1), 121–128.

National Association of Social Workers. (1982). Changes in NASW family policy. *NASW News, 27*(2), 10.

National Association of Social Workers. (1992). Case management in health, education, and human service settings. In S. Rose (Ed.), *Case management and social work practice.* White Plains, NY: Longman.

National Association of Social Workers. (1996). *The National Association of Social Workers code of ethics.* Washington, DC: Author.

National Institute on Alcohol Abuse and Alcoholism. (2000). *10th Special report to the U.S. Congress on alcohol and health.* Washington, DC: National Institute of Health.

National Organization for Human Service Education (2000). *Ethical standards of human service professionals.* Narragansett, RI: Author.

National Program Office on Self-Determination. (1998). *The Robert Wood Johnson Foundation initiative in self-determination for persons with developmental disabilities* [On-line]. Princeton, NJ: The Robert Wood Johnson Foundations. Available: http://www.self-determination.org.

National Victim Center (1992). *Rape in America: A report to the nation. Report prepared by the crime victims research and treatment center.* Charleston: Medical University of South Carolina.

Neiding, P. H., & Friedman, D. H. (1984). *Spouse abuse: A treatment program for couples.* Champaign, IL: Research Press.

Netting, F. E., Kettner, P. M., & McMurtry, S. L. (1993). *Social work macro practice.* New York: Longman.

Norman, E., & Mancuso, A. (1980). *Women's issues and social work practice.* Itasca, IL: Peacock.

North, C. S., & Smith, E. M. (1994). Comparison of white and nonwhite homeless men and women. *Social work 39*(6), 639–647.

Northen, H. (1982). *Clinical social work.* New York: Columbia University Press.

Northen, H. (1987). Assessment in direct practice. In *Encyclopedia of social work* (18th ed., vol. 1, pp. 171–183). Silver Spring, MD: National Association of Social Workers.

Northwood, L. K. (1964). Deterioration of the inner city. In N. E. Cohen (Ed.), *Social work and social problems* (pp. 201–269). New York: National Association of Social Workers.

Norton, D. (1978). *The dual perspective.* New York: Council on Social Work Education.

Nunnally, E., & Moy, C. (1989). *Communication basics for human service professionals.* Newbury Park, CA: Sage.

Okun, B. F. (1996). *Understanding diverse families: What practitioners need to know.* New York: Guilford.

Okun, B. F. (1997). *Effective helping: Interviewing and counseling techniques* (5th ed.). Pacific Grove, CA: Brooks/Cole.

Orton, G. L. (1997). *Strategies for counseling with children and their parents.* Pacific Grove, CA: Brooks/Cole.

Osborne, O., Pinkleton, N., Carter, C., & Richards, H. (1983). Development of African American curriculum content in psychiatric and mental health nursing. In J. C. Chunn, P. J. Dunston, & F. Ross-Sheriff, *Mental health and people of color* (pp. 335–376). Washington, DC: Howard University Press.

Papalia, D. E., Olds, S. W., & Feldman, R. D. (2001). *Human development* (8th ed.) New York: McGraw-Hill.

Parad, H. J., & Parad, L. G. (Eds.). (1990). *Crisis intervention book 2: The practitioner's source book for brief therapy.* Milwaukee, WI: Family Service America.

Parsons, R. D., & Wicks, R. J. (1994). *Counseling strategies and intervention techniques for the human services* (4th ed.). Boston: Allyn & Bacon.

Patti, R. J., & Resnick, H. (1972). Changing the agency from within. *Social work, 17*(4), 48–57.

Patti, R. J., & Resnick, H. (1980). Changing the agency from within. In H. Resnick & R. J. Patti (Eds.), *Change from within: Humanizing social welfare organizations* (pp. 217–230). Philadelphia: Temple University Press.

Perez, J. E. (1979). *Family counseling theory and practice.* New York: Van Nostrand Reinhold.

Perez, R. M., DeBord, K. A., & Bieschke, K. J. (2000). *Handbook of counseling and psychotherapy with lesbian, gay, and bisexual clients.* Washington, DC: American Psychological Association.

Perkinson, R. R. (1997). *Chemical dependency counseling: A practical guide.* Thousand Oaks, CA: Sage.

Peters, H. (1982). The legal rights of gays. In A. E. Moses & R. O. Hawkins (Eds.), *Counseling lesbian women and gay men: A life issues approach* (pp. 21–26). St. Louis: Mosby-Year Book.

Philleo, J., & Brisbane, F. L. (1995). *Cultural competence for social workers: A guide for alcohol and other drug abuse prevention professionals working with ethnic/racial communities.* Washington, DC: Department of Health and Human Services.

Phillips, W. (1996). Culturally competent practice: Understanding Asian family values. *The roundtable, 10*(1), 1–3.

Pierce, D. M. (1989). Farewell to alms: Women's fare under welfare. In J. Freeman (Ed.), *Women: A feminist perspective* (pp. 493–506). Palo Alto, CA: Mayfield.

Pietrzak, J., Ramler, M., Renner, T., Ford, L., & Gilbert, N. (1990). *Practical program evaluation.* Newbury Park, CA: Sage.

Pincus, A., & Minahan, A. (1973). *Social work practice: Model and method.* Itasca, IL: Peacock.

Pitter, G. E. (1992, September). Policing cultural celebrations. *FBI law enforcement bulletin, 61*(9), 10–14.

Plasse, B. R. (1995). Parenting groups for recovering addicts in a day treatment center. *Social Work, 40*(1), 65–74.

Pollard, W. L. (1995). Civil rights. In *Encyclopedia of social work* (19th ed., vol. 1, pp. 494–502). Washington, DC: NASW Press.

Polowy, C. I., & Gorenberg, C. (1997). Legal issues: Recent developments in confidentiality and privilege. In *Encyclopedia of social work 1997 supplement* (pp. 179–190). Washington, DC: NASW Press.

Proctor, E. K., & Davis, L. E. (1996). The challenge of racial difference: Skills for clinical practice. In P. L. Ewalt, E. M. Freeman, S. A. Kirk, & D. L. Poole (Eds.), *Multicultural issues in social work.* Washington, DC: NASW Press.

Proctor, E. K., Davis, L. E., & Vosler, N. R. (1995). Families: Direct practice. In *Encyclopedia of social work* (19th ed., vol. 2, pp. 941–950). Washington, DC: NASW Press.

Pryor, C. B., Kent, C., McGunn, C., & LeRoy, B. (1996). Redesigning social work in inclusive schools. *Social work, 41*(6), 668–695.

Pyke, S. W., & Kahill, S. P. (1983). Sex differences in characteristics presumed relevant to professional productivity. *Psychology of women quarterly, 8*(2), 189–192.

Quinn, A. E. (1993). Child protective services and intensive family preservation: A primary relationship. In E. S. Morton and R. K. Grigsby (Eds.), *Advancing family preservation practice*. Newbury Park, CA: Sage.

Raber, M. J. (1996). Job loss and dislocated workers: A stage theory model for treatment. *Employee assistance quarterly, 12*(2), 19–31.

Radloff, L. (1975). Sex differences in depression: The effects of occupation and marital status. *Sex roles, 1*(3), 249–265.

Randall, T. (1990). Domestic violence intervention calls for more than treating injuries. *Journal of the American Medical Association, 264,* 939–940.

Random House Webster's college dictionary (1999, 2nd ed.). New York: Random House.

Raskin, M. S., & Daley, D. C. (1991). Assessment of addiction problems. In M. S. Raskin and D. C. Daley (Eds.), *Treating the chemically dependent and their families* (pp. 22–56). Newbury Park, CA: Sage.

Rathus, S. A., Nevid, J. S., & Fichner-Rathus, L. (2000). *Human sexuality in a world of diversity* (4th ed.). Boston: Allyn & Bacon.

Rauch, J. B. (Ed.). (1993). *Assessment: A sourcebook for social work practice*. Milwaukee: Families International.

Rauch, J. B., & Tivoli, L. (1989). Social workers' knowledge and utilization of genetic services. *Social work, 34*(1), 55–56.

Reamer, F. G. (1987). Values and ethics. In *Encyclopedia of social work* (18th ed., vol. 2, pp. 801–809). Silver Spring, MD: National Association of Social Workers.

Reamer, F. G. (1990). *Ethical dilemmas in social service* (2nd ed.). New York: Columbia University Press.

Reamer, F. G. (1995a). Ethics and values. In *Encyclopedia of social work* (19th ed., vol. 1, pp. 893–902). Washington, DC: NASW Press.

Reamer, F. G. (1998). *Ethical standards in social work*. Washington, DC: NASW Press.

Reid, W. (1978). *The task-centered system*. New York: Columbia University Press.

Reid, W., & Epstein, L. (1972). *Task centered casework*. New York: Columbia University Press.

Reid, W. J. (1985). *Family problem solving*. New York: Columbia University Press.

Reid, W. J. (1987). Task-centered approach. In A. Minahan (Editor-in-chief), *Encyclopedia of social work* (18th ed., vol. 2, pp. 757–765). Silver Spring, MD: NASW.

Reid, W. J. (1995). Research overview. In *Encyclopedia of social work* (19th ed., vol. 3, pp. 2040–2054). Washington, DC: NASW Press.

Reisch, M., & Lowe, J. I. (2000). Of means and ends revisited: Teaching ethical community organizing in an unethical society. *Journal of community practice, 7*(1), 19–38.

Renz-Beaulaurier, R. (1998). Empowering people with disabilities: The role of choice. In L. M. Gutierrez, R. J. Parsons, & E. O. Cox (Eds.), *Empowerment in social work practice: A sourcebook* (pp. 73–84). Pacific Grove, CA: Brooks/Cole.

Renzetti, C. M., & Curran, D. J., (1995). *Women, men, and society* (3rd ed.). Boston: Allyn & Bacon.

Renzetti, C. M., & Curran, D. J. (1999). *Women, men, and society* (4th ed.). Boston: Allyn & Bacon.

Resnick, H. (1980a). Effecting internal change in human service organizations. In H. Resnick & R. J. Patti (Eds.), *Change from within: Humanizing social welfare organizations* (pp. 187–199). Philadelphia: Temple University Press.

Resnick, H. (1980b). Tasks in changing the organization from within. In H. Resnick & R. J. Patti (Eds.), *Change from within: Humanizing social welfare organizations* (pp. 200–216). Philadelphia: Temple University Press.

Resnick, M. (1976). *Wife beating counselor training manual no. 1*. Ann Arbor, MI: NOW/WIFE Assault.

Richardson, E. (1981). Cultural and historical perspectives in counseling American Indians. In D. W. Sue, *Counseling the culturally different* (pp. 216–255). New York: John Wiley.

Richmond, M. (1917). *Social diagnosis*. New York: Free Press.

Ridley, C. R. (1995). *Overcoming unintentional racism in counseling and therapy*. Thousand Oaks, CA: Sage.

Robert, H. M. (1989). *Robert's rules of order*. New York: Berkeley Books.

Roberts, A. R. (Ed.). (1996). *Helping battered women*. New York: Oxford University Press.

Roberts, A. R. (2000). An overview of crisis theory and crisis intervention. In A. R. Roberts (Ed.), *Crisis intervention handbook: Assessment, treatment, and research* (2nd ed., pp. 3–30). New York: Oxford.

Roberts-DeGennaro, M. (1987). Developing case management as a practice model. *Social casework, 68*(8), 466–470.

Robison, W., & Reeser, L. C. (2000). *Ethical decision making in social work*. Boston: Allyn & Bacon.

Roffman, R. A. (1987). Drug use and abuse. In *Encyclopedia of social work* (18th ed., vol. 1, pp. 477–487). Silver Spring, MD: National Association of Social Workers.

Rose, R. (Feb. 1995). Hook editors with a pro-caliber release. *NASW News,* 5.

Rose, S. D. (1981). Assessment in groups. *Social work research & abstracts, 17*(1), 29–37.

Rotella, E. J. (1998). Women and the American economy. In S. Ruth (Ed.), *Issues in feminism: An introduction to women's studies* (4th ed., pp. 346–359). Mountain View, CA: Mayfield.

Rotella, E. J. (2001). Women and the American economy. In S. Ruth (Ed.), *Issues in feminism: An introduction to women's studies* (5th ed., pp. 393-397). Mountain View, CA: Mayfield.

Rothman, J., Erlich, J. L., & Tropman, J. E. (1995). *Strategies of community intervention*. Itasca, IL: Peacock.

Rothman, J. C. (1998). *From the front lines: Student cases in social work ethics*. Boston: Allyn & Bacon.

Rubin, A. (1992). Case management. In S. Rose (Ed.), *Case management and social work practice*. White Plains, NY: Longman.

Rubin, H. & Rubin, I. (1986). *Community organizing and development.* Columbus, OH: Merrill.

Ruth, S. (1998). *Issues in feminism: An introduction to women's studies* (4th ed., pp. 334–345). Mountain View, CA: Mayfield.

Rzepnicki, T. L., Schuerman, J. R., & Littell, J. H. (1991). Issues in evaluating intensive family preservation services. In E. M. Tracy, D. A. Haapala, J. M. Kinney, & P. J. Pecora (Eds.), *Intensive family preservation services: An instructional sourcebook* (pp. 71–93). Cleveland, OH: Case Western Reserve University.

Sager, C. J., Brown, H. S., Crohn, H., Engel, T., Rodstein, E., & Walker, L. (1983). *Treating the remarried family.* New York: Brunner/Mazel.

Saleebey, D. (1997). *The strengths perspective in social work practice* (2nd ed.). New York: Longman.

Saleebey, D. (Ed.) (2002). *The strengths perspective in social work practice* (3rd ed.). Boston: Allyn & Bacon.

Sapiro, V. (1999). *Women in American society: An introduction to women's studies* (4th ed.). Mountain View, CA: Mayfield.

Satir, V. M. (1972). *Peoplemaking.* Palo Alto, CA: Science and Behavior Books.

Saunders, D. G. (1995). Domestic violence: Legal issues. In *Encyclopedia of social work* (19th ed., vol. 1, pp. 789–795). Washington, DC: NASW Press.

Scannapieco, M., & Jackson, S. (1996). Kinship care: The African American response to family preservation. *Social work, 41*(2), 190–195.

Scheidel, T., & Crowell, L. (1979). *Discussing and deciding: A deskbook for group leaders and members.* New York: Macmillan.

Schene, P. (1996). Child abuse and neglect policy: History, models, and future directions. In J. Briere et al., *The APSAC handbook on child maltreatment,* pp. 385–397. Thousand Oaks, CA: Sage.

Schiele, J. H. (1996). Afrocentricity: An emerging paradigm in social work practice. *Social work, 41*(3), 284–294.

Schiele, J. H. (1999). Afrocentricity: An emerging paradigm in social work practice. In P. L. Ewalt, E. M. Freeman, A. E. Fortune, D. L. Poole, & S. L. Witkin (Eds.), *Multicultural issues in social work: Practice and research.* Washington, DC: NASW Press.

Schlesinger, E. G., & Devore, W. (1995). Ethnic-sensitive practice. In R. L. Edwards (Editor-in-chief), *Encyclopedia of social work* (19th ed., vol. I, pp. 902–908). Washington, DC: NASW Press.

Schmitt, B. (1980). The child with non-accidental trauma. In C. H. Kempe (Ed.), *The battered child,* pp. 128–146. Chicago: University of Chicago Press.

Schreiner, T. (1984). A revolution that has just begun. *USA Today,* May 29, 40.

Schwab, D. P. (1984). Using job evaluation to obtain pay equity. In *Comparable worth: Issue for the 80's: A consultation for the U.S. Commission on Civil Rights, 1*(June 6–7), 83–92. Washington, DC: U.S. Government Printing Office.

Schwaber, F. H. (1985). Some legal issues related to outside institutions. In H. Hidalgo et al. (Eds.), *Lesbian and gay issues: A resource manual for social workers* (pp. 92–99). Silver Spring, MD: National Association of Social Workers.

Seabury, B. A. (1987). Contracting and engaging in direct practice. In *Encyclopedia of social work* (18th ed., vol. 1,

pp. 339–345). Silver Spring, MD: National Association of Social Workers.

Sermabeikian, P. (1994). Our clients, ourselves: The spiritual perspective and social work practice. *Social work 39*(2), 178–183.

Severson, M. M., & Bankston, T. V. (1995). Social work and the pursuit of justice through mediation. *Social work, 40*(5), 683–691.

Shaw, S. M., & Lee, J. (2001). *Women's voices, feminist visions: Classic and contemporary readings.* Mountain View, CA: Mayfield.

Sheafor, B. W., Horejsi, C. R., & Horejsi, G. A. (1997). *Techniques and guidelines for social work practice* (4th ed.). Boston: Allyn and Bacon.

Sheafor, B. W., Horejsi, C. R., & Horejsi, G. A. (2000). *Techniques and guidelines for social work practice,* 5th ed. Boston: Allyn & Bacon.

Sheafor, B. W., & Landon, P. S. (1987). Generalist perspective. In *Encyclopedia of social work* (18th ed., vol. 1, pp. 660–669). Silver Spring, MD: National Association of Social Workers.

Shelton, J., & Ackerman, J. M. (1974). *Homework in counseling and psychotherapy.* Springfield, IL: Charles C. Thomas.

Sherman, S. N. (1977). Family services: Family treatment. In *Encyclopedia of social work* (Vol. 1, pp. 435–440). Silver Spring, MD: National Association of Social Workers.

Shulman, L. (1992). *The skills of helping individuals, families, and groups.* (3rd ed.) Itasca, IL: Peacock.

Shulman, L. (1999). *The skills of helping individuals, families, and groups.* (4th ed.). Itasca, IL: Peacock.

Sieber, S. (1981). *Fatal remedies.* New York: Plenum.

Siegel, L. M., Attkisson, C. C., & Carson, L. G. (1987). Need identification and program planning in the community context. In F. M. Cox, J. L. Erlich, J. Rothman, & J. Tropman (Eds.), *Strategies of community organization* (pp. 71–97). Itasca, IL: Peacock.

Simon, B. (1994). *The empowerment tradition in American social work.* New York: Columbia University Press.

Sinclair, L. (1993). Making ethical decisions. In K. K. Kirst-Ashman and G. H. Hull, Jr., *Understanding generalist practice.* Chicago: Nelson-Hall.

Siporin, M. (1975). *Introduction to social work practice.* New York: Macmillan.

Skidmore, R. A. (1990). *Social work administration: Dynamic management and human relationships.* Englewood Cliffs, NJ: Prentice-Hall.

Smith, L. A., & Thrasher, S. P. (1993). A practice approach for working with overwhelmed African-American families. *Black caucus, 1,* 1–10.

Smolowe, J. (1995, July 31). Noble aims, mixed results. *Time,* pp. 54–55.

Sosin, M., & Caulum, S. (1989). Advocacy: A conceptualization for social work practice. In B. R. Compton & B. Galaway (Eds.), *Social work processes* (pp. 533–540). Belmont, CA: Wadsworth.

Spickard, P. R., Fong, R., & Ewalt, P. L. (1995). Undermining the very basis of racism—Its categories. *Social work, 40*(5), pp. 581–584.

Star, B. (1987). Domestic violence. In A. Minahan (Ed.), *Encyclopedia of social work* (18th ed., vol. 1, pp. 463–476). Silver Spring, MD: NASW Press.

Stein, T. J. (1981). Macro and micro level issues in case management. In *Case management: State of the art. Proceedings of the national case management conference,* National Conference on Social Welfare, Indianapolis, IN. Washington, DC: Administration on Developmental Disabilities.

Stoddard, S., Jans, L., Ripple, J. M., & Kraus, L. (1998). *Chartbook on work and disability in the United States, 1998.* Berkeley, CA: InfoUse.

Stout, K. D., & McPhail, B. (1998). *Confronting sexism & violence against women: A challenge for social work.* New York: Longman.

Strand, V. C. (1995). Single parents. In *Encyclopedia of social work* (19th ed., vol. 3, pp. 2157–2164). Washington, DC: NASW Press.

Straus, M. A. (1993). Physical assaults by wives: A major social problem. In R. J. Gelles & D. R. Loseke (Eds.), *Current controversies on family violence,* 67–87. Newbury Park, CA: Sage.

Street, E. (1994). *Counseling for family problems.* Thousand Oaks, CA: Sage.

Stromberg, A. H., & Harkess, S. (1988). *Women working.* Mountain View, CA: Mayfield.

Strom-Gottfried, K. (2000, May). Ensuring ethical practice: An examination of NASW Code Violations, 1986–97. *Social work, 45*(3), 251–261.

Strong, B. (1983). *The marriage and family experience.* New York: West.

Strong, B., & DeVault, C. (1997). *Human sexuality* (2nd ed.). Mountain View, CA: Mayfield.

Strong, B., DeVault, C., & Sayad, B. W. (1999). *Human sexuality: Diversity in contemporary America* (3rd ed.). Mountain View, CA: Mayfield.

Takahashi, R. (1994, Winter). Ethnic/cultural/racial terminology. *News & views, 2,* 7.

Tamura, T., & Lau, A. (1992). Connectedness versus separateness: Applicability of family therapy to Japanese families. *Family process, 31,* 319–340.

Tarasoff v. *The Regents of the University of California,* 551 P. 2d 334 (Cal. 1976).

Taylor-Brown, S. (1995). HIV/AIDS: Direct practice. In *Encyclopedia of social work* (19th ed., vol. 2, pp. 1291–1305). Washington, DC: NASW Press.

Thompson, C. L., & Rudolph, L. B., (2000). *Counseling children* (5th ed.). Pacific Grove, CA: Brooks/Cole.

Thompson, D. G. (1977). *Writing long-term and short-term objectives.* Champaign, IL: Research Press.

Thorman, G. (1982). *Helping troubled families: A social work perspective.* New York: Aldine.

Thornborrow, N. M., & Sheldon, M. B. (1995). Women in the labor force. In J. Freeman (Ed.), *Women: A feminist perspective* (5th ed.). Mountain View, CA: Mayfield.

Toomey, B. G. (1987). Sexual assault services. In *Encyclopedia of social work* (18th ed., vol. 2, pp. 569–575). Silver Spring, MD: National Association of Social Workers.

Toseland, R. W. (1995). Aging: Direct practice. In *Encyclopedia of social work* (19th ed., vol. 1, pp. 153–159). Washington, DC: NASW Press.

Toseland, R. W., & Rivas, R. F. (1995). *An introduction to group work practice* (2nd ed.). Boston: Allyn & Bacon.

Toseland, R. W., & Rivas, R. F. (1998). *An introduction to group work practice* (3rd ed.). Boston: Allyn & Bacon.

Tower, C. C. (1989). *Understanding child abuse and neglect.* Boston: Allyn & Bacon.

Tracy, E. M. (1995). Family preservation and home-based services. In *Encyclopedia of social work* (19th ed., vol. 2, pp. 973–983). Washington, DC: NASW Press.

Tracy, E. M., Haapala, D. A., Kinney, J. M., & Pecora, P. J. (1991). Intensive family preservation services: A strategic response to families in crisis. In E. M. Tracy, D. A. Haapala, J. M. Kinney, & P. J. Pecora (Eds.) *Intensive family preservation services: An instructional sourcebook,* pp. 1–13. Cleveland, OH: Case Western Reserve University.

Tully, C. T. (1995). Lesbians overview. *Encyclopedia of social work* (19th ed., vol. 2, pp. 1591–1596). Washington, DC: NASW Press.

Tully, C. T. (2000). *Lesbians, gays, & the empowerment perspective.* New York: Columbia University Press.

U.S. Bureau of the Census (1987). *Male–female differences in work experience, occupation, and earnings, 1984.* Washington, DC: U.S. Government Printing Office.

U.S. Bureau of the Census (1998). *Statistical abstract of the United States 1998* (118th ed.). Washington, DC: U.S. Department of Commerce.

U.S. Bureau of the Census (2000a). *Resident population estimates of the United States by sex, race, and Hispanic origin: April 1, 1990 to July 1, 1999 with short-term projection to July 1, 2000.* Washington, DC: Author.

U.S. Bureau of the Census (2000b). *Projections of the resident population by race, Hispanic origin, and nativity: Middle series, 2050–2070.* Washington, DC: Author.

U.S. Bureau of Indian Affairs (2000). *Answers to frequently asked questions.* http://www.doi.gov/bia/oirm.faq.htm._ Author.

U.S. Department of Commerce (1998). *Statistical abstract of the United States: 1998.* Washington, DC: Author.

U.S. Department of Commerce (2000). *Statistical abstract of the United States: 2000.* Washington, DC: Author.

U.S. Department of Health, Education, and Welfare (1979). *Resource materials: A curriculum on CAN DHEW.* Public No. (OHDS) 79–30221. September, 1979.

U.S. Department of Justice (1994). *Violence against women.* Washington, DC: Author.

U.S. Department of Labor (1991). *Employment and earnings.* Washington, DC: U.S. Government Printing Office.

U.S. House of Representatives (1988). *Women, violence, and the law.* Washington, DC: U.S. Government Printing Office.

U.S. Merit Systems Protection Board (BSPB) (1981). *Sexual harassment in the work place: Is it a problem?* Washington, DC: U.S. Government Printing Office.

U.S. News & World Report. "Law: How women lawyers fare," Jan. 15, 1996, 14.

University of Wisconsin Board of Regents (1981). Regent Policy 81–2 *Sexual harassment policy statement and implementation:* Res. 2361 adopted 5/8/81. Madison, WI: Office of the Secretary of the Board of Regents.

Unson, D. O. (1992). *Counseling Asians: An intergenerational perspective.* Unpublished manuscript, University of Wisconsin–Eau Claire.

Van Den Bergh, N. (1995). Employee assistance programs. *Encyclopedia of social work* (19th ed., vol. 1, pp. 842–849). Washington, DC: NASW Press.

Van Den Bergh, N., & Cooper, L. B. (Eds.) (1986). *Feminist visions for social work*. Washington, DC: NASW Press.

Van Den Bergh, N., & Cooper, L. B. (1987). Feminist social work. In *Encyclopedia of social work* (19th ed., vol. 1, pp. 610–618). Silver Spring, MD: National Association of Social Workers.

Van Wormer, K., Wells, J., & Boes, M. (2000). *Social work with lesbians, gays, and bisexuals: A strengths perspective*. Boston: Allyn & Bacon.

Visher, F. B., & Visher, J. S. (1988). Treating families with problems associated with remarriage and step relationships. In C. S. Chilman, E. W. Nunnally, & F. M. Cox (Eds.), *Variant family forms* (pp. 222–244). Newbury Park, CA: Sage.

Vosler, N. K. (1990). Assessing family access to basic resources: An essential component of social work practice. *Social work, 37*(5), 434–441.

Voss, R. W., Douville, V., Little Soldier, A., & White Hat, A. (1999). Wo'Lakol Kiciyapi: Traditional philosophies of helping and healing among the Lakotas: Toward a Lakota-Centric practice of social work. *Journal of multicultural social work, 7* (1/2), 73–93.

Walker, L. E. (1979a). *The battered woman*. New York: Harper & Row.

Wall, L. (2000, September 10). Proud pairs: Milwaukee's same-sex registry marks one-year anniversary. *The Milwaukee journal sentinel*, L1–2.

Warheit, G. J., Bell, R. A., & Schwab, J. J. (1977) *Planning for change: Needs assessment approaches*. Washington, DC: National Institute of Mental Health.

Warren, R. B., & Warren, D. E. (1984). How to diagnose a neighborhood. In F. Cox, J. L. Erlich, J. Rothman, & J. E. Tropman (Eds.), *Tactics and techniques of community practice* (2nd ed., pp. 27–40). Itasca, IL: Peacock.

Weatherley, R. A., & Cartoof, V. G. (1988). Helping single adolescent parents. In C. Chilman, E. Nunnally, & F. Cox (Eds.), *Variant family forms* (pp. 39–55). Newbury Park, CA: Sage.

Weaver, G. (1992, September). Law enforcement in a culturally sensitive society. *FBI law enforcement bulletin, 61*(9), 1–7.

Wegscheider, S. (1981). *Another chance: Hope and health for the alcoholic family*. Palo Alto, CA: Science Behavior Books.

Weitzman, L. J. (1985). *The divorce revolution*. New York: Free Press.

Wells, E. (1987). Food stamp program. In A. Minahan (Editor-in-chief), *Encyclopedia of social work* (18th ed., vol. 1, pp. 628–634). Silver Spring, MD: NASW.

Wells, S. J. (1995). Child abuse and neglect overview. In *Encyclopedia of social work* (Vol. 1, pp. 346–353). Washington, DC: NASW Press.

Westra, M. (1996). *Active communication*. Pacific Grove, CA: Brooks/Cole.

White, G. D., Nielsen, G., & Johnson, S. M. (1972). Timeout duration and the suppression of deviant behavior in children. *Journal of applied behavior analysis, 5*(2), 111–120.

Whithan, F. L., & Mathy, R. M. (1986). *Male homosexuality in four societies*. New York: Praeger.

Whittaker, J. K., & Tracy, E. M. (1989). *Social treatment: An introduction to social work practice*. New York: Aldine de Gruyter.

Wicks, R. J., & Parsons, R. D. (1984). *Counseling strategies and intervention techniques for the human services*. New York: Longman.

Williams, E. E., & Ellison, F. (1996). Culturally informed social work practice with American Indian clients: Guidelines for non-Indian social workers. *Social work, 41*(2), 147–151.

Williams, J. B. (1987). Diagnostic and statistical manual (DSM). In *Encyclopedia of social work* (18th ed., vol. 1, pp. 389–393). Washington, DC: National Association of Social Workers.

Williams, J. B. W. (1995). Diagnostic and statistical manual of mental disorders. In *Encyclopedia of social work* (pp. 729–739). Washington, DC: National Association of Social Workers.

Williams, M., Unrau, Y. A., & Grinnell, R. M. (1998). *Introduction to social work research*. Itasca, IL: Peacock.

Wolk, J. L., Sullivan, W. P., & Hartmann, D. J. (1994). The managerial nature of case management. *Social work, 39*(2), 152–159.

Wolock, I., & Horowitz, B. (1984). Child maltreatment as a social problem: The neglect of neglect. *American journal of orthopsychiatry, 54*(4), 530–543.

Wong, H. Z., Kim, L. I., Lim, D. T., & Morishima, J. K. (1983). The training of psychologists for Asian and Pacific American communities. In J. C. Chunn, P. J. Dunston, and F. Ross-Sheriff (Eds.), *Mental health and people of color* (pp. 23–41). Washington, DC: Howard University Press.

Woodman, N. J. (1995). Lesbians: Direct practice. In *Encyclopedia of social work* (19th ed., vol. 2, pp. 1597–1604). Washington, DC: NASW Press.

Woodside, M., & McClam, T. (1998). *Generalist case management*. Pacific Grove, CA: Brooks/Cole.

Worden, M. (1994). *Family therapy basics*. Pacific Grove, CA: Brooks/Cole.

Worden, M. (1999). *Family therapy basics*. (2nd ed.). Pacific Grove, CA: Brooks/Cole.

Yegidis, B. L., & Weinbach, R. W. (1996). *Research methods for social workers*. Boston: Allyn & Bacon.

Yessian, M. R., & Broskowski, A. (1983). Generalists in human service systems: Their problems and prospects. In R. M. Kramer & H. Specht (Eds.), *Readings in community organization practice* (pp. 180–198). Englewood Cliffs, NJ: Prentice-Hall.

York, R. O., Denton, R. T., & Moran, J. R. (1990). Congruence between specializations in graduate school and post-graduate employment patterns for social workers. *Journal of teaching in social work, 4*(1), 3–15.

Zander, A. (1983). *Making groups effective*. San Francisco: Jossey-Bass.

Zastrow, C., & Kirst-Ashman, K. K. (2001). *Understanding human behavior and the social environment* (5th ed.). Chicago: Nelson-Hall.

Zuniga, M. E. (1992). Using metaphors in therapy: Dichos and Latino clients. *Social work, 37*(1), 55–60.

Zuniga, M. E. (1995). Aging: Social work practice. In *Encyclopedia of social work* (Vol. 1, pp. 173–183). Washington, DC: NASW Press.

Zuravin, S. J., & Taylor, R. (1987). *Family planning behaviors and child care adequacy*. Final report submitted to the U.S. Department of Health and Human Services, Office of Population Affairs (Grant FPR 000028001-1).

Name Index

Subject Index

A

AA (Alcoholics Anonymous), 218, 219–220, 226
AB design, 241
ABC design, 242–243
Ableism, 67
Abusers of children, 200–201
Accountability, 234
Acculturation
 of Asian Americans, 84
 definition of, 74, 327
 of Native Americans, 75
Action groups, 191
Action steps
 in an intervention contract, 183
 specifying, 179
Action system, 405
 definition of, 9
Ad hoc committees, 375
Adaptation
 concept for empowering the elderly, 207
 as an ecological perspective concept, 10
Addiction, 218
Adversary, assessing the, 425
Advocacy
 assessment in, 422–425
 and battered women, 117
 case, 393–394, 416–417
 cause (class), 393, 417–418
 and child maltreatment, 207
 definition of, 416
 and the elderly, 207–208
 and feminism, 99
 and the Generalist Intervention Model, 416
 goals of, 418
 guidelines for, 427
 indications of, 419
 and intervention, 426–429
 legislative, 429–434
 and organizational and community change, 410–411
 planning in, 425–426
 realities of, 419–421
 skills useful in, 418
 and social action, 392–394
 targets of, 418–419
Advocates
 definition of, 20

knowledge required by, 421–422
 role in social work, 17, 21, 291
AFDC (Aid to Families with Dependent Children), 121, 314
Affirmative action, 124–125
Afghan immigrants, 292
African Americans
 and importance of church, 72, 81
 communication patterns, 81
 working with families, 352–354
 family strengths, 352
 family experiences, 81
 helping styles, 82–83
 impact of history and oppression on, 353
 inhuman treatment, 68, 80
 macro-level approaches, 83
 number in U.S. population, 66
 terms, 81
Afrocentricity, 82
Ageism
 definition of, 27
Agencies
 characteristics of, 440–441
 contact persons in, 441
 eligibility criteria of, 440
 sponsorship of groups, 154–155
Agenda of a meeting, 375
Aggression, 97
Aggressive members in groups, 376
Aid to Families with Dependent Children (AFDC), 121, 314
AIDS, 144
 confidentiality and, 50
Al-Anon, 218, 220
Alaskan natives, 292
Alateen, 220
Alcohol, 217
Alcohol abuse
 assessing, 145, 147, 223–224
 and substance abuse, 216–220
Alcoholic, 218
Alcoholics Anonymous (AA), 218, 219–220, 226
Alcoholism
 assessment, 147
 and child maltreatment, 201
 definition of, 217, 220
 and family relationships, 222
 implementation with, 224–226
 intervention, 222–223

phases of, 220
 terms related to, 217–218
Amendment (to a motion), 375
American Psychiatric Association (APA), 144, 217, 220
American Sign Language (ASL), 88
Americans with Disabilities Act, 55, 68
 impact of, 70
 physical or mental impairments, definition of, 68
 reasons for creation, 69
Anglo, 78, 90
Antabuse, 220
Anticipatory planning, 213, 215
Anxiety disorders, 144
AODA. See Alcohol abuse
APA (American Psychiatric Association), 144, 217, 220
Appeals
 avenues of, 421–422
 legal, 428
Asian Americans and Pacific Islanders
 attending skills when working with, 84–85
 and importance of church, 72
 communication patterns, 84
 family centering, 83
 filial piety and, 83
 inhuman treatment of, 68
 U.S. population of, 66
 racist behavior toward, 68
 within-group differences, 84
Assertiveness, 102–106
 assessing, 145
 Rathus Assertiveness Schedule (RAS), 145–146
Assessment (GIM step), 24–28, 134–138
 of adversary, 425
 in advocacy, 422–425
 of alcohol and substance dependence and, 223–224
 how to approach, 135
 and child maltreatment, 203
 client-in-situation, 26
 of clients, 425
 gathering data for, 143
 of community needs, 159
 during crisis intervention, 211–212
 versus diagnosis, 134

diversity, aspects of, 27, 72
empowerment and strengths, purpose of, 164
of families. *See* Family assessment
goals of, 137–138
instruments for, 144–147
in macro practice, 159–164
in mezzo practice, 154–159
from a micro practice perspective, 138
of needs. *See* Needs assessment
and personal values, 324
steps of, 136
questions to ask during, 143
with women, 96
Assimilation, 75, 84, 89, 292, 327
Attending skills, 77, 377–378
Attention deficit hyperactivity disorder, 342
Attentive listening, 270–271
Authenticity, 90
Authority-based practice, 233
Autonomy, 207
fostering, 448
Aztecs, 75

B
BAB design, 242–243
Bargaining. *See* Negotiation
Baseline, 236–237
Battered women, 112
battering cycle, 114
counseling, 115–118
description of, 113
macro practice on behalf of, 118
perpetrators, 113
profile of, 113
why does she stay, 114–115
B design, 241
Behavior modification, 318
Behavior therapy, 342
Behavioral indicators of physical abuse, 198–199
Bilingualism, 79
Bills, influencing passage of, 432–433
Bipolar disorders, 144, 365
Blocker role, 376–377
Boards of directors, 361
Body positioning,
Boundaries
definition of, 7
in family systems, 309
in stepfamilies, 326
Brainstorming, 373–374
Broker
with alcohol and substance abuse, 219–220
definition of, 20, 439
being an effective, 439–440

importance in generalist practice, 439
with groups, 366
with micro systems, 290
and planned change process, 445–448
Budgeting, 398–399
Building on clients' strengths. *See* NOHSE
Bureau of Indian Affairs, 75
Burmese, 83

C
CA (Cocaine Anonymous), 219
Care of clients, continuity of, 448
Case advocacy, 394, 416–417
Case conferences, 362
Case consultation, 383
Case management, 448–461
and assessment, 451–454
definition of, 448–450
and evaluation, 459
and generalist practice, 450–451
and implementation, 457–459
planning in, 454–457
principles of, 448
termination in, 459
Case manager/coordinator
definition of, 20
human services role, 291
Cause advocacy, 394–395, 417–418
Cerebral palsy, 167
Change agent system, 9
Chicano, 78
Chief enabler, 222
Child abuse. *See* Child maltreatment
Child force, 205
Child maltreatment, 197–209
definitions and indicators of, 197–198
mezzo and macro practice, 207, 209
perpetrators of, 200–201
victims of, 200
Child management methods, 341–342
Child neglect, 199
Child–parent relationship difficulties, 318
Child Protective Services (CPS), 201, 206
Child Welfare League of America (CWLA), 346, 401
Chippewa, 76
Chronic phase of alcoholism, 220
Civil Rights Act, Title VII, 124
Civil War, 68
Clarification, 283
Clarity of an objective, 177
Class advocacy. *See* Cause advocacy
Client-initiated silence, 293

Client satisfaction questionnaires, 245–247
Client system, 9
Clients
assessing the, 425, 445
confronting, 294
difficulties in role performance, 170
empowerment of, 276–277
identifying, 445
involuntary, 295–296
involvement during intervention process, 168
lying by, 297
realities about, 421
rights of, 421
self determination. *See* Self determination
support groups of, 452–454
Clinical disorders, 144
Coaching, 381–382
Coalitions, 409–410
Cocaine Anonymous (CA), 219
Coercive power, 423
Cognitive disabilities, 40, 68
Cognitive therapy with Asian Americans, 86
Collaboration, 406–407
Color blindness, 71
Coming out, 349–350
Committees and commissions, 361–362, 375
Communication
avenues of, 307–308
within families, 148, 338–339
and family assessment, 304–308
problems within a marriage, 319
Communities
assessment of needs in, 159–164
format for analyzing, 161–162
Community, 391, 392
Community change, 391–394, 410–412
Community forum approach, 408
Community organization, traditional focus, 392
Community pressure for change, 428
Comparable worth, 126
Competence, concept of empowering the elderly, 207
Compromise, decision making by, 370, 372
Compromiser role, 376
Concurrent validity, 237
Condemnation, avenue of communication, 307
Conditions of an objective, 177–178
Confessor role, 377
Confidentiality
and AIDS, 50
and cultural competence, 71
ethical principle, 38, 47, 49

IN-BOOK SURVEY

At Brooks/Cole, we are excited about creating new types of learning materials that are interactive, three-dimensional, and fun to use. To guide us in our publishing/development process, we hope that you'll take just a few moments to fill out the survey below. Your answers can help us make decisions that will allow us to produce a wide variety of videos, CD-ROMs, and Internet-based learning systems to complement standard textbooks. If you're interested in working with us as a student Beta-tester, be sure to fill in your name, telephone number, and address. We look forward to hearing from you!

In addition to books, which of the following learning tools do you currently use in your counseling/human services/social work courses?

_____ **Video** _____ in class _____ school library _____ own VCR

_____ **CD-ROM** _____ in class _____ in lab _____ own computer

_____ **Macintosh disks** _____ in class _____ in lab _____ own computer

_____ **Windows disks** _____ in class _____ in lab _____ own computer

_____ **Internet** _____ in class _____ in lab _____ own computer

How often do you access the Internet? _____

My own home computer is a:

_____

The computer I use in class for counseling/human services/social work courses is a:

_____

If you are NOT currently using multimedia materials in your counseling/human services/social work courses, but can see ways that video, CD-ROM, Internet, or other technologies could enhance your learning, please comment below:

_____

_____

_____

Other comments (optional):

_____

Name _____ Telephone_____

Address _____

School _____

Professor/Course _____

You can fax this form to us at (650) 592-9081 or detach, fold, secure, and mail.

FOLD HERE

BUSINESS REPLY MAIL

FIRST CLASS   PERMIT NO. 358   PACIFIC GROVE, CA

POSTAGE WILL BE PAID BY ADDRESSEE

ATT: *Marketing*

**The Wadsworth Group
10 Davis Drive
Belmont, CA 94002**

FOLD HERE